The Wars in Vietnam, Cambodia and Laos, 1945–1982

War/Peace Bibliography Series #18
Richard Dean Burns, Series Editor

The Wars in Vietnam, Cambodia and Laos, 1945–1982

A Bibliographic Guide

Richard Dean Burns and Milton Leitenberg

ABC-Clio Information Services

Santa Barbara, California

Oxford, England

Library of Congress Cataloging in Publication Data

Burns, Richard Dean.
    The Wars in Vietnam, Cambodia and Laos, 1945–1982.

    (War/peace bibliography series; 18)
    Includes index.
    1.   Vietnamese Conflict, 1961–1975—Bibliography.
2.   Indochina—History—1945–   —Bibliography.
3.   Indochina—History, Military—Bibliography.
I.   Leitenberg, Milton.   II. Title.
Z3228.V5B87 1983 [DS557.7] 016.959704'3 80-13246
ISBN 0–87436–310–1

10 9 8 7 6 5 4 3 2 1

ABC-Clio Information Services
2040 Alameda Padre Serra, Box 4397
Santa Barbara, California 93103

Clio Press Ltd.
55 St. Thomas Street
Oxford, OX1 1JG, England

Manufactured in the United States of America

The War/Peace Bibliography Series

Richard Dean Burns, Editor

This Series has been developed in cooperation with the Center for the Study of Armament and Disarmament, California State University, Los Angeles.

#1 *Songs of Protest, War and Peace*
A Bibliography and Discography
R. Serge Denisoff

#2 *Warfare in Primitive Societies*
A Bibliography
William Tulio Divale

#3 *The Vietnam Conflict*
Its Geographical Dimensions, Political
Traumas and Military Developments
Milton Leitenberg and
Richard Dean Burns

#4 *The Arab-Israeli Conflict*
A Historical, Political, Social and
Military Bibliography
Ronald M. DeVore

#5 *Modern Revolutions and Revolutionists*
A Bibliography
Robert Blackey

#6 *Arms Control and Disarmament*
A Bibliography
Richard Dean Burns

#7 *The United States in World War I*
A Selected Bibliography
Ronald Schaffer

#8 *Uncertain Judgment*
A Bibliography of War Crimes Trials
John R. Lewis

#9 *The Soviet Navy, 1941–1978*
A Guide to Sources in English
Myron J. Smith, Jr.

#10 *The Soviet Air and Strategic Rocket
Forces, 1939–1980*
A Guide to Sources in English
Myron J. Smith, Jr.

#11 *The Soviet Army, 1930–1980*
A Guide to Sources in English
Myron J. Smith, Jr.

#12 *The Secret Wars*
A Guide to Sources in English
Volume I: Intelligence, Propaganda and
Psychological Warfare, Resistance
Movements, and Secret Operations,
1939–1945
Myron J. Smith, Jr.

#13 *The Secret Wars*
A Guide to Sources in English
Volume II: Intelligence, Propaganda and
Psychological Warfare, Covert
Operations, 1945–1980
Myron J. Smith, Jr.

About the War/Peace Bibliography Series

WITH THIS BIBLIOGRAPHICAL SERIES, the Center for the Study of Armament and Disarmament, California State University, Los Angeles, seeks to promote a wider understanding of martial violence and the alternatives to its employment. The Center, which was formed by concerned faculty and students in 1962–63, has as its primary objective the stimulation of intelligent discussion of war/peace issues. More precisely, the Center has undertaken two essential functions: (1) to collect and catalogue materials bearing on war/peace issues; and (2) to aid faculty, students, and the public in their individual and collective probing of the historical, political, economic, philosophical, technical, and psychological facets of these fundamental problems.

This bibliography series is, obviously, one tool with which we may more effectively approach our task. Each issue in this series is intended to provide a comprehensive "working," rather than definitive, bibliography on a relatively narrow theme within the spectrum of war/peace studies. While we hope this series will prove to be a useful tool, we also solicit your comments regarding its format, contents, and topics.

— *Richard Dean Burns*
Series Editor

Contents

Chapter One
General Reference Aids

Chapter Two
Southeast Asia: Cambodia, Laos and Thailand

Chapter Three
Vietnam: From the First to the Third Indochina Wars

Chapter Four
United States and the Politics of Intervention

Chapter Five
Congress, International Law and Negotiations

Chapter Six
Strategy, Tactics and Support Efforts

Chapter Seven
Combat Operations

Chapter Eight
The Costs of War: Ecocide, POWs, War Crimes and Casualties

Chapter Nine
The War at Home

List of Maps

List of Tables

Preface

THIS REVISED EDITION expands both the format and the number of references contained in the initial volume. We have added statistics, chronologies and maps providing ready access to information not always easily located.

The enlarged "Contents" is designed to provide quick access to themes, episodes and personalities, while the added cross-references will guide the researcher to related materials. The occasional interjection of brief comments following reference items is aimed at clarifying the reference's essential theme.

Another added feature is the inclusion of chapter and section "introductions" which suggest basic works. Where markedly differing viewpoints exist, an attempt has been made to cross-reference them. We hope that these comments and cross-references will be taken for what they were meant to be—suggestions of where differing views may be found—not as an attempt to introduce any particular thesis into the *Guide*.

If the *Guide* contains any "thesis" at all, it is a belief that none of the conventional wisdom cited below, whether from an "interventionist" or "antiwar" writer, is beyond rigorous, objective reexamination. Since Milton Leitenberg and I have been separated by thousands of miles, it has fallen my lot to prepare these comments and cross-references and I therefore accept full responsibility for them.

We are greatly indebted to Lillemor Lindh, who assisted in the compiling of the initial volume, to Mary Gormly, who reviewed the entire volume with the critical eye of a reference librarian, and to Frances R. Burns, who provided us with valuable assistance in organizing the manuscript. Our appreciation is also extended to Beverly Wachel, who transformed rough notes into typescript, and to John Wagner, who undertook the trying task of copyediting the massive manuscript. Finally, we wish to acknowledge the assistance we received from the many librarians in the California State University system, especially Robert Rose, Leah Freeman, Jo Whitlatch and Randy Hensley. We, of course, accept full responsibility for any errors or ommissions.

— *Richard Dean Burns*

Introduction

HANOI'S MILITARY TRIUMPH in 1975 ended three decades of war in Indochina that had begun with the end of Japanese occupation in 1945 and the subsequent French attempt to reestablish their colonial prerogatives. During the First Indochina War (1946–1954) the Vietnamese struggled to eject the French. This conflict—which many Vietnamese feel began in the 1880s—ended with the signing of the Geneva Accords in 1954 and the temporary separation of Vietnam into Northern and Southern halves.

The Second Indochina War (1961–1975)—by far the most violent—was a civil war between the two separated halves of Vietnam complicated by American, Soviet and Chinese intervention. Under Presidents John F. Kennedy and Lyndon B. Johnson, American combat forces slowly increased in numbers and gradually undertook expanded military operations. The early United States decision to employ its technological advantage, rather than large armies, led to such destruction of the countryside that critics labelled these operations "ecocide." Under increasing public and congressional pressure to end American involvement, President Richard M. Nixon reduced U.S. ground operations in Vietnam and relied on airpower and bombing to end the war. The 1973 armistice saw the accelerated withdrawal of U.S. ground forces, an end to all U.S. military operations, and restrictions on U.S. military aid to South Vietnam.

In 1977 President Jimmy Carter initiated contacts with the victorious authorities in Hanoi in hopes of normalizing relations. The United States was to acknowledge that "North" Vietnam no longer held any American prisoners of war or the bodies of any "missing-in-action" servicemen, while Vietnam understood that it should no longer press for the multi-billion-dollar economic aid package that the Nixon administration had offered during peace negotiations. United States–Vietnamese negotiations were close to completion when they were abruptly interrupted by renewed fighting in Indochina.

Hanoi's victory in 1975 had led most observers to assume that the long skein of war in Indochina was at an end. They believed that after thirty years of conflict the Vietnamese would relish their independence, rejoice at the unification of their country, and turn their energies to repairing the ravages of war. But after a brief respite, war broke out again in 1977 when the Vietnamese invaded Cambodia, and China responded by attacking Vietnam. Indochina thus began its third cycle of war since the end of World War II.

From any vantage point, these conflicts leave a bewildering array of historical questions with vast ramifications for the present and the future. The remarks that follow are designed to focus on some of the issues, especially those emerging from the protracted, violent Second Indochina War, which have aroused controversy and which are delineated in this *Guide*.

First Indochina War

American involvement in Indochinese affairs began during World War II when its agents enlisted the support of Vietnamese nationals, including Ho Chi Minh, to harass the Japanese. Few people on this side of the Pacific understood that Japan's invasion of Indochina had merely interrupted a continuing struggle by native forces to gain their independence from the French. Believing colonialism outmoded, President Franklin D. Roosevelt argued against the reestablishment of the prewar empires in Asia. He did not sympathize with the French desire to regain control of their overseas territories and repeatedly urged that Indochina be given independence.

What actually transpired in Indochina following Japan's surrender is still a matter of historical contention. During the war, the Japanese lacked sufficient troops to patrol outlying regions; consequently, the Vietminh were able to rally and organize nationalists of all political persuasions. When the war ended, the Vietminh moved quickly into Hanoi, created the Democratic Republic of Vietnam, and declared their independence. The French, after briefly recognizing the Vietminh regime, staged a coup and regained control of the major Vietnamese cities with the assistance of British and Japanese forces.

Although General Douglas MacArthur complained that the use of Japanese military forces to defeat our former allies was disgraceful, the United States did nothing. The *Pentagon Papers* revealed that Ho Chi Minh tried to interest President Harry S. Truman in the plight of the Vietminh government during 1945–1946, but Truman chose not to intervene because of America's desire to enlist France's support in revitalizing Europe and because of Ho's communist background.[1]

After several failed attempts at negotiation, the French fleet bombarded the Vietnamese sections of Haiphong in November 1946, killing some 6,000 citizens. The Vietminh retaliated on December 20 with an unsuccessful attack upon French positions in Hanoi. The Vietminh forces then slipped away into the jungles and mountains to continue the struggle for independence; The First Indochina War had begun.

Although the United States proclaimed a hands-off attitude, it was soon indirectly involved. American military and economic aid sent to France under NATO and various other European-oriented programs began, inevitably, to find its way to Southeast Asia. Two factors prevented Washington from protesting the misuse of American aid: the outbreak of the Korean War redirected the attention of American policymakers toward Asia generally, and the American people, caught up in foreign policy initiatives justified on the appeal to anticommunism, accepted programs aimed at "containing" alleged foes everywhere with little critical examination. In 1950, Washington recognized the French puppet regime in Indochina headed by Emperor–playboy Bao Dai and began to supply the French forces openly.

At the urging of Secretary of State John Foster Dulles, the Eisenhower administration intensified support of French military efforts in Indochina. To prevent the collapse of French forces in early 1954, Washington officials, among them Vice-President Richard Nixon, Dulles and the U.S. Joint Chiefs of Staff, pressed for direct American military intervention. Eisenhower refused one proposal, Project Vulture, calling for the use of American tactical nuclear weapons to aid the French besieged at Diem Bien Phu, primarily because he could not obtain congressional or British support for joint action. The embittered French were forced to accept a cease-fire and acknowledge Vietnamese independence in July 1954 at Geneva.

The French withdrawal from Indochina in 1955–1956 left a great-power political vacuum promptly filled by the United States. The records and memoirs of the mid-1950s indicate that Dulles sponsored American efforts to abrogate the Geneva settlement; subsequently, the new Kennedy administration sanctioned this policy. These efforts involved, in part, sabotaging North Vietnamese facilities, terrorizing North Vietnamese Catholics into fleeing to the South, establishing an *Armeé Clandestine* in Laos, and supplying illegal arms and advisors to South Vietnam. Eisenhower also endorsed President Diem's refusal to hold talks with Ho regarding reunification, including the nationwide elections prescribed by the Geneva Accords.

The Eisenhower administration initiated the curious, ever-shifting public statements "justifying" America's involvement and interest in Indochina. On April 7, 1954, the President linked the "falling domino" principle to Southeast Asia, a principle used earlier by the Truman administration with regard to the Near East. He stressed Indochina's "production of materials that the world needs," an infrequent official justification of American involvement, and emphasized "the possibility that many human beings might [without U.S. action] pass under a dictatorship that is inimical to the free world."[2] The Pentagon Papers gathered most of Washington's official statements on the "Justification of the War"; they appear in the back of each volume of the Senator Gravel Edition.

Second Indochina War

The Second Indochina War began with the initiation of suppression campaigns by Diem that contravened various sections of the Accords, the subsequent decision of pro-unification forces to form the National Liberation Front, and President John F. Kennedy's breach of the Geneva restrictions as the civil war went increasingly against Diem. The American decision to increase its participation seems to have been dictated more by a desire to stand up to the Soviet Union and (according to Secretary of State—Dean Rusk) to China, and to demonstrate the administration's "credibility"—a word which would appear more and more frequently in the justification for U.S. military involvement in Vietnam—than by any specific American interests in Southeast Asia. As American military involvement increased, South Vietnam's Buddhists, and then Washington, became disillusioned with the performance of President Diem and his family. On November 1, 1963, Diem was overthrown and assassinated in a palace coup; within the month, President Kennedy was also dead.

When the Vietcong (as the Vietminh were now commonly called) pressed toward victory in the South, President Lyndon B. Johnson had to choose between withdrawing or augmenting American forces in the country. The records indicate little discussion of withdrawal; Johnson appeared determined that the United States would not be forced out of Southeast Asia. As soon as the elections of 1964 had registered a landslide victory for the "moderate" Johnson against the "radical" Senator Barry Goldwater, the President expanded American military operations to include limited and controlled aerial bombing of the North. Although Marine Corps units were deployed to Vietnam as "defensive measures" in early 1965, it was not until congressional endorsement was extended in the Tonkin Gulf Resolution of August 1964 that Johnson greatly increased American military forces.

Employing the policy of "graduated response," attributed to presidential advisor W.W. Rostow, President Johnson sought to convince the Hanoi regime that it could not reunify Vietnam by force and to accept the existence of South Vietnam as an independent nation. This policy greatly miscalculated the determination of the North Vietnamese regime and of the Southern Vietcong.

The war intensified and casualties mounted in a contest for which many Americans could not find a satisfactory purpose. International criticism was strong; many Western countries and NATO allies opposed U.S. action. As the bloodshed increased, Johnson was sharply attacked by domestic opponents of the war. Choosing to ignore the arguments of these "doves," the administration justified its policies on various grounds: three previous presidents had pledged American aid to South Vietnam; Vietnam represented a test case in America's opposition to the "new Communist strategy" of national liberation movements sponsored by Peking; this was a struggle for freedom against aggression by terror; America's "credibility" was being tested; if South Vietnam fell to the communists, the rest of Southeast Asia would, like "falling dominoes," come under Peking's domination. Perhaps the most curious theme to come from Washington was that the United States must make Hanoi abide by the Geneva Accords of 1954—the very agreements that Washington itself had consistently ignored.

The simplistic nature of the "official" justifications for the war failed to convince critics. They questioned whether Washington should try to "save" the Vietnamese people by virtually destroying their nation, whether Ho was really a puppet of international communism—as the Administration portrayed him to be—or whether America should assume the role of world policeman by intervening in "domestic" quarrels. In early 1968, Senator Eugene McCarthy challenged Johnson's policies in the Democratic presidential primaries. After a poor showing in the New Hampshire primary, Johnson withdrew from the race. He halted the bombing of North Vietnam and began formal peace talks in Paris during his final months in office. The presidential contest resulted in an "interventionist" of 1954 moving into the White House—Richard M. Nixon.

During the campaign Nixon claimed to possess a secret plan to end the war, but it was soon apparent that the new administration had nothing new to offer. Nixon sought to mollify domestic dissent by pulling out American ground forces, thereby reducing American casualties. But in order to maintain a favorable military situation, the administration ordered the accelerated training and equipping of South Vietnamese forces and a greatly increased use of bombing.

At the same time, the Nixon administration expanded its bombing into Cambodia (26 percent of its territory was under saturation bombing, with 2 million people killed, wounded or displaced) and intensified its bombing in Laos (over four times that of the previous years and eight times more than dropped on Japan in World War II). It is little wonder that Americans came to be considered the "new barbarians." Nixon's reliance on aerial bombing to continue the war caused critics to label his operations the "Third Indochina War." In four years, this bombing more than doubled the death and destruction from military activities of the Kennedy–Johnson years.

The large-scale North Vietnamese invasion ("Easter Offensive") of the South, on March 30, 1972, resulted in renewed American bombing of the North and, on May 8, the mining of Haiphong harbor. The South Vietnamese military did not respond well to this new challenge, but American airpower halted the North's drive and inflicted heavy losses in men and material upon the invading forces. Hanoi announced on October 26 that it would adhere to the cease-fire sketched out by negotiators if the agreement was signed by October 31. Obviously, this move was timed to bring pressure on Richard Nixon before the presidential election of November 7. President Nixon assured the American people that only a few minor details were left to be adjusted, but he insisted that he would not sign under pressure.

After receiving his mandate in the November election, Nixon sent Special Advisor Henry Kissinger to Paris to complete negotiation with North Vietnam's Le Duc Tho. The secret Kissinger–Tho discussions collapsed on December 16, 1972, and Nixon ordered the bombing (December 18–30) of North Vietnam's industrial heartland; areas in and around Hanoi were particularly hard hit. On January 8, 1973, the Kissinger–Tho talks were resumed in Paris and on January 24, a cease-fire was initiated, but few observers expected the Indochina struggle to halt simply because Kissinger and Tho had agreed upon a cease-fire.

Second Indochina War: Tactics and Weapons

America's military tactics and weapons policies in Vietnam, Laos and Cambodia during the Second Indochina War employed the conventional and the novel, and received nearly as much criticism as did the political maneuvering[3] surrounding the U.S. military involvement in Indochina. In the early 1960s, the nation's military program and strategic theories placed great emphasis upon the ability of its armed forces to contain "wars of national liberation," and to maintain a strategic nuclear deterrent. Many military and civilian officials welcomed the opportunity, in 1964–65, to demonstrate in Vietnam that they had the tactics and equipment necessary to beat down "brushfire wars." According to *Armed Forces Management* (November 1965), "Just as Vietnam has become a test-bed for the proof-testing and debugging of new hardware, new tactical concepts, new logistics systems, so is it a test of the validity of Defense's basic policy—not an exception to it."

These new tactics included the extensive use of airborne (helicopter) troops on "search and destroy" missions, the designation for artillery and aircraft of widespread "free-fire zones," the intentional "population relocation" programs designed to clear free-fire zones, the extensive use of air power in support and interdiction missions, and the use of CS gas, crop and forest destroying herbicides, and weather modification programs. American military forces also become heavily engaged in pacification programs designed to "win the hearts and minds" of the South Vietnamese peasants; unfortunately, this program's acronym (WHAM) was often too vividly parodied by operational tactics such as "search and destroy missions," B-52 "carpet bombing," and ground-strafing gunships.

Among the innovative weapons systems employed in Vietnam were new delivery systems for the application of CS gas and herbicides; light-gathering and heat-gathering devices for nighttime; ground-based, anti-personnel targeting; laser-guided and television-guided bombs; and ground-based sensors ("electronic battlefield") which detected personnel and motor traffic and telemetered this information through circling aircraft to ground-based computers which called in air strikes. The Air Force also made extensive use of special aircraft for airborne tactical control and electronic countermeasures over the China Sea and North Vietnam. Even more bizarre and unprecedented was the use of meteorological warfare designed to cause an additional amount of rainfall. Other less dramatic devices, lightships which lit up the night sky and "gunships" with multibarreled, rapid-fire machine guns (6,000 rpm per gun), also came into general use with awesome results.

The United States' virtually unimpeded use of airpower in Indochina was one of the war's most striking and controversial features. During World War II the U.S. dropped slightly over 2 million tons of bombs in all theaters and during the Korean War it dropped a little less than 1 million tons, but during the Second Indochina War American airplanes dropped more than 7 million tons of bombs. More than one-half of this tonnage was dropped during the Nixon administration. When all other forms of bombardment (artillery shelling, rocket attacks, etc.) are combined, the total tonnage of explosives used by the United States in Indochina reaches 14 million tons, seven times the amount expended by the United States in World War II.

Serious legal questions and widespread diplomatic protest was raised by the United States' use of some 7,000 tons of CS gas. Although the United States was not at that time a signatory to the Geneva Protocol of 1925 (prohibiting the use of gas warfare), American presidents beginning with Franklin Roosevelt had affirmed the United States' intention to abide by it. Despite this position, Vietnam witnessed the first battlefield use of gas since Italy's Ethiopian campaign and Japan's assault on China in the late 1930s. Critics argued that renewed use of gas on the battlefield would weaken the international restraints against the employment of more toxic chemical weapons in future wars. In response to strong opposition, particularly that marshalled in the United Nations General Assembly, Washington agreed to curtail its use of CS gas.

The United States also employed herbicides for the destruction of food crops and for the destruction of extensive forest areas. Although only minor herbicidal operations had been carried out before as military operations (by the British in Malaya and the French in Algeria) and despite the fact that little was known about the ultimate impact of such operations, the U.S. applied some 83,000 tons of herbicides in Vietnam. In food-denial and area-denial programs, herbicides were employed at strengths twelve to fifteen times that used in commercial agricultural operations. During the crop destruction program, from 1962 until the end of 1970, some 10 percent of all the cultivated land in South Vietnam was "treated." Additionally, data from American sources indicates that 20,000 square kilometers (5 1/2 million acres) of forest were in part destroyed by aerial spraying. This included the destruction of some 300,000 acres comprising one-half of the total coastal and delta mangrove forests, and 4 million acres of mature upland forest, about one-fifth the total forest area of South Vietnam (roughly the size of Massachusetts). This was justified at the time with the careless euphemism that the program was a "test of our enlarged military capability."

The assault upon Vietnam's ecology was expanded by the U.S. army engineers' use of specially designed bulldozers (the "Rome Plows," so named because they were built in Rome, Georgia) to scrape other forest areas clear of vegetation. This program stripped the land at the rate of 1,000 acres a day; by mid-1971 some 750,000 acres had been cleared, resulting in a denuded area roughly the size of Rhode Island. South Vietnam's ecological problems were also complicated by heavy bombing, particularly by B-52s. It has been estimated that these activities left some 23 million craters which buried the thin topsoil and created swampy, unplowable conditions.

While the total impact of this unprecedented disruption of Vietnam's basic ecology is still to be assessed, it was feared that the combination of programs (especially the herbicides) could bring about a permanent change in the basic soil structure. It is for these reasons that critics of American military technology and tactics labelled its programs "ecocide."

Second Indochina War: Costs and Consequences

The toll of dead, wounded and missing-in-action was staggering. Preliminary statistics place American casualties at 46,000 killed (with an additional 10,000 nonbattlefield deaths) and over 300,000 wounded. South Vietnamese military losses were 215,000 killed and 603,000 wounded, a ratio of one killed to three wounded. Over 415,000 South Vietnamese civilians were killed and approximately 1,021,500 were wounded. North Vietnamese and "Vietcong" losses were 1,075,000 killed, with numbers of wounded not known. (If one used the 1:3 ratio, this would imply over 3 million wounded.) Approximately ten times the number of North and South Vietnamese were killed and wounded as were Americans. The more than 300,000 military personnel, engineers and air defense specialists China claims to have sent into North Vietnam apparently suffered "thousands" of casualties, both killed and wounded, as a result of U.S. aerial bombing raids.

Casualty figures for Laos and Cambodia are less complete. It has been estimated that some 700,000 Cambodian civilians were either killed or wounded by March 1975, with 99 percent of the Cambodian civilian casualties occurring outside Phnom Penh. Civilian casualties accounted for 90 percent or more of those killed in Indochina.

United States aircraft losses have been placed at 4,900 helicopters and 3,700 fixed-wing aircraft; nearly 1,100 of the latter were lost over North Vietnam. The monetary cost of the war to the American taxpayers was around 225.2 billion dollars in direct outlays. The total cost of veterans and survivors benefits and interest payments may amount to as much as three times the sum of the direct outlays.

The various military programs also caused the violent displacement of large numbers of the Indochinese population. Aerial bombing and the establishment of free-fire zones have accounted for the majority of these refugees. At the time of the cease-fire in 1973 about one-third of the South Vietnamese, Laotian and Cambodian populations were classified as refugees: 8.5 million South Vietnamese out of a population of 20 million; 1 million Laotians out of about 3 million; and 2 million Cambodians out of 7 million. By January 1975 these figures had reached 11.7 million South Vietnamese, 2 million Laotians and 3.4 million Cambodians. Some 17.1 million people had become refugees in Indochina in the ten years between 1965 and 1975. A return to economic normalcy would be extremely difficult as rubber plantations and commercial forests were destroyed in the South, as was industry in the North; crater-pocked cropland posed a difficult reclamation task in both the North and South. The destruction of bridges, railroads, tunnels and buildings was extensive. Numerous towns in both North and South Vietnam were leveled.

Efforts to extend the control of the Saigon government through the establishment of strategic hamlets, and relocation and pacification programs were often not a military success, and caused serious social damage. The disruption was augmented by the Vietcong practice of selective assassination and by its American-sponsored counterpart, "Operation Phoenix" which, as part of the pacification program, "neutralized" some 84,000 members of the suspected "VC infrastructure" in South Vietnam—21,000 of these individuals were killed between 1967 and 1971.

Most wars have had atrocities and Vietnam was no exception. The United States was charged with violating the Geneva convention (1925) on gas warfare as a result of its use of tear gas and herbicides, with ignoring the traditional immunities of noncombatants because of its "free-fire" zones and bombing tactics, and with ignoring the prisoner-of-war rules because of the torture of North Vietnamese and Vietcong POWs. American battlefield discipline collapsed at My Lai and, so critics have claimed, elsewhere. In turn the United States claimed that the North Vietnamese and Vietcong were guilty of war crimes for their execution of civilians at Hue during the Tet offensive, for their practice of impressing civilians as supply-bearers, for their mistreatment and torture of American POWs (especially pilots), and for their employment of "blind" weapons (such as rockets) against urban noncombatants.

It would appear, however, that the vastly greater amount of questionable conduct, regarding injury and damage must be lodged against the United States. The preponderance of charges stems from the abundance of military firepower available to the United States and from the inability to impose (or, indeed, to recognize the need for) restraint in applying its modern arsenal.

At the beginning of the Second Indochina War, American combat personnel performed with enthusiasm, but the protracted combat, with battlefield objectives becoming less clearly related to the conclusion of the war, had unexpected adverse effects. Morale gradually deteriorated until some units refused orders to engage the enemy. Racial disputes broke out between white and black servicemen and assaults called "fragging," upon officers and noncommissioned officers, became prevalent. Drug use was also a problem; marijuana use was widespread, especially in rear areas, and the extensive use of heroin became a matter of grave concern to military leaders. The Army was much harder hit by the decline of morale than either the Air Force or the Navy.

Much as been written about the military, political and social effects of this violent struggle. But some of the most important studies may not be written. Whether the critics of the war fairly evaluated the problems encountered by the United States' armed services or not, most observers anticipated that American military leaders faced a sizeable, yet vital task in reevaluating the many facets of this lengthy contest. Which strategies and tactics worked? Which weapons systems accomplished their objectives? Even more importantly, which ones did *not* work, and why? If this task had been undertaken honestly and candidly, the armed services and the nation would have benefitted. Unfortunately the defensiveness of most military writers and the redirection of policymakers to new issues have largely removed questions related to the Second Indochina War from the agenda of military analysis.

The evidence also suggests that the policymakers in succeeding administrations never understood one essential factor: at no point during American involvement in Vietnam did American leadership exhibit any genuine understanding of the essential political nature of the Second Indochina War. A former State Department expert on the Far East has clearly delineated the problem: "By the evidence, the policymakers in Washington never really understood, from beginning to end, what the Indochinese revolution was all about—that it was inherently a political, not a military struggle. Blinded by this error, the United States tried to dominate and suppress the Indochinese revolutionaries—and failed ingloriously. Whether it can repair its position in Asia will depend on whether it has learned the lesson of its eleven-year Indochinese war: Asia is not to be molded after American patterns.[4] He might also have added an admonition credited to General (then Secretary of State) George C. Marshall, that any political problem continually defined in military terms soon becomes a military problem.

Third Indochina War

Peace did not come to Indochina with either America's 1973 withdrawal or Hanoi's 1975 victory. In 1977, a serious dispute erupted between the neighboring communist states of Vietnam and Kampuchea (Cambodia), which ultimately influenced relations between Vietnam and China. Border issues remaining from the days of French occupation had been part of the contention, but these issues were minor compared to contemporary political disputes, territorial ambitions and security considerations.

Immediately after the conclusion of the Second Indochina War, both Vietnam and Kampuchea attempted large and forcible programs to move their populations back into the countryside to produce basic agricultural staples. These policies were designed to reverse the extreme concentrations of population in Phnom Penh, Saigon and other large urban centers. These concentrations resulted from American saturation bombing of the countryside, the persistent Vietcong policy of forcing firefights within villages and hamlets, and the general urban shift in progress since 1945. In both Kampuchea and Vietnam, the population relocation programs caused social upheaval, individual deprivation and considerable loss of life.

Fighting broke out when Vietnam invaded Kampuchea on December 25, 1978. Two months later China retaliated by attacking Vietnam. This renewed warfare resulted from several factors, but Vietnam's desire to reunite the three Indochina states under its control loomed large. By the end of 1979, the Vietnamese appeared to have accomplished their objective. They had 30,000 troops garrisoned in Laos; occupation forces installed in Kampuchea; and a stalemate on their border with China. Hanoi was soon to discover that the price of conquest and empire was high. The prolonged occupation of Kampuchea, required to suppress local resistence, required some 200,000 troops and added a heavy burden to Vietnam's depleted economy.

China's limited, but bloody, military incursion along Vietnam's northern border began on February 19, 1979. China's displeasure stemmed from Vietnam's desire for hegemony over Indochina, dependence upon the Soviet Union, and mistreatment of its resident Chinese. Chinese officials had sought to play down the Sino–Soviet dispute in its dealings with Hanoi, and had shown restraint in commenting on Vietnam's imperial ambitions; but when the *hua giao* (Vietnamese of Chinese extraction) began to flee Vietnam in 1978, the Chinese publically accused Hanoi of persecuting its Chinese residents. While an uneasy armistice existed along the China–Vietnam border by the end of 1979, relations between the two neighbors remained strained. The Chinese demanded that Vietnam withdraw its troops from Kampuchea and Laos, and reduce its connection with the Soviet Union as a price for a return to peaceful relations.

The extent to which the Third Indochina War was linked to great-power considerations is not clear; but some connections seem likely. For example, Hanoi invaded Kampuchea a month after signing a friendship treaty with the Soviet Union (November 3, 1978), and China attacked Vietnam about a month after normalizing its relations with the United States. Chinese leaders have been concerned about the Soviet–Vietnamese relationship and the effect that this situation has on the general Sino–Soviet dispute.

Ironically, the United States found itself with a new Indochina problem as the Vietnamese encouraged or intimidated its resident Chinese to flee. These new refugees, the so-called "boat people," caught the attention of the American media, and immigration laws were amended to allow some of these displaced individuals to enter the United States.

Conclusions

The Indochina saga appears to be a continuing one. Its various wars affected the emotions and politics of peoples and governments around the world. The impact of these wars upon the United States and Southeast Asia has been especially traumatic.

The interminable duration and ever-mounting destructiveness of the Second Indochina War caused many Americans, especially the younger generation, to reevaluate the American Cold War attitudes and policies, its emphasis on military over public priorities, and its moral conscience. In these Americans, the conflict aroused a sense of dissatisfaction which manifested itself in emotional and political dissent. In other Americans, the response to the conflict was a less dramatic but equally significant defense of the old order, of national honor, and of American commitment to anticommunism. Writing in 1982—seven years after the end of the war—it is interesting to see how quickly the issues involved in the U.S. military intervention in Vietnam lost their currency as a touchstone of U.S. foreign policy decision-making.

The purpose of this *Guide* is to facilitate the extraction, from historical sources, of the knowledge that should be transformed into political policy. The novelist Saul Bellow wrote in his book *Humboldt's Gift* that to be an American is to go "... uncorrected by the main history of human suffering." This is similar to a more famous dictum by the American philosopher George Santayana: "Those who are ignorant of history are condemned to repeat it." The hope of the editors is that this will not happen.

— *Milton Leitenberg*

NOTES

1. See the Senator Gravel Edition of *The Pentagon Papers*, 5 vols. (Boston: Beacon, 1971–1972).

2. Each volume of *The Pentagon Papers*, cited above, has appended a list of "official justifications" for American involvement in the Vietnam conflict.

3. For a documented development of these arguments, see Milton Leitenberg, "America in Vietnam: Statistics of a War," *Survival* 14:6 (1972): 268–274.

4. O. Edmund Clubb, "The Cease-Fire," *Nation* 216:7 (Feb. 12, 1973): 201.

Chronology

xxx   The Wars in Vietnam, Cambodia and Laos, 1945–1982

pledge of aid to Diem; increases U.S. advisors to 18,000 and permits their entry into combat

1962
February 3: Diem begins "strategic hamlet" program

February 8: U.S. Military Advisory Command, Vietnam, formed under General Hawkins

July 23: Geneva Pact reached, neutralizing Laos

August: First Australian military personnel arrive in South Vietnam

1963
January 2: South Vietnamese defeated at Battle of Ap Bac

June 3: Buddhist disturbances in Hue

November 2: Diem overthrown and killed by junta led by General Duong Van Minh

1964
January 30: General Nguyen Khanh overthrows Minh junta

April 25: General Westmoreland appointed to succeed General Hawkins as commander of Military Advisory Command, Vietnam

May: Pathet Lao take Plain of Jars again; U.S. begins bombing of Pathet Lao

June 30: General Maxwell Taylor becomes U.S. Ambassador to South Vietnam

August 2 & 4: Gulf of Tonkin incident; Congress authorizes "all necessary measures"

1965
February 7: U.S. begins bombing of North Vietnam following a Vietcong raid on Pleiku

March 8: First U.S. combat troops land in South Vietnam

March 24–25: First "teach-in" held at University of Michigan

June: Nguyen Cao Ky becomes premier; on 15th, U.S. troops launch their first ground operation against Vietcong

July 12: Moscow announces military aid for North Vietnam

July 14: First U.S. plane brought down by a SAM over North Vietnam

November 4: U.S. forces reach 154,000

November 14: First U.S. combat operations against North Vietnamese army at Ia Drang

December 24: U.S. begins second bombing pause; Hanoi calls for adherence to Geneva Accords

1966
January 31: Bombing of North Vietnam resumed

February 6–8: Honolulu Conference

between President Johnson and Premier Ky

March–June: Buddhist uprising against Ky

April 21: U.S.S.R. complains again that Chinese delaying aid to North Vietnam; Chinese deny the charge on May 3

April 23: First major air battle over North Vietnam

July 25: Ky urges invasion of North Vietnam

July 30: Congressional protest begins

August 21: President Johnson says he informed Ky U.S. forces would be withdrawn and aid halted if North invaded

August 28: U.S.S.R. admits training North Vietnamese pilots; a week later it acknowledges the training of SAM crews

October 26: President Johnson visits Cam Ranh Bay

December 8: U.S. forces reach 362,000

December 23: President Johnson orders U.S. planes not to bomb within ten miles of Hanoi

1967
April: Massive antiwar demonstrations throughout U.S.

May 18: "Free-fire" zone created near Demilitarized Zone at 17th parallel

September 3: Nguyen Van Thieu elected president of South Vietnam; takes office October 31

1968
January 15: Bombing of Haiphong area suspended

January 21: Siege of Khe Sanh begins

January 31–February 26: Vietcong Tet offensive

February 6: Fall of Lang Vei

February 10: U.S. resumes bombing of Haiphong

March 19: A Shau Valley Operation begins, lasts until May 17

March 31: President Johnson announces he will not seek reelection; orders cessation of bombing of North Vietnam except near DMZ

March: General Westmoreland succeeded by General Abrams

April 1: Clark Clifford succeeds Robert McNamara as secretary of defense

April 3: North Vietnam accepts U.S. offer to negotiate

April 7: Khe Sanh siege lifted; abandoned on July 5

May 13: Peace talks begin in Paris

October 31: President Johnson orders halt to bombing of North Vietnam; bombing in Laos intensified

1969

January 25: Four-party peace talks open in Paris

March 16: My Lai incident occurs

May: President Nixon begins gradual withdrawal of 500,000 U.S. forces from Vietnam

July 25: Nixon Doctrine announced

September 3: Death of Ho Chi Minh

October 15 & November 15: Nationwide "Moratorium" demonstrations, the November protest is largest to date

November–December: President Nixon announces "Vietnamization" program

1970

March 18: Prince Sihanouk ousted from Cambodian government by Lon Nol

April 29: South Vietnamese forces invade Cambodia

May 1: U.S. troops enter Cambodia; widespread protests, particularly on campuses

May 5: Kent State students killed

May 15: Jackson State University students killed

June 24: U.S. Senate repeals the Tonkin Gulf Resolution by vote of 81 to 0

June 29: Last U.S. troops leave Cambodia

November 21: U.S. commando raid on Son Tay POW camp in North Vietnam

1971

February 8–March 25: South Vietnamese troops invade Laos

April 27: Largest nationwide antiwar demonstration

October 3: Thieu reelected president of South Vietnam

1972

March 23: Paris peace talks resumed

March 30: North Vietnam and Vietcong "Easter Offensive" begins

April 5: Siege of An Loc begins, relieved June 12

April 6: U.S. bombing of North Vietnam resumed

April 28: Dong Ha captured by Vietcong

May 1: Quang Tri captured by North Vietnamese

May 4: Paris peace talks suspended, resumed July 13

May 9: Nixon orders mining of North Vietnamese ports including Haiphong,

increases bombing of North Vietnam

May 10: Martial law declared in South Vietnam

June 28: General Weyland relieves General Abrams

September 15: Quang Tri retaken by South Vietnamese

October 26: Hanoi announces willingness to accept cease-fire and return American POWs

November 7: Nixon overwhelmingly reelected president

December 16: Kissinger breaks off Paris peace talks

December 18–30: Heavy U.S. bombing campaigning around Hanoi and Haiphong

1973

January 8: Paris peace talks resumed

January 15: Nixon halts bombing of North Vietnam

January 23: Cease-fire agreement initialed in Paris

January: Separate Laotian cease-fire concluded

January 28: Cease-fire comes into effect

June 24: Graham Martin becomes U.S. Ambassador to South Vietnam

July 3: Congress cuts off funds for bombing of Cambodia; last missions flown on August 15

November–December: North Vietnamese division carries out first "strategic raids" in Quang Duc province

November 7: Congress overrides Nixon's veto of War Powers Act

November 14: Khmer Rouge attack Phnom Penh

1974

February: South Vietnamese attack Vietcong areas around Saigon; in April Vietcong and North Vietnamese forces counterattack

April 3–4: Congress reduces U.S. aid to South Vietnam

April 12: South Vietnam withdraws from Paris bilateral talks; subsequently North Vietnam walks out of Joint Military Commission in Saigon

August 9: Nixon resigns; Ford becomes president

October: North Vietnamese decide on a tentative, piecemeal winter–spring offensive

November: Khmer Rouge cut land routes to Phnom Penh; U.S. begins massive air and river supply efforts

December 14–15: North Vietnamese launch first phase of winter– spring offensive in Mekong Delta

1975
January 7: Phuoc Binh falls to North Vietnamese forces in second phase of campaign

January: U.S.S.R. increases military aid to North Vietnam and encourages offensive; U.S. denounces cease-fire accord on grounds North Vietnamese have already violated it

March 1: North Vietnamese launch third phase of offensive in Central Highlands

March 14: Ban Me Thuot falls; South Vietnamese military collapse begins

March 25: Hue falls

March 30: Danang falls

April 17: Khmer Rouge capture Phnom Penh, Lon Nol flees

April 30: Saigon falls, last Americans flee

December: Pathet Lao formally take power in Laos

1977
January: Initial conflict on Cambodia–Vietnam border

July: Signing of Laotian–Vietnamese Friendship Treaty; Vietnamese troops garrisoned in Laos

1978
August: Cambodia–Vietnam border war heats up

December: Vietnam launches all-out push to occupy all of Cambodia

1979
February: People's Republic of China attacks Vietnam

The Wars in Vietnam, Cambodia and Laos, 1945–1982

❧ Chapter One ❧
General Reference Aids

THE VOLUME OF PUBLISHED ITEMS on the Vietnamese conflict and modern Southeast Asia makes compiling a definitive list difficult. This guide collects and organizes important contemporary and retrospective books, dissertations, research papers and essays.

The general reference aids in this chapter—bibliographies, guides, indexes, documentary collections, journals, atlases and yearbooks—list additional research materials. Some of these, particularly *America: History and Life* (63), ABC POL SCI (61), and *Recently Published Articles* (64), are especially valuable in locating books and essays printed after the *Guide* went to press.

Phan Thien Chau's *Vietnamese Communism* (38) is a particularly useful Vietnamese source. The author has interpreted his topic broadly and has included many Western-language items in his well-arranged, comprehensive volume. Western-language materials, as well as Vietnamese-language sources, are listed in the *Bibliography of Asian Studies* (the September issue of the *Journal of Asian Studies*). Before 1966, see the Association of Asian Studies' *Cumulative Bibliography of Asian Studies, 1941–1970* (6–9). John Chen's *Vietnam: A Comprehensive Bibliography* (14) indexes 2,300 books and pamphlets, mostly in Western languages, and is arranged in alphabetical order by author. While this *Guide* updates our original volume (27), it does not repeat every item, although we have retained those items we felt to be still of value. Finally, Michael Cotter's *Vietnam: A Guide to Reference Sources* (15) is a very useful tool, particularly for the advanced researcher.

Specialized bibliographies and other reference tools are located throughout the *Guide*; we assume the researcher will be better served with these reference items located close to their related specialized topic.

Many of the contemporary essays appearing in "opinion" journals were repetitive; we have not attempted to include them all. They can be located in the *Reader's Guide* (71), *PAIS* (70) and other periodical indexes. Although we have included several items from the *New York Times Magazine* and the *New York Review of Books*, both still may be profitably mined for contemporary views; the same is true for *Dissent, Army, Air Force & Space Digest* and many other journals. We have also found that the *Congressional Record* is a valuable, but often overlooked, source of contemporary newspaper articles and pamphlets. When an issue or episode becomes a controversial public topic, representatives and senators frequently request that such items—favorable to their personal views—be reprinted in the *Congressional Record*; for example see Chapter 7, "Easter Offensive, 1972," the section on "Bombing of Dikes."

The *Pentagon Papers* (130–132) represent the single most valuable collection of documents readily available to the researcher. The three editions should be compared, since no single edition contains all items. The *Pentagon Papers* must be employed cautiously as the collection was prepared by Department of Defense civilians who concentrated on materials in their files and largely ignored those in the White House and State Department. Perhaps the best evaluation of this collection is by Kahin (2912).

Subsequent to the publication of the *Pentagon Papers*, many additional documents have been declassified and made available to researchers. These are indexed by the *Declassified Documents Quarterly* (119).

Hanoi has not made available internal documents related to policymaking, nor is it to be expected that such materials will be accessible to historians in the near future. However, published essays, proclamations and other documents for the years 1945 to 1973 have been collected, together with Western materials, by Porter (133).

Chronologies

A source of brief scattered chronologies (1945–1965) is the Pentagon Papers, *the Senator Gravel Edition (131). Also see U.S. Senate, Committee on Foreign Relations, Background Information Relating to Southeast Asia and Vietnam (137–143), which contains an extensive chronology (June 1948–August 1973).*

1. Great Britain. Central Office of Information. Reference Division. *Viet Nam, Laos and Cambodia: Chronology of Events, 1968–70.* London: HMSO, 1970.

2. Hunt, David. "Chronology of the Vietnam War." *Radical America* 8:1/2 (1974): 182–184.

3. *Naval and Maritime Chronology, 1961–1971.* Annapolis, MD: Naval Institute Press, 1972.

4. Staaversen, Van J., and H.S. Wolk. "Southeast Asia Political–Military Chronology, 1948–1967." *Air Force Magazine* 50 (Mar. 1967): 137–138, 141–142.

5. U.S. Air Force. *Chronology of SEA Conflict, 1945–1967.* Wright–Patterson AFB, OH: Air Force Logistics Command, Historical Research Division, Apr. 1969.

Bibliographies

Other, more specialized, bibliographies have been placed elsewhere under the appropriate subject headings.

Books
6. Association of Asian Studies. *Cumulative Bibliography of Asian Studies, 1941–1965: Author Bibliography.* 4 vols. Boston: G.K. Hall, 1970.

7. _____. *Cumulative Bibliography of Asian Studies, 1941–1965: Subject Bibliography.* 4 vols. Boston: G.K. Hall, 1970.

8. _____. *Cumulative Bibliography of Asian Studies, 1966–1970: Author Bibliography.* 3 vols. Boston: G.K. Hall, 1972.

9. _____. *Cumulative Bibliography of Asian Studies, 1966–1970: Subject Bibliography.* 3 vols. Boston: G.K.

Hall, 1972. The annual bibliography previously printed in the *Journal of Asian Studies* has been detached and is printed as a separate annual volume; the one for 1975 was printed in 1978.

10. Auvade, Robert. *Bibliographie critique des oeuvres parues sur l'Indochine française.* Paris: G-P Maisonneuve & Larose, 1965.

11. Berton, Peter, and Alvin Z. Rubinstein. *Soviet Works on Southeast Asia: A Bibliography of Non-Periodical Literature.* Los Angeles: University of Southern California Press, 1967.

12. Birnbaum, Eleazar, ed. *Books on Asia from the Near East to Far East.* Toronto: University of Toronto Press, 1971.

13. Bixler, Paul. *Southeast Asia: Bibliographic Directions in a Complex Area.* Middletown, CT: Choice, 1974.

14. Chen, John H.M. *Vietnam: A Comprehensive Bibliography.* Metuchen, NJ: Scarecrow, 1973.

15. Cotter, Michael. *Vietnam: A Guide to Reference Sources.* Boston: G.K. Hall, 1977. This is a valuable tool for advanced researchers.

16. Council on Foreign Relations. *Foreign Affairs Bibliography: A Selected and Annotated List of Books on International Relations.* 5 vols. New York: Harper; Bowker, 1933– . These volumes, covering 1919–1972, are supplemented by book notes in *Foreign Affairs.*

17. Embree, John F., and Lillian O. Dotson. *Bibliography of the Peoples and Cultures of Mainland Southeast Asia.* New Haven, CT: Yale University Press, 1950.

18. Hay, S.N., and M.M. Case. *Southeast Asian History: A Bibliographic Guide.* New York: Praeger, 1962.

19. Hobbs, Cecil C., ed. *Southeast Asia: An Annotated Bibliography of Selected Reference Sources in Western Languages.* Washington, DC: Library of Congress, 1964.

20. _____, et al., eds. *Indochina: A Bibliography of the Land and the People.* Washington, DC: Library of Congress, 1950.

21. Johnson, Donald C. *A Guide to Reference Materials on Southeast Asia.* New Haven, CT: Yale University Press, 1970.

22. Jumper, Roy. *Bibliography on the Political and Administrative History of Vietnam, 1802–1962: Selected and Annotated.* Saigon: Michigan State University, Vietnam Advisory Group, 1962.

23. Keyes, Jane G., ed. *A Bibliography of North Vietnamese Publications in the Cornell University Library.*

Data Paper no. 47. Ithaca, NY: Cornell University, Southeast Asia Program, 1962.

24. _____. *A Bibliography of Western-Language Publications Concerning North Vietnam in the Cornell University Library*. Data Paper no. 63, supplement to no. 47. Ithaca, NY: Cornell University, Southeast Asia Program, 1966.

25. Lafont, Pierre B. *Bibliographie du Laos*. Paris: École Française d'Extrême Orient, 1964.

26. Legler, Anton, and Frieda Bauer. *Der Krieg in Vietnam: Bericht und Bibliographie*. 5 vols. Frankfurt: Bernard und Graefe, 1969–1979.

27. Leitenberg, Milton, and Richard Dean Burns. *The Vietnam Conflict: Its Geographical Dimensions, Political Traumas, & Military Developments*. Santa Barbara, CA: ABC-Clio, 1973.

28. McKinstry, John. *Bibliography of Laos and Ethnically Related Areas*. Laos Project Paper no. 22. Los Angeles: University of California, Department of Anthropology, 1961.

29. _____. *Bibliography of Laos and Ethnically Related Areas to 1961*. Berkeley: University of California Press, 1962.

30. McVey, Ruth. *Bibliography of Soviet Publications on Southeast Asia as Listed in the Library of Congress Monthly Index of Russian Acquisitions*. Data Paper no. 34. Ithaca, NY: Cornell University, Southeast Asia Program, 1959.

31. Michigan State University. Vietnam Project. *What to Read on Vietnam: A Selected Annotated Bibliography*. 2d ed. New York: Institute of Pacific Relations, 1960.

32. Morrison, Gayle. *A Guide to Books on Southeast Asian History (1961–1966)*. Santa Barbara, CA: ABC-Clio, 1967.

33. Nguyen The Anh. *Bibliographie critique sur les relations entre Vietnam et l'Occident des origines à 1954*. New York: Adler, 1967.

34. Nunn, G. Raymond. *Asia: A Selected and Annotated Guide to Reference Works*. Cambridge, MA: MIT Press, 1971.

35. _____, ed. *South and Southeast Asia: A Bibliography of Bibliographies*. Honolulu: University of Hawaii, East–West Center, 1966.

36. O'Brien, P.A., ed. *Vietnam*. Bibliographic Series 4, no. 113. Adelaide: State Library of South Australia, 1968.

37. Oey, Giok Po. *Checklist of the Vietnamese Holdings of the Watson Collection, Cornell University Libraries,*

as of June 1971. Data Paper no. 84. Ithaca, NY: Cornell University, Southeast Asia Program, 1971.

38. Phan Thien Chau. *Vietnamese Communism: A Research Bibliography*. Westport, CT: Greenwood, 1975.

39. Ramsey, Russell W., ed. *Some Keys to the Vietnam Puzzle*. Bibliography Series, no. 7. Gainesville: University of Florida Libraries, 1968.

40. Thrombley, Woodworth G., and William J. Siffin. *Thailand: Politics, Economy, and Socio-Cultural Setting: A Selective Guide to the Literature*. Bloomington: Indiana University Press, 1972.

41. Tregonning, K.G. *Southeast Asia: A Critical Bibliography*. Tucson: University of Arizona Press, 1969.

42. United Nations. Dag Hammarskjöld Library. *Lower Mekong Basin: Selected Bibliography*. 2 vols. New York, 1969.

43. _____. E.C.A.F.E. Mekong Documentation Centre. *Cambodia: A Select Bibliography*. Bangkok, 1967.

44. U.S. Army. *Insular Southeast Asia: A Bibliographic Survey*. DA Pamphlet 550–12. Washington, DC: GPO, 1971.

45. _____. *Peninsular Southeast Asia: A Bibliographic Survey of Literature*. DA Pamphlet 550–14. Washington, DC: GPO, 1972.

46. U.S. Department of State. *The Republic of Vietnam: A Bibliography*. Washington, DC: External Research Staff, 1963.

47. U.S. Military Assistance Institute Library. *Vietnam: A Selected Bibliography*. Arlington, VA, 1965.

48. *University of California Holdings on Vietnam*. Berkeley: University of California, Center for South and Southeast Asia Studies, May 1968.

Essays

49. Bezacier, L. "Liste des travaux relatifs au Vietnam publiés par L'École Française d'Extrême-Orient." *France-Asie* 13 (Oct.–Nov. 1958): 535–553.

50. Braestrup, Peter. "Vietnam as History." *Wilson Quarterly* 2 (Spring 1978): 178–187.

51. Clammer, John R. "French Studies on the Chinese in Indochina: A Bibliographical Survey." *Journal of Southeast Asian Studies* 12 (Mar. 1981): 15–26.

52. Dunn, Joe P. "In Search of Lessons: The Development of a Vietnam Historiography." *Parameters* 9 (Dec. 1979): 28–40.

53. Fall, Bernard B. "Recent Publications on Indochina." *Pacific Affairs* 29 (Mar. 1956): 57–64.

54. Gallo, P.J. "Understanding the Vietnam War: A Bibliographic Essay." *New University Thought* 6 (May–June 1968): 29–34.

55. Ginsburgs, George. "Soviet Sources on the Law of North Vietnam." *Asian Survey* 13 (July 1973): 659–676; (Oct. 1973): 980–988.

56. Leifer, Michael. "Vietnam and the Premises of Intervention: A Review Article." *Pacific Affairs* 45 (Summer 1973): 268–272.

57. Marr, David. "Vietnamese Sources on Vietnam." *Bulletin of Concerned Asian Scholars* 4 (Winter 1972): 119–124.

58. Pike, Douglas. "Writing on Vietnam." *Problems of Communism* 30 (Nov.–Dec. 1981): 60–64.

59. Polner, Murray. "Vietnam War Stores." *Trans-Action* 6 (Nov. 1968): 8–20.

60. "Vietnam Bibliography." *New York University Law Review* 45 (June 1970): 749–759.

Guides and Indexes

The following guides and indexes are valuable aids for updating this volume.

GUIDES

61. *ABC POL SCI: A Bibliography of Contents: Political Science & Government.* Santa Barbara, CA: ABC-Clio, 1969– .

62. *Air University Library Index to Military Periodicals.* Maxwell Air Force Base, AL: Air University Library, 1949– .

63. *America: History and Life; A Guide to Periodical Literature.* Santa Barbara, CA: ABC-Clio, 1963– .

64. American Historical Association. *Recently Published Articles.* Washington, DC, 1976– . Three to four numbers appear each year.

65. *Historical Abstracts. Part B: Twentieth Century Abstracts (1914–).* Santa Barbara, CA: ABC-Clio, 1955– .

66. *Index to Foreign Legal Periodicals and Collections of Essays.* Chicago: William D. Murphy, 1960– .

67. *Index to Periodical Articles Related to Law.* New York: Glenville, 1959– .

68. *International Bibliography of Economics.* Chicago: Aldine, 1955– .

69. *International Political Science Abstracts.* Oxford: Basil Blackwell, 1951– .

70. *Public Affairs Information Service (PAIS) Bulletin.* New York: PAIS, 1951– .

71. *Reader's Guide to Periodical Literature.* New York: H.W. Wilson, 1905– .

72. *Social Science and Humanities Index.* New York: H.W. Wilson, 1913– .

INDEXES TO NEWSPAPERS

73. *The Christian Science Monitor Index.* Corvallis, OR: Helen M. Cropsey, 1960– .

74. *Index to The Times.* London: The Times, 1809– .

75. *The New York Times Index.* New York: The New York Times, 1913– .

76. *The Wall Street Journal Index.* New York: Dow-Jones, 1958– .

Journals

77. Nguyen Kuan Dao, and K. Richard Gardner. *Bibliography of Periodicals Published in Vietnam.* East Lansing: Michigan State University, Vietnam Project, 1958– .

78. Yale University Library. Southeast Asia Collection. *Checklist of Southeast Asia Serials.* New Haven, CT, 1969– .

OFFICIAL AND SEMI-OFFICIAL

79. *Current Digest of the Soviet Press.* New York: Joint Committee on Slavic Studies, 1949– .

80. *Current Notes on International Affairs.* Canberra, Australia: Department of External Affairs, 1936– .

81. *External Affairs*. Ottawa: Department of External Affairs, 1948– .

82. *External Affairs Review*. Wellington, New Zealand: Department of External Affairs, 1951– .

83. Foreign Broadcast Information Service (FBIS). *Daily Report*. Washington, DC: Library of Congress, 1947– .

84. *Free China Review*. Taipei: Republic of China, 1951– .

85. *International Affairs: A Monthly Journal of Political Analysis*. Moscow: Izvestia Printing Office, 1955– .

86. *Peking Review: A Magazine of Chinese News and Views*. Peking: People's Republic of China, 1958– .

87. *SEATO Record*. Bangkok: SEATO Headquarters, 1962– .

88. *South Vietnam in Struggle*. Hanoi: South Viet Nam National Front for Liberation, 1966– . [biweekly]

89. *Soviet Documents: Current Statements, Speeches, Reports, and Editorials*. New York: Crosscurrent Press, 1963– .

90. U.S. Department of State. *U.S. Department of State Bulletin*. Washington, DC: GPO, 1939– .

91. U.S. Mission in Viet Nam. *Viet-Nam Documents and Research Notes*, nos. 1–117. Saigon: U.S. Information Service, Oct. 1967–Apr. 1974.

92. _____. *Vietnam Information Notes*. Washington, DC: GPO, 1967– .

93. *Vietnam*. Hanoi: Democratic Republic of Vietnam, 1957. [monthly]

94. *Vietnam Courier*. Hanoi: Democratic Republic of Vietnam, 1963– . [weekly; monthly after June 1972]

95. *Vietnam Economic Report*. Saigon: Vietnam Council on Foreign Relations, 1970– . [monthly]

96. *Vietnam Magazine*. Saigon: Vietnam Council on Foreign Relations, 1967– . [monthly]

97. *Vietnam Newsletter*. Saigon: Vietnam Council on Foreign Relations, 1968– . [weekly]

98. *Vietnam Review*. Washington, DC: Embassy of Vietnam, 1962– . [quarterly]

99. *Vietnamese Studies*. Hanoi: Democratic Republic of Vietnam, 1964– . [supersedes *Vietnam Advances*]

ACADEMIC AND PUBLIC OPINION

100. *Asia Recorder: A Weekly Digest of Outstanding Asian Events with Index*. New Delhi: Sankaran, 1955– .

101. *Asian Survey: A Monthly Review of Contemporary Asian Affairs*. Berkeley: University of California Press, 1961– .

102. *Australian Outlook*. Melbourne: Australian Institute of International Affairs, 1947– .

103. *Bulletin of Concerned Asian Scholars*. Charlemont, ME, 1969– .

104. *China Mainland Review*. Hong Kong: University of Hong Kong, 1966– .

105. *China Quarterly*. London: Congress of Cultural Freedom, 1960– .

106. *Contemporary Japan: A Review of Far Eastern Affairs*. Tokyo: Foreign Affairs Association of Japan, 1932– .

107. *Eastern Economist*. New Delhi: Eastern Economist, 1943– .

108. *Facts on File: A Weekly News Guide, with Cumulative Index*. New York: Facts on File, 1940– .

109. *Far Eastern Economic Review*. Hong Kong: Far Eastern Economic Review, 1946– .

110. *Indochina Chronicle*. Washington, DC: Indochina Resource Center, July 1971– . [monthly newsletter]

111. *Kessing's Contemporary Archives*. London: Kessing's Publications, 1931– . [weekly summary with index]

112. *Pacific Affairs: An International Review of the Far East and Pacific Area*. Vancouver: University of British Columbia, 1928– .

113. *Pakistan Horizon*. Karachi: Pakistan Institute of International Affairs, 1948– .

114. *Thoi-Bao-Ga*. Cambridge, MA, Jan. 1970– . [monthly newsletter]

115. *Viet Report: An Emergency News Bulletin on Southeast Asian Affairs*. New York: Viet Report, June 1965–1968.

116. *Vietnam Perspectives*. New York: American Friends of Vietnam, 1965– . [irregular]

117. *Vital Speeches of the Day*. Pelham, NY: City News Publishing, 1934– .

Documentary Collections

The Pentagon Papers *represent the most extensive and valuable printed collection relating to U.S. involvement in the Indochina conflict. For evaluations of the* Papers, *see (2912).*

118. *Cumulative Subject Index to the Monthly Catalog of United States Government Publications, 1900–1971.* 14 vols. Washington, DC: Carrollton, 1972.

119. *Declassified Documents Quarterly.* Washington, DC: Carrollton, 1975– . This guide to recently declassified government documents is keyed to microfiche copies of the documents themselves.

120. United Nations. Dag Hammarskjöld Library. *United Nations Documents Index.* New York, 1950– .

COLLECTIONS

121. Australia. Department of External Affairs. *Vietnam, Nov. 1966 to June 1967.* Canberra, 1967.

122. Cameron, Allan W., ed. *Vietnam Crisis: A Documentary History, 1940–1956.* Ithaca, NY: Cornell University Press, 1971.

123. CBS News. *Face the Nation: The Collected Transcripts from the CBS Radio and Television Broadcasts, 1954–1971.* 14 vols. New York: Holt Information Systems, 1972. [indexed]

124. Cole, A.B., et al., eds. *Conflict in Indo China and International Repercussions: A Documentary History 1945–1955.* Ithaca, NY: Cornell University Press, 1956.

125. Council on Foreign Relations. *Documents on American Foreign Relations.* New York: Harpers, 1952– . [annual]

126. Freyberg, Jutta von, and Kurt Steinhaus, eds. *Dokumente und Materialen der Vietnamischen Revolution.* 2 vols. Frankfurt: Marxistische Blatter, 1969.

127. Gettleman, Marvin E., ed. *Vietnam: History, Documents and Opinions on a Major World Crisis.* New York: Fawcett World Library, 1965, 2d ed. New York: Mentor, 1970.

128. Great Britain. Foreign Office. *Documents Relating to British Involvement in the Indo-China Conflict, 1954–1965.* Miscellaneous no. 25, Cmnd. 2834. London: HMSO, 1965.

129. Maki, J.M., ed. *Conflict and Tension in the Far East: Key Documents 1894–1960.* Seattle: University of Washington Press, 1961.

130. *The Pentagon Papers: As Published by The New York Times.* Edited by Neil Sheehan, et al. New York: Quadrangle Books, 1971. This is the best introduction to the *Papers.*

131. *The Pentagon Papers.* The Senator Gravel Edition. 5 vols. Boston: Beacon, 1971–1972. Volume 5 contains an index and commentaries.

132. [Pentagon Papers]. U.S. Department of Defense. *United States-Vietnam Relations, 1945–1967.* 12 vols. Washington, DC: GPO, 1971. This collection contains materials not in the Senator Gravel Edition.

133. Porter, Gareth, ed. *Vietnam: The Definitive Documentation of Human Decisions.* 2 vols. Stanfordville, NY: Coleman, 1979. This is a valuable collection of selected documents, essays, etc., many of which have been printed elsewhere; however, the presumptions of the title are suspect.

134. *Public Papers of the Presidents of the United States.* Washington, DC: GPO, 1945– ; 1957– . Included are the papers of all presidents from Truman to Carter.

135. U.S. Department of State. *American Foreign Policy: Current Documents.* Washington, DC: GPO, 1957– . [annual]

136. _____. *American Foreign Policy, 1950–55: Basic Documents.* 2 vols. Washington, DC: GPO, 1957.

137. U.S. Senate. Committee on Foreign Relations. *Background Information Relating to Southeast Asia and Vietnam.* 89th Cong., 1st sess., Jan. 14, 1965.

138. _____. *Background Information Relating to Southeast Asia and Vietnam.* 89th Cong., 2d sess., Mar. 1966.

139. _____. *Background Information Relating to Southeast Asia and Vietnam.* 90th Cong., 1st sess., July 1967.

140. _____. *Background Information Relating to Southeast Asia and Vietnam.* 90th Cong., 2d sess., Mar. 1968.

141. _____. *Background Information Relating to Southeast Asia and Vietnam.* 91st Cong., 1st sess., Mar. 1969.

142. _____. *Background Information Relating to Southeast Asia and Vietnam.* 91st Cong., 2d sess., June 1970.

143. _____. *Background Information Relating to Southeast Asia and Vietnam.* 7th rev. ed. 93d Cong., 2d sess., 1975.

Other References

ATLASES

144.   Gernsheimer, Jacob S., and Howard M. Potter. *Historical Atlas of Indochina, 100 BC to the Present.* West Point, NY: United States Military Academy, Department of Social Sciences, 1970.

145.   Hall, D.G.E. *Atlas of South East Asia.* New York: St. Martin's Press, 1964.

146.   United Nations. *Atlas of Physical, Economic and Social Resources of the Lower Mekong Basin.* Prepared for the U.N. Economic Commission for Asia and the Far East. Washington, DC, 1968.

147.   U.S. Central Intelligence Agency. Office of Basic and Geographic Intelligence. *South Vietnam: Provincial Maps.* Washington, DC, 1967.

148.   U.S. Department of State. Office of Geography. *South Vietnam and the South China Sea: Official Standard Names Approved by the United States Board of Geographic Names.* Gazetteer no. 58. Washington, DC: GPO, 1962. [revised in 1971]

BIOGRAPHICAL DATA

149.   *Biographical Directory of the American Congress, 1774–1971.* Washington, DC: GPO, 1971.

150.   *Biographical Index: A Cumulative Guide to Biographical Material in Books and Magazines.* New York: H.W. Wilson, 1949– .

151.   *Current Biography.* New York: H.W. Wilson, 1940– .

152.   *International Who's Who.* London: Europe Publications, 1935– . This title is just one of several Who's Who series.

153.   Tilman, Robert O. *International Biographical Directory of Southeast Asia Specialists.* Ann Arbor, MI: Association for Asian Studies, Interuniversity Southeast Asia Committee, 1970.

154.   _____. *International Biographical Directory of Southeast Asian Specialists, 1969.* Athens: Ohio University, Center for International Studies, 1969.

155.   U.S. Department of State. *Biographical Information on Prominent Nationalist Leaders in French Indochina.* R & A no. 3336. Washington, DC: Interim Research & Intelligence Service, Research Analysis Branch, Oct. 25, 1945.

156.   _____. Office of External Research. *Who's Who In North Vietnam.* Washington, DC, 1972.

157.   _____. Office of Intelligence Research. *Political Alignments of Vietnamese Nationalists.* No. 3708. Washington, DC: GPO, 1949.

158.   *VWP-DRV Leadership, 1960 to 1973.* Pt. I: *The Party*; Pt. II: *The Government.* Viet Nam Documents & Notes, no. 114. Saigon: U.S. Mission, 1973.

YEARBOOKS

159.   *Annuaire Statistique de l'Indochine.* Hanoi and Saigon: Direction des Affaire Économiques, Service de la Statistique Générale, 1927–1949.

160.   *Annual Statistical Bulletin.* Saigon: United States Operations Mission, Agency for International Development, 1958– .

161.   Council on Foreign Relations. *The United States in World Affairs.* New York: Harpers, 1932– .

162.   *Far Eastern Economic Review. Yearbook.* Hong Kong: Far Eastern Economic Review, 1960– .

163.   London Institute of World Affairs. *Year Book of World Affairs.* London: Stevens and Sons, 1947– .

164.   *The New International Year Book: A Compendium of the World's Progress for the Year.* New York: Funk & Wagnalls, 1932– .

165.   *Political Handbook and Atlas of the World.* New York: Harper & Row; Simon & Schuster, 1927– . [annual]

166.   United Nations. Statistical Office. *Statistical Year Book.* New York, 1949– .

167.   _____. *Yearbook of International Trade Statistics.* New York, 1949– .

168.   *Yearbook on International Communist Affairs.* Stanford, CA: Hoover Institution, 1967– .

Southeast Asia Studies

The fate of institutes and centers dealing with Southeast Asian studies has been rather gloomy since the end of the Second Indochina War.

169. Chatterji, B.R. "Recent Advances in Southeast Asian Studies: Modern Indochina." *International Studies* 1 (July 1959): 110–115; (Apr. 1960): 115–119.

170. Lagow, Larry D. "A History of the Center for Vietnamese Studies at Southern Illinois University, 1969–1976." Ph.D. dissertation, Southern Illinois University at Carbondale, 1978.

171. Nguyen Khai Kham. *Vietnamese Studies and Their Relationships to Asian Studies.* Vietnam: Directorate of National Archives & Libraries, 1964.

172. Phan Thien Chau, ed. *Viet Studies in North America: Personnel, Programs, Resources.* Ann Arbor, MI: Association for Asian Studies, Southeast Asia Regional Council, Vietnam Studies Group, 1976.

❧ Chapter Two ❧
Southeast Asia: Cambodia, Laos and Thailand

THE SIGNIFICANCE of the Second Indochina conflict ranged beyond the borders of Vietnam as the nations of Southeast Asia felt its consequences. Three of these states—Cambodia, Laos and, to a lesser extent, Thailand—were caught up in its violence. The major Cold War powers—the U.S., the U.S.S.R. and China—found their global hostilities and interests reflected in the uneasy Southeast Asian situation.

In Washington, alarmed presidents likened potential "free world" losses to "falling dominoes." If communist insurgents won in Vietnam, Southeast Asian states would subsequently fall to other like-minded insurgents, and then nations more distant—such as Indonesia, Australia, the Philippines and Japan—would succumb to similar pressures. The communist superpowers carried their own particular phobias into Southeast Asian politics. The Sino-Soviet conflict prompted the aggressive wooing of local communist parties in return for allegiance to Peking or Moscow. This fratricidal contest contributed to the Third Indochina War (see Chapter 3).

Dwight Eisenhower initially linked the "domino theory" to the Indochina crisis; see Kail (373) for this and subsequent official echoes of the thesis. Perhaps the best critique of this idea is Brodie's essay (364). SEATO was largely the outgrowth of fears for the future of U.S. influence in Southeast Asia. Washington's hopes for this "collective security" pact (1954–1975) never materialized because SEATO nations did not possess the industrial-military potential, political maturity or similarity of goals that was NATO's inheritance. At this writing, no adequate account of SEATO exists; however, the essays by Eckel (464) and Millar (480) are useful. Accounts of U.S. aid programs to this region are still fragmentary and inadequate; those that we have found are scattered throughout the *Guide* under various countries.

The Sino-Soviet conflict's impact on the Second Indochina War has not always been fully understood. A recent series of essays, collected by Zasloff and Brown (392), provides a good introduction, as does Funnell's article (396). References to Peking and Moscow's competition for Hanoi's allegiance can be found in Chapter 3, where we list materials that focus on the more general aspirations and policies of each toward Southeast Asia. For an introduction to China's hopes, see Gurtov (407) and Martin (409).

Cambodia (later Kampuchea) fared badly in the Second Indochina War. Pounded by massive U.S. aerial bombardment, ravished by a bloody civil war and brutalized by an immoderate, victorious revolutionary government, the Cambodians survived only to endure a subsequent invasion and occupation by their traditional Vietnamese enemies. Accounts of this sequence are listed in this and subsequent chapters. Osborne's many solid essays and books deal with the historical dimensions. Burchett's volumes are very sympathetic to the insurgents, as is that of Caldwell and Tan (512). Rogers (584) and Nixon (619–624) present the U.S. justification for its 1970 incursion and bombing and the best critique is Shawcross's study (572).

The brutal forced relocation of Cambodia's urban population ordered by the Khmer Rouge is, at the least, controversial. Barron and Paul (625) accuse the communist regime of "genocide," which is certainly a misuse of the term; while Hildebrand and Porter (627) defend Khmer Rouge policies, a defense which became less convincing as additional evidence became available.

Laos figured prominently in Hanoi's strategy and U.S. counteractions. The North Vietnamese used the western slope of the Laotian panhandle as a supply route (the so-called Ho Chi Minh trail) and as a sanctuary to rest and regroup their forces. The U.S. responded with an air interdiction strategy that called for heavy aerial bombing of the supply line and suspected military positions. (See Chapter 7 for combat operations.)

The initial Laotian crisis of 1960–1961 resulted in a "neutralization" convention inspired by John F. Kennedy which did little to lessen the violence. Books by Dommen (695) and Fall (697) provide excellent overviews of the effort, while Porter (744) and Langer and Zasloff (828) argue over which side was most responsible for the convention's failure. Laotian communists (Pathet Lao), heavily reinforced by North Vietnamese forces, were contested on the populous Plain of Jars by a CIA-financed "secret army" composed of Laotian rightists, Meo tribesmen and Thai "volunteers." Studies by Langer (841) and Zasloff (833) are valuable introductions to the organization and policies of the Pathet Lao, while Stevenson's volume (781) and Haney's essay (792) are fine critiques of U.S. policy toward Laos. Branfman's essays (815) are very critical of the American bombing campaign.

Thailand sided with the U.S. in the Second Indochina War and subsequently provided the U.S. Air Force with secure bases from which to operate over Vietnam, Cambodia and Laos. Additionally, the Thais contributed a modest number of combat forces in return for generous American aid. Listed below are a number of books and essays, including dated general surveys, that will provide some insight into Thailand's attitude toward the conflict; however, a solid account of Thailand's role (1961–1973) has yet to be written. At the conclusion of the 1973 armistice and upon the withdrawal of Americans from Vietnam, the Thais moved quickly to adopt a "neutral" stance. However, at this writing the Thais still have insurgency problems and it is not yet clear what the future holds for them.

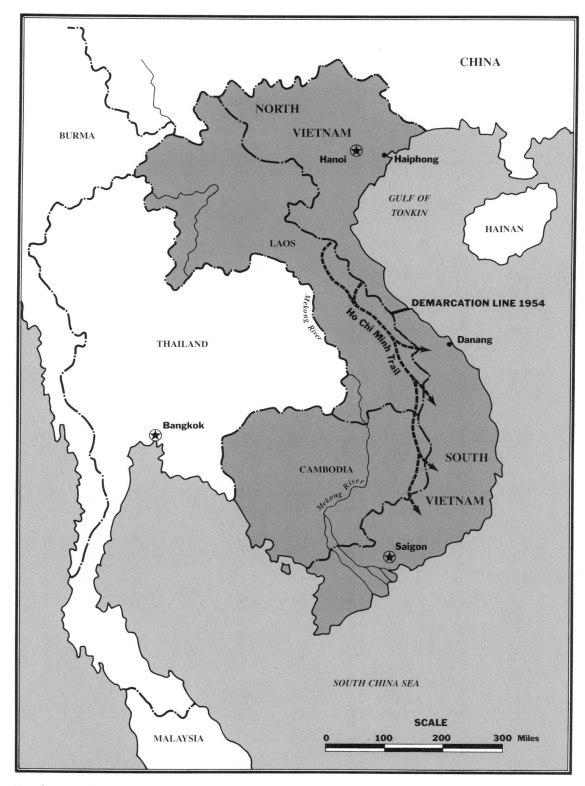

Southeast Asia

Reprinted by permission of the author from *Guide to American Foreign Relations since 1700*, ed. by Richard Dean Burns, The Society for Historians of American Foreign Relations (Santa Barbara, CA: ABC-Clio, 1983), p.903. © 1980 by SHAFR.

Southeast Asia

Listed here are books and essays that provide information about the general Southeast Asian setting.

Books

173.   Ball, W. MacMahon. *Nationalism and Communism in East Asia*. Melbourne, Australia: Melbourne University Press, 1952.

174.   Bloodworth, Dennis. *An Eye for the Dragon: Southeast Asia Observed, 1954–1970*. New York: Farrar, Straus & Giroux, 1970.

175.   Buchanan, Keith. *The Southeast Asian World*. New York: Taplinger, 1967.

176.   Burling, Robbins. *Hill Farms and Padi Fields: Life in Mainland Southeast Asia*. Englewood Cliffs, NJ: Prentice-Hall, 1965.

177.   Buss, Claude A. *Contemporary Southeast Asia*. New York: Van Nostrand Reinhold, 1970.

178.   Butwell, Richard A. *Southeast Asia Today—and Tomorrow: A Political Analysis*. New York: Praeger, 1964.

179.   Cady, John F. *The History of Post-War Southeast Asia: Independence Problems*. Athens: Ohio University Press, 1975.

180.   _____. *Southeast Asia: Its Historical Development*. New York: McGraw-Hill, 1964.

181.   _____. *Thailand, Burma, Laos and Cambodia*. Englewood Cliffs, NJ: Prentice-Hall, 1966.

182.   Coedes, George. *The Making of Southeast Asia*. Berkeley: University of California Press, 1966.

183.   Conway, Gordon, and Jeff Conway. *Ecology and Resource Development in Southeast Asia*. New York: Ford Foundation, 1973.

184.   Crozier, Brian. *South-East Asia in Turmoil*. New York: Penguin Books, 1965.

185.   Dobby, E.H.G. *Southeast Asia*. London: University of London Press, 1950.

186.   Elsbree, W.M. *Japan's Role in Southeast Asian Nationalist Movements*. Cambridge, MA: Harvard University Press, 1963.

187.   Embree, J., and W.L. Thomas, Jr. *Ethnic Groups of Northern Southeast Asia*. New Haven, CT: Yale University Press, 1950.

188.   Fifield, Russell H. *The Diplomacy of Southeast Asia: 1945–1958*. New York: Harper, 1958.

189.   Fischer, A. *South-East Asia: A Social, Economic, and Political Geography*. 2d ed. New York: E.P. Dutton, 1965.

190.   Fryer, Donald W. *Emerging Southeast Asia: A Study in Growth and Stagnation*. New York: McGraw-Hill, 1970.

191.   Golay, F.H., et al. *Underdevelopment and Economic Nationalism in Southeast Asia*. Ithaca, NY: Cornell University Press, 1969.

192.   Gordon, Bernard K. *The Dimensions of Conflict in Southeast Asia*. Englewood Cliffs, NJ: Prentice-Hall, 1966.

193.   Great Britain. Central Office of Information. *Vietnam, Laos and Cambodia: Chronology of Events, 1945–68*. London: British Information Service, 1968.

194.   Hall, D.G.E. *History of Southeast Asia*. New York: St. Martin's Press, 1955.

195.   _____. *A History of Southeast Asia*. 3d ed. London: Macmillan, 1968.

196.   Jacoby, E.H. *Agrarian Unrest in Southeast Asia*. New York: Columbia University Press, 1949.

197.   Jumper, Roy, and Marjorie Weiner Normand. *Governments and Politics of Southeast Asia*. 2d ed. Ithaca, NY: Cornell University Press, 1964.

198.   Kahin, George McT. *The Asian-African Conference, Bandung, Indonesia, April 1955*. Ithaca, NY: Cornell University Press, 1956.

199.   _____, and John W. Lewis. *Governments and Politics of Southeast Asia*. Ithaca, NY: Cornell University Press, 1964.

200.   Kunstadter, Peter, ed. *Southeast Asian Tribes, Minorities, and Nations*. 3 vols. Princeton, NJ: Princeton University Press, 1967.

201.   Lyon, Peter. *War and Peace in Southeast Asia*. London: Oxford University Press, 1969.

202.   McAlister, John T., ed. *Southeast Asia: The Politics of National Integration* New York: Random House, 1973.

203. McGee, T.G. *The Southeast Asian City: A Social Geography of the Primate Cities of Southeast Asia*. New York: Praeger, 1967.

204. Pluvier, Jan M. *South East Asia From Colonialism to Independence*. New York: Oxford University Press, 1974.

205. Rose, Saul. *Britain and South-East Asia*. Baltimore: Johns Hopkins University Press, 1962.

206. Sar Desai, D.R. *Indian Foreign Policy in Cambodia, Laos and Vietnam 1947–1964*. Berkeley: University of California Press, 1969.

207. Schaaf, C.H., and R.H. Fifield. *The Lower Mekong: Challenge to Cooperation in Southeast Asia*. Princeton, NJ: Van Nostrand, 1963.

208. Schecter, J.L. *The New Face of Buddha: The Rise of Buddhism as a New Political Force in Southeast Asia*. New York: Coward, McCann & Geoghegan, 1967.

209. Scott, James C. *The Moral Economy of the Peasant: Rebellion and Subsistence in Southeast Asia*. New Haven, CT: Yale University Press, 1976.

210. Shaplen, Robert. *Time Out of Hand: Revolution and Reaction in Southeast Asia*. New York: Harper & Row, 1969.

211. Smith, R.M. *Government and Politics of Southeast Asia*. Ithaca, NY: Cornell University Press, 1964.

212. Thompson, Virginia, and Richard Adloff. *The Left Wing in Southeast Asia*. New York: Sloane, 1950.

213. _____. *Minority Problems in Southeast Asia*. Stanford, CA: Stanford University Press, 1955.

214. Tow, William T. "Southeast Asian Security in the Post-Vietnam Era: A Study Concerning Strategies of Opportunity and Retraction." Ph.D. dissertation, University of Southern California, 1977.

215. Trager, Frank N., ed. *Marxism in Southeast Asia: A Study of Four Countries*. Stanford, CA: Stanford University Press, 1959.

216. Trumbull, Robert. *The Scrutable East: A Correspondent's Report on Southeast Asia*. New York: David McKay, 1964.

217. Vandenbosch, Amry, and Mary Belle Vandenbosch. *Australia Faces Southeast Asia*. Lexington: University of Kentucky Press, 1967.

218. Vandenbosch, Amry, and Richard Butwell. *The Changing Face of Southeast Asia*. Lexington: University of Kentucky Press, 1966.

219. Waddell, J.R.E. *An Introduction to South-East Asian Politics*. New York: Wiley, 1972.

220. Warner, Denis. *Reporting Southeast Asia*. Sydney, Australia: Angus & Robertson, 1966.

221. Williams, Lea E. *The Future of the Overseas Chinese in Southeast Asia*. New York: McGraw-Hill, 1966.

FRENCH INDOCHINA (HISTORICAL)

222. Ajalbert, Jean. *Les Nuages sur l'Indochine*. Paris: Louis-Michaud, 1912.

223. Alberti, Jean B. *L'Indochine d'sutrefois et d'aujourd'hui*. Paris: Société d'Éditions Géographiques, Maritimes et Coloniales, 1934.

224. Balny d'Avricourt, Adrien. *L'enseigne Balny et la conquête du Tonkin: Indochine, 1873*. Paris: Éditions France Empire, 1973.

225. Barthouet, Arnaud. *La Tragédie Franco-indochinoise*. Paris: Delmas, 1948.

226. Bauchar, René (pseudonym of Jean Charbonneau). *Rafales sur l'Indochine*. Paris: Fournier, 1946.

227. Bernard, Paul. *Le Problème économique indochinois*. Paris: Nouvelles Éditions Latines, 1934.

228. Bising, James A. "The Admiral's Government: A History of the Naval Colony That Was French Cochinchina, 1862–1879." Ph.D. dissertation, New York University, 1972.

229. Cady, John F. *The Roots of French Imperialism in Eastern Asia*. Ithaca, NY: Cornell University Press, 1954.

230. Cultru, P. *Histoire de la Cochincine française des origines à 1883*. Paris: Challamel, 1910.

231. Cunningham, Alfred. *The French in Tonkin and South China*. London: Sampson Low, 1902.

232. Daufès, E. *La Garde indigène de l'Indochine de sa création à nos jours*. 2 vols. Avignon, France: Seguin, 1933–1934.

233. Gosselin, Charles. *L'Empire d'Annam*. Paris: Perrin, 1904.

234. Goudal, Jean. *Labor Conditions in Indochina*. Geneva: International Labour Office, 1938.

235. Gourdon, Henri. *L'Indochine*. Paris: Librairie Larousse, 1951.

236. Lancaster, Donald. *The Emancipation of French Indochina.* London: Oxford University Press, 1961.

237. Levy, Roger. *L'Indochine et ses traites.* Paris: Centre d'Études de Politique Étrangère, 1947.

238. Marchand, Jean. *L'Indochine en guerre (1870–1954).* Paris: Pouzet, 1955.

239. Marr, David G. *Vietnamese Anticolonialism, 1885–1925.* Berkeley: University of California Press, 1971.

240. Masson, André. *Histoire du Vietnam.* 4th ed. Paris: Presses Universitaires de France, 1972. [originally titled *Histoire de l'Indochine*]

241. Robequain, D. *The Economic Development of French Indochina.* London: Oxford University Press, 1944.

242. Roberts, Stephen H. *History of French Colonial Policy, 1870–1925.* 2 vols. London: P.S. King, 1929.

243. Sarrault, Albert. *La Mise en valeur des colonies françaises.* Paris: Payot, 1923.

244. Shütze, Günter. *Der Schumtzige Krieg: Frankreichs Kolonialpolitik in Indochina.* Munich: Editions R. Oldenbourg, 1959.

245. Taboulet, Georges. *La geste française en Indochine: Histoire par les textes de la France en Indochine des origines à 1914.* 2 vols. Paris; Adrien-Maisonneuve, 1955–1956.

246. Tate, D.J.M. *The Making of Modern South-East Asia.* Vol. I: *The European Conquest.* London: Oxford University Press, 1971.

247. Thompson, Virginia. *French Indochina.* London: Allen & Unwin, 1937.

Essays
Cited here is a sampling of essays written on Southeast Asian affairs since 1968; they were selected to supplement the books listed above.

248. Allison, John M. "Japan's Relations with Southeast Asia." *Asia,* no. 17 (Winter 1970): 34–59.

249. Bose, Tarun C. "American and Soviet Interests in Asia: Conflict and Co-operation." *International Studies* 10 (July–Oct. 1968): 48–108.

250. Buchan, Alastair. "The Indochina War and World Politics." *Foreign Affairs* 53 (July 1975): 638–650.

251. Bull, Hedley. "The New Balance of Power in Asia and the Pacific." *Foreign Affairs* 49 (July 1971): 669–681.

252. Bundy, William P. "New Tides in Southeast Asia." *Foreign Affairs* 49 (Jan. 1971): 187–200.

253. Chopra, Maharaj K. "New Winds Over Southeast Asia." *Military Review* 48 (Sept. 1968): 10–18.

254. Clubb, Oliver E. "The New Power Imbalance in Southeast Asia." *Current History* 69 (Dec. 1975): 209–211ff.

255. Dubnic, Vladimir Reisky de. "The Global Realignment of Forces and the Indochina Question." *Orbis* 18 (Summer 1974): 535–552.

256. Duncanson, Dennis J. "Whither Indochina?" *Asian Affairs* 2 (June 1971): 131–139.

257. "The Economic Effects of the Vietnamese War in East and Southeast Asia." *Quarterly Economic Review,* special issue no. 3 (Nov. 1968).

258. Ellithorpe, Harold. "Why Fear Grips Southeast Asia." *National Review* 24 (Mar. 3, 1972): 221–223.

259. Fairbairn, Geoffrey, and Graeme Duncan. "Vietnam and the Future of Southeast Asia." *Australian Outlook* 23 (Apr. 1969): 18–45.

260. Fifield, Russell H. "Multipolarity and Southeast Asia: A Post-Vietnam Perspective." *Australian Outlook* 30 (Aug. 1976): 304–322.

261. ———. "Power Relations Among the Southeast Asian States." *Asian Affairs* [U.S.] 4 (Jan.–Feb. 1977): 151–171.

262. ———. "The Thirty Years War in Indochina: A Conceptual Framework." *Asian Survey* 17 (Sept. 1977): 857–879.

263. Gordon, Bernard K. "Regionalism and Instability in Southeast Asia." *Orbis* 10 (Summer 1966): 438–457.

264. Grant, Bruce. *The Security of South-East Asia.* Adelphi Papers no. 142. London: International Institute for Strategic Studies, 1978.

265. Gurtov, Melvin. *Southeast Asia After Withdrawal from Vietnam.* P–4413. Santa Monica, CA: Rand Corp., Aug. 1970.

266. ———. *Southeast Asia Tomorrow: Problems and Prospects.* RM–5910. Santa Monica, CA: Rand Corp., May 1969. [reprinted by Johns Hopkins University Press, 1970]

267. Halperin, Morton H. "After Vietnam: Security

and Intervention in Asia." *Journal of International Affairs* 22:2 (1968): 236–246.

268. Hanks, Lucien M. "Corruption and Commerce in Southeast Asia." *Trans-Action* 8 (May 1971): 18–25.

269. Hoadley, J. Stephen. "Military Officers in Southeast Asian Politics and Economics." *Asian Profile* 3 (Feb. 1975): 73–82.

270. Hodges, H.S., and G.R. Webb. "The Climates of Southeast Asia." *Australian Army Journal*, no. 228 (May 1968): 29–44.

271. Keyes, Charles F. "Peoples of Indochina: The War-Worn Human Fabric of Southeast Asia Has Survived Many Strains." *Natural History Magazine* 79 (Oct. 1970): 41–53.

272. Kirk, Donald. "War and the Indochinese: Scars to Live in History." *Far Eastern Economic Review* 74 (Dec. 25, 1971): 24–26.

273. Kroef, J.M. van der. "The Gorton Manner: Australia, Southeast Asia, and the U.S." *Pacific Affairs* 42 (Fall 1969): 311–333.

274. Mahajani, Usha. "India and Southeast Asia: Splendid Isolation, Active Intervention or Detached Involvement?" *United Asia* [India] 22 (May–June 1970): 105–124.

275. Maruyama Shizuo. "A New World in Southeast Asia." *Japan Quarterly* 16 (Apr.–June 1969): 170–179.

276. Matthews, Lloyd J. "'Farewell the Tranquil Mind': Security and Stability in the Post-Vietnam Era." *Parameters* 5:2 (1976): 2–13.

277. Naya Seiji. "The Vietnam War and Some Aspects of Its Economic Impact on Asian Countries." *Developing Economies* 9 (Mar. 1971): 31–57.

278. Nuechterlein, Donald E. "Prospects for Regional Security in Southeast Asia." *Asian Survey* 8 (Sept. 1968): 806–816.

279. Osborne, Milton E. "Post Vietnam: The End of an Era in Southeast Asia?" *International Affairs* [London] 45 (Apr. 1969): 223–233.

280. Pauker, Guy J. *New Centers of Power in the Pacific Basin 1985–1995.* P–5849. Santa Monica, CA: Rand Corp., 1977. This book covers primarily Indonesia and Vietnam.

281. _____. *Prospects for Regional Hegemony in Southeast Asia: Statement Presented to the Subcommittee on Future Foreign Policy Research and Development of the House International Relations Committee.* P–5630 Santa Monica, CA: Rand Corp., Apr. 1976.

282. Pike, Douglas. "Conceptions of Asian Security: Indochina." *Asian Forum* 8 (Autumn 1976): 77–84.

283. Poole, Peter A. "The Vietnamese in Cambodia and Thailand: Their Role in Interstate Relations." *Asian Survey* 14 (Apr. 1974): 325–337.

284. Scott, James C. "Patron-Client Politics and Political Change in Southeast Asia." *American Political Science Review* 66 (Mar. 1972): 91–113.

285. Shippee, John. "Southeast Asia and the Superpowers: Structural Obstacles to Learning from History." *Journal of Peace Research* 13:2 (1976): 131–148.

286. Solomon, Robert L. *Boundary Concepts and Practices in Southeast Asia.* RM–5936–1–ARPA. Santa Monica, CA: Rand Corp., Dec. 1969. [reprinted in *World Politics* 23 (Oct. 1970): 1–23]

287. Stockwin, H. "Asia and the Backlash of Vietnam." *Far Eastern Economic Review* 88 (Apr. 25, 1975): 53–56.

288. Thee, Marek. "The International System After Vietnam." *Bulletin of Peace Proposals* 4:4 (1973): 375–382.

289. Tiwari, S.N. "Prospect of Indo-Australian Role in Southeast Asia." *United Asia* [India] 20 (July–Aug. 1968): 218–226.

290. "Vietnam and Southeast Asia." *Current History* 56 (Feb. 1969): Entire issue.

291. Wanandi, Josef. "Politico-Security Dimensions of Southeast Asia." *Asian Survey* 17 (Aug. 1977): 771–792.

292. Weinstein, Walter. "The Meaning of National Security in Southeast Asia." *Bulletin of the Atomic Scientists* 34 (Nov. 1978): 20–28.

MEKONG DELTA

293. Croizat, Victor J. *The Mekong River Development Project: Some Geographical Historical and Political Considerations.* P–3616. Santa Monica, CA: Rand Corp., June 1967.

294. Gentil, Pierre. *Remous du Mekong.* Paris: Charles Lavauzelle, 1950.

295. Hanna, Willard A. *The Mekong Project.* 4 pts. Southeast Asia Series. New York: American Universities, Field Staff Report, 1968.

296. _____. *The Rediscoveries of the Mekong.* 7 pts. Southeast Asia Series. New York: American Universities, Field Staff Report, 1970.

Southeast Asia: Cambodia, Laos and Thailand   21

297. Jenkins, David. "The Lower Mekong Scheme." *Asian Survey* 8 (June 1968): 456–464.

298. Jones, Emily, and Alan Jones. "Taming the Mekong." *Far Eastern Economic Review* 49 (Sept. 2, 1965): 418–420.

299. Sewell, W.R. Derrick. "The Mekong Scheme: Guidelines for a Solution to Strife in Southeast Asia." *Asian Survey* 8 (June 1968): 448–455.

300. _____, and G.F. White. "The Lower Mekong." *International Conciliation*, no. 558 (May 1966).

301. Suryanarayan, V. "The Mekong Project: A Case of International Cooperation for Economic Development in Southeast Asia." *United Asia* [India] 25 (Mar.–Apr. 1974): 84–90.

302. "Whatever Happened to Ambitious Plans to Harness the Untamed Mekong River." *U.S. News and World Report* 73 (Sept. 25, 1972): 43.

303. White, Peter T. "The Mekong: River of Terror and Hope." *National Geographic* 134 (Dec. 1968): 737–787.

U.S. and Southeast Asia

These accounts deal with U.S. activities in Southeast Asia generally; specific activities are listed under appropriate title below.

Books, Dissertations and Reports

304. Bernabe, Gilbert A. "Southeast Asia and National Security Objectives: An Examination of 1950 Policies." Ph.D. dissertation, Claremont Graduate School, 1977.

305. Chomsky, Noam. *At War with Asia*. New York: Random House, 1969.

306. Farley, Miriam S. *United States Relations with Southeast Asia*. New York: American Institute of Pacific Relations, 1955.

307. Fifield, Russell H. *Americans in Southeast Asia: The Roots of Commitment*. New York: Crowell, 1973.

308. _____. *Southeast Asia in United States Policy*. New York: Praeger, 1963.

309. Friedman, Edward, and Mark Sheldon, eds. *America's Asia: Dissenting Essays on Asian–American Relations*. New York: Vintage, 1971.

310. Ichord, Robert F. "Southeast Asian Oil and United States Foreign Policy." Ph.D. dissertation, University of Hawaii, 1975. This work covers the post-armistice period.

311. Kalb, Marvin L., and Elie Abel. *Roots of Involvement: The U.S. in Asia, 1784–1971*. New York: Norton, 1971.

312. Kirk, Donald. *Wider War: The Struggle for Cambodia, Thailand and Laos*. New York: Praeger, 1971.

313. Larson, Donald R., and Arthur Larson. *Vietnam and Beyond: A New American Foreign Policy and Program*. Durham, NC: Duke University, Rule of Law Research Center, 1965.

314. McMahon, Robert J. "The United States and Decolonization in Southeast Asia: The Case of Indonesia, 1945–1949." Ph.D. dissertation, University of Connecticut, 1977.

315. Ohn, Byunghoon. "United States and Southeast Asia, 1945–1954: The Evolution of American Policy in Southeast Asia." Ph.D. dissertation, University of Kentucky, 1966.

316. Purdy, David M. "American Southeast Asian Foreign Policy." Ph.D. dissertation, University of Georgia, 1972.

317. Reischauer, Edwin O. *Beyond Vietnam: The United States and Asia*. New York: Vintage, 1968.

318. Sylvester, John F. *Eagle and the Dragon*. Philadelphia: Dorrance, 1965.

319. Tongdhummachart, Kramol. "American Policy in Southeast Asia: With Special Reference to Burma, Thailand and Indochina, 1945–1960." Ph.D. dissertation, University of Virginia, 1962.

320. U.S. House. Committee on Armed Services. *Report of Special Subcommittee Following Visit to Southeast Asia, April 7–19, 1966*. 89th Cong., 2d sess., July 19, 1966.

321. _____. Committee on Foreign Affairs. Hearings; *The Future U.S. Role in Asia and in the Pacific*. 90th Cong., 2d sess., Feb.–Apr. 1968.

322. _____. *Report of the Special Study Mission to East and Southeast Asia*. House Rpt. 91–30. 91st Cong., 1st sess., Mar. 6, 1969.

323. _____. Report; *United States Policy Toward Asia*. 89th Cong., 2d sess., May 19, 1966.

324. _____. *Special Study Mission to Southeast Asia and the Pacific: Report by Hon. Walter H. Judd, Minnesota, Chairman; Hon. Marguerite Stitt Church, Illinois; Hon. E. Ross Adair, Indiana; Hon. Clement J. Zablocki, Wisconsin*. 83d Cong., 2d sess., Jan. 29, 1954.

325. U.S. Senate. Committee on Foreign Relations. "*Report of Senator Mike Mansfield on a Study Mission to the Associated States of Indochina: Vietnam, Cambodia and Laos.*" 83d Cong., 1st sess., 1953.

326. _____. *Report on Indochina: Report of Senator Mike Mansfield on a Study Mission to Vietnam, Cambodia, Laos.* 83d Cong., 2d sess., Oct. 15, 1954.

327. _____. Report; *Vietnam, Cambodia and Laos: Report by Senator Mike Mansfield.* 84th Cong., 1st sess., Oct. 6, 1955.

328. _____. Staff Report; *Thailand, Laos, and Cambodia: January 1972.* 92d Cong., 2d sess., 1972.

329. _____. Staff Report; *Thailand, Laos, Cambodia and Vietnam, April 1973.* 93d Cong., 1st sess., 1973.

Essays

330. Bell, Coral. "Security in Asia: Reappraisals after Vietnam." *International Journal* [Toronto] 24 (Winter 1968): 1–12.

331. Bowles, Chester. "Five Major Blunders by the U.S. in Asia." *Saturday Review* 54 (Nov. 6, 1971): 28–31.

332. Brand, H. "On 'Containment' in Asia." *Dissent* 14 (Mar.–Apr. 1967): 140–144.

333. Bundy, William P. "The Nixon Policies in Asia and the Pacific." *Pacific Community* [Japan] 2 (Oct. 1970): 77–86.

334. Darling, Frank C. "United States Policy in Southeast Asia: Permanency and Change." *Asian Survey* 14 (Aug. 1974): 608–626.

335. Finkelstein, Lawrence S. *American Policy in Southeast Asia.* New York: American Institute of Public Relations, 1951.

336. Fleming, D.F. "What Is Our Role in East Asia?" *Western Political Quarterly* 18 (Mar. 1965): 73–86.

337. Griffith, W.E. "Containing Communist China." *Air Force Magazine* 48 (July 1965): 46–47.

338. Gurtov, Melvin. *Southeast Asia after Withdrawal from Vietnam.* P–4413. Santa Monica, CA: Rand Corp., Aug. 1970.

339. Hunter, Robert E., and Philip Windsor. "Vietnam and United States Policy in Asia." *International Affairs* [London] 44 (Apr. 1968): 202–213.

340. Johnstone, William C. "U.S. Policy in Southeast Asia: What's Ahead?" *Current History* 50 (Feb. 1966): 106–111.

341. Landon, Kenneth P. "Southeast Asia and United States Foreign Policy." *United Asia* [India] 17 (July–Aug. 1965): 267–277.

342. Mackie, J.A.C. "United States Interests in Southeast Asia." *Australian Outlook* 32 (Aug. 1978): 205–223.

343. Pauker, Guy J. *New American Perspectives on Southeast Asia.* P–5557. Santa Monica, CA: Rand Corp., Dec. 1975.

344. "Prospect for Southeast Asia: A Symposium of United States Foreign Policy." *Saturday Review* 48 (Oct. 30, 1965): 25–37.

345. Shaplen, Robert. "Southeast Asia: Before and After." *Foreign Affairs* 53 (Apr. 1975): 533–557. This article discusses the spread of democracy throughout the region.

346. Shuck, L. Edward, Jr. "The United States in Southeast Asia." *Current History* 71 (Dec. 1976): 193–196.

347. Thee, Marek. "War and Peace in Indochina: U.S. Asian and Pacific Policies." *Journal of Peace Research* 10:1/2 (1973): 51–70.

348. Thompson, W. Scott. "The Indochinese Debacle and the United States." *Orbis* 29 (Fall 1975): 990–1011.

349. Trager, Frank N. "Alternative Futures for Southeast Asia and United States Policy." *Orbis* 15 (Spring 1971): 381–402.

350. Volskii, Dmitrii A. "U.S. Military Expansion in South-East Asia." *International Affairs* [Moscow] 14 (Feb. 1968): 47–51.

351. Weinstein, Franklin B. "The United States and the Security of Southeast Asia." *Bulletin of the Atomic Scientists* 34 (Dec. 1978): 26–32.

352. _____. "U.S.–Vietnam Relations and the Security of Southeast Asia." *Foreign Affairs* 56 (July 1978): 842–856.

AID PROGRAMS

For general materials on U.S. Military Assistance Programs, see Richard Dean Burns, Arms Control & Disarmament: A Bibliography, Santa Barbara, CA: ABC-Clio, 1977, 308–309; see also Chapter 4 under "Nixon Doctrine." Specific aid programs are listed below under various countries.

353. Bell, David E. "Investment Opportunities in Southeast Asia." *Vital Speeches* 31 (Nov. 1, 1964): 61–62.

354. Black, Eugene R. *Alternative in Southeast Asia.* Foreword by Lyndon B. Johnson. New York: Praeger, 1969.

355. Hayes, Samuel P. *The Beginning of American Aid to Southeast Asia: The Griffin Mission of 1950.* Lexington, MA: Heath, 1971.

356. Johnson, Lyndon B. "Southeast Asian Aid." *Current History* 49 (Nov. 1965): 303–304ff.

357. Jordan, Amos A. *Foreign Aid and the Defense of Southeast Asia.* New York: Praeger, 1962.

358. Mason, Lionel. "Arming Indochina." *Far Eastern Economic Review* 71 (Feb. 13, 1971): 21–28.

359. Montgomery, John D. *The Politics of Foreign Aid: American Experience in Southeast Asia.* New York: Praeger, 1962.

360. "Mutual Defense Assistance in Indochina: Agreement Between the United States of America and Cambodia, Laos and Vietnam." *Treaties and Other International Acts,* no. 2447. Washington, DC: GPO, 1953.

361. Roseman, Alvin. "Thailand, Laos and Cambodia: A Decade of Aid." *Current History* 49 (Nov. 1965): 271–277, 306–307.

362. _____. "U.S. Economic Commitment in Southeast Asia." *Current History* 54 (Jan. 1968): 7–14ff.

363. U.S. House. Committee on Government Operations. Hearings; *Economy and Efficiency of U.S. Aid Programs in Laos and Cambodia.* 92d Cong., 1st sess., 1971.

DOMINO THEORY

Eisenhower first linked the domino principle to the Indochina crisis in 1953; the loss of Indochina (later South Vietnam) to communism would be followed by the loss of Burma, Thailand, Malaya, Indonesia and by the endangering of Australia, New Zealand, the Philippines and Japan.

364. Brodie, Bernard. "The Domino Theory." *Revue Militaire Générale* [Paris] 10 (Nov. 1972): 468–478.

365. Cooke, Alistair. "Falling Dominoes." *Listener* 83 (May 7, 1970): 604.

366. Critchley, Julian, ed. *The Domino Theory: Laos and Cambodia.* London: Atlantic Information Centre for Teachers, 1970.

367. Donnelly, Dorothy J.C. *American Policy in Vietnam, 1949–1965: A Perceptual Analysis of the Domino Theory and Enemy Based on the Pentagon Papers.* Ph.D. dissertation, University of Pittsburgh, 1980.

368. Fleming, D.F. "Vietnam: The Crashing Dominoes." *New World Review* 36 (Summer 1968): 8–16.

369. Fritchey, Clayton. "New Appraisal of the Old Domino Game." *Harper's* 232 (Apr. 1966): 46.

370. Girling, J.L.S. "Vietnam and the Domino Theory." *Australian Outlook* 21 (Apr. 1967): 61–70.

371. Gittings, John. "Will the Dominos Fall?" *Far Eastern Economic Review* 60 (Apr. 7–13, 1968): 53–54.

372. Griswold, Laurence. "A Scattering of Dominoes." *Sea Power* 18 (June 1975): 14–19.

373. Kail, F.M. "The Domino Principle." In his *What Washington Said: Administrative Rhetoric and the Vietnam War, 1949–1969.* New York: Harper & Row, 1973, 84–95. This chapter contains official statements on the domino theory.

374. Leifer, Michael. "After Vietnam: Will the Dominoes Fall?" *New Society* 24 (Apr. 12, 1973): 70–72.

375. Murphy, Rhoads. "China and the Dominoes." *Asian Survey* 6 (Sept. 1966): 510–515.

376. Parker, Maynard. "Asia: How Stand the Dominoes?" *Newsweek* 78 (Sept. 27, 1971): 47ff.

377. Roth, David F. "Political Changes in Asia After Vietnam: Some Thoughts and Alternatives to Dominoes." *Asia Quarterly* [Brussels], no. 1 (1977): 3–16.

378. Silverman, Jerry M. "The Domino Theory: Alternatives to a Self-Fulfilling Prophecy." *Asian Survey* 15 (Nov. 1975): 915–939.

379. "Toppling the Domino Theory." *Far Eastern Economic Review* 88 (Apr. 25, 1975): 36ff.

380. Trager, Frank N. "After Vietnam: Dominoes and Collective Security." *Asian Affairs* [U.S.] 2 (May 1975): 265–275.

381. Zagoria, Donald S. "Who's Afraid of the Domino Theory?" *New York Times Magazine* (Apr. 21, 1968): 28–29ff.

China, Soviet Union and Communism

Russian and Chinese encouragement of Marxist parties and insurgency in Southeast Asia is examined here; more specific topics, such as the role of Vietnam in the Sino–Soviet split, and Russian and Chinese aid to Hanoi, are located in Chapter 3 under "North Vietnam, 1954–1975," "Relations with Communist States."

Books

382. Barnett, A. Doak, ed. *Communist Strategies in Asia: A Comparative Analysis of Governments and Parties.* New York: Praeger, 1963.

383. Beloff, Max. *Soviet Policy in the Far East, 1944–1951.* London: Oxford University Press, 1953.

384. Brimmell, Jack H. *Communism in Southeast Asia: A Political Analysis.* New York: Oxford University Press, 1959.

385. Clubb, Oliver E. *The United States and the Sino–Soviet Bloc in Southeast Asia.* Washington, DC: Brookings Institution, 1962.

386. Dai Shen-Yu. *Peking, Moscow, and the Communist Parties of Colonial Asia.* Cambridge, MA: MIT, Center for International Studies, 1954.

387. Fairbairn, Geoffrey. *Revolutionary Warfare and Communist Strategy: The Threat to Southeast Asia.* London: Faber, 1968.

388. Girling, J.L.S. *People's War: Conditions and Consequences in China and Southeast Asia.* New York: Praeger, 1969.

389. Pye, Lucian W. *Guerrilla Communism in Malaya: Its Social and Political Meaning.* Princeton, NJ: Princeton University Press, 1956.

390. Scalapino, Robert A., ed. *The Communist Revolution in Asia: Tactics, Goals and Achievements.* Englewood Cliffs, NJ: Prentice-Hall, 1965.

391. Trager, Frank N., ed. *Marxism in Southeast Asia: A Study of Four Countries.* Stanford, CA: Stanford University Press, 1959.

392. Zasloff, Joseph J., and MacAlister Brown, eds. *Communism in Indo-China: New Perspectives.* Toronto: Lexington Books, 1975.

Essays

393. Benda, Harry J. "Communism in Southeast Asia." *Yale Review* 45 (Mar. 1956): 417–429.

394. Butwell, Richard. "Communist Liaison in Southeast Asia." *United Asia* [India] 16 (Nov.–Dec. 1954): 146–151.

395. Candlin, A.H.S. "The Communist Threat to South and Southeast Asia." *Brassey's 1964* (1964): 83–95; *Brassey's 1967* (1967): 211–223.

396. Funnell, Victor C. "Vietnam and the Sino–Soviet Conflict, 1965–1976." *Studies in Comparative Communism* 11 (Spring–Summer 1978): 142–169. This is the most comprehensive study to date.

397. Gurtov, Melvin. "Sino–Soviet Relations and Southeast Asia: Recent Developments and Future Possibilities." *Pacific Affairs* 43 (Winter 1970): 491–505.

398. Horn, Robert C. "Moscow and Peking in Post-Indochina Southeast Asia." *Asian Affairs* [U.S.] 4 (Sept.–Oct. 1976): 14–40.

399. Kroef, Justus M. van der. "Southeast Asia: The Arc of Communist Insurrection." *South Atlantic Quarterly* 66 (Autumn 1967): 497–519.

400. McConaughy, John B. "Communist Strategy in Southeast Asia." *Military Review* 42 (May 1962): 39–53.

401. Speed, F.W. "South East Asia Now." *Army Quarterly and Defence Journal* [Great Britain] 106:2 (1976): 226–235. Speed discusses Chinese and Soviet military and political strategy.

402. Thornton, Richard C. "Peking–Moscow Rivalry in Southeast Asia." *Issues & Studies* 16 (Oct. 1980): 38–48.

403. White, Ralph K. "The [Vietnam] Conflict as Seen by the Communists." *Journal of Social Issues* 22 (July 1966): 44–64.

404. Williams, J.E. "The Colombo Conference and Communist Insurgency in South and South-East Asia." *International Relations* 4 (May 1972): 94–107.

405. Wilson, Dick. "Sino–Soviet Rivalry in Southeast Asia." *Problems of Communism* 23 (Sept.–Oct. 1974): 39–51.

CHINA AND SOUTHEAST ASIA

The war in Vietnam was also traumatic for China; see "Third Indochina War," in Chapter 3.

Books

406. Ambekar, G.V., and V.D. Divekar, eds. *Documents on China's Relations with South and Southeast Asia (1949–1962)*. Bombay: Allied, 1964.

407. Gurtov, Melvin. *China and Southeast Asia: The Politics of Survival*. Lexington, MA: Heath, 1971.

408. McCabe, Robert K. *Storm Over Asia: China and Southeast Asia; Thrust and Response*. New York: New American Library, 1967.

409. Martin, Edwin W. *Southeast Asia and China: The End of Containment*. Boulder, CO: Westview, 1977.

410. Purcell, Victor. *The Chinese in Southeast Asia*. 2d ed. London: Oxford University Press, 1965.

Essays

411. Dai Shen-Yu. "Peking and Indochina's Destiny." *Western Political Quarterly* 7 (Sept. 1954): 346–368.

412. Fall, Bernard B. "Red China's Aims in South Asia." *Current History* 43 (July 1962): 136–141.

413. Fitzgerald, C.R. "China and South East Asia After Vietnam." *Plural Societies* 6 (Winter 1975): 3–16.

414. Gordon, Bernard K. "The Southeast Asian View of China." *Current History* 55 (Sept. 1968): 165–170ff.

415. Guillon, J. Les peuples d'Asie en lutte pour leur indépendance nationale: Chine et Sud-Est Asiatique." *Cahiers du Communisme* 25 (Nov. 1948): 1273–1286.

416. Gurtov, Melvin. "China's Policies in Southeast Asia: Three Studies." *Studies in Comparative Communism* 3 (July–Oct. 1970): 13–46.

417. Kalicki, J.H. "Sino–American Relations Despite Indochina." *World Today* [London] 27 (Nov. 1971): 472–478.

418. Kroef, Justus M. van der. "The Continuing Partnership: People's China and Asian Insurgency." *SEATO Record* 11 (Feb. 1972): 5–19.

419. McColl, Robert W. "A Political Geography of Revolution: China, Vietnam, and Thailand." *Journal of Conflict Resolution* 11 (June 1967): 153–167.

420. Pan, Stephen C.Y. "China and Southeast Asia." *Current History* 57 (Sept. 1969): 164–168ff.

421. Tretiak, Daniel. "Changes in Chinese Attention to Southeast Asia, 1967–1969: Their Relevance for the Future of the Area." *Current Science: Developments in Mainland China* 7 (Nov. 1969): 1–17.

422. Wit, Daniel. "The Sino–American Clash of Interests in Southeast Asia." *United Asia* [India] 17 (July–Aug. 1965): 287–293.

SOVIET UNION AND SOUTHEAST ASIA

For Soviet assistance in the Vietnam conflict, see Chapter 3 under "North Vietnam, 1954–1975," "Relations with Communist States."

423. Alexeyev, E., and V. Zhurkin. "U.S.A.: Wanton Escalation." *International Affairs* [Moscow] 11 (Aug. 1965): 59–63.

424. Buszynski, Les. "The Soviet Union and Southeast Asia Since the Fall of Saigon." *Asian Survey* 21 (May 1981): 536–550.

425. Girling, J.L.S. "Russia and Indochina in International Perspective." *International Affairs* [London] 49 (Oct. 1973): 608–616.

426. Horelick, Arnold L. "The Soviet Union's Asian Collective Security Proposal: A Club in Search of Members." *Pacific Affairs* 47 (Fall 1974): 269–285.

427. Horn, Robert C. "Changing Soviet Policies and Sino–Soviet Competition in Southeast Asia." *Orbis* 17 (Summer 1973): 493–526.

428. ———. "Moscow's Southeast Asian Offensive." *Asian Affairs* [U.S.] 2 (Mar.–Apr. 1975): 217–240.

429. Howard, Peter. "Soviet Policies in Southeast Asia." *International Journal* [Toronto] 23 (Summer 1968): 435–455.

430. Jukes, Geoffrey. "The Soviet Union and Southeast Asia." *Australian Outlook* 31 (Apr. 1977): 174–184.

431. Kashin, Alexander. "The Soviet Offensive in Asia." *Studies on the Soviet Union* 5:3 (1966): 1–10.

432. McLane, Charles B. *Soviet Strategies in Southeast Asia: An Exploration of Eastern Policy Under Lenin and Stalin*. Princeton, NJ: Princeton University Press, 1966.

433. Parker, F. Charles. "Vietnam and Soviet–Asian Strategy." *Asian Affairs* [U.S.] 4 (Nov.–Dec. 1976): 94–116.

434. Quested, J. "Russian Interest in Southeast Asia:

Outlines and Sources, 1803–1970." *Journal of Southeast Asian Studies* 1 (Sept. 1970): 48–60.

435.   Thomas, J.R. "Soviet Russia and Southeast Asia." *Current History* 55 (Nov. 1968): 575–580.

Regional Organizations and Proposals

For a plan put forward by the U.S.S.R., see Horelick (426).

NEUTRALIZATION

During the Second Indochina War, private proposals were advanced for "neutralizing" Southeast Asia by having the major powers refrain from exercising military or political influence in the region.

436.   Chandola, Harish. "Mirage of Neutral Southeast Asia." *Economic and Political Weekly* 7 (Jan. 15, 1972): 104–105.

437.   Darby, Phillip. "Stability Mechanisms in South-East Asia: Balance of Power and Neutralisation." *International Affairs* [London] 49 (Apr. 1973): 204–218.

438.   Fairbairn, Geoffrey. "The Neutralisation of South-East Asia: Reflections on a New Concept." *Current Affairs Bulletin* 50 (June 1973): 23–30.

439.   Girling, J.L.S. "A Neutral Southeast Asia?" *Australian Outlook* 27 (Aug. 1973): 123–133.

440.   Millet, Stanley, et al. "Can Vietnam be Neutralized? An Analysis of Experts." *War/Peace Report* 4 (Apr. 1964): 3–10.

441.   Shafie, M. Ghazali bin. "The Neutralisation of Southeast Asia." *Pacific Community* 3 (Oct. 1971): 110–117.

442.   "Southeast Asia: The Neutralisation Proposals." *Current Notes on International Affairs* [Canberra, Australia] 43 (Oct. 1972): 498–504.

443.   U.S. Senate. Committee on Foreign Affairs. Staff Study; *Neutralization in Southeast Asia: Problems and Prospects.* 89th Cong., 2d sess., 1966.

444.   Young, Kenneth T. "Neutralism in Laos and Cambodia." *International Studies Quarterly* 14 (Jan. 1970): 219–226.

ASEAN, 1967–

The Association of Southeast Asian Nations (ASEAN) has become the major organization in the area with the demise of SEATO.

445.   Ali, Mehrunnisa. "The Changing Stance of ASEAN Towards Its Communist Neighbors." *Pakistan Horizon* 29:2 (1976): 33–56.

446.   Crone, Donald. "Emerging Trends in Control of Foreign Investments in ASEAN." *Asian Survey* 21 (Apr. 1981): 417–426.

447.   Fifield, Russell H. "The Association of Southeastern Asian Nations (ASEAN): Image and Reality." *Asian Survey* 19 (Dec. 1979): 1199–1208.

448.   Galbraith, Francis J. "ASEAN Today: Feeling the Heat." *Asian Affairs* [U.S.] 8 (Sept.–Oct. 1980): 31–40.

449.   Gordon, Bernard K. "Asian Perspectives on Security: The ASEAN Region." *Asian Forum* 8 (Autumn 1976): 62–76.

450.   Hill, H. Monte. "Community Formation Within ASEAN." *International Organization* 32 (Spring 1978): 569ff.

451.   Kroef, Justus M. van der. "ASEAN, Hanoi, and the Kampuchean Conflict: Between 'Kuantan' and a 'Third Alternative.'" *Asian Survey* 21 (May 1981): 515–535.

452.   _____. "Hanoi and ASEAN: A New Confrontation in Southeast Asia?" *Asia Quarterly* [Brussels], no. 4 (1976): 245–269.

453.   Leifer, Michael. "The Paradox of ASEAN: A Security Organization Without the Structure of an Alliance." *Round Table*, no. 271 (July 1978): 261–269.

454.   Melchor, Alejandro, Jr. "Assessing ASEAN's Viability in a Changing World." *Asian Survey* 18 (Apr. 1978): 422–436.

455.   Nicholas, Rhondda. "ASEAN and the Pacific Community Debate: Much Ado About Something?" *Asian Survey* 21 (Dec. 1981): 1197–1210.

456.   Pollard, Vincent K. "ASA and ASEAN, 1961–1967: South-East Asian Regionalism." *Asian Survey* 10 (Mar. 1970): 244–255.

457.   Shee Poon-Kim. "A Decade of ASEAN, 1967–1977." *Asian Survey* 17 (Aug. 1977): 753–770.

458.   Simon, Sheldon W. "The ASEAN States: Obstacles to Security Cooperation." *Orbis* 22 (Summer 1978): 415–434.

459. ———. "China, Vietnam and ASEAN: The Politics of Polarization." *Asian Survey* 19 (Dec. 1979): 1171–1188.

460. Soedjatmoko. "Southeast Asia and Security." *Military Review* 50 (July 1970): 40–48.

461. Stirling, John. "ASEAN: The Anti-Domino Factor." *Asian Affairs* [U.S.] 7 (May–June 1980): 273–287.

462. Wilborn, Thomas L. "ASEAN, 1985–2000: A U.S. Role to Influence Its Shape." *Parameters* 8 (Sept. 1978): 17–29.

SEATO, 1954–1975

The United States formed SEATO at the end of the First Indochina War to provide security for South Vietnam, Cambodia and Laos. At the urging of Thailand and the Philippines, it was agreed, on September 24, 1975, to dissolve SEATO.

463. Clubb, Oliver E. "Vietnam and the End of the SEATO Decade." *Correspondent* 33 (Winter 1965): 14–18.

464. Eckel, Paul E. "SEATO: An Ailing Alliance." *World Affairs* 134 (Fall 1971): 97–114.

465. Fifield, Russell H. "U.S. Objectives and Treaty Organization in Asia and the Western Pacific." *Naval War College Review* 18 (Apr. 1966): 4–14.

466. Greene, Fred. *U.S. Policy and the Security of Asia.* New York: McGraw-Hill, 1968.

467. Hasluck, Paul. "Vietnam and SEATO." *Current Notes on International Affairs* [Canberra, Australia] 37 (May 1966): 257–260.

468. Ingersoll, Robert S. "Department Discusses Continued Need for Manila Pact and SEATO." *U.S. Department of State Bulletin* 70 (Apr. 1, 1974): 345–348.

469. Institute for Defense Analyses. *SEATO Before and After a Vietnam Settlement.* Research Paper P–517. Arlington, VA, June 1969.

470. Joyce, J.A. "SEATO: False Alibi." *Christian Century* 84 (Nov. 8, 1967): 1424–1429. Joyce seeks to justify U.S. military intervention.

471. Kahin, George McT. "Cutting the US Out of SEATO." *New Republic* 169 (Oct. 13, 1973): 18–21.

472. Kim, Benedict Sang-Joon. "The United States and SEATO." Ph.D. dissertation, Yale University, 1964.

473. Kroef, Justus M. van der. "Will the Dominoes Stand?" *National Review* 24 (Nov. 10, 1972): 1245–1246ff.

474. Lee, L. "Review of the Southeast Asia Treaty Organization." *Asian Outlook* 8 (Mar. 1973): 14–17.

475. Leifer, M. "Cambodia and SEATO." *International Journal* [Toronto] 17 (Spring 1962): 122–132.

476. Lyon, Peter. "SEATO in Perspective." *Yearbook of World Affairs, 1965.* London: Stevens, 1965, 113–136.

477. McCloud, Donald G. "United States Policies Toward Regional Organizations in Southeast Asia." *World Affairs* 133 (Sept. 1970): 133–145.

478. Magnien, M. "Une Opération montér par L'O.T.A.S.E., au Laos." *Cahiers du Communisme* 35 (1959): 919–923.

479. Mendez, Mauro. "SEATO 'Fortifies Morale' in S.E. Asia." *SEATO Record* 4 (Oct. 1965): 3–6.

480. Millar, T.B. "The Five-Power Defence Agreement and Southeast Asian Security." *Pacific Community* [Japan] 3 (Jan. 1972): 341–351.

481. Miller, Roger J. "Is SEATO Obsolete?" *U.S. Naval Institute Proceedings* 94 (Nov. 1968): 56–63. Miller portrays SEATO's inability to respond to threats.

482. Modelski, George A. "Indochina and SEATO." *Australian Outlook* 13 (Mar. 1959): 27–54.

483. ———, ed. *SEATO: Six Studies.* Melbourne, Australia: F.W. Cheshire, 1962.

484. Nairn, Ronald C. "SEATO: A Critique." *Pacific Affairs* 41 (Spring 1968): 5–18.

485. Neuchterlein, Donald E. "Thailand and SEATO: A Ten-year Appraisal." *Asian Survey* 4 (Dec. 1964): 1174–1181.

486. Rhitharom, Chati. "The Making of the Thai–U.S. Military Alliance and the SEATO Treaty of 1954: A Study in Thai Decision-Making." Ph.D. dissertation, Claremont Graduate School, 1976.

487. Rogers, William P. "SEATO Council Meeting, Canberra: Statement, with Text of Communique, June 28, 1972." *U.S. Department of State Bulletin* 67 (Aug. 7, 1972): 159–164.

488. Rubin, Alfred P. "SEATO and American Legal Obligations concerning Laos and Cambodia." *International and Comparative Law Quarterly* 20 (July 1971): 500–518.

489. Snyder, Joel J. "SEATO's Capabilities for Counter-subversion." *Air University Review* 21 (Sept.–Oct. 1970): 51–60.

490. "Southeast Asia Collective Defense Treaty, Signed at Manila, on 8 September 1954." *United Nations Treaty Series* 209: 28–36.

491. Trager, Frank N. "The United States, SEATO and the Defense of Southeast Asia." *United Asia* [India] 17 (July–Aug. 1965): 278–286.

492. Turner, Nicholas. "Southeast Asia: Crumbling Cornerstone." *Far Eastern Economic Review* 60 (Apr. 14–20, 1968): 161–162.

493. U.S. Senate. Committee on Foreign Relations. Hearings; *The Southeast Asia Collective Defense Treaty.* 83d Cong., 2d sess., 1954.

Cambodia (Kampuchea)

If Cambodia was able to avoid conflict during the First Indochina War, it could not do so in the Second or Third Indochina Wars. Listed here are materials dealing with the politics and economics of Cambodia (later Kampuchea). Chapter 7, "Combat Operations," also has materials relating to U.S. activities in this country; also see the "Third Indochina War, 1978– " section in Chapter 3.

Books

494. Audric, John *Angkor and the Khmer Empire.* London: R. Hale, 1972.

495. _____. *Siam.* New York: Barnes & Noble Books, 1970.

496. Burchett, Wilfred G. *Mekong Upstream: A Visit to Laos and Cambodia.* Berlin: Seven Seas Publishers, 1959.

497. Ghosh, Manomohan. *A History of Cambodia: From the Earliest Time to the End of the French.* Saigon: J.K. Gupta, 1960.

498. Munson, Frederick P. *Area Handbook for Cambodia.* DA Pamphlet 550–50. Washington, DC: GPO, 1968.

499. Osborne, Milton E. *The French Presence in Cochinchina and Cambodia: Rule and Response (1859–1905).* Ithaca, NY: Cornell University Press, 1969.

500. Preschez, Phillippe. *Essai sur la démocratique du Cambodge.* Paris: Fondation Nationale des Sciences Politiques, Centre d'Études des Relations Internationales, 1961.

501. U.S. Department of State. Geographic Names Division. *Cambodia: Official Standard Names.* 2d ed. Washington, DC: GPO, 1971.

502. Williams, Maslyn. *The Land in Between: The Cambodian Dilemma.* New York: Morrow, 1970.

503. Willmott, W.E. *The Chinese in Cambodia.* Vancouver: University of British Columbia, 1967.

Essays

504. Adloff, R., and V. Thompson. "Cambodia Moves Toward Independence." *Far Eastern Survey* 22 (Aug. 1953): 105–111.

505. Field, Michael. "Cambodia Between East and West." *New Leader* 43 (Jan. 4, 1960): 18–20.

506. Kirk, Donald. "Cambodia's Economic Crisis." *Asian Survey* 11 (Mar. 1971): 238–255.

507. Leifer, Michael. "Cambodia and Her Neighbors." *Pacific Affairs* 34 (Winter 1961–1962): 361–374.

508. Norton, R.P.W. "Cambodian Economy: Doing It Their Way." *Far Eastern Economic Review* 71 (Mar. 27, 1971): 80–82.

509. Osborne, Milton E. "Peasant Politics in Cambodia: The 1916 Affair." *Modern Asian Studies* 12 (Feb. 1978): 217–244.

510. Thomson, R.S. "Establishment of the French Protectorate Over Cambodia." *Far Eastern Quarterly*, no. 4 (1945): 313–340.

CAMBODIAN FOREIGN POLICY

Prince Sihanouk sought to keep Cambodia "neutral" as NLF and NVA forces used his country as a pipeline (the "Sihanouk Trail") for military supplies. General Lon Nol deposed Sihanouk on March 18, 1970, allegedly encouraged by the United States, and aligned with the United States and South Vietnam.

Books and Documents

511. Burchett, Wilfred G. *The Second Indochina War: Cambodia and Laos.* New York: International Publishers, 1970.

512. Caldwell, Malcolm, and Lek Tan. *Cambodia in the Southeast Asian War.* New York: Monthly Review Press, 1973.

513.   Government of Cambodia. *Documents on Vietcong and North Vietnamese Aggression Against Cambodia* (1970). Phnom Penh: Ministry of Information, 1970.

514.   Great Britain. Secretary of State for Foreign Affairs. *Recent Diplomatic Exchanges Concerning the Proposal for an International Conference on the Neutrality and Territorial Integrity of Cambodia.* Cmnd. 2678. London: HMSO, 1965.

515.   Kosut, Hal, ed. *Cambodia and the Vietnam War.* New York: Facts on File, 1971.

516.   Laurent, Maurice. *L'Armée au Cambodge et dans les pays en voie de développement du Sud-est Asiatique.* Paris: Presses Universitaires de France, 1968.

517.   Leifer, Michael. *Cambodia: The Search for Security.* New York: Praeger, 1967.

518.   Osborne, Milton E. *Politics and Power in Cambodia: The Sihanouk Years.* Camberwell, Australia: Longmans, 1973.

519.   Simon, Sheldon W. *War and Politics in Cambodia: A Communications Analysis.* Durham, NC: Duke University Press, 1974.

520.   Smith, Roger M. *Cambodia's Foreign Policy.* Ithaca, NY: Cornell University Press, 1965.

521.   U.S. House. Committee on International Relations. Hearings; *The Vietnam–Cambodia Emergency, 1975.* 4 pts. 94th Cong., 1st and 2d sess., 1976.

Essays

522.   Chandler, David P. "Cambodia's Strategy of Survival." *Current History* 57 (Dec. 1969): 344–348, 366.

523.   _____. "Changing Cambodia." *Current History* 59 (Dec. 1970): 333–338.

524.   Chopra, Maharaj K. "Cambodia's Search for Firm Borders." *Military Review* 49 (Nov. 1969): 3–9.

525.   Gordon, Bernard K. "Cambodia: Shadow Over Angkor." *Asian Survey* 9 (Jan. 1969): 58–68.

526.   Leifer, Michael. "Cambodia: In Search of Neutrality." *Asian Survey* 3 (Jan. 1963): 55–60.

527.   _____. "Cambodia: The Politics of Accommodation." *Asian Survey* 4 (Jan. 1964): 674–679.

528.   _____. "A New Orientation for Cambodia?" *World Today* [London] 25 (June 1969): 234–237.

529.   _____. "Peace and War in Cambodia." *Southeast Asia* 1 (Winter–Spring 1971): 59–73.

530.   _____. "Rebellion or Subversion in Cambodia?" *Current History* 56 (Feb. 1969): 88–93ff.

531.   Marsot, Alain-Gerard. "China's Aid to Cambodia." *Pacific Affairs* 43 (Sept. 1969): 189–198.

532.   O'Ballance, Edgar. "Cambodia on a Tightrope." *United Service Institution of India Journal* 95 (July–Sept. 1966): 150–158. O'Ballance focuses on political and military problems.

533.   Osborne, Milton E. "Beyond Charisma: Princely Politics and the Problem of Political Succession in Cambodia." *International Journal* [Toronto] 24 (Winter 1968–1969): 109–121.

534.   _____. "Regional Disunity in Cambodia." *Australian Outlook* 22 (Dec. 1968): 317–333.

535.   Pike, Douglas E. *Cambodia's War.* Southeast Asia Perspective, no. 1. New York: American Friends of Vietnam, 1971.

536.   Reddi, V.M. "Cambodian Neutralism." *International Studies* 2 (Oct. 1960): 190–205.

537.   Simon, Jean-Pierre. "Cambodia: Pursuit of Crisis." *Asian Survey* 5 (Jan. 1965): 49–53.

538.   Simon, Sheldon W. "The Role of Outsiders in the Cambodian Conflict." *Orbis* 19 (Spring 1975): 209–230.

539.   Smith, Roger M. "Cambodia: Between Scylla and Charybdis." *Asian Survey* 8 (Jan. 1968): 72–79.

540.   _____. "Cambodia's Neutrality and the Laotian Crisis." *Asian Survey* 1 (July 1961): 17–24.

541.   Stark, Gail D. "Cambodia Beset." *Nation* 202 (Apr. 17, 1966): 445–449.

542.   Szaz, Z.M. "Cambodia's Foreign Policy." *Far Eastern Survey* 24 (Oct. 1955): 151–158.

543.   Taussig, H.C. "Neutral Cambodia." *Eastern World* 11 (Sept. 1957): 32–35.

Norodom Sihanouk

Sihanouk believed that the CIA carried out a covert campaign of sabotage and assassination aimed at ousting him.

544.   Allman, T.D. "Sihanouk: Victim of Detente." *Far Eastern Economic Review* 82 (Oct. 1, 1973): 13–14.

545.   Armstrong, John P. *Sihanouk Speaks.* New York: Walker, 1964.

546.   Barre, Jean. "Sihanouk's Neutral Way." *Far Eastern Economic Review* 53 (July 21, 1966): 110–113.

547.   Cassella, Alessandro. "With Sihanouk in Peking." *Nation* 212 (Mar. 8, 1971): 205–208.

548.   Girling, J.L.S. *Cambodia and the Sihanouk Myths.* Occasional Paper no. 7. Singapore: Institute of Southeast Asian Studies, 1971.

549.   "Interview with Prince Norodom Sihanouk, Head of State of Cambodia." *Far Eastern Economic Review* 50 (Dec. 9, 1965): 456–458.

550.   Manee, Walton C. "Cambodia's Controversial Sihanouk." *World Affairs* 130 (Oct.–Dec. 1967): 147–151.

551.   Nghiem Xuan Thien. "Cambodia and Sihanouk's Role in China's Hands." *Contemporary Review* 224 (Feb. 1974): 93–100.

552.   Sihanouk, Norodom. "Aspects of Cambodian Neutrality." *Free World Review* 4 (Summer 1958): 11–12.

553.   _____. "Cambodia Neutral: The Dictate of Necessity." *Foreign Affairs* 36 (July 1958): 582–586.

554.   _____. "The Future of Cambodia." *Foreign Affairs* 49 (Oct. 1970): 1–10.

555.   _____. "My Overthrow and Resistance." *Ramparts* 11 (July 1972): 19–23, 42–47.

556.   _____. *My War with the CIA.* As told to Wilfred Burchett. New York: Pantheon, 1972.

557.   _____. "Russians Don't Want Hanoi to Win." *Far Eastern Economic Review* 74 (Dec. 25, 1971): 19–21.

558.   "Sihanouk, the Man We May Have to Settle for in Cambodia." *New York Times Magazine* (Aug. 12, 1973): 14ff.

Lon Nol

559.   Allman, T.D. "Anatomy of a Coup." *Far Eastern Economic Review* 67 (Apr. 9, 1970): 17–22.

560.   Baczynskyj, Boris. "Cambodia: Lon Nol's Private War." *Far Eastern Economic Review* 77 (July 1, 1972): 23–24.

561.   Halasz, Louis. "Lon Nol: Tactics for Survival." *Far Eastern Economic Review* 86 (Dec. 13, 1974): 22–23. Halasz focuses on Cambodia and the U.N.

562.   Kamm, Henry. "Lon Nol Reads No Newspapers and Never Uses a Telephone." *New York Times Magazine* (Dec. 13, 1970): 28–29ff.

563.   Kirk, Donald. "Why They Call Lon Nol 'The Mayor of Pnompenh.'" *New York Times Magazine* (June 27, 1971): 27ff.

564.   Scott, Peter D. "Cambodia: Why the Generals Won." *New York Review of Books* (June 19, 1970): 28–33.

U.S. ACTIVITIES IN CAMBODIA

The best survey of U.S. involvement in Cambodia is Shawcross (572).

565.   Barnes, William S. "United States Recognition Policy and Cambodia." *Boston University Law Review* 50 (Spring 1970): 117–129. [special issue: "U.S. Intervention in Cambodia"]

566.   Batchelder, Sydney H., Jr., and D.A. Quinlan. "Operation Eagle Pull." *Marine Corps Gazette* 60 (May 1976): 47–60. The authors describe the emergency evacuation of American citizens from Cambodia in 1975.

567.   "Cambodia: Growing Base for Vietnam Reds." *U.S. News and World Report* 63 (Dec. 11, 1967): 62–63.

568.   George, T.J.S. "Cambodia: A Long War to Come." *Far Eastern Economic Review* 68 (May 21, 1970): 63–66.

569.   Mataxis, Theodore C. "Cambodia: A New Model for Military Assistance." *Army* 23 (Jan. 1973): 25–30.

570.   Rush, Kenneth. "Department Supports Request for Emergency Appropriations for Security Assistance for Israel and Cambodia." *U.S. Department of State Bulletin* 69 (Nov. 26, 1973): 64–65.

571.   Sanders, Sol W. "Close-up of a Red 'Sanctuary': Cambodia and Its Leaky Border." *U.S. News and World Report* 60 (Jan. 3, 1966): 48–49.

572.   Shawcross, William. *Sideshow: Kissinger, Nixon and the Destruction of Cambodia.* New York: Simon & Schuster, 1979. This is the best survey to date.

573.   U.S. Agency for International Development. *The American Aid Program in Cambodia: A Decade of Cooperation, 1951–61.* Washington, DC: GPO, 1961.

574.   U.S. General Accounting Office. *Report on the Payment of Phantom Troops in the Cambodian Military Forces.* B–169832. Washington, DC, 1973.

575.   U.S. International Cooperation Administration. *Cambodia: Fact Sheet, Mutual Security in Action.* Department of State Publication 6931. Far Eastern Series 85. Washington, DC: GPO, 1960.

576. U.S. Library of Congress. *United States Policy Toward Cambodia, April 1970–June 1973: Statements by President Nixon, Dr. Henry Kissinger, and the Secretaries of State and Defense.* DS 558C2, 73–114E. Washington, DC: Congressional Research Service, 1973.

U.S. Bombing of Cambodia

B-52s secretly attacked a ten-mile-wide strip of Cambodia under Operation Menu from March 18, 1969 to August 15, 1973. Congress, invoking the War Powers Act (see Chapter 5), terminated the bombing.

577. "Americans Opposed to Bombing in Laos, Cambodia by 2-to-1 Margin." *Gallup Opinion Index*, no. 95 (May 1973): 16–19.

578. "Bombing Halt: Cambodia Compromise Brings Bitterness." *CQ Weekly Report* 31 (Aug. 11, 1973): 2205–2210.

579. "Bombing in Cambodia, Laos." *Gallup Opinion Index*, no. 98 (Aug. 1973): 6.

580. Carhart, T.M. *The Impact of U.S. Domestic Law on the Last Days of American Presence in Vietnam.* P–5583. Santa Monica, CA: Rand Corp., May 1975. Carhart focuses on the War Powers Act of 1973.

581. "Investigation of Secret Cambodian Bombing: A Preliminary Report." *Congressional Record* 119 (July 23, 1973): 25275–25277. [from *New York Times Magazine*]

582. Millet, Stephen M. "The Air Force, the Courts, and the Controversial Bombing of Cambodia." *Air University Review* 27 (July–Sept. 1976): 80–88. Millet finds it a political, not a judicial issue.

583. "Nixon Defends Secret Bombing of Cambodia in 1969." *CQ Weekly Report* 31 (Aug. 25, 1973): 2299.

584. Rogers, William P. "Department Discusses Presidential Authority to Continue U.S. Air Combat Operations in Cambodia." *U.S. Department of State Bulletin* 68 (May 21, 1973): 652–655.

585. Schanberg, Sydney H.A. "A Cambodian Landscape: Bomb Pits, Rubble, Ashes." *Congressional Record* 119 (May 29, 1973): S9799–9700.

586. "Secret Bombing of Cambodia: ABC's of a Growing Dispute." *U.S. News and World Report* 75 (Aug 13, 1973): 64–65.

587. "Senate Votes 63–19 to End U.S. Combat Role in Cambodia." *CQ Weekly Report* 31 (June 2, 1973): 1347–1348.

588. Sokan, I.U. "The U.S. Onslaught upon the Cambodian People." *World Peace Council* 3 (May–June 1973): 21–22.

589. Szulc, Tad. "Mum's the War: More Hushed-Up Mischief in Asia." *New Republic* 169 (Aug. 18–25, 1973): 19–21.

590. U.S. House. Committee on Judiciary. Hearings; *Bombing of Cambodia.* Pursuant to H.R. 803. 93d Cong., 2d sess., 1974. These hearings investigated whether Nixon violated his constitutional authority in ordering the bombing of Cambodia; the charge was considered during the impeachment hearings.

591. U.S. Senate. Committee on Foreign Relations. Staff Report; *U.S. Air Operation in Cambodia, April 1973.* 93d Cong., 1st sess., 1973.

592. "War Powers: Military Activities in Cambodia." *International Legal Materials* 12 (July 1973): 783–821. [July 25–Aug. 4, 1973]

593. "The White Paper on Secret Operations in Laos and Cambodia." *Congressional Record* 119 (Sept. 10, 1973): S16197–S16204.

U.S. Military Incursion, 1970

For the military side, see Chapter 7, "Combat Operations."

594. Allman, T.D. "Cambodia: Better Dead Than Red." *Far Eastern Economic Review* 68 (May 7, 1970): 21–24.

595. "And So We Leave Cambodia." *Newsweek* 76 (July 13, 1970): 16–22.

596. "Cambodian Situation." *Gallup Opinion Index*, no. 60 (June 1970): 3–7.

597. Case, W. "Beyond Vietnam to Indo-China: The Legal Implications of the United States' Incursions into Cambodia and Laos." *Journal of International Law* 3 (Spring 1971): 163ff.

598. Egan, Richard. "Sixty Days in Cambodia: A Summing Up: The Gains, the Losses, and the Out-Look Now in Southeast Asia." *Congressional Record* 116 (June 29, 1970): 21915–21916. [from *National Observer*]

599. Falk, Richard A., et al. "Symposium on the United States Military Action in Cambodia, 1970." *American Journal of International Law* 65 (Jan. 1971): 1–83.

600. Fox, Donald T., ed. *The Cambodian Incursion ... Legal Issues.* 15th Hammarskjöld Forum. New York: Oceana, 1971.

601. Grant, Jonathan S., et al., eds. *Cambodia: The Widening War in Indochina*. New York: Washington Square Press, 1971.

602. Kaiser, Robert. "'Getting Into the Enemy's System': The Cambodian Operation as Limited Tactic." *Interplay* 3 (July 1970): 26–28.

603. Kalicki, J.H. "Sino–American Relations after Cambodia." *World Today* [London] 26 (Sept. 1970): 383–393.

604. Kosygin, A.N. "Kosygin Condemns U.S.A. on Cambodia." *Current Digest of the Soviet Press* 22 (June 2, 1970): 1–4ff.

605. Lacouture, Jean. "From the Vietnam War to an Indochina War." *Foreign Affairs* 48 (July 1970): 617–628.

606. Lowenfeld, A.F., et al. "Hammarskjöld Forum: Expansion of the Vietnam War into Cambodia—The Legal Issues." *New York Law Review* 45 (June 1970): 625–678.

607. Maxey, David R. "How Nixon Decided to Invade Cambodia." *Look* 34 (Aug. 11, 1970): 22–25.

608. Poole, Peter A. *The Expansion of the Vietnam War Into Cambodia: Action and Response by Governments of North Vietnam, South Vietnam, Cambodia and the United States*. Athens: Ohio University, Center for International Studies, 1970.

609. _____. "The Vietnamization of Cambodia." *Washington Monthly* 3 (Apr. 1971): 17–24.

610. Schurmann, Franz. "Cambodia: Nixon's Trap." *Nation* 210 (June 1, 1970): 651–656.

611. Smith, Russell H. "The Presidential Decision on the Cambodian Operation: A Case Study in Crisis Management." *Air University Review* 22 (Sept.–Oct. 1971): 45–53.

612. Stevenson, John R. "United States Military Action in Cambodia: Questions of International Law." *U.S. Department of State Bulletin* 62 (June 22, 1970): 765–770.

613. U.S. House. Committee on Appropriations. Hearings; *U.S. Operations in Cambodia and Summary of Fiscal Year 1971 Budget*. Department of Defense Appropriation for 1971, Pt. 6. 91st Cong., 2d sess., 1970.

614. "The U.S. Intervention in Cambodia." *Orbis* 14 (Summer 1970): 257–260.

615. "U.S. Intervention in Cambodia: Legal Analyses of the Event and Domestic Repercussions." *Boston University Law Review* 50 (Spring 1970): 1–188.

616. U.S. Senate. Committee on Foreign Relations. Staff Report; *Cambodia: May 1970*. Washington, DC: GPO, June 7, 1970.

617. _____. Staff Report; *Cambodia: December 1970*. Washington, DC: GPO, Dec. 16, 1970.

Nixon's Defense

618. Gregg, Richard B., and Gerald A. Hauser. "Richard Nixon's April 30, 1970 Address on Cambodia: The 'Ceremony' of Confrontation." *Speech Monographs* 40 (Aug. 1973): 167–181.

619. Nixon, Richard M. "The Cambodian Sanctuary Operation: An Interim Report." *U.S. Department of State Bulletin* 62 (June 22, 1970): 761–764.

620. _____. "The Cambodia Strike: Defensive Action for Peace." *U.S. Department of State Bulletin* 62 (May 18, 1970): 617–621.

621. _____. "A Report on Progress in Vietnam." *U.S. Department of State. Bulletin* 62 (May 11, 1970): 601–604.

622. _____. "A Report on the Conclusion of the Cambodian Operation." *U.S. Department of State Bulletin* 63 (July 20, 1970): 65–75.

623. _____. "Text of President's News Conference on Cambodia." *CQ Weekly Report* 28 (May 15, 1970): 1315–1318.

624. _____. "Text of President's Speech on Cambodian Operation." *CQ Weekly Report* 28 (June 12, 1970): 1559–1560.

KHMER ROUGE

The Cambodian communists, aided by North Vietnam, won a prolonged civil war. Events following this victory are difficult to ascertain, yet considerable evidence suggests that the consequences of the new government's atrocities were more devastating than U.S. bombings. Pol Pot's short-lived regime demonstrated once again that it is possible, even without modern military technology, to brutalize a society.

Books and Dissertations

625. Barron, John, and Anthony Paul. *Murder of a Gentle Land: The Untold Story of Communist Genocide in Cambodia*. New York: Reader's Digest Press, 1977.

626. Carr, Earl A. "The Origins and Precipitating Factors of the Khmer Revolution, 1945–1975." Ph.D. dissertation, Southern Illinois University at Carbondale, 1977.

627. Hildebrand, George C., and D. Gareth Porter. *Cambodia: Starvation and Revolution.* New York: Monthly Review Press, 1976. The authors present a favorable view of Pol Pot's regime.

628. Ponchaud, François. *Cambodia: Year Zero.* Translated by N. Amphoux. New York: Holt, Rinehart & Winston, 1978.

Essays (Previctory)

629. Allman, T.D. "Cambodia: Deeper into the Mire." *Far Eastern Economic Review* 83 (Jan. 7, 1974): 18–20.

630. ———. "When Khmers Kill Khmers." *Far Eastern Economic Review* 67 (Apr. 9, 1970): 5–7.

631. "America's War Ends, but Cambodia's Ordeal Goes On." *U.S. News and World Report* 75 (Aug. 27, 1973): 17–18.

632. "Cambodia: A New Leader Emerges From the Shadows." *Far Eastern Economic Review* 84 (May 13, 1974): 26–27.

633. "Cambodia: Time is Running Out. . . ." *U.S. News and World Report* 78 (Mar. 24, 1975): 13–15.

634. Cerovic, Vasilije. "The War in Cambodia." *Review of International Affairs* [Belgrade] 24 (May 5, 1973): 31–32.

635. Davis, N. "Cambodia: Choosing the Peace Team." *Far Eastern Economic Review* 88 (Apr. 4, 1975): 12–13.

636. Gayn, Mark. "Domino: Cambodia Consulting the Stars." *New York Times Magazine* (Apr. 22, 1973): 13ff.

637. Gordon, Bernard K., and Kathryn Young. "The Khmer Republic: That Was the Cambodia that Was." *Asian Survey* 11 (Jan. 1971): 26–40.

638. Greenway, H.D.S. "Cambodia." *Atlantic* 233 (Jan. 1974): 6–8ff.

639. "The Khmer Republic Prince Sihanouk's Deposition and Subsequent Events." *Current Notes on International Affairs* [Canberra, Australia] 42 (Nov. 1971): 595–604.

640. Norton, R.P.W. "The Popular War." *Far Eastern Economic Review* 72 (June 12, 1971): 7–8.

641. Poole, Peter A. "Cambodia: Will Vietnam Truce Halt Drift to Civil War?" *Asian Survey* 13 (Jan. 1973): 76–82.

642. Quinn, Kenneth M. "Political Change in Wartime: The Khmer Krohom Revolution in Southern Cambodia, 1970–1974." *Naval War College Review* 28 (Spring 1976): 3–31.

643. Snitowsky, Mike. "Phnom Penh's New Power Men." *Far Eastern Economic Review* 85 (July 1, 1974): 18.

644. Starner, Frances L. "Cambodia: Twilight of a Limited War." *Far Eastern Economic Review* 81 (Aug. 13, 1973): 10–13.

645. Summers, Laura. "The Cambodian Civil War." *Current History* 63 (Dec. 1972): 259–262ff.

Essays (Postvictory)

646. "Cambodia After Victory: Pointers to a Neutral Future." *Far Eastern Economic Review* 88 (May 9, 1975): 20.

647. Carney, Timothy, ed. *Communist Party Power Kampuchea (Cambodia): Documents and Discussion.* Data Paper no. 106. Ithaca, NY: Cornell University, South East Asian Program, 1977.

648. Chandler, David P. "Notes and Comment: The Constitution of Democratic Kampuchea (Cambodia): The Semantics of Revolutionary Change." *Pacific Affairs* 49 (Fall 1976): 506–515.

649. Davis, N. "Dodging Death: A Daily Exercise." *Far Eastern Economic Review* 91 (Mar. 21, 1976): 11–12. Davis focuses on the threat of starvation.

650. Dunbar, Ian. "Following Peking's Revolutionary Model." *Far Eastern Economic Review* 88 (May 23, 1975): 22–23.

651. Ea Meng-Try. "Kampuchea: A Country Adrift." *Population and Development Review* 7 (June 1981): 209–228.

652. Ebihara, May. "Perspectives on Sociopolitical Transformations in Cambodia/Kampuchea." *Journal of Asian Studies* 41 (Nov. 1981): 63–72.

653. Jackson, Karl D. "Cambodia 1977: Gone to Pot." *Asian Survey* 18 (Jan. 1978): 76–90.

654. Kiernan, Ben. "Social Cohesion in Revolutionary Cambodia." *Australian Outlook* 30 (Dec. 1976): 371–386.

655. Kroef, Justus M. van der. "Political Ideology in Democratic Kampuchea." *Orbis* 22 (Winter 1979): 1007–1032.

656. Lacouture, Jean. "The Bloodiest Revolution." *New York Review of Books* (Mar. 31, 1977): 9–10.

657. ———. "Cambodia: Corrections." *New York Review of Books* (May 26, 1977): 46.

658. Laurie, J. "Spelling Out a 'Controlled Solution.'"

Far Eastern Economic Review 87 (Mar. 21, 1975): 12–13.

659. Leifer, Michael. "Kampuchea in 1980: The Politics of Attrition." *Asian Survey* 21 (Jan. 1981): 93–101.

660. Poole, Peter A. "Cambodia: Khmer Communist Party in Perspective." *Asian Thought and Society* 3 (Dec. 1978): 351ff.

661. _____. "Cambodia 1975: The GRUNK Regime." *Asian Survey* 16 (Jan. 1976): 23–30.

662. Quinn, Kenneth M. "Cambodia 1976: Internal Consolidation and External Expansion." *Asian Survey* 17 (Jan. 1977): 43–54.

663. Simon, Sheldon W. "Cambodia: Barbarism in a Small State Under Siege." *Current History* 75 (Dec. 1978): 197–201.

664. _____. "Kampuchea: Pawn in a Political Chess Match." *Current History* 79 (Dec. 1980): 170–174.

665. Summers, Laura. "Consolidating the Cambodian Revolution." *Current History* 69 (Dec. 1975): 218–223ff.

666. _____. "Defining the Revolutionary State in Cambodia." *Current History* 71 (Dec. 1976): 213–217.

667. Willmott, W.E. "Analytical Errors of the Kampuchean Communist Party." *Pacific Affairs* 54 (Summer 1981): 209–227.

Laos

Laos was drawn into the Second Indochina War when the first North Vietnamese forces moved into its territory in July 1959. U.S.–Soviet efforts resulted in the "neutralization" of Laos in 1962; at the same time the CIA entered Laos to organize a native army to fight the Laotian communists—the Pathet Lao. Later, Hanoi used Laotian territory to send supplies and men into South Vietnam (along the "Ho Chi Minh Trail"); the United States retaliated with an intense aerial bombing of the supply line. For more on the military dimension, see Chapter 7, "Combat Operations."

Books and Dissertations

668. Berval, R., et al. *Kingdom of Laos: The Land of the Million Elephants and the White Parasol.* Saigon: France-Asie, 1959.

669. Chittenden, G.M. "Laos and the Powers, 1954–1962." Ph.D. dissertation, University of London, 1969.

670. Deschamps, J.M. *Tam Tam sur le Mekong avec les guerillas Laotiens.* Saigon: C. Arden, 1948.

671. Gosselin, Charles. *Le Laos et le Protectorate Français.* Paris: Perrin, 1900.

672. Great Britain. Central Office of Information. Reference Division. *Laos.* London: HMSO, 1970.

673. Halpern, A.M. *Government, Politics and Social Structure in Laos.* New Haven, CT: Yale University Press, 1964.

674. Lebar, F.M., and A. Suddard, eds. *Laos: Its People, Its Society, Its Culture.* rev. ed. New Haven, CT: Human Relations Area Files, 1967.

675. LeBoulanger, Paul. *Histoire du Laos français: Essai d'une étude chronologique des principautés laotiennes.* Franborough, England: Gregg, 1969.

676. Manich, Jumsai M.L. *History of Laos.* Bangkok: Chalermnit Press, 1967.

677. Meeker, Oden. *The Little World of Lao.* New York: Scribner's, 1959.

678. Rose, Saul, ed. *Politics in Southern Asia: Independence and Political Rivalry in Laos, 1945–1961.* London: Macmillan, 1963.

679. Sasorith, Katay. *Le Laos.* Paris: Berger-Levrault, 1953.

680. Sisouk Na Champassak. *Storm Over Laos: A Contemporary History.* New York: Praeger, 1961. This is an account by a Laotian representative to the ICC from 1954 to 1961.

681. Toye, Hugh. *Laos: Buffer State or Battleground?* New York: Oxford University Press, 1968.

682. Whitaker, Donald P., et al. *Area Handbook for Laos.* rev. ed. DA Pamphlet 550–58. Washington, DC: GPO, 1972.

Essays

683. Adams, Nina S. "Patrons, Clients and Revolutionaries: The Lao Search for Independence, 1945–54." In *Laos: War and Revolution,* edited by N. S. Adams and Alfred W. McCoy. New York: Harper & Row, 1970, 100–120.

684. Boun Oum Na Champassak, Prince. "Allocution à l'occasion de le signature des conventions

Franco–Laotiennes." *France-Asie*, no. 46/47 (Jan.–Feb. 1950): 629–631.

685.   Duparc, Charles-Henri. "Le problème politique Laotien." *Politique Étrangère* 12 (Nov. 1947): 529–556.

686.   Fredman, H.B. *The Role of the Chinese in Lao Society*. P–2161. Santa Monica, CA: Rand Corp., 1961.

687.   Halpern, A.M. *The Lao Elite: A Study of Tradition and Innovation*. RM–2636–RC. Santa Monica, CA: Rand Corp., Nov. 1960.

688.   Mookerji, Sudhansu B. "Twenty-five Years of Laotian Independence (1946–1970)." *United Asia* [India] 22 (Sept.–Oct. 1970): 269–273.

689.   Simmonds, E.H.S. "Independence and Political Rivalry in Laos, 1945–1961." In *Politics of Southern Asia*, edited by Saul Rose. New York: St. Martin's Press, 1963.

690.   Stephens, Michael D. "Laos and the Sino–Laotian Boundary." *Asian Review* 3 (Apr. 1966): 39–44.

691.   U.S. Department of State. The Geographer. *Laos–Vietnam Boundary*. International Boundary Study no. 35, rev. ed. Washington, DC: GPO, 1966.

692.   "Who's Who in Laos." *World Today* [London] 16 (Sept. 1960): 365–367.

NEUTRALIZATION, 1960–1962

President Kennedy persuaded the U.S.S.R. to join in pressuring the Laotian communists and China into accepting the neutralization of Laos at the Geneva Conference of 1962; the idea was to remove Laotian politics from Cold War influences. However, the agreement was short-lived.

693.   Great Britain. Secretary of State for Foreign Affairs. *Declaration and Protocol on the Neutrality of Laos, Geneva, July 23, 1962*. Treaty Series no. 27 (1963), Cmnd. 2025. London: HMSO, 1963.

694.   _____. *International Conference on the Settlement of the Laotian Question, May 12, 1961–July 23, 1962*. Cmnd. 1828. London: HMSO, 1962.

Books
695.   Dommen, Arthur J. *Conflict in Laos: The Politics of Neutralization*. rev. ed. New York: Praeger, 1971.

696.   Epstein, Israel, and Elsie Fairflax-Cholmeley. *Laos in the Mirror of Geneva*. Peking; New World Press, 1961.

697.   Fall, Bernard B. *Anatomy of a Crisis: The Laotian Crisis of 1960–1961*. New York: Doubleday, 1969.

698.   Lall, Arthur S. *How Communist China Negotiates*. New York: Columbia University Press, 1968.

699.   Modelski, George A. *International Conference on the Settlement of the Laotian Questions, 1961–62*. Vancouver: University of British Columbia Press, 1962.

700.   People's Republic of China. *Concerning the Situation in Laos*. Peking: Foreign Languages Press, 1959.

Essays
701.   Beech, Keys. "How Uncle Sam Fumbled in Laos." *Saturday Evening Post* 234 (Apr. 22, 1961): 28ff.

702.   Black, Edwin F. "Laos: A Case Study of Communist Strategy." *Military Review* 44 (Dec. 1964): 49–59.

703.   Burnham, James. "Laos and Containment: With Editorial Comment." *National Review* 10 (Apr. 8, 1961): 207–213.

704.   Cousins, Norman. "Report from Laos." *Saturday Review* 44 (Feb. 18, 1961): 12–18.

705.   Crozier, Brian. "Peking and the Laotian Crisis: A Further Appraisal." *China Quarterly*, no. 11 (July–Sept. 1962): 116–123.

706.   _____. "Peking and the Laotian Crisis: An Interim Appraisal." *China Quarterly*, no. 7 (July–Sept. 1961): 128–137.

707.   Czyzak, John J., and Carl F. Salans. "The International Conference on Laos and the Geneva Agreement of 1962." *Journal of Southeast Asian History* 7 (Sept. 1966): 27–47.

708.   Elegant, Robert S. "The Laos Blunder." *New Leader* 44 (June 5, 1961): 5–6.

709.   Fall, Bernard B. "The International Relations of Laos." *Pacific Affairs* 30 (Mar. 1957): 22–34.

710.   _____. "The Laos Tangle." *International Journal* [Toronto] 16 (Spring 1961): 138–157.

711.   _____. "Laos: Will Neutralism Work?" *New Republic* 147 (July 2, 1963): 17–19.

712.   Farley, Miriam S. "Peking and the Laotian Crisis: A Further Appraisal." *China Quarterly*, no. 11 (July–Sept. 1962): 116–123.

713.   Fredman, H.B. *Laos in Strategic Prospective*. P–2330. Santa Monica, CA: Rand Corp., June 1961.

714.   Goldbloom, M.J. "Our Strange Game in Laos." *Progressive* 23 (Dec. 1959): 22–25.

715.   Gross, Leo. "The Question of Laos and the Double

Veto in the Security Council." *American Journal of International Law* 54 (Jan. 1960): 118–131.

716.   Halpern, A.M., and H.B. Fredman. *Communist Strategy in Laos*. RM–2561. Santa Monica, CA: Rand Corp., June 1960.

717.   Henderson, William D., and Frank N. Trager. "Laos: The Vientiane Agreement." *Journal of Southeast Asian History* 8 (Sept. 1967): 257–267.

718.   ———. "Showdown at Geneva: Cease-fire in Laos." *New Leader* 44 (May 22, 1961): 9–11.

719.   Hill, Kenneth L. "President Kennedy and the Neutralization of Laos." *Review of Politics* 31 (July 1969): 353–369.

720.   Kellogg, M.K. "The Laos Question: Double What Veto?" *Virginia Law Review* 45 (Dec. 1959): 1352–1360.

721.   Lederer, William J. "The Laos Fraud." In his *A Nation of Sheep*. New York: Norton, 1961, 11–26. Lederer addresses the Lao crisis of 1959–1960.

722.   Lee Chae-Jin. "Communist China and the Geneva Conference on Laos: A Reappraisal." *Asian Survey* 9 (July 1969): 522–539.

723.   Magnien, M. "Aventure américaine au Laos." *Cahiers dur Communisme* 37 (1961): 179–184.

724.   Mahajani, Usha. "President Kennedy and United States Policy in Laos, 1961–63." *Journal of Southeast Asian Studies* 2 (Sept. 1971): 87–99.

725.   Morley, Lorna. "Menaced Laos." *Editorial Research Reports* 2 (Sept. 23, 1959): 717–734.

726.   Patrick, Richard. "Presidential Leadership in Foreign Affairs Reexamined: Kennedy and Laos Without Radical Revisionism." *World Affairs* 140 (Fall 1978): 245–258.

727.   Pelz, Stephen E. "'When Do I Have Time to Think?' John F. Kennedy, Roger Hilsman and the Laotian Crisis of 1962." *Diplomatic History* 3 (Spring 1979): 215–229. For a subsequent exchange of letters between Pelz and Hilsman, see *Diplomatic History* 3 (Summer 1979): 345–348.

728.   Perazic, Elizabeth. "Little Laos Next Door to Red China." *National Geographic* 117 (Jan. 1960): 46–69.

729.   Ritvo, Herbert. "A Neutral Laos: The Danger." *New Leader* 44 (Apr. 10, 1961): 6.

730.   Rousset, Pierre. "Reappraisal in Laos." *Current History* 42 (Jan. 1962): 8–14.

731.   Souvanna Phouma. "Laos: Le fond du problème." *France-Asie* 17 (Mar.–Apr. 1961): 1824–1826.

732.   Trager, Frank N. "Dilemma in Laos." *America* 105 (July 8, 1961): 506–511.

733.   U.S. Department of State. *The Situation in Laos.* Washington, DC: GPO, 1959.

734.   Warner, Denis. "Crisis in Laos: Sham Battle in a Real War." *Reporter* 21 (Nov. 12, 1959): 25–27.

735.   ———. "The Loss of Laos." *Reporter* 25 (July 6, 1961): 21–24.

736.   White, Peter T. "Report on Laos." *National Geographic* 120 (Aug. 1961): 241–274.

737.   Wilde, James. "The Russians in Laos." *Time* 77 (Mar. 10, 1961): 26.

738.   Wright, Philip. "Laos: Wrong Place for a War." *Reporter* 24 (Feb. 16, 1961): 26–30.

Violations of Convention

Everyone appears to have violated the Laos convention. D. Gareth Porter (744) catalogues U.S. and rightist forces' actions while ignoring the North Vietnamese and Pathet Lao; Langer and Zasloff (828) show a reverse myopia; Stevenson (781, 180–199) provides a more balanced view.

739.   Dommen, Arthur J. "Neutralization Experiment in Laos." *Current History* 48 (Feb. 1965): 89–94ff. See Dommen's book (230–260) for violations.

740.   Laos. Ministry of Foreign Affairs. *North Vietnamese Interference in Laos.* Vientiane, 1965.

741.   ———. *White Book on Violations of the Geneva Accords of 1962.* Vientiane, 1966.

742.   ———. *White Book on Violations of the Geneva Accords of 1962.* Vientiane, 1968.

743.   ———. *White Book on Violations of the Geneva Accords of 1962.* Vientiane, 1970.

744.   Porter, D. Gareth. "After Geneva: Subverting Laotian Neutrality." In *Laos: War and Revolution*, edited by N.S. Adams and Alfred W. McCoy. New York: Harper & Row, 1970, 179–212.

745.   Simmonds, E.H.S. "Breakdown in Laos." *World Today* [London] 20 (July 1964): 285–292.

746. "U.S. Reviews North Vietnamese Violations of Agreement on Laos." *U.S. Department of State Bulletin* 58 (June 24, 1968): 817–820.

INDOCHINA CONFLICT AND LAOS

The following list of articles deals generally with the impact of the war on Laos and contains materials dealing with U.S. involvement.

747. Adloff, R., and V. Thompson. "Laos: Background of Invasion." *Far Eastern Survey* 22 (May 1953): 62–66. The authors describe the events which led to the Vietminh invasion of 1953.

748. Allman, T.D. "The Military Situation in Laos: There's No Third Man." *Far Eastern Economic Review* 65 (July 13–19, 1969): 168–170.

749. _____. "The War in Laos: Plain Facts." *Far Eastern Economic Review* 75 (Jan. 8, 1972): 16–18.

750. Dommen, Arthur J. "Laos in the Second Indochina War." *Current History* 59 (Dec. 1970): 326–332ff.

751. _____. "Laos: The Troubled 'Neutral.'" *Asian Survey* 7 (Jan. 1967): 74–80.

752. _____. "Laos: Was the War a Conspiracy?" *Current History* 63 (Dec. 1972): 267–270ff.

753. Duncanson, Dennis J. *Laos Emancipated.* Southeast Asian Perspectives, no. 5. New York: American Friends of Vietnam, 1972.

754. Duskin, Edgar W. "Laos." *Military Review* 48 (Mar. 1968): 3–10.

755. Galle, Wernar R. "At the Front in Laos." *Swiss Review of World Affairs* 19 (Oct. 1969): 12–15.

756. Girling, J.L.S. "Laos: Falling Domino?" *Pacific Affairs* 43 (Fall 1970): 370–383.

757. Hannoteaux, Guy. "The Savage Peace: The War in Laos." *Far Eastern Economic Review* 62 (Nov. 17–23, 1968): 405–407.

758. Kumpa, Peter J. "Insurgency in Laos: Vientiane Plays it Cool." *Far Eastern Economic Review* 59 (Mar. 24–30, 1968): 597–600.

759. Langer, Paul F. "Laos: Preparing for a Settlement in Vietnam." *Asian Survey* 9 (Jan. 1969): 69–74.

760. _____. "Laos: Search for Peace in the Midst of War." *Asian Survey* 8 (Jan. 1968): 80–86 [based on his Rand paper, P–3748, Dec. 1967]

761. _____. "The Soviet Union, China, and the Revolutionary Movement in Laos." *Studies in Comparative Communism* 6 (Spring–Summer 1973): 66–98.

762. Langland, S.G. "Laos Factor in A Vietnam Equation." *International Affairs* [London] 45 (Oct. 1969): 631–647.

763. Lumsden, M. *Laos: Refugee and Civilian War Casualty Problems.* Institute of Psychology, Department of Social Psychology, N–5001. Bergen, Norway, 1971.

764. Pace, Eric. "Laos: Continuing Crises." *Foreign Affairs* 43 (Oct. 1964): 64–74.

765. Ronk, D.E. "The Distorted War In Laos." *War/Peace Report* 11 (Oct. 1971): 19–20.

766. Simmonds, E.H.S. "Laos and the War in Vietnam." *World Today* [London] 22 (May 1966): 199–206.

767. _____. "The Problem of Laos." *World Today* [London] 26 (May 1970): 189–196.

768. Smith, Charles. "Pressures on Laos." *Asian Affairs* [U.S.] 57 (Oct. 1970): 285–292.

769. Stanton, Thomas H. "Conflict in Laos: The Village Point of View." *Transition*, no. 18 (Apr. 1969): 23–43.

770. Tilford, Earl H., Jr. "Two Scorpions in a Cup: American and Soviet Airlift to Laos." *Aerospace Historian* 27 (Fall 1980): 151–162.

771. Trager, Frank N. "Importance of Laos in Southeast Asia." *Current History* 46 (Feb. 1964): 107–111.

772. Urrows, Elizabeth. "Recurring Problems in Laos." *Current History* 57 (Dec. 1969): 361–363, 367.

773. Warner, Denis. "The Catastrophic Non-War in Laos." *Reporter* 30 (June 13, 1964): 21–24.

774. Zasloff, Joseph J. "Laos: The Forgotten War Widens." *Asian Survey* 10 (Jan. 1970): 65–72.

U.S. ACTIVITIES IN LAOS

While U.S. military and economic aid was given to Laos in the 1950s, the CIA waged its so-called secret war there, from 1962 to 1973, against the Pathet Lao and NVA by supplying a 30,000-man native Armée Clandestine. Some forty to fifty CIA agents, with a minimum annual budget of $300 million and their own air force (Air America), directed the military actions; see Chapter 6, under "Intelligence and Reconnaissance." The Stevenson account (781) and the Haney essay (792) provide excellent introductions.

Books, Dissertations and Reports

775. Adams, Nina S., and Alfred W. McCoy, eds. *Laos: War and Revolution*. New York: Harper & Row, 1970. Although they are often one-sided, these essays are well worth reading.

776. Bergot, Erwin. *Mourir au Laos*. Paris: Éditions France-Empire, 1965.

777. Branfman, Fred, ed. *Voices From the Plain of Jars*. New York: Harper & Row, 1972.

778. Burchett, Wilfred G. *The Furtive War: The United States in Vietnam and Laos*. New York: International Publishers, 1963.

779. Dengler, Dieter. *Escape From Laos*. San Rafael, CA: Presidio Press, 1979.

780. Goldstein, Martin E. *American Policy Toward Laos*. Rutherford, NJ: Fairleigh Dickinson University Press, 1973. [based on his University of Pennsylvania Ph.D. dissertation, 1968]

781. Stevenson, Charles A. *The End of Nowhere: American Policy toward Laos since 1954*. Boston: Beacon, 1972.

782. U.S. Senate. Committee on Foreign Relations. Hearings; *United States Security Agreements and Commitments Abroad: Kingdom of Laos*. Oct. 20–22, 28, 1969. 91st Cong., 1st sess., 1970.

783. _____. Report; *Laos: April 1971*. 92d Cong., 1st sess., 1971.

Essays

784. Abrams, Arnold. "The Once-hidden War: Escalation in Laos." *New Leader* 53 (Feb. 16, 1970): 8–10.

785. Bartlett, Merrill L. "Intervention in Laos." *Marine Corps Gazette* 58 (Sept. 1974): 18–23.

786. Branfman, Fred. "The President's Secret Army: A Case Study; the CIA in Laos, 1962–1972." In *The CIA File*, edited by R.L. Borosage and J.D. Marks. New York: Grossman, 1976, 46–78.

787. Campbell, Alex. "In Hot Pursuit: Reactions to U.S. Pursuit of North Vietnamese Inside Borders." *New Republic* 158 (Jan. 13, 1968): 19–21.

788. "Concern Grows over U.S. Commitment in Laos." *CQ Weekly Report* 27 (Oct. 24, 1972): 2069–2074.

789. Cranston, Senator. Alan. "Laos: Next Step in the Big Muddy." *Nation* 210 (Mar. 30, 1970): 363–366.

790. Ellsberg, Daniel. "Laos: What Nixon is up to." *New York Review of Books* (Mar. 11, 1971): 13ff.

791. Grant, Zalin B. "Report from Laos, the Hidden War." *New Republic* 158 (Apr. 20, 1968): 17–19.

792. Haney, Walt. "The Pentagon Papers and the United States Involvement in Laos." In *The Senator Gravel Edition: The Pentagon Papers, Critical Essays*. Vol. 5. Boston: Beacon, 1972, 248–293. This is an excellent essay; its footnotes provide a critical review of the literature.

793. Munthe-Kass, Harold. "The US and Laos: Are There More than Two Vietnams?" *Far Eastern Economic Review* 66 (Oct. 19–25, 1969): 226–228.

794. Nixon, Richard M. "Scope of the U.S. Involvement in Laos." *U.S. Department of State Bulletin* 62 (Mar. 30, 1970): 405–409.

795. Paul, Roland A. "Laos: Anatomy of an American Involvement." *Foreign Affairs* 49 (Apr. 1971): 533–547.

796. Rusk, Dean. "Why Laos is Critically Important." *U.S. Department of State Bulletin* 51 (July 6, 1964): 3–5.

797. Scott, Peter D. "Air America: Flying the U.S. into Laos." *Ramparts* 8 (Feb. 1970): 39–42. This article focuses on a CIA-owned and operated airline.

798. "Senate Subcommittee Details U.S. Involvement in Laos." *CQ Weekly Report* 28 (May 8, 1970): 1243–1246.

799. Shaplen, Robert. "Our Involvement in Laos." *Foreign Affairs* 48 (Apr. 1970): 478–493.

800. Starner, Frances L. "Flight of the CIA." *Far Eastern Economic Review* 78 (Oct. 7, 1972): 23–26.

801. Warner, Denis. "Our Secret War in Laos." *Reporter* 32 (Apr. 22, 1965): 23–26.

U.S. Aid Programs

Charges of corruption and waste may be found in the Committee on Government Operations' 7th Report (812).

802. Clark, Joel. "The Foreign Exchange Operations Fund for Laos: An Interesting Experiment in Monetary Stabilization." *Asia Survey* 6 (Mar. 1964): 134–149.

803. "Economic Cooperation Agreement and Notes Between the United States of America and Laos." *Treaties and Other International Acts Series*, no. 2344. Washington, DC: GPO, 1952.

804. Kirby, Robert L. "American Military Airlift During the Laotian Civil War, 1958–1963." *Aerospace Historian* 24 (Mar. 1977): 1–10.

805. Leerburger, F.J. "Laos: Case Study of U.S. Foreign Aid." *Foreign Policy Bulletin* 38:5 (1959): 61–63.

806. Schancke, Don. *Mister Pop.* New York: McKay, 1970. This is an account of a fascinating American who was part of U.S. aid programs in this region.

807. U.S. Department of State. *Laos Fact Sheet: Mutual Security in Action.* Publication no. 6842. Washington, DC: GPO, 1959.

808. U.S. General Accounting Office. Report; *Examination of Economics and Technical Assistance Program for Laos* [for Fiscal Years 1955–57]. Washington, DC, 1958.

809. _____. Report; *Follow-up Review of Economic and Technical Assistance Program for Laos.* Washington, DC, 1959.

810. _____. Report; *Legislative Ceiling on Expenditures in Laos Reduced Costs but the Ceiling was Exceeded.* Washington, DC, 1974.

811. U.S. House. Committee on Foreign Affairs. Hearings; *Mutual Security Program in Laos.* 85th Cong., 2d sess., May 7–8, 1958.

812. U.S. House. Committee on Government Operations. Hearings; *United States Aid Operations in Laos.* 86th Cong., 1st sess., Mar. 11 and June 1, 1959. These hearings contain the "Porter Harding Report," which was critical of the U.S. aid program.

813. U.S. Senate. Committee on Foreign Relations. Hearings; *Aid Activities in Laos.* 93d Cong., 1st sess., 1972.

814. _____. Hearings; *United States Security Agreements and Commitments Abroad.* Pt. 2: *Kingdom of Laos.* 91st Cong., 1st sess., 1970, 365–606.

U.S. Bombing of Laos

U.S. air operations in Laos were conducted secretly from June 1964 to March 1970, thereafter openly until Congress ordered a halt in mid-1973; see Chapter 7, under "Aerial Bombing" and Chapter 5, "Congress and Vietnam Intervention," especially the section, "War Powers Act, 1973."

815. Branfman, Fred. "Laos: No Place to Hide?" *Bulletin of Concerned Asian Scholars* 2 (Fall 1970): 15–46.

816. _____. "The Wild Blue Yonder Over Laos." *Washington Monthly* 3 (July 1971): 28–43.

817. Everingham, John. "Let Them Eat Bombs." *Washington Monthly* 4 (Sept. 1972): 10–16.

818. Freel, William F. "Laos: Secret War and Crucial Test." *Navy* 13 (Apr. 1970): 26–31.

819. Hersh, Seymour M. "An American Who Once Picked the Targets Tells: How We Ran the Secret Air War in Laos." *New York Times Magazine* (Oct. 29, 1972): 18–19ff.

Meo Tribesmen

As early as 1961 the CIA had armed some 9,000 Meo tribesmen (L'Armée Clandestine) to fight the Pathet Lao and NVA; later, this number was expanded. Today remnants of this army are refugees in Thailand.

820. Garrett, W.E. "No Place to Run: The Hmong of Laos." *National Geographic* 145 (Jan. 1974): 78–111.

821. Lemoine, Jacques. *Un village Hmong Vert du haut Laos.* Paris: Éditions du centre nationale de la recherche scientifique, 1972.

822. Marks, Thomas A. "The Meo Hill Tribe Problem in North Thailand." *Asian Survey* 13 (Oct. 1973): 929–944.

823. "Meo Culpa." *New Republic* 164 (Apr. 10, 1971): 11–12.

824. Osburn, G.M.T. "Government and the Hill Tribe of Laos." In *Southeast Asian Tribes, Minorities and Nations,* edited by Peter Kunstadter. Princeton, NJ: Princeton University Press, 1967, 259–270.

825. Ward, J. Thomas. "U.S. Aid to Hill Tribe Refugees in Laos." In *Southeast Asian Tribes, Minorities and Nations,* edited by Peter Kunstadter. Princeton, NJ: Princeton University Press, 1967, 295–306.

PATHET LAO

Studies of the Laotian communist party are infrequent; perhaps the best surveys are found in the writings of Langer and Zasloff (828) and in Zasloff (833).

Books

826. Caply, Michael. *Guérilla au Laos.* Paris: Presses de la Cité, 1966.

827. *In the Liberated Zone of Laos.* Hanoi: Foreign Languages Publishing House, 1968.

828. Langer, P.F., and J.J. Zasloff. *North Vietnam and the Pathet Lao: Partners in the Struggle for Laos.* Cambridge, MA: Harvard University Press, 1970.

829. McKeithen, Edwin T. *The Role of the North Viet-*

namese Cadres in the Pathet Lao Administration of Xieng Khouang Province. New York: Scribner's, 1959.

830.   Manich, Jumsai M.L. *Battle of Vientiane of 1960: With Historical Background Leading to the Battle.* Bangkok: Prayura Phisnaka, 1961. This book describes the Kong Le coup.

831.   Phoumi, Vongvichit. *Laos and the Victorious Struggle of the Lao People against U.S. Neo-Colonialism.* Hanoi: Neo Lao Haksat Publications, 1969.

832.   Scalapino, R., and B. Fall, eds. *The Communist Revolution in Asia: The Pathet Lao; A Liberation Movement.* Englewood Cliffs, NJ: Prentice-Hall, 1965.

833.   Zasloff, Joseph J. *The Pathet Lao: Leadership and Organization.* Lexington, MA: Lexington Books, 1973.

Essays
834.   Bhadkamkar, Ashok B. "North Vietnamese Interference in Laos." *Current Notes on International Affairs* [Canberra, Australia] 36 (Dec. 1965): 817–823.

835.   Butwell, Richard. "From Feudalism to Communism in Laos (1954–1975)." *Current History* 69 (Dec. 1975): 223–226ff.

836.   Champassak, Sisouk Na. "The Emergence of an Asian Communist Coalition." *Annals of the American Academy of Political and Social Science* 349 (Sept. 1963): 117–129.

837.   Chapelier, G., and J. Van Malderghem. "Plain of Jars: Social Changes Under Five Years of Pathet Lao Administration." *Asia Quarterly* [Brussels], no. 1 (1971): 61–90.

838.   Fall, Bernard. "The Pathet Lao: A 'Liberation' Movement." In *The Communist Revolution in Asia.* 2d ed., edited by Robert A. Scalapino. Englewood Cliffs, NJ: Prentice-Hall, 1969, 185–211.

839.   Hafner, J.A. "The Pathet Lao and Change in Traditional Economics of the Mao and Kha, 1958–1961." *Papers of Michigan Academy of Science, Arts, and Letters* 50 (1965): 431–436.

840.   Jonas, A., and G.K. Tanham. "Laos: A Phase in Cyclic Regional Revolution." *Orbis* 5 (Spring 1961): 64–73.

841.   Langer, Paul F. *Comments on Bernard Fall's "The Pathet Lao: A 'Liberation' Party."* P–3751. Santa Monica, CA: Rand Corp., Feb. 1969.

842.   _____. *The Soviet Union, China and the Pathet Lao: Analysis and Chronology.* P–4765. Santa Monica, CA: Rand Corp., Jan. 1972.

843.   _____, and Joseph J. Zasloff. *The Northern Vietnamese Adviser in Laos: A First Hand Account.* RM–5688–ARPA. Santa Monica, CA: Rand Corp., June 1968.

844.   _____. *Revolution in Laos: The North Vietnamese and the Pathet Laos.* RM–5935–ARPA. Santa Monica, CA: Rand Corp., Sept. 1969.

845.   Mikheyev, Y. "Laotian Patriots: Years of Struggles and Victories (1945–1975)." *International Affairs* [Moscow] 21 (Nov. 1975): 42–48.

846.   Phoumi Vongvichit. "Thirty Years of Struggle, Second Year of Freedom." *World Marxist Revolution* [Canada] 19 (Nov. 1976): 81–89.

847.   Stuart-Fox, Martin. "The Lao Revolution: Leadership and Policy Differences." *Australian Outlook* 31 (Aug. 1977): 279–288.

PEACE ACCORDS

The peace agreement was reached in September of 1973.

848.   Brown, MacAlister, and Joseph J. Zasloff. "Laos 1973: Wary Steps Toward Peace." *Asian Survey* 14 (Feb. 1974): 166–174.

849.   _____. "Laos 1974: Coalition Government Shoots the Rapids." *Asian Survey* 15 (Feb. 1975): 174–183.

850.   Coiffait, Max. "Laotian Leaders Search for Peace." *Pacific Community* [Japan] 2 (Oct. 1970): 179–188.

851.   Dommen, Arthur J. "Toward Negotiations in Laos." *Asian Survey* 11 (Jan. 1971): 41–50.

852.   George, T.J.S. "Laos, the Latest Peace Domino." *Far Eastern Economic Review* 79 (Feb. 26, 1973): 12–13.

853.   Jenkins, Chris. "Laos: Showing the Way to Peace." *Indochina Chronicle*, no. 29 (Nov. 23, 1973): 1–19.

854.   Jenkins, David. "Laos: Peace and the Numbers Game." *Far East Economic Review* 82 (Nov. 26, 1973): 29–31.

855.   Karnow, Stanley. "The Fragile Accord: Defusing Laos." *New Republic* 168 (Mar. 10, 1973): 15–17.

856.   "Lao Government of Vientiane-Lao Patriotic Forces: Agreement on Cease-fire in Laos." *International Legal Materials* 12 (Mar. 1973): 397–406.

857. "Lao Patriotic Forces' Just Stand on Peaceful Settlement of Lao Issue." *Peking Review* 15 (Nov. 3, 1972): 12–14.

858. "Laos: No Progress at Peace Talks and Significant Communist Military Advances." *Asia Research Bulletin* 2 (Dec. 1972): 1383–1385.

859. "Laos: Protocol Agreement to the Ceasefire." *Australian Foreign Affairs Record* 44 (Oct. 1973): 674–687.

860. "Laos: The Silent Surrender." *Far Eastern Economic Review* 88 (May 23, 1975): 10–11.

861. Peagam, Norman. "Laos' Princes of Peace." *Far Eastern Economic Review* 84 (Apr. 8, 1974): 14–16.

862. _____. "Laos: The Third Time Around." *Far Eastern Economic Review* 84 (Apr. 15, 1974): 12–15.

863. "Protocol to Agreement on Laos (Sept. 14, 1973)." *Asia Research Bulletin* 3 (Nov. 1973): 2262–2266.

864. Sergeyev, A. "Peace and National Accord for Laos." *International Affairs* [Moscow] 19 (May 1973): 78–80.

865. Zasloff, Joseph J. "Laos 1972: The War, Politics and Peace Negotiations." *Asian Survey* 13 (Jan. 1973): 60–75.

POSTWAR ACTIVITIES

Vietnam's role in Laotian affairs is not yet fully evident; however, in 1979 it was estimated that 30,000 to 45,000 Vietnamese troops remained there. Some evidence also suggests that small groups of Laotian "freedom fighters" are still challenging the Pathet Lao and the Vietnamese.

866. Andelman, David A. "Laos After the Takeover." *New York Times Magazine* (Oct. 24, 1976): 14–15ff.

867. Bedlington, Stanley S. "Laos in 1980: The Portents Are Ominous." *Asian Survey* 21 (Jan. 1981): 102–111.

868. Brown, MacAlister, and Joseph J. Zasloff. "Dependency in Laos." *Current History* 75 (Dec. 1978): 202–207. The authors side with Vietnam against Cambodia and China.

869. _____. "Laos 1976: Faltering First Steps Toward Socialism." *Asian Survey* 17 (Feb. 1977): 107–115.

870. _____. "Laos 1977: The Realities of Independence." *Asian Survey* 18 (Feb. 1978): 164–174.

871. _____. "Laos 1978: The Ebb and Flow of Adversity." *Asian Survey* 19 (Feb. 1979): 95–103.

872. _____. "New Stages of Revolution in Laos." *Current History* 71 (Dec. 1976): 218–221ff.

873. Chanda, Nayan. "Laos: Back to the Drawing Board." *Far Eastern Economic Review* 101 (Sept. 8, 1978): 32–34.

874. _____. "The Sounds of Distant Gunfire." *Far Eastern Economic Review* 102 (Dec. 8, 1978): 34–38.

875. Dommen, Arthur J. "Communist Strategy in Laos." *Problems of Communism* 24 (July–Aug. 1975): 53–66.

876. Hiebert, Murray. "'Socialist Transformation' in Laos." *Current History* 79 (Dec. 1980): 175–179.

877. Kroef, Justus M. van der. "Laos: Paradoxes and Dilemmas of Survival." *Asian Thought and Society* 5 (Sept. 1980): 160–174.

878. Mikheyev, Y. "Laos: Toward Building Socialism." *International Affairs* [Moscow] 24 (Feb. 1978): 40–45.

879. Stuart-Fox, Martin. "The Initial Failure of Agriculture Cooperativization in Laos." *Asia Quarterly*, no. 4 (1980): 273–294.

880. _____. "Laos: A Small State Involved in Neighbor's Conflict." *Round Table*, no. 282 (Apr. 1981): 163–169.

881. _____. "Laos: The First Five-Year Plan." *Asia Thought and Society* 6 (Sept.–Nov. 1981): 272–276.

882. Zasloff, Joseph J. "Laos: The Lao Peoples Revolutionary Party: The Ruling Party in Laos." *Asian Thought and Society* 4 (Apr. 1979): 116–118.

Thailand

As one of the prophesied "dominoes," Thailand sided with the United States in the Second Indochina War. Noted for their ability to survive international storms, the Thais chose to provide the United States with its Southeast Asian "sanctuary" (airbases), and to make a modest troop contribution; in return, the United States provided the Thais with substantial economic aid and a pledge for security assistance. Since the withdrawal of the United States from Vietnam, Thailand has sought closer relations with China in order to offset the new Vietnamese threat on its northern border.

Books

883.   American University. *Area Handbook for Thailand.* DA Pamphlet 550–53. Washington, DC: GPO, 1971.

884.   Basche, James. *Thailand: Land of the Free.* New York: Taplinger, 1971.

885.   Blanchard, Wendell. *Thailand: Its People, Its Society, Its Culture.* New Haven, CT: Human Relations Area Files, 1958.

886.   Busch, Noel F. *Thailand: An Introduction to Modern Siam.* Princeton, NJ: Van Nostrand, 1959.

887.   Darling, Frank C. *Thailand and the United States.* Washington, DC: Public Affairs Press, 1965.

888.   _____. *The United States in Thailand.* Ithaca, NY: Cornell University Press, 1966.

889.   Insor, D. *Thailand: A Political, Social, And Economic Analysis.* New York: Praeger, 1963.

890.   Nuechterlein, Donald E. *Thailand and the Struggle for Southeast Asia.* Ithaca, NY: Cornell University Press, 1965.

891.   Poole, Peter A. *The Vietnamese in Thailand.* Ithaca, NY: Cornell University Press, 1970.

892.   Riggs, Fred W. *Thailand: The Modernization of a Bureaucractic Policy.* Honolulu: East–West Center Press, 1966.

893.   Siffin, William J. *The Thai Bureaucracy: Institutional Change and Development.* Honolulu: East–West Center Press, 1966.

894.   Suthiwart-Narueput, Smairob. "A Strategy for Survival of Thailand: Reappraisal and Readjustment in Her Alliances (1969–76)." Ph.D. dissertation, University of Oklahoma, 1980.

895.   Sutton, Joseph L., ed. *Problems of Politics and Administration in Thailand.* Bloomington: Indiana University, Institute of Training for Public Service, 1962.

896.   U.S. Department of State. *Background Notes: Thailand.* Washington, DC: GPO, 1966.

897.   Wilson, David A. *Politics in Thailand.* Ithaca, NY: Cornell University Press, 1962.

898.   _____. *The United States and the Future of Thailand.* New York: Praeger, 1970.

Essays

899.   Buszynski, Leszek. "Thailand, the Soviet Union, and the Kampuchean Imbroglio." *World Today* [London] 38 (Feb. 1982): 66–72.

900.   Butwell, Richard. "Thailand after Vietnam." *Current History* 57:340 (1969): 339–343, 368–369.

901.   Darling, Frank C. "Thailand in 1977: The Search for Stability and Progress." *Asian Survey* 18 (Feb. 1978): 153–163.

902.   _____. "Thailand in the 1980s." *Current History* 79 (Dec. 1980): 185–188.

903.   Keyes, Charles F. "Buddhism and National Integration in Thailand." *Journal of Asian Studies* 30 (May 1971): 551–567.

904.   Lohr, Chester H. "What is the Outlook for Thailand?" *Naval War College Review* 21 (Sept. 1968): 92–125.

905.   Martin, Graham. "Thailand and Southeast Asia." *U.S. Department of State Bulletin* 66 (Feb. 6, 1967): 193–199.

906.   Martin, James V., Jr. "Thai–American Relations in World War II." *Journal of American Studies* 22 (Aug. 1963): 451–467.

907.   Neher, Clark D. "Thailand: Toward Fundamental Change." *Asian Survey* 11 (Feb. 1971): 131–138.

908.   Piker, Steven. "Sources of Stability and Instability in Rural Thai Society." *Journal of Asian Studies* 27 (Aug. 1968): 777–790.

909.   Shaplen, Robert. "Letter from Bangkok." *New Yorker* 43 (Mar. 18, 1967): 135–172.

910.   _____. "Letter from Thailand." *New Yorker* 51 (July 14, 1975): 75ff.

911.   _____. "Letter from Thailand." *New Yorker* 54 (July 24, 1978): 43ff.

912.   "Symposium on Northeast Thailand." *Asian Survey* 6 (July 1966): 349–380.

913.   Textor, Robert B. "The 'Loose Structure' of Thai Society: A Paradigm Under Pressure." *Pacific Affairs* 50 (Fall 1977): 467–472.

914.   Wilson, David A. "China, Thailand and the Spirit of Bandung." *China Quarterly* 30 (Apr.–June 1967): 149–169; (July–Sept. 1967): 96–127.

915.   _____. "Thailand—Scandal and Progress." *Asian Survey* 5 (Feb. 1965): 108–112.

916.   Young, Stephan B. "The Northeastern Thai Village: A Nonparticipatory Democracy." *Asian Survey* 8 (Nov. 1968): 873–886.

Politics

917.   Darling, Frank C. "American Influence on the Evolution of Constitutional Government in Thailand." Ph.D. dissertation, American University, 1961.

918.   _____. "Modern Politics in Thailand." *Review of Politics* 24 (Apr. 1962): 163–182.

919.   _____. "Political Parties in Thailand." *Pacific Affairs* 44 (Summer 1971): 228–241.

920.   _____. "Student Protest and Political Change in Thailand." *Pacific Affairs* 47 (Spring 1974): 5–19.

921.   _____. "Thailand: Return to Military Rule." *Current History* 71 (Dec. 1976): 197–200.

922.   _____. "Thailand in 1976: Another Defeat for Constitutional Democracy." *Asian Survey* 17 (Feb. 1977): 116–132.

923.   Girling, J.L.S. "Politics Amalgamated: The Thai Example." *Australian Outlook* 24 (Dec. 1971): 263–276.

924.   _____. "Strong-Man Tactics in Thailand: The Problems Remain." *Pacific Community* [Japan] 3 (Apr. 1972): 531–542.

925.   _____. "Thailand: The Coup and its Implications." *Pacific Affairs* 50 (Fall 1977): 387–405.

926.   Heinze, Ruth-Inge. "Ten Days in October: Students vs the Military." *Asian Survey* 14 (June 1974): 491–508.

927.   Hindley, Donald. "Thailand: The Politics of Passivity." *Pacific Affairs* 41 (Fall 1968): 355–371.

928.   Marks, Thomas A. "The Communist Party and the Strategy of the United Front in Thailand Since October, 1976." *Asia Quarterly* [Brussels], no. 1 (1980): 3–18.

929.   _____. "The Military and Politics in Thailand: An Analysis of Two October Coups (1976 & 1977)." *Issues & Studies* 14 (Jan. 1978): 58–90.

930.   Mezey, Michael L. "The 1971 Coup in Thailand: Understanding Why the Legislature Fails." *Asian Survey* 13 (Mar. 1973): 306–317.

931.   Neher, Clark D. "Constitutionalism and Elections in Thailand." *Pacific Affairs* 43 (Summer 1970): 240–257.

932.   _____. "Political Corruption in a Thai Province." *Journal of Developing Areas* 11 (July 1977): 479–492.

933.   Neuchterlein, Donald E. "Thailand After Sarit." *Asian Survey* 4 (May 1964): 842–850.

934.   Prizzia, Ross. "Thailand: Elections and Coalition Government." *Asia Quarterly* [Brussels], no. 3 (1976): 192–208; no. 4 (1976): 281–295.

935.   U.S. House. Committee on Foreign Affairs. Hearings; *Political Situation in Thailand.* 93d Cong., 1st sess., 1974.

936.   Zimmerman, Robert F. "Student 'Revolution' in Thailand: The End of the Thai Bureaucractic Policy?" *Asian Survey* 14 (June 1974): 509–529.

Economy and Modernization

For items on U.S. aid, see "U.S. and Thailand," in this chapter.

Books and Dissertations

937.   Charupat Ruangsuwan. "The Use of Military Forces for National Development in Thailand." Ph.D. dissertation, Claremont Graduate School, 1977.

938.   Chaupen Puckahtikom. "Balance of Payments and Monetary Developments: Thailand, 1947–1973." Ph.D. dissertation, University of Rochester, 1977.

939.   Ingram, James C. *Economic Change in Thailand, 1850–1970.* rev. ed. Stanford, CA: Stanford University Press, 1971.

940.   Jacobs, Norman. *Modernization Without Development: Thailand as an Asian Case Study.* New York: Praeger, 1971.

941.   Kanala Sukhabaniji Eksaengsri. "Political Change and Modernization: Northeast Thailand's Quest for Identity and Its Potential Threat to National Security." Ph.D. dissertation, State University of New York, Binghamton, 1977.

942.   Muscat, Robert J. *Development Strategy in Thailand: A Study of Economic Growth.* New York: Praeger, 1966.

943.   Nairn, Ronald C. *International Aid to Thailand: The New Colonialism?* New Haven, CT: Yale University Press, 1966.

944.   Nakahara, Joyce, and Ronald A. Wilson. *Development and Conflict in Thailand.* Data Paper no. 80. Ithaca, NY: Cornell University, Southeast Asia Program, 1971.

945.   Silcock, T.H., ed. *Thailand: Social and Economic Studies in Development.* Durham, NC: Duke University Press, 1967.

946.   Skinner, G. William, and A. Thomas Kirsch, eds. *Change and Persistence in Thai Society.* Ithaca, NY: Cornell University Press, 1975.

947.   Trescott, Paul B. *Thailand's Monetary Experience: The Economics of Stability.* New York: Praeger, 1971.

948.   Van Roy, Edward. *Economic Systems of Northern Thailand.* Ithaca, NY: Cornell University Press, 1971.

Essays

949.   Ayal, Eliezer B. "Private Enterprise and Economic Progress in Thailand." *Journal of Asian Studies* 26 (Nov. 1966): 5–14.

950.   Chalirm Vudhikosit. "Thailand and the Balance of Trade Problem." *Pacific Community* [Japan] 2 (Jan. 1971): 377–390.

951.   Jenkins, David. "The New Frontier." *Far Eastern Economic Review* 80 (June 4, 1973): 25–28. Jenkins focuses on modernization and insurgency in northeast Thailand.

952.   Lin, Sein, and Bruce Esposito. "Agrarian Reform in Thailand: Problems and Prospects." *Pacific Affairs* 49 (Fall 1976): 425–442.

953.   Simonet, P.A. "Harmonious Development in Thailand." *Finance and Development* 3 (Sept. 1966): 194ff.

954.   Stifel, Laurence D. "Technocrats and Modernization in Thailand." *Asian Survey* 16 (Dec. 1976): 1184–1196.

THAILAND AND THE INDOCHINA WAR

955.   Alpern, Stephen I. "Thailand's Changing Attitude Toward Communist China: Diplomacy of Adaptability." *Military Review* 54 (Mar. 1974): 85–93.

956.   Astri Suhrki. "Smaller-Nation Diplomacy: Thailand's Current Dilemmas." *Asian Survey* 11 (May 1971): 429–444.

957.   "Background Papers: Background to the Security Situation on the Thai–Laos Border." *Asia Research Bulletin* 2 (July 1972): 1059–1066.

958.   Darling, Frank C. "The Role of Laos in the Defense Strategy of Thailand." *Pacific Community* [Japan] 3 (Apr. 1972): 516–530.

959.   _____. "Thailand: De-escalation and Uncertainty." *Asian Survey* 9 (Feb. 1969): 115–121.

960.   _____. "Thailand: Stability and Escalation." *Asian Survey* 8 (Feb. 1968): 120–126.

961.   Fulham, Parke. "A Land at Peace? Country's Internal Situation and Its Foreign Relations." *Far Eastern Economic Review* 51 (Feb. 10, 1966): 235–236.

962.   Hanna, Willard A. "Thailand's Strategic Northeast: Defense and Development." *American Universities Field Staff Reports Service: Southeast Asia Series* 14 (1966).

963.   Hough, Richard L. "Development and Security in Thailand: Lessons From Other Asian Countries." *Asian Survey* 9 (Mar. 1969): 178–187.

964.   Kroef, Justus M. van der. "Thailand between Two Millstones." *Contemporary Review* 209 (July 1966): 20–24.

965.   Kroesen, Frederick J. "The Precarious Position of Thailand." *Military Review* 44 (Dec. 1964): 60–69.

966.   Murphy, Charles J.V. "Thailand's Fight to the Finish." *Fortune* 72 (Oct. 1964): 122–127, 266–274.

967.   Olson, John V. "Thai Ranger School." *Armor* 80 (May–June 1971): 43–46.

968.   Parker, Maynard. "Untying Thailand." *Foreign Affairs* 51 (Jan. 1973): 327–339.

969.   Santos, A.B. "Thailand: The Next Domino?" *Far Eastern Economic Review* 60 (Apr. 7, 1968): 56–57.

970.   Sar Desai, D.R. "Die Rolle der Thais und der Vietnamesen in Kambodscha." *Europa-Archiv* 26 (Jan. 10, 1971): 30–38.

971.   Shirk, Paul R. "Thai–Soviet Relations." *Asian Survey* 9 (Sept. 1969): 682–693.

972.   Warren, W. "Cool Hand in Thailand." *New York Times Magazine* (Oct. 5, 1975): 42ff.

973.   Wilson, Dick. "Thailand: The Next Domino?" *Spectator*, no. 7199 (June 17, 1966): 752–753.

974.   Young, Kenneth T. "Thailand and the Cambodian Conflict." *Current History* 59 (Dec. 1970): 351–355ff.

Refugees

Increasing numbers of Vietnamese, Laotian and Cambodian refugees fled to Thailand after 1975.

975.   Jenkins, David. "Refugees: Thailand's Enduring

Dilemma." *Far Eastern Economic Review* 80 (Apr. 30, 1973): 27–28.

976. Poole, Peter A. "Thailand's Vietnamese Minority." *Asian Survey* 7 (Dec. 1967): 886–895.

977. ———. "Thailand's Vietnamese Refugees: Can They Be Assimilated?" *Pacific Affairs* 40 (Fall–Winter 1967–1968): 324–332.

INSURGENCY IN THAILAND

978. Aertker, Samuel R., et al. "Communist Terrorist Camp: Thailand–Malaysian Frontier." *Military Review* 46 (June 1966): 39–46.

979. Ali, S.M. "Thailand: Guarding the 'Land of the Free.'" *Far Eastern Economic Review* 69 (Dec. 26, 1970): 25–27.

980. Bartlett, Merrill L. "The Communist Insurgency in Thailand." *Marine Corps Gazette* 57 (Mar. 1973): 42–49.

981. Bell, Peter F. "Thailand's Northeast: Regional Underdevelopment, 'Insurgency,' and Official Response." *Pacific Affairs* 42 (Spring 1969): 47–54.

982. Casella, Alessandro. "Communism and Insurrection in Thailand." *World Today* [London] 26 (May 1970): 197–208.

983. Girling, J.L.S. "Northeast Thailand: Tomorrow's Vietnam?" *Foreign Affairs* 46 (Jan. 1968): 388–397.

984. Hewison, Kevin J. "Revolutionary Warfare in Thailand: A Comment." *Australian Outlook* 34 (Aug. 1980): 197–208.

985. "Insurgency–Counterinsurgency in Thailand." *Psychological Opportunities*, no. 64 (Oct. 30, 1967): 18–25.

986. Karnow, Stanley. "The Looking Glass War: Insurgency in Thailand." *Far Eastern Economic Review* 58 (Dec. 21, 1967): 539–542ff.

987. Klare, Michael T. "Thailand: Counterinsurgency's Proving Ground." *Nation* 212 (Apr. 26, 1971): 527–531.

988. Kroef, Justus M. van der. "Communism and Political Instability in Thailand." *Issues & Studies* 12 (Sept. 1976): 74–102.

989. ———. "Guerrilla Communism and Counterinsurgency in Thailand." *Orbis* 18 (Spring 1974): 106–139. [survey of the topic from the 1950s to 1974]

990. ———. "Organizing Counter-Insurgency: The

Thai Experience." *South-East Asian Spectrum* 2 (Jan. 1974): 45–53.

991. Kuebler, Jeanne. "Thailand: New Red Target." *Editorial Research Reports* (Sept. 15, 1965): 665–682.

992. Lomax, Louis E. *Thailand: The War That Is, The War That Will Be.* New York: Vintage, 1967.

993. Lo Shih-fu. "The Thai Communists: Two-Front Warfare." *Issues & Studies* 8 (Mar. 1972): 57–67.

994. Lovelace, Daniel D. "'Peoples War' and Chinese Foreign Policy: Thailand as a Case Study of Overt Insurgent Support." Ph.D. dissertation, Claremont Graduate School, 1971.

995. Luther, Hans U. "Thailand: Counterinsurgency or Rural Development." *Asia Research Bulletin* 2 (Nov. 1972): 1295–1298.

996. Menos, Dennis. "Thailand Insurgency: A New Cause?" *Military Review* 47 (Aug. 1967): 32–40.

997. Morell, David, and Chai-anan Samudaranija. "Thailand's Revolutionary Insurgency: Changes in Leadership Potential." *Asian Survey* 19 (Apr. 1979): 315–332.

998. Myers, Bruce F. "Thailand: Peking's Next Rural Base Area in 'Encirclement.'" *Naval War College Review* 19 (June 1967): 23–51.

999. Nuechterlein, Donald E. "Thailand: Another Vietnam?" *Asian Survey* 7 (Feb. 1967): 126–130.

1000. O'Neil, Wayne. "Who Says Thailand's Next?" *New Republic* 164 (Jan. 9, 1971): 25–27.

1001. Parker, Maynard. "Squeeze Play in Thailand." *Reporter* 25 (Aug. 11, 1966): 16–18. The author reports the reactions of Thai communists.

1002. Peagam, Norman. "The Grassroots of a Rebellion." *Far Eastern Economic Review* (May 9, 1975): 27–30. The author argues that insurgency is fueled by the nonethnic Thai population, not Marxism.

1003. Randolph, R. Sean, and W. Scott Thompson. "Thai Insurgency: Contemporary Developments." *Washington Papers* 9:81 (1981): Entire issue.

1004. Starner, Frances L. "Thai Insurgency: Tribal Guerrillas." *Far Eastern Economic Review* 78 (Dec. 9, 1972): 26–28.

1005. Stuart-Fox, Martin. "Factors Influencing Relations Between the Communist Parties of Thailand and Laos." *Asian Survey* 19 (Apr. 1979): 333–352.

1006. ———. "Tensions Within the Thai Insurgency." *Australian Outlook* 33 (Aug. 1979): 182–197.

1007.   Tanham, George K. *Assessing U.S. Counterinsurgency: Trial in Thailand.* New York: Crane, Russak, 1974.

1008.   Thomson, John R. "Thailand's Communists: The Burning Mountain." *Far Eastern Economic Review* 60 (Apr. 21, 1968): 218–220.

1009.   _____. "Thailand's Communists: The Mountains Are Steeper." *Far Eastern Economic Review* 60 (Apr. 7, 1968): 139–142.

1010.   Wei-jiun Chow. "Chinese Communists Trying to Turn Thailand into Second Vietnam: Activities of the Thai Communist 'Liberation Army' and Its 'Ten Policy' Statement." *Asian Outlook* 4 (Mar. 1969): 23–44.

1011.   Wit, Daniel. *Thailand: Another Vietnam?* New York: Scribner's, 1968.

1012.   Zimmerman, Robert F. "Insurgency in Thailand." *Problems of Communism* 25 (May–June 1976): 18–39.

U.S. AND THAILAND

1013.   Allman, Timothy. "US–Thailand: The Lovers Part." *Far Eastern Economic Review* 69 (Aug. 13, 1970): 23–25.

1014.   Bartlett, Merrill L. "Post Vietnam: U.S. and Thailand (1974–1975)." *Marine Corps Gazette* 60 (Jan. 1976): 24–29.

1015.   Caswell, John D. "The Changing Thai–United States Alliance: Implications for the Nixon Doctrine in Asia." *Naval War College Review* 24 (Oct. 1971): 59–75.

1016.   Darling, Frank C. "American Policy in Thailand." *Western Political Quarterly* 15 (Mar. 1962): 93–110.

1017.   _____. "A New American Policy in Thailand." *Air University Review* 21 (July–Aug. 1970): 58–64.

1018.   Gordon, Bernard K. "Thailand: Its Meaning for the U.S." *Current History* 52 (Jan. 1967): 16–21, 53–54.

1019.   Karnow, Stanley. "Thailand and the U.S.: Up in Arms." *Far Eastern Economic Review* 58 (Dec. 24, 1967): 583–585ff.

1020.   Marks, Thomas A. "Thai Security During the 'American Era,' 1960–1976." *Issues & Studies* 15 (Apr. 1979): 61–88.

1021.   Nibondh Sasidhorn. "The United States and Extraterritoriality in Thailand: Some Unique Aspects of American–Thai Relations." Ph.D. dissertation, Indiana University, 1960.

1022.   "The Nixon Doctrine and Thailand." *SEATO Record* 10 (Apr. 1967): 15–17.

1023.   Randolph, Raymond S. "Diplomacy and National Interest: Thai–American Security Cooperation in the Vietnam Era." Ph.D. dissertation, Fletcher School of Law and Diplomacy, 1978.

1024.   Rice, Irvin M. "Thailand's Relations with the United States: A Study in Foreign Involvement." Ph.D. dissertation, American University, 1956.

1025.   Santos, A.B. "Thai–U.S. Relations: The Fretful Wife." *Far Eastern Economic Review* 60 (Apr. 28, 1968): 263–265.

1026.   Sethachuay, Vivat. "United States–Thailand Diplomatic Relations During World War II." Ph.D. dissertation, Brigham Young University, 1977.

1027.   Sirikrai, Surachai. "Thai–American Relations in the Laotian Crisis of 1960–1962." Ph.D. dissertation, State University of New York, Binghamton, 1980.

1028.   Thompson, W. Scott. *Unequal Partners: Philippine and Thai Relations with the United States, 1965–1975.* Lexington, MA: Heath, 1975.

1029.   Toru Yano. "Sarit and Thailand's 'Pro-American Policy.'" *Developing Economies* 6 (Sept. 1968): 284–299.

1030.   Unger, Leonard. "The United States and Thailand in a New Era." *U.S. Department of State Bulletin* 68 (Mar. 19, 1973): 330–334.

1031.   U.S. Senate. Committee on Foreign Relations. Hearings; *United States Security Agreements and Commitments Abroad: Kingdom of Thailand.* (Nov. 10–14, 1969) 91st Cong., 1st sess., 1970, 607–917.

1032.   Vankataramani, M.S. "The United States and Thailand: The Anatomy of Super-Power Policy-Making, 1948–1963." *International Studies* [India] 12:1 (1973): 57–110.

1033.   Wehner, Wolfgang. "American Involvement in Thailand." *Journal of Contemporary Asia* 3:3 (1973): 292–305.

U.S. Aid Programs

1034.   Hanks, Lucien M. "American Aid Is Damaging Thai Society." *Trans–Action* 5 (Oct. 1968): 29–34.

1035.   Parker, Maynard. "Americans in Thailand: Counterinsurgency Activities of Armed Forces, USIS and AID." *Atlantic* 218 (Dec. 1966): 51–58.

1036. Randolph, R. Sean. "The Limits of Influence: American Aid to Thailand, 1965–70." *Asian Affairs* [U.S.] 6 (Mar.–Apr. 1979): 243–263.

1037. U.S. Department of State. *Agreement Respecting Military Assistance between the Government of the United States of America and the Government of Thailand.* Signed at Bangkok, October 17, 1950. Treaties and Other International Acts Series 2434. Washington, DC: GPO, 1953.

1038. U.S. General Accounting Office. *Problems in Coordinating Multilateral Assistance to Thailand.* ID–76–6. Washington, DC, 1975.

1039. _____. *United States Assistance to the Government of Thailand for Deployment of Thai Forces to Vietnam.* B–133258. Washington, DC, 1972.

1040. Viksnins, George J. "United States Military Spending and the Economy of Thailand, 1967–1972." *Asian Survey* 13 (May 1973): 441–457.

U.S. Bases in Thailand

For general accounts of U.S. aerial activities from Thai bases, see "Air War," Chapter 7.

1041. Campbell, Alex. "The Future of the US Military Presence." *New Republic* 160 (Apr. 5, 1969): 14–17.

1042. Casella, Alessandro. "U.S.–Thai Relations." *World Today* [London] 26 (Mar. 1970): 118–125. This article examines a secret 1965 agreement which permitted U.S. bases in Thailand.

1043. Critchfield, Richard. "Bombers Nesting in Thailand." *Nation* 217 (Oct. 1, 1973): 293–295.

1044. Grant, Zalin B. "What Are We Doing in Thailand?" *New Republic* 160 (May 24, 1969): 19–21.

1045. Nivolon, François. "U.S. Bases in Thailand: Unbreakable Thais?" *Far Eastern Economic Review* 60 (Apr. 14, 1968): 173–175.

1046. Schell, Orville. "Thailand: Privileged Sanctuary." *New Republic* 157 (Sept. 30, 1967): 16–19.

1047. "The War: Relentless Pressure." *Time* 90 (Oct. 13, 1967): 34–35. This article includes a map of air bases in Thailand.

❧ Chapter Three ❧

Vietnam: From the First
to the Third Indochina Wars

THE PEOPLES that compose modern Vietnam come from a misty, shrouded past that has prompted a great deal of historical speculation. Whether the Vietnamese come from Chinese or Thai stock, or both, they have known a great deal of strife and struggle. Much of this turmoil and war has been to achieve independence, first from the Chinese and, later, from the French. When free from external constraints, the Vietnamese have fought for empire. The second half of the twentieth century has witnessed the Vietnamese pursuit of both independence and empire.

World War II gave Vietnamese nationalists an opportunity to make a bid for independence. The fine monograph by McAlister (1104) examines the roots of this movement and offers insights which help explain subsequent events. Pike (1109) offers an informative survey of Vietnamese communism, with particular emphasis on organizational techniques. Researchers seeking materials on the U.S. response to this resurgent independence movement during World War II should see the section entitled "Roosevelt and Truman Years, 1941–1952" in Chapter 4.

Ho Chi Minh's efforts in 1945–1946 to win some measure of independence from France failed, and the First Indochina War began. A standard account of the political dimensions of these initial negotiations and the ensuing conflict is given by Hammer (1128), while Irving (1129) analyzes the dynamics of French policy, and Chen (1154) discusses China's ideological and military contributions. The military dimension is described by Fall (1195), Bodard (1123) and O'Ballance (1204). Fall's classic description of the critical battle of Dien Bien Phu (1220) explains the French willingness to negotiate an end to the war. Randle's analytical study of the ensuing Geneva Conference of 1954 (1244) is detailed and thorough; he emphasizes the vagueness of the armistice clauses as a cause of future misunderstandings. The role of the United States in the First Indochina War is discussed in Chapter 4, under "The Eisenhower Years, 1953–1960," where sources are to be found describing President Eisenhower's thoughts on intervention and Secretary Dulles' views on the Geneva armistice.

For the sake of convenience, materials pertaining to the internal affairs of both Vietnams during the Second Indochina War are listed in this section. During the Diem era (1954–1963), South Vietnam searched for a sense of nationhood but found internal turmoil, frequently sparked by religious groups. Scigliano (1322) describes many of the efforts of Americans to advise regarding political and economic reform, while Denis Warner (1501) and Bouscaren (1482) provide useful biographies of President Diem. Additionally, Geoffrey Warner (1502) subsequently used the *Pentagon Papers* to review the role of the United States in the coup that removed Diem from power and took his life. While President Nguyen Van Thieu has yet to offer his memoirs, his vice-president (and former president), Nguyen Cao

Ky (1506), has published his. Providing a critical view from a Saigon insider, General Tran Van Dinh takes both South Vietnamese leadership and American interference to task for inhibiting the development of a stable, vigorous government in the South (1402).

The success of North Vietnam is due in no small measure to the stamina of Ho Chi Minh, the cohesion of his ruling Politburo and the organization of the Party. These combined to form an operational trinity: organization, mobilization and motivation. Honey (1628) and Turner (1115) provide unsympathetic views of Vietnamese communism, while more congenial interpretations are to be found in the Ph.D. dissertations scattered throughout the "North Vietnam, 1954–1975" section; however, we await a comprehensive analysis of North Vietnam during the Second Indochina War.

We know little about the individuals who led the Hanoi government to victory. Lacouture's biography of Ho Chi Minh (1681), one of several that use essentially the same materials, focuses on Ho's charisma and nationalism. Fall's edition of Ho's writings (1673) is adequate. Vo Nguyen Giap, the victorious general of the First Indochina War, has written extensively about strategy and politics; some of his English-language volumes are listed in this chapter, but the ones focusing on military matters are found in Chapter 7.

Much confusion has arisen over the use of the terms "Vietminh," "Vietcong" (VC) and "National Liberation Front" (NLF). In brief, Vietminh referred to all Vietnamese insurgents, communists, and noncommunists, North and South, opposed to the French; in 1960, the insurgents in the south, increasingly communist, were reorganized into the National Liberation Front or, as it was sometimes called, the NLF South Vietnam. The term Vietcong appeared in *Saigon Press* accounts after 1956, and has generally been used to refer to the militarily active southern insurgents ("guerrillas"). Pike's study (1757) may be compared with Fitzgerald's sympathetic treatment (1902–1904).

The unified Socialist Republic of Vietnam, which followed Hanoi's victory in 1975, and the subsequent Third Indochina War, are too new to have generated any lengthy analysis at this writing. Both episodes have prompted some misgivings and disappointment. Jean Lacouture, writing after the initial unified election, criticized the listing of only "approved" candidates and the brushing aside of southern NLF leadership: "Is there but one social truth with one man, one tendency, one ideology representing an entire society that is multiple by definition?"

Finally, the Third Indochina War seems to have accelerated a display of the ancient Vietnamese prejudice against China and things Chinese. The encouraged or forced emigration of Vietnamese citizens of Chinese origins (the so-called Boat People) is the most cruel and dramatic exercise of this prejudice. But more than this, the new conflict offers some clues to the territorial ambitions of the Vietnamese leaders. If the Second Indochina War was—as opponents frequently claimed—the American exercise of capitalist imperialism, then the Third Indochina War may be seen as Vietnam's indulgence in socialist imperialism.

TABLE I

Casualties of First Indochina War

French Forces*	
Killed in action, dead (noncombat) or missing	92,797
Wounded	76,369
Evacuated for medical reasons	48,673

Vietminh/Civilian	
Estimates vary from 45,000 to 1,000,000	

Source: Douglas Pike, *Viet Cong* (Cambridge, MA: MIT Press, 1966), p.49.

*These include French, Foreign Legion, African, and Indochinese.

Vietnam: General Accounts

Listed here are a few of the general histories of Vietnam. For general accounts of U.S. involvement, see Chapter 4. Buttinger (1053) and Smith (1078) provide introductions to Vietnam's past.

Books

1048. Bain, Chester A. *Vietnam: The Roots of the Conflict.* Englewood Cliffs, NJ: Prentice-Hall, 1967.

1049. Bergman, Arlene E. *Women of Viet Nam.* San Francisco: Peoples' Press, 1975. [also printed as *La Femme au Vietnam.* Hanoi: Foreign Languages Publishing House, 1976]

1050. Blanchet, M.T. *La Naissance de l'état associé du Vietnam.* Paris: Genin, 1954.

1051. Buell, Hal. *Vietnam: Land of Many Dragons.* New York: Dodd, 1968.

1052. Buttinger, Joseph. *The Smaller Dragon: A Political History of Vietnam.* New York: Praeger, 1958.

1053. _____. *Vietnam: A Dragon Embattled.* 2 vols. New York: Praeger, 1967.

1054. _____. *Vietnam: A Political History.* New York: Praeger, 1968. The Buttinger accounts are adequate introductions to Vietnamese history and politics.

1055. Cairns, James F. *The Eagle and the Lotus: Western Intervention in Vietnam, 1847–1971.* 2d ed. Melbourne, Australia: Lansdowne Press, 1971.

1056. Chesneaux, Jean. *Contribution à l'histoire de la nation vietnamienne.* Paris: Éditions Sociales, 1955.

1057. _____. *La Culture et les hommes: Contribution à l'histoire de la nation vietnamienne.* Paris: Éditions Sociales, 1965.

1058. _____. *Le Vietnam études de politique et d'histoire.* Paris: F. Maspero, 1968.

1059. Crawford, Ann [Caddell]. *Customs and Culture of Vietnam.* Illustrations by Han Dinh Cam. Rutland, VT: C.E. Tuttle, 1966.

1060. Do Van Minh. *Vietnam: Where East and West Meet.* 2d rev. ed. New York: Paragon Book Reprint Corporation, 1968.

1061. Duncanson, Dennis J. *Government and Revolution in Vietnam.* New York: Oxford University Press, 1968.

1062. Hammer, Ellen Joy. *Vietnam: Yesterday and Today.* New York: Rinehart & Winston, 1966.

1063. Iredell, F. Raymond. *Viet-Nam: The Country and the People.* New York: American Press, 1966.

1064. Isoart, P. *Le Phénomène national vietnamien de l'indépendance unitaire à l'indépendance fractionnée.* Paris: Librarie Générale de Droit et de Jurisprudence, 1961.

1065. _____. *Le Vietnam.* Paris: Armand Colin, 1970.

1066. Jumper, Roy, and Nguyen Thi Hue. *Notes on the Political and Administrative History of Viet Nam, 1802–1962.* Saigon: Michigan State University, Vietnam Advisory Group, 1962.

1067. Le Thanh Khoi. *3000 Jahre Vietnam.* Munich: Kindler Verlag, Leinen, 1969.

1068. _____. *Le Viet-Nam: Histoire et civilisation.* Paris: Éditions de Minuit, 1955.

1069. Mus, Paul. *Viet-Nam: Sociologie d'une guerre.* Paris: Éditions du Seuil, 1950.

1070. Newman, B. *Background to Vietnam.* London: R. Hale, 1965.

1071. Nguyen Phut Tan. *A Modern History of Vietnam, 1802–1954.* Saigon: Khai-Trr, 1964.

1072. Nguyen Thain Binh. *Vietnam: The Problem and a Solution.* Paris: Vietnam Democratic Party, 1962.

1073. Nguyen Van Thai, and Nguyen Van Mung. *A Short History of Vietnam.* Saigon: Times Publishing, 1958.

1074. Pettit, Clyde E. *The Experts: 100 Years of Blunder in Indochina.* Secausus, NJ: Lyle Stuart, 1975.

1075. Popkin, Samuel L. *The Rational Peasant: The Political Economy of Rural Society in Vietnam.* Berkeley: University of California Press, 1979.

1076. Porter, D. Gareth. "Imperialism and Social Structure in Twentieth Century Vietnam." Ph.D. dissertation, Cornell University, 1976.

1077. Sheehan, Susan. *Ten Vietnamese.* New York: Knopf, 1967.

1078. Smith, Ralph B. *Viet-Nam and the West.* Ithaca, NY: Cornell University Press, 1971.

1079. Thich Nhat Hanh. *Vietnam: Lotus in a Sea of Fire.* New York: Hill & Wang, 1967.

1080. Tran Van Tung. *Viet-nam.* New York: Praeger, 1959.

1081.   Vella, Walter F., ed. *Aspects of Vietnamese History*. Honolulu: University Press of Hawaii, 1973.

Essays

These essays on general Vietnamese history and society may be supplemented by use of the Journal of Asian Studies *bibliographies (6–9).*

1082.   Adams, John, and Nancy Hancock. "Land and Economy in Traditional Vietnam." *Journal of Southeast Asian Studies* 1 (Sept. 1970): 90–98.

1083.   Lam Le Trinh. "Village Councils: Yesterday and Today." *Viet-My* [Saigon] (Aug. 1958): 36–44; (Sept. 1958): 59–70.

1084.   Mus, Paul. "The Role of the Village in Vietnamese Politics." *Pacific Affairs* 22 (Sept. 1949): 265–272.

1085.   Osborne, Milton E. "Truong Vinh Ky and Phan Thanh Gian: The Problem of a Nationalist Interpretation of 19th Century Vietnamese History." *Journal of Asian Studies* 30 (Nov. 1970): 81–94.

Vietnam: Historical Accounts

These accounts emphasize the period prior to the beginning of the modern Vietnamese conflicts; see also "French Indochina (Historical)" in Chapter 2.

1086.   Ayme, G. *Monographie du le térritoire militaire.* Hanoi: Imprimerie d'Extrême-Orient, 1930.

1087.   Deschamp, Hubert, and Paul Chavet, eds. *Gallieni, pacificateur.* Paris: Presses Universitaires de France, 1949.

1088.   Hammersmith, Jack L. "American Attempts to Prevent a War 'Over Vietnam': The Experience of John Russell Young, 1882–1885." *Historian* 38 (Feb. 1976): 253–267.

1089.   McAleavy, Henry. *Black Flags in Vietnam: The Story of a Chinese Intervention.* New York: Macmillan, 1968.

1090.   Montaigu, Fernand de. *La Colonisation française dans l'est de la Cochinchine.* Limoges: Perrette, 1929.

1091.   Ngo Vinh Long. *Before the Revolution: The Vietnamese Peasants Under the French.* Cambridge, MA: MIT Press, 1973.

1092.   Nguyen Dang Thuc. *Democracy in Traditional Vietnamese Society.* Saigon: Department of National Education, 1960.

1093.   Robaud, Louis. *Viet-Nam: La Tragédie indochinoise.* Paris: Valois, 1931.

1094.   Rouyer, Charles E. *Histoire militaire et politique de l'Annam et du Tonkin depuis 1799.* Paris: Lavauzelle, 1906.

1095.   Taylor, Keith W. "The Birth of Vietnam: Sino–Vietnamese Relations to the Tenth Century and the Origins of Vietnamese Nationhood." Ph.D. dissertation, University of Michigan, 1976.

1096.   Yu, Insun. "Law and Family in Seventeenth and Eighteenth Century Vietnam." Ph.D. dissertation, University of Michigan, 1978.

Struggle: Revolution and Independence

These general accounts should be supplemented with the more specific ones which follow in this chapter and the next. Duiker (1101) and McAlister (1104) provide excellent accounts of the early years of the First Indochina War which contain many insights into the dynamics of the struggle for independence.

1097.   Cannon, Terry. *Vietnam: A Thousand Years of Struggle.* San Francisco: Peoples' Press, 1969.

1098.   Chaffard, Georges. *Les Deux Guerres du Vietnam.* Paris: La Table Ronde, 1969.

1099.   Chandler, David P. "*Post mortes* on the Wars in Indochina." *Journal of Asian Studies* 40 (Nov. 1980): 77–86.

1100.   Chau, Phan T. *The Racial Factor in the Indo-China Conflict.* Denver: Center on International Race Relations, 1971.

1101.   Duiker, William J. *The Rise of Nationalism in Vietnam, 1900–1941.* Ithaca, NY: Cornell University Press, 1975.

1102.   Jenkins, Brian M. "Patterns of Conflict in Vietnamese History." *Conflict* 2:3 (1980): 279–310.

1103.   Lamb, Helen B. *Vietnam's Will to Live:*

Resistance to Foreign Aggression From Early Times Through the Nineteenth Century. New York: Monthly Review Press, 1973.

1104.   McAlister, John T., Jr. *Vietnam: Origins of Revolution.* New York: Knopf, 1969.

1105.   _____, and Paul Mus. *The Vietnamese and Their Revolution.* New York: Harper & Row, 1970.

1106.   Nguyen Khac Vien. *The Long Resistance, 1858–1975.* Hanoi: Foreign Languages Publishing House, 1975.

1107.   _____. *Tradition and Revolution in Vietnam.* Edited by D. Marr and J. Werner. Translated by L. Yarr, J. Werner and Tran Tuong Nhu. Berkeley: Indochina Resource Center, 1974.

1108.   Pham Coung, and Nguyen Van Ba. *Revolution in the Village: Nam Hong, 1945–1975.* Hanoi: Foreign Languages Publishing House, 1976.

1109.   Pike, Douglas. *History of Vietnamese Communism.* Stanford, CA: Hoover Institution Press, 1978. This is a useful survey emphazing organizational techniques.

1110.   Rousset, Pierre. *Le parti communiste Vietnamien: Contribution à l'étude du mouvement communiste au Vietnam.* Paris: F. Maspero, 1973.

1111.   Si Kuen Lee. "Foreign Intervention and the Use of Mesogenous Peasant Nationalism: The Case of Vietnam." Ph.D. dissertation, New York University, 1977. The title refers to the communist use of mesogenous peasant nationalism.

1112.   Slingsby, H.G. *Vietnam Fights Back.* Christchurch, New Zealand: Caxton, 1972.

1113.   Suant, Jacques. *Vietnam '45–'72: La Guerre d'indépendance.* Paris: B. Arthaud, 1972.

1114.   Truong Buu Lam. *Patterns of Vietnamese Response to Foreign Intervention 1858–1900.* Southeast Asia Studies Monograph Series no. 11. New Haven, CT: Yale University Press, 1967.

1115.   Turner, Robert F. *Vietnamese Communism: Its Origins and Development.* Stanford, CA: Hoover Institution Press, 1975. The author views communists as usurpers of nationalism.

1116.   Weidemann, Diethelm, and Renate Wunsche. *Vietnam 1945–1970: Der nationale und soziale Befreiungskampf des vietnamesichen Volkes.* Berlin: Deutscher Verlag der Wissenschaften, 1971. The authors present a communist view of the growth of the people's power in Vietnam.

1117.   Young, Stephen B. "Communism and Nationalism in Vietnam (a review essay)." *Problems of Communism* 30 (Mar.–Apr. 1981): 80–87.

EARLY REVOLUTIONARY MOVEMENTS

1118.   Duiker, William J. "The Red Soviets of Nghe-Tinh: An Early Communist Rebellion in Vietnam." *Journal of Southeast Asian Studies* 4 (Sept. 1973): 186ff.

1119.   Indochine. Gouvernement Général de l'Indochine. Direction des Affaires Politiques et de la Sureté Générale. *Contribution à l'Histoire des Mouvements politiques de l'Indochine francaise, documents*—Vol. IV: *Le "dong-Duong Cong-San Dang" ou "Parti Communiste Indochinois."* Hanoi: IDEO, 1933. [covers 1925 to 1933]

1120.   Osborne, Milton E. "Continuity and Motivation in the Vietnamese Revolution: New Light From the 1930's." *Pacific Affairs* 47 (Spring 1974): 37–55.

1121.   Sacks, I. Milton. "Marxism in Viet Nam." In *Marxism in Southeast Asia: A Study of Four Countries,* edited by Frank N. Trager. Stanford, CA: Stanford University Press, 1959, 102–170. [surveys 1930 to 1945]

1122.   Vanlande, René. *L'Indochine sous la menace communiste.* Paris: J. Peyronnet, 1930.

First Indochina War

The First Indochina War (1945–1954) found the French ultimately agreeing to withdraw after their defeat at Dien Bien Phu. For convenience, we have divided the conflict into two phases: World War II to 1946 and 1947 to 1954. Works cited in previous sections can be valuable here, especially such good surveys as McAlister (1104), Bodard (1123) and Hammer (1062).

1123.   Bodard, Lucien. *The Quicksand War: Prelude to Vietnam.* Boston: Little, Brown, 1967. [a translation of his *La Guerre d'Indochine: L'enlisement.* Paris: Gallimard, 1963; and *La Guerre d'Indochine: L'humiliation.* Paris: Gallimard, 1965]

1124.   Catroux, Georges. *Deux actes du drame indochinois: Hanoi, juin 1940; Dien Bien Phu, mars-mai 1954.* Paris. Librairie Plon, 1959.

1125.   Chen, King C. *Vietnam and China, 1938–1954.* Princeton, NJ: Princeton University Press, 1969. Chen discusses China's ideological and military contributions.

1126.   Fall, Bernard B. *Political Development of Viet-Nam, V-J Day to the General Cease-Fire.* Ann Arbor, MI: University Microfilms, 1966.

1127.   Great Britain. *Documents Relating to British Involvement in the Indo-China Conflict, 1945–1965.* Accounts and Papers, Cmnd. 2834. London: HMSO, Dec. 1965.

1128.   Hammer, Ellen J. *The Struggle for Indochina, 1940–1955.* Stanford, CA: Stanford University Press, 1956.

1129.   Irving, Ronald E. *The First Indochina War: French and American Policy, 1945–1954.* London: C. Helm, 1975. [based on his "The M.R.P. and French Policy in Indochina, 1945–1954." Ph.D. dissertation, Oxford University, 1968] This article is particularly useful for understanding French policy.

1130.   Lancaster, Donald. *The Emancipation of French Indochina.* New York: Oxford University Press, 1961.

1131.   Nguyen, Lien V. "American Perceptions of the Chinese Role in Vietnam, 1946–1954." Ph.D. dissertation, University of South Carolina, 1979.

1132.   Sainteny, Jean. *Histoire d'une paix manquée.* Paris: Amiot Dumont, 1953.

1133.   Salisbury-Jones, Sir Guy. *So Full a Glory.* London: Widenfield & Nicholson, 1954.

1134.   Schutze, Gunter. *Der Schumsige Krieg Frankreichs Kolonialpolitik in Indochina.* Munich: Editions R. Oldenbourg, 1959.

1135.   Starobin, Joseph R. *Eyewitness in Indo-China.* New York: Cameron & Kahn, 1954.

1136.   *A Translation From the French: Lessons of the War in Indochina.* 3 vols. RM–5271–PR. Santa Monica, CA: Rand Corp., 1967.

FIRST PHASE, 1940–1946

For the U.S. role in the initial phase, see Chapter 4, the "Roosevelt and Truman Years, 1941–1952" section.

Books

1137.   *Breaking Our Chains: Documents on the Vietnamese Revolution of August, 1945.* Hanoi: Foreign Languages Publishing House, 1960. This book is very important source of information.

1138.   Decoux, Jean. *À la Barre de l'Indochine: Histoire de mon gouvernement général, 1940–45.* Paris: Librairie Plon, 1952.

1139.   Duçoroy, Maurice. *Ma Trahison en Indochine.* Paris: Les Éditions Internationales, 1949.

1140.   Gaudel, André. *L'Indochine française en face du Japon.* Paris: Susse, 1947.

1141.   Gaultier, Marcel. *Prisons japonais.* Monte Carlo, Monaco: Regain, 1950.

1142.   Hertrich, Jean-Michael. *Doc-Lap! L'indépendance ou la mort.* Paris: Vigneau, 1946.

1143.   Institute Franco-Suisse d'Études Coloniales. *France and Viet-Nam: The Franco–Vietnamese Conflict According to Official Documents.* Geneva: Éditions du Milieu du Monde, 1947.

1144.   LeBourgeois, Jacques. *Saigon sans la France: Des japonais au Viet-Minh.* Paris: Librairie Plon, 1949.

1145.   Martin, Françoise. *Heures tragiques au Tonkin: 9 mars 1945–18 mars 1946.* Paris: Berger-Levrault, 1948.

1146.   Mordant, General. *Au Service de la France en Indochine: 1941–1945.* Saigon: Imprimerie Française d'Outre-Mer, 1950.

1147.   Mountbatten, Louis, Earl of Burma. *Post Surrender Tasks: Section E of the Report to the Combined Chiefs of Staff by the Supreme Allied Commander South East Asia, 1943–1945.* London: HMSO, 1969.

1148.   Naville, Pierre. *La Guerre du Viet-Nam.* Paris: Éditions de la Revue Internationale, 1949.

1149.   Rosie, George. *The British in Vietnam: How the Twenty-Five Year War Began.* London: Panther, 1970.

1150.   Sabattier, G. *Le Destin de l'Indochine: Souvenir et documents, 1941–1951.* Paris: Librairie Plon, 1952.

1151.   Truong Chinh. *The August Revolution* (1945). 2d ed. Hanoi: Foreign Languages Publishing House, 1962. Written in September of 1946, the book has been reprinted in various forms.

1152.   _____. *The Resistence Will Win.* 3d ed. Hanoi: Foreign Languages Publishing House, 1966. This valuable work on early events was, based on an essay written in 1946–1947.

Essays

1153.   Bridges, Flora. "Behind the Indo-Chinese Revolts." *Current History* 10 (May 1946): 429–434.

1154.   Chen, King C. "The Chinese Occupation of Vietnam, 1945–46." *France-Asie/Asia* 196 (1969): 3–28.

1155.   Devillers, Philippe. "Vietnamese Nationalism and French Policies." In *Asian Nationalism and the West*, edited by William L. Holland. New York: Macmillan, 1953, 197–265.

1156.   Fonde, J.J. "Giap et le maquis de Cho ru (mars 1945-mars 1946)." *Revue Historique des Armées* 2 (1976): 112–127.

1157.   Garrett, C.W. "In Search of Grandeur: France and Vietnam, 1940–1946." *Review of Politics* 29 (July 1967): 303–323.

1158.   Huynh Kim Khanh. "The Vietnamese August Revolution Reinterpreted." *Journal of Asian Studies* 30 (Aug. 1971): 761–782.

1159.   Issacs, Harold R. *New Cycle in Asia.* New York: Macmillan, 1947, 156–175.

1160.   _____. *No Peace for Asia.* New York: Macmillan, 1947, 134–176.

1161.   Jubelin, A. "The Haiphong 'Misunderstanding' of March 6, 1946." *U.S. Naval Institute Proceedings* 83 (Aug. 1957): 846–856.

1162.   Nayan Chanda. "The Franco–Japanese War." *Far Eastern Economic Review* 96 (June 24, 1977): 62–63. The author focuses on trade in Vietnam.

1163.   Shaplen, Robert. "Indochina: Tides of Revolt." *Newsweek* 28 (Aug. 19, 1946): 41–43.

1164.   Smith, Ralph B. "The Japanese Period in Indochina and the Coup of 9 March 1945." *Journal of Southeast Asian Studies* 9 (Sept. 1978): 268ff.

SECOND PHASE, 1947–1954

Political

Books and Pamphlets
1165.   Despuech, Jacques. *Le Trafic des piastres.* Paris: Éditions des Deux-Rives, 1953.

1166.   Devillers, Philippe. *Histoire du Vietnam de 1940 à 1952.* Paris: Éditions du Seuil, 1952.

1167.   Graham, Andrew. *Interval in Indochina.* New York: St. Martin's Press, 1956.

1168.   Gurtov, Melvin. *The First Vietnam Crisis: Chinese Communist Strategy and United States Involvement, 1953–1954.* New York: Columbia University Press, 1967.

1169.   Laurent, Arthur. *La Banque de l'Indochine et la piastre.* Paris: Éditions des Deux-Rives, 1954.

1170.   U.S. Department of State. *Indochina: The War in Viet-Nam, Cambodia, and Laos.* Department of State Publication 5092. Far Eastern Series 58. Washington, DC, 1953.

1171.   U.S. Mutual Security Agency. *Dateline Saigon: Our Quiet War in Indochina.* Washington, DC: GPO, 1952.

1172.   Vermeersch, Jeannette. *Paix immédiate au Viet-Nam discours pronouncé à l'assemblée nationale le 27 janvier 1950 par Jeannette Vermeersch suivi d'une déclaration de Maurice Thorez.* Paris: Parti Communiste Francais, 1950.

Essays
1173.   Birns, J. "Indo China: It is a Rich, Beautiful Colony Which France May Lose." *Life* 26 (Mar. 7, 1949): 97–107.

1174.   Buu Loc. "Aspects of the Vietnamese Problem." *Pacific Affairs* 25 (Sept. 1952): 235–247.

1175.   Duncan, David Douglas. "The Year of the Snake." *Life* 35 (Aug. 3, 1953): 73–84.

1176.   Hammer, Ellen J. "The Bao Dai Experiment." *Pacific Affairs* 23 (Mar. 1950): 58ff.

1177.   _____. "Blueprinting a New Indochina." *Pacific Affairs* 21 (Sept. 1948): 252–263.

1178.   Katzenbach, E.L., Jr. "Indo-China: A Military-Political Appreciation." *World Politics* 4 (Jan. 1952): 186–218.

1179.   _____, and M.O. Williams. "Portrait of Indochina." *National Geographic* 99 (Apr. 1951): 461–490.

1180.   Lacouture, Jean. "Vietnam: The Lessons of War." *New York Review of Books* (Mar. 3, 1966): 3–5. Lacouture maintains that American leaders should examine errors made by the French between 1945 and 1956.

1181.   Moore, W.R. "Strife-Torn Indochina." *National Geographic* 98 (Oct. 1950): 499–510.

1182.   Sheldon, George. "The Case for Vietnam." *Commonweal* 45 (Jan. 31, 1947): 393–397; (Mar. 7, 1947): 516–517.

1183.   Soustelle, Jacques. "Indochina and Korea: One Front." *Foreign Affairs* 29 (Oct. 1950): 56–66.

1184.   Tran Ngoc Hung. "The Role of the Indo-Chinese Communist Party in the Evolution of the Viet Minh,

1945–1951." *Australian Quarterly* 26 (Sept. 1954): 87–98.

Military

The French Expeditionary Corps in Indochina (1953–1954) consisted of 235,721 regulars (no draftees), 2,460 female personnel and 115,477 Indochinese troops; the Armed Forces of the Associated States had 257,130 men under arms. No figures are available for Vietminh guerrillas. Additional sources include "Situation militaire en Indochine," in Revue militaire d'Information *(France), monthly; the* Army Quarterly and Defence Journal *(Great Britain); and the* Army Quarterly *(Great Britain). For U.S. policies, see Chapter 4, under "Eisenhower Years, 1953–1960." Bodard (1123), Fall (1195) and O'Ballance (1204) provide the best surveys of military activities during this period.*

Books

1185.   Anley, Henry. *In Order to Die*. London: Burke, 1955.

1186.   Blanchet, André. *Au Pays des Ballila jaunes: Relations d'un correspondant de guerre en Indochine*. Saint-Étienne: Éditions Dorian, 1947.

1187.   Chassin, L.M. *Aviation Indochine*. Paris: Amiot Dumont, 1954.

1188.   Chezel, Guy de. *Parachute en Indochine*. Paris: Sirenes, 1947.

1189.   Cooper, Killigrew, et al. *Case Studies in Insurgency and Revolution Warfare: Vietnam, 1941–1954*. Washington, DC: American University, Special Operations Research Office, 1964.

1190.   Dannaud, J.P. *Guerre morte*. Paris: George Lang, 1954.

1191.   Darcourt, Pierre. *De Lattre au Viet-Nam: Une année de victoire*. Paris: La Table Ronde, 1965.

1192.   Demariaux, Jean-Claude. *Les Secrets des îles Poulo-Condore: Le grand bagne indochinois*. Paris: J. Payronnet, 1956.

1193.   Dinfreville, Jacques [pseudonym]. *L'Opération Indochine*. Paris: Les Éditions Internationales, 1953.

1194.   Ély, Paul. *Mémoires: L'Indochine dans la tourmente*. Paris: Librairie Plon, 1964.

1195.   Fall, Bernard B. *Street without Joy: Insurgency in Indochina*. 4th ed. London: Pall Mall Press, 1965.

1196.   Ferrandi, Jean. *Les Officiers français face au Vietminh, 1945–1954*. Paris: Fayard, 1966.

1197.   Goeldhieux, Claude. *Quinze mois prionnier chez les Viets*. Paris: Armand Colin, 1960.

1198.   Gronier, Maurice. *Riz et Pruneaux: Avec les Commandos dans la Brousse d'Indochine*. Paris: Émile-Paul, 1950.

1199.   Halle, Gunther. *Legion Étrangère*. East Berlin: Volk und Welt, 1952.

1200.   Leroy, Jean. *Un Homme dans la rizière*. Paris: Éditions de Paris, 1955.

1201.   Mordal, Jacques. *Marine Indochine*. Paris: Amiot Dumont, 1953.

1202.   Navarre, General Henri. *Agonie de l'Indochine, 1953–1954*. Paris: Librairie Plon, 1956.

1203.   Ngo Van Chien. *Journal d'un combattant Viet-Minh*. Paris: ÉDITIONS DU Seuil, 1955.

1204.   O'Balance, Edgar. *The Indo-China War, 1945–54: A Study in Guerilla Warfare*. London: Faber & Faber, 1964.

1205.   Paret, Peter. *French Revolutionary Warfare from Indochina to Algeria: The Analysis of a Political and Military Doctrine*. New York: Praeger, 1964.

1206   Rissen, René. *Jungle Mission*. New York: Crowell, 1957.

1207.   _____. *Le Silence du ciel*. Paris: Éditions de la Pensée Moderne, 1956.

Essays

1208.   Fall, Bernard B. "Indochina: The Last Year of the War—Communist Organization and Tactics." *Military Review* 36 (Oct. 1956): 48–56.

1209.   _____. "The Last Year of the War—The Navarre Plan." *Military Review* 36 (Dec. 1956): 48–56.

1210.   Howard, John D. "GCMA (Groupements de Commandos Mixtes Aéropretés) GMI (Groupement Mixte d'Intervention): A French Experience in Indochina." *Military Review* 56 (Apr. 1976): 76–81.

1211.   Martin, H.G. "The War in Indochina." *Brassey's Annual* (1954): 241–254.

1212.   Number not used.

1213.   O'Ballance, Edgar. "The Fighting in Tongking, 1952–53." *Army Quarterly* 47 (Jan. 1954): 188–196.

1214. Sanders, Ricford M. "The 1954 Indochina Crisis." *Military Review* 58 (Apr. 1978): 68–78.

1215. Thompson, Scott W. "Lessons From the French in Vietnam." *Naval War College Review* 27 (Mar.–Apr. 1975): 43–52.

1216. Zasloff, Joseph J. *Role of the Sanctuary in Insurgency: Communist China's Support to the Vietminh, 1946–1954.* RM–4618–PR. Santa Monica, CA: Rand Corp., May 1967.

Dien Bien Phu

This battle, initiated by the French but won by the Vietminh, ended political support in France for the war. Both the political and military dimensions of this battle have been well studied. The books by Fall (1220) and Roy (1228) are considered the standard accounts. An interesting account usually overlooked is Hanson Baldwin, "Lessons of Dienbienphu: Too Little and Too Late," New York Times, May 16, 1954.

1217. Backlund, Donald R. "Stalingrad and Dien Bien Phu: Two Cases of Failure in Strategic Resupply." *Aerospace Historian* 17 (Summer–Fall 1970): 60–68.

1218. Bell, J.C. "Dien Bien Phu: Giap's Last Win?" *Military Review* 48 (Feb. 1968): 84–91.

1219. Dejean, Maurice. "The Meaning of Dien Bien Phu." *U.S. Naval Institute Proceedings* 80 (July 1954): 717–725.

1220. Fall, Bernard B. *Hell in a Very Small Place: The Siege of Dien Bien Phu.* New York: Lippincott, 1967.

1221. Gabriel, Richard A. *The Tactical and Strategic Failures of Dien Bien Phu.* Fort Huachuca, AZ: U.S. Army Intelligence School Archives, 1976.

1222. Grauwin, Paul. *Doctor at Dien Bien Phu.* New York: John Day, 1955.

1223. Laniel, Joseph. *Le Drame indochinois: De Dien-Bien-Phu au pari de Genève.* Paris: Librairie Plon, 1957.

1224. Long, William F. "The Spectre of Dien Bien Phu." *Military Review* 46 (Oct. 1966): 35–39.

1225. Pahwa, P.K. "Artillery in the Battle of Dien Bien Phu." *Journal of the Royal Artillery* 98 (Sept. 1971): 109–116.

1226. Parham, David M. "Siege at Dien Bien Phu." *Conflict* (Oct. 1973): 4–27.

1227. Renald, Jean. *L'Enfer de Dien Bien Phu.* Paris: Flammarion, 1954.

1228. Roy, Jules. *The Battle of Dien Bien Phu.* Translated by Robert Baldich. New York: Harper & Row, 1965.

1229. Simcock, William. "Dien Bien Phu: Yesterday's Battlefield." *Canadian Army Journal* 12 (July 1958): 35–46.

1230. Stanley, G.F.C. "Dien Bien Phu in Retrospect." *International Journal* [Toronto] 10 (Winter 1954–1955): 38–50.

1231. Vo Nguyen Giap. *Dien Bien Phu.* Hanoi: Foreign Languages Publishing House, 1962.

GENEVA ACCORDS, 1954

This armistice, signed July 20, 1954, divided Vietnam and recommended reunification via internationally supervised elections in both North and South. South Vietnam's decision that "fair" elections could not be held, apparently accepted by the United States, led to renewed conflict. Considerable dispute arose as to what obligations the United States incurred in the accords; see Devillers and Lacouture (1239) and Randle (1244) for fine accounts of the conference.

Documents

1232. Democratic Republic of Vietnam. *Documents relatifs à l'exécution des accords de Genève concernant le Viet-Nam.* Hanoi: Ministry of Foreign Affairs, 1956. [also printed in English]

1233. Falk, Richard A., ed. [Text of accords]. *The Vietnam War and International Law.* 4 vols. Princeton, NJ: Princeton University Press, 1968, I, 543–573.

1234. Great Britain. *Documents Relating to the Discussion of Korea and Indo-China at the Geneva Conference (April 27–June 15, 1954).* Parliamentary Papers 31 (Accounts and Papers, Vol. 12) Cmnd. 9186. London: HMSO, June 1954.

1235. ———. *Further Documents Relating to the Discussion of Indo-China at the Geneva Conference* (June 16–July 21, 1954). Parliamentary Papers 31 (Accounts and Papers, Vol. 12) Cmnd. 9239. London: HMSO, Aug. 1954.

1236. ———. *Vietnam and Geneva Agreements: Documents Concerning Discussions Between Representatives of Her Majesty's Government and the Government of the Union of Soviet Socialist Republics Held in London in April and May 1956, March 30–May 8, 1956.* Parliamentary papers 45. Cmnd. 9763. London: HMSO, 1956.

Books and Dissertations

1237.   Democratic Republic of Vietnam. *Facts and Dates on the Problem of the Reunification of Viet-Nam.* Hanoi: Foreign Languages Publishing House, 1956.

1238.   _____. *On the Reestablishment of Normal Relations between the Northern and Southern Zones of Vietnam.* Hanoi: Foreign Languages Publishing House, 1955.

1239.   Devillers, Philippe, and Jean Lacouture. *End of a War: Indochina, 1954.* New York: Praeger, 1969. [translation of their *La Fin d'une guerre: Indochine, 1954.* Paris: Éditions du Seuil, 1960]

1240.   Eden, Anthony. *Full Circle: The Memoirs of Rt. Hon. Sir Anthony Eden.* London: Cassell, 1960. This is a detailed account by a participant in the events described.

1241.   Frederic-Dupont. *Mission de la France en Asie.* Paris: Éditions France Empire, 1956.

1242.   Guillain, Robert. *La Fin des illusions: Notes d'Indochine, févier–juillet 1954.* Paris: Centre d'Études de Politique Étrangère, 1954.

1243.   Ngo Ton Dat. "The Geneva Partition of Vietnam and the Question of Reunification." Ph.D. dissertation, Cornell University, 1963. This account was written by a participant from the Republic of Vietnam.

1244.   Randle, Robert F. *Geneva 1954: The Settlement of the Indochinese War.* Princeton, NJ: Princeton University Press, 1969. Randle provides a fine analysis of issues and problems.

1245.   Republic of Vietnam. *The Problem of Reunification of Vietnam.* Saigon: Ministry of Information, 1958.

1246.   Ronning, Chester A. *A Memoir of china in War and Revolution.* New York: Pantheon Books, 1974. Ronning was a Canadian diplomat present at the 1954 Geneva Conference.

1247.   Vo Nguyen Giap. *On the Implementation of the Geneva Agreements: Excerpts from a Report in the Fourth Session of the National Assembly, March 1955.* Hanoi: Foreign Languages Publishing House, 1955.

Essays

1248.   Bator, V. "Geneva, 1954: The Broken Mold." *Reporter* 34 (June 30, 1966): 15–18.

1249.   Buu Hoan. "Vietnam: Economic Consequences of the Geneva Peace." *Far Eastern Economic Review* 25 (Dec. 11, 1958): 753–757.

1250.   Deutscher, Isaac. "How the Russians Bet a Little in Asia to Win a Lot in Europe." *Reporter* 2 (Sept. 23, 1954): 19–22.

1251.   Durdin, Peggy. "Uncle Ho's Disciplined Joy." *New Yorker* 31 (Dec. 17, 1955): 140–147.

1252.   Fall, Bernard B. "The Cease-Fire in Indochina: An Appraisal." *Far Eastern Survey* 23 (Sept. 1954): 135–139; (Oct. 1954): 152–155.

1253.   _____. "That Geneva Agreement: How the French Got Out of Vietnam." *New York Times Magazine* 28 (May 2, 1965): 113–119.

1254.   Hannon, J.S., Jr. "A Political Settlement for Vietnam: The 1954 Geneva Conference and Its Current Implications." *Virginia Journal of International Law* 8 (Dec. 1967): 20–65.

1255.   Hogan, W.C., and P. Hogan. "The Road to Geneva." *U.S. Naval Institute Proceedings* 81 (Feb. 1955): 135ff.

1256.   Holmes, John W. "Geneva, 1954." *International Journal* [Toronto] 22 (Summer 1967): 457–483.

1257.   Landon, Kenneth P. "The 1954 Geneva Agreements." *Current History* 50 (Feb. 1966): 79–84.

1258.   Ton That Thien. "The Geneva Agreements and Peace Prospects in Vietnam." *India Quarterly* 12 (Oct.–Dec. 1956): 375–388.

1259.   Weinstein, Franklin B. *Vietnam's Unheld Elections: The Failure to Carry Out the 1956 Reunification Elections and the Effects on Hanoi's Present Outlook.* Data Paper no. 60. Ithaca, NY: Cornell University, Southeast Asia Program, 1966.

1260.   Zagare, Frank C. "The Geneva Conference of 1954: A Case of Tacit Deception." *International Studies Quarterly,* 23 (Sept. 1979): 390– 411.

International Control Commission (ICC)

The ICC was responsible for supervising the enforcement of the armistice terms, particularly the military prohibitions. For an excellent description of the composition of the ICC and an evaluation of its effectiveness, see Wainhouse (1273).

1261.   Australia. Department of External Affairs. "Special Report of the International Control Commission in Vietnam." *Current Notes on International Affairs* 33 (June 1962): 25–35.

1262.   Bridle, Paul. *Canada and the International Commissions in Indochina, 1954–1972.* Toronto: Canadian Institute of International Affairs, 1973.

1263.   Dai, Poeliu. "Canada's Role in the International Commission for Supervision and Control in Viet Nam."

Canadian Year Book of International Law 4 (1966): 161–177.

1264. Hannon, J.S., Jr. "The International Control Commission Experience and the Role of an Improved International Supervisory Body in the Vietnam Settlement." *Virginia Journal of International Law* 9 (Dec. 1968): 20–65.

1265. Holmes, John W. "Techniques of Peacekeeping in Asia." In *China and the Peace of Asia*, edited by A. Buchan. New York: Praeger, 1965, 231–249.

1266. Maneli, Mieczyslav. *War of the Vanquished: A Polish Diplomat in Vietnam*. New York: Harper & Row, 1971.

1267. Martin, Paul. *Canada and the Quest for Peace*. New York: Columbia University Press, 1967, Chapter 2.

1268. Murti, B.S.N. *Vietnam Divided: The Unfinished Struggle*. New York: Asia Publishing House, 1964.

1269. Naravane, A.S. "The International Commission for Vietnam." *Journal of the United Service Institution of India* 94 (Apr. 1964): 159–167.

1270. Ross, Douglas. "In the Interests of Peace: Perception and Response in the History of Canadian Foreign Policy Decision-making Concerning the International Commission for Supervision and Control for Vietnam, 1954–1965." Ph.D. dissertation, University of Toronto, 1979. This dissertation supercedes all previous works.

1271. Thakur, Ramesh. "Peacekeeping and Foreign Policy: Canada, India, and the International Commission in Vietnam, 1954–1965." *British Journal of International Studies* 6 (July 1980): 125–153.

1272. Thee, Marek. *Notes of a Witness: Laos and the Second Indochinese War*. New York: Vintage, 1973.

1273. Wainhouse, David. *International Peace Observation: A History and Forecast*. Baltimore: Johns Hopkins Press, 1966, 489–524.

ICC Official Reports

1274. International Commission for Supervision and Control in Vietnam. *1st and 2d Interim Reports, August 11–December 10, 1954*. Cmnd. 9461. London: HMSO, 1955.

1275. _____. *3d Interim Report, February 11–April 10, 1955*. Cmnd. 9499. London: HMSO, 1955.

1276. _____. *4th Interim Report, April 11–August 10, 1955*. Cmnd. 9654. London: HMSO, 1955.

1277. _____. *5th Interim Report, August 11–December 10, 1955*. Cmnd. 9706. London: HMSO, 1956.

1278. _____. *6th Interim Report, December 11, 1955–July 31, 1956*. Cmnd. 31. London: HMSO, 1956.

1279. _____. *7th Interim Report, August 1, 1956–April 30, 1957*. Cmnd. 335. London: HMSO, 1957.

1280. _____. *8th Interim Report, May 1, 1957–April 30, 1958*. Cmnd. 509. London: HMSO, 1958.

1281. _____. *9th Interim Report, May 1, 1958–January 31, 1959*. Cmnd. 972. London: HMSO, 1959.

1282. _____. *10th Interim Report, February 1, 1959–January 31, 1960*. Cmnd. 1040. London: HMSO, 1960.

1283. _____. *11th Interim Report, February 1, 1960–February 28, 1961*. Cmnd. 1551. London: HMSO, 1961.

1284. _____. *Special Report, June 2, 1962*. Cmnd. 1775. London: HMSO, 1962.

1285. _____. *Special Report, February 13, 1965*. Cmnd. 2609. London: HMSO, 1965.

1286. _____. *Special Report, February 27, 1965*. Cmnd. 2634. London: HMSO, 1965.

1287. International Commission for Supervision and Control in Cambodia. *1st Progress Report, December 31, 1954*. Cmnd. 9458. London: HMSO, 1955.

1288. _____. *2d Progress Report, January 1–March 31, 1955*. Cmnd. 9534. London: HMSO, 1955.

1289. _____. *3d Interim Report, April 1–July 28, 1955*. Cmnd. 9579. London: HMSO, 1955.

1290. _____. *4th Interim Report, July 29–September 30, 1955*. Cmnd. 9671. London: HMSO, 1955.

1291. _____. *5th Interim Report, October 1, 1955–December 31, 1956*. Cmnd. 253. London: HMSO, 1957.

1292. _____. *6th Interim Report, 1957*. Cmnd. 526. London: HMSO, 1958.

1293. _____. *7th Interim Report, 1958*. Cmnd. 887. London: HMSO, 1959.

1294. _____. *Report of the ICC on the Aggressions against Cambodia by the American–South-Vietnamese Forces*. Phnom Penh: Ministère des Affaires Étrangères, 1964.

1295. International Commission for Supervision and Control in Laos. *1st Interim Report, January 15, 1955.* Cmnd. 9455. London: HMSO, 1955.

1296. _____. *2d Interim Report, January 1–June 30, 1955.* Cmnd. 9630. London: HMSO, 1955.

1297. _____. *3d Interim Report, July 1, 1955–May 16, 1957.* Cmnd. 314. London: HMSO, 1957.

1298. _____. *4th Interim Report, May 17, 1957–May 31, 1958.* Cmnd. 541. London: HMSO, 1958.

Charges of Violations

See the ICC Official Reports, above, which list a considerable number of specific violations, as well as the general lack of cooperation found by the supervisors.

1299. Bo Ngoai Giao. *Infiltration d'éléments armés communists et introduction clandestine d'armes du Nord au Sud Vietnam.* Saigon: Ministère des Affaires Étrangères, Républic du Vietnam, 1967.

1300. Democratic Republic of Vietnam. *Facts and Figures Concerning U.S. and U.S. Agents' Sabotage Activities in North Viet-Nam.* Hanoi: Ministry of Foreign Affairs, 1963.

1301. _____. *La Politique d'intervention et d'aggression des Étas-Unis au Sud.* Hanoi: Ministry of Foreign Affairs, 1962.

1302. Karpikhim, A. "The U.S.A. Sabotages the Geneva Agreements on Indochina." *International Affairs* [Moscow] 5 (Aug. 1959): 57–62.

1303. Republic of Vietnam. *Violations of the Geneva Agreements by the Viet-Minh Communists.* Saigon, 1959.

1304. U.S. Department of State. *Aggression From the North: The Record of North Vietnam's Campaign to Conquer South Vietnam.* Publication No. 7839. Far East Series 130. Washington, DC: GPO, 1965.

Refugees

In the moving of people after the armistice, the Catholics in North Vietnam attempted to move South to escape anticipated religious persecution. See also "North Vietnam, 1954–1975," the section on "Economics," in this chapter, for discussion on the land reform program and the bloodshed involved in its execution.

1305. Dooley, Thomas A. "BUI CHU Means Valiant." *U.S. Naval Institute Proceedings* 82 (Jan. 1956): 44–47.

This article focuses on the situation as Catholics from Bui Chu province sought to move south.

1306. _____. *Dr. Tom Dooley's Three Great Books: Deliver Us From Evil, Edge of Tomorrow, and The Night They Burned the Mountain.* New York: Farrar, Straus & Cudahy, 1960. The first book is by a young U.S. Navy doctor who assisted in taking North Vietnamese Catholics south in 1956; the last book deals with Dooley in Laos.

1307. Porter, D. Gareth. "Catholic Bloodbath in Vietnam?" *Commonweal* 97 (Oct. 13, 1972): 37–41.

1308. Samuels, Gertrude. "Passage to Freedom in Vietnam." *National Geographic* 107 (June 1955): 858–874.

1309. "Study Refutes Claim of Massacre of Vietnamese Catholics: 1950's Bloodbath Myth." *Christian Century* 89 (Oct. 4, 1972): 979ff.

South Vietnam, 1954–1975

For two turbulent decades, political elites, religious sects and, finally, the military in South Vietnam sought to create a viable state; in the end, each failed to develop a sense of purpose and nationhood. The items cited in this section relate the efforts and problems attendant to this undertaking.

Books and Reports

1310. Broekmeijer, M.W.J.M. *South Vietnam: Victim of Misunderstanding.* Bilthoven, Netherlands: H. Nelissen, 1967.

1311. Chaffard, Georges. *Indochine: Dix ans d'indépendance.* Paris: Calmann-Lévy, 1964.

1312. Fishel, Wesley R., ed. *Problems of Freedom: South Vietnam Since Independence.* Chicago: Free Press of Glencoe, 1961.

1313. Laurin, Pierre. *Sud Vietnam: La Fin d'une mystification.* Paris: Nouvelles Éditions Latines, 1973.

1314. Le Chau. *Bauernrevolution in Sudvietnam.* Munich: Trikant Verlag, Restexemplare, 1968.

1315. Lindholm, Richard W., ed. *Vietnam: The First Five Years.* East Lansing: Michigan State University Press, 1959. Also see Michigan State Assistance Group, below.

1316. Nguyen Cong Vien. *Seeking the Truth: The Inside Story of Viet Nam after the French Defeat.* New York: Vantage, 1967.

1317. Nguyen Kien. *Le Sud-Vietnam depuis Dien-Bien-Phu.* Paris: F. Maspero, 1963.

1318. Nguyen Thai. *Is South Vietnam Viable?* Manila: Carmelo & Bauermann, 1962.

1319. O'Daniel, John W. *The Nation That Refused to Starve: The Challenge of the New Vietnam.* New York: Coward, McCann & Geoghegan, 1960. O'Daniel was the general in charge of the first U.S. Military Mission.

1320. Pomonti, Jean-Claude. *La Rage d'être Vietnamien: Portraits du Sud.* Paris: Éditions du Seuil, 1974.

1321. Schrock, J.L. *Minority Groups in the Republic of Vietnam.* Washington, DC: American University, 1966.

1322. Scigliano, Robert. *South Vietnam: Nation Under Stress.* Boston: Houghton Mifflin, 1964.

1323. Serong, F.P. *The Future of South Vietnam.* New York: National Strategy Information Center, 1971.

1324. Smith, Harvey H., et. al. *Area Handbook for South Vietnam.* DA Pamphlet 550–55. Washington, DC: GPO, 1967. [previous editions appeared in 1957, 1962 and 1964]

Essays

1325. Ascoli, Max. "The Prodigal Nation." *Reporter* 35 (Sept. 8, 1966): 22–23.

1326. Berregan, Darrell. "The Ordeal of South Vietnam." *Reporter* 14 (Sept. 20, 1956): 29–33.

1327. Carver, George A., Jr. "The Real Revolution in South Vietnam." *Foreign Affairs* 43 (Apr. 1956): 387–408.

1328. Cary, S. "Three Months in Vietnam." *Progressive* 29 (Oct. 1965): 12–15.

1329. Corley, Francis J. "Progress in Vietnam." *America* 99 (May 10, 1958): 191–193.

1330. _____. "Vietnam since Geneva." *Thought* [Fordham University Quarterly] 33 (1958–1959): 515–568.

1331. Dorsey, John T., Jr. "South Vietnam in Perspective." *Far Eastern Survey* 27 (Dec. 1958): 177–182.

1332. Duong Van Minh. "A Question of Confidence." *Foreign Affairs* 47 (Oct. 1968): 84–91.

1333. Fitzgerald, Frances. "The Tragedy of Saigon." *Atlantic Monthly* 218 (Dec. 1966): 59–67.

1334. Furness, B. "Progress in Vietnam." *New Republic* 156 (Mar. 18, 1967): 7–9. This essay questions official U.S. reports of social, economic and political progress in Vietnam.

1335. Henderson, William D. "South Vietnam Finds Itself." *Foreign Affairs* 35 (Jan. 1957): 283–294.

1336. Ladejinsky, W. "Vietnam: The First Five Years." *Reporter* 21 (Dec. 24, 1959): 20–23.

1337. Langguth, A. Jack. "Saigon Tries to Live in a Hurry." *New York Times Magazine* (Aug. 8, 1965): 12ff.

1338. McClure, Brooks. "The South Vietnam Nobody Knows." *Air Force & Space Digest* 53 (Oct. 1970): 45–51.

1339. Miller, Haynes. "A Bulwark Built on Sand." *Reporter* 19 (Nov. 13, 1958): 11–16.

1340. Nguyen Ngoc Bich. "Vietnam: An Independent Viewpoint." *China Quarterly* 9 (Jan.–Mar. 1962): 105–111.

1341. Schmid, Peter. "Free Indochina Fights Against Time." *Commentary* 22 (Jan. 1955): 18–29.

1342. Shaplen, Robert. "Profiles: We Have Always Survived." *New Yorker* 48 (Apr. 15, 1972): 51–107. The author takes a fatalistic view of the coming armistice.

1343. Sochurek, Howard. "Slow Train Through Viet Nam's Hope." *National Geographic* 126 (Sept. 19, 1964): 412–444.

1344. Takashi Oka. "What the South Vietnamese Want." *New Republic* 158 (Mar. 23, 1968): 22–29.

1345. Warner, Denis. "Behind the Battlefront: A Search for Stability." *Reporter* 34 (Feb. 24, 1966): 25–29.

1346. Werth, A. "America's Colony in Hell." *Nation* 202 (June 13, 1966): 702–704. Werth sees the conflict in Vietnam as the biggest danger to world peace since the end of World War II.

1347. White, Peter T. "Behind the Headlines in Viet Nam." *National Geographic* 131 (Feb. 1967): 149–193.

1348. _____. "Saigon: Eye of the Storm." *National Geographic* 127 (June 1965): 835–872.

WAR RESUMES

Much of the material on this topic can be found in later chapters; see especially those sections dealing with combat operations in Chapter 7.

1349. Browne, R.S. "The Civil War in Vietnam." *Liberation* 9 (Sept. 1964): 7–12.

1350. Child, Frank C. "Vietnam: The Eleventh Hour." *New Republic* 145 (Dec. 4, 1961): 14–16.

1351. Emerson, Gloria. "The Consequences for South Vietnam: Each Day Is a Separate Ordeal." *Saturday Review* 55 (Dec. 1972): 52–57.

1352. Fishel, Wesley R. "Communist Terror in South Vietnam: The Diem Regime Has Undertaken Bold Measures." *New Leader* 43 (July 4, 1960): 14–15.

1353. _____. "Free Vietnam Since Geneva: Factors in the Rollback of Communism without War." *Yale Review* 49 (Sept. 1959): 68–79.

1354. Opinion Research Corporation. *The People of South Vietnam: How They Feel About the War, a CBS News Public Opinion Survey.* Princeton, NJ, 1967.

1355. Republic of Vietnam. *The Measure of Aggression: A Documentation of the Communist Effort to Subvert South Vietnam.* Saigon, 1966.

1356. _____. *The Problem of Reunification of Vietnam.* Saigon: Ministry of Information, 1958.

1357. Research Analysis Corporation. *Survey of Casualties, Republic of Vietnam Military Forces, 1962.* Tech Paper RAC–TP–167 (FOV). McLean, VA, 1965.

1358. Richer, Edward. "Peace Activism in Vietnam." *Studies on the Left* 6 (Jan.–Feb. 1966): 54–63.

1359. Rose, Jerry A. "The Fight for Rice in Divided Vietnam." *Reporter* 29 (Oct. 12, 1961): 37–38.

1360. Sanders, Sol W. "Appraisal from Saigon: Can South Vietnam Survive After the GI's Leave?" *U.S. News and World Report* 69 (Sept. 28, 1970): 72–74.

1361. Tanham, George K. "The Communist Challenge in the Provinces." *Vietnam Perspectives* 1:2 (1965): 4–18.

1362. Ton That Thien. "So Easy Without Thieu." *Far Eastern Economic Review* 70 (Oct. 10, 1970): 30–31. This article points out that while many did not like President Thieu, they wanted even less to live under a communist banner.

1363. Vann, John P. "Where Peace Is Returning in Vietnam." *U.S. News and World Report* 70 (May 31, 1971): 29–31.

1364. "Le Vietnam: Entre la Guerre et la Paix." *Tiers Monde* 11 (Apr.–Sept. 1970): Entire issue.

1365. White, Peter T., and W.E. Garrett. "South Viet Nam Fights the Red Tide." *National Geographic* 120 (Oct. 1961): 445–489.

POLITICS AND GOVERNMENT

1366. Browne, R.S. "The Junta Has the Cards: The U.S. Holds the Trump." *New Republic* 157 (July 22, 1967): 11–12.

1367. Butwell, Richard. "The Many-Sided Politics of South Vietnam." *Current History* 56 (Feb. 1969): 71–76ff.

1368. Corley, Francis J. "The President in the Constitution of the Republic of Vietnam." *Pacific Affairs* 34 (Summer 1961): 165–174.

1369. Donnell, John C. "Expanding Political Participation: The Long Haul From Villagism to Nationalism." *Asian Survey* 10 (Aug. 1970): 688–704.

1370. _____, and Charles A. Joiner, eds. *Electoral Politics in South Vietnam.* Lexington, MA: Lexington Books, 1974.

1371. Finkle, Jason L., and Tran Van Dinh. *Provincial Government in Viet Nam: A Study of Vinh Long Province.* Saigon: Michigan State University, Vietnam Advisory Group, 1961.

1372. Fishel, Wesley R. "Vietnam's Democratic One-Man Rule." *New Leader* 42 (Nov. 2, 1959): 10–13.

1373. Goodman, Allan E. "Government and the Countryside: Political Accommodation and South Vietnam's Communal Groups." *Orbis* 13 (Summer 1969): 502–525. [based on his Rand study, P–3924, Sept. 1968]

1374. _____. *Politics in War: The Bases of Political Community in South Vietnam.* Cambridge, MA: Harvard University Press, 1973. Although overly optimistic, this is the only well-researched account for 1967–1971.

1375. Grant, J.A.C. "The Vietnam Constitution of 1956." *American Political Science Review* 56 (June 1958): 437–463.

1376. Hess, David L. "The Educated Vietnamese Middle Class of Metropolitan Saigon and Their Legacy of Confucian Authority, 1954–1975." Ph.D. dissertation, New York University, 1977.

1377. Hickey, Gerald C. *Accommodation and Coalition in South Vietnam.* P–4213. Santa Monica, CA: Rand Corp., Jan. 1970.

1378. _____. *Accommodation in South Vietnam: The Key to Sociopolitical Solidarity.* P–3707. Santa Monica, CA: Rand Corp., Oct. 1967.

1379. Honey, P.J. "The Problem of Democracy in Vietnam." *World Today* [London] 16 (Feb. 1960): 71–79.

1380. Jumper, Roy. "Mandarin Bureaucracy and Politics in South Vietnam." *Pacific Affairs* 30 (Mar. 1957): 44–58.

1381. Kahin, George M. "Political Polarization in South Vietnam: U.S. Policy in the Post-Diem Period." *Pacific Affairs* 52 (Winter 1979–1980): 647–673.

1382. King, Peter. "The Political Balance in Saigon." *Pacific Affairs* 44 (Fall 1971): 401–420.

1383. Krich, Claudia A. "Vietnam: The Sickness." *Progressive* 38 (Nov. 1974): 35–37. Kirch focuses on corruption.

1384. Luce, Don. "How Thieu Rules." *New Republic* 162 (Feb. 28, 1970): 17–18.

1385. Morris, Stephen. "The Social Basis of Politics in Vietnam: The Nguyen Van Thieu Government." *Australian Outlook* 27 (Aug. 1973): 140–154. See Thayer's rejoinder (1399).

1386. Nivolon, François. "Politics in South Vietnam: Saigon's Political Challenge." *Far Eastern Economic Review* 65 (July 27, 1969): 280– 283.

1387. Osborne, Milton E. "The Vietnamese Perception of the Identity of the State." *Australian Outlook* 23 (Apr. 1969): 7–17.

1388. Palmer, Joe M. "Political Negotiations in Vietnam." *Military Review* 46 (Sept. 1966): 62–69. Palmer discusses negotiations for domestic leadership.

1389. Race, Jeffrey. "South Vietnam Politics: Of Hearts and Minds." *Far Eastern Economic Review* 64 (Apr. 20–26, 1969): 246–248.

1390. Sacks, M. "Restructuring Government in South Vietnam." *Asian Survey* 7 (Aug. 1967): 515–526.

1391. Scigliano, Robert. "The Electoral Process in South Vietnam: Politics in an Underdeveloped State." *Midwest Journal of Political Science* 4 (May 1960): 138–161.

1392. _____. "Political Parties in South Vietnam under the Republic." *Pacific Affairs* 33 (June 1960): 327–346.

1393. Silverman, Jerry M. "Political Elites in South Vietnam: A National and Provincial Comparison." *Asian Survey* 10 (Apr. 1970): 290–307.

1394. _____. "Political Presence and Electoral Support in South Vietnam." *Asian Survey* 14 (May 1974): 397–417.

1395. _____. "Politics in South Vietnam." *Current History* 57 (Dec. 1969): 321–326.

1396. Smuckler, Ralph H., et al. *Report on the Police of Vietnam.* Saigon: Michigan State University, Vietnam Advisory Group, 1955.

1397. Sola Pool, Ithiel de. "Political Alternatives to the Viet Cong." *Asian Survey* 7 (Aug. 1967): 555–556.

1398. Sosmena, Gaudioso C., Jr. "Vietnamese Village Government: Attempts in Local Autonomy." *Philippine Journal of Public Administration* 14 (Jan. 1970): 41–54.

1399. Thayer, Carlyle A. "The Social Basis of Politics in Vietnam: A Rejoinder." *Australian Outlook* 27 (Dec. 1973): 262–271.

1400. Tippin, Gerald L. "The Army as a Nation-Builder." *Military Review* 50 (Oct. 1970): 11–19.

1401. Tolischus, O.D. "Elections in Vietnam." *New Leader* 48 (Aug. 16, 1965): 8–9.

1402. Tran Van Dinh. *Our Endless War: Inside Vietnam.* San Rafael, CA: Presidio Press, 1978. In this article, a South Vietnamese general discusses the political muddle in Saigon; he is critical of both U.S. meddling and South Vietnamese political immaturity.

1403. U.S. Military Assistance Command, Vietnam. Office of the Staff Judge Advocate. *The Constitution of Vietnam: An Analysis and Comparison.* Saigon, 1967.

1404. Wurfel, David. "The Saigon Political Elite: Focus on Four Cabinets." *Asian Survey* 7 (Aug. 1967): 527–539.

1405. Young, Kenneth T. "United States Policy and Vietnamese Political Viability, 1954–67." *Asian Survey* 7 (Aug. 1967): 507–514.

Election of 1967

This was the national election which was supposed to show the American public a democratic South Vietnam; Thieu and Ky chose to take no chances and eliminated opposition candidates. We have also included background items relating to the South Vietnamese election process in general.

1406. Close, Alexandra. "The Voters of Vietnam." *Far Eastern Economic Review* 57 (Sept. 10–16, 1967): 505–506.

1407. Kirk, Donald. "The Thieu Presidential Campaign: Background and Consequences of the Single-Candidacy Phenomenon." *Asian Survey* 12 (July 1972): 609–624.

1408. Nguyen Tuyet Mai. "Electioneering: Vietnamese Style." *Asian Survey* 2 (Nov. 1962): 11–18. [Contains background material]

1409. Penniman, Howard R. *Elections in South Vietnam.* Washington, DC: American Enterprise Institute for Public Research, 1972.

1410. Purnell, K.H. "Vietnam Elections: Marching Out the Horses." *Nation* 205 (Sept. 25, 1967): 267–269.

1411. "Republic of Viet-Nam: Elections." *Current Notes on International Affairs* [Canberra, Australia] 38 (Sept. 1967): 349–370.

1412. Silverman, Jerry M. "South Vietnam: The Symbolic Nature of Election Campaign Appeals." *Journal of Southeast Asian Studies* 3 (Mar. 1972): 44–62.

1413. Taillefer, Jean. "Les Élections au Sud-Vietnam." *France-Asie/Asia* 21 (Spring–Summer 1967): 447–458.

1414. Tran Van Dinh. "South Vietnam's Captive Vote." *New Republic* 157 (Sept. 2, 1967): 15–16.

1415. Warner, Denis. "Vietnam Prepares for Elections." *Reporter* 35 (Aug. 11, 1966): 12ff.

1416. Young, Stephen M. "The New 'Democracy' in Vietnam." *Progressive* 31 (July 1967): 10–11.

Political Freedom and Repression

South Vietnamese leaders, Diem and Thieu especially, curtailed personal freedoms and imprisoned all who opposed them, whether communist or not. Antiwar critics often cited the controversial "tiger cages" of Con Son as examples of South Vietnam's harsh and unjust practices; however, they rarely took notice of North Vietnamese restrictions of civil liberties.

1417. Branfman, Fred. "South Vietnam's Police and Prison System: the U.S. Connection." In *Uncloaking the CIA,* edited by Howard Frazier. New York: Free Press, 1978, 101–125.

1418. _____. "Vietnam: The POW's We Left Behind." *Ramparts* 12 (Dec. 1973): 11–14. Branfman focuses on South Vietnamese political prisoners.

1419. Brown, Holmes, and Don Luce. *Hostages of War: Saigon's Political Prisoners.* Washington, DC: Indochina Mobile Education Project, 1973.

1420. Buttinger, Joseph. "Thieu's Prisoners." *New York Review of Books* (June 14, 1973): 20–24.

1421. Casella, Alexander. "Saigon's Prisoners." *Far Eastern Economic Review* 78 (Dec. 23, 1972): 24–25.

1422. Coffey, Raymond. "Vietnam's Not-so-Free Press." *Saturday Review* 50 (Oct. 14, 1967): 122–123, 131.

1423. Corley, Francis J. "Freedom in Indo-China: A Review Article." *Pacific Affairs* 34 (Winter 1961): 375–380.

1424. Debris, Jean-Pierre, and André Menras. *Rescapes des bagnes de Saigon: Nous accusons.* Paris: Les Éditeurs Français Réunis, 1973. The authors discuss political prisoners.

1425. Drinan, Robert F. "Political Freedom in Vietnam." *America* 120 (Aug. 1969): 821–831.

1426. Ellsberg, Daniel. "Diemism and U.S. Army: Impact of the Arrest, Trial and Imprisonment of Tran Ngoc Chau." In U.S. Senate. Committee on Foreign Relations. Hearings; *Impact of War in Southeast Asia on the U.S. Economy.* Pt. 2. 91st Cong., 2d sess., 1970, 334–365.

1427. Fox, Tom. "Devil's Island Off Vietnam." *Commonweal* 90 (July 11, 1969): 432–435.

1428. Front Solidarite Indochine. *Saigon: Les Prisonniers par le Front Solidarité Indochine.* Paris: F. Maspero, 1973.

1429. *In Thieu's Prisons.* Hanoi: Foreign Languages Publishing House, 1973.

1430. Millet, Stanley. "Terror in Vietnam: An American's Ordeal at the Hands of Our 'Friends.'" *Harper's* 225 (Sept. 1962): 31–39.

1431. Nguyen Khac Vien. "With Survivors From Saigon Jails." *Crime and Social Justice* 2 (Fall–Winter 1974): 48–53.

1432. *Political Prisoners in South Vietnam.* London: Amnesty International Publications, 1973.

1433. Porter, D. Gareth. "Saigon's Secret Police." *Nation* 210 (Apr. 27, 1970): 498–500.

1434. "Thieu–Ky Brand of Freedom." *Progressive* 34 (Feb. 1970): 14–16.

1435. "The Tiger Cages of Con Son." *Life* 69 (July 17, 1970): 26–29.

1436. United Nations. Report; *The Violation of Human Rights in South Viet Nam.* U.N. Document A/5630, 1963.

1437. U.S. House. Committee on Foreign Affairs. Hearings; *Political Prisoners in South Vietnam and the Philippines.* 93d Cong., 2d sess., May 1–June 5, 1974.

1438. _____. Hearings; *The Treatment of Political Prisoners in South Vietnam by the Government of the Republic of South Vietnam.* 93d Cong., 1st sess., Sept. 13, 1973.

Religion and Politics

The Buddhists' militant protest of South Vietnamese politics, especially those of Diem, led to conflict, arrests and death.

1439. Fairbanks, H.G. "Diem and the Buddhists." *Commonweal* 78 (July 26, 1963): 452–454.

1440. Fall, Bernard B. "The Political–Religious Sects of Viet-Nam." *Pacific Affairs* 28 (Sept. 1955): 235–252.

1441. Gheddo, Piero. *The Cross and the Bo-Tree: Catholics and Buddhists in Vietnam.* Translated by Charles U. Quinn. New York: Sheed & Ward, 1970.

1442. Hope, Marjorie. "Vietnam Perspectives: The Buddhist Way: Guns, Butter, or Chinh Nghia?" *War/Peace Report* 6 (Aug.–Sept. 1966): 14–16.

1443. Howe, Irving. "The Buddhist Revolt in Vietnam." *Dissent* 13 (May–June 1966): 227–229.

1444. "An Interview with the Buddhists Vo Van Ai and Thich Nhat Hanh." *War/Peace Report* 9 (June–July 1969): 13ff.

1445. Joiner, Charles A. "South Vietnam's Buddhist Crisis: Organization for Charity, Dissidence, and Unity." *Asian Survey* 4 (July 1964): 915–928.

1446. Jumper, Roy. "Sects and Communism in South Vietnam." *Orbis* 3 (Spring 1959): 85–96.

1447. Luu Quoc. "The Buddhists' and Students' Politics of Peace and Sovereignty in South Vietnam, 1964–1968." *Cornell Journal of Social Relations* 6 (Spring 1971): 98–114.

1448. Morgan, K.W. "The Buddhists: The Problem and the Promise." *Asia* 4 (Winter 1966): 503–518.

1449. Nakamura Hajime. "The Buddhist Protest." *Japan Quarterly* 13 (Oct.–Dec. 1966): 439–443.

1450. Roberts, Adam. "Buddhism and Politics in South Vietnam." *World Today* [London] 21 (June 1965): 240–250.

1451. _____. "The Buddhists, the War and the Viet-cong." *World Today* [London] 22 (May 1966): 214–222.

1452. Scigliano, Robert. "Vietnam: Politics and Religion." *Asian Survey* 4 (Jan. 1964): 666–673.

1453. Thich Nhat Hanh. "On the War by a Buddhist Monk: A Buddhist Poet in Vietnam." *New York Review of Books* (June 9, 1966): 4–5.

1454. Warner, Denis. "The Divided Buddhists of South Vietnam." *Reporter* 34 (June 16, 1966): 22–24.

1455. _____. "How Much Power Does Tri Quang Want?" *Reporter* 34 (May 5, 1966): 11–14.

1456. _____. "Vietnam's Militant Buddhists." *Reporter* 31 (Dec. 3, 1964): 29–31.

1457. Wirmark, Bo. *The Buddhists in Vietnam: An Alternative View of the War.* Brussels: War Resisters International, 1974. [also printed as Rpt. no. 9, Uppsala University, Sweden, Department of Peace and Conflict Research, 1974]

1458. Wulff, Erich. "The Buddhist Revolt: Diem's New Opponents Deserve U.S. Support." *New Republic* 149 (Aug. 31, 1963): 11–14.

Social Aspects

1459. Buttinger, Joseph. "The Ethnic Minorities in the Republic of Vietnam." In *Problems of Freedom: South Vietnam Since Independence*, edited by Wesley R. Fishel. Chicago: Free Press of Glencoe, 1961, 99–121.

1460. Coffey, Raymond. "Vietnam: The People, No." *Progressive* 30 (Feb. 1966): 11–13. Coffey discusses South Vietnam's social action project.

1461. Collins, J.L., et al. *Medical Problems of South Viet Nam.* Boston: Physicians for Social Responsibility, 1967.

1462. Finkle, Jason L. *A Profile of N.I.A. Students.* Saigon: Michigan State University, Vietnam Advisory Group, May 1961.

1463. Marti, Jill. "Mascots of War." *Ramparts* 10 (Jan. 1972): 52–53. An account of a 13-year-old boy working for Americans as an interpreter.

1464. Nicolaus, Martin. "The Professor, the Policeman and the Peasant." *Viet-Report* 2 (Feb. 1966): 16–21.

1465. Pepper, W.F. "The Children of Vietnam." *Ramparts* 5 (Jan. 1957): 53–60.

1466. Pomonti, Jean-Claude. "Despair Among South Vietnam's Young People." *Atlas* 19 (July 1970): 21–22.

1467. Reimann, H.A. "Medicine in Saigon." *Medical Opinion & Review* 3 (Aug. 1967): 86–90.

1468. Smith, N.I. "Education in the Republic of Vietnam." *Australian Army Journal*, no. 244 (Sept. 1969): 33–59.

Public Administration

1469. Allen, Luther A., and Pham Ngoc An. *A Vietnamese District Chief in Action*. Saigon: Michigan State University, Vietnam Advisory Group, 1961.

1470. Andrews, S. "Red Tape and Broken Promises." *Reporter* 34 (May 5, 1966): 14–16. Andrews probes the inability of the Saigon government to deliver promised programs.

1471. Armbruster, Frank E. *A Military and Police Security Program for South Vietnam*. HI–881/2 RR. Croton-on-Hudson, NY: Hudson Institute, 1967.

1472. Jumper, Roy. "Problems of Public Administration in South Vietnam." *Far Eastern Survey* 26 (Dec. 1957): 183–190.

1473. Montgomery, John D., and N.I.A. Case Development Seminar. *Cases In Vietnamese Administration*. Saigon: Michigan State University, Vietnam Advisory Group, 1959.

1474. Nghiem Dang. *Viet-Nam: Politics and Public Administration*. Honolulu: East–West Center Press, 1966.

1475. Rose, Dale L. *The Vietnamese Civil Service System*. Saigon: Michigan State University, Vietnam Advisory Group, 1961.

1476. Scigliano, Robert, and Wayne W. Snyder. "The Budget Process in South Vietnam." *Pacific Affairs* 33 (Mar. 1960): 48–60.

1477. Woodruff, Lloyd W. *Local Administration in Vietnam*. Saigon: Michigan State University, Vietnam Advisory Group, 1961.

1478. Zasloff, Joseph J., and Nguyen Khac Nhan. *A Study of Administration in Binh Minh District*. Saigon: Michigan State University, Vietnam Advisory Group, 1961.

PERSONALITIES

1479. *No Other Road to Take: Memoir of Mrs. Nguyen Thi Dinh*. Translated by Mai Elliott. Data Paper no. 102. Ithaca, NY: Cornell University, Department of Asian Studies, Southeast Asia Program, 1976.

1480. *Who's Who of the Republic of South Viet Nam*. Saigon: Gai Phong Editions, 1969.

Ngo Dinh Diem/Madame Nhu

The first pro-Western strong man of South Vietnam, Ngo Dinh Diem, was killed in a 1963 coup. Allegations have been leveled that the United States was involved, at least morally, in Diem's death.

1481. Borin, V.L. "Who Killed Diem and Why." *National Review* 16 (June 2, 1964): 441–446.

1482. Bouscaren, Anthony T. *The Last of the Mandarins: Diem of Vietnam*. Pittsburgh: Duquesne University Press, 1965. Bouscaren provides a sympathetic view of Diem.

1483. Hagan, R. "The Ngos." *Correspondent* 29 (Nov. 12, 1963): 3–9.

1484. Henderson, W., and Wesley R. Fishel. "The Foreign Policy of Ngo Dinh Diem." *Vietnam Perspectives* 2:1 (1966): 3–30.

1485. Huynh Sanh Thong. "Greatest Little Man in Asia." *Nation* 192 (Feb. 18, 1961): 140–142.

1486. Karnow, Stanley. "Diem Defeats His Own Best Troops." *Reporter* 24 (Jan. 19, 1961): 24–29.

1487. _____. "The Edge of Chaos." *Saturday Evening Post* 236 (Sept. 28, 1963): 27–36.

1488. _____. "The Fall of the House of Ngo Dinh." *Saturday Evening Post* 236 (Dec. 21, 1963): 75–79.

1489. Luce, Clare Boothe. "The Lady is for Burning: The Seven Deadly Sins of Madame Nhu." *National Review* 15 (Nov. 5, 1963): 395–399.

1490. "Ngo Dinh Diem, President of the Republic of Vietnam." *Far Eastern Economic Review* 26 (May 28, 1959): 744–746.

1491. Nguyen Minh Vy. "L'Inamovible famille Diem." *Democratic Nouvelle* 10 (Oct. 1963): 14–19.

1492. Oosten, Fernand. "Ngo Dinh Diem, der Viet Cong und die Amerikaner." *Aussenpolitik* 14 (Sept. 1963): 624–633.

1493. Porter, D. Gareth. "The Diemist Restoration." *Commonweal* 90 (July 11, 1969): 435–437.

1494. Scheer, Robert. "Hang Down Your Head Tom Dooley." *Ramparts* 3 (Jan. 2, 1965): 23–28. Many American Catholics were glad to see an end to Diem's "Catholic Despotism."

1495. Shaplen, Robert. "Nine Years After a Fateful Assassination: The Cult of Diem." *New York Times Magazine* (May 14, 1972): 16ff.

1496. _____. "A Reporter in Vietnam: Diem." *New Yorker* 38 (Sept. 22, 1962): 103–131.

1497. Sharron, Marc. "The Fall of the House of Ngo: A Case Review." *Institute of Applied Psychology Review* 4 (Summer 1964): 83–92.

1498. Sparks, Will. "A New Role for Mme. Nhu." *New Leader* 46 (Nov. 25, 1963): 8–10.

1499. U.S. Senate. Committee on Foreign Relations. *U.S. Involvement in Overthrow of Diem, 1963.* Staff Study No. 3. 92d Cong., 2d sess., July 20, 1972. [based on the *Pentagon Papers*]

1500. Warner, Denis. "Agony in Saigon: The Lady and the Cadaver." *Reporter* 26 (Oct. 10, 1963): 39–42.

1501. _____. *The Last Confucian.* New York: Macmillan, 1963. The title refers to Diem.

1502. Warner, Geoffrey. "The United States and the Fall of Diem." *Australian Outlook* 28 (Dec. 1974): 245–258; 29 (Apr. 1975): 3–17.

1503. West, M.L. "The Tragedy of Diem and the Paradox of Asia." *America* 112 (Mar. 13, 1965): 342–356.

Nguyen Cao Ky/Nguyen Van Thieu

1504. Buckley, Kevin P. "No One Can Be Sure What Thieu Is Thinking." *New York Times Magazine* (Mar. 2, 1969): 28ff.

1505. Morrow, Michael. "The Movement to Replace Thieu–Ky with a 'Reconciliatory Government.'" *War/Peace Report* 10 (Jan. 1970): 8–11.

1506. Nguyen Cao Ky. *Twenty Years and Twenty Days.* New York: Stein & Day, 1976. [memoirs of Ky]

1507. Nguyen Van Thieu. "Our Military Struggle: Relief and Struggle." *Vital Speeches* 34 (Apr. 15, 1968): 392–394.

1508. Shawcross, William. "How Thieu Hangs On." *New York Review of Books* (July 18, 1977): 16–20.

1509. "Thieu: An Interview with Oriana Fallaci." *New Republic* 168 (Jan. 20, 1973): 16–25.

1510. Ton That Thien. "Ky's Election Victory." *Far Eastern Economic Review* 53 (Sept. 22, 1966): 561–563.

1511. Tran Van Dinh. "The Ky Question." *New Republic* 156 (Jan. 21, 1967): 21–23.

1512. _____. "Ky vs. Buddhists: Round 2." *New Republic* 156 (May 13, 1967): 15–19.

1513. _____. "Thieu and Ky: The Rivalry of Puppets." *Nation* 206 (Jan. 29, 1968): 136–139.

ECONOMICS

1514. Anderson, K.P. *A Model of External and Internal Price Equilibrium in South Vietnam.* P–4433. Santa Monica, CA: Rand Corp., Aug. 1970.

1515. Barber, C.H. "Business Boom in Saigon." *Far Eastern Economic Review* 51 (Mar. 10, 1966): 443–444, 447.

1516. Barton, Clifton G. "Credit and Commercial Control: Strategies and Methods of Chinese Businessmen in South Vietnam (1967–1975)." Ph.D. dissertation, Cornell University, 1977.

1517. Buu Hoan. "The South Vietnamese Economy in the Transition to Peace and After." *Asian Survey* 11 (Apr. 1971): 305–320.

1518. Child, Frank C. *Essays on Economic Growth, Capital Formation, and Public Policy in Viet–Nam.* Saigon: Michigan State University, Vietnam Advisory Group, 1961.

1519. Cole, David C. "Financing Provincial and Local Government in the Republic of Vietnam." Ph.D. dissertation, University of Michigan, 1959.

1520. Crawford, William R. "The Impact of Political Violence on Marketing Development in South Vietnam, 1955 through 1972." Ph.D. dissertation, University of Alabama, 1976.

1521. Development and Resources Corporation. *Export Prospects for the Republic of Vietnam.* New York: Praeger, 1971.

1522. Faltermeyer, E.K. "The Surprising Assets of South Vietnam's Economy." *Fortune* 73 (Mar. 1966): 110–121.

1523. Goodman, Allan E. "The End of the War as a Setting for the Future Development of South Vietnam." *Asian Survey* 11 (Apr. 1971): 341–351.

1524. Goodrich, Carter. *Toward the Economic Development of Viet Nam.* New York: United Nations, 1956.

1525. Hallinan, T. *Economic Prospects of the Republic of Vietnam.* P–4224. Santa Monica, CA: Rand Corp., Nov. 1969.

1526. Hendry, James B. "Economic Development Under Conditions of Guerrilla Warfare: The Case of Viet Nam." *Asian Survey* 2 (June 1962): 1–12.

1527. Heymann, H., Jr. *Imposing Communism on the Economy of South Vietnam: A Conjectured View.* P–4569. Santa Monica, CA: Rand Corp., Jan. 1971.

1528. International Bank for Reconstruction and Development. International Development Association. *Current Economic Position and Prospects of the Republic of South Vietnam.* Washington, DC, 1974.

1529. Lilienthal, David E. "Postwar Development in Vietnam." *Foreign Affairs* 47 (Jan. 1969): 321–333. See Williams' critique (1543).

1530. Linder, Willy. "Economic Crisis in South Vietnam." *Swiss Review of World Affairs* 20 (May 1970): 4–7.

1531. Lindholm, Richard W. *Economic Development Policy with Emphasis on Viet-Nam.* Eugene: University of Oregon Press, 1964.

1532. Logan, William J.C. "How Deep Is the Green Revolution in South Vietnam?" *Asian Survey* 11 (Apr. 1971): 321–330.

1533. McCulloch, Frank. "For Profiteers, What a Lovely War: In a Black Market, Vietnamese and Americans Do a Flourishing Business in Corruption." *Life* 67 (Aug. 1, 1969): 46–48ff.

1534. Musolf, Lloyd D. "Public Enterprise and Development Perspectives in South Vietnam." *Asian Survey* 3 (Aug. 1963): 357–372.

1535. Republic of Vietnam. *The Economic Promise of the Republic of Vietnam.* Saigon: Ministry of Finance, 1973.

1536. Smith, Desmond. "Saigon: Drowning in Dollars." *Nation* 203 (Dec. 5, 1966): 602–605.

1537. Starner, Frances L. "South Vietnam: A Need to Devalue." *Far Eastern Economic Review* 69 (July 16, 1970): 22–23ff.

1538. Taylor, Milton C. *The Taxation of Income in Vietnam.* Saigon: Michigan State University, Vietnam Advisory Group, 1959.

1539. Trued, M.N. "South Vietnam's Industrial Development Center." *Pacific Affairs* 33 (Sept. 1960): 250–267.

1540. U.S. Department of State. Bureau of Intelligence and Research. *Dollar Leakage in Vietnam.* Research Memo RES–12–66. Washington, DC, 1966.

1541. U.S. House. Committee on Government Operations. Hearings; *Inequitable Current Exchange Rates in Vietnam.* 92d Cong., 1st sess., 1971.

1542. _____. Twenty-Sixth Report; *A Review of the Inequitable Monetary Rate of Exchange in Vietnam.* House Rpt. no. 91–1228. 91st Cong., 2d sess., 1970.

1543. Williams, Albert P., Jr. "South Vietnam's Development in a Postwar Era: A Commentary on the Thuc–Lilienthal Report." *Asian Survey* 11 (Apr. 1971): 352–370. [based on Williams' Rand paper P–4563, Jan. 1971]

1544. Woodruff, Lloyd W. *Local Finance in South Vietnam: A Study of 25 Villages in the Two Southern Regions.* Saigon: Michigan State University, Vietnam Advisory Group, 1961.

Rural Vietnam

1545. Black, Edwin. "Village in Vietnam." *U.S. Naval Institute Proceedings* 91 (Sept. 1965): 121–123. Black reviews Hickey's book.

1546. Brown, James, Jr., and Jay S. Salkin. "Underemployment in Rural South Vietnam: A Comment and a Discussion of Family Labor." *Economic Development and Cultural Change* 23 (Oct. 1974): 151–160.

1547. Bullington, James R., and James D. Rosenthal. "The South Vietnamese Countryside: Non-Communist Political Perceptions." *Asian Survey* 10 (Aug. 1970): 651–661.

1548. Dowdy, Homer E. *The Bamboo Cross: Christian Witness in the Jungles of Viet Nam.* New York: Harper & Row, 1964. Dowdy also describes rural tribes and their clashes with the VC.

1549. Goodman, Allan E. "The Political Implications of Rural Problems in South Vietnam: Creating the Public Interest." *Asian Survey* 10 (Aug. 1970): 672–687.

1550. Hendry, James B. *The Small World of Khanh Hau.* Chicago: Aldine, 1964.

1551. Hickey, Gerald C. *The Highland People of South Vietnam: Social and Economic Development.* RM–5281/1. Santa Monica, CA: Rand Corp., Aug. 1967.

1552. _____. *The Major Ethnic Groups of the South Vietnamese Highlands.* RM–4041–ARPA. Santa Monica, CA: Rand Corp., Apr. 1964.

1553. _____. *Some Recommendations Affecting the Prospective Role of Vietnamese Highlanders in Economic Development.* P–4708. Santa Monica, CA: Rand Corp., Sept. 1971.

1554. _____. *Village in Vietnam.* New Haven, CT: Yale University Press, 1964. Hickey discusses the village of Khanh Hau.

1555. Honda Katsuichi. *Vietnam: A Voice from the Villages.* Tokyo: Committee for the English Publication of "Vietnam: A Voice from the Villages," 1968.

1556. Manke, Hugh I. "The Expulsion of I.V.S.—Another Casualty of the War." *War/Peace Report* 11 (Dec. 1971): 7–9. Man59): 85–96.

1557. *Quiet Warriors Supporting Social Revolution in Viet-Nam.* U.S. Department of State Publication 8041. Far Eastern Series 140. Washington, DC: GPO, Apr. 1966.

1558. Stroup, Robert H., and Richard E. Gift. "Underemployment in Rural South Vietnam: Reply." *Economic Development and Cultural Change* 23 (Oct. 1974): 161–162.

1559. Woodruff, Lloyd W. *The Study of a Vietnamese Rural Community: Administration Activity.* 2 vols. Saigon: Michigan State University, Vietnam Advisory Group, 1960.

Land Reform

See also Chapter 6, under "Pacification," the "Strategic Hamlet Program" section.

1560. Bredo, William. "Agrarian Reform in Vietnam: Vietcong and Government of Vietnam Strategies in Conflict." *Asian Survey* 10 (Aug. 1970): 738–750.

1561. Burr, Jewett M. "Land to the Tiller: Land Redistribution in South Viet Nam 1970–1973." Ph.D. dissertation, University of Oregon, 1976.

1562. Cherry, B. "Digging In: Does the Granting of Legal Title Also Confer a Will to Defend the Land?" *Far Eastern Economic Review* 76 (June 24, 1972): 22ff.

1563. Gittinger, J. Price. *Studies on Land Tenure in Vietnam: Terminal Report.* Saigon: United States Operations Mission to Vietnam, 1959.

1564. Hendry, James B. "Land Tenure in South Vietnam." *Economic Development and Cultural Change* 9 (Oct. 1960): 27–44.

1565. Koffman, Louis A. "Photogrammetry for Land Reform: Vietnam." *Military Engineer* 62 (May–June 1970): 188–191.

1566. Mitchell, Edward J. *Land Tenure and Rebellion: A Statistical Analysis of Factors Affecting Government Control in South Vietnam.* RM–5181–ARPA Santa Monica, CA: Rand Corp., June 1967. [abridged; see also his summary in *Asian Survey* 7 (Aug. 1967): 577–580]

1567. Montgomery, John D. "Land Reform as a Means to Political Development in Vietnam." *Orbis* 12 (Spring 1968): 19–38.

1568. Morrock, Richard. "Agrarian 'Reform' in South Vietnam." *Monthly Review* 16 (Nov. 1964): 442–446.

1569. Nguyen Khac Nhan. "Policy of Key Rural Agrovilles." *Asian Culture* [Saigon] 3 (July–Dec. 1961): 29–49.

1570. Peterson, Jeffery G. "The Political and Military Uses of Land Reform in Wartime Vietnam: Precedences, 1960–1968." Ph.D. dissertation, University of Miami, 1975.

1571. Prosterman, Roy L. "Land Reform in South Vietnam: A Proposal for Turning the Tables on the Viet Cong." *Cornell Law Review* 53 (Nov. 1967): 26–44.

1572. _____. "Land-to-Tiller in South Vietnam: The Tables Turn." *Asian Survey* 10 (Aug. 1970): 751–764.

1573. Race, Jeffrey. "South Vietnam: The Battle Over Land." *Far Eastern Economic Review* 69 (Aug. 20, 1970): 19–22.

1574. _____. "South Vietnam's Peasants: Land Without Hope?" *Far Eastern Economic Review* 60 (May 12, 1968): 349–352.

1575. Salter, MacDonald. "The Broadening Base of Land Reform in South Vietnam." *Asian Survey* 10 (Aug. 1970): 724–737.

1576. U.S. House. Committee on Government Operations. Report No. 1142; *Land Reform in Vietnam.* [20th Rpt.] 90th Cong., 2d sess., 1968.

1577. Wiegersma, Nancy A. "Land Tenure and Land Reform: A History of Property and Power in Vietnam." Ph.D. dissertation, University of Maryland, 1976.

1578. Woodside, Alexander. "Decolonization and Agricultural Reform in South Vietnam." *Asian Survey* 10 (Aug. 1970): 705–723.

1579. Wurfel, David. "Agrarian Reform in the Republic of Vietnam." *Far Eastern Economic Survey* 26 (June 1957): 81–92.

U.S. AID

Between 1966 and 1972, the United States sent $101 billion to South Vietnam, while Russia sent $2.4 billion and China $1.7 billion to North Vietnam. In 1973, the United States sent $5.26 billion to South Vietnam; Russia sent $175 million and China $115 million to North Vietnam. (Source: CIA and Department of Defense, as cited in New York Times, *Aug. 8, 1974.)*

1580. "Aid to Thieu: Deadlock on Aid." *Congressional Record* 118 (Oct. 11, 1972): 34841-34854. [NARMIC report by Le Anh Tu]

1581. *Aid to Vietnam.* New York: American Friends of Vietnam, 1959.

1582. Barrows, Leland. "American Economic Aid to Vietnam." *Viet-My* [Saigon] 1 (1956): 29–40.

1583. Bennet, John T. *Political Implications of Economic Change: South Vietnam: SEADAG Papers on Development and Development Policy Problems, No. 19.* New York: The Asia Society, 1967.

1584. Bresse, Gerald. *The Great City and Economic Development in Southeast Asia: SEADAG Papers on Problems of Development in Southeast Asia, No. 29.* New York: The Asia Society, 1968.

1585. Fishel, Wesley R. "American Aid to Vietnam." *Current History* 49 (Nov. 1965): 294–299.

1586. Gaud, W.S. "AID Report on Viet-Nam Commodity Programs." *U.S. Department of State Bulletin* 56 (Feb. 6, 1967): 200–216.

1587. Genin, P. "L'Aide américaine au Sud-Vietnam." *Les Cahiers de la République* 6:30 (1961): 51–56.

1588. Gran, Guy. "American Welfare Abroad: Aid to South Vietnam." *Indochina Chronicle*, no. 24 (Apr. 8, 1973): 1–15.

1589. Grant, James P. "AID's Proposed Program for Viet Nam in Fiscal Year 1969." *U.S. Department of State Bulletin* 58 (May 6, 1968): 594–598.

1590. Hendry, James B. "American Aid in Vietnam: The View from a Village." *Pacific Affairs* 33 (Dec. 1960): 387–391.

1591. Holbik, Karel. "U.S. Aid to Vietnam." *Inter Economics* 7 (July 1968): 242–246.

1592. Hotham, David. "U.S. Aid to Vietnam—A Balance Sheet." *Reporter* 17 (Sept. 19, 1957): 30–33.

1593. Moseley, G.V.H., III. "U.S. Aid to Indo-China." *New Leader* 41 (Feb. 24, 1958): 13–14.

1594. Smith, R.L. "The Lessons of Vietnam: A Study of Problems Faced by U.S. Aid Programs." *Challenge* 8 (Nov. 1959): 7–12.

1595. Taylor, Milton C. "South Vietnam: Lavish Aid, Limited Progress." *Pacific Affairs* 34 (Fall 1961): 242–256.

1596. United Nations. Economic Survey Mission to the Republic of Viet-Nam. Report; *Toward the Economic Development of the Republic of Vietnam.* FAO Rpt. no. 539. New York, 1959.

1597. U.S. General Accounting Office. Report; *Economic and Technical Assistance Program for Vietnam* [for fiscal years 1955–57]. Washington, DC, 1958.

1598. _____. Report; *Suggestions for Changes in U.S. Funding and Management of Pacification and Development Programs in Vietnam.* Washington, DC: Comptroller General of the U.S., 1972.

1599. _____. Report; *United States Assistance to the Government of Vietnam for Its Roads and Highway System.* B–159451. Washington, DC, 1974.

1600. U.S. House. Committee on Government Operations. Hearings; *U.S. Assistance Programs in Vietnam.* 92d Cong., 1st sess., July 15–21, Aug. 2, 1971.

1601. _____. Report; *The Commercial (Commodity) Import Program for Vietnam (Follow-up Investigation), Fifth Report.* House Rpt. no. 610. 90th Cong., 1st sess., 1967.

1602. _____. Report; *An Investigation of the U.S. Economic and Military Assistance Programs in Vietnam.* House Rpt. no. 2257. 89th Cong., 2d sess., 1966.

1603. _____. Report; *A Review of the Inequitable Monetary Rate of Exchange in Vietnam.* Rpt. 91–1228. 91st Cong., 2d sess., June 25, 1970.

1604. U.S. Senate. Committee on Foreign Relations. Hearings; *Foreign Assistance Act of 1968, Part 1: Vietnam.* 90th Cong., 2d sess., Mar. 11–12, 1968.

1605. _____. Hearings; *Supplemental Foreign Assistance Fiscal Year 1966–Vietnam.* 89th Cong., 2d sess., 1966.

1606. _____. Report; *United States Aid Program in Vietnam.* 86th Cong., 2d sess., 1960.

Michigan State University Project

Shortly after the end of the First Indochina War, the United States commissioned Michigan State University to supply technical assistance; charges have been leveled that the CIA was connected with the MSU project.

1607. Hinckle, Warren, et al. "Michigan State: University on the Make." *Ramparts* 4 (Apr. 1966): 11–21.

1608. Horowitz, Irving L. "Michigan State and the CIA: A Dilemma for Social Science." *Bulletin of the Atomic Scientists* 22 (Sept. 1966): 26–29.

1609. Scigliano, Robert, and G.H. Fox. *Technical*

Assistance in Vietnam: The Michigan State University Experience. New York: Praeger, 1965.

1610. Sheinbaum, Sam. "University on the Make: Or, How Michigan State University Helped Arm Madame Nhu." *Ramparts* 7 (Jan. 25, 1969): 52– 60.

Nongovernmental Assistance

See also Chapter 8, under "Civilian Casualties."

1611. Beechy, Atlee, and Winifred Beechy. *Vietnam: Who Cares?* Scottdale, PA: Herald Press, 1968. The authors focus on church and civilian relief.

1612. Brown, Lester R. *Seeds of Change: The Green Revolution and Development in the 1970's.* New York: Praeger, 1970.

1613. Hope, Samuel R. "Vietnam Christian Service." *Journal of Presbyterian History* 47:2 (1969): 103–123.

1614. Kolko, Gabriel. "The United States Effort to Mobilize World Bank Aid to Saigon (1971–1974)." *Journal of Contemporary Asia* [Sweden] 5:1 (1975): 42–52.

1615. "Nonmilitary Aid to Vietnam." In *Allied Participation in Vietnam*, edited by Stanley R. Larsen and James L. Collins, Jr. Washington, DC: GPO, 1975, 160–170.

1616. Schwengel, Fred, and William Cowger. "Report of the Volunteers for Vietnam." *Congressional Record* 116 (Aug. 12, 1970): 28539–28551.

North Vietnam, 1954–1975

Hanoi officials did not waver in their determination to unify Vietnam. When they failed to gain unification at the ballot box, following the Geneva armistice of 1954, they renewed guerilla activities and, later, committed troops to achieve victory. The North Vietnamese successfully identified their cause with local "nationalism," but their ability to persist in their cause was due in large measure to party organization. Anyone researching North Vietnam will find Phan Thieu Chau's bibliography (38) quite valuable. For the views of Western visitors, see Chapter 4, under "Personal Experiences in Vietnam."

Books and Dissertations

1617. Betz, Christiaan J. "Vietnam: Social Transformation From Confucianism to Communism." Ph.D. dissertation, California Institute of Asian Studies, 1977.

1618. Burchett, Wilfred G. *North of the 17th Parallel.* Hanoi: Red River Publishing House, 1957.

1619. _____. *Vietnam North.* New York: International Publishers, 1966.

1620. Chaliand, Gerard. *The Peasants of North Vietnam.* Baltimore: Penguin Books, 1969.

1621. *The Democratic Republic of Viet Nam.* Hanoi: Foreign Languages Publishing House, 1975.

1622. Diamond, Dick. *The Walls Are Down.* Hanoi: Foreign Languages Publishing House, 1958.

1623. Duiker, William J. *The Communist Road to Power in Vietnam.* Boulder, CO: Westview Press, 1980.

1624. Fall, Bernard B. *Le Viet-Minh: La République démocratique du Viet-Nam 1945–1960.* Paris: Armand Colin, 1960.

1625. Fox, Len. *Friendly Vietnam.* Hanoi: Foreign Languages Publishing House, 1958.

1626. Gerassi, John. *North Vietnam: A Documentary.* London: Allen & Unwin, 1968.

1627. Hoang Van Chi. *From Colonialism to Communism: A Case History of North Vietnam.* New York: Praeger, 1964.

1628. Honey, Patrick J., ed. *North Vietnam Today: Profile of a Communist Satellite.* New York: Praeger, 1962.

1629. Raffaeli, J. *Hanoi, capitale de la survie.* Paris: Grasset, 1967.

1630. Salmon, Malcolm. *Focus on Indo-China.* Hanoi: Foreign Languages Publishing House, 1961.

1631. Tongas, Gérard. *J'ai vécu dans l'enfer communiste au Nord Viet-Nam et j'ai choisi la liberté.* Paris: Nouvelles Éditions Debresse, 1960.

1632. Tran Mai Nam. *The Narrow Strip of Land.* Hanoi: Foreign Languages Publishing House, 1969. The story of a journey.

1633. U.S. Army. *Area Handbook for North Vietnam.* 3d ed. DA Pamphlet 550–57. Washington, DC: GPO, 1967.

1634. Weiss, Peter. *Notes on the Cultural Life of the Democratic Republic of Vietnam.* New York: Dell, 1970. [translated from German]

Essays

1635. Chesneaux, Jean. "The Historical Background of Vietnamese Communism." *Government and Opposition* 4 (Winter 1969): 118–135.

1636. Colvin, John. "Hanoi in My Time." *Washington Quarterly* 4 (Spring 1981): 138–156.

1637. Dommen, Arthur J. "The Future of North Vietnam." *Current History* 58 (Apr. 1970): 229–232ff.

1638. Elliott, David W.P. "North Vietnam Since Ho." *Problems of Communism* 24 (July–Aug. 1975): 35–52.

1639. Fall, Bernard B. "North Vietnam: A Profile." *Problems of Communism* 14 (July–Aug. 1965): 13–25.

1640. ______. "North Viet-Nam's Constitution and Government." *Pacific Affairs* 33 (Sept. 1960): 282–290.

1641. ______. "The Other Side of the 17th Parallel." *New York Times Magazine* (July 10, 1966): 4ff.

1642. ______. *The Viet-Minh Regime*. Ithaca, NY: Cornell University Southeast Asia Program and the Institute of Pacific Relations, 1956.

1643. Gurtov, Melvin. *Indochina in North Vietnamese Strategy*. P–4605. Santa Monica, CA: Rand Corp., Mar. 1971.

1644. Honey, P.J. "North Vietnam's Party Congress." *China Quarterly*, no. 4 (Oct.–Dec. 1960): 66–75.

1645. Hunebele, D. "Nord-Vietnam: Une expérience isoliteé dans le camp communiste." *Réalités*, no. 146 (Jan. 1963): 78–85.

1646. Lacouture, Jean. "Inside North Vietnam." *New Republic* 146 (May 21, 1962): 17–20.

1647. Landon, Kenneth P. "North Vietnam Today and Tomorrow." *Current History* 56 (Feb. 1969): 77–81ff.

1648. Langer, Paul F. *The Minor Asian Communist States: Outer Mongolia, North Korea and North Vietnam*. P–2981. Santa Monica, CA: Rand Corp., Sept. 1964.

1649. Mori Kyozo. "The Logic and Psychology of North Vietnam." *Japan Quarterly* 13 (July–Sept. 1967): 286–296.

1650. Pike, Douglas. "North Vietnam in the Year 1972." *Asian Survey* 14 (Jan. 1973): 46–59.

1651. Turley, William S. "Women in the Communist Revolution in Vietnam." *Asian Survey* 12 (Sept. 1972): 793–805.

1652. Woodside, Alexander. "Problems of Education in the Chinese and Vietnamese Revolutions." *Pacific Affairs* 49 (Winter 1976–1977): 648–666.

POLITICS AND GOVERNMENT

The Vietnam Workers' Party (Lao Dong) is the major political apparatus in Hanoi.

1653. *Documents of the Third National Congress of the Viet Nam Workers' Party*. 4 vols. Hanoi: Foreign Languages Publishing House, 1960.

1654. Kellen, Konrad. *Nineteen Seventy One and Beyond: The View from Hanoi*. P–4634–1. Santa Monica, CA: Rand Corp., June 1971. Kellen describes the attitudes and actions of the Lao Dong.

1655. Mau, Michael P. "The Political Evolution of the Village-Commune in North Vietnam, 1802–1970." Ph.D. dissertation, University of Pennsylvania, 1977.

1656. ______. "Training of Cadres in the Lao Dong Party of North Vietnam, 1960–1967." *Asian Studies* 9 (Apr. 1969): 281–296.

1657. *An Outline History of the Viet Nam Workers' Party* (1930–1975). Hanoi: Foreign Languages Publishing House, 1976.

1658. Phan Thien Chau. "Leadership in the Viet Nam Workers' Party: The Process of Transition." *Asian Survey* 12 (Sept. 1972): 772–782.

1659. Pike, Douglas E. "Operational Code of the North Vietnamese Politburo." *Asia Quarterly* [Brussels], no. 1 (1971): 91–102.

1660. Porter, D. Gareth. "How Scholars Lie." *Worldview* 16 (Dec. 1973): 22–27. Porter describes the cultivated misunderstanding of Hanoi's leadership.

1661. Rogers, Robert F. "Policy Differences Within the Hanoi Leadership." *Studies in Comparative Communism* 9 (Spring–Summer 1976): 108–128.

1662. Spinks, Charles N., et al. *The North Vietnamese Regime: Institutions and Problems*. Washington, DC: American University, Center for Research in Social Systems, 1969.

1663. *Third National Congress of the Vietnamese Trade Union*. Hanoi: Lao Dong, 1974.

1664. Turley, William S. "Army, Party and Society in the Democratic Republic of Vietnam: Civil-Military Relations in a Mass-Mobilization System." Ph.D. dissertation, University of Washington, 1972.

1665. _____. "Civil-Military Relations in North Vietnam." *Asian Survey* 9 (Dec. 1969): 879–899.

1666. _____. "The Democratic Republic of Vietnam and the 'Third Stage' of the Revolution." *Asian Survey* 14 (Jan. 1974): 78–88.

1667. _____, ed. *Vietnamese Communism in Comparative Perspective.* Boulder, CO: Westview Press, 1981.

1668. Weil, Herman H. "Can Bureaucracies be Rational Actors? Foreign Policy Decision-Making in North Vietnam." *International Studies Quarterly* 19 (Dec. 1975): 432–468.

PERSONALITIES

Ho Chi Minh

1669. Adams, Nina S. "Man in the Middle." *New York Review of Books* (Sept. 11, 1969): 42–44. [review article]

1670. Azeau, H. *Ho Chi Minh: Dernière chance.* Paris: Flammarion, 1969.

1671. Bain, Chester A. "Ho Chi Minh: Master Teacher." *Texas Quarterly* 16:3 (1973): 6–15.

1672. Fall, Bernard B. "Ho Chi Minh, Like it or Not." *Esquire* 68 (Nov. 1967): 120–121, 201–211.

1673. _____, ed. *Ho Chi Minh on Revolution: Selected Writings, 1920–1964.* New York: Praeger, 1967.

1674. Fenn, Charles. *Ho Chi Minh: A Biographical Introduction.* New York: Scribner's, 1973.

1675. Halberstam, David. *Ho.* New York: Random House, 1971.

1676. Ho Chi Minh. *Action et révolution, 1920–1967.* Edited by C. Capitan-Peter. Paris: Union Générale d'Éditions, 1968.

1677. _____. *Against U.S. Aggression for National Salvation.* Hanoi: Foreign Languages Publishing House, 1967.

1678. _____. *On Lenin and Leninism: Selected Speeches and Articles.* Moscow: Novosti Press, 1971.

1679. _____. *On Revolution: Selected Writings, 1920–1966.* New York: Praeger, 1967.

1680. _____. *Selected Works.* 4 vols. Hanoi: Foreign Languages Publishing House, 1960–1962. This work form the basis of most biographies of Ho Chi Minh.

1681. Lacouture, Jean. *Ho Chi Minh: A Political Biography.* New York: Random House, 1968.

1682. _____. "Uncle Ho Defies Uncle Sam." *New York Times Magazine* (Mar. 28, 1965): 25ff.

1683. Marr, David G., ed. *Reflections from Captivity: Phan Boi Chau's Prison Notes and Ho Chi Minh's Prison Diary.* Athens: Ohio University Press, 1978.

1684. Mus, Paul. *Ho Chi Minh, le Vietnam, L'Asie.* Edited by Annie Nguyen Nguyet Ho. Paris: Éditions du Seuil, 1971.

1685. Neumann-Hoditz, Reinhold. *Portrait of Ho Chi Minh: An Illustrated Biography.* Translated by J. Hargreaves. New York: Herder & Herder, 1972.

1686. Nguyen Khac Huyen. *Vision Accomplished? The Enigma of Ho Chi Minh.* New York: Macmillan, 1971.

1687. Pasquel-Rageau, C. *Ho Chi Minh.* Paris: Éditions Universitaires, 1970.

1688. Rageau, Christine. "Ho Chi Minh et l'international communiste." *Partisans* 48 (June–Aug. 1969): 44–55.

1689. Rolph, Hammond M. "Ho Chi Minh: Fifty Years of Revolution." *Studies in Comparative Communism* 1 (July–Oct. 1968): 55–103.

1690. Sainteny, Jean. *Ho Chi Minh and His Vietnam: A Personal Memoir.* Translated by H. Briffault. Chicago: Cowles, 1972.

1691. Schurmann, Franz. "Eulogy to Ho Chi Minh." *Ramparts* 8 (Nov. 1969): 52–60.

1692. Shaplen, Robert. "The Enigma of Ho Chi Minh." *Reporter* 12 (Jan. 27, 1955): 11–19.

1693. Stuhlmann, Manfred. *Ho Chi Minh: Ein Leben für Vietnam.* Berlin: Dietz Verlag, 1960.

1694. Sully, François. "Life Under Uncle Ho." *Newsweek* 60 (Aug. 27, 1962): 34–38.

1695. Truong Chinh. *President Ho-chi-Minh: Beloved Leader of the Vietnamese People.* Hanoi: Foreign Languages Publishing House, 1966.

1696. Warbey, William. *Ho Chi Minh and the Struggle for an Independent Vietnam.* London: Merlin, 1972.

1697. Woodis, Jack, ed. *Ho Chi Minh: Selected Articles and Speeches, 1920–1967.* New York: International Publishers, 1970.

Pham Van Dong

1698. Lacouture, Jean. "Uncle Ho's 'Best Nephew': Pham Van Dong, Prime Minister of North Vietnam and the Man Behind Hanoi's Delegates in Paris." *New York Times Magazine* (May 19, 1968): 26–27, 112–115.

1699. Pham Van Dong. "The Foreign Policy of the Democratic Republic of Vietnam." *International Affairs* [Moscow] (July 1958): 19–22.

1700. _____. *Twenty-five Years of National Struggle and Construction.* Hanoi: Foreign Languages Publishing House, 1970.

Le Duan

1701. Critchfield, Richard. "New Man in Hanoi: First Party Secretary Le Duan." *New Leader* 52 (Sept. 15, 1969): 3–6.

1702. Le Duan. *On the Socialist Revolution in Viet Nam.* 3 vols. Hanoi: Foreign Languages Publishing House, 1965.

1703. _____. *Some Present Tasks.* Hanoi: Foreign Languages Publishing House, 1974.

1704. _____. *This Nation and Socialism Are One.* Edited by Tran Van Dinh. Chicago: Vanguard Press, 1977.

1705. _____. *The Vietnamese Revolution: Fundamental Problems, Essential Tasks.* Hanoi: Foreign Languages Publishing House, 1970. This is a significant statement made on the fortieth anniversary of the Party.

Vo Nguyen Giap

For the military strategy of Vo Nguyen Giap, see Chapter 6.

1706. Vo Nguyen Giap. *Banner of People's War: The Party's Military Line.* Preface by Jean Lacouture. New York: Praeger, 1970.

1707. _____. *Big Victory, Great Task: North Vietnam's Minister of Defense Assesses the Course of the War.* New York: Praeger, 1968.

1708. _____. *Once Again We Will Win.* Hanoi: Foreign Languages Publishing House, 1960.

1709. _____. *People's War, People's Army: The Viet Cong Insurrection Manual for Underdeveloped Countries.* New York: Praeger, 1962.

1710. _____. *The South Vietnam People Will Win.* Hanoi: Foreign Languages Publishing House, 1965.

ECONOMICS

1711. Charriere, Jacques. "Socialism in North Vietnam." *Missouri Review* (Feb. 1966): 19–41.

1712. Ello, Paul S. "The Commissar and the Peasant: A Comparative Analysis of Land Reform and Collectivization in North Korea and North Vietnam." Ph.D. dissertation, University of Iowa, 1967.

1713. Gittinger, J. Price. "Communist Land Policy in North Viet Nam." *Far Eastern Survey* 27 (Aug. 1959): 113–126.

1714. Honey, P.J. "Food Crisis in North Vietnam." *Far Eastern Economic Review* 41 (Aug. 15, 1963): 493–495.

1715. Kaye, William. "A Bowl of Rice Divided: The Economy of North Vietnam." *China Quarterly*, no. 13 (Jan.–Mar. 1962): 82–93.

1716. Moise, Edwin E. "Land Reform in China and North Vietnam: Revolution at the Village Level." Ph.D. dissertation, University of Michigan, 1977. Moise discusses the land reform carried out in North Vietnam from 1953 to 1956.

1717. Nguyen Ho Dinh. "Les Communistes, les Catholiques et les Cooperateurs au Nord-Vietnam." *Communauté* 37 (Jan.–June 1975): 152–182. The author focuses on agricultural cooperatives.

1718. Nguyen Xuan Lai. "The Economy of the D.R.V. Facing the Trial of War." *Vietnamese Studies*, no. 17 (1968): 75–109.

1719. Shadbad, Theodore. "Economic Developments in North Vietnam." *Pacific Affairs* 31 (Mar. 1958): 36–53.

1720. Tran Nhu Trang. "The Transformation of the Peasantry in North Vietnam." Ph.D. dissertation, University of Pittsburgh, 1972.

1721. Truong Chinh. *Resolutely Taking the North Viet Nam Countryside to Socialism Through Agricultural Co-operation.* Hanoi: Foreign Languages Publishing House, 1959.

1722. Vo Nhan Tri. "Wartime Economy of the D.R.V." *International Affairs* [Moscow] 15 (Feb. 1969): 27–33.

Casualties of Land Reform

North Vietnam carried out a land reform program between 1953 and 1956, during which hundreds of peasants were executed; disagreement has arisen over just how many were killed.

1723. Moise, Edwin E. "Land Reform and Land Reform Errors in North Vietnam." *Pacific Affairs* 49

(Spring 1976): 70–92. Moise claims 5,000 peasants were executed, not tens of thousands as others claim.

1724. Porter, D. Gareth. *The Myth of the Bloodbath: North Vietnam's Land Reform-Reconsidered.* Interim Rpt. no. 2. Ithaca, NY: Cornell University, International Relations of East Asia Project, 1972. [reprinted in *Congressional Record* 118 (Oct. 17, 1972): 36880ff]

1725. U.S. Senate. Committee on the Judiciary. Hearings; *The Human Cost of Communism in Vietnam. II: The Myth of No Bloodbath.* 93d Cong., 1st sess., Jan. 5, 1973. [claims deaths ranged in tens of thousands]

WAR RESUMES, 1955–1973

1726. *American Imperialism's Intervention in Vietnam.* Hanoi: Foreign Languages Publishing House, 1955.

1727. "Answers to a Mystery: Why North Vietnam Fights On." *U.S. News and World Report* 71 (Aug. 9, 1971): 40–41.

1728. Chaffard, Georges. "Morale in North Vietnam: From Here to November." *Far Eastern Economic Review* 60 (Apr. 7, 1968): 63–64.

1729. Durbrow, Elbridge. "Hanoi's Intensified Aggression, 1959." *Air War College Supplement* 6 (Nov. 1967): 1–24.

1730. Gurtov, Melvin. *Hanoi on War and Peace.* P–3696. Santa Monica, CA: Rand Corp., 1967.

1731. Hayden, Tom, and B. Reade. "Grasping for Values in Vietnam: Direct Reports North and South." *Renewal* 6 (Apr. 1966): 4–19.

1732. Honey, P.J. "Hanoi and the Vietnam War." *Mizen* 9 (Jan.–Feb. 1967): 1–9.

1733. ———. "North Viet Nam's Model of Strategy and Tactics for Revolution." *Studies on the Soviet Union* 6:2 (1966): 8–26.

1734. Hoskins, J. Robert. "Hard-Line Demands Victory: Exclusive Report from Hanoi." *Look* 34 (Dec. 26, 1970): 20–25.

1735. Latimer, Thomas K. "Hanoi's Leaders and Their South Vietnam Policies, 1954–1968." Ph.D. dissertation, Georgetown University, 1972.

1736. Nguyen Khac Vien, ed. *North Vietnamese Medicine Facing the Trials of War.* Hanoi: Vietnamese Studies, 1967.

1737. "Red Losses Heavy, but End Not Near." *U.S. News and World Report* 69 (July 20, 1970): 13–14.

1738. Rogers, Robert F. "Risk Taking in Hanoi's War Policy: An Analysis of Militancy versus Manipulation in a Communist Party-State's Behavior in a Conflict Environment." Ph.D. dissertation, Georgetown University, 1974.

1739. Spitz, Allan. "The North Vietnamese Regime: Expansion versus Consolidation." *Asian Studies* 8 (Jan. 1970): 25–37.

1740. Steiner, H.A. "Viet-Nam: Civil War Again?" *New Republic* 133 (July 18, 1955): 11–13.

1741. Tanham, George K. *Communist Revolutionary Warfare: The Vietminh in Indo China.* rev. ed. New York: Praeger, 1967.

1742. Truong Chinh. *Primer for Revolt: The Communist Takeover in Vietnam.* New York: Praeger, 1963.

1743. Wallace, James N. "Hanoi's Formula: How to Win While Losing." *U.S. News and World Report* 68 (Apr. 6, 1970): 44–46.

1744. Zorza, Victor. "In Hanoi, the Doves Have Beaten the Hawks." *Atlas* 19 (June 1970): 15–20.

U.S. Bombing of North Vietnam

This theme is extensively explored in materials found in Chapter 7, under "Air War."

1745. Baggs, Andrew H. "Bombing, Bargaining and Limited War: North Vietnam, 1965–1968." Ph.D. dissertation, University of North Carolina, 1972.

1746. Barrymaine, Norman. "Bomb Damage in North Vietnam Described." *Aviation Week* 85 (Dec. 26, 1966): 47ff.

1747. Burchett, Wilfred G. "Hanoi and the Bombs." *Eastern Horizon* 6 (May 1967): 38–40.

1748. Cameron, J., and F. Greene. "The Bombing as Viewed from Hanoi." *Progressive* 30 (Feb. 1966): 37–39.

1749. Fall, Bernard B. "The Air Raids: Leftover Puzzles." *New Republic* 155 (July 16, 1966): 7–8. Fall gives the North's reaction to raids on petroleum areas.

1750. Friedman, P.L. "Work and Watch the Sky: Life Today in North Vietnam." *Nation* 217 (Dec. 10, 1973): 626–628.

1751. Hoeffding, Oleg. *Bombing North Vietnam: An Appraisal of Economic and Political Effects.* RM–5213-1-ISA. Santa Monica, CA: Rand Corp., 1968.

1752. Van Duke, Jon M. *North Vietnam's Strategy for*

Survival. Palo Alto, CA: Pacific Books, 1972. The author discusses over seven years of U.S. bombing.

1753. Van Tien Dung. "People's War Against Air War of Destruction." *Vietnamese Studies* 20 (Dec. 1968): 63–86.

1754. *Vietnam: Destruction, War Damage.* Hanoi: Foreign Languages Publishing House, 1977.

1755. "What 2 1/2 Years of Bombing Has Done to North Vietnam." *U.S. News and World Report* 63 (Sept. 11, 1967): 34–35.

VIETCONG

These items deal more specifically with Vietcong political and organizational structures than with military operations; for the latter, see Chapter 7, under "VC/NVA Operations."

Books and Dissertations

1756. Hosmer, Stephen T. *Viet Cong Repression and Its Implications for the Future.* Lexington, MA: Heath, 1970. [based on his Rand study R–475/1–ARPA, June 1970]

1757. Pike, Douglas. *Viet Cong: The Organization and Techniques of the National Liberation Front of South Vietnam.* Cambridge, MA: MIT Press, 1966. This is an encyclopedic work based on some 800 captured documents and some 100 interviews with defecting VC, a very useful source book.

1758. Record, Jeffrey. "The Viet Cong: Shadow and Substance." Ph.D. dissertation, Johns Hopkins University, 1972.

Essays

1759. Buckley, Tom. "What Life's Like in Vietcong Territory." *New York Times Magazine* (Nov. 23, 1969): 48–49ff.

1760. Carver, George A., Jr. "The Faceless Viet Cong." *Foreign Affairs* 44 (Apr. 1960): 347–372.

1761. Duiker, William J. "Revolutionary Youth League: Cradle of Communism in Vietnam." *China Quarterly,* no. 50 (July–Sept. 1972): 475–499.

1762. Duncanson, Dennis J. "How ... and Why ... the Viet Cong Holds Out." *Encounter* [Great Britain] 27 (Dec. 1966): 79–80.

1763. _____. "The Vitality of the Viet Cong." *Survival* 9 (Jan. 1967): 14–18.

1764. Gration, P.C. "Development of Viet Minh Political Power." *Australian Army Journal* (July 1972): 3–16.

1765. Grose, Peter. "Vietcong's 'Shadow Government.'" *New York Times Magazine* (Jan. 24, 1965): 10–11, 64–67.

1766. Halberstam, David. "Voices of the Vietcong." *Harper's* 236 (Jan. 1968): 45–52.

1767. Kelly, Gail. "Origins and Aims of the Viet Cong." *New Politics* 5 (Winter 1966): 5–16.

1768. Lacouture, Jean. "Charlie's Long March." *Ramparts* 30 (July 1966): 11–14.

1769. Leites, Nathan. *The Viet Cong Style of Politics.* RM–5487/1–ISA/ARPA. Santa Monica, CA: Rand Corp., May 1969.

1770. Rolph, Hammond M. "The Viet Cong: Politics at Gunpoint." *Communist Affairs* 4 (July–Aug. 1966): 3–13.

1771. Rose, Jerry A. "The Elusive Viet Cong: 25,000 Guerillas, 3,000,000 Sympathizers." *New Republic* 148 (May 4, 1963): 19–26.

1772. Schesch, Adam. "Who Are the 'Viet Cong'?" *Progressive* 32 (Sept. 1968): 35–39.

1773. Schultz, Richard T. "The Limits of Terrorism in Insurgency Warfare: The Case of the Viet Cong." *Polity* 11 (Fall 1978): 67–91.

1774. Sully, François. "A Kind of Co-existence with the Viet Cong." *New Republic* 157 (Aug. 10, 1967): 11–12.

1775. Warnenska, Monika. "Dans la jungle avec les partisans." *Nouvelle Revue Internationale* 9 (Jan. 1966): 202–209.

1776. Weiss, J.H. "How Hanoi Controls the Vietcong." *Reporter* 38 (Jan. 11, 1968): 27–28.

1777. Zasloff, Joseph J. *Political Motivation of the Viet Cong: The Vietminh.* KRM–4703/2–ISA/ARPA. Santa Monica, CA: Rand Corp., May 1968.

NATIONAL LIBERATION FRONT

Books and Dissertations

1778. Berman, Paul. *Revolutionary Organization: Institution Building Within the People's Liberation Armed Forces.* Lexington, MA: Heath, 1974.

1779. Do Young Chang. "Nature and Characteristics of the Communist Revolution in South Vietnam." Ph.D. dissertation, University of Michigan, 1969.

1780. Heneghan, G.M. *Nationalism, Communism, and the National Liberation Front of Vietnam: Dilemma for American Foreign Policy.* Ph.D. dissertation, Stanford University, 1970.

1781. Hodges, Donald C. *NLF: National Liberation Fronts, 1960/1970.* New York: Morrow, 1972.

1782. *South Viet Nam Congress of People's Representatives for the Formulation of the Provisional Revolutionary Government of the Republic of South Viet Nam.* South Vietnam: Giai Phong Editions, 1969.

1783. South Viet Nam National Front for Liberation. *Three Documents of the National Liberation Front.* Edited by Gabriel Kolko. Boston: Beacon, 1970. [includes a manifesto and the NLF's program]

1784. Thayer, Carlyle A. "The Origins of the National Front for the Liberation of South Vietnam." Ph.D. dissertation, Australian National University, 1977.

1785. *Viet-Nam Fatherland Front: Resolutions, Manifesto, Programme and Statutes.* rev. ed. Hanoi: Foreign Languages Publishing House, 1972. The "Fatherland Front" succeeded the Vietminh and Lien Viet fronts.

1786. Vuglen, S.M. *National Liberation Movements: Communist Conspiracy or Political Realities?* Flanders, NJ: O'Hare Books, 1968.

Essays
1787. Arnett, Peter. "The National Liberation Front." *Current History* 56 (Feb. 1969): 82–87, 116.

1788. Burchett, Wilfred G. "Lunch with President Tho." *Eastern Horizon* 6 (Jan. 1967): 38–41. The title refers to Nguyen Huu Tho, president of the NLF.

1789. Davis, L.L., and A. Adams. "The NLF: South Vietnam's Other Government." *Minority of One* 10 (Oct. 1968): 12–16.

1790. Fishel, Wesley R. "The National Liberation Front." *Vietnam Perspectives* 1:1 (1965): 8–16.

1791. Honda Katsuichi. *The National Liberation Front.* Tokyo: Committee for the English Publication of "Vietnam: A Voice from the Villages," 1968.

1792. Honey, Patrick J. "The National United Front in Vietnam." *Studies in Comparative Communism* 2 (Jan. 1969): 69–95.

1793. Hunt, David. "Villagers at War: The National Liberation Front in My Tho Province, 1965–1967." *Radical America* 8 (Jan.–Apr. 1974): 31–184.

1794. Lamont, N.S. "On Communist Organization and Strategy in South Vietnam." *Public and International Affairs* 3 (Spring 1965): 32–50.

1795. Langguth, A.J. "The Lengthening Shadow of the N.L.F." *New York Times Magazine* (Apr. 7, 1968): 28–31ff.

1796. *Leaders of the PRG-NLF and Affiliated Organizations.* Viet Nam Documents and Research Notes, no. 105. Saigon: U.S. Mission, May 1972.

1797. *The Leadership of the PRG, the NFLSV and Their Affiliated Organization.* Viet Nam Documents and Research Notes, no. 111. Saigon: U.S. Mission, 1973. [PRG—Provisional Revolutionary Government]

1798. Minear, Richard. "Douglas Pike and the NLF." *Bulletin of Concerned Asian Scholars* 2 (Oct. 1969): 44–47.

1799. Munk, Michael. "Why the Vietnamese Support the NLF." *New Politics* 4 (Spring 1965): 18–25.

1800. Pike, Douglas. "How Strong Is the NLF?" *Reporter* 34 (Feb. 24, 1966): 20–24.

1801. "Program of the National Liberation Front." *New World Review* 36 (Winter 1968): 102–115.

1802. *Provisional Revolutionary Government of the Republic of South Viet Nam.* Pts. I–IV. Viet Nam Documents and Research Notes, no. 101. Saigon: U.S. Mission, Jan. 1972.

1803. Selden, Mark. "The National Liberation Front and the Transformation of the Vietnamese Society." *Bulletin of Concerned Asian Scholars* 2 (Oct. 1969): 34–43.

1804. Stern, S. "A Talk with the Front." *Ramparts* 6 (Nov. 1967): 31–33.

1805. Warner, Denis. "The NLF's New Program." *Reporter* 37 (Oct. 5, 1967): 23–30.

RELATIONS WITH COMMUNIST STATES

See Le Duan (1705) for Hanoi's cautious, independent position in the beginning of the Sino–Soviet split.

1806. Albinski, Henry S. "Chinese and Soviet Policies in the Vietnam Crisis." *Australian Quarterly* 40 (Mar. 1968): 65–74.

1807. Chen, King C. "North Vietnam in the Sino–Soviet Dispute, 1962–64." *Asian Survey* 4 (Sept. 1964): 1023–1036.

1808. Deutscher, Isaac. "Russian vs. China: Clash over Viet Nam." *Nation* 201 (July 27, 1963): 3–4. Deutscher early recognized a problem that has persisted.

1809. Donnell, J.C., and M. Gurtov. *North Vietnam: Left of Moscow Right of Peking.* P–3794. Santa Monica, CA: Rand Corp., Feb. 1968.

1810. Ghosh, S.K. "Relations Between North Vietnam, China and the Soviet Union." *India Quarterly* 31 (Apr.–June 1975): 136–158.

1811. Honey, Patrick J. *Communism in North Vietnam: Its Role in the Sino–Soviet Dispute.* Cambridge, MA: MIT Press, 1963.

1812. Kux, Ernst. "Ho Chi Minh Between Moscow and Peking." *Swiss Review of World Affairs* 14 (Apr. 1964): 11–14.

1813. Le Duan. *On Some Present International Problems.* 2d ed. Hanoi: Foreign Languages Publishing House, 1964.

1814. Lin Kuo-hsiung. "Peking–Moscow Competition in North Vietnam Today." *Issues & Studies* 8 (Dec. 1971): 30–39.

1815. London, Kurt L. "Vietnam: A Sino–Soviet Dilemma." *Russian Review* 26 (Jan. 1967): 26–37.

1816. O'Ballance, Edgar. "Sino–Soviet Influence on the War in Vietnam." *Contemporary Review* 210 (Feb. 1967): 70–76.

1817. Papp, Daniel. *Vietnam: The View from Moscow, Peking and Washington.* Jefferson, NC: McFarland, 1981.

1818. Rupen, Robert A. "Vietnam and the Sino–Soviet Dispute: A Summary." *Studies on the Soviet Union* 6:2 (1966): 99–118.

1819. _____, and Robert Ferrell, eds. *Vietnam and the Sino–Soviet Dispute.* New York: Praeger, 1967.

1820. Tai Sung An. "The Sino–Soviet Dispute and Vietnam." *Orbis* 9 (Summer 1965): 426–436.

1821. Zagoria, Donald S. *The Viet-Nam Triangle: Moscow, Peking, Hanoi.* New York: Pegasus, 1968. [still insightful]

China

1822. Bernal, M. "North Vietnam and China: Reflections on a Visit." *New York Review of Books* (Aug. 12, 1971): 16–20.

1823. Chen, King C. "Hanoi vs. Peking: Policies and Relations, a Survey." *Asian Survey* 12 (Sept. 1972): 806–817.

1824. Dakovic, Vojo. "Chinese Policy and the War in Vietnam." *Review of International Affairs* [Belgrade] 17 (Jan. 20, 1966): 9–10.

1825. Deshpande, G.P. "China and Vietnam." *International Studies* [India] 12 (Oct.–Dec. 1973): 568–581.

1826. Glaubitz, Joachim. "Relations Between Communist China and Vietnam." *Studies on the Soviet Union* 6:2 (1966): 57–67.

1827. Grossman, Bernhard. "The Influence of the War in Vietnam on the Economy of Communist China." *Studies on the Soviet Union* 6:2 (1966): 68–73.

1828. Harding, H., and M. Gurtov. *The Purge of Lo Jui-ch'ing: The Politics of Chinese Strategic Planning.* R–548–PR. Santa Monica, CA: Rand Corp., Feb. 1971. The authors describe China's Vietnam policy in 1965.

1829. Hsin-Hung Ou. "Communist China's Foreign Policy Toward the War in Vietnam, 1965–1973." Ph.D. dissertation, Southern Illinois University, 1977.

1830. Lee, C.J. "Some Chinese Communist Attitudes Toward the Vietnam War." *Vietnam Perspectives* 2 (Feb. 1967): 3–14.

1831. Lichtheim, George. "Vietnam and China." *Commentary* 39 (May 1965): 56–59.

1832. Markhinin, Evgeny. *Peking and the Vietnam People's Struggle.* Moscow: Novosti Press, 1973.

1833. Mozingo, D.P., and T.W. Robinson. *Lin Piao on "People's War": China Takes a Second Look at Vietnam.* RM–4814–PR. Santa Monica, CA: Rand Corp., Nov. 1965.

1834. Nguyen Thai. "The Two Vietnams and China." *Harvard Review* 2 (Fall–Winter 1963): 26–32.

1835. Ojha, I.C. "China and North Vietnam: The Limits of the Alliance." *Current History* 54 (Jan. 1968): 42–47.

1836. Raymond, David A. "Communist China and the Vietnam War." *Asian Affairs* [U.S.] 18 (Nov.–Dec. 1974): 83–99.

1837. Sar Desai, D.R. "China and Peace in Vietnam." *Military Review* 44 (Dec. 1969): 56–61.

1838. Snow, Edgar. "China and Vietnam." *New Republic* 155 (July 30, 1966): 12–14.

1839. Tao, Jay. "Mao's World Outlook: Vietnam and the Revolution in China." *Asian Survey* 8 (May 1968): 416–432.

1840. Turner, Robert F. "Red China's Role in Vietnam." *Washington Report* WR–69–9 (Mar. 3, 1969): Entire issue.

1841. *U.S. Aggression Has No Bounds and Our Counter to Aggression Has No Bounds.* Peking: Foreign Languages Press, 1966.

1842. Woodside, Alexander. "Peking and Hanoi: Anatomy of a Revolutionary Partnership." *International Journal* [Toronto] 24 (Winter 1968–1969): 65–85.

U.S.S.R.

1843. Attwood, William. "Why Vietnam Worries the Russians." *Look* 31 (July 11, 1967): 23–25.

1844. Ballis, W.B. "Relations Between the U.S.S.R. and Vietnam." *Studies on the Soviet Union* 6:2 (1966): 43–56.

1845. Cameron, Allen W. "The Soviet Union and Vietnam: The Origins of Involvement." In *Soviet Policy in Developing Countries*, edited by W. Raymond Duncan. Waltham, MA: Ginn-Blaisdell, 1970, 166–205.

1846. Dallin, Alexander. "Moscow and Vietnam." *New Leader* 48 (May 10, 1965): 5–8.

1847. Kalb, Marvin. "The Kremlin Dilemma Over Vietnam." *Reporter* 33 (July 1, 1965): 22–23.

1848. Kapchenko, N. "In the Interests of Strengthening Peace in Vietnam." *International Affairs* [Moscow] 19 (May 1973): 42–46.

1849. McGovern, Raymond L. "Moscow and Hanoi." *Problems of Communism* 14 (May–June 1967): 68ff.

1850. McLane, Charles B. "The Russians and Vietnam: Strategies in Indirection." *International Journal* [Toronto] 24 (Winter 1968–1969): 47–64.

1851. Morris, Roger. "Russia's Stake in Vietnam." *New Republic* 152 (Feb. 13, 1965): 13–15.

1852. Pike, Douglas. "The USSR and Vietnam: Into the Swamp." *Asian Survey* 19 (Oct. 1979): 1159–1170. [also printed as a pamphlet by Army War College Strategic Studies Institute, May 1980]

1853. Smith, Jessica. "How the Soviet State and People Help Vietnam." *New World Review* 38 (Fall 1970): 97–104.

1854. Thornton, Richard C. "Soviet Strategy and the Vietnam War." *Asian Affairs* [U.S.] 1 (Mar.–Apr. 1974): 205–228.

1855. Turner, Nicholas. "The Soviet Stake in Vietnam." *Far Eastern Economic Review* 54 (Oct. 27, 1966): 180–182.

1856. *The World Accuses: Escalation of U.S. Crimes in Vietnam.* Moscow: Novosti Press, 1968.

1857. Zimmerman, William, and Robert Axelrod. "The 'Lessons' of Vietnam and Soviet Foreign Policy." *World Politics* 34 (Oct. 1981): 1–24.

Aid

1858. "China's Aid to Vietnam in Fighting U.S. Aggression Further Ceases to be Subject to any Bonds or Restrictions: Chinese Government Statement." *Peking Review* 9 (July 8, 1966): 19–20.

1859. "More and More Soviet Arms Keep War Going." *U.S. News and World Report* 62 (Apr. 3, 1967): 31–32.

1860. Parry, Albert. "Soviet Aid to Vietnam." *Reporter* 36 (Jan. 12, 1967): 28–32. [widely reprinted: *Survival* 9 (Mar. 1967): 76–82; *Military Review* 47 (June 1967): 13–22]

1861. Prybyla, Jan S. "Soviet and China Economic Aid to North Vietnam." *China Quarterly*, no. 27 (July–Sept. 1966): 84–100.

Post-Armistice Interlude, 1973–1975

The short-lived armistice did not stop the fighting in South Vietnam, nor provide enough time to see if the numerous postwar plans for South Vietnam were feasible.

1862. Barton, David, et al. "The Second Year of the Paris Peace Agreement." *Indochina Chronicle* 38 (Jan.–Feb. 1975): 1–19.

1863. Branfman, Fred. "Nuovi modi di intervento in Indochina." *Ponte* [Italy] 29:2/3 (1973): 259–275.

Branfman discusses U.S. military and economic aid to South Vietnam after the Paris armistice.

1864. Bunker, Ellsworth. "Optimism Over South Vietnam: 'The Potential Is Very Great.'" *U.S. News and World Report* 74 (May 21, 1973): 78–80.

1865. Butterfield, F. "Who was This Enemy." *New York Times Magazine* (Feb. 4, 1973): 8ff.

1866. Carey, Alex. "Clockwork Vietnam: (1) Gaining Physical Control." *Meanjin Quarterly* 32 (Mar. 1973): 45–54.

1867. _____. "Clockwork Vietnam: (2) The Social Engineers Take Over." *Meanjin Quarterly* 32 (Dec. 1973): 406–418.

1868. Clubb, Oliver E. "Indochina and U.S. Aid." *Worldview* 16 (May 1973): 43–46.

1869. Evans, Les. "What Has Been Settled in Vietnam?" *International Socialist Review* 34:2 (1973): 12–15ff.

1870. Fitzgerald, Frances. "A Reporter At Large: Journey to North Vietnam." *New Yorker* 51 (Apr. 28, 1975): 96–119.

1871. Gayn, Mark. "The Problems of Transition to a Settlement in Vietnam." *International Perspectives* [Canada], no. 1 (1973): 14–19.

1872. Goodman, Allan E. "Toward a Political Settlement in Vietnam: Assessing the First Eighteen Months of the Postwar Years." *Orbis* 18 (Fall 1974): 809–837.

1873. Hasdorff, James C. "Vietnam in Retrospective: An Interview with Ambassador Frederick E. Nolting, Jr." *Air University Review* 25 (Jan.–Feb. 1974): 2–10.

1874. Haviland, H. Field, et al. *Vietnam After the War: Peacekeeping and Rehabilitation*. Washington, DC: Brookings Institution, 1968.

1875. Jenkins, B. *After the War*. P–4996. Santa Monica, CA: Rand Corp., Apr. 1973. Jenkins presents a hypothetical scenario of what might happen.

1876. Kolko, Gabriel. "Strategia del governo Nixon nel Vietnam." *Ponte* [Italy] 29:2/3 (1973): 276–300. Kolko discusses U.S. aid to South Vietnam after the armistice.

1877. Levy, David W. "The Debate Over Vietnam: One Perspective." *Yale Review* 63 (Spring 1974): 333–346. [discusses U.S. aid]

1878. Lumsden, M. "The Politics of Reconstruction in Indochina." *Instant Research on Peace and Violence*, no. 1 (1972): 17–33.

1879. National Action/Research on the Military-Industrial Complex [NARMIC]. *The Third Force in South Vietnam*. Philadelphia, 1975.

1880. Nayan Chanda. "A Permanent State of Misery." *Far Eastern Economic Review* 86 (Oct. 11, 1974): 12–14.

1881. "Post-war Aid: The Going Will be Rough on Capital Hill." *CQ Weekly Report* 31 (Feb. 3, 1973): 188–190.

1882. "The Question of U.S. Reconstruction Aid for North Vietnam: Pro and Con." *Congressional Digest* 52 (June–July 1973): Entire issue.

1883. Rondinelli, Dennis A. "Postwar Reconstruction in Vietnam: The Case for an Urbanization Policy." *Asian Forum* 5 (July–Sept. 1973): 1–15.

1884. Salmon, Malcolm. "Revolutionary Spirit in the Ruins." *Far Eastern Economic Review* 86 (Dec. 6, 1974): 37–40.

1885. Selden, Mark. "'A Terribly Delicate Matter': Multinational Aid to Saigon." *Nation* 218 (Apr. 6, 1974): 422–424.

1886. Shipler, D.K. "Hooked on Vietnam." *New York Times Magazine* (Sept. 8, 1974: 30ff. Shipler focuses on hundreds of Americans who decided to stay in Vietnam.

1887. _____. "No Room for Peace: Possible Futures for Indochina." *Worldview* 17 (Apr. 1974): 25–29.

1888. Silverman, Jerry M. "South Vietnam and the Return to Political Struggle." *Asian Survey* 14 (Jan. 1974): 65–77.

1889. Starner, Frances L. "Economies: Vietnam's Uncertain Future." *Far Eastern Economic Review* 80 (Apr. 30, 1973): 61–63.

1890. Thayer, Carlyle A. "The Democratic Republic of Vietnam in 1974: The Politics of Transition." *Asian Survey* 15 (Jan. 1975): 61–69.

1891. Tran Van Dinh. "Viet Nam 1974: A Revolution Unfulfilled." *Pacific Community* [Japan] 5 (Apr. 1974): 435–444.

1892. U.S. House. Committee on Foreign Affairs. Hearings; *Report on the Situation in the Republic of Vietnam*. 93d Cong., 2d sess., 1974.

1893. _____. Report; *Vietnam: A Changing Crucible*. House Rpt. no. 93–1196. 93d Cong., 2d sess., 1974.

1894. U.S. Senate. Committee on Armed Services. Report; *Southeast Asia*. 94th Cong., 1st sess., 1975.

1895. _____. Committee on Foreign Relations. Staff Report; *Vietnam: May 1974.* 93d Cong., 2d sess., 1974.

1896. "Will The U.S. Bail Out North Vietnam?" *U.S. News and World Report* 76 (Feb. 19, 1973): 22–24.

WAR CONTINUES, 1973–1975

Although a lull in combat existed between ARVN and NVA forces, considerable fighting continued between ARVN and NLF units within South Vietnam during the cease-fire."

1897. Blair, G.L., and R. Goldensohn. "No Peace, No Honor." *Liberation* 17 (May 1973): 4–5.

1898. Branfman, Fred. "Indochina: The Illusion of Withdrawal: Behind the Celebrations of Progress a Policy of Covert War." *Harper's* 243 (May 1973): 65–76.

1899. _____. "Vietnam: The Aftermath." *Progressive* 37 (Nov. 1973): 29–33.

1900. Butterfield, F. "Peace is Still at Hand." *New York Times Magazine* (Nov. 11, 1973): 37ff.

1901. Caterini, Dino J. "Old Wars in New Rhetoric." *Progressive* 38 (May 1974): 45–48.

1902. Fitzgerald, Frances. "Can the War End?" *New York Review of Books* (Feb. 22, 1973): 13–14.

1903. _____. "The Offensive, View from Vietnam." *New York Review of Books* (May 10, 1973): 6–14.

1904. _____. "Vietnam: Behind the Lines of the 'Ceasefire' War." *Atlantic* 233 (Apr. 1974): 4–18.

1905. Frisbee, John L. "The Communist Buildup in Vietnam." *Air Force Magazine* 57 (Apr. 1974): 32–35.

1906. Goodman, Allan E. "South Vietnam: War Without End." *Asian Survey* 15 (Jan. 1975): 70–84. [refers to 1973–1974]

1907. Luce, Don. "The War Goes on in Vietnam." *War/Peace Report* 13 (June 1974): 24–26.

1908. Lugern, Joel. *Viet-nam des poussières par millions, 1972–1975: Le Cessez-le-feu, la guerre oubliée, la libération.* Les Sables-d'Olonne, France: Éditions le Cercle d'or, 1975.

1909. McFadden, Dave. *We Call This War a Ceasefire.* Philadelphia: National Action/Research on the Military-Industrial Complex [NARMIC], Apr. 1973.

1910. Ngo Vinh Long. "Vietnam: Cease-fire That Never Was." *Ramparts* 12 (Jan. 1974): 12–15.

1911. Parker, Maynard. "Vietnam: The War That Won't End." *Foreign Affairs* 53 (Jan. 1975): 352–374.

1912. Serong, F.P. "Vietnam's Menacing Cease-Fire." *Conflict Studies* 6 (Nov. 1974): 1–19.

1913. Spurr, Russell. "South Vietnam . . . and the Killing Goes On and On." *Far Eastern Economic Review* 85 (July 22, 1974): 24–25.

1914. Stone, I.F. "Toward a Third Indochina War." *New York Review of Books* (Mar. 8, 1973): 16–20.

1915. Timmes, Charles J. "Vietnam Summary: Military Operations After the Cease-Fire Agreement." *Military Review* 56 (Aug. 1976): 63–75. [January 1973–April 30, 1975]

1916. "The Vietnam Dove of Peace Flew the Coop: How? Why?" *War/Peace Report* 13 (Jan.–Feb. 1973): 20–21.

FINAL CAMPAIGN, 1975

This section deals with political aspects; for the military side, see Chapter 7.

1917. Buckley, Kevin P. "Memoirs of Defeat, Long Ago." *New Republic* 172 (May 3, 1975): 5–6.

1918. Butterfield, F. "How South Vietnam Died: By the Stab in the Front." *New York Times Magazine* (May 25, 1975): 30ff.

1919. Chace, James. "Reappraisal Without Agony." *New Republic* 172 (May 3, 1975): 23–25.

1920. Davis, S. "The U.S. Is Told: Look Before Leaping." *Far Eastern Economic Review* 88 (Apr. 25, 1975): 22.

1921. Donnell, John C. "South Vietnam in 1975: The Year of Communist Victory." *Asian Survey* 16 (Jan. 1976): 1–13.

1922. "Everything is Over." *Far Eastern Economic Review* 88 (Apr. 25, 1975): 18–19.

1923. Hoffman, Stanley. "The Sulking Giant." *New Republic* 172 (Mar. 5, 1975): 15–17.

1924. Holbrooke, Richard. "Pushing Sand." *New Republic* 172 (May 3, 1975): 10–12.

1925. Hosmer, Stephen T., et al. *The Fall of South Vietnam: Statements by Vietnamese Military and Civilian Leaders.* R–2208–OSD. Santa Monica, CA: Rand Corp., Aug. 1978. South Vietnamese leaders were convinced to the end that the United States would at least reenter the conflict with its airpower.

1926. _____. *The Fall of South Vietnam: Statements by Vietnamese Military and Civilian Leaders.* New York: Crane, Russak, 1980.

1927. Issacs, Harold R. "Our SOB's." *New Republic* 172 (May 3, 1975): 4–5. Issacs argues that the United States failed because it did not find a sound government in South Vietnam.

1928. Kirk, Donald. "The Final Tragedy of Vietnam." *New Leader* 58 (Apr. 28, 1975): 12–13.

1929. Lewis, Anthony. "Hubris, National and Personal." *New Republic* 172 (May 3, 1975): 17–19. The rushed ending evokes many thoughts and memories.

1930. Marks, John D. "Leaving Vietnam: The One Man We Remembered." *Washington Monthly* 7 (Apr. 1975): 26–29.

1931. Murray, J.E. "Vietnam: The Map Turns Red." *Air Force Magazine* 58 (Feb. 1975): 32–33.

1932. Nayan Chanda. "Requiem for an Old Order." *Far Eastern Economic Review* 88 (June 6, 1975): 10–19.

1933. _____. "Thieu: Fighting for Survival." *Far Eastern Economic Review* 88 (Apr. 25, 1975): 20–21.

1934. Peters, Charles. "Leaving Vietnam: The Others We Forgot." *Washington Monthly* 7 (Apr. 1975): 30–33.

1935. Ravenal, Earl C. "Consequences of the End Game in Vietnam." *Foreign Affairs* 53 (July 1975): 651–667.

1936. Rovere, Richard. "Letter From Washington." *New Yorker* 51 (Apr. 21, 1975): 140–142ff. Rovere describes the evacuation of Americans from South Vietnam.

1937. Shaplen, Robert. "Letter from Saigon." *New Yorker* 50 (Jan. 6, 1975): 64–75. Shaplen reports some signs of noncommunist nationalism.

1938. _____. "Letter from Saigon." *New Yorker* 51 (Apr. 21, 1975): 124–138. By April 14, Saigon was the capital of a lost cause.

1939. _____. "A Reporter At Large: Saigon Exit." *New Yorker* 51 (May 19, 1975): 94ff.

1940. "South Vietnam Capitulation: A Comparison of Radio Free Europe and Radio Liberty Coverage with Soviet and East European Media Coverage." In U.S. Senate. Committee on Foreign Relations. Hearings; *Foreign Relations Authorization, FY 1976 and FY 1977.* 94th Cong., 1st sess., 1975, 128–132.

1941. Steel, Ronald. "Lies and Whimpers." *New Republic* 172 (May 3, 1975): 21–22. Everyone in Washington knew Saigon had to fall.

1942. Stuart, Douglas B. "The Fall of Vietnam: A Soldier's Retrospection." *Parameters* 11 (June 1981): 28–36.

1943. Tucker, Robert W. "Vietnam: The Final Reckoning." *Commentary* 59 (May 1975): 27–34.

1944. Warner, Denis. *Not With Guns Alone: How Hanoi Won the War.* London: Sheed, Andrews & McMeel, 1977.

Vietnam: Reunification and Rebuilding

On April 25, 1976, the new rulers of unified Vietnam held a typical communist (single-party) election resulting in complete domination by Hanoi leaders. The Socialist Republic of Vietnam promptly negotiated a treaty with the Soviet Union.

1945. Austerlitz, M. "Vietnamizing South Vietnam." *New York Times Magazine* (Aug. 25, 1976): 32ff.

1946. Burchett, Wilfred. *Vietnam: Un + Un = Un.* Paris: F. Maspero, 1977.

1947. Casella, Alexander. "Unity: 'Only a Matter of Time.'" *Far Eastern Economic Review* 85 (July 8, 1974): 24–26.

1948. Devillers, Philippe. "The Struggle for the Unification of Vietnam." *China Quarterly*, no. 9 (Jan.–Mar. 1962): 2–23.

1949. Elliott, David W.P. "Revolutionary Re-integration: A Comparison of the Foundation of Post-Liberation Political Systems in North Vietnam and China." Ph.D. dissertation, Cornell University, 1976.

1950. Fishel, Wesley R. "One Vietnam or Two?" *Virginia Quarterly Review* 50 (Summer 1974): 348–367.

1951. Fitzgerald, Frances. "Vietnam: Reconciliation." *Atlantic* 233 (June 1974): 14–16ff.

1952. Friang, Brigitte. *La Mousson de la liberté: Vietnam du colonialisme au Stalinisme.* Paris: Librairie Plon, 1976.

1953. Gordon, Max. "Two Vietnams or One?" *New Republic* 157 (July 22–29, 1967): 36–37.

1954. *The Reunification of Vietnam: Documents of the Political Consultative Conference on National Reunification.* Hanoi: Foreign Languages Publishing House, 1975.

1955. *The Socialist Republic of Viet Nam: Structure and Basis: Documents of the First Session of the National Assembly of Reunified Viet Nam, June–July 1976.* Hanoi: Foreign Languages Publishing House, 1976.

1956. Tai Sung An. "The All-Vietnam National Assembly: Significant Development." *Asian Survey* 17 (May 1977): 432–439.

1957. Thayer, Carlyle A. "North Vietnam in 1975: National Liberation Reunification and Socialist Construction." *Asian Survey* 16 (Jan. 1976): 14–22.

1958. Tran Van Dinh. "Vietnam in the Year of the Dragon: Reunification, Reunion and Socialist Reconstruction." *Monthly Review* 28 (Jan. 1976): 19–33.

AVOIDANCE OF A BLOODBATH

Some American hawks argued that if Saigon fell to the communists there would be reprisals and executions of Vietnamese who assisted the government and the United States during the Second Indochina War.

1959. Carroll, John S. "After We Get Out, Will There be a Bloodbath in South Vietnam?" *New York Times Magazine* (Oct. 15, 1972): 38ff.

1960. Nutt, Anita L. *On the Question of Communist Reprisals in Vietnam.* P–4416. Santa Monica, CA: Rand Corp., Aug. 1970.

1961. Pfaff, William. "Reflections: The Bloodbath." *New Yorker* 48 (Oct 21, 1972): 80ff.

1962. Porter, D. Gareth, and Len E. Ackland. "Vietnam: The Bloodbath Argument." In *Moral Argument and the War in Vietnam,* edited by Paul T. Menzel. Nashville, TN: Aurora, 1971, 144–146.

1963. Rosenfeld, Stephen S. "Vietnam Reprisals Theory Disputed." *Congressional Record* 118 (Aug. 7, 1972): 27015–27016. [reprinted from *Washington Post,* June 19, 1972]

1964. Springer, W.L. "The Vietcong Strategy of Terror." *Congressional Record* 116 (May 28, 1970): 17542.

POSTWAR EVENTS

1965. Amnesty International Report. *Report of an Amnesty International Mission to the Socialist Republic of Viet Nam, 10–21 December 1979.* London, 1981. Some 20,000 persons were thought to be held in "reeducation" camps.

1966. Bingham, S. "Vietnam's Catholics Debate the Future." *Reporter* 38 (June 13, 1978): 37–39.

1967. Cameron, Allan W. *Indochina: Prospects After "the End."* Washington, DC: American Enterprise Institute for Public Policy Research, 1976.

1968. Casella, Alexander. "Dateline Vietnam: Managing the Peace." *Foreign Policy,* no. 30 (Spring 1978): 170–191.

1969. Chomsky, Noam, and Edward S. Herman. "Distortions at Fourth Hand." *Nation* 223 (June 25, 1977): 789–794. The authors contest the *New York Times* account of May 1, 1977 about "painful problems of peace" in Vietnam.

1970. Davis, Neil, and Robert Shaplen. "Letter from Saigon." *New Yorker* 51 (Oct. 6, 1975): 130–155.

1971. Davis, S. "The Men Most Likely to …?" *Far Eastern Economic Review* 87 (Mar. 28, 1975): 11–12.

1972. Duncanson, Dennis J. "Social Control in Liberated Indochina." *World Today* [London] 33 (June 1977): 232–240.

1973. Fifield, Russell H. "The Liquidation of a War: The United States and Vietnam." *Asia Quarterly* [Brussels], no. 3 (1978): 209–228.

1974. Fitzgerald, Frances. "The End is the Beginning." *New Republic* 172 (May 3, 1975): 7–8.

1975. ———. "Punch In! Punch Out! East Quick!" *New York Times Magazine* (Dec. 28, 1975): 8ff.

1976. Gelinas, André. "Life in the New Vietnam." *New York Review of Books* (Mar. 17, 1977): 21–27.

1977. Glazunov, Y. "Vietnam's Road to Socialism." *International Affairs* [Moscow] 24 (Sept. 1978): 23–30.

1978. Goodstadt, Leo. "Repairing a Rural Base." *Far Eastern Economic Review* 91 (Feb. 13, 1976): 95–96.

1979. Hammer, Ellen J. "Indochina: Communist But Nonaligned." *Problems of Communism* 25 (May–June 1976): 1–17.

1980. ———. "Perspective on Vietnam." *Problems of Communism* 25 (Jan.–Feb. 1976): 81–84.

1981. Heinl, Robert D., Jr. "Armed Resistance Is Far From Over in Vietnam." *Sea Power* 20 (Oct. 1977): 36–37.

1982. Lacouture, Jean. "Vietnam: After the Debacle." *New York Review of Books* (May 1, 1975): 34ff.

1983. Le Hoang Trong. "Survival and Self-Reliance: A Vietnamese Viewpoint." *Asian Survey* 15 (Apr. 1975): 281–301.

1984. Martin, Earl S. "The New Vietnam: An Opposing View." *New York Review of Books* (May 12, 1977): 45–46.

1985. ———. *Reaching the Other Side: The Journal of an American Who Stayed to Witness Vietnam's Postwar Transition.* New York: Crown, 1978. Martin stayed with a friend on the revolutionary side.

1986. Nayan Chanda. "South Vietnam Sits It Out." *Far Eastern Economic Review* 91 (Mar. 21, 1976): 13.

1987. Osborne, John. "In the Beginning." *New Republic* 172 (May 10, 1975): 9–12.

1988. Pike, Douglas. "Inside Vietnam: The Recycling of a Society." *Strategic Review* 6 (Summer 1978): 48–55.

1989. ———. "Vietnam in 1980: The Gathering Storm?" *Asian Survey* 21 (Jan. 1981): 84–92.

1990. Porter, D. Gareth. "The Revolutionary Government in Vietnam." *Current History* 69 (Dec. 1975): 232–235ff.

1991. ———. "Vietnam's Long Road to Socialism." *Current History* 71 (Dec. 1976): 209–212ff.

1992. Smith, Richard M., and Ron Moreau. "Vietnam: A Year Later." *Newsweek* 87 (May 23, 1976): 40–41.

1993. Spurr, Russell. "A Town Called Ho Chi Minh (Saigon)." *Far Eastern Economic Review* 88 (May 9, 1975): 10–11.

1994. Thayer, Carlyle A. "Vietnam: Beleaguered Outpost of Socialism." *Current History* 79 (Dec. 1980): 165–169.

1995. Turley, William S. "Vietnam Since Reunification." *Problems of Communism* 26 (Mar.–Apr. 1977): 36–54.

1996. U.S. House. Committee on International Affairs. Hearings; *Human Rights in Vietnam.* 95th Cong., 1st sess., June 16–26, 1977.

1997. Young, Stephen B. "Vietnamese Marxism: Transition in Elite Ideology." *Asian Survey* 19 (Aug. 1979): 770–780.

REBUILDING THE ECONOMY

A major postwar issue was whether the United States should assist in rebuilding Vietnam's economy; Congress showed no real interest, and the American public was not enthusiastic for such an undertaking.

1998. Brown, David G. "The Development of Vietnam's Petroleum Resources." *Asian Survey* 16 (June 1976): 553–570.

1999. Cordier, Andrew W., and Ruth B. Russell. "Next: A Two-Stage Blueprint of an Aid Program for Vietnam." *International Perspectives* [Canada], no. 1 (1973): 19–21.

2000. Duiker, William J. "Ideology and Nation-Building in the Democratic Republic of Vietnam." *Asian Survey* 17 (Apr. 1977): 413–431.

2001. Lindland, Bobbe. "POW/MIA Families Oppose Aid, Trade, etc. with Vietnam." *Armed Forces Journal International* 113 (Feb. 1976): 10–11.

2002. McCarthy, Eugene J. "Aid to Vietnam." *Commonweal* 98 (Apr. 20, 1973): 151–153.

2003. Nayan Chanda. "Rebuilding Shattered Vietnam." *Far Eastern Economic Review* 91 (Feb. 13, 1976): 92–98.

2004. Niehaus, Marjorie. *A Chronology of Selected Statements by Administration Officials on the Subject of Postwar Reconstruction Aid to Indochina: April 7, 1965–April 4, 1973.* JX 1435 US ASIA 73–64. Washington, DC: Library of Congress, Congressional Research Service, Apr. 4, 1973.

2005. Nivolon, François. "Hanoi's Next Victory: An Emphasis on Reconstruction, Not Military Adventures." *Atlas* 23 (June 1976): 23–25.

2006. Pike, Douglas. "Vietnam During 1976: Economics in Command." *Asian Survey* 17 (Jan. 1977): 34–42.

2007. ———. "Vietnam in 1977: More of the Same." *Asian Survey* 18 (Jan. 1978): 68–75.

2008. St. John, R.B. "Marxist-Leninist Theory and Organization in South Vietnam." *Asian Survey* 20 (Aug. 1980): 812–828.

2009. Smith, Rolph. "Vietnam's Fourth Party Congress." *World Today* [London] 33 (May 1977): 195–202. [revised five-year plan, 1976–1980]

2010. Thayer, Carlyle A. "Dilemmas of Development in Vietnam." *Current History* 75 (Dec. 1978): 221–230.

2011. U.S. Senate. Committee on Appropriations. Report; *The United States and the Rehabilitation and*

Reconstruction of Indochina: A Summary Report; Japan—Cambodia—Laos—South Vietnam—North Vietnam, by Sen. Edward W. Brooke. 93d Cong., 1st sess., June 15, 1973.

Third Indochina War, 1978–

Socialist Vietnam's invasion and occupation of Cambodia in 1978 opened the Third Indochina War, as China subsequently initiated hostilities in early 1979. Ancient territorial ambitions, racial prejudices and communist party rivalries played a major role in triggering these new hostilities. It is doubtful if either of these two military actions have been concluded; they may well fester and prolong tensions and hostilities in Indochina. An unfortunate by-product of this conflict has been Vietnam's apparent decision to persuade or intimidate its citizens of Chinese extraction to leave the country.

2012. Donnell, John C. "Vietnam: Continuing Conflicts and Diminishing Options." *Asian Thought & Society* 4 (Apr. 1979): 39–59.

2013. _____. "Vietnam: Vietnam versus China and Cambodia, Nearing a Flash Point?" *Asian Thought & Society* 3 (Sept. 1978): 225ff.

2014. Dutter, Lee E., and Raymond S. Kania. "Explaining Recent Vietnamese Behavior." *Asian Survey* 20 (Sept. 1980): 931–943.

2015. Elliott, David W.P., ed. *The Third Indochina Conflict.* Boulder, CO: Westview Press, 1980.

2016. Hickey, Gerald. "Peace: A New Experience." *New Republic* 172 (May 3, 1975): 26. Hickey discusses euphoric expectations of peace that were not to be.

2017. Horn, Robert C. "Soviet–Vietnamese Relations and the Future of Southeast Asia." *Pacific Affairs* 51 (Winter 1978–1979): 585–605.

2018. Leighton, Marian. "Vietnam and the Sino–Soviet Rivalry." *Asian Affairs* [U.S.] 6 (Sept.–Oct. 1978): 1–31.

2019. Niehaus, Marjorie. "Vietnam 1978: The Elusive Peace." *Asian Survey* 19 (Jan. 1979): 85–94.

2020. "Treaty of Friendship and Cooperation Between the Union of Soviet Socialist Republics and the Socialist Republic of Vietnam." *International Legal Materials* 17 (Nov. 1978): 1485–1487. [also in *International Affairs* (Moscow) 25 (Jan. 1979): 146–147]

2021. Turley, William S., and Jeffrey Race. "The Third Indochina War." *Foreign Policy*, no. 38 (Spring 1980): 92–116.

VIETNAM–CAMBODIA CONFLICT

A good essay on the historical dimensions is given by Osborne (2044).

Documents
2022. "Kampuchea–Vietnam: Treaty of Peace, Friendship and Cooperation." *International Legal Materials* 18 (Mar. 1979): 394–396. This document reveals Vietnam's terms to its puppet government in Cambodia.

2023. U.S. Department of State. Office of the Geographer. *Cambodia–Vietnam Boundary.* International Boundary Study, no. 155. Washington, DC: GPO, Mar. 5, 1976.

Essays
2024. "Cambodia: The Killing Ground." *Far Eastern Economic Review* 103 (Jan. 19, 1979): 10–14, 18–22. This is a special section of the issue; see also subsequent issues for additional accounts.

2025. Chandler, David P. "The Tragedy of Cambodian History." *Pacific Affairs* 52 (Fall 1979): 410–419.

2026. Chomsky, Noam, Hans J. Morgenthau, and Michael Walzer. "Vietnam and Cambodia." *Dissent* 25 (Fall 1978): 386–391. The authors present differing views.

2027. "Fallen Domino." *Nation* 228 (Jan. 20, 1979): 25–26. This article focuses on the occupation of Cambodia.

2028. Ferrante, A. "End of a Tunnel Looks Dark in Phnom Penh." *Maclean's* 92 (Jan. 15, 1979): 26–27.

2029. "Hanoi Engulfs Its Neighbor." *Time* 113 (Jan. 22, 1979): 32–33.

2030. "Hanoi's Power Play." *Newsweek* 93 (Jan. 22, 1979): 29, 32–34.

2031. Jackson, Karl D. "Cambodia 1978: War, Pillage, and Purge in Democratic Kampuchea." *Asian Survey* 19 (Jan. 1979): 72–84.

2032. Kahin, George McT. "The Secret War." *New Republic* 172 (May 3, 1975): 13–14. Kahin gives an early discussion of Vietnam–Cambodia tensions.

2033. Kamm, Henry. "The Agony of Cambodia." *New York Times Magazine* (Nov. 19, 1978): 40–42, 142–160.

[see the *New York Times* for subsequent articles by Kamm]

2034. Kershaw, Roger. "Unlimited Sovereignty in Cambodia: The View From Bangkok." *World Today* [London] 35 (Mar. 1979): 101–109.

2035. Leifer, Michael. "The International Dimensions of the Cambodian Conflict." *International Affairs* [London] 51 (Oct. 1975): 531–543.

2036. Leighton, Marian K. "Perspectives on the Vietnam–Cambodia Border Conflict." *Asian Survey* 18 (May 1978): 448–457.

2037. Mack, Andrew. "America's Role in the Destruction of Kampuchea." *Politics* 16 (May 1981): 135–140. [a review essay]

2038. Mendenhall, Joseph A. "Communist Vietnam and the Border War: Victim or Aggressor?" *Strategic Review* 6 (Summer 1978): 56–61.

2039. Miller, C. "Vietnam's Bid for Hegemony." *Atlas* 26 (Jan. 1979): 16–18.

2040. Mohan, Jitendra. "Why Vietnam Invaded Kampuchea." *Economic and Political Weekly* 16 (Jan. 24, 1981): 121–125.

2041. Nayan Chanda. "Words, Not Deeds, From Peking." *Far Eastern Economic Review* 102 (Dec. 22, 1978): 17–18. The author discusses the lack of Chinese aid to Cambodia.

2042. Orlov, Stephen. "The New Cambodia War." *Economic and Political Weekly* 16 (Jan. 31, 1981): 145–149.

2043. _____. "Vietnam's Rule Over Kampuchea Threatens Regional Stability." *International Perspective* (May–June 1981): 6–10.

2044. Osborne, Milton E. "Kampuchea and Viet Nam: A Historical Perspective." *Pacific Community* [Japan] 9 (Apr. 1978): 249–263.

2045. "The Peking Approach." *Far Eastern Economic Review* 91 (Mar. 21, 1976): 12. Senator Mansfield discusses his political estimates of the situation.

2046. Shawcross, William. "Cambodia's Latest Convulsion." *New Republic* 180 (Mar. 24, 1979): 14–16.

2047. _____. "The Third Indochina War." *New York Review of Books* (Apr. 6, 1978): 15–22. A debate with Gareth Porter regarding this essay appeared in the *New York Review of Books* (July 20, 1978): 48–49.

2048. Simon, Sheldon W. "Cambodia: Barbarism in a Small State Under Seige." *Current History* 75 (Dec. 1978): 197–210.

2049. _____. "New Conflict in Indochina." *Problems of Communism* 27 (Sept.–Oct. 1978): 20–36.

2050. Tai Sung An. "Turmoil in Indochina: The Vietnam–Cambodian Conflict." *Asian Affairs* [U.S.] 5 (Mar.–Apr. 1978): 245–264.

2051. Tang, Peter S.H. "Kampuchea: Soviet–Vietnamese Subjugation and International Responsibility." *Asian Thought & Society* 6 (Sept.–Nov. 1981): 268–271.

2052. [United Nations]. "Call for Withdrawal of Foreign Troops From Kampchea Not Adopted." *U.N. Chronicle* 16 (Feb. 1979): 5–19.

2053. _____. "Security Council Adjourns Consideration of Southeast Situation: Its Implication." *U.N. Chronicle* 16 (Mar. 1979): 5–17.

2054. Wallace, James N. "New Indo-China Struggle: Communist vs Communist." *U.S. News and World Report* 85 (Dec. 18, 1978): 33–34.

2055. Zasloff, Joseph J., and MacAlister Brown. "The Passion of Kampuchea." *Problems of Communism* 28 (Jan.–Feb. 1979): 28–44.

VIETNAM–CHINA CONFLICT

Communist party rivalry, historical animosity, racial prejudices and general suspicions fueled the Vietnam–China conflict. Materials on China's Southeast Asian policies, and its relations with Hanoi, appear throughout the Guide.

2056. Buszynski, Les. "Vietnam Confronts China." *Asian Survey* 20 (Aug. 1980): 829–843.

2057. Chen, King C. "The Sino–Vietnamese Dispute." *Asian Thought & Society* 3 (Sept. 1978): 218–219.

2058. "China–Vietnam: The Costly Lesson." *Far Eastern Economic Review* 103 (Mar. 9, 1979): 12–18.

2059. Duncanson, Dennis J. "China's Vietnam War: New and Old Strategic Imperatives." *World Today* [London] 35 (June 1979): 241–248.

2060. Garver, John W. "Sino–Vietnamese Conflict and Sino–American Rapprochement." *Political Science Quarterly* 96 (Fall 1981): 445–464.

2061. Goodstadt, Leo. "Race, Refugees and Rice:

China and the Indo-China Triangle." *Round Table*, no. 271 (July 1978): 253–268.

2062.   Haggerly, J.J. "The Chinese–Vietnamese Border War of 1979." *Army Quarterly and Defence Journal* [Great Britain] (June 1979): 265–272.

2063.   Jencks, Harlan W. "China's 'Punitive' War on Vietnam: A Military Assessment." *Asian Survey* 19 (Aug. 1979): 801–900.

2064.   Larkin, Bruce. "China and Asia: The Year of the China–Vietnam War." *Current History* 76 (May–June 1979): 53–61.

2065.   Lawson, Eugene K. "China's Vietnam War and It's Consequences: A Comment." *China Quarterly*, no. 88 (Dec. 1981): 691–696.

2066.   Leifer, Michael. "Post Mortem on the Third Indochina War." *World Today* [London] 35 (June 1979): 249–258.

2067.   Nelson, Charles R. "The Sino–Viet War: Causes, Conduct, and Consequences." *Parameters* 9 (Sept. 1979): 23–30.

2068.   Nguyen Manh Hung. "The Sino–Vietnam Conflict: Power Play Among Communist Neighbors." *Asian Survey* 19 (Nov. 1979): 1037–1052.

2069.   Pike, Douglas. "Communist vs. Communist in Southeast Asia." *International Security* 4 (Summer 1979): 20–38.

2070.   Porter, Gareth. "Asia's New Cold War." *Nation* 226 (Sept. 9, 1978): 209–212.

2071.   ———. "The Sino–Vietnamese Conflict in Southeast Asia." *Current History* 75 (Dec. 1978): 193–196.

2072.   Simon, Sheldon W. "Peking and Indochina: The Perplexity of Victory." *Asian Survey* 16 (May 1976): 401–410.

2073.   Tan Kuang. "Chinese Communist Subversion of Indo-China Intensified." *Asian Outlook* 9 (June 1974): 18–21.

2074.   Thakur, Ramesh. "Coexistence to Conflict: Hanoi–Moscow–Peking Relations and the China Vietnam War." *Australian Outlook* 34 (Apr. 1980): 64–74.

2075.   Thee, Marek. "The China–Indochina Conflict: Notes on the Background and Conflict Resolution: The Case of Neutrality." *Journal of Peace Research* 17:2 (1980): 223–234.

2076.   ———. "Red East in Conflict: The China/Indo-china Wars." *Journal of Peace Research* 16:2 (1979): 93–100.

2077.   Tretiak, Daniel. "China's Vietnam War and Its Consequences." *China Quarterly*, no. 80 (Dec. 1979): 740–767.

2078.   "Vietnam–China Confrontation." *Far Eastern Economic Review* 101 (July 14, 1978): 6–10, 15–17.

2079.   "Vietnam–China War." *Southeast Asia Chronicle*, no. 68 (Dec. 1979): 1–28.

2080.   Woodside, Alexander. "Nationalism and Poverty in the Breakdown of Sino–Vietnamese Relations." *Pacific Affairs* 52 (Fall 1979): 381–409.

2081.   Yahuda, Michael B. "Chinese Foreign Policy After Victories in Indochina." *World Today* [London] 31 (Aug. 1975): 291–298.

Spratly Islands Dispute

These isles in the South China Sea are claimed by both China and Vietnam.

2082.   Cheng Huan. "A Matter of Legality." *Far Eastern Economic Review* 83 (Feb. 25, 1974): 25ff.

2083.   Hungdah Chiu, and Choon-ho Park. "Legal Status of the Paracel and Spratly Islands." *Ocean Development and International Law* 3:1 (1975): 1–28.

2084.   Katchen, Martin H. "The Spratly Islands and the Law of the Sea: 'Dangerous Ground' for Asian Peace." *Asian Survey* 17 (Dec. 1977): 1167–1181.

2085.   Kux, Ernst. "The Conflict in the South China Sea." *Swiss Review of World Affairs* 23 (Mar. 1974): 6–7.

Boat People

The "encouraged" departure of ethnic Chinese citizens of Vietnam, usually by boat, and the refusal of other Southeast Asian nations to accept them is but another manifestation of racial hostility. The number of deaths that have occurred will never be known. Pugash (2097) shows the problems of these refugees in finding a place to live. See also Chapter 8, under "Refugees: Post-Armistice."

2086.   "Agony of the Boat People." *Newsweek* 94 (July 2, 1979): 42–50.

2087.   "Barring the Boat People." *Time* 112 (Dec. 4, 1978): 46ff.

2088. Butler, David, et al. "Calling All Boat People." *Newsweek* 94 (Aug. 13, 1979): 30–33.

2089. Clugston, M. "Moral Problem of Refugees." *New Republic* 180 (Feb. 10, 1979): 15–17.

2090. "Damn the Refugee and Full Speed Ahead." *Commonweal* 105 (Sept. 1, 1978): 49–50. This article gives accounts of ships failing to stop to take aboard refugees.

2091. "Exodus." *Far Eastern Economic Review* 102 (Dec. 22, 1978): 8–13, 17, 18. [special section of this issue]

2092. "A Helping Hand." *Newsweek* 94 (July 30, 1979): 51–53.

2093. Kroef, Justus M. van der. "The Vietnamese Refugee Problem." *World Affairs* 142 (Summer 1979): 3–16.

2094. Lonchon-Gamma/Liaison. "Save Us! Save Us!" *Time* 114 (July 9, 1979): 28–32.

2095. Osborne, Milton E. "The Indochinese Refugees: Causes and Effects." *International Affairs* [London] 56 (Jan. 1980): 37–53.

2096. "Paddle, Homeless Masses: Vietnamese Boat People." *America* 139 (Dec. 23, 1978): 468–469.

2097. Pugash, James Z. "The Dilemma of the Sea Refugees: Rescue Without Refuge." *Harvard International Law Journal* 18 (Summer 1977): 577–604.

2098. Samuels, G. "Journey of the Boat People." *New Leader* 62 (Feb. 12, 1979): 10–11.

2099. Tran Van Dinh. "Are the Vietnamese Anti-Chinese?" *New Republic* 159 (Feb. 3, 1968): 18–21.

2100. U.S. Senate. Committee on the Judiciary. Study Mission Report; *Refugee and Humanitarian Problem in Vietnam.* 95th Cong., 2d sess., Aug. 1978.

2101. "The Voice of Joan Baez." *Newsweek* 94 (Aug. 13, 1979): 27–28. The article complains that antiwar activists showed no interest in subsequent refugees.

2102. Wain, Barry. "The Indochina Refugee Crisis." *Foreign Affairs* 58 (Fall 1979): 160ff.

2103. Willenson, K., et al. "Floodtide of Refugees." *Newsweek* 92 (Dec. 11, 1978): 51–52.

❦ Chapter Four ❦

United States and the Politics of Intervention

HOW DID THE UNITED STATES become involved in the Indochina conflict? During the long years of the Second Indochina War, writers continually sought the basic cause, or the most significant cause, of the American commitment. They argued that it stemmed from the exigencies of domestic politics (no president or party wanted to "lose" Indochina); that it flowed from bureaucratic failure; or that it evolved from an arrogance of power.

Barnet (2111) indicts the bureaucracy ("national security managers"), while Kolko (2133) and many of the "New Left" argue that intervention was the natural product of American imperialism. Most presidents, Kail (2381) notes, verbally found strategic considerations important as they spoke vaguely of "falling dominoes" and new "Munichs." Fulbright's *The Arrogance of Power* warns against assuming that power means virtue. Conventional wisdom during the 1960s and early 1970s preferred to use the quagmire thesis—Schlesinger (2142) and Rovere (2646)—to describe America's floundering into the Indochina morass. Gelb and Betts (2380) and Ellsberg (2237) have argued contrarily, that each president from Truman to Johnson foresaw the pitfalls of intervention but felt driven by the vicissitudes of domestic politics to maintain the status quo in Indochina, despite the risks and costs. Brodie (2114) criticizes both the quagmire thesis and the domestic politics argument by challenging American perceptions of the essential relationship between war and politics.

In 1979 many signs—renewed student interest and increased numbers of books, essays, movies and television dramas—pointed to a desire to restudy the Indochina conflict. These undertakings, especially the academic writings, are continuing the inevitable process of historical revisionism, a process particularly painful, as always, for the ideologues.

The antirevisionist plea "to struggle against the rewriting of the history of the [Vietnam] war" may well become the cry of the old New Left, but it will find few disciples. This is not to say that the current phase of revisionism has found the "truth," because it will, in turn, suffer from the pens of the next generation.

The lack of an adequate survey of the Second Indochina conflict has been rectified by Herring (2108). His account can be profitably supplemented with Millett's collection of essays (2109) to provide the materials necessary for a university-level class on the war. Much work still needs to be done to illuminate the roles of individuals. Halberstam's large, rambling discourse (2128) contains a number of exceptional biographical vignettes; apart from these, we are left largely with personal accounts.

This chapter contains a number of special topics. A few writers have sought to find a "historical parallel" to the Vietnam conflict with, at best, only partial success. It is rather surprising that so few people found such a parallel between Vietnam and either the American Revolution or the Spanish Civil War (1936–1939). Most writers tried to draw comparisons with the Korean War, particularly in the so-called "limited war" aspects. In drawing this parallel, one must keep in mind the fact that neither side in the Korean conflict adopted that strategy initially; they came to accept it only after they realized the high costs, or impossibility, of achieving victory.

Lessons from the Vietnam conflict began to be drawn long before American withdrawal. We have included here a number of essays which relate for the most part to the political dimensions of our involvement. (Chapter 6 begins with similar essays and books which focus on the military lessons.)

The "*Pentagon Papers* affair" has an interesting history quite apart from the documents themselves. (We have listed the documents in Chapter 1.) Two trials evolved from their release. The *New York Times* found itself defending the freedom of the press against the federal government's claim for the primacy of national security secrecy; the two men who made the papers available to the press, Daniel Ellsberg and Anthony Russo, were charged with violating national security laws. We have presented materials on both trials, although the true course of the latter might be traced more effectively in the *Los Angeles Times* via its index.

Overviews

Books on this topic have been divided into two segments: those contemporary to the Vietnam era and those more retrospective.

Retrospective Books

2104. Brown, Weldon A. *The Last Chopper: The Denouncement of the American Role in Vietnam, 1963–1975*. Port Washington, NY: Kennikat, 1976.

2105. _____. *Prelude to Disaster: The American Role in Vietnam, 1940–1963*. Port Washington, NY: Kennikat, 1976.

2106. Buttinger, Joseph. *Vietnam: The Unforgettable Tragedy*. New York: Horizon, 1977. This is a survey of "lessons to be learned."

2107. Charlton, Michael, and Anthony Moncrieff. *Many Reasons Why: The American Involvement in Vietnam*. New York: Hill & Wang, 1978. This is a summary of BBC broadcasts.

2108. Herring, George C. *America's Longest War: The United States and Vietnam, 1950–1975*. New York: Wiley, 1979.

2109. Millett, Alan R., ed. *A Short History of the Vietnam War*. Bloomington, IN: Indiana University Press, 1978.

2110. Warner, Denis. *Certain Victory: How Hanoi Won the War*. Kansas City: Sheed, Andrews & McMeel, 1978.

Contemporary Books

2111. Barnet, Richard J. *Roots of War: The Men and Institutions Behind U.S. Foreign Policy*. New York: Atheneum, 1971. Barnet presents a radical critique.

2112. Berrier, Hilaire du. *Background to Betrayal (1939–1965)*. Belmont, MA: Western Islands, 1965. The author presents a right-wing view of French and U.S. failures.

2113. Brandon, Henry. *Anatomy of Error: The Inside Story of the Asian War on the Potomac, 1954–1969*. Boston: Gambit, 1969.

2114. Brodie, Bernard. *War and Politics*. New York: Macmillan, 1973. America's foremost strategic analyst critiques the "quagmire" and "domestic impetus" theses of U.S. involvement in Vietnam.

2115. Bromely, Dorothy D. *Washington and Vietnam: An Examination of the Moral and Political Issues*. Dobbs Ferry, NY: Oceana, 1966. Bromely surveys official and journalistic views.

2116. Chomsky, Noam. *American Power and the New Mandarins*. New York: Pantheon Books, 1969.

2117. Committee of Concerned Asian Scholars. *The Indochina Story*. New York: Bantam, 1970.

2118. _____. *Indochina Story: A Critical Appraisal of American Involvement in Southeast Asia*. New York: Pantheon Books, 1971.

2119. Cooper, Chester L. *The Lost Crusade: America in Vietnam*. New York: Dodd, Mead, 1970. Cooper was a second-level official during the JFK and LBJ years.

2120. Critchfield, Richard. *The Long Charade: Political Subversion in the Vietnam War*. New York: Harcourt, Brace & World, 1968.

2121. Cronkite, Walter. *Vietnam Perspective: CBS News Special Report*. New York: Pocket, 1965. This is a brief, balanced account of key events in the early 1960s.

2122. Devillers, P., and Jean Lacouture. *Viet Nam: De la guerre française à la guerre américaine*. Paris: Éditions du Seuil, 1969.

2123. Fall, Bernard B. *Last Reflections on a War*. Garden City, NY: Doubleday, 1967.

2124. _____. *The Two Vietnams: A Political and Military Analysis*. 2d ed. New York: Praeger, 1967.

2125. _____. *Viet-Nam Witness, 1953–66*. New York: Praeger, 1966.

2126. Fitzgerald, Frances. *Fire in the Lake: The Vietnamese and the Americans in Vietnam*. New York: Atlantic Monthly Press (Little, Brown), 1972 [for an extended review, see Nguyen Khac Vien, *Radical America* 8:3 (1974): 87–107].

2127. Groulart, Claude de. *L'Aigle et le dragon: Vietnam 54–73*. Paris: Rossel, 1973.

2128. Halberstam, David. *The Best and the Brightest*. New York: Random House, 1972. This book is massive and rambling, but often perceptive with vivid sketches of policymakers. For extensive reviews, see *Asian Affairs* 3 (Apr. 1976): 263–272; and *Naval War College Review* 26:1 (1973): 42–53.

2129. _____. *The Making of a Quagmire, (1954–65)*. New York: Random House, 1964. Halberstam reveals the frustration of newsmen in Saigon.

2130.   Harris, Louis. *The Anguish of Change*. New York: W.W. Norton, 1973.

2131.   Honey, Patrick J. *Genesis of a Tragedy: The Historical Background to the Vietnam War*. London: Benn, 1968.

2132.   Kahin, George McT., and John W. Lewis. *The United States in Vietnam*. New York: Dial Press, 1966.

2133.   Kolko, Gabriel. *The Roots of American Foreign Policy*. Boston: Beacon, 1969. Kolko gives a radical critique.

2134.   Lacouture, Jean. *Vietnam Between Two Truces*. New York: Random House, 1966.

2135.   Luther, Hans U. *Der Vietnam Konflikt Darstellung and Dokumentation*. Berlin: Colloquium Verlag, 1969.

2136.   McCarthy, Joseph E. *Illusion of Power: American Policy Toward Viet-Nam, 1954–1966*. New York: Carlton Press, 1967. This book contains criticism by a career army officer.

2137.   McCarthy, Mary. *The Seventeenth Degree*. New York: Harcourt, Brace Jovanovich, 1974. [collected essays on Vietnam; see G.O. Taylor, "Cast a Cold 'I': Mary McCarthy on Vietnam." *Journal of American Studies* [Great Britain] 9:1 (1975): 103–114.]

2138.   Melano, H.J.M. *The Viet-Nam Story*. Willingboro, NJ: Alexia Press, 1969.

2139.   Mohn, A.H. *Vietnam*. Oslo: Gyldendal Norsk Forlag, 1965.

2140.   Morgenthau, Hans J. *Vietnam and the United States*. Washington, DC: Public Affairs Press, 1965.

2141.   Podwal, Mark H. *The Decline and Fall of the American Empire*. New York: Darien House, 1971.

2142.   Schlesinger, Arthur M., Jr. *The Bitter Heritage: Vietnam and American Democracy, 1941–1966*. Boston: Houghton Mifflin, 1966. Schlesinger presents an early liberal critique.

2143.   Schoenbrun, David. *Vietnam: How We Got In, How to Get Out*. New York: Atheneum, 1968.

2144.   Scott, Peter D. *The War Conspiracy: The Secret Road to the Second Indochina War*. New York: Bobbs-Merrill, 1972.

2145.   Shaplen, Robert. *Lost Revolution: The U.S. in Vietnam*. New York: Harper & Row, 1965.

2146.   _____. *Lost Revolution: U.S. in Vietnam, 1946–1966*. rev. ed. New York: Harper & Row, 1966.

2147.   _____. *The Road from War: Vietnam 1965–1970*. New York: Harper & Row, 1970.

2148.   _____. *The Road from War: Vietnam, 1965–1971*. New York: Harper & Row, 1971.

2149.   Stone, Isidor F. *Polemics and Prophecies, 1967–1970*. New York: Random House, 1970.

2150.   Thomas, James A. *Holy War*. New Rochelle, NY: Arlington House, 1974. Thomas argues that the United States failed in Vietnam because of military hierarchy and some civilians.

Essays

For general surveys, see also "'Lessons' of the Vietnam War," in this chapter.

2151.   Baral, Jaya Krishna. "US Involvement in Vietnam: From Cold War to 1960." *China Report* [India] 12:3 (1976): 28–52.

2152.   Kattenburg, Paul M. "Viet Nam and U.S. Diplomacy, 1940–1970." *Orbis* 15 (Fall 1971): 818–841.

2153.   Maruyama Shizuo. "America's Logic and Vietnam's Logic." *Japan Quarterly* 22 (July–Sept. 1975): 205-213. The author presents views on the war, peace accords, democracy and balance of power.

2154.   Maslin, V., and G. Lokshin. "Indo-China Fifteen Years After Geneva." *International Affairs* [Moscow] 15 (Aug. 1969): 69–73.

2155.   Massengale, Eugene W. "We Did Not Lose in Vietnam." *Worldview* 18 (Dec. 1975): 20–26. [U.S.–Asia, 1949–1975]

2156.   Thee, Marek. "The Indochina Wars: Great Power Involvement: Escalation and Disengagement." *Journal of Peace Research* 13:2 (1976): 117–130.

2157.   Warner, Geoffrey. "The United States and Vietnam, 1945–65." *International Affairs* [London] 48 (July 1972): 379–394; (Oct. 1972): 593–615.

Edited Collections

2158.   Boettiger, John R., ed. *Vietnam and American Foreign Policy*. Boston: Heath, 1968.

2159.   Brown, Sam, and Len A. Ackland, eds. *Why Are We Still in Vietnam?* New York: Random House, 1970.

2160.   Fishel, Wesley R., ed. *Vietnam: Anatomy of a Conflict*. Itasca, IL: Peacock, 1968.

2161.   Frizzell, Donaldson D., and W. Scott Thompson, eds. *The Lessons of the Vietnam War*. New York: Crane, Russak, 1977.

2162.   Garrett, Banning, and Katerine Barkley, eds. *Two, Three . . . Many Vietnams: A Radical Reader on the Wars in Southeast Asia and the Conflicts at Home.* San Francisco: Canfield, 1971.

2163.   Gettleman, Marvin E., et al., eds. *Conflict in Indochina.* New York: Vintage, 1970.

2164.   Gregg, R.W., and C.W. Kegley, Jr., eds. *After Vietnam.* New York: Anchor, 1971.

2165.   Isard, Walter, ed. *Vietnam: Some Basic Issues and Alternatives.* Cambridge, MA: Schenkman, 1969.

2166.   Kim, Jung-gun, ed. *Essays on the Vietnam War.* Greenville, NC: East Carolina University Press, 1970.

2167.   Krause, Patricia A., ed. *Anatomy of an Undeclared War.* Boston: Beacon, 1972.

2168.   Ly Qui Chung, ed. *Between Two Fires: The Unheard Voices of Vietnam.* New York: Praeger, 1970.

2169.   Manning, Robert, and Michael Janeway, eds. *Who We Are: An Atlantic Chronicle of the United States and Vietnam.* Boston: Little, Brown, 1969.

2170.   Murray, Rubin, ed. *Vietnam.* London: Eyre & Spottiswoode, 1965.

2171.   Pfeffer, Richard M., ed. *No More Vietnams? The War and the Future of American Foreign Policy.* New York: Harper & Row, 1968.

2172.   Raskin, Marcus G., and Bernard B. Fall, eds. *The Vietnam Reader: Articles and Documents on American Foreign Policy and the Vietnam Crisis.* New York: Vintage, 1965.

2173.   Ray, Sibnarayan, ed. *Vietnam Seen from East and West: An International Symposium.* New York: Praeger, 1966.

2174.   Rezazadeh, Reza, ed. *VietNam: The Alternatives for American Policy.* Platteville: Wisconsin State University Press, 1965.

2175.   Sobel, Lester A., ed. *South Vietnam: Communist–U.S. Confrontation in Southeast Asia (1961–1973).* 7 vols. Interim History Series. New York: Facts on File, 1975.

2176.   Sweezy, Paul M., ed. *Vietnam: The Endless War: From Monthly Review, 1954–1970.* New York: Monthly Review Press, 1970.

2177.   Wells, J.M., and M. Wilhelm, eds. *The People vs. Presidential War.* New York: Dunellen, 1970.

HISTORICAL COMPARISONS

These essays attempt, with varying degrees of success, to put the Vietnam conflict in historical perspective. Surprisingly few analogies to America's own revolution and the Spanish Civil War (1936–1939) were written. For presidential affirmation of the "Munich analogy," see Kail (2381), 95–104.

2178.   Chang Jim Park. "American Foreign Policy in Korea and Vietnam: Comparative Case Studies." *Review of Politics* 37 (Jan. 1975): 20–47.

2179.   Drummond, S. "Korea and Vietnam: Some Speculations about the Possible Influences of the Korean War on American Policy in Vietnam." *Army Quarterly and Defence Journal* [Great Britain] 97:1 (1968): 65–71.

2180.   Elowitz, Larry. "Korea and Vietnam: Limited War and the American Political System." Ph.D. dissertation, University of Florida at Gainesville, 1972.

2181.   _____, and John W. Spanier. "Korea and Vietnam: Limited War and the American Political System." *Orbis* 18 (Summer 1974): 510–534.

2182.   Fall, Bernard B. "Vietnam: The New Korea." *Current History* 50 (Feb. 1966): 85–90, 117–119.

2183.   Haggerty, J.J. "South Vietnam and the Munich Crossroad." *Army Quarterly and Defence Journal* [Great Britain] 96:2 (1968): 224–235.

2184.   Hoffman, Stanley. "Vietnam: An Algerian Solution?" *Foreign Policy*, no. 2 (1971): 3–37.

2185.   Howe, Irving. "Vietnam and Israel." *Dissent* 17 (May 1970): 401–404.

2186.   "Indo-China: America's Algeria." *Dissent* 10 (Summer 1963): 204–214.

2187.   McGuire, C.T., and C. Ogburn. "Vietnam and Korea: An Exchange of Views." *New Republic* 157 (Dec. 2, 1967): 15–18.

2188.   McWilliams, Wilson C., and Dennis Hale. "Spain and Vietnam: Comparing Two Civil Wars." *Commonweal* 48 (Sept. 16, 1966): 575–577.

2189.   Morgenthau, Hans J. "Asia: The American Algeria." *Commentary* 32 (July 1961): 43–47.

2190.   _____. "Vietnam Another Korea?" *Commentary* 33 (May 1962): 369–374.

2191.   Pohl, James W. "The American Revolution and the Vietnamese War: Pertinent Military Analogies." *History Teacher* 7 (Feb. 1974): 255–265.

2192. Van Alstyne, Richard W. "Vietnam War in Historical Perspective." *Current History* 65 (Dec. 1973): 241–246, 273–274.

"LESSONS" OF THE VIETNAM WAR

These essays, written between 1970 and 1982, seek to assess or predict the consequences or lessons of U.S. intervention in the Vietnam War. The essays are obviously tentative, but they do offer themes which bear reflection. See also Chapter 6, under "Strategy and Tactics."

2193. Ball, George W. "Have We Learned or Only Failed." *New York Times Magazine* (Apr. 1, 1973): 12ff. Ball is a former presidential advisor.

2194. Beaulac, Willard L. "No More Vietnams?" *U.S. Naval Institute Proceedings* 98 (Dec. 1972): 18–25. Will the United States be afraid to intervene when it is necessary?

2195. Carl, Walter L. "The Lesson of the Vietnam War." *Journal of Human Relations* 18:3 (1970): 1030–1039.

2196. Ellsberg, Daniel. *Some Lessons from Failure in Vietnam.* P–4036. Santa Monica, CA: Rand Corp., July 1969.

2197. Falk, Richard A. "What We Should Learn from Vietnam." *Foreign Policy* 1 (Winter 1970–1971): 98–128. [reprinted in R.W. Gregg and C.W. Kegley, Jr., eds. *After Vietnam.* New York: Anchor, 1971, 324– 339]

2198. Frey, Cynthia, Barton J. Bernstein, Richard Flacks, Stanley Rothman, and Guenter Levy. "The Drawing of Conclusions." *Center Magazine* [Center for the Study of Democratic Institutions, Santa Barbara, CA] 12 (May 1979): 31–41.

2199. Garrett, Stephen A. "The Lessons of Vietnam." *Center Magazine* [Center for the Study of Democratic Institutions, Santa Barbara, CA] 4:4 (July–Aug. 1971): 10–20.

2200. Goldstein, Walter. "The Lessons of the Vietnamese War." *Bulletin of the Atomic Scientists* 26 (Feb. 1970): 41–45.

2201. Greenbacker, John E. "The Lesson of Vietnam." *U.S. Naval Institute Proceedings* 99 (Aug. 1973): 18–25.

2202. Gurtov, Melvin, and Konrad Kellen. *Vietnam: Lessons and Mislessons.* P–4084. Santa Monica, CA: Rand Corp., June 1969.

2203. Hobsbawm, Eric. "Why America Lost the Vietnam War." *Listener* 87 (May 18, 1972): 639–641.

2204. Lake, Anthony. *The Vietnam Legacy: The War, American Society and the Future of American Foreign Policy.* New York: New York University Press, 1976.

2205. Lake, Antonia, and Anthony Lake. "Coming of Age Through Vietnam." *New York Times Magazine* (July 20, 1975): 9ff.

2206. Lomperis, Timothy J. "A Conceptual Framework for Deriving the 'Lessons of History': The U.S. Involvement in Viet Nam (1960–1975) as a Case Study." Ph.D. dissertation, Duke University, 1981.

2207. Maruyama Shizuo. "The Vietnam War—An Evaluation." *Japan Quarterly* 20 (Apr.–June 1973): 151–158.

2208. Nguyen Khac Vien. "The Vietnamese Experience and the Third World." *Bulletin of Concerned Asian Scholars* 6 (Sept.–Oct. 1974): 7–11.

2209. Phan Quang Dan. "The Vietnam Experience." *Asian Affairs* [U.S.] 4 (Mar.–Apr. 1977): 255–271.

2210. Rabinowitch, Eugene. "After Vietnam, What?" *Science and Public Affairs* 26 (June 1973): 13–15.

2211. Ravenal, Earl C. "Was Vietnam a 'Mistake'?" *Asian Survey* 14 (July 1974): 589–607.

2212. Sanders, Sol W., and William D. Henderson. "The Consequences of 'Vietnam.'" *Orbis* 21 (Spring 1977): 61–76.

2213. Sarkesian, Sam C. "Revolution and the Limits of Military Power: The Haunting Specter of Vietnam." *Social Science Quarterly* 56 (Mar. 1976): 673–688.

2214. Siracusa, Joseph M. "Lessons of Vietnam and Future of American Foreign Policy." *Australian Outlook* 30 (Aug. 1976): 227–237.

2215. ———. "The United States, Viet-Nam, and the Cold War: A Reappraisal." *Journal of Southeast Asian Studies* 5 (Mar. 1974): 82–101.

2216. "Symposium on the Vietnam Experience." *Armed Forces and Society* 2 (Spring 1976): 340–420. Each symposium item is also listed in the *Guide.*

2217. Thompson, W. Scott. "The Indochinese Debacle and the United States." *Orbis* 19 (Fall 1975): 990–1911.

2218. Tyson, James L. "Economic Lessons From the Defeat of South Vietnam." *Asia Quarterly* [Brussels], no. 1 (1977): 41–51.

2219. "Vietnam: What Lesson?" *Columbia Journalism Review* 9 (Winter 1970–1971): 1–64. [special issue]

2220. Watt, D.C. "Lessons of the American Defeat in Vietnam." *Journal of the Royal Services Institute for Defence Studies* 118 (June 1973): 35–38.

2221. Weise, Eric. "Mr. 'X', Russia, and Vietnam." *Modern Age* 19 (Fall 1975): 397–406. Weise argues that Kennan's 1946 "containment" thesis was proven by Vietnam.

2222. Yarmolinsky, A. "Some Lessons of Vietnam." *Round Table* 245 (Jan. 1972): 85–92.

REVISIONISM

While many revisionist items appear throughout the Guide, this section contains a few that focus more directly on this theme.

2223. Hoffmann, Stanley, et al. "Vietnam Reappraised." *International Security* 5 (Summer 1981): 3–26.

2224. Kaiser, David E. "Vietnam: Was the System the Solution? A Review Essay." *International Security* 4 (Spring 1980): 199–218.

2225. Nardin, Terry, and Jerome Slater. "Vietnam Revisted: Review Article." *World Politics* 33 (Apr. 1981): 436–448.

2226. Pelz, Stephen. "Alibi Alley: Vietnam as History." *Reviews in American History* 8:1 (1980): 139–141.

2227. Young, Marilyn B. "Revisionists Revised: The Case of Vietnam." *Society for Historians of American Foreign Relations Newsletter* 10:2 (1979): 1–10.

Politics and Vietnam

The selections contained in this section are primarily expressions of opinions or examinations of specific strategies.

GENERAL

Books
2228. Andres, Gunther. *Eskalation des Verbrechens: Aus einem ABC der amerikanischen Aggression gegen Vietnam.* Berlin: Unron Verlag, 1971.

2229. Armbruster, Frank E., et al. *Can We Win in Vietnam?* New York: Praeger, 1968.

2230. Beal, C.W. *The Realities of Vietnam: A Ripon Society Appraisal.* Washington, DC: Public Affairs Press, 1968.

2231. Burchett, Wilfred G. *Vietnam Will Win!* New York: Guardian Books, 1968.

2232. Chaumont, Charles Marie. *Analyse critique de l'intervention américaine au Vietnam.* Brussels: Commission permanente d'enquête pour le Vietnam, 1968.

2233. Chomsky, Noam. *For Reasons of State.* New York: Random House, 1973.

2234. Draper, Theodore. *Abuse of Power.* New York: Viking Press, 1966.

2235. Ellsberg, Daniel. *Escalating in a Quagmire.* Cambridge, MA: MIT Center of International Studies, Sept. 1970.

2236. ———. *Kahn on Winning in Vietnam: A Review.* P–3965. Santa Monica, CA: Rand Corp., Nov. 1968.

2237. ———. *Papers on the War.* New York: Simon & Schuster, 1972.

2238. Ennis, Thomas E. *Vietnam: Land without Laughter.* Morgantown, WV: West Virginia University, Cooperative Extension Service, 1966.

2239. Fishel, Wesley R. *The U.S. and Vietnam.* Pamphlet no. 391. New York: Public Affairs Commission, 1966.

2240. ———. *Vietnam: Is Victory Possible?* Headline Series. New York: Foreign Policy Association, Feb. 1964.

2241. Glyn, Alan. *Witness to Viet Nam: The Containment of Communism in South East Asia.* London: Johnson, 1968.

2242. Goodwin, Richard N. *Triumph or Tragedy: Reflections on Vietnam.* New York: Random House, 1966.

2243. Gordon, Bernard K. *Toward Disengagement in Asia: A Strategy for American Foreign Policy.* Englewood Cliffs, NJ: Prentice-Hall, 1969.

2244. Hassler, R. Alfred. *Saigon, USA.* New York: R.W. Baron, 1970.

2245. Herman, E.S., and R.B. DuBoff. *America's Vietnam Policy: The Strategy of Deception.* Washington, DC: Public Affairs Press, 1966.

2246. Horlemann, J., and P. Gang. *Vietnam: Genesis eines Konflikts*. Frankfurt: Editions Suhrkamp 133, 1966.

2247. Kang, Pilwon. *The Road to Victory in Vietnam*. New York: Exposition Press, 1970.

2248. Labin, Suzanne. *Sellout in Vietnam?* Springfield, VA: Crestwood, 1966.

2249. Lane, Thomas A. *America on Trial: The War for Vietnam*. New Rochelle, NY: Arlington House, 1971.

2250. Lederer, William J. *Our Own Worst Enemy*. New York: W.W. Norton, 1968.

2251. Levchenko, Irina Nikolavena. *Land Aflame*. Moscow: Progress Publishers, 1969.

2252. Liska, George. *War and Order: Reflections on Vietnam and History*. Baltimore: Johns Hopkins Press, 1968.

2253. Little, David. *American Foreign Policy and Moral Rhetoric: The Example of Vietnam*. New York: Council on Religion and International Affairs, 1969.

2254. Luce, Don, and John Sommer. *Viet Nam: The Unheard Voices*. Ithaca, NY: Cornell University Press, 1969.

2255. Lyons, Daniel S. *Vietnam Crisis*. New York: Twin Circle Publishing, 1967.

2256. McCarthy, Mary. *Vietnam*. New York: Harcourt, Brace and World, 1967.

2257. Milstein, Jeffery S. *Dynamics of the Vietnam War: A Quantitative Analysis and Predictive Computer Simulation*. Columbus: Ohio State University Press, 1974.

2258. Monroe, Malcolm. *The Means Is the End In Vietnam*. White Plains, NY: Murlagan, 1968.

2259. Scheer, Robert. *How the United States Got Involved in Viet Nam*. Santa Barbara, CA: Center for the Study of Democratic Institutions, 1965.

2260. Shinso Shibata. *Lessons of the Vietnam War: Philosophical Considerations of the Vietnam Revolution*. Amsterdam: Gruner, 1973.

2261. Sivaram, M. *The Vietnam War: Why?* Rutland, VT: Tuttle, 1966.

2262. Stavins, R., R. Burnel, and M.G. Raskin. *Washington Plans An Aggressive War*. New York: Random House, 1971.

2263. Sully, François. *We the Vietnamese: Voices from Vietnam*. New York: Praeger, 1971.

2264. Trager, Frank N. *Why Vietnam?* New York: Praeger, 1966.

2265. Vien, N.C. *Seeking the Truth*. New York: Vintage, 1967.

2266. Warbey, William. *Vietnam the Truth*. London: Merlin, 1965.

2267. Weil, Charles A. *Curtains Over Vietnam*. Jericho, NY: Exposition Press, 1969.

2268. White, Ralph K. *Nobody Wanted War: Misperception in Vietnam and Other Wars*. rev. ed. New York: Doubleday, 1970.

2269. Zils, Maria Susanne. *Vietnam: Hand ohne Frieden*. Weilheim/Oberbayern, West Germany: O.W. Barth-Verlag, 1965.

2270. Zinn, Howard. *Vietnam: The Logic of Withdrawal*. Boston: Beacon, 1967.

Essays

2271. Abel, Lionel. "The Position of Noam Chomsky." *Commentary* 47 (May 1969): 35–44.

2272. _____. "Reply (to Noam Chomsky)." *Commentary* 48 (Apr. 1969): 26–43.

2273. Bruen, John D. "Repercussions from the Vietnam Mobilization Decision." *Parameters* 2 (Spring–Summer 1972): 30–39.

2274. Buchan, Alastair. "Vietnam: Reasons and Rationales." *Encounter* [Great Britain] 40 (Apr. 1973): 30–35.

2275. Buttinger, Joseph. "How We Sank Into Vietnam." *Dissent* 19 (Spring 1972): 407–441.

2276. Chan, Steve. "Temporal Delineation of International Conflicts: Poisson Results from the Vietnam War, 1963–65." *International Studies Quarterly* 22 (June 1978): 237–265.

2277. Chomsky, Noam. "Vietnam, the Cold War and Other Matters." *Commentary* 48 (Apr. 1969): 12–26.

2278. _____. "Vietnam: How Government Became Wolves." *New York Review of Books* (June 15, 1972): 23–31. Chomsky gives a record of U.S. policy from the *Pentagon Papers*.

2279. Claymore, John. "Vietnamization of the Foreign Service." *Foreign Service Journal* 48 (Jan. 1971): 14–17.

2280. Darling, Frank C. "American Policy in Vietnam:

Its Role in the Quakeland Theory and International Peace." *Asian Survey* 2 (Aug. 1971): 818–839.

2281. DeManiel, D.R. "Will China Intervene in Vietnam?" *Australian Army Journal*, no. 202 (Mar. 1966): 33–40.

2282. Draper, Theodore. "The American Crisis: Vietnam, Cuba and the Dominican Republic." *Commentary* 43 (Jan. 1967): 27–43.

2283. Fairlie, Henry. "We Knew What We Were Doing When We Went Into Vietnam." *Washington Monthly 5* (Mar. 1973): 7–26.

2284. Fall, Bernard B. "The Second Indochina War." *International Affairs* [London] 41 (Jan. 1965): 59–73.

2285. Fleming, D.F. "Vietnam and After." *Western Political Quarterly* 21 (Mar. 1968): 141–151.

2286. Gelb, Leslie H. "On Schlesinger and Ellsberg: A Reply." *New York Review of Books* (Dec. 2, 1971): 31. Gelb argues that U.S. policy was influenced by the domino theory and anticommunism.

2287. Gester, Friedrich W. "Linguistic Aspects of the Vietnam War." *Amerikastudien/American Studies* [West Germany] 20:2 (1975): 307–319.

2288. Gittings, John. "United States and Vietnam: The Roots of the Agony." *Far Eastern Economic Review* 62 (Nov. 10, 1968): 368–372.

2289. Honey, Patrick J. *Vietnam: If the Communists Won.* Southeast Asian Perspectives, no. 2. New York: American Friends of Vietnam, 1971.

2290. Hoopes, Townsend. "Legacy of the Cold War in Indochina." *Foreign Affairs* 48 (July 1970): 601–616.

2291. Johnstone, William C. "The Political-Strategic Significance of Vietnam." *Current History* 56 (Feb. 1969): 65–70.

2292. Kramer, Helmut, and Helfried Bauer. "Imperialism, Intervention Capacity, and Foreign Policy Making: On the Political Economy of the U.S. Intervention in Indochina." *Journal of Peace Research* 9:4 (1972): 285–302.

2293. Langguth, A.J. "1964: Exhilaration, 1968: Frustration, 1970: Hopelessness." *New York Times Magazine* (Oct. 4, 1970): 26–27ff.

2294. Lansdale, Edward G. "Viet Nam: Do We Understand Revolution?" *Foreign Affairs* 43 (Oct. 1964): 75–86.

2295. Le Borgne, J. "Dix ans de politique americaine au Vietnam." *Revue de Défence Nationale* 20 (Oct. 1964): 1613–1631.

2296. Lens, Sidney. "How It 'Really' All Began." *Progressive* 37 (June 1973): 20–24.

2297. _____. "The Myth of Chinese Aggression." *Liberation* 11 (Summer 1966): 35–37.

2298. Lewy, Guenter. "Vietnam: New Light on the Question of American Guilt." *Commentary* 65 (Feb. 1978): 29–49. [see also Lewy's book (3553)]

2299. Lifton, Robert J. "The 'Gook Syndrome' and 'Numed Warfare.'" *Saturday Review* 55 (Dec. 1972): 66–72.

2300. McDermott, John. "Portent for the Future: Welfare Imperialism in Vietnam." *Nation* 203 (July 25, 1966): 76–88.

2301. McMahon, John F. "Vietnam: Our World War II Legacy." *Air University Review* 19 (Sept.–Oct. 1968): 59–66. To foster and preserve freedom in Southeast Asia is, according to McMahon, the American legacy of Vietnam.

2302. Milstein, Jeffery S., and W.C. Mitchell. "Dynamics of the Vietnam Conflict: A Quantitative Analysis and Predictive Computer Simulation." *Peace Research Reviews* 3:5 (1969): 64ff.

2303. Mirsky, Jonathan. "Decisions for War." *Saturday Review* 55 (Aug. 19, 1972): 54–56.

2304. Murakami Hideo. "'Vietnam' and the Question of Chinese Aggression." *Journal of Southeast Asian History* 7 (Sept. 1966): 11–16.

2305. Nicholas, H.G. "Vietnam and the Traditions of American Foreign Policy." *International Affairs* [London] 44 (Apr. 1968): 189–201.

2306. Nolting, F.E. "The Turning Point: The Origin and Development of U.S. Commitment in Viet-Nam." *Foreign Service Journal* 45 (July 1968): 18–20.

2307. O'Meara, P., Jr. "Vietnam in Perspective." *Armor* 84 (Nov.–Dec. 1975): 8–14.

2308. Osborne, Milton E. "Viet-Nam: The Origins of Crisis." *Behind the Headlines.* Toronto: Canadian Institute of International Affairs, Sept. 1965.

2309. Race, Jeffrey. "The Origins of the Second Indochina War." *Asian Survey* 10 (May 1970): 359–382.

2310. Randle, Robert F. "The Transformation of the Context of the Indochina Wars." In *From War to Peace: Essays in Peacemaking and War Termination*, edited by David S. Smith. New York: Columbia University Press, 1974.

2311. Ray, Jayanta K. "America in Vietnam: A Study of

Entrenched Interests." *India Quarterly* 31:2 (1975): 209–222.

2312. Reinhardt, G.C. *America's Crossroads—Vietnam*. P–3710. Santa Monica, CA: Rand Corp., Oct. 1967.

2313. Scheer, Robert, and Warren Hinckle. "The 'Vietnam Lobby.'" *Ramparts* 4 (July 1965): 16–24.

2314. Schlesinger, Arthur M., Jr. "Eyeless in Indochina." *New York Review of Books* (Oct. 21, 1971): 23–32. Schlesinger maintains that U.S. policy came from ignorance, misjudgment and muddle; see Gelb's reply, (2286).

2315. _____. "Vietnam and the End of the Age of Superpowers." *Harper's* 238 (Mar. 1969): 41–49.

2316. Sullivan, Michael P. "Symbolic Involvement as a Correlate of Escalation: The Vietnam Case." In *Peace, War, and Numbers*, edited by Bruce M. Russett. Beverly Hills, CA: Sage, 1972, 185–212.

2317. Swenson, Mark E. "The U.S. Involvement in Vietnam: How and Why." *Air Force & Space Digest* 52 (June 1969): 32–38.

2318. Taylor, Maxwell D. "Post-Vietnam Role of the Military in Foreign Policy." *Air University Review* 19 (Sept.–Oct. 1968): 50–58.

2319. Thee, Marek. "The International System After Vietnam." *Bulletin of Peace Proposals*, no. 4 (1973): 375–382.

2320. Trivers, Howard. "Myths, Slogans, and Vietnam: Specious Abstraction and Foreign Policy." *Virginia Quarterly Review* 48 (Winter 1972): 1–23. Trivers explores the fallacy of misplaced concreteness.

2321. Voth, A. "Vietnam: Studying a Major Controversy." *Conflict Resolution* 11 (Dec. 1967): 431–443.

2322. Warner, Geoffrey. "Escalation in Vietnam: The Precedent of 1954." *International Affairs* [London] 41 (Apr. 1965): 267–277.

2323. Watt, Alan. "The Geneva Agreements 1954 in Relation to Vietnam." *Australian Quarterly* 39 (June 1967): 7–23.

2324. White, Ralph K. "Misperception of Aggression in Vietnam." *Journal of International Affairs* 21:1 (1967): 123–140.

2325. Whiting, Allen S. "How We Almost Went to War With China." *Look* 33 (Apr. 29, 1969): 76–79. Whiting describes a series of shooting incidents between 1964 and 1967.

2326. Wolk, H.S. "Vietnam and the Warfare State Complex." *Air Force & Space Digest* 50 (Apr. 1967): 39–43.

PERSONAL EXPERIENCES IN VIETNAM

These books and essays record some of the visits of correspondents to Vietnam, particularly to Hanoi and Saigon. Soldiers' experiences are listed separately in Chapter 6.

Books

2327. Aptheker, Herbert. *Mission to Hanoi*. New York: International Publishers, 1966. Aptheker is a member of the American Communist party.

2328. Arrowsmith, P., ed. *To Asia in Peace: Story of a Non-Violent Action Mission to Indo-China*. London: Sidswick & Jackson, 1972.

2329. Berrigan, Daniel. *Night Flight to Hanoi: War Diary with 11 Poems*. New York: Macmillan, 1968. Berrigan was an antiwar activist.

2330. Bertolino, Jean. *Vietnam sanslant, 1967–1968: Au sud et au nord du 17e parallele*. Paris: Stock, 1968.

2331. Bonosky, Philip. *Beyond the Borders of Myth: From Vilnius to Hanoi*. New York: Praxis, 1967.

2332. Briand, Rena. *No Tears to Flow: Woman at War*. Melbourne, Australia: Heineman, 1969.

2333. Cameron, James. *Here is Your Enemy: Complete Report from North Vietnam*. New York: Holt, Rinehart & Winston, 1966. Cameron was a pro-Hanoi British journalist.

2334. Coe, Charles. *Young Men in Vietnam*. New York: Four Winds Press, 1968.

2335. Emerson, Gloria. *Winners and Losers: Battles, Retreats, Gains, Losses, and Ruins from a Long War*. New York: Harcourt, Brace, 1976.

2336. Falabella, J. Robert. *Vietnam Memoirs: A Passage to Sorrow*. New York: Pageant Press International, 1971.

2337. Fallaci, Oriana. *Nothing and So Be It*. Translated by I. Quigly. Garden City, NY: Doubleday, 1972. Fallaci is an Italian journalist.

2338. Feinberg, Abraham L. *Rabbi Feinberg's Hanoi Diary*. Don Mills, Ontario: Longmans, 1968. Feinberg was a Canadian visitor to Vietnam.

2339. Field, Michael. *The Prevailing Wind: Witness in Indo-China*. London: Methuen, 1965.

2340. Herr, Michael. *Dispatches*. New York: Knopf, 1977. Written by a correspondent for *Esquire* in South Vietnam, the book takes an irreverent look at the life of the 'grunts'.

2341. Higgins, Marguerite. *Our Vietnam Nightmare*. New York: Harper & Row, 1965. Higgins was a correspondent.

2342. Hope, Bob. *Five Women I Love: Bob Hope's Vietnam Story*. New York: Doubleday, 1966.

2343. Jones, James. *Viet Journal*. New York: Delacorte Press, 1974. Jones gives "One man's view" based on an officially sponsored trip.

2344. Just, Ward S. *To What End? Report From Vietnam*. Boston: Houghton Mifflin, 1968. Just was a correspondent.

2345. Kirk, Donald. *Tell It to the Dead: Memories of a War*. Chicago: Nelson-Hall, 1977. Kirk was a correspondent.

2346. Labin, Suzanne. *Vietnam: An Eye-Witness Account*. Springfield, VA: Crestwood, 1964. Labin was a pro-interventionist.

2347. Lansdale, Edward G. *In the Midst of Wars: An American's Mission to Southeast Asia*. New York: Harper & Row, 1972. Lansdale discusses government military assistance programs.

2348. Lynd, Staughton, and Thomas Hayden. *The Other Side*. New York: New American Library, 1967.

2349. McGrady, Mike. *Dove in Vietnam*. New York: Funk & Wagnalls, 1968.

2350. Munson, Glenn, ed. *Letters From Viet Nam*. New York: Parallax, 1966 [appeared in *This Week*]

2351. Portisch, Hugo. *Eyewitness in Vietnam*. Translated by M. Glenny. London: Bodley Head, 1967.

2352. Ray, Michele. *The Two Shores of Hell*. Translated by E. Abbot. New York: McKay, 1968.

2353. Sager, Peter. *Report from Vietnam*. Bern: Swiss Eastern Institute, 1968.

2354. Salisbury, Harrison E. *Behind the Lines— Hanoi: December 23, 1966–January 7, 1967*. New York: Harper & Row, 1967. This trip by a senior editor of the *New York Times* prompted a Senate hearing; see Committee on Foreign Relations, *Harrison E. Salisbury's Trip to North Vietnam*, 90th Cong., 1st sess., Feb. 2, 1967.

2355. Scholl-Latour, Peter. *Death in the Rice Fields*. New York: Orbis, 1981.

2356. Sontag, Susan. *Trip to Hanoi*. New York: Farrar, Straus & Giroux, 1969.

2357. Spruille, Jane Polk. *The Line is Drawn: Extracts from the Letters of Captain J. P. Spruille, U.S. Army*. Washington, DC: GPO, 1964.

2358. Tregaskis, Richard B. *Vietnam Diary*. New York: Holt, Rinehart & Winston, 1963. Tregaskis was a veteran correspondent.

2359. West, Richard. *Sketches from Vietnam*. New York: International Publications Services, 1968.

2360. Willwerth, James. *Eye in the Last Storm: A Reporter's Journal of One Year in Southeast Asia*. New York: Grossman, 1972.

2361. Young, Perry D. *Two of the Missing: A Reminiscence of Some Friends in the War*. New York: Coward, McCann & Geoghegan, 1975. This journalist's friends were lost in Cambodia in 1970.

Essays

2362. Berrigan, Daniel. "Mission to Hanoi." *Worldview* 11 (Apr. 1968): 6–11.

2363. Brown, J.P. "A Visit to the North Vietnamese." *Christian Century* 85 (Jan. 3, 1968): 18–21.

2364. Chomsky, Noam. "In North Vietnam: A Special Supplement." *New York Review of Books* (Aug. 13, 1970): 16–23.

2365. Dellinger, Dave. "North Viet Nam: Eyewitness Report." *Liberation* 11 (Dec. 1966): 3–15.

2366. Higgins, Marguerite. "Saigon Summary." *America* 110 (Jan. 4, 1964): 18–21.

2367. Just, Ward S. "Vietnam Notebook." *Harper's* 236 (Apr. 1968). This book contains the highlights of a Vietnam experience by a crack correspondent.

2368. Koch, Chris. "The View from North Vietnam." *War/Peace Report* 5 (Nov. 1965): 4–7.

2369. Kraft, Joseph. "Letter From Hanoi." *New Yorker* 48 (Aug. 12, 1972): 58ff.

2370. Lewis, Anthony. "North Vietnam: A Visit to a Hospital." *Atlantic* 229 (Aug. 1972): 6ff.

2371. _____. "'You Americans Do Not Understand Vietnam' They Kept Telling Me ... Journal of a Correspondent in North Vietnam." *New York Times Magazine* (June 18, 1972): 9ff.

2372. Livingston, David, et al. "Labor Mission to Hanoi." *Nation* 214 (Apr. 24, 1972): 520–522.

2373. Shoenbrun, David. "Journey to North Vietnam." *Saturday Evening Post* 240 (Dec. 16, 1967): 21–25ff.

2374. Sochwick, Howard. "Slow Train through Viet Nam's War." *National Geographic* 126 (Sept. 1964): 412–444.

2375. Taylor, Edmond. "Back From Vietnam." *Reporter* 34 (Jan. 27, 1966): 23–26.

2376. "Vietnam Diary: Notes from the Journal of a Young American in Saigon." *Reporter* 34 (Jan. 13, 1966): 25–27.

2377. Witze, Claude. "Report from Vietnam." *Air Force & Space Digest* 47 (Aug. 1964): 12–16.

Presidential Policies and Critics

The arrangement of materials by presidential administration is designed to illuminate the evolution of American policymaking toward Southeast Asia. The same groupings reveal the development of public criticism. As it is impossible to list all critical arguments, a review of the Reader's Guide, PAIS *and the* New York Times Index *will be helpful.*

Documents
See also Chapter 1, under "Documentary Collections," especially for the Pentagon Papers *collections.*

2378. U.S. Department of State. *A Threat to Peace: North Vietnam's Efforts to Conquer South Vietnam.* Publication no. 7308. Far Eastern Series 110. Washington, DC: GPO, 1961.

POLICYMAKING, 1941–1973

Books and Dissertations
2379. Garrett, Stephan A. "An Intellectual Analysis of Foreign Policy Arguments: The Vietnam Debate." Ph.D. dissertation, University of Virginia, 1968.

2380. Gelb, Leslie H., and Richard K. Betts. *The Irony of Vietnam: The System Worked.* Washington, DC:

Brookings Institution, 1979. The decisionmaking process worked, but U.S. foreign policy failed.

2381. Kail, F.M. *What Washington Said: Administration Rhetoric and the Vietnam War, 1949–1969.* New York: Harper & Row, 1973. Kail provides a useful analysis of presidential policy justifications.

2382. Kenney, Henry J. "The Changing Importance of Vietnam in United States Policy, 1949–1969." Ph.D. dissertation, American University, 1974.

2383. Kenney, Stephen F. "Vietnam Decision-making: A Psychological Perspective on American Foreign Policy." Ph.D. dissertation, Boston University, 1978.

2384. McCarthy, Joseph E. "The Concept and Evolution of American Foreign Policy Toward Viet-Nam, 1954–1963." Ph.D. dissertation, University of Maryland, 1965.

2385. Nacht, Michael L. "Vietnam Policy: Some Theoretical Perspectives." Ph.D. dissertation, Columbia University, 1973.

2386. _____. *The War in Vietnam: The Influence of Concepts on Policy.* ACIS Working Paper no. 26. Los Angeles: UCLA, Center for International and Strategic Affairs, July 1980.

2387. Poole, Peter A. *Eight Presidents and Indochina.* Huntington, NY: Krieger, 1978.

2388. Roskin, Michael G. "Turning Inward: The Effects of Vietnam on U.S. Foreign Policy." Ph.D. dissertation, American University, 1972.

2389. Selter, Robert V. "The Truman–Johnson Analog: A Study of Presidential Rhetoric in Limited War." Ph.D. dissertation, Wayne State University, 1976.

2390. Sigford, Rolf N. "The Rhetoric of the Vietnam War: Presidents Johnson and Nixon." Ph.D. dissertation, University of Minnesota, 1973.

2391. Stempel, John D. "Policy/Decision-making in the Department of State: The Vietnamese Problem, 1961–1965." Ph.D. dissertation, University of California, Berkeley, 1965.

2392. Thompson, James C. "Disaster in Foreign Policy: Organizational Response to Failure." Ph.D. dissertation, University of Michigan, 1975.

2393. Welch, Susan K. "Groups and Foreign Policy Decisions: The Case of Indochina, 1950–1956." Ph.D. dissertation, University of Illinois at Urbana—Champaign, 1970.

2394. Wilson, Melford A., Jr. "Criticism and the Policy Maker's Reaction: United States Policy on Vietnam,

1961–1966." Ph.D. dissertation, American University, 1969.

2395. Zant, Thomas. "The Concept of National Interest and Its Application to United States Policy in Vietnam." Ph.D. dissertation, University of Missouri, Columbia, 1973.

Essays
2396. "Actors: An Analysis of United States Decision Making in Vietnam." In J. R. Handelman, et al., *Vietnam/The Middle East/The Environment Crisis*. Chicago: Rand McNally, 1974.

2397. Bundy, McGeorge. "Vietnam, Watergate and Presidential Powers." *Foreign Affairs* 58 (Winter 1980): 397–407.

2398. Gelb, Leslie H. "Vietnam: The System Worked." *Foreign Policy*, no. 3 (Summer 1971): 140–167. This is a preview of the book he coauthored with Richard Betts (2380).

2399. Goldstein, Walter. "The American Political System and the Next Vietnam." *Journal of International Affairs* 25:1 (1971): 91–119.

2400. Holsti, Ole R., and James N. Rosenau. "Vietnam, Consensus, and the Belief Systems of American Leaders." *World Politics* 32 (Oct. 1979): 1–56.

2401. Joseph, Paul I. "The Making of United States Policy in Vietnam." *Socialist Revolution* 3 (May–June 1973): 113–156.

2402. Karnow, Stanley. "Grand Illusion." *New Republic* 172 (May 3, 1975): 8–10. Karnow describes policymakers influenced by Munich and World War II.

2403. Landau, D. "Behind the Policy Makers: RAND and the Vietnam War." *Ramparts* 11 (Nov. 1972): 26–37.

2404. Meaney, Neville. "From the Pentagon Papers: Reflections on the Making of America's Vietnam Policy." *Australian Outlook* 26 (Aug. 1972): 163–192.

2405. Morgenthau, Hans J. "The Elite Protects Itself." *New Republic* 172 (May 3, 1975): 20–21.

2406. Mueller, John E. "The Search for the 'Breaking Point' in Vietnam: The Statistics of a Deadly Quarrel." *International Studies Quarterly* 24 (Dec. 1980): 497–531.

2407. Record, Jeffrey. "The Perception of American Interests In Vietnam." *SAIS Review* 14 (Winter 1970): 17–24.

2408. Thomson, James C., Jr. "Getting Out and Speaking Out." *Foreign Policy*, no. 13 (1973–1974): 49–69.

Thomson points out that while officials may oppose policies, most hesitate to resign in order to speak out.

2409. _____. "How Could Vietnam Happen? An Autopsy." *Atlantic* 221 (Apr. 1968): 47–53.

Roosevelt and Truman Years, 1941–1952

For Truman's public presidential papers, see (134); see also the Pentagon Papers *(130–132) and Porter (133) for additional pertinent documents. The U.S. Department of State's* Foreign Relations *volumes have included many valuable papers for the 1940s and early 1950s. See also Chapter 3, under "Struggle: Revolution and Independence," for events in Vietnam during this period.*

2410. Stapleton, Margaret L. *The Truman and Eisenhower Years, 1945–1960: A Selective Bibliography*. Metuchen, NJ: Scarecrow, 1973.

2411. Stewart, William J. *The Era of Franklin D. Roosevelt: A Selected Bibliography of Periodical, Essay and Dissertation Literature, 1945–1971*. Hyde Park, NY: Franklin D. Roosevelt Library, n.d. This work contains excellent background material on FDR's foreign policy.

PERSONALITIES, POLICIES AND POLITICS

2412. Acheson, Dean. *Present at the Creation: My Years in the State Department*. New York: W.W. Norton, 1969. Covering 1941 to 1953, these memoirs are essential for understanding the man and his policies; the book includes a few direct comments about Vietnam.

2413. Drachman, Edward R. *United States Policy Toward Vietnam, 1940–1945*. Rutherford, NJ: Fairleigh Dickinson University Press, 1970.

2414. Eggleston, Noel C. "America's First Withdrawal From Indochina (1945–52)." *Research Studies* 44:3 (1976): 217–228.

2415. _____. "The Roots of Commitment: United States Policy Toward Vietnam, 1945–1950." Ph.D. dissertation, University of Georgia, 1977.

2416. Fall, Bernard B. "La politique américaine au Viet Nam." *Politique Étrangère* 20 (July 1955): 299–322. Fall focuses on FDR's anticolonialism.

2417. Garfield, Gene J. "The Genesis of Involvement: The Truman Decision to Assist the French in Indochina." Ph.D. dissertation, Southern Illinois University, 1972.

2418. Habibuddin, S.M. "Franklin D. Roosevelt's Anti-Colonial Policy Towards Asia: Its Implications for India, Indo-China and Indonesia." *Journal of Indian History* [India] 53:3 (1975): 497–522.

2419. Herring, George C. "The Truman Administration and the Restoration of French Sovereignty in Indochina." *Diplomatic History* 1 (Spring 1977): 97–117.

2420. Hess, Gary R. "The First American Commitment in Indochina: The Acceptance of the 'Bao Dai Solution,' 1950." *Diplomatic History* 2 (Fall 1978): 331–350.

2421. _____. "Franklin Roosevelt and Indochina." *Journal of American History* 59 (Sept. 1972): 353–368.

2422. _____. "United States Policy and the Origins of the French–Viet Minh War, 1945–46." *Peace & Change* 3:2/3 (1975): 21–33.

2423. Hoang Nguyen. *U.S. Aggressive Activities Against Viet-Nam.* Peking: Cultural Press, 1950.

2424. Kahler, John K. "The Genesis of the American Involvement in Indo-China, 1940–1954." Ph.D. dissertation, University of Chicago, 1964.

2425. Katz, Mark N. "The Origins of the Vietnam War, 1945–1948." *Review of Politics* 42:2 (1980): 131–151.

2426. LeFeber, Walter. "Roosevelt, Churchill, and Indochina, 1942–1945." *American Historical Review* 80 (Dec. 1975): 1277–1295.

2427. Marvel, W. Macy. "Drift and Intrigue: United States Relations with the Viet-Minh, 1945." *Millenium* [London] 4 (Spring 1975): 10–27.

2428. Patti, Archimedes L.A. *Why Vietnam? Prelude to America's Albatross.* Berkeley: University of California Press, 1980. Patti, a former OSS officer, describes U.S.–Vietnamese cooperation during World War II.

2429. Thorne, Christopher. "Indochina and Anglo–American Relations, 1942–1945." *Pacific Historical Review* 45 (Feb. 1976): 73–96.

2430. U.S. Senate. Committee on Foreign Relations. *The United States and Vietnam: 1944–1947.* Staff Study no. 2. 92d Cong., 2d sess., Apr. 3, 1972. [based on the *Pentagon Papers*]

2431. White, David H. "American Soldiers and the Franco–Viet Minh Struggle in Indo-China, 1945." *Proceedings of the French Colonial Historical Society* 1 (1975): 108–115.

Eisenhower Years, 1953–1960

For Eisenhower's public presidential papers, see (134); the Pentagon Papers *(130–132) will also have pertinent documents. See also Chapter 3, "Geneva Accords, 1954."*

2432. Branyan, Robert L., and Lawrence Larsen. *The Eisenhower Administration, 1953–1961: A Documentary History.* 2 vols. New York: Random House, 1971. This is a valuable work on general foreign policy.

2433. Vexler, Robert I., ed. *Dwight D. Eisenhower, 1890–1969: Chronology, Documents, Bibliographical Aids.* Dobbs Ferry, NY: Oceana, 1970.

PERSONALITIES AND POLICIES

John Foster Dulles

2434. Beal, John R. *John Foster Dulles: A Biography.* New York: Harper, 1957.

2435. Berding, Andrew. *Dulles on Diplomacy.* Princeton, NJ: Van Nostrand, 1965. This work is important for understanding Dulles's views.

2436. Drummond, R., and C. Coblentz. *Duel at the Brink: John Foster Dulles' Command of American Power.* New York: Doubleday, 1960.

2437. Gerson, Louis. *John Foster Dulles.* New York: Cooper Square, 1967.

2438. Goold-Adams, Richard. *John Foster Dulles: A Reappraisal.* New York: Appleton-Century-Crofts, 1962. This is a good survey of the Dulles period.

2439. Guchin, Michael A. *John Foster Dulles: A Statesman and His Times.* New York: Columbia University Press, 1972.

2440. Hostetter, John H. "John Foster Dulles and the French Defeat in Indochina." Ph.D. dissertation, Rutgers University, 1972.

2441. Jones, Henry P. "John Foster Dulles and United States Involvement in Vietnam." Ph.D. dissertation, University of Oklahoma, 1972.

2442. Ladenburger, John F. "The Philosophy of International Politics of John Foster Dulles, 1919–1952." Ph.D. dissertation, University of Connecticut, 1969.

Dwight D. Eisenhower

2443. Albertson, Dean. *Eisenhower as President.* New York: Hill & Wang, 1963.

2444. Capitanchik, David B. *The Eisenhower Presidency and American Foreign Policy.* London: Routledge & Paul, 1969.

2445. Donovan, Robert J. *Eisenhower: The Inside Story.* New York: Harper, 1956.

2446. Eisenhower, Dwight D. *The White House Years: Mandate for Change, 1953–1956.* New York: Doubleday, 1963.

2447. _____. *The White House Years: Waging Peace, 1956–1961.* New York: Doubleday, 1965.

2448. Hughes, Emmet John. *The Ordeal of Power: A Political Memoir of the Eisenhower Years.* New York: Atheneum, 1963.

2449. Larson, Arthur. *Eisenhower: The President Nobody Knew.* New York: Scribner's, 1968.

2450. Parmet, Herbert S. *Eisenhower and the American Crusades.* New York: Macmillan, 1972. Parmet revises the picture of the U.S. role in the 1954 crisis.

Others

2451. Robertson, W.S. "Progress in Free Viet-Nam." *U.S. Department of State Bulletin* 34 (June 11, 1956): 972–974.

2452. Taylor, Maxwell D. *The Uncertain Trumpet.* New York: Harper, 1959. More on Taylor can be found below in this chapter, under "Johnson Years, 1964–1978."

POLITICS

Particularly valuable, although dated, is Bator (2453). See also Chapter 3, under "Michigan State University Project."

2453. Bator, Victor. *Vietnam: A Diplomatic Tragedy.* Dobbs Ferry, NY: Oceana, 1965. [covers 1953 to 1956]

2454. Corley, Francis J. "Vietnam Since Geneva." *Fordham University Quarterly* 33 (Winter 1958–1959): 515–568.

2455. Crozier, Brian. "Indo-China: The Unfinished Struggle." *World Today* [London] 12 (Dec. 1956): 17–26.

2456. _____. "The International Situation in Indochina." *Pacific Affairs* 29 (Dec. 1956): 309–323.

2457. Do Vang Ly. "The Emergency of Vietnam." *Foreign Affairs Reports* 7 (Jan. 1958): 1–19.

2458. Dunn, William B. *American Policy and Vietnamese Nationalism, 1950–1954.* Chicago: University of Chicago Press, 1960.

2459. _____. "How the West Could Win Vietnam's Support." *Foreign Policy Bulletin* 33 (May 15, 1954): 1–2.

2460. Ennis, Thomas E. "Vietnam: Our Outpost in Asia." *Current History* 31 (July 1956): 33–38.

2461. "Interview with General Nathan F. Twining." *U.S. News and World Report* 35 (Dec. 25, 1953): 40–45.

2462. Jumper, Roy. "The Communist Challenge to South Vietnam." *Far Eastern Survey* 25 (Nov. 1956): 161–168.

2463. Karpikhim, A. "The United States Takes Over in South Viet-Nam." *International Affairs* [Moscow] 2 (Apr. 1956): 83–91.

2464. MacAllister, Robert J. "The Great Gamble: United States Policy Toward South Viet Nam from July, 1954, to July, 1956." Ph.D. dissertation, University of Chicago, 1958.

2465. Ridgway, Matthew B. "My Battles in War and Peace." *Saturday Evening Post* 229 (Jan. 21, 1956): 17–19, 46–48.

2466. _____. *Soldier: The Memoirs of Matthew B. Ridgway.* New York: Harper, 1956.

2467. _____, and Harold H. Martin. "A 1956 Warning on Land War in Asia." *U.S. News and World Report* 60 (Jan. 3, 1966): 32–34.

1954 INCIDENT

During the battle for Diem Bien Phu, Dulles and Nixon raised the question of U.S. military intervention.

2468. Childs, Marquis. *The Ragged Edge: The Diary of a Crisis.* New York: Doubleday, 1955.

2469. "Intervention in Indo-China: Radford Knows What He Wants, But Will His Policy Work?" *New Republic* 130 (June 14, 1954): 3–7.

2470. Kennedy, John F. "What Should the U.S. Do in Indo-China?" *Foreign Policy Bulletin* 33 (May 15, 1954): 4, 6.

2471. Roberts, Chalmers H. "The Day We Didn't Go to War." *Reporter* 11 (Sept. 14, 1954): 31–35.

2472. Shepley, James. "How Dulles Averted War." *Life* 40 (Jan. 16, 1956): 70–80.

Kennedy Years, 1961–1963

For Kennedy's public presidential papers, see (134); see also the Pentagon Papers *(130–132) for additional pertinent documents.*

2473. *The Kennedy Presidential Press Conferences.* Introduction by David Halberstam. New York: Coleman, 1978. These press conferences contain many references to Vietnam.

PERSONALITIES AND POLICIES

Materials on personalities have been grouped by individuals.

Roger Hilsman

2474. Greenfield, M. "The Kiss and Tell Memoirs." *Reporter* 37 (Nov. 30, 1967): 14–20. Greenfield reviews Hilsman's memoirs.

2475. Hilsman, Roger. *To Move a Nation: The Politics of Foreign Policy in the Administration of John F. Kennedy.* New York: Doubleday, 1967. Hilsman provides valuable information on counterinsurgency planning and anti-Diem attitudes.

John F. Kennedy

2476. Beck, Kent M. "The Kennedy Image: Politics, Camelot, and Vietnam." *Wisconsin Magazine of History* 58 (Autumn 1974): 45–55.

2477. Blair, Joan, and Clay Blair, Jr. *The Search for J.F.K.* New York: Putnam's, 1976. The authors give a personality study of Kennedy.

2478. Galbraith, John Kenneth. *Ambassador's Journal: A Personal Account of the Kennedy Years.* Boston: Houghton Mifflin, 1969. Galbraith includes letters to JFK about Vietnam policy.

2479. Galloway, John, ed. *The Kennedys and Vietnam.* New York: Facts on File, 1971. [addresses John F. Kennedy, Robert F. Kennedy and Edward M. Kennedy]

2480. Hurley, R.M. *President John F. Kennedy and Vietnam, 1961–1963.* Ph.D. dissertation, University of Hawaii, 1970.

2481. Jeffries, Jean. "Why Vietnam is Kennedy's War." *National Review* 20 (Apr. 23, 1968): 396–397, 411.

2482. Kennedy, John F. "America's Stake in Vietnam." *Vital Speeches* 22 (Aug. 1, 1956): 617–619.

2483. _____. *The Strategy of Peace.* New York: Harper, 1960.

2484. Nurse, Ronald J. "America Must Not Sleep: The Development of John F. Kennedy's Foreign Policy Attitudes, 1947–1960." Ph.D. dissertation, Michigan State University, 1971.

2485. Schlesinger, Arthur M., Jr. *A Thousand Days: John F. Kennedy in the White House.* Boston: Houghton Mifflin, 1965.

2486. Sorensen, Theodore C. *Kennedy.* New York: Harper & Row, 1965.

2487. Stavins, Ralph. "Kennedy's Private War." *New York Review of Books* (July 22, 1971): 20ff.

2488. Walton, Richard J. *Cold War and Counter-Revolution: The Foreign Policy of John F. Kennedy.* New York: Viking Press, 1972.

2489. Wicker, Tom. *JFK and LBJ: The Influence of Personality Upon Politics.* New York: William Morrow, 1968.

Adlai E. Stevenson

2490. Johnson, Walter, ed. *The Papers of Adlai E. Stevenson.* 8 vols. Boston: Little, Brown, 1972– .

2491. Martin, John B. *The Life of Adlai E. Stevenson.* 2 vols. Garden City, NY: Doubleday, 1976–1977. The second volume is important for the JFK and LBJ years.

Others

2492. Bowles, Chester. *Promises to Keep.* New York: Harper & Row, 1971.

2493. Heavner, T.J.C. "The Viet-Nam Situation." *U.S. Department of State Bulletin* 49 (Sept. 9, 1963): 393–398.

2494. Mecklin, John. *Mission in Torment: An Intimate Account of the U.S. Role in Vietnam.* New York: Doubleday, 1965. Mecklin paints a vivid picture of the turmoil in the U.S. embassy in Saigon.

2495. Rusk, Dean. "The Stake in Viet-Nam." *U.S. Department of State Bulletin* 48 (May 13, 1963): 727–735. For more on Rusk, see in this chapter the "Johnson Years, 1964–1968."

POLITICS

2496. Bainton, R.H., et al. "An Open Letter to President John F. Kennedy." *Minority of One* 4 (June 1962): 7.

2497. Barber, Sandra P. "A Role Simulation: Escalation of U.S. Troop Commitment in Vietnam, October 1961." *Teaching Political Science* 5 (July 1978): 405–420.

2498. Black, Edwin F. "The Master Plan for Conquest in Vietnam." *Military Review* 43 (June 1963): 51–57. The title refers to Hanoi's plans.

2499. Buchan, Alastair. "Questions About Vietnam." *Encounter* [Great Britain] 30 (Jan. 1968): 3–12.

2500. Burrows, Larry. "Stark Color of the Vicious Struggle in Vietnam: We Wade Deeper into Jungle War." *Life* 54 (Jan. 25, 1963): 22–30.

2501. Chaffard, Georges. "Peace Through Neutrality." *Atlas* 6 (Nov. 1963): 289–291.

2502. Cook, H.C.B. "The Situation in Vietnam." *Royal United Service Institution Journal* 107 (Aug. 1962): 220–229.

2503. Deane, Hugh. *The War in Vietnam.* New York: Monthly Review Press, 1963.

2504. Edwards, Theodore. "Kennedy's War in Vietnam." *International Socialist Review* 24 (Summer 1963): 84–87.

2505. Elegant, Robert S. "The Task in Vietnam." *New Leader* 46 (Nov. 25, 1963): 5–7.

2506. Goshal, Kumar. "War in South Vietnam." *New World Review* 31 (Oct. 1963): 8–14.

2507. Kearney, V.S., and F.J. Buckley. "Vietnam Dilemma." *America* 109 (Sept. 7, 1963): 237–240.

2508. Kristol, Irving. "Facing the Facts in Vietnam." *New Leader* 46 (Sept. 30, 1963): 7–8.

2509. Ngo Dinh Thuc. "What's Really Going on in Vietnam." *National Review* 15 (Nov. 5, 1963): 388–390.

2510. Orshefsky, M. "Despite Battlefield Setbacks There Is Hope—*With Caution.*" *Life* 54 (Jan. 25, 1963): 31–32.

2511. Osmanski, R.A. "Report on Viet Nam." *Army* 14 (Dec. 1963): 56ff.

2512. Quillot, R. "Vietnamese Powder Keg." *Atlas* 5 (Mar. 1963): 158–160.

2513. Rose, Jerry A. "Dead End in Vietnam: We Can't Win, But We Need Not Lose." *New Republic* 149 (Oct. 12, 1963): 15–18.

2514. Schecter, J.L. "Bitter Harvest in Vietnam." *Progressive* 27 (Oct. 1963): 10–15.

2515. Scigliano, Robert. "Vietnam: A Country at War." *Asian Survey* 3 (Jan. 1963): 48–54.

2516. Simpson, Howard R. "A Dirty Dangerous Business." *Foreign Service Journal* 40 (Apr. 1963): 46–50.

2517. "U.S. Imperialism and Vietnam." *Political Affairs* 42 (Nov. 1963): 1–7.

2518. Vernon, Hilda. "Vietnam: U.S. Guilt and Dilemma." *Labour Monthly* 45 (Nov. 1963): 515–518.

2519. Warner, Denis. "The Many-Fronted War in South Vietnam." *Reporter* 27 (Sept. 13, 1962): 33–35.

2520. Worthington, Peter. "Vietnam: School for U.S. Guerrillas." *Nation* 196 (Mar. 2, 1963): 179–180.

Johnson Years, 1964–1968

For Johnson's public presidential papers, see (134); see also the Pentagon Papers *(130–132) for additional pertinent documents.*

2521. *The Johnson Presidential Press Conferences.* 2 vols. Introduction by Doris Kearns Goodwin. New York: Coleman, 1978. These press conferences contain many references to Vietnam.

PERSONALITIES AND POLICIES

For convenience, we have grouped materials by and about major personalities in this section.

George W. Ball

2522. Ball, George W. "The Issue in Viet-Nam." *U.S. Department of State Bulletin* 54 (Feb. 14, 1966): 239–246.

2523. _____. "Top Secret: The Prophecy the President Rejected [in 1964]." *Atlantic* 230:1 (July 1972): 35–49. LBJ often referred to Ball as "our Dove."

2524. _____. "We Should De-Escalate the Importance of Vietnam." *New York Times Magazine* (Dec. 21, 1969): 6–7ff.

McGeorge Bundy

2525. Brandon, Henry. "State of Affairs: Bundy and Beyond." *Saturday Review* 49 (Jan. 22, 1966): 18.

2526. Frankel, Max. "The Importance of Being Bundy." *New York Times Magazine* (Mar. 28, 1965): 32–33.

2527. Kraft, Joseph. "The Two Worlds of McGeorge Bundy." *Harper's* 231 (Nov. 1965): 106–118.

2528. Morgenthau, Hans J. "Bundy's Doctrine of War Without End." *New Republic* 159 (Nov. 2, 1968): 18–20.

Clark Clifford

2529. Anderson, P. "Clark Clifford 'Sounds and Alarm.'" *New York Times Magazine* (Aug. 8, 1971): 8ff.

2530. Clifford, Clark M. "Set a Date in Vietnam: Stick to It. Get Out." *Life* 68 (May 22, 1970): 34–38.

2531. _____. "A Viet Nam Appraisal: The Personal History of One Man's View and How It Evolved." *Foreign Affairs* 47 (July 1969): 601–622.

2532. U.S. Senate. Committee on Armed Services. Hearings; *Nomination of Clark M. Clifford to Be Secretary of Defense*. 90th Cong., 2d sess., Jan. 25, 1968.

Hubert Humphrey

2533. Cousins, Norman. "Journeys With Humphrey: Memoir of a Mission That Failed." *Saturday Review* 61 (Mar. 4, 1978): 10–18.

2534. Engelmayer, Sheldon D., and Robert J. Wagman, eds. *Hubert Humphrey: The Man and His Dreams*. New York: Methuen, 1978.

2535. Humphrey, Hubert. "United States Tasks and Responsibilities in Asia." *U.S. Department of State Bulletin* 55 (Apr. 4, 1966): 523–528.

2536. Wechsler, J.A. "Humphrey At War With Himself." *Progressive* 19 (July 1966): 10–13.

Lyndon B. Johnson

2537. Bradley, George L. "A Critical Analysis of Lyndon Johnson's Peace Rhetoric, 1963–1969." Ph.D. dissertation, University of Kansas, 1974.

2538. Casey, Francis M. "The Vietnam Policy of Lyndon Baines Johnson in Response to the Theory of the Protracted Conflict as Applied in the Politics of Indochina: A Case Study of Threat Perception and Assessment in the Crisis Management Process of a Pluralistic Society." Ph.D. dissertation, Claremont Graduate School, 1976.

2539. Deakin, James. *LBJ's Credibility Gap*. Washington, DC: Public Affairs Press, 1968.

2540. Evans, Rowland, and Robert Novak. *Lyndon B. Johnson: The Exercise of Power*. New York: New American Library, 1966.

2541. Fairlie, Henry. "Johnson and the Intellectuals: A British View." *Commentary* 40 (Oct. 1965): 49–55.

2542. Geyelin, Philip. *Lyndon B. Johnson and the World*. New York: Praeger, 1966.

2543. Goldman, Eric F. *The Tragedy of Lyndon Johnson*. New York: Knopf, 1969.

2544. _____. "The Wrong Man From the Wrong Place at the Wrong Time Who May Live in History." *New York Times Magazine* (Jan. 5, 1969): 24ff.

2545. Graff, Henry F. "How Johnson Makes Foreign Policy." *New York Times Magazine* (July 4, 1965): 4ff.

2546. _____. *The Tuesday Cabinet: Deliberation and Decision on Peace and War under Lyndon B. Johnson*. Englewood Cliffs, NJ: Prentice-Hall, 1970. Graff relates personal conversations with Johnson and top officials, 1965–1968.

2547. Grice, George L. "We Are a People of Peace, But . . . : A Rhetorical Study of President Lyndon B. Johnson's Statements on United States Military Involvement in Vietnam." Ph.D. dissertation, University of Texas at Austin, 1976.

2548. Hayes, James T. "Lyndon Baines Johnson's Public Defense of the Vietnam War, 1964–1969: The Evolution of a Rhetorical Position." Ph.D. dissertation, University of Wisconsin, Madison, 1975.

2549. Heren, Louis. *No Hail, No Farewell*. New York: Harper & Row, 1970.

2550. Johnson, Gerald W. "The Superfluity of L.B.J." *American Scholar* 37 (Spring 1968): 221–226.

2551. Johnson, Lyndon B. "Answering Aggression in Viet-Nam." *U.S. Department of State Bulletin* 57 (Oct. 23, 1967): 519–522.

2552. _____. "The Defense of Viet-Nam: Key to the Future of Free Asia." *U.S. Department of State Bulletin* 56 (Apr. 3, 1967): 534–539.

2553. _____. "Lyndon Johnson Discusses With Walter Cronkite of CBS News, His Decision to Halt the Bombing of North Vietnam and Withdraw From the Presidential Election." *Listener* 83 (Feb. 12, 1970): 210–212.

2554. _____. "Our Objective in Vietnam." *U.S. Department of State Bulletin* 55 (Sept. 12, 1966): 368–371.

2555. _____. "Pattern for Peace in Southeast Asia." *U.S. Department of State Bulletin* 52 (Apr. 26, 1965): 606–610.

2556. _____. "The U.S. Commitment to Peace—A Shield for Threatened Nations." *U.S. Department of State Bulletin* 57 (Dec. 25, 1967): 851–854.

2557. _____. "United States Takes Measures to Repel Attack Against U.S. Forces in Southeast Asia." *U.S. Department of State Bulletin* 51 (Aug. 24, 1964): 272–281.

2558. _____. *The Vantage Point: Perspectives of the Presidency, 1963–1969*. New York: Holt, Rinehart & Winston, 1971. Although dull, this work is essential for an understanding of the period; among the review essays on this work, see "LBJ's The Vantage Point." *Social Science Quarterly* 53 (Sept. 1972): 394–416.

2559. _____. "Viet-Nam: The Struggle to be Free." *U.S. Department of State Bulletin* 54 (Mar. 14, 1966): 390–396.

2560. _____. "Viet-Nam: The Third Face of War." *U.S. Department of State Bulletin* 52 (May 31, 1965): 838–841.

2561. _____. "The Vietnam War: The Objectives of the United States." *Vital Speeches* 34 (Sept. 15, 1968): 712–716.

2562. _____. "We Will Stand in Viet-Nam." *U.S. Department of State Bulletin* 53 (Aug. 16, 1965): 262–265.

2563. _____. "Why We Are in Vietnam." *U.S. News and World Report* 63 (Oct. 16, 1967): 80–82.

2564. Johnson, Sam H. *My Brother, Lyndon*. New York: Cowles, 1971.

2565. Joseph, Paul I. "March 1968: A Study of Vietnam Decision-Making." Ph.D. dissertation, University of California, Berkeley, 1975. Joseph describes the events which influenced LBJ's March 31, 1968, speech withdrawing from the presidential race.

2566. Kearns, Doris. *Lyndon Johnson and the American Dream*. New York: Harper & Row, 1976. Kearns provides an extremely valuable insight into LBJ's personality and values.

2567. _____. "Lyndon Johnson's Political Personality." *Political Science Quarterly* 91 (Fall 1976): 385–410.

2568. King, Larry L. "Machismo In the White House: L.B.J. and Vietnam." *American Heritage* 27 (May 1976): 98–101. King contends that the Kennedy White House group was also big on machismo.

2569. Miller, Lawrence W., and Lee Sigelman. "Is the Audience the Message? A Note on LBJ's Vietnam Statements." *Public Opinion Quarterly* 42 (Spring 1978): 71–80.

2570. Mutnick, Jeffery. "American Intervention in Vietnam: The Public Image Presented by Lyndon Baines Johnson." Ph.D. dissertation, Indiana University, 1978.

2571. Partney, Gerald D. "Lyndon Johnson's Speaking on the Vietnam War: Argumentative Appeals and Rhetorical Strategies." Ph.D. dissertation, University of Iowa, 1975.

2572. Pryor, Bernard B. "Role and Perception: A Case Study of a President's Use of the Concept of Democracy as the Rationale for the Conduct of War in Vietnam." Ph.D. dissertation, Claremont Graduate School, 1975.

2573. Robert, Charles. "Inside Story: L.B.J.'s Switch on Vietnam." *Newsweek* 73 (Mar. 10, 1969): 31–33.

2574. _____. *LBJ's Inner Circle*. New York: Delacorte Press, 1965.

2574a. Schandler, Herbert Y. *The Unmaking of a President: Lyndon Johnson and Vietnam*. Princeton, NJ: Princeton University Press, 1977. An excellent book, it focuses on the decisions of March 1968.

2575. Sherril, Robert. *The Accidental President*. New York: Grossman, 1967.

2576. Sidey, Hugh. *A Very Personal Presidency: LBJ in the White House*. New York: Atheneum, 1968.

2577. Sigelman, Lee. "The Commander in Chief and the Public: Mass Response to Johnson's March 31, 1968 Bombing Halt Speech." *Journal of Political and Military Sociology* 8 (Spring 1980): 1–14.

2578. Sproule, James M. "The Case for a Wider War: A Study of the Administration Rationale for Commitment to Vietnam, 1964–1967." Ph.D. dissertation, Ohio State University, 1973.

2579. Steinburg, Alfred. *Sam Johnson's Boy: A Close-up of the President from Texas*. New York: Macmillan, 1968.

2580. Turner, Kathleen J. "The Effects of Presidential–Press Interaction on Lyndon B. Johnson's Vietnam

War Rhetoric." Ph.D. dissertation, Purdue University, 1978.

2581. Valenti, Jack. *A Very Human President.* New York: W.W. Norton, 1975.

2582. Wolfenstein, E. Victor. "The Two Wars of Lyndon Johnson." *Politics and Society* 4:3 (1974): 357–396.

2583. Workman, Randall H. "Lyndon B. Johnson and Vietnam: The Rhetorical Influence of Presidential Power." Ph.D. dissertation, Indiana University, 1978.

Henry Cabot Lodge, Jr.

2584. Lodge, Henry Cabot. "Ambassador Lodge Discusses Viet-Nam in New York Times Interview." *U.S. Department of State Bulletin* 56 (May 22, 1967): 795–800.

2585. _____. *As It Was: An Inside View of Politics and Power in the '50s and '60s.* New York: W.W. Norton, 1976.

2586. _____. "How the World's Hottest Spot Looks to Me." *Life* 56 (Apr. 17, 1964): 38D–38F.

2587. _____. "If We Are Persistent, the Outlook Is Good: Ambassador Lodge Reports on Southeast Asia." *Army* 15 (Aug. 1964): 80–81.

2588. _____. *The Storm Has Many Eyes: A Personal Narrative.* New York: W.W. Norton, 1973. [sketchy and apologetic]

Robert S. McNamara

2589. Burnham, James. "McNamara's Non-War." *National Review* 19 (Sept. 19, 1967): 1012–1014.

2590. McNamara, Robert S. "Secretary McNamara Discusses Buildup of Forces in Vietnam." *U.S. Department of State Bulletin* 53 (July 5, 1965): 12–19.

2591. _____. "South Vietnam: The United States Policy." *Vital Speeches* 30 (Apr. 15, 1964): 394–399.

2592. Roherty, James M. *Decisions of Robert S. McNamara: A Study of the Role of the Secretary of Defense.* Coral Gables, FL: University of Miami Press, 1970.

2593. Trewhitt, Henry L. *McNamara: His Ordeal in the Pentagon.* New York: Harper & Row, 1971.

2594. Wicker, Tom. "The Awesome Twosome." *New York Times Magazine* (Jan. 30, 1966): 8ff. Wicker focuses on Lyndon Johnson and Robert McNamara.

Walt W. Rostow

2595. Rostow, Walt W. "Dangers That Remain in the Vietnam War." *U.S. News and World Report* 71 (Nov. 8, 1971): 80–85.

2596. _____. *Diffusion of Power.* New York: Macmillan, 1972.

2597. _____. "Why We Should Not Abandon Our Role in Asia." *Congressional Record* 116 (June 30, 1970): S10244–S10246.

2598. _____. "Will We Snatch Defeat from the Jaws of Victory?" *Naval War College Review* 24 (Sept. 1971): 3–18.

Dean Rusk

2598a. Cohen, Warren I. *Dean Rusk.* Totowa, N.J.: Cooper Square, 1980.

2599. Forte, David F. "The Policies and Principles of Dean Rusk." Ph.D. dissertation, University of Toronto, 1974.

2600. Frankel, Max. "The President's 'Just-a-Minute' Man." *New York Times Magazine* (Sept. 12, 1965): 48–49.

2601. Henry, John B., II., and William Espinosa. "The Tragedy of Dean Rusk." *Foreign Policy*, no. 8 (Fall 1971): 166–189.

2602. Kraft, Joseph. "Washington Insight: The Enigma of Dean Rusk." *Harper's* 236 (July 1965): 100–103.

2603. Rusk, Dean. "Background of U.S. Policy in Southeast Asia." *U.S. Department of State Bulletin* 54 (May 30, 1966): 830–834.

2604. _____. "Communist Aggression: Vietnam." *Vital Speeches* 35 (Oct. 15. 1968): 2–6.

2605. _____. "Firmness and Restraint in Viet-Nam." *U.S. Department of State Bulletin* 57 (Nov. 27, 1967): 703–705.

2606. _____. *The Heart of the Problem: Secretary Rusk and General Taylor Review Viet-Nam Policy in Senate Hearings.* Washington, DC: GPO, 1966.

2607. _____. "Keeping Our Commitment to Peace." *U.S. Department of State Bulletin* 54 (Apr. 4, 1966): 514–521.

2608. _____. "Secretary Rusk Discusses Viet-Nam Situation on 'Face the Nation' Program." *U.S. Department of State Bulletin* 52 (Mar. 29, 1965): 442–448.

2609. _____. "Secretary Rusk Redefines United States

Policy on Vietnam for Student Leaders." *U.S. Department of State Bulletin* 56 (Jan. 23, 1967): 133–136.

2610. _____. "Secretary Rusk Reviews Efforts to Reach Peaceful Settlement in Southeast Asia." *U.S. Department of State Bulletin* 53 (July 5, 1965): 5–12.

2611. _____, and R.S. McNamara. "Political and Military Aspects of U.S. Policy in Vietnam." *U.S. Department of State Bulletin* 53 (Aug. 30, 1965): 342–356.

2612. Rusk Dean, and Maxwell D. Taylor. "The U.S. Commitment in Viet-Nam: Fundamental Issues." *U.S. Department of State Bulletin* 54 (Mar. 7, 1966): 346–362.

2613. _____. "Viet-Nam: Four Steps to Peace." *U.S. Department of State Bulletin* 53 (July 12, 1965): 50–55.

2614. Rusk, Dean, et al. "Viet-Nam: Winning the Peace." *U.S. Department of State Bulletin* 53 (Sept. 13, 1965): 431–444.

2615. "Rusk vs Senators: The War Explained." *U.S. News and World Report* 64 (Mar. 25, 1968): 74–78.

2616. Stupak, Ronald J. "Dean Rusk on International Relations: An Analysis of His Philosophical Perceptions." *Australian Outlook* 25 (Apr. 1971): 13–28.

Maxwell D. Taylor

2617. Taylor, Maxwell D. "The Cause in Vietnam Is Being Won." *New York Times Magazine* (Oct. 15, 1967): 36–37.

2618. _____. "Lessons of Vietnam." *U.S. News and World Report* 73 (Nov. 27, 1972): 22–26.

2619. _____. *Swords and Plowshares*. New York: W.W. Norton, 1972. [a detailed memoir]

2620. Warner, Denis. "Vietnam: General Taylor Faces an All-Out War." *Reporter* 31 (Aug. 13, 1964): 50–53.

Others

2621. Bundy, William P. "American Policy in South Vietnam and Southeast Asia." *U.S. Department of State Bulletin* 52 (Feb. 8, 1965): 168–175.

2622. _____. "The Path to Vietnam: A Lesson in Involvement." *U.S. Department of State Bulletin* 57 (Sept. 4, 1967): 275–287.

2623. _____. "The Path to Vietnam: Ten Decisions." *Orbis* 11 (Fall 1967): 647–663.

2624. _____. "A Perspective on U.S. Policy in Vietnam." *U.S. Department of State Bulletin* 52 (June 21, 1965): 1001–1005.

2625. _____. "Reality and Myth Concerning South Viet Nam." *U.S. Department of State Bulletin* 52 (June 7, 1965): 890–896.

2626. _____. "Why U.S. Is in Vietnam: An Official Explanation." *U.S. News and World Report* 63 (Dec. 18, 1967): 48–49.

2627. Bunker, Ellsworth. "Report on Vietnam." *U.S. Department of State Bulletin* 57 (Dec. 11, 1967): 781–784.

2628. Christian, George. *The President Steps Down: A Personal Memoir of the Transfer of Power*. New York: Macmillan, 1970. Christian was a presidential assistant.

2629. Eder, Richard. "A Quiet American Goes to Vietnam." *New York Times Magazine* (Mar. 26, 1967): 28ff. The title refers to Ellsworth Bunker.

2630. Goldberg, Arthur J. "The Search for Peace." *Thought* [Fordham University Quarterly] 41:160 (1966): 45–51.

2631. _____. "United States Peace Aims in Viet-Nam." *U.S. Department of State Bulletin* 56 (Feb. 27, 1967): 310–316.

2632. Graff, Henry F. "Teach-In on Vietnam by . . . the President, the Secretary of State, the Secretary of Defense and the Under-Secretary of State." *New York Times Magazine* (Mar. 20, 1966): 25.

2633. Grant, Donald. "Goldberg's Dilemma." *Progressive* 30 (July 1966): 22–24. The dilemma is whether to leave the Supreme Court to go to the U.N.

2634. Johnson, Harold K. "The Defense of Freedom in Viet-Nam." *U.S. Department of State Bulletin* 52 (Feb. 8, 1965): 176–180. Johnson was the chief of JCS.

2635. _____. "End of Vietnam War in Sight?" *U.S. News and World Report* 63 (Sept. 11, 1967): 44–48.

2636. Johnson, U. Alexis. "The Issues and Goal in Vietnam." *U.S. Department of State Bulletin* 54 (Apr. 4, 1966): 529–536.

2637. Katzenbach, Nicholas. "The Complex and Difficult Problems in Vietnam." *U.S. Department of State Bulletin* 57 (Nov. 6, 1967): 602–604.

2638. _____. "Vietnam and the Independence of Southeast Asia." *U.S. Department of State Bulletin* 58 (Feb. 12, 1968): 201–205.

2639. MacArthur, Douglas, II. "The Free World Stake in Viet-Nam." *U.S. Department of State Bulletin* 55 (Nov. 14, 1966): 745–750.

2640. Moyers, Bill D. "One Thing We Learned in Vietnam." *Foreign Affairs* 46 (July 1968): 657–664.

2641. Rostow, Eugene V. "A Certain Restlessness About Viet-Nam." *U.S. Department of State Bulletin* 58 (Mar. 25, 1968): 405–416.

POLITICS

Books and Dissertations

2642. Gavin, James M. *Crisis Now*. New York: Random House, 1968.

2643. Hoopes, Townsend. *The Limits of Intervention: An Inside Account of How the Johnson Policy of Escalation in Vietnam Was Reversed*. rev. ed. New York: McKay, 1973.

2644. Milstein, Jeffrey S. "The Escalation of the Vietnam War, 1965–1967: A Quantitative Analysis and Predictive Computer Simulation." Ph.D. dissertation, Stanford University, 1970.

2645. Roberts, Charles W. *LBJ's Inner Circle*. New York: Delacorte Press, 1965.

2646. Rovere, Richard. *Waist Deep in the Big Muddy: Personal Reflections on 1968*. Boston: Little, Brown, 1968. The title refers to the "Quagmire thesis."

Essays

2647. Armstrong, Hamilton Fish. "Power in a Sieve." *Foreign Affairs*. 46 (Apr. 1968): 467–475.

2648. Ashmore, Harry, et al. "Vietnam: Matters for the Agenda." *A Center Occasional Paper* [Center for the Study of Democratic Institutions, Santa Barbara, CA] 1 (June 1968): 2–62.

2649. Baldwin, Hanson W. "The Case for Escalation." *New York Times Magazine* (Feb. 27, 1966): 22, 79–82.

2650. _____. "The Case for Mobilization." *Reporter* 34 (May 19, 1966): 20–33.

2651. _____. "We Must Choose: (1) 'Bug-Out' (2) Negotiate (3) Fight." *New York Times Magazine* (Feb. 21, 1965): 9.

2652. _____. "What We Must Do To Win in Asia." *Reader's Digest* 87 (Nov. 1965): 111–116.

2653. _____. "Why Not Blockade North Vietnam?" *Reader's Digest* 88 (Mar. 1966): 58–62.

2654. Basich, Thomas. "Vietnam: The Confusion and the Commitment." *Dialog* 6 (Winter 1967): 34–43.

2655. Brogan, Dennis W. "Naiveté versus Reality in Vietnam." *Atlantic Monthly* 220 (July 1967): 48–55.

2656. Carthew, A. "Vietnam Is Like an Oriental Western." *New York Times Magazine* (Jan. 23, 1966); 8ff.

2657. Clifford, J.W. "Some Fallacies about the Vietnam War." *Catholic World* 203 (Sept. 1966): 361–364.

2658. Critchfield, Richard. "Lessons of Vietnam." *Annals of the American Academy of Political and Social Science* 380 (Nov. 1968): 125–134.

2659. Cutrona, Joseph F.H. "Peace in Vietnam: An Acceptable Solution." *Military Review* 46 (Nov. 1966): 60–68.

2660. Elegant, Robert S. "Vietnam: An American Tragedy." *New Leader* 47 (Sept. 28, 1964): 5–7.

2661. Elston, G.A. "Vietnam: Some Basic Considerations." *Catholic World* 205 (May 1967): 78–82.

2662. "The Emerging Victory in Asia." *Fortune* 74 (Aug. 1966): 97ff. This article describes LBJ's optimistism about victory in Vietnam.

2663. Fairbanks, H.G. "Facing Hard Facts in Vietnam." *Catholic World* 199 (May 1964): 891–895.

2664. Fall, Bernard B. "If Ho Chi Minh's Army Moves South in Force—." *New York Times Magazine* (Sept. 5, 1965): 7ff.

2665. _____. "Our Options in Vietnam." *Reporter* 30 (Mar. 12, 1964): 17–22.

2666. _____. "Vietnam: The Agonizing Reappraisal." *Current History* 48 (Feb. 1965): 95–102, 166.

2667. _____. "Vietnam in the Balance." *Foreign Affairs* 45 (Oct. 1966): 1–18.

2668. _____. "The Year of the Hawks." *New York Times Magazine* (Dec. 12, 1965): 46.

2669. Fishel, Wesley R. "The Eleventh Hour in Vietnam." *Asian Survey* 5 (Feb. 1965): 98–107.

2670. _____. "The U.S. and Vietnam." *United Asia* [India] 17 (Nov.–Dec. 1965): 374–384.

2671. _____. "Vietnam: The Broadening War." *Asian Survey* 6 (Jan. 1966): 49–58.

2672. Ford, D.F. "Misadventure in Vietnam: 'The Only War We've Got.'" *Nation* 199 (Aug. 24, 1964): 66–68.

2673. _____. "With the 'Redskins' in Vietnam." *Nation* 199 (July 27, 1964): 29–31. The title employs the U.S. slang for Montagnards.

2674. Gange, John. "Misadventure in Vietnam: The Mix of Fact and Truth." *Nation* 199 (Aug. 24, 1964): 63–66.

2675. Gavin, James M. "We Can Get Out of Vietnam."

Saturday Evening Post 241 (Feb. 24, 1968): 23–25. Gavin describes the enclave concept.

2676.   Gilpatric, R.L. "Will Vietnam Lead to World War III?" *New York Times Magazine* (May 30, 1965): 11.

2677.   Graham, Dominick. "Vietnam and the Crisis in War." *Yale Review* 55 (June 1966): 391–402.

2678.   Grant, Donald. "Vietnam: Alternative to Disaster." *Nation* 198 (May 25, 1964): 521–523.

2679.   Harries, Owen. "Should the U.S. Withdraw from Asia?" *Foreign Affairs* 47 (Oct. 1968): 15–25.

2680.   Harrigan, Anthony. "We Can Win in Southeast Asia." *National Review* 17 (Mar. 9, 1965): 187–188.

2681.   Head, Simon. "LBJ's Vietnam Options." *Far Eastern Economic Review* 58 (Oct. 26, 1967): 182–188.

2682.   Heller, Walter W. "Getting Ready For Peace." *Harper's* 236 (Apr. 1968): 57–62. Heller gives an economist's view of the impact of the Vietnam War.

2683.   Hilsman, Roger. "Must We Invade the North?" *Foreign Affairs* 47 (Apr. 1968): 425–441.

2684.   _____. "The Policy Proposals: 'Strength and Conciliation.'" *Bulletin of the Atomic Scientists* 21 (June 1965): 41–42.

2685.   Hinterhoff, E. "What Seems to Be a Right Solution for the Crisis in Vietnam?" *Contemporary Review* 208 (May 1966): 240–245.

2686.   Howe, Irving. "Vietnam: The Costs and Lessons of Defeat." *Dissent* 12 (Spring 1965): 151–156.

2687.   Kahin, George McT., and John W. Lewis. "Escalation and East Asia." *Bulletin of the Atomic Scientists* 23 (Jan. 1967): 20–24.

2688.   Kamath, M.V. "Vietnam: Victim of Power Politics." *United Asia* [India] 17 (May–June 1965): 193–198.

2689.   Kennan, G.F. "Kennan on Vietnam." *New Republic* 154 (Feb. 26, 1966): 19–30.

2690.   _____, and Maxwell D. Taylor. "The Vietnam Debate." *Survival* 8 (Apr. 1966): 108–114.

2691.   "Kosygin's Visit to Hanoi: American Bombings." *Current Digest of the Soviet Press* 17 (Mar. 3, 1965): 3–12.

2692.   Kraft, Joseph. "A Way Out of Vietnam." *Harper's* 229 (Dec. 1964): 33ff.

2693.   Lansdale, Edward G. "Viet Nam: Still the Search for Goals." *Foreign Affairs* 47 (Oct. 1968): 92–98.

2694.   Lefever, Ernest W. "Vietnam: Joining the Issues." *Catholic World* 205 (May 1967): 72–77.

2695.   Lowenthal, Richard. "The Vietnamese Agony." *Encounter* [Great Britain] 26 (Jan. 1966): 54–59.

2696.   Melby, J.F. "Can the West Win in South Vietnam?" *Orbis* 7 (Winter 1964): 873–876.

2697.   Mirsky, J. The War Is Over." *Ramparts* 6 (Dec. 1967): 1–8.

2698.   Morgenthau, Hans J. "Vietnam: Shadow and Substance." *New York Review of Books* (Sept. 16, 1965): 3–7. Morgenthau was an early critic of the war.

2699.   _____. "We Are Deluding Ourselves in Vietnam." *New York Times Magazine* (Apr. 18, 1965): 25.

2700.   _____. "What Are U.S. Interests In Vietnam?" *War/Peace Report* 5 (Dec. 1965): 5–6.

2701.   _____. "Who Makes Those Commitments?" *New Republic* 160 (June 14, 1969): 16–18.

2702.   Moriarty, J.K. "Politics of Delusion." *Commonweal* 86 (Sept. 22, 1967): 574–580.

2703.   Murphy, Charles J.V. "Vietnam Hangs on U.S. Determination." *Fortune* 69 (May 1964): 159–162, 227–232.

2704.   Pfaff, William. "No Victory in Vietnam." *Commonweal* 82 (Apr. 23, 1965): 135–137.

2705.   Raskin, Marcus G. "America's Night of the Generals." *Ramparts* 6 (July 1967): 15–19.

2706.   Renfield, R.L. "A Policy for Vietnam." *Yale Review* 16 (June 1967): 481–505.

2707.   Rovere, Richard. "Reflections: Half Out of Our Tree." *New Yorker* 43 (Oct. 28, 1967): 60ff.

2708.   Scott, George C. "Sorry About That." *Esquire* 64 (Dec. 1965): 208ff. An actor measures his performance against those in Vietnam.

2709.   Selton, Robert W. "Rational Victor U.S." *U.S. Naval Institute Proceedings* 94 (Feb. 1968): 26–32.

2710.   Shaplen, Robert. "Viet Nam: Crisis of Indecision." *Foreign Affairs* 46 (Oct. 1967): 95–110.

2711.   Skorov, A. "McNamara's Dirty War." *International Affairs* [Moscow] 10 (Aug. 1964): 61–64.

2712.   Smith, R.S. "Viet-Nam: The War That Is Not a War." *Foreign Service Journal* 42 (Jan. 1965): 18–21.

2713.   Soloveytchik, G. "Loss and Gain [Problems of

LBJ]." *Contemporary Review* 212 (May 1968): 230–237.

2714. _____. "President Johnson's Problems." *Contemporary Review* 209 (Sept. 1966): 120–126.

2715. Starner, Frances L. "LBJ's Doctrine for Asia." *Far Eastern Economic Review* 53 (Sept. 29, 1966): 635–637.

2716. Stone, Marvin L. "Is U.S. Trapped in a 'Hopeless War'?" *U.S. News and World Report* 61 (Dec. 5, 1966): 40–49.

2717. Stucki, Lorenz. "From a Report on Indochina." *Swiss Review of World Affairs* 14 (June 1964): 12–15.

2718. Thompson, Robert. "Squaring the Error." *Foreign Affairs* 46 (Apr. 1968): 442–453.

2719. Thompson, W.F.K. "Vietnam Task." *Royal United Service Institution Journal* 113 (Nov. 1968): 344–345.

2720. Tucker, Robert W., et al. "Commentary: Experts Respond to the President's Foreign Policy Speech at Johns Hopkins." *Johns Hopkins Magazine* 15 (Apr. 1965): 5ff.

2721. Van der Haag, Ernest. "Vietnam: After All Is Said and Done." *National Review* 18 (Nov. 29, 1966): 1210–1212, 1237.

2722. Veilly, M. "Faire le Viet ou faire l'Américain." *Revue Militaire Générale* 6 (Mar. 1968): 377–387.

2723. "Vietnam's Growing Burden: The Policeman Seeks Support." *Round Table* 222 (Mar. 1966): 155–160.

2724. Warner, Denis. "The Stepped-Up War: The Price of Victory." *Reporter* 30 (Apr. 1966): 18–21. Warner maintains that if the U.S. had not intervened in the spring of 1965, the Vietcong would have won.

2725. _____. "Vietnam: The Need for a Loyal Opposition." *Reporter* 37 (Dec. 14, 1967): 23–25.

2726. _____. "Vietnam: The Politics of 'Peace.'" *Reporter* 32 (Apr. 8, 1965): 40–42.

2727. "Why U.S. Risks Big War in Asia?" *U.S. News and World Report* 58 (Mar. 15, 1965): 31–34.

2728. Number not used.

2729. Witze, Claude. "A Rough Road to Peace." *Air Force Magazine* 48 (Mar. 1965): 17–18.

Johnson Critics

See also Chapter 9, under "Antiwar Movement."

2730. Bolitzer, Bernard. "For the Immediate Withdrawal of American Troops." *New Politics* 4 (Winter 1965): 18–24.

2731. Deakin, James. "Big Brass Lamb: Each in His Own Way Has This to Say About the War in Vietnam: 'Nuts!'" *Esquire* 68 (Dec. 1967): 145ff. Former Marine Commandant David Shoup announces his opposition to the war.

2732. Fleming, D.F. "Can We Play God in Asia?" *Progressive* 29 (June 1965): 12–14. Fleming was a professional critic.

2733. "Going Up?" *New Republic* 157 (Oct. 28, 1967): 5–7. This is a rebuttal to the official rationale for escalation.

2734. Huberman, L., and P.M. Swezy. "The Road to Ruin." *Monthly Review* 16 (Apr. 1965): 785–801. The authors write from an American socialist viewpoint.

2735. Krech, David. "Passion in Clear Reason." *Nation* 202 (Mar. 28, 1966): 362–364.

2736. Marder, Murray. "Our Crumbling Credibility." *Progressive* 30 (Aug. 1966): 11–14.

2737. Oglesby, Carl. "Let Us Shape the Future." *Liberation* 10 (Jan. 1969): 11–14. Oglesby is a former president of the SDS.

2738. _____. "Vietnamism Has Failed." *Commonweal* 90 (Mar. 21, 1969): 11–12.

2739. Thomas, Norman. "Let the President Call for Immediate Cease Fire." *New Politics* 4 (Winter 1965): 4–11.

2740. Toynbee, Arnold J. "The Failure of American Foreign Policy." *Fact* 2 (Sept.–Oct. 1965): 2–7. This is a dissent by a leading British historian.

2741. U.S. Senate. Committee on Foreign Relations. Hearings; *Present Situation in Vietnam*. 90th Cong., 2d sess., 1968. General David M. Shoup testifies.

2742. Whalen, R.J. "The Elusive General Gavin." *Harper's* 235 (Nov. 1967): 107–118. Whallen looks at Gavin's enclave plan.

2743. "Why No War Declaration? Growing Mystery of Vietnam." *U.S. News and World Report* 62 (May 22, 1967): 31–33.

2744. Zinn, Howard. "Vietnam: The Logic of Withdrawal." *Nation* 204 (Feb. 6, 1967): 170–175. Zinn was a vociferous, persistent critic of the war.

Johnson Supporters

2745.   Howard, Anthony. "At the White House, Intellectual-in-Residence." *New York Times Magazine* (Mar. 12, 1967): 34ff. The title refers to John P. Roche.

2746.   Kissin, S.F. "Why the U.S. Deserves Our Support." *Venture* 19 (Mar. 1967): 19–22.

2747.   "Only Five Minutes to Darkness in Vietnam." *Life* 59 (July 23, 1965): 54–61.

2748.   Ramsey, Paul. "Is Vietnam a Just War?" *Dialog* 6 (Winter 1967): 19–29.

2749.   _____. "Vietnam: Dissent from Dissent." *Christian Century* 83 (July 20, 1966): 909–913.

2750.   Roche, John P. "The Liberals and Vietnam." *New Leader* 48 (Apr. 26, 1965): 16–20.

2751.   _____. "A Professor Votes for Mr. Johnson." *New York Times Magazine* (Oct. 24, 1965): 45.

2752.   _____. "Why I Oppose Vietnam Critics." *Air Force Magazine* 49 (Apr. 1966): 55–56.

2753.   Scalapino, Robert A. "We Cannot Accept a Communist Seizure of Vietnam." *New York Times Magazine* (Dec. 11, 1966): 46–47, 133–140.

2754.   Smith, Nelle Van D., ed. *We Care: Inspirational Messages.* New York: William Frederick, 1968.

2755.   Swearingen, Roger. "The Vietnam Critics in Perspective." *Communist Affairs* 4 (May 6, 1966): 7–9.

2756.   U.S. House. Committee on Un-American Activities. Report; *Communist Origin and Manipulation of Vietnam Week, April 8–15, 1967.* House Rpt. no. 186. 90th Cong., 1st sess., 1967.

2757.   Wegaman, Philip. "The Vietnam War and Paul Ramsey's Conscience." *Dialog* 6 (Autumn 1967): 292–298. For a response, see (2748).

2758.   Wood, W.W. "The Betrayed: Our Men in Uniform Want to Win in Vietnam." *American Opinion* 12 (Jan. 1969): 1–16.

GULF OF TONKIN: EPISODE AND RESOLUTION

Most accounts are based on the Senate's 1968 hearings. Also listed below, Austin (2759), Goulden (2766) and *Windchy (2774; probably the best) are surveys of the major issues.*

2759.   Austin, Anthony. *The President's War: The Story of the Tonkin Gulf Resolution and How the Nation Was Trapped in Vietnam.* Philadelphia: Lippincott, 1971.

2760.   Cherwitz, Richard D. "Lyndon Johnson and the 'Crisis' of Tonkin Bay: A President's Justification of War." *Western Journal of Speech Communication* 42:2 (1978): 93–104.

2761.   _____. "The Rhetoric of the Gulf of Tonkin: A Study of the Crisis Speaking of President Lyndon B. Johnson." Ph.D. dissertation, University of Iowa, 1978.

2762.   Duncan, D. "The Tonkin Gulf Incident: Provocation—Consciously or Carelessly?" *Pacific* 58 (May–June 1968): 15–17.

2763.   Finney, John. "Tonkin Gulf Attack." *New Republic* 158 (Jan. 27, 1968: 19–22.

2764.   _____. "The Tonkin Verdict." *New Republic* 158 (Mar. 9, 1968): 17–19.

2765.   Galloway, John. *The Gulf of Tonkin Resolution.* Rutherford, NJ: Fairleigh Dickinson University Press, 1970.

2766.   Goulden, Joseph C. *Truth is the First Casualty: The Gulf of Tonkin Affair, Illusion and Reality.* Chicago: Rand McNally, 1969.

2767.   "McNamara Testifies on Tonkin Gulf Attacks." *CQ Weekly Report* 26 (Mar. 1, 1968): 384–386.

2768.   Roberts, Adam. "The Fog of Crisis: The 1964 Tonkin Gulf Incidents." *World Today* [London] 26 (May 1970): 209–217.

2769.   Schmidt, John W. "The Gulf of Tonkin Debates, 1964 and 1967: A Study in Argument." Ph.D. dissertation, University of Minnesota, 1969.

2770.   Stone, I.F. "The Tonkin Bay Mystery." *New York Review of Books* (Mar. 28, 1968): 5–12.

2771.   U.S. Senate. Committee on Foreign Relations. Hearings; *The Gulf of Tonkin: The 1964 Incidents: Pt. I Feb. 20, 1968; Pt. II (Dec. 16, 1968).* 90th Cong., 2d sess., 1969.

2772.   _____. Hearings; *Termination of Southeast Asia Resolution.* Rpt. no. 91–872 [by Fulbright]. 91st Cong., 2d sess., May 15, 1970.

2773.   _____. Committee on Foreign Relations and the Committee on Armed Services. Joint Hearings; *Southeast Asia Resolution.* 88th Cong., 2d sess., Aug. 6, 1964. The title refers to the Tonkin Gulf Resolution.

2774.   Windchy, Eugene G. *Tonkin Gulf.* New York: Doubleday, 1971.

2775.   Wise, David. "Remember the Maddox." *Esquire* 69 (Apr. 1968): 123–127ff.

TET OFFENSIVE: POLITICAL IMPACT

For the impact upon U.S. public opinion, see Schandler, The Unmasking of a President (2574a); for media coverage, see Braestrup, Big Story (5579). Military activities are covered in Chapter 7.

2776.   "Hanoi Attacks and Scores a Major Psychological Blow." *Newsweek* 71 (Feb. 24, 1968): 23–24.

2777.   Henry, John B., II. "February 1968." *Foreign Policy*, no. 4 (Fall 1971): 3–33.

2778.   Hodgkin, Liz. "Peoples' War Comes to the Towns: Tet 1968." *Marxism Today* 22 (May 1978): 147–153.

2779.   Oberdorfer, Don. *Tet!* New York: Doubleday, 1971.

2780.   Phan Quang Dan. "The Communist Tet Offensive: An Assessment." *Congressional Record* 114 (Apr. 19, 1968): S4316–4318.

ELECTION OF 1968

The Tet offensive and Senator McCarthy's accomplishment in the New Hampshire primary led to Robert Kennedy's entrance into the presidential race and Johnson's withdrawal. March 1968 was a crucial month in U.S. politics and military strategy. See Chapter 5, "Congressional Opinions," for more on Kennedy.

2781.   Brody, Richard A. "How the Vietnam War May Effect the Election." *Trans-Action* 5 (Oct. 1968): 16–23.

2782.   Chester, Lewis, Godfrey Hodgson, and Bruce Page. *An American Melodrama: The Presidential Campaign of 1968.* New York: Viking Press, 1969.

2783.   Clery, R. "Le Vietnam et les élections américaines de 1968." *Revue de Défense Nationale* 24:3 (1968): 508–517.

2784.   Converse, Philip E., et al. "Continuity and Change in American Politics: Parties and Issues in the 1968 Election." *American Political Science Review* 63 (Dec. 1969): 1083–1105.

2785.   Halberstam, David. "McCarthy and the Divided Left." *Harper's* 238 (Mar. 1968): 32–44.

2786.   _____. *The Unfinished Odyssey of Robert Kennedy.* New York: Random House, 1968. Additional items on RFK can be found under "Congressional Opinions" in Chapter 5.

2787.   Herzog, Arthur. *McCarthy for President.* New York: Viking Press, 1969.

2788.   Hoopes, Townsend. "LBJ's Account of March, 1968." *New Republic* 163 (Mar. 14, 1970): 17–19.

2789.   Joyner, Conrad. "Eugene McCarthy and the Vision of American Politics." *Polity* 3:4 (1971): 550–556.

2790.   Larner, Jeremy. *Nobody Knows: Reflections on the McCarthy Campaign of 1968.* New York: Macmillan, 1970.

2791.   McCarthy, Eugene J. *The Year of the People.* Garden City, NY: Doubleday, 1969.

2792.   Mailer, Norman. *Miami and the Siege of Chicago.* New York: New American Library, 1971. The riots at the 1968 Democratic convention in Chicago damaged Humphrey's chances.

2793.   Schlesinger, Arthur M., Jr. *Robert Kennedy and His Times.* Boston: Houghton Mifflin, 1978. Schlesinger gives new information on Vietnam and counterinsurgency strategies.

2794.   _____. "Vietnam and the 1968 Elections." *New Leader* 50 (Nov. 6, 1967): 5–12.

2795.   Schreiber, E.M. "Vietnam Policy Preferences and Withheld 1968 Presidential Polls." *Public Opinion Quarterly* 37 (Spring 1973): 91–98.

2796.   Stavis, Ben. *We Were the Campaign: New Hampshire to Chicago for McCarthy.* Boston: Beacon, 1969.

2797.   White, Theodore H. *The Making of the President, 1968.* New York: Atheneum, 1969.

2798.   Witcover, Jules. *85 Days: The Last Campaign of Robert Kennedy.* New York: G.P. Putnam's Sons, 1969.

Nixon Years, 1969–1974

For Nixon's public presidential papers, see (134).

2799.   *The Nixon Presidential Press Conferences.* Introduction by Helen Thomas. New York: Coleman,

1978. Nixon's dislike of the press was evident during these press conferences.

PERSONALITIES AND POLICIES

See Chapter 5, under "Negotiations," for additional items relating to Kissinger and Nixon.

Henry A. Kissinger

2800.   Brown, Seyon. *The Crises of Power: An Interpretation of United States Foreign Policy During the Kissinger Years.* New York: Columbia University Press, 1979.

2801.   Bundy, McGeorge. "Vietnam, Watergate and Presidential Powers." *Foreign Affairs* 58 (Jan. 1979–1980): 397–407. An LBJ advisor reviews Kissinger's *White House Years.*

2802.   Girling, J.L.S. "'Kissingerism': The Enduring Problems." *International Affairs* [London] 51 (July 1975): 323–343.

2803.   Graubard, Stephen R. *Kissinger: Portrait of a Mind.* New York: W.W. Norton, 1974. This book is helpful in understanding Kissinger's views.

2804.   Gray, Francine du Plessix. "Kissinger: The Swinging Sphinx." *Ramparts* 11 (Dec. 1972): 33–34, 58–62.

2805.   Kalb, Marvin, and Bernard Kalb. *Kissinger.* Boston: Little, Brown, 1974. This work is thorough and generally sympathetic.

2806.   [Kissinger, Henry]. "Secretary Kissinger Responds to Senator Kennedy on Indochina Policy Issues." *U.S. Department of State Bulletin* 70 (Apr. 22, 1974): 425–431.

2807.   _____. *The White House Years.* Boston: Little, Brown, 1979. Kissinger gives his views on the Vietnam negotiations.

2808.   Kraft, Joseph. "In Search of Kissinger." *Harper's* 242 (Jan. 1971): 54–61.

2809.   Landau, David. *Kissinger: The Uses of Power.* Boston: Houghton Mifflin, 1972.

2810.   _____. "The Real Kissinger?" *New York Review of Books* (Feb. 22, 1973): 37–38. This is a letter to the editor.

2811.   McDonald, William W. "Henry Kissinger: The Man, the Mystique, and the Foreign Policy." *Research Studies* 43:4 (1975): 264–276.

2812.   Montgomery, John D. "The Education of Henry Kissinger." *Journal of International Affairs* 29:1 (1975): 49–62.

2813.   Morris, Roger. *Uncertain Greatness: Henry Kissinger and American Foreign Policy.* New York: Harper & Row, 1977. This is a complex appraisal by a former insider.

2814.   Sanders, Sol W. "Dr. Kissinger's Asia: Balance or Vertigo?" *Asian Affairs* [U.S.] 1 (Sept.–Oct. 1973): 1–16.

2815.   Sewell, James P. "Master Builder or Captain of the Dike? Notes on the Leadership of Kissinger." *International Journal* [Toronto] 31 (Autumn 1976): 648–665.

2816.   Stoessinger, John G. *Henry Kissinger: The Anguish of Power.* New York: W.W. Norton, 1976.

2817.   Walker, Stephen C. "The Interface Between Beliefs and Behavior: Henry Kissinger's Operational Code and the Vietnam War." *Journal of Conflict Resolution.* 21:1 (1977): 129–168.

Richard M. Nixon

2818.   Allen, Gary. *Richard Nixon: The Man Behind the Mask.* Boston: Western Islands, 1971.

2819.   Evans, Rowland. *Nixon in the White House: The Frustrations of Power.* New York: Vintage, 1972.

2820.   Harrington, Michael. "Anatomy of Nixonism." *Dissent* 19 (Fall 1972): 563–578.

2821.   Hughes, Arthur J. *Richard M. Nixon.* New York: Dodd, Mead, 1972.

2822.   Keogy, James. *President Nixon and the Press.* New York: Funk & Wagnalls, 1972.

2823.   Mazlish, Bruce. *In Search of Nixon.* New York: Basic Books, 1972. Mazlish attempts psychohistory.

2824.   Murphy, William F. "Rhetorical Processes and Patterns in the Nixon Addresses on Vietnam and Related News Coverage." Ph.D. dissertation, University of Pittsburgh, 1979.

2825.   Nixon, Richard M. "Asia After Vietnam." *Foreign Affairs* 46 (Oct. 1967): 111–125.

2826.   _____. "The Pursuit of Peace in Viet-Nam." *U.S. Department of State Bulletin* 61 (Nov. 24, 1969): 437–443.

2827.   _____. "A Report on Progress in Vietnam." *U.S. Department of State Bulletin* 62 (May 11, 1970): 601–604. See Chapter 2, under "Cambodia (Kampuchea)," the section on "U.S. Military Incursion, 1970," for additional statements.

2828. _____. *RN: The Memoirs of Richard Nixon.* New York: Grosset & Dunlap, 1978. Nixon includes candid views on foreign affairs.

2829. _____. *Setting the Course.* New York: Funk & Wagnalls, 1970.

2830. _____. "Strengthening the Total Fabric of Peace." *U.S. Department of State Bulletin* 61 (Oct. 6, 1969): 297–302.

2831. _____. "A Vietnam Plan: The Silent Majority." *Vital Speeches* 36 (Nov. 15, 1969): 66–70.

2832. Safire, William. *Before the Fall: An Inside View of the Pre-Watergate White House.* Garden City, NY: Doubleday, 1975. Although a former speechwriter, Safire was only on the fringe of foreign policymaking.

2833. Szulc, Tad. *The Illusion of Peace: Foreign Policy in the Nixon–Kissinger Years.* New York: Viking Press, 1979.

2834. Van Der Linden, Frank. *Nixon's Quest for Peace.* Washington, DC: Luce, 1972.

2835. Wills, Garry. *Nixon Agonistes: The Crisis of the Self Made Man.* New York: Mentor, 1970. This is a valuable work on Nixon's personality.

Others

2836. Richardson, E.L. "The Foreign Policy of the Nixon Administration: Its Aims and Strategy." *U.S. Department of State Bulletin* 61 (Sept. 22, 1969): 257–260.

2837. Rogers, William P. *Viet-Nam in Perspective.* Department of State Publication no. 8462. Washington, D.C.: GPO, 1969.

POLITICS

Books
2838. Bell, Coral. *The Diplomacy of Detente: The Kissinger Era.* New York: St. Martin's Press, 1977.

2839. Brandon, Henry. *The Retreat of American Power.* Garden City, NY: Doubleday, 1973.

2840. Brodine, Virginia, and Mark Selden. *Open Secret: The Kissinger–Nixon Doctrine in Asia.* New York: Harper & Row, 1972.

2841. Corson, William R. *Consequences of Failure.* New York: W.W. Norton, 1974. Corson maintains that the American people must understand and admit that

Vietnam was a failure and overcome the temptation to retreat into isolationism.

2842. Herman, E.S., and R.B. DuBoff. *How to Coo Like a Dove While Fighting to Win: The Public Relations of a Nixon Policy in Vietnam.* New York: Clergy and Laymen Concerned about Vietnam, 1969.

2843. Osgood, Robert E., et al. *Retreat From Empire? The First Nixon Administration.* Baltimore: Johns Hopkins University Press, 1975.

Essays
2844. Arnett, P., and W. Burchett. "The Final Chapter in Vietnam: A Political or Military Denouncement?" *War/Peace Report* 11 (Dec. 1971): 3–7.

2845. Ashmore, Harry S. "The Policy of Illusion; the Illusion of Policy." *Center Magazine* [Center for the Study of Democratic Institutions. Santa Barbara, CA] 3 (May–June 1970): 2–10.

2846. "Back to Bombing." *New Republic* 166 (Jan. 1, 8, 1972): 9–10.

2847. Barnet, Richard J. "How Hanoi Sees Nixon." *New York Review of Books* (Jan. 29, 1970): 19ff.

2848. Berthoff, A.E. "Mumbling and Fumbling, or Lying?" *Bulletin of the Atomic Scientists* 26 (Oct. 1970): 49–50.

2849. Bookman, John T. "War Rationale." *Contemporary Review* 214 (Mar. 1969): 113–116.

2850. Buckley, Tom. "Is This Written in the Stars? See It Through with Nguyen Van Thieu." *New York Times Magazine* (Sept. 26, 1971): 14.

2851. Bunker, Ellsworth. "A Close Look at Progress inside Vietnam." *U.S. News and World Report* 67 (Nov. 17, 1969): 46–52.

2852. Cao Van Vien. "Vietnam: What Next? The Strategy of Isolation." *Military Review* 52 (Apr. 1972): 22–30.

2853. Chomsky, Noam. "Indochina: The Next Phase." *Ramparts* 10 (May 1972): 60–65.

2854. Davies, John P. "No More Vietnams: The End of Intervention?" *Worldview* 12 (Dec. 1969): 5–9.

2855. Duncanson, Dennis J. "Vietnam Without Polemics." *Royal Central Asian Journal* 56 (Feb. 1969): 20–29.

2856. Geyer, G.S. "The Illusion Dies." *Progressive* 33 (Feb. 1969): 18–21. Many still believed we were winning the war.

2857. Girling, J.L.S. "Nixon's 'Algeria': Doctrine and

Disengagement in Indochina." *Pacific Affairs* 44 (Winter 1971–1972): 527–544.

2858.   Ha Nhu Chi. "The Situation in Vietnam." *Pacific Community* [Japan], no. 3 (1969): 232–237.

2859.   Halberstam, David. "President Nixon and Vietnam." *Harper's* 238 (Jan. 1969): 22–23.

2860.   Henderson, John T. "Leadership Personality and War: The Cases of Richard Nixon and Anthony Eden." *Political Science* 28 (Dec. 1976): 141–170.

2861.   Hoopes, Townsend. "The Fight for the President's Mind: And the Men Who Won It." *Atlantic* 224 (Oct. 1969): 97–104.

2862.   _____. "How to Set a Date for Getting Out of Vietnam." *New York Times Magazine* (June 9, 1971): 20ff.

2863.   Horowitz, David. "Nixon's Vietnam Strategy." *Ramparts* 11 (Aug. 1972): 17–20.

2864.   Huglin, Henry C. "Our Gains from Success in Vietnam." *Air University Review* 20 (Mar.–Apr. 1969): 71–78.

2865.   Jenkins, Brian. *Forecasting Vietnam's Future: The Next Stage in the War.* P–4904. Santa Monica, CA: Rand Corp., Sept. 1972.

2866.   Kirk, Donald. "Who Wants to Be the Last American Killed in Vietnam?" *New York Times Magazine* (Sept. 19, 1971): 9ff.

2867.   Klare, Michael. "The Great South Asian War." *Nation* 209 (Mar. 9, 1970): 265–273.

2868.   Kolko, Gabriel. "Nixon's Vietnam Strategy." *Commonweal* 98 (Mar. 1973): 55–59.

2869.   _____. "Vietnam and the Future of U.S. Foreign Policy." *Liberation* 17 (May 1973): 8–17.

2870.   Lacouture, Jean. "Toward an End to the Indochina War?" *Pacific Community* [Japan] 3 (Jan. 1972): 328–340.

2871.   Lewis, J.W., and J.S. Werner. "The 'New State' in Vietnam." *Bulletin of the Atomic Scientists* 25 (Jan. 1969): 21–29.

2872.   Loomis, W. "It's No Longer LBJ's War." *Data* 14 (July 1969): 15–17.

2873.   McCombs, P.A. "Letter from Saigon: How Can We Lose in Vietnam, Having Won?" *National Review* 22 (Dec. 29, 1970): 1399–1402.

2874.   Morgenthau, Hans J. "The New Escalation in Vietnam." *New Republic* 166 (May 20, 1972): 9–10.

2875.   "Nixon's Handling of Vietnam." *Gallup Opinion Index*, no. 64 (Oct. 1970): 4.

2876.   Novak, Michael. "Vietnam's Tomorrow: The Points for Withdrawal." *Commonweal* 91 (Oct. 1969): 45–47.

2877.   Rhyne, R.F. "[Military] Victory in Vietnam." *Military Review* 50 (Feb. 1970): 37–47.

2878.   Ridgway, Matthew B. "Indochina: Disengaging." *Foreign Affairs* 49 (July 1971): 583–592.

2879.   Smith, Gaines. "How Ho Started the War: A History Lesson for Richard Nixon." *New Guard* 12 (May 1972): 10–12.

2880.   Stone, I.F. "Will the War Go On until 1976?" *New York Review of Books* (Sept. 21, 1972): 14–16.

2881.   Swenson, Mark E. "Which Way Out?" *Air Forces & Space Digest* 52 (Nov. 1969): 43–45.

2882.   Thompson, Robert. "Vietnam: Which Way Out?" *Survival* 11 (May 1969): 142–145.

2883.   Van der Haag, Ernest. "The Honorable Alternative." *National Review* 21 (Nov. 18, 1969): 1167–1168.

2884.   "The Vietnam War—Prospect and Retrospect: An Interview with George McT. Kahin." *Center Magazine* [Center for the Study of Democratic Institutions, Santa Barbara, CA] 5 (Mar.–Apr. 1972): 24–32.

2885.   Watt, D.C. "American Policy and Vietnam." *Political Quarterly* 43 (Jan.–Mar. 1972): 89–102.

2886.   Whitney, Craig R. "Giap Teaches Us a Lesson: But It's over Our Heads." *New York Times Magazine* (Sept. 24, 1972): 16–17, 76–84.

2887.   "Why Vietnam War Drags On." *U.S. News and World Report* 74 (Jan. 1, 1973): 9–12.

2888.   "Will the Leaders Now Lead?" *New Republic* 167 (Dec. 30, 1972): 7–8.

2889.   Witze, Claude. "Is the Enemy in Hanoi?" *Air Force Magazine* 53 (July 1970): 12–13.

2890.   Zinn, Howard. "Vacating the Premises in Vietnam." *Asian Survey* 9 (Nov. 1969): 862–867.

NIXON DOCTRINE

The Nixon Doctrine is sometimes referred to as the "Guam Doctrine" after the location of its announcement.

2891.   Anthony, William H. "Public Diplomacy and the Nixon Doctrine: Reaction by Foreign and American

Media and the U.S. Information Agency's Role." Ph.D. dissertation, George Washington University, 1976.

2892. Barber, James A. "The Nixon Doctrine and the Navy." *Naval War College Review* 23 (June 1971): 5–15.

2893. Butwell, Richard. "The Nixon Doctrine in Southeast Asia." *Current History* 61 (Dec. 1971): 321–326.

2894. "Cambodia: Nixon Doctrine Under Fire in Congress." *CQ Weekly Report* 28 (Dec. 18, 1970): 3008–3013.

2895. Dower, John W. "Asia and the Nixon Doctrine: 10 Points of Note." *Bulletin of Concerned Asian Scholars* 2 (Fall 1970): 47–70.

2896. Girling, J.L.S. "The Guam Doctrine." *International Affairs* [London] 46 (Jan. 1970): 48–62.

2897. Gleason, Robert L. "Quo Vadis? The Nixon Doctrine and Air Power." *Air University Review* 23 (Sept.–Oct. 1972): 45–56.

2898. Green, Marshall. "The Nixon Doctrine: A Blueprint for the 1970's." *U.S. Department of State Newsletter*, no. 117 (Jan. 1971): 2–4.

2899. Gurtov, Melvin. "The Nixon Doctrine and Southeast Asia." *Pacific Community* [Japan] 4 (Oct. 1972): 18–29.

2900. Leifer, Michael. "The Nixon Doctrine and the Future of Indochina." *Pacific Community* [Japan] 2 (July 1971): 742–753.

2901. "The Nixon Doctrine: Vietnam and America." *Far Eastern Economic Review* 66 (Nov. 13, 1969): 363–364ff.

2902. "President Nixon and President Thieu Confer at Midway Island." *U.S. Department of State Bulletin* 60 (June 30, 1969): 549–554.

2903. "President Nixon's Round the World Trip." *U.S. Department of State Bulletin* 61 (Aug. 25, 1969): 147–176.

2904. Ravenal, Earl C. "The Nixon Doctrine and Our Asian Commitments." *Foreign Affairs* 49 (Jan. 1971): 201–217.

2905. _____. "The Political–Military Gap." *Foreign Policy*, no. 3 (Summer 1971): 140–167. This article is highly critical of the Nixon Doctrine.

2906. Rennagel, William C. "Organizational Responses to the President: The Military Response to the Nixon Doctrine." Ph.D. dissertation, Ohio State University, 1977.

2907. Sidey, Hugh. "Question of Belief in Hanoi and at Home." *Life* 67 (Oct. 10, 1969): 4.

2908. U.S. Senate. Committee on Foreign Relations. Report; *Perspective on Asia: The New U.S. Doctrine and Southeast Asia.* 91st Cong., 1st sess., 1969.

PENTAGON PAPERS CASE

The Pentagon Papers *must be used with caution, for they emphasize Defense Department accounts and stress military matters. Other dimensions are inadequately treated; see Kahin (2912) for the assets and deficiencies of the various editions.*

2909. *Anatomy of an Undeclared War: Congressmen and Other Authorities Respond to the Pentagon Papers.* New York: International Universities Press, 1972.

2910. Andrus, David J. "The Origins of American Involvement in Vietnam: A Thematic Analysis of the Pentagon Papers." Ph.D. dissertation, University of Southern California, 1975.

2911. Horowitz, Irving L. "The Pentagon Papers and Social Sciences." *Trans-Action* 8 (Nov. 1971): 37–39.

2912. Kahin, George McT. "The Pentagon Papers: A Critical Evaluation." *American Political Science Review* 69 (June 1975): 675–684.

2913. Koning, Hans. "Did the Pentagon Papers Make Any Difference?" *Saturday Review* 54 (June 10, 1972): 13–15.

2914. McGovern, George S., and John P. Roche. "Pentagon Papers: A Discussion." *Political Science Quarterly* 87 (June 1972): 173–191.

2915. Schlesinger, Arthur M., Jr. "The Quagmire Papers." *New York Review of Books* (Dec. 16, 1971): 41–42.

2916. Sheehan, Neil. "The Press and the Pentagon Papers." *Naval War College Review* 24 (Nov.–Dec. 1972): 8–12.

2917. Turner, Robert F. "Myths of the Vietnam War: The Pentagon Papers Reconsidered." *Southeast Asian Perspectives*, no. 7 (Sept. 1972): Entire issue.

2918. Ullman, Richard H. "The Pentagon's History as 'History.'" *Foreign Policy* 4 (Fall 1971): 150–156.

2919. Waskow, Arthur I. "The Politics of the Pentagon Papers." *Peace & Change: A Journal of Peace Research* 17 (Fall 1972): 1–10.

2920. Westerfield, H. Bradford. "What Use Are Three

Versions of the Pentagon Papers?" *American Political Science Review* 69 (June 1975): 685–696.

Trials Involving the Pentagon Papers

Two basic trials involved the Pentagon Papers: *the first involved the decision of the* New York Times *to print the initial volume of the papers, while the second was the trial of Daniel Ellsberg and Anthony Russo for their role in "leaking" the documents. Check newspaper indexes and the* Reader's Guide *for additional information on the latter trial.*

2921.   Falk, Richard A. "The Nuremberg Defense in the Pentagon Papers Case." *Columbia Journal of Transitional Law* 13:2 (1974): 208–238.

2922.   Goodale, James C., ed. *The New York Times Company vs United States, a Documentary History: The Pentagon Papers Litigation.* 2 vols. New York: Arno, 1971.

2923.   Pember, Don R. "The 'Pentagon Papers' Decision: More Questions Than Answers." *Journalism Quarterly* 48 (Autumn 1971): 403–411.

2924.   Schrag, Peter. "Heresy in Los Angeles." *New York Review of Books* (Mar. 22, 1973): 24–26. The title refers to the Ellsberg and Russo trial.

2925.   "Symposium: The National Interest and the Pentagon Papers." *Partisan Review* 39 (Summer 1972): 336–375.

2926.   Unger, Sanford J. *The Papers and the Papers: An Account of the Legal and Political Battle Over the Pentagon Papers.* New York: E.P. Dutton, 1972.

2927.   _____. "Pentagon Papers Trial." *Atlantic* 230 (Nov. 1972): 22–34.

Ellsberg and Russo Trials

The Ellsberg and Russo trials took place in Los Angeles and resulted in a mistrial when the judge acknowledged possible misconduct.

2928.   Arnold, M. "Daniel Ellsberg at the Trial of Anthony J. Russo." *Esquire* 81 (Jan. 1974): 72–77.

2929.   "Case Dismissed." *New Republic* 168 (May 26, 1973): 9.

2930.   "Ellsberg & Russo Show." *National Review* 25 (Apr. 27, 1973): 401–402ff.

2931.   "Ellsberg on the Stand." *Newsweek* 81 (Apr. 23, 1973): 22–23.

2932.   Farrell, B. "Ellsberg Mask." *Harper's* 247 (Oct. 1973): 79–80ff.

2933.   Pincus, William. "Getting to the Bottom of the CIA Coverup: The Break-in at the Office of Daniel Ellsberg's Psychiatrist." *New Republic* 171 (Sept. 28, 1974): 11–13.

ELECTIONS OF 1972

McGovern placed great emphasis in his campaign on "getting the United States out of Vietnam."

2934.   Hayden, Tom. "How to Vote for the Vietnamese." *Ramparts* 11 (Oct. 1972): 40–44.

2935.   Hess, Stephen. "Foreign Policy and Presidential Campaigns." *Foreign Policy*, no. 8 (Fall 1972): 3–22.

2936.   Jeffries, Jean. "McGovern on Vietnam: Slipping and Sliding." *New Guard* 12 (Nov. 1972): 7–8.

2937.   Kolodney, David. "Vietnam and the Elections: Old Myths and New Realities." *Ramparts* 10 (Apr. 1972): 4ff.

2938.   "McGovern's Peace Plan" *New Republic* 167 (Oct. 21, 1972): 11.

2939.   Reisner, Will. "McGovern's Bid for the Peace Vote." *International Socialist Review* 33 (Jan. 1972): 6–7, 40–41.

2940.   Rostow, Walt W. "Aftermath, Losing Big: A Reply." *Esquire* 78 (Dec. 1972): 10–12.

2941.   "Terms for Ending the War: What the Candidates Say." *U.S. News and World Report* 73 (Oct. 23, 1972): 28–29.

2942.   White, Theodore H. *The Making of the President, 1972.* New York: Atheneum, 1973.

❦ Chapter Five ❦

Congress, International Law and Negotiations

CONGRESS WAS CAUGHT between persistent executive demands to support White House actions and a growing public outcry to "stop the war." Since the late 1940s, Congress had grown accustomed to following executive leadership in foreign affairs, particularly when national security and Cold War issues were involved. Moreover, once armed with the 1964 Gulf of Tonkin Resolution, neither President Lyndon Johnson, nor his successor, Richard Nixon, were inclined to ask the legislators to decide fundamental Vietnam issues; nor were the legislators, at first, eager to challenge presidential initiatives by demanding a larger voice in these matters. However, by the time the 1973 armistice was signed, Congress had begun to reassert itself on policy issues.

Congressional dissenters were slow to come forward. By 1967, a small band of legislators led by J. William Fulbright, chairman of the Senate's prestigious Committee on Foreign Relations, had begun to publicly question the purpose and practicality of American involvement in Indochina. While the public dissent of individuals such as Fulbright (2976–2981) extended an aura of legitimacy to the antiwar movement, it accomplished little more.

In 1969, antiwar legislators mustered sufficient votes to begin using the appropriations process to limit executive action. A proviso was added to the Defense Appropriation Act of 1970 declaring that none of its funds could be used to finance the introduction of American ground troops into Laos and Thailand. The public uproar over the Cambodian incursion of 1970 prompted legislative enactment of the first substantive limitation on presidential initiatives in Indochina. The so-called "Cooper-Church resolution" (passing the Senate by a 58–37 margin) prohibited the reintroduction of American ground forces into Cambodia. Other, more ambitious legislative schemes—such as the "Hatfield–McGovern bill," which sought to unilaterally withdraw all U.S. forces from Vietnam by June 20, 1971—were defeated. The War Powers Act of 1973 is Congress' legacy from the Indochina War. This law limits the authority of presidents to commit troops overseas beyond a stipulated time without congressional approval.

To date, there is no adequate published survey of congressional responses to the issues of the Indochina conflict; however, anyone seeking information about legislative actions should examine the several dissertations relating to this theme.

Legal experts spent considerable effort in futile arguments over the legality of American intervention. It was a sign of our society that we would seek a legal answer to a political issue. In such matters as armed intervention, governments have never had much difficulty in offering legal pretexts to justify their actions. Readers interested in this topic will find that Falk's volumes (3065) collect most of the arguments, while Moore's account (3069) presents the ablest brief for the interventionists.

The search for a political formula to terminate the Indochina conflict began even before large numbers of Americans joined the fighting. Indeed, contrary to some views, American military strategy approved by President Johnson was geared to that objective. In his memoirs, the *Vantage Point* (2558), Johnson listed seventy-two separate initiatives and fourteen complete or partial bombing halts between May 1965 and March 1968, all aimed at opening negotiations.

"Peace" was not at issue—all sides desired it; the fundamental question was on whose terms peace would be achieved. Put simply, Presidents Johnson and Nixon wanted a settlement that would guarantee an independent, secure South Vietnam. The North Vietnamese insisted on a unified Vietnam on their terms.

Ashmore and Boggs (3186) deal interestingly with America's early efforts to open negotiations, but the best account to date is Goodman's (3191), which covers most diplomatic episodes between 1963 and 1973. Kissinger's memoirs (2807) provide his view of the final negotiations.

The ill-fated 1973 armistice was apparently violated by both sides from its inception. South Vietnam found the recognized Vietcong-controlled areas within its borders intolerable, while the North Vietnamese began preparing for the final military conquest of the South. The reputation of the Nobel Peace Prize was not enhanced when the 1973 award was given to the authors of the armistice—Kissinger and Le Duc Tho.

Congress and Vietnam Intervention

Except for Senators Gruening and Morse, Congress initially went along with presidential policies. Early in 1965, and later in the hearings of the Senate Foreign Relations Committee under Senator Fulbright, more congressional critics began to appear. However, it was not until 1970 that congressional impact became significant. We have listed below studies on the Congress and Vietnam, some individual statements and some basic congressional documents.

2943. Burt, Richard, and Geoffrey Kemp, eds. *Congressional Hearings on American Defense Policy, 1947–1971: An Annotated Bibliography.* Lawrence: University Press of Kansas, 1974.

CONGRESS AND POLICYMAKING

2944. American Enterprise Institute for Public Policy Research. *What Pace Withdrawal?* Washington, DC, 1970. [The McGovern–Hatfield Amendment]

2945. Bader, W.B. "Congress and National Strategy." *Naval War College Review* 22 (Feb. 1970): 9–18.

2946. Baldwin, David A. "Congressional Initiative in Foreign Policy." *Journal of Politics* 28 (Nov. 1966): 754–773.

2947. Buckwalter, Doyle W. "The Congressional Concurrent Resolution: A Search for Foreign Policy Influences." *Midwest Journal of Political Science* 14 (Aug. 1970): 434–458.

2948. Burstein, Paul. "Senate Voting on the Vietnam War, 1964–1973: From Hawk to Dove." *Journal of Political and Military Sociology* 7 (Fall 1979): 271–282.

2949. _____, and William Freudenburg. "Ending Vietnam War: Components of Change in Senate Voting on Vietnam War Bills." *American Journal of Sociology* 82 (Mar. 1977): 991–1006.

2950. Caim, Robert S. "Rhetors' Guilt Placement at Senate Hearings, 1970–1972: Illocutionary Acts on the Vietnamese War." Ph.D. dissertation, Temple University, 1973.

2951. Christopher, L.S. *Limiting U.S. Involvement in the Indochina War: A Digest of Ammendments Proposed and/or Passed in the Ninety-First and the Ninety-Second Congress.* Washington, DC: Library of Congress, Congressional Research Service, 1972.

2952. Committee for a Vote on the War. *The Amendment to Fund the War: Report of the Steering Committee of the Congressional Committee for a Vote on the War.* Washington, DC, 1970.

2953. "Congressional Majority Challenges Nixon on War." *CQ Weekly Report* 31 (June 30, 1973): 1707–1709. [Laos and Cambodia bombings]

2954. Dvorin, Eugene P., ed. *The Senate's War Powers: Debate on Cambodia from the Congressional Record.* Chicago: Markham, 1971.

2955. Fanning, Louis A. *Betrayal in Vietnam.* New Rochelle, NY: Arlington House, 1976. Cited elsewhere, this book features the "stab-in-the-back" thesis: Hanoi did not win, Congress lost the war; see Chapter 6, under "Admirals and Generals," for more on this theme.

2956. Frye, A. "Congress: The Virtues of Its Vices." *Foreign Policy*, no. 3 (Summer 1971): 108–128.

2957. Goldberg, Ronald A. "The Senate and Vietnam: A Study in Acquiescence." Ph.D. dissertation, University of Georgia, 1972.

2958. Hamre, John J. "Congressional Dissent and American Foreign Policy: Constitutional War-Making in the Vietnam Years." Ph.D. dissertation, Johns Hopkins University, 1978.

2959. Javits, Senator Jacob K. "The Congressional Presence in Foreign Relations." *Foreign Affairs* 48 (Jan. 1970): 221–234.

2960. Moyer, Henry W., Jr. "Congressional Voting on Defense in World War II and Viet Nam: Toward a General Ideological Explanation." Ph.D. dissertation, Yale University, 1976.

2961. Rosenberg, Michael P. "Congress and the Vietnam War: A Study of Critics of the War in 1967 and 1968." Ph.D. dissertation, New School for Social Research, 1973.

2962. "Senate Postpones Vote On End-the-War Legislation." *CQ Weekly Report* 30 (May 6, 1972): 989–991.

2963. Senate Republican Policy Committee. *The War in Vietnam.* Washington, DC: Public Affairs Press, 1967.

2964. "Strikes Against North Vietnam Spark War Policy Debate." *CQ Weekly Report* 28 (Nov. 27, 1970): 2874–2875.

2965. "Vietnam and the Congressional Record: An Analytical Symposium." *Michigan Quarterly Review* 7 (Sept. 1968): 151–165.

2966. "Vietnam Debate: Dirksen vs. Fulbright." *New Leader* 50 (Oct. 23, 1967): 9–19.

2967. "The Vietnam War: Growing Congressional Opposition." *CQ Weekly Report* 30 (Apr. 22, 1972): 874–876.

2968. "What U.S. Should Do about Vietnam: Survey of Key Senators." *U.S. News and World Report* 66 (Feb. 10, 1969): 29–32.

2969. Williams, C. Dickerman. "The Cooper–Church Amendment: Is It Constitutional." *National Review* 22 (July 14, 1970): 731–733. Williams questions the constitutionality of prohibiting funds for the Cambodian campaign.

CONGRESSIONAL OPINIONS

This section includes sample statements by individual legislators and/or accounts about them.

Senator Frank Church

2970. Church, Frank. "Interview [on Vietnam]." *Ramparts* 3 (Jan.–Feb. 1965): 17–22.

2971. _____. "Vietnam: Disengagement Now." *Vital Speeches* 36 (Nov. 1, 1969): 34–39.

2972. _____. "War Without End." *Congressional Record* 116, Pt. 10 (May 1, 1970): 13829.

Senator Joseph S. Clark

2973. U.S. Senate. Committee on Foreign Relations. Report; *China and the Vietnam War—Will History Repeat?* 90th Cong., 2d sess., Mar. 19, 1968.

2974. _____. Report; *Stalemate in Vietnam*. 90th Cong., 2d sess., 1968.

Senator J. William Fulbright

2975. Fairlie, Henry. "The Senator [Fulbright] and World Power: Letter from America." *Encounter* [Great Britain] 30 (May 1968): 57–66.

2976. Fulbright, J. William. *The Arrogance of Power.* New York: Random House, 1967.

2977. _____. *The Crippled Giant: American Foreign Policy and Its Domestic Consequences.* New York: Random House, 1972.

2978. _____. "The Higher Patriotism." *Progressive* 30 (July 1966): 10–13. Fulbright defends the right to criticize presidential policies.

2979. _____. *Old Myths and New Realities: And Other Commentaries.* New York: Random House, 1964.

2980. _____. "We Must Negotiate Peace in Vietnam." *Saturday Evening Post* 239 (Apr. 9, 1966): 10–14.

2981. _____, ed. *The Vietnam Hearings.* New York: Vintage, 1966.

2982. Johnson, Haynes B., and Bernard M. Gwertzman. *Fulbright: The Dissenter.* Garden City, NY: Doubleday, 1968.

Senator Ernest H. Gruening

2983. Gruening, Ernest H. "The Reality of Vietnam." *Progressive* 30 (Feb. 1966): 15–17.

2984. _____, and H.B. Beaser. *Vietnam Folly.* Washington, DC: National Press, 1967.

Senator Vance Hartke

2985. Hartke, Vance. *The American Crisis in Vietnam.* New York: Bobbs-Merrill, 1968.

2986. _____. "Vietnam Costs More Than You Think." *Saturday Evening Post* 240 (Apr. 1967): 10ff.

2987. _____. "Where Are the Peacemakers?" *Progressive* 30 (Sept. 1966): 13–14.

Senator Edward M. Kennedy

See also, "Kennedy Years, 1961–1963" in Chapter 4, for other materials.

2988. Kennedy, Edward M. "A Fresh Look at Vietnam." *Look* 30 (Feb. 8, 1966): 21–23.

2989. _____. "The 'Other War' in Vietnam." *New Leader* 50 (Nov. 20, 1967): 6–9.

Senator Robert F. Kennedy

See also, "Kennedy Years, 1961–1963" and "Election of 1968" in Chapter 4.

2990. Cutbrith, Craig W. "A Strategic Perspective: Robert F. Kennedy's Dissent on the Vietnam War, 1966–1968." Ph.D. dissertation, Bowling Green State University, 1976.

2991. Kennedy, Robert F. "Comment [on P. Findley's 'End the Vietnam War through the Rule of Law']." *Social Science* 43 (June 1968): 138–139.

2992. _____. "Senator Robert Kennedy Explains His

Position." *U.S. News and World Report* 60 (Mar. 14, 1966): 68–70.

2993. _____. *To Seek a Newer World.* New York: Doubleday, 1967.

2994. _____. "What We Can Do to End the Agony of Vietnam." *Look* 31 (Nov. 28, 1967): 34–46.

2995. Newfield, Jack. *Robert Kennedy: A Memoir.* New York: E.P. Dutton, 1969.

2996. Weintraub, Arnold N. "The Public Statements and Speeches of Robert F. Kennedy on the Vietnam War Issue." Ph.D. dissertation, University of Nebraska, Lincoln, 1975.

2997. Zeiger, Henry A. *Robert F. Kennedy: A Biography.* New York: Meredith, 1968.

Senator Mike Mansfield

2998. Mansfield, Mike. "Reprieve in Vietnam." *Harper's* 212 (Jan. 1956): 46–51.

2999. U.S. Senate. Committee on Foreign Relations. *Two Reports on Vietnam and Southeast Asia to the President of the United States,* by Senator Mansfield. 93d Cong., 1st sess., 1973.

3000. _____. Report; *Viet Nam and Southeast Asia.* 88th Cong., 1st sess., 1963.

3001. _____. Report; *The Vietnam Conflict: The Substance and the Shadow,* by Mansfield and others, Jan. 6, 1966. 89th Cong., 2d sess., 1966.

Senator Gale W. McGee

3002. McGee, Gale W. *The Responsibilities of World Power.* Washington, DC: National Press, 1968. McGee supports Johnson.

3003. _____. "Vietnam: A Living Example for Implementing the American Spirit." *Vital Speeches* 26 (May 1, 1960): 440–443.

Senator George S. McGovern

See also Chapter 4, under "Election of 1972."

3004. McGovern, George S. "Affirmative Alternative in Vietnam." *Progressive* 29 (Mar. 1965): 12–14.

3005. _____. "The Lessons of Vietnam." *Progressive* 31 (May 1967): 12–17.

3006. _____. "A Proposal for Vietnam." *New York Review of Books,* (July 7, 1966): 5–6.

3007. _____. "Vietnam: The Time Is Now." *Progressive* 33 (Sept. 1969): 13–16.

3008. _____. "We Can Solve the Vietnam Dilemma." *Saturday Review* 48 (Oct. 16, 1965): 37–38.

3009. _____. "Why Don't You Speak Out, Senator?" *New Republic* 156 (Mar. 18, 1967): 10–11.

Senator Wayne Morse

3010. Benton, M.J.G. "Wayne Morse and Vietnam: A Study of the Role of Dissenter." Ph.D. dissertation, University of Denver, 1968.

3011. Morse, Wayne. "American Foreign Policy and Vietnam." *North American Review* 4 (Sept. 1967): 6–10.

3012. _____. "Humpty Dumpty in Vietnam." *Progressive* 28 (Aug. 1964): 13–16.

3013. _____. "Protests Against Vietnam Policy." *Vital Speeches* 32 (Nov. 15, 1965): 74–78.

3014. _____. *The Truth About Vietnam: Report on the U.S. Senate Hearings.* Analysis by W. Morse. Edited by F.M. Robinson and E. Kemp. San Diego, CA: Greenleaf Classics, 1966.

3015. Neal, William P. "Senator Wayne L. Morse and the Quagmire of Vietnam, 1964–1968." Ph.D. dissertation, University of Oregon, 1979.

3016. "Senator Morse's Advice and Dissent." *New York Times Magazine* (Apr. 17, 1966): 24ff.

Others

3017. Brooke, Senator Edward W. "The United States and Vietnam." *World Affairs* 130 (Apr.–June 1967): 5–12.

3018. Docking, Senator Robert. "Viet Nam: An Observer's Report." *Washburn Law Journal* 7 (Winter 1968): 187–193.

3019. Findley, Congressman Paul. "End the Vietnam War through the Rule of Law." *Social Science* 43 (June 1968): 133–138.

3020. Goodell, Senator Charles E. "Setting a Deadline for Withdrawal." *Current,* no. 115 (Feb. 1970): 30–32.

3021. Hatfield, Senator Mark O. *Not Quite So Simple.* New York: Harper & Row, 1968.

3022. Hickenlooper, Senator B.B., and Congressman John B. Rhodes. "The War in Vietnam." *Congressional Record* 113 (May 9, 1967): S6585.

3023. Javits, Senator Jacob K. "The United States and Europe: After Vietnam." *Atlantic Community Quarterly* 6 (Fall 1968): 361–367.

3024. McCarthy, Senator Eugene J. *The Limits of Power: America's Role in the World.* New York: Holt, Rinehart & Winston, 1967.

3025. McClosky, Congressman Paul N., Jr. "Special Indochina Section: Introduction." *Washington Monthly* 3 (Apr. 1971): 4–7.

3026. Muskie, Senator Edmund S. "Muskie's Timetable: Out of Indochina in 18 Months." *New York Times Magazine* (July 5, 1970): 8ff.

3027. Stoler, Mark A. "What Did He *Really* Say? The 'Aiken Formula' for Vietnam Revisited." *Vermont History* 46 (Spring 1978): 100–108.

3028. Zablocki, Congressman Clement J. "Recent Events in South Vietnam: Who Is Responsible?" *Vital Speeches* 30 (Dec. 15, 1963): 133–134.

3029. _____. *Report on Vietnam*, by Clement J. Zablocki. 89th Cong., 2d sess., 1966.

WAR POWERS ACT, 1973

This act limits the authority of the president to commit troops without congressional authority; consequently, Congress voted on June 30, 1973, to cut off funds for all U.S. military activity in Indochina, effective August 15, 1973.

3030. Barrett, Raymond J. "The War Powers: Constitutional Crisis." *U.S. Naval Institute Proceedings* 99 (Nov. 1973): 18–25.

3031. "Bombing and War Powers: Congress Prepares to Act." *CQ Weekly Report* 31 (Apr. 21, 1973): 923–927. Continued bombing in Laos and Cambodia provided support for the act.

3032. Butler, Francis P. "The Executive Power to Make War: The Power to Deceive." Ph.D. dissertation, University of Utah, 1975.

3033. "Congress, the President and the Power to Commit Forces to Combat." *Harvard Law Review* 81 (June 1968): 1771–1805.

3034. Darling, W. Stuart, and D. Craig Mense. "Rethinking the War Powers Act." *Presidential Studies Quarterly* 7 (Spring–Summer 1977): 126–135.

3035. Dauses, Wolf. "Vietnam in Retrospect: President, Congress, and the Question of War Powers." *Political Studies* 21 (Nov.–Dec. 1973): 631–643.

3036. King, Donald E., and Arthur B. Leavens. "Curbing the Dog of War: The War Powers Resolution." *Harvard International Law Journal* 18 (Winter 1977): 55–96.

3037. Latzer, Barry. "The Constitutional Authority of the President to Commence Hostilities Without a Congressional Declaration of War." Ph.D. dissertation, University of Massachusetts, 1977. Latzer provides the background to the War Powers Act.

3038. Levin, N. Gordon, Jr. "Nixon, the Senate & the War." *Commentary* 50 (Nov. 1970): 69–84.

3039. Moore, John N. "The National Executive and the Use of the Armed Forces Abroad." *Naval War College Review* 28 (Jan. 1969): 28–38.

3040. Reveley, W. Taylor, III. "Presidential War-Making: Constitutional Prerogative or Usurpation?" *Virginia Law Review* 10 (Nov. 1969): 1243–1305.

3041. Thomson, Harry G. "The War Powers Resolution of 1973: Can Congress Make It Stick?" *World Affairs* 139 (Summer 1976): 3–9.

3042. U.S. House. Committee on Foreign Affairs. Hearings; *War Powers Legislation.* 92d Cong., 1st sess., June 1–2, 1971.

3043. U.S. Senate. Committee on Foreign Relations. *Documents Relating to the War Powers of Congress, the President's Authority as Commander-in-Chief and the War in Indochina.* 91st Cong., 2d sess., July 1970.

3044. Velel, L.R. "The War in Viet Nam: Unconstitutional, Unjustifiable, and Jurisdictionally Attackable." *Kansas Law Review* 16 (1968): 449–503.

3045. Windchy, Eugene G. "The Right to Make War." *New Republic* 166 (Jan. 29, 1972): 19–23.

3046. Wormuth, F.D. "The Vietnam War, the President versus the Constitution." *A Center Occasional Paper* [Center for the Study of Democratic Institutions, Santa Barbara, CA] 1:3 (1968).

CONGRESSIONAL HEARINGS AND REPORTS

Other hearings and reports are listed under appropriate subjects throughout the Guide.

3047. U.S. House. Committee on Armed Services. Special Subcommittee on National Defense Posture. *Review of the Vietnam Conflict and Its Impact on U.S. Military*

Commitments Abroad. 90th Cong., 2d sess., Aug. 24, 1968.

3048. _____. Committee on Foreign Affairs. Hearings; *Legislation on the Indochina War, June 22–July 12, 1971.* 92d Cong., 1st sess., 1971.

3049. _____. *Report of the Special Study Mission to Asia,* by L.L. Wolff and J.H. Burke. 91st Cong., 2d sess., Apr. 22, 1970.

3050. _____. *Report of the Special Study Mission to South and Southeast Asia,* by R. Taft, Jr. 91st Cong., 1st sess., May 5, 1969.

3051. _____. *Report of the Special Study Mission to East and Southeast Asia,* by E. R. Roybal. 90th Cong., 2d sess., Dec. 1968.

3052. _____. *Report of the Special Study Mission to East and Southeast Asia,* by E. R. Roybal. 91st Cong., 1st sess., Feb. 18, 1969.

3053. U.S. Senate. Committee on Foreign Relations. Hearings; *Briefing on Vietnam,* by Secretary of State Rogers and Secretary of Defense M. Laird. 91st Cong., 1st sess., Nov. 18–19, 1969.

3054. _____. Hearings; *Causes, Origins, and Lessons of the Vietnam War.* 92d Cong., 2d sess., May 9–11, 1972.

3055. _____. Hearings; *Situation in Vietnam.* 86th Cong., 1st sess., July 30–31, 1959.

3056. _____. Hearings; *Situation in Vietnam.* 86th Cong., 1st sess., Dec. 7–8, 1960.

3057. _____. Report; *Impact of the Vietnam War.* Prepared by the Library of Congress. 92d Cong., 1st sess., June 30, 1971.

3058. _____. Staff Report; *Vietnam: December 1969.* 91st Cong., 2d sess., Feb. 2, 1970.

3059. _____. Staff Study. *Vietnam Commitments, 1961.* Staff Study based on the *Pentagon Papers.* 92d Cong., 2d sess., Mar. 20, 1972.

U.S. Intervention and International Law

Questions involving international and domestic law have been raised in regard to U.S. intervention and other issues as well.

3060. Blaustein, Albert P. "Current Legal Bibliography: Viet Nam." *Law Library Journal* 61 (Winter 1968): 20–22.

3061. United Nations. Dag Hammarskjöld Library. *International Law and the Vietnam Conflict: Selected References.* LIB/BIBLIO/69/2. New York, 1969.

Books and Pamphlets

3062. Carhart, T.M. *The Impact of U.S. Domestic Law on the Last Days of American Presence in Vietnam.* P–5583. Santa Monica, CA: Rand Corp., May 1975.

3063. Daugherty, William J. "The Courts, the Constitution, and the War in Vietnam: A Legal Interpretation of Presidential Warmaking." Ph.D. dissertation, Claremont Graduate School, 1979.

3064. Falk, Richard A. *The Six Legal Dimensions of the Vietnam War.* Research Monograph no. 34. Princeton, NJ: Princeton University, Center of International Studies, 1968.

3065. _____, ed. *The Vietnam War and International Law.* 4 vols. Princeton, NJ: Princeton University Press, 1968–1976. These volumes contain published essays, some of which are listed below, comprising the best collection on international law issues.

3066. Hull, Roger, and J. Novogrod. *Law and Vietnam.* Dobbs Ferry, NY: Oceana, 1968.

3067. Kozhevnikov, Fedor I., and V.I. Menzhinskii. *U.S. Aggression in International Law.* Moscow: Novosti Publishing House, 1968.

3068. Lawyer's Committee on American Policy Towards Vietnam. *Vietnam and International Law: An Analysis of the Legality of U.S. Military Involvement.* Flanders, NJ: O'Hare Books, 1967.

3069. Moore, John Norton. *Law and the Indo-China War.* Princeton, NY: Princeton University Press, 1972.

3070. Possony, Stefan I. *Aggression and Self-Defense: The Legality of U.S. Action in South Vietnam.* FPRI Monograph Series no. 6. Philadelphia: University of Pennsylvania, Foreign Policy Research Institute, 1966.

3071. Wu, L.H. *Recent Court Cases on the Legality of the Vietnam War and the Bombing in Cambodia.* Washington, DC: Library of Congress, 1973.

Essays

3072. Alford, Neill H., Jr. "The Legality of American Military Involvement in Vietnam: A Broader Perspective." *Yale Law Journal* 75 (June 1966): 1109–1121.

3073. Andonian, J.K. "Law and Vietnam." *American Bar Association Journal* 54 (May 1968): 457–459.

3074.   Bickel, Alexander M. "The Constitution and the War." *Commentary* 54 (July 1972): 49–55.

3075.   _____. "Vietnam: An Unconstitutional War?" *Current*, no. 142 (July–Aug. 1972): 3–14.

3076.   Deutsch, Eberhard. "Legality of the War in Vietnam." *Washburn Law Journal* 7 (1968): 153–186.

3077.   Falk, Richard A. "International Law and the United States' Role in the Viet Nam War." *Yale Law Journal* 75 (June 1966): 1122–1160.

3078.   _____. "International Law and the United States' Role in Vietnam: A Response to Professor Moore." *Yale Law Journal* 76 (Aug. 1967): 1095–1158. This debate with Moore established the basic elements of the question.

3079.   _____. "U.S. in Vietnam: Rationale and Law." *Dissent* 13 (May–June 1966): 275–284.

3080.   Friedmann, Wolfgang. "Law and Politics in the Vietnamese War: Commentary." *American Journal of International Law* 6 (July 1967): 776–784.

3081.   Holton, Thomas. "Peace in Vietnam Through Due Process: An Unexplored Path." *American Bar Association Journal* 54 (Jan. 1968): 45–47.

3082.   Lobel, William N. "Legality of the United States' Involvement in Vietnam: A Pragmatic Approach." *University of Miami Law Review* 23 (Summer 1969): 792–814.

3083.   Meeker, Leonard C. "The Legality of United States Participation in the Defense of Viet Nam." *U.S. Department of State Bulletin* 54 (Mar. 28, 1966): 474–489.

3084.   _____. "Viet-Nam and the International Law of Self-Defense." *U.S. Department of State Bulletin* 56 (Jan. 9, 1967): 54–63.

3085.   Messing, J.H. "American Actions in Vietnam: Justifiable in International Law?" *Stanford Law Review* 19 (June 1967): 1307–1336.

3086.   Moore, John Norton. "International Law and the United States' Role in Viet Nam: A Reply [to R.A. Falk]." *Yale Law Journal* 76 (May 1967): 1051–1094. Moore argued the legality of U.S. intervention.

3087.   _____. "Law and Politics in the Vietnamese War: A Response to Professor Friedman." *American Journal of International Law* 61 (Oct. 1967): 1039–1053.

3088.   _____. "The Lawfulness of Military Assistance to the Republic of Vietnam." *American Journal of International Law* 61 (Jan. 1967): 1–34.

3089.   Murphy, C.F., Jr. "Indochina: Lingering Issues of Law and Policy." *Duquesne Law Review* 10 (Winter 1971): 155ff.

3090.   _____, and M.Q. Sibley. "War in Vietnam: A Discussion." *Natural Law Forum* 12 (1967): 196–209.

3091.   Partan, D.G. "Legal Aspects of the Vietnam Conflict." *Boston University Law Review* 46 (1966): 281–316.

3092.   Robertson, D.W. "Debate Among American International Lawyers About the Vietnam War." *Texas Law Review* 46 (July 1968): 898–913.

3093.   Schick, R.B. "Some Reflections on the Legal Controversies Concerning America's Involvement in Vietnam." *International and Comparative Law Quarterly* 17 (Oct. 1968): 953–995.

3094.   Sorenson, John L. "Vietnam: Just a War, or a Just War?" *Dialogue: A Journal of Mormon Thought* 2:4 (1967): 65–100.

3095.   "Symposium of Lawyers on Indochina, May 20, 1970." *Congressional Record* 116 (May 28, 1970): S7967–S7975.

3096.   Wright, Quincy. "Legal Aspects of the Viet-Nam Situation." *American Journal of International Law* 60 (Oct. 1966): 750–769.

Other Nations View U.S. Intervention

The following sample of foreign opinion may provide an introduction to this significant theme. Entries are grouped by national or geographic entity.

GREAT BRITAIN AND THE COMMONWEALTH

Australia

3097.   Albinski, Henry S. *Politics and Foreign Policy in Australia: The Impact of Vietnam and Conscription.* Durham, NC: Duke University Press, 1970.

3098.   Australia. Department of External Affairs. *Viet-Nam, Australia and Asia: Attitudes of Asian Countries to Viet-Nam and Australia's Role There.* Canberra, 1967.

3099. _____. *Viet-Nam, November 1966 to June 1967.* Canberra: Goverment Printer, 1967. [selected documents, issued periodically]

3100. _____. *"Viet Nam Since the 1954 Geneva Agreements."* Canberra, 1964.

3101. _____. "Vietnam: Documents on Communist Aggression." *Current Notes on International Affairs* [Canberra, Australia] 33 (Jan. 1962): 27–40.

3102. Cooksey, Robert. "Australian Public Opinion and Vietnam Policy." *Dissent* [Melbourne, Australia] 22 (1968): 5–11.

3103. Findley, P.T. *Protest Politics and Psychological Warfare: The Communist Role in the Anti-Vietnam War and Anti-Conscription Movement in Australia.* Melbourne: Hawthorn Press, 1968.

3104. Freudenberg, Graham. "The Australian Labor Party and Vietnam." *Australian Outlook* 33 (Aug. 1979): 157–165.

3105. Grenville, Kenneth. *The Saving of South Vietnam.* Sydney, Australia: Alpha Books, 1972.

3106. Groenewegen, P.D. "The Public Finance of Australia's Participation in the Vietnam War." *Australian Quarterly* 42 (Dec. 1970): 63–73.

3107. Rawson, D.W. "The Vietnam War and the Australian Party System." *Australian Outlook* 23 (Apr. 1969): 58–67.

3108. Read, Susan. "How Electors Confounded the Pundits: The Vietnam War, 1969." *Politics* 10 (Nov. 1975): 200–206.

3109. Speed, F.W. "Australia in Southeast Asia." *Army Quarterly & Defence Journal* [Great Britain] 96 (Apr. 1968): 30–37.

3110. Warner, Denis. "Australia Votes to Stay in Vietnam." *Reporter* 35 (Dec. 29, 1966): 29–31.

3111. Watt, Alan. *Vietnam: An Australian Analysis.* Melbourne: F.W. Cheshire, 1968.

Canada

3112. "Bases of Canada's Policy on Vietnam." *External Affairs* [Ottawa] 19 (Apr. 1967): 131–135.

3113. "Canada and Vietnam." *International Canada* 4 (Feb. 1973): 33–41.

3114. Culhane, Claire. *Why Is Canada in Vietnam? The Truth about Our Foreign Aid.* Toronto: NC Press, 1972.

3115. Holmes, John W. "Canada and the Vietnam War." In *War and Society in North America,* edited by J.L. Granatstein and R.D. Cuff. Toronto: Nelson, 1971, 184–199.

3116. Macraw, J., and P. Smoker. "A Vietnam Simulation: A Report on the Canadian/English Joint Project." *Journal of Peace Research* 1 (1967): 1–25.

3117. Martin, Paul. "Canada's Approach to the Vietnam Conflict." *External Affairs* [Ottawa] 19 (June 1967): 221–234.

3118. Rigin, Y. "Canada and the War in Viet-Nam." *International Affairs* [Moscow] 14 (May 1968): 57–62.

3119. Singh, L.P. "Canada, the United States and Vietnam." *Journal of Commonwealth Political Studies* 6 (July 1968): 125–148.

3120. Taylor, Charles. *Snow Job: Canada, the United States and Vietnam (1954–1973).* Toronto: Anansi, 1974.

3121. Thakur, Ramesh C. "Canada, India and the Vietnam War: Peacekeeping, Foreign Policy and International Politics." Ph.D. dissertation, Queen's University at Kingston (Canada), 1978.

Great Britain

3122. Fletcher, James. "British Support on Vietnam?" *National Review* 18 (Apr. 19, 1966): 167–168.

3123. _____. "The English and the Vietnam War." *National Review* 19 (June 27, 1967): 684–687, 706.

EUROPE

3124. Ben, Phillip. "How the Europeans See the War." *New Republic* 156 (May 13, 1967): 7–8.

3125. "Europe and Vietnam." *Interplay* 1 (Mar. 1968): 5–13.

3126. Fall, Bernard B. "Vietnam: European View Points." *New Republic* 153 (Aug. 21, 1965): 13–15.

3127. Geisenheyner, Stefan. "How Europeans View the War in Vietnam." *Air Force & Space Digest* 49 (Mar. 1966): 31–32.

3128. Hoffman, Stanley. "Vietnam and Western Europe." *New Republic* 164 (Jan. 30, 1971): 18–23.

3129. Huizinga, J.H. "A European's View of the Vietnam War." *Reporter* 36 (Mar. 9, 1967): 30–36.

3130. Radio Free Europe. Audience & Public Opinion

Research Department. *Identification North or South Vietnam in Eastern Europe*. Munich, 1968.

3131.   Reese, Gunter. "Between Verdicts: German Students; View of the War." *Motive* 2 (Aug. 1967): 48–52.

3132.   Terrill, Ross. "The Polish Consensus." *New Republic* 156 (May 27, 1967): 17–22.

3133.   U.S. House. Committee on Foreign Affairs. Hearings; *European Reaction to U.S. Policies in Vietnam*. 93d Cong., 1st sess., Jan. 4, 17, 1973.

France

3134.   Devillers, Philippe. "French Policy and the Second Vietnam War." *World Today* [London] 23 (June 16, 1967): 249–262.

3135.   Lacouture, Jean. "General DeGaulle and Vietnam." *New Republic* 154 (Mar. 12, 1966): 19–21.

3136.   Leifer, Michael. "De Gaulle and Vietnam: A Conception of Political Pathology." *International Journal* [Toronto] 23 (Spring 1969): 221–233.

3137.   Steel, Ronald. "De Gaulle on Vietnam." *Commonweal* 80 (Apr. 24, 1964): 141–143.

3138.   Sullivan, Marianna P. "De Gaulle's Policy Toward the Conflict in Vietnam, 1963–1969." Ph.D. dissertation, University of Virginia, 1971.

3139.   _____. *France's Vietnam Policy: A Study in French–American Relations*. Westport, CT: Greenwood, 1978. [covers 1963 to 1973]

Sweden

The Swedish prime minister was the most outspoken European critic of President Johnson's policies.

3140.   Link, Ruth. "Ambassador Holland and the Swedes." *Crisis* 78 (Mar. 1971): 43–48.

3141.   Schiff, Martin. "The United States and Sweden: A Troubled Relationship." *American Scandinavian Review* 61:4 (1973): 367–372.

ASIA

3142.   Fuse, Toyomasa. "An Asian's View of the American–Vietnam Crisis." *Journal of Human Relations* 13:4 (1965): 492–504.

3143.   Honda Katsuichi. *Vietnam War: A Report Through Asian Eyes*. Translated by K. Miulla. Tokyo: Mirai-sha, 1972.

3144.   Hu Shing. "A Republic of China View of the War in Vietnam." *Military Review* 50 (Aug. 1970): 58–65.

3145.   Ingles, Jose D. "The Philippine Position on the Vietnam Question." *Philippine Studies* 14 (Oct. 1966): 633–652.

3146.   Se Jin Kim. "South Korea's Involvement in Vietnam and Its Economic and Political Impact." *Asian Survey* 10 (June 1970): 519–532.

3147.   Sethi, J.D. "India, China and the Vietnam War." *India Quarterly* 22 (Apr.–June 1966): 154–176.

India

3148.   Parimal Kumar Das. *India and the Vietnam War*. New Delhi: Young Asia Publications, 1972.

3149.   Power, Paul F. "India and Vietnam." *Asian Survey* 7 (Oct. 1967): 740–751.

3150.   Sar Desai, D.R. "South Asia and the Vietnam War." *United Asia* [India] 20 (July–Aug. 1968): 210–217.

3151.   Thakur, Ramesh. "India's Vietnam Policy, 1946–1979." *Asian Survey* 19 (Oct. 1979): 957–976.

Japan

3152.   "The ASAHI Poll on Vietnam." *Japan Quarterly* 12 (Oct.–Dec. 1965): 463–466.

3153.   Brown, Raymond L. "The Japanese and Vietnam." *Contemporary Review* 208 (May 1966): 234–236.

3154.   Kesavan, K.V. "The Vietnam War As an Issue in Japan's Relations with the United States." *International Studies* [India] 16 (Oct.–Dec. 1977): 501–520.

3155.   Olson, Lawrence. *Vietnam: Notes on the Japanese Reaction*. East Asia Series 12:2 (Japan). New York: American University Field Staff, 1965.

3156.   Osamu, Kuno. "The Vietnam War and Japan." *Japan Quarterly* 20 (Apr.–June 1973): 143–150.

3157.   Shinjiro Tanaka. "The 'Whys' of Vietnam." *Japan Quarterly* 12 (Oct.–Dec. 1965): 454–462.

3158.   Storry, Richard. "Repercussions in Japan." *Studies on the Soviet Union* 6:2 (1966): 74–82.

OTHER VIEWS

3159.   Duncanson, Dennis J. "Vietnam and Foreign

Powers." *International Affairs* [London] 45 (July 1969): 413–423.

3160.   Mitgang, Herbert. "The Mexican War Dove." *New Republic* 156 (Feb. 11, 1967): 23–24.

3161.   "Vietnam: French, American and Vietnamese Views." *Orbis* 10 (Fall 1966): 669–672.

3162.   Woolf, Cecil, and John Bagguley, eds. *Authors Take Sides on Vietnam: Two Questions on the War in Vietnam Answered by Authors of Several Nations.* New York: Simon & Schuster, 1967.

3163.   "The World Looks at Vietnam." *Atlas* 12 (Nov. 1966): 19–26.

United Nations and the Conflict

In the mid-1960s some critics argued that the Vietnam dispute ought to be resolved by the U.N.; Washington was not interested in the idea, and although Hanoi gave official and private support to the suggestion, their real intentions were not tested.

3164.   Bargman, Abraham. "Can the U.N. Act on Vietnam?" *War/Peace Report* 7 (Oct. 1967): 12–13.

3165.   Bloomfield, Lincoln P. "Ending the War in Vietnam: What Role for the UN?" *Current*, no. 100 (Oct. 1968): 45–48.

3166.   _____. *The U.N. and Vietnam.* New York: Carnegie Endowment for International Peace, 1968.

3167.   Cousins, Norman. "Double Jeopardy: U.N. and Vietnam." *Saturday Review* 48 (Mar. 27, 1965): 20.

3168.   Goldberg, Arthur J. "Ambassador Goldberg Submits Viet-Nam Question to U.N. Security Council." *U.S. Department of State Bulletin* 54 (Feb. 15, 1956): 229–239.

3169.   _____. "The Responsibility of the United Nations in the Search for Peace in Viet-Nam." *U.S. Department of State Bulletin* 57 (Nov. 20, 1967): 667–672.

3170.   Gordon, Max. "Vietnam, the U.S. and the UN Charter." *Vista* 6 (Nov.–Dec. 1970): 35–38.

3171.   Grant, Donald. "Vietnam: The View from the United Nations." *Progressive* 30 (Apr. 1966): 18–21.

3172.   Lawrence, David. "It's the Duty of the U.N. to Make Peace in Vietnam." *U.S. News and World Report* 72 (May 22, 1972): 104.

3173.   Long, Russell J. "Vietnam: What Role for the U.N.: The Strategy of a Truce." *Nation* 202 (Feb. 28, 1966): 227–229.

3174.   Mezerik, A.G., ed. *Viet Nam and the U.N., 1967: National and International Policy.* New York: International Review Service, 1967.

3175.   Pilkington, Betty. "Vietnam: The U.N. Peeks In." *Nation* 197 (Nov. 2, 1963): 273–275.

3176.   Rajan, M.S., and T. Israel. "The United Nations and the Conflict in Vietnam." *International Studies* [India] 12 (Oct.–Dec. 1973): 511–540.

3177.   Reuss, H.S. "Let the U.N. Handle It: Peacekeeping in Vietnam." *Commonweal* 82 (July 23, 1965): 523–526.

3178.   Schacter, Oscar. "Intervention and the United Nations." *Stanford Journal of International Studies* 3 (1968): 5–12.

3179.   Stephen, Jacobs, and Marc Poirier. "The Right to Veto United Nations Membership Applications: The United States Veto of the Viet-Nams." *Harvard International Law Journal* 17 (Summer 1976): 581–608.

3180.   Stevenson, Adlai E. "Security Council Hears U.S. Charge of North Vietnamese Attacks." *U.S. Department of State Bulletin* 51 (Aug. 24, 1964): 272–275.

3181.   "United States Accepts U.N. Secretary-General's Proposal for Ending the Vietnam Conflict." *U.S. Department of State Bulletin* 56 (Apr. 17, 1967): 624–626.

3182.   U.S. Senate. Committee on Foreign Relations. Hearings; *Submission of the Vietnam Conflict to the United Nations.* 90th Cong., 1st sess., Oct. 26, 27 and Nov. 2, 1967.

3183.   "U Thant's Path to Peace." *Progressive* 30 (Aug. 1966): 3–4.

3184.   "Vietnam: Statements by Secretary-General on Recent Developments." *U.N. Monthly Chronicle* 2 (May 1965): 21–24.

3185.   Weill-Tucherman, Anne. "Vietnam at the U.N." *Nation* 202 (Feb. 14, 1966): 169. [editorial]

Negotiations

Formal and informal negotiations were carried on throughout the war years as Washington and Hanoi jockeyed for the advantage. There was no shortage of intermediaries, "peace feelers" or private peace plans; however, Washington officials were frequently charged by antiwar critics with missing opportunities to end the war. Goodman (3191) provides an excellent introduction to the peace talks; see also "Retrospective Essays," later in this chapter.

3186.   Ashmore, Harry, and William Boggs. *Mission to Hanoi: A Chronicle of Double-Dealing in High Places.* New York: Putnam, 1968.

3187.   Cousins, Norman. "How the U.S. Spurned Three Chances for Peace in Vietnam." *Look* 33 (July 29, 1969): 45–48.

3188.   Critchley, Julian, and Betty Hunt. *The Vietnam War Negotiations.* London: World and School Crisis Papers, 1968.

3189.   Duff, P. *The Credibility Gap: A Chronological Record of Attempts to Achieve a Political Solution Leading to Peace in Vietnam.* London: International Confederation for Disarmament and Peace, 1967.

3190.   Gittings, John. "Vietnam: The Record of Proposals to Negotiate." *World Today* [London] 21 (Dec. 1965): 503–506.

3191.   Goodman, Allan E. *The Lost Peace: America's Search for a Negotiated Settlement of the Vietnam War.* Stanford, CA: Stanford University Press, 1978. This is the best study available.

3192.   Hopkins, Waring C. "An Historical Analogy: Geneva 1954 and Paris 1968." *Naval War College Review* 21 (Sept. 1968): 88–91.

3193.   Kahn, Herman, et al. *War Termination Issues and Concepts.* Croton-on Hudson, NY: Hudson Institute, 1968.

3194.   Kraslow, David, and Stuart H. Loory. *The Secret Search for Peace in Vietnam.* New York: Random House, 1968.

3195.   McCullouch, Frank. "Peace Feelers: This Frail Dance of the Seven Veils." *Life* 64 (Mar. 22, 1968): 32–38.

3196.   Niksch, Larry A. *Cease Fire in Vietnam: A Chronology of Statements by the United States, South Viet-*nam, North Vietnam, and the NLF/PRG. Washington, DC: Library of Congress, Legislative Reference Service, 1970.

3197.   Parimal Kumar Das. "The Indo-Chinese Crisis and India's Efforts Toward Peace Making, 1959–1966." *International Studies* [India] 10 (Jan. 1969): 303–320.

3198.   Radvanyi, Janos. *Delusion and Reality: Gambits, Hoaxes and Diplomatic One-Upmanship in Vietnam.* South Bend, IN: Gateway, 1978. The author reviews Soviet and East European peace initiatives.

3199.   Schurmann, Franz, et al. *The Politics of Escalation in Vietnam: A Citizens White Paper, A Study of United States Responses to Pressures for a Political Settlement of the Vietnam War, November 1963–July 1966.* Greenwich, CT: Fawcett, 1966.

3200.   Schwartz, H., et al. "An Interview With Theodore Von Laue: The Semantic Curtain of 'Negotiations.'" *Minority of One* 8 (Nov. 1966): 2–6.

3201.   Thee, Marek. *Convergent Points in the Search for Peace in Vietnam.* Oslo: International Peace Research Institute, 1969.

3202.   ———. "Vietnam: The Subtle Art of Negotiations." *Bulletin of Peace Proposals* 3:2 (1972): 163–171.

3203.   ———, ed. *Vietnam Peace Proposals, Documents 1954–1968.* Oslo: International Peace Research Institute, Mar. 1969.

3204.   Thies, Wallace J. *When Governments Collide: Coercion and Diplomacy in the Vietnam Conflict, 1964–1969.* Berkeley: University of California Press, 1981.

3205.   Tran Chanh Thanh. *From Geneva '54 to Paris '69, Have Words Lost All of Their Meanings?* Saigon: Vietnam Council on Foreign Relations, 1969.

3206.   U.S. House. Committee on Foreign Affairs. Hearings; *Termination of Hostilities in Indochina.* 92d Cong., 2d sess., 1972.

3207.   U.S. Senate. Committee on Foreign Relations. Hearings; *Vietnam Policy Proposals.* 91st Cong., 2d sess., 1970.

3208.   Van Thai, V. *Fighting and Negotiating on Vietnam: A Strategy.* RM–5997–ARPA. Santa Monica, CA: Rand Corp., July 1969.

Retrospective Essays

3209.   Baral, Jaya Krishna. "Paris Talks on Vietnam and American Diplomacy." *International Studies* [India] 14 (Apr.–June 1975): 375–396.

3210.   Grinter, Lawrence E. "Bargaining Between Saigon and Washington: Dilemmas of Linkage Politics During War." *Orbis* 18 (Fall 1974): 837–868. Grinter provides a significant analysis of how and why U.S. influence declined in Saigon between 1961 and 1971.

3211.   Pillar, Paul R. "Negotiating Peace: The Making of Armistice Agreements." Ph.D. dissertation, Princeton University, 1978. Pillar details the creation of armistice agreements for the War of 1812, the Korean War, the Algerian insurrection and the French and American wars in Vietnam.

3212.   Radvanyi, Janos. "Vietnam War Diplomacy: Reflections of a Former Iron Curtain Official." *Parameters* 10 (Sept. 1980): 8–15.

3213.   Scheidig, Robert E. "A Comparison of Communist Negotiating Methods." *Military Review* 54 (Dec. 1974): 79–89. The author compares the methods of Korea and Vietnam.

3214.   Thies, Wallace J. "Searching for Peace: Vietnam and the Question of How Wars End." *Polity* (Spring 1975): 304–333.

3215.   Zagare, Frank C. "Deception in Three-Person Games: An Analysis of Strategic Misrepresentation in Vietnam." Ph.D. dissertation, New York University, 1977. Zagare focuses on the Geneva Conference of 1954 and the Paris peace talks of 1969 to 1973.

3216.   _____. "A Game-Theoretic Analysis of the Vietnam Negotiations: Preferences and Strategies." *Journal of Conflict Resolution* 21 (Dec. 1977): 663–684.

PRIVATE PEACE PROPOSALS

"At any one time," Max Frankel wrote (3225), "there are usually more peace plans than bombs in the air." Unfortunately, most of these plans failed to consider the objectives and ambitions of either Hanoi or Washington. Listed below are some of these peace proposals. See the section entitled "Antiwar Movement" in Chapter 9, for more suggestions for peace.

3217.   American Friends Service Committee. *Peace in Vietnam: A New Approach in South East Asia.* New York: Hill & Wang, 1966.

3218.   _____. *La Tragédie vietnamiènne vue par des Quakers américaines: Propositions nouvelles pour la paix.* Paris: Les Éditions du Pavillon, 1967.

3219.   Barnet, Richard J. "An Administration Critic Presents His Version of the Winning Scenario for the Last Act in Vietnam." *New York Times Magazine* (Feb. 4, 1968): 26–27ff.

3220.   Burns, J.M. "A Way Out in Vietnam." *Harper's* 233 (Aug. 1968): 34–35.

3221.   Cavers, D., et al. *A Workable Plan for a Peaceful Settlement in Southeast Asia Offered as a Proposal to the United Nations to Resolve the War in Vietnam and Bring Peace to the Entire Area.* New York: National Research Council of Peace Strategy, 1965.

3222.   Devillers, Philippe. "Preventing the Peace: Report from an Intermediary." *Nation* 203 (Dec. 5, 1966): 597–603.

3223.   Eden, Anthony. *Toward Peace in Indochina.* London: Oxford University Press, 1966. [an extract appears in *Harper's* 233 (Aug. 1966): 36–43]

3224.   Falk, Richard A. "An End for the Vietnam War: A Plan and Rationale." *Congressional Record* 115 (May 19, 1969): 12994–12998.

3225.   Frankel, Max. "How Long Will it Last?" *New York Times Magazine* (Apr. 30, 1967): 28ff.

3226.   Galbraith, John Kenneth. *How to Get Out of Vietnam: A Workable Solution to the Worst Problem of Our Time.* New York: New American Library, 1967. [an extract appears in *New York Times Magazine* (Nov. 12, 1967): 29–30ff; see also William P. Bundy, "Bundy Comments on Galbraith's Plan" in the same issue: 31ff]

3227.   Glazer, Nathan. "Vietnam: The Case for Immediate Withdrawal." *Commentary* 51 (May 1971): 33–37.

3228.   "Harriman [W. Averell] Suggests a Way Out of Vietnam." *New York Times Magazine* (Aug. 24, 1969): 24–25ff. See I.F. Stone's plea (3237) below.

3229.   Kennedy, Edward M. "Halt the Bombing: Mutual Withdrawal." *Vital Speeches* 34 (Sept. 15, 1968): 717–719. See "Congressional Opinions," above, this chapter, for other congressional suggestions.

3230.   Kiester, E. "Canada's Chester Ronning: One Man's Attempt to Bring Peace to Vietnam." *Parade* (June 4, 1967): 26–28.

3231.   Landauer, Carl. "A Dove's Peace Proposal." *New Leader* 52 (Oct. 27, 1969): 3–5.

3232.   Lieurance, Peter R. "Negotiation Now! The National Committee for a Political Settlement in Vietnam." In *From War to Peace: Essays in Peacemaking and War Termination*, edited by David S. Smith. New York: Columbia University Press, 1974, 171–201.

3233.   McCarthy, Mary. "Vietnam: Solutions." *New York Review of Books* (Nov. 9, 1967): 3–8.

3234.   Marcovich, M. "Pugwash and Vietnam—1967:

A Memoir." *Pugwash Newsletter* 13 (Apr. 1974): 203–207.

3235. Schlesinger, Arthur M., Jr. "A Middle Way Out of Vietnam." *New York Times Magazine* (Sept. 18, 1966): 47ff.

3236. Smith, H. "The Paris Talks Started 471 Days Ago . . . Harriman Suggests a Way Out of Vietnam." *New York Times Magazine* (Aug. 24, 1969): 24.

3237. Stone, I.F. "An Appeal to Averell Harriman." *New York Review of Books* (June 19, 1969): 5–7. See also Smith (3236) and Harriman (3228).

3238. Vu Van Thai. "A Regional Solution for Vietnam." *Foreign Affairs* 46 (Jan. 1968): 347–361.

3239. White, G.F. "Vietnam: The Fourth Course." *Bulletin of the Atomic Scientists* 20 (Dec. 1964): 6–10. White focuses on regional development.

3240. White, Theodore H. "A Proposal to End the Vietnam Fighting." *Saturday Review* 53 (Mar. 21, 1970): 23–25ff.

3241. Woito, R. *Vietnam Peace Proposals.* Berkeley: World Without War Council, 1967.

NORTH VIETNAM'S POSITION

Hanoi's basic objective was to "unify" Vietnam under its control; any suggested "flexibility" in the North's negotiating position only reflected Hanoi's assessment of how the basic goal could best be accomplished.

3242. Burchett, Wilfred G. "How Hanoi and the N.L.F. See Chances for Peace." *War/Peace Report* 7 (Nov. 1967): 3–6.

3243. _____. "Negotiations on Vietnam? How It Looks from the 'Other Side.'" *War/Peace Report* 6 (Nov. 1966): 3–5.

3244. _____. "Why North Vietnam Rejects 'Unconditional Negotiations.'" *War/Peace Report* 5 (Dec. 1965): 7–9.

3245. "D.R.V.N. Government Statement on Negotiations on Vietnam Problem." *Peking Review* 15 (Nov. 3, 1972): 6–10.

3246. Falk, Richard A. *A Vietnam Settlement: The View from Hanoi.* Princeton, NJ: Princeton University, Center of International Studies, 1968.

3247. "Ho Keeps Saying 'No': Two Years, 45 Peace 'Feelers.'" *U.S. News and World Report* 62 (Apr. 10, 1967): 42.

3248. Honey, Patrick J. "North Vietnam and Peace Negotiations." *China New Analysis* 726 (Sept. 20, 1968): 1–7.

3249. "An Interview with Ha Van Lau." *War/Peace Report* 9 (June–July 1969): 12–13. Ha Van Lau was the Hanoi deputy delegate to the Paris talks.

3250. "An Interview with Mme. Nguyen Thia Binh." *War/Peace Report* 9 (June–July, 1969): 7–11. Mm. Binh was the NLF delegate to the Paris talks.

3251. Jenkins, Brian. *Why the North Vietnamese Keep Fighting.* P–4395. Santa Monica, CA: Rand Corp., Aug. 1970.

3252. Kahin, George McT. "Negotiations: The View from Hanoi." *New Republic* 165 (Nov. 6, 1971): 13–16.

3253. _____. "The NLF's Terms for Peace." *New Republic* 157 (Oct. 14, 1967): 13–17.

3254. Lacouture, Jean. "How to Talk to Mr. Ho." *Ramparts* 5 (Oct. 1966): 42–46.

3255. Lens, Sidney. "What Hanoi Wants." *Progressive* 31 (Sept. 1967): 18–20.

3256. Moskin, J. Robert. "The Hard-Line Demand: Victory-Exclusive Report from Hanoi." *Look* 34 (Dec. 29, 1970): 20–25.

3257. Osborne, Milton E. "Hanoi's Aims: Vietnam or Indochina?" *Pacific Community* [Japan] 3 (Jan. 1971): 330–341.

3258. Roberts, Adam. "Hanoi's Offer to Talk." *World Affairs* 24 (May 1968): 176–178.

3259. "Text of the North Vietnam Seven-Point Peace Plan." *Survival* 13 (Sept. 1971): 314–315.

3260. Tombough, William W. "Some Thoughts on Negotiations with the North Vietnamese." *Forum* 22 (Spring–Summer 1975): 49–58. [covers 1972 to 1974]

SOUTH VIETNAM'S POSITION

In the later stages of negotiating the armistice, Saigon officials provided some of the most serious obstacles; they wanted defomote guarantees from the U.S.

3261. Downs, Hunton. "Diplomacy: Saigon in Retrospect." *Ramparts* 6 (Dec. 1967): 12–19, 22.

3262. Falk, Richard A. "Saigon Notwithstanding." *Nation* 208 (June 2, 1969): 689–693.

3263. Grant, Zalin B. "Why Saigon Wants No Early Cease-Fire." *New Republic* 159 (Dec. 21, 1968): 15–17.

3264.   Hudson, Richard. "Time for a Coup in Saigon." *War/Peace Report* 9 (June–July 1969): 3–6.

3265.   Joiner, Charles A. "South Vietnam: The Politics of Peace." *Asian Survey* 9 (Feb. 1969): 138–155.

3266.   Langguth, A.J. "Thieu and Ky Think About the Unthinkable." *New York Times Magazine* (Apr. 14, 1968): 21ff.

3267.   Nguyen Huu Chi. "Negotiations or Surrender?" *Vital Speeches* 35 (Mar. 1, 1969): 318–320.

3268.   Sanders, Sol W. "Why Saigon Fears Nixon Peace Plan." *U.S. News and World Report* 66 (June 30, 1969): 28–29.

3269.   Schanberg, Sydney H.A. "The Saigon Follies, or Trying to Head Them Off at Credibility Gap." *New York Times Magazine* (Nov. 12, 1972): 38ff.

3270.   Silverman, Jerry M. "South Vietnam and the Elusive Peace." *Asian Survey* 13 (Jan. 1979): 19–45.

JOHNSON YEARS, 1964–1968

President Johnson opened formal talks with Hanoi. See also Chapter 4 for more on negotiations during these years.

Official Statements

3271.   Bunker, Ellsworth. "U.S. Reaffirms Goals of Vietnam Peace Talks." *U.S. Department of State Bulletin* 59 (Nov. 25, 1968): 537.

3272.   Goldberg, Arthur J. "Persevering for Peace." *U.S. Department of State Bulletin* 56 (June 5, 1967): 838–844.

3273.   Harriman, W. Averell. "Vietnam Peace Talks: Harriman Gives Official U.S. Position." *U.S. News and World Report* 64 (May 27, 1968): 90–91.

3274.   Johnson, Lyndon B. "A Bid for Peace ... and a Rebuff." *U.S. News and World Report* 62 (Apr. 3, 1967): 26–27. This article contains the full text of the Johnson and Ho Chi Minh letters.

3275.   _____. "Essentials of Honorable Peace in Vietnam." *U.S. Department of State Bulletin* 59 (Sept. 9, 1968): 275–279.

3276.   _____. "LBJ Declares He Won't Run: Halts North Vietnam Raids." *CQ Weekly Report* 26 (Apr. 5, 1968): 721–724.

3277.   _____. "President Johnson's Proposal for Negotiation on Vietnam Rejected by Ho Chi Minh." *U.S.*

Department of State Bulletin 56 (Apr. 10, 1967): 595–597.

3278.   Johnson, Walter. "The U Thant–Stevenson Peace Initiatives in Vietnam, 1964–1965." *Diplomatic History* 1 (Summer 1977): 285–295.

3279.   Sevareid, Eric. "The Final Troubled Hours of Adlai Stevenson." *Look* 29 (Nov. 30, 1965): 81–86.

General

3280.   Acheson, Dean. "Negotiate with the Reds?" *U.S. News and World Report* 63 (Dec. 18, 1967): 50–51.

3281.   "After the [Bombing] Pause: Motion or Progress?" *Newsweek* 67 (Feb. 14, 1966): 17–23.

3282.   Browne, Malcolm W. "Are Negotiations Possible? No." *War/Peace Report* 7 (Jan. 1967): 6–7.

3283.   Buttinger, Joseph. "Can the Negotiations Bring Peace to Vietnam?" *Dissent* 15 (July–Aug. 1968): 296–300.

3284.   "Can Vietnam be Neutralized?" *War/Peace Report* 4 (Apr. 1964): 3–7.

3285.   Cooper, Chester L. "The Complexities of Negotiation." *Foreign Affairs* 46 (Apr. 1968): 454–466.

3286.   Cousins, Norman. "Why Don't They Negotiate?" *Saturday Review* 48 (Dec. 25, 1965): 24, 62.

3287.   Donhoff, Marion. "In the Shadow of Vietnam: The Great Powers More Rigid, Asia More Flexible." *International Affairs* [London] 42 (Oct. 1966): 609–618.

3288.   Draper, Theodore. "How Not to Negotiate." *New York Review of Books* (May 4, 1967): 17–29.

3289.   Durbrow, Elbridge. "Negotiating with the Communists: Firmness Is the Key." *Air Force & Space Digest* 51 (Sept. 1968): 48–52.

3290.   Fallers, L.A., et al. "The Policy Proposals: 'A Negotiated Stalemate.'" *Bulletin of the Atomic Scientists* 21 (June 1965): 42–44.

3291.   Fraleigh, Arnold. "How to Fail in Negotiations Without Really Trying." *New Republic* 154 (Jan. 1, 1966): 9.

3292.   Great Britain. Foreign Office. *Recent Exchange concerning Attempts to Promote a Negotiated Settlement of the Conflict in Viet-Nam.* London: HMSO, 1965.

3293.   Halberstam, David. "Bargaining with Hanoi." *New Republic* 158 (May 11, 1968): 14–16.

3294. Hudson, Richard. "The Nearest to Negotiations Yet." *War/Peace Report* 7 (Mar. 1967): 3–4.

3295. Huntington, Samuel P. "The Bases of Accommodation." *Foreign Affairs* 46 (July 1968): 642–656.

3296. Ikle, Fred C. "The Real Negotiations on South Vietnam." *Reporter* 32 (June 3, 1965): 15–19.

3297. Jencks, Christopher. "Negotiations Now? Reflections on a Meeting with the Enemy." *New Republic* 157 (Oct. 7, 1967): 19–23.

3298. Kahn, Herman. "If Negotiations Fail." *Foreign Affairs* 46 (July 1968): 627–641.

3299. Mecklin, John. "Should We Negotiate in Vietnam?" *New Leader* 50 (Mar. 13, 1967): 14–19.

3300. Nguyen Van Ba. "Bases for a Valid Settlement." *Vietnamese Studies* 18/19 (Sept. 1968): 303–334.

3301. Nicolson, Nigel. "Diplomatic Initiative on Vietnam." *Listener* 74 (July 22, 1965): 111–112, 142.

3302. Phan Quang Dan. "We Must Contact Our Opponents." *War/Peace Report* 8 (Aug.–Sept. 1968): 12–16.

3303. Reicher, Reuben. *Une Paix immédiate au Viet-Nam: Est-elle possible?* Paris: S.G.R.A.D.I., 1966.

3304. Sanders, Sol W. "Why the Communists Need a Truce." *U.S. News and World Report* 65 (Nov. 4, 1968): 64–66.

3305. Swomley, John M., Jr. "Peace Negotiations and President Johnson." *Minority of One* 10 (Sept. 1968): 10–12.

3306. Trager, Frank N. "Back to Geneva '54? An Act of Political Folly!" *Vietnam Perspectives* 1:1 (1965): 1–7.

3307. Tran Van Dinh. "Are Negotiations Possible? Yes." *War/Peace Report* 7 (Jan. 1967): 7–10.

3308. _____. "Reunification: Key to Peace in Vietnam." *War/Peace Reports* 6 (Dec. 1966): 3–4.

3309. Williams, Geoffrey. "America Seeks to Negotiate." *Contemporary Review* 213 (Aug. 1968): 84–85, 89.

3310. "With United States Winning in Vietnam, Reds Don't Talk Peace: What's Holding Them Up?" *U.S. News and World Report* 59 (Nov. 8, 1965): 44–45.

Paris Talks—First Phase

See also Chapter 7, under "Air War," for negative views.

3311. Barnet, Richard J. "The North Vietnamese in Paris: The Impasse." *New York Review of Books* (Oct. 24, 1968): 7.

3312. Belovski, Dimce. "The Paris Talks." *Review of International Affairs* [Belgrade] 19 (June 5, 1968): 6–8.

3313. Burchett, Wilfred G. "The Paris Talks: Report." *New World Review* 36 (Fall–Winter 1968): 3–16.

3314. _____. "The Paris Talks and the War." *Liberation* 13 (Oct. 1968): 29–31.

3315. _____. "Vietnam: One Year of the Peace Talks." *New World Review* 37:2 (1969): 2–9.

3316. Davis, Derek. "What Price Peace at Paris?" *Far Eastern Economic Review* 60 (May 26–June 1, 1968): 473–476.

3317. Hayden, Tom. "The Impasse in Paris." *Ramparts* 3 (Aug. 24, 1968): 18–21.

3318. Kahin, George McT. "Impasse at Paris." *New Republic* 159 (Oct. 12, 1968): 23–26.

3319. Lenart, Edith R. "Paris Talks: Stubbornly Last Summer." *Far Eastern Economic Review* 63 (Dec. 29, 1968): 18–20.

3320. Mustafa, Zubeida. "The Paris Peace Talks." *Pakistan Horizon* 22:1 (1969): 29–38.

3321. Shaplen, Robert. "Seats at the Table." *New Yorker* 44 (Nov. 16, 1968): 193–206.

3322. _____. "Until the Chairs Rot." *New Yorker* 45 (July 5, 1969): 36–57.

3323. Terrill, Ross. "Making Peace at Paris: A Special Report on the Negotiations." *Atlantic Monthly* 222 (Dec. 1968): 4–33.

3324. _____. "A Report on the Paris Talks." *New Republic* 159 (July 13, 1968): 15–18.

Bombing Pause

President Johnson withdrew from renomination and halted bombing of North Vietnam on March 31, 1968.

3325. Grant, Zalin B. "The Bombing Halt." *New Republic* 159 (Nov. 9, 1968): 13–15.

3326. Greene, Wallace M. "The Bombing 'Pause': Formula for Failure." *Air Force Magazine* 59 (Apr. 1976): 36–39.

3327. Johnson, Lyndon B. "United States Halts the

Bombing of North Vietnam." *U.S. Department of State Bulletin* 59 (Nov. 18, 1968): 517–519.

3328.   Shaplen, Robert. "A Reporter at Large." *New Yorker* 44 (Nov. 16, 1968): 193–200ff. Shaplen gives Hanoi's reaction.

NIXON YEARS, 1969–1973

Nixon and his foreign affairs advisor, Henry Kissinger, conducted the negotiations which concluded the formal armistice. These negotiations included the bombing of Haiphong and Hanoi; see Chapter 7, under "Aerial Blitz, 1972," for this action. See also Chapter 4, under "Presidential Policies and Critics," for accounts of Nixon and Kissinger. Kissinger's memoirs (2807) shed additional light on the issues and decisions of this period.

Official Statements

3329.   Irwin, John N., II. "Vietnam: Ending U.S. Involvement in the War." *U.S. Department of State Bulletin* 64 (May 31, 1971): 711–714.

3330.   Kissinger, Henry A. "The Viet Nam Negotiation." *Foreign Affairs* 47 (Jan. 1969): 211–234. This was written before he joined Nixon's staff.

3331.   Nixon, Richard M. "Indochina: An Equitable Proposal for Peace." *U.S. Department of State Bulletin* 66 (Feb. 14, 1972): 181–185.

3332.   _____. "President Nixon Hails Saigon Proposals for Political Settlement in South Vietnam." *U.S. Department of State Bulletin* 61 (July 28, 1969): 61–62.

3333.   _____. "The War in Vietnam: Peace Negotiations." *Vital Speeches* 36 (June 1, 1969): 482–484.

3334.   U.S. Department of State. *Viet-Nam: The Negotiating Process.* Publication no. 8629. Washington, DC: GPO, 1972.

General

3335.   "After One Year of Truce Moves." *U.S. News and World Report* 66 (Apr. 7, 1969): 26–28.

3336.   Baldwin, Frank. "A 'Korean Solution' for Vietnam?" *New Republic* 163 (July 18, 1970): 19–21.

3337.   Chomsky, Noam. "Nixon's Peace Offer." *Ramparts* 10 (Apr. 1972): 12–14ff.

3338.   Cousins, Norman. "Vietnam: The Spurned Peace." *Saturday Review* 52 (July 26, 1969): 12–16ff.

3339.   Davis, Rennie, et al. "The Statement of Ngo Cong

Duc: The Way to End the War." *New York Review of Books* (Nov. 5, 1970): 17–18.

3340.   Dickson, P. "The War of the Words." *Progressive* 36 (Apr. 1972): 36–39.

3341.   Fulbright, Senator J. William. "Signals for Peace in 1969." *Congressional Record* 118 (Aug. 15, 1972): 28225–28240.

3342.   Goodman, Allan E. "Ending the Vietnam Conflict: Expectations in Hanoi and Saigon." *Orbis* 16 (Fall 1972): 632–645.

3343.   _____. "Is It Too Late to End the Vietnam War?" *Southeast Asia* 1 (Fall 1971): 365–377.

3344.   Kahin, George McT. "Nixon's Peace Plan: No Basis for Negotiation." *New Republic* 166 (Feb. 12, 1972): 12–14.

3345.   Kleiman, Robert. "The Vance Plan for a Vietnam Cease-Fire." *New York Times Magazine* (Sept. 21, 1969): 30–31ff. Cyrus Vance later became secretary of state under President Carter.

3346.   Kolko, Gabriel. "Vietnam: La Guerre et la diplomatic américaine depuis janvier 1968." *Partisans* 48 (June–Aug. 1969): 81–106.

3347.   Kung Hsien-wu. "Why Does the United States Make Concessions in the War in Vietnam?" *Asian Outlook* 4 (June 1969): 40–44.

3348.   Morganthau, Hans J. "Between Hanoi and Saigon: Kissinger's Next Test." *New Leader* 55 (Nov. 13, 1972): 5–6.

3349.   Osborne, John. "Vietnam: The President's Fading Hope." *New Republic* 161 (Sept. 27, 1969): 17–19.

3350.   Starobin, Joseph R. "What Nixon Isn't Admitting." *New York Review of Books* (Dec. 18, 1969): 44ff. [Senator Fulbright's report, see (3341) above]

3351.   Stone, I.F. "The Hidden Traps in Nixon's Peace Plan." *New York Review of Books* (Mar. 9, 1972): 13–17.

3352.   "The Strategy and Tactics of Peace in Vietnam." *Time* 93 (Mar. 28, 1969): 18–20ff.

3353.   Tran Van Dinh. "The Only Road to Peace." *Progressive* 36 (Jan. 1972): 35–38.

3354.   Vielly, M. "L'Enjeu des negociations sur le Vietnam." *Revue de Défense Nationale* 25:1 (1969): 44–54.

3355.   "Vietnam: Peace Talks, Bombing, 1969 Secret Study." *CQ Weekly Report* 30 (Apr. 29, 1972): 923–927.

3356.   Wallace, James N. "Vietnam Dilemma: A First-

Hand Explanation." *U.S. News and World Report* 66 (June 16, 1969): 26–29.

3357. Wolf, Charles, Jr. "Vietnam Prospects and Precepts." *Asian Survey* 9 (Mar. 1969): 157–162.

Paris Talks—Second Phase

Nixon and Kissinger conducted this phase during 1969 and 1970.

3358. Buttinger, Joseph. "Toward Peace at Paris?" *Dissent* 16 (Mar.–Apr. 1969): 108–112.

3359. Devillers, Philippe. "The Paris Negotiations on Vietnam." *World Today* [London] 25 (Aug. 1969): 339–350.

3360. Grant, Zalin B. "Why the Paris Talks Are Getting Nowhere." *New Republic* 163 (Oct. 10, 1970): 17–19.

3361. Kahin, George McT. "Why Is the U.S. So Afraid of Coalition? Going Nowhere in Paris." *New Republic* 163 (Dec. 26, 1970): 11–12.

3362. Lenart, Edith R., "Paris Talks: End Game in Paris." *Far Eastern Economic Review* 65 (Aug. 3–9, 1969): 370–372.

3363. Rinalfo, Robert. "A Report on the Paris Peace Talks." *Journal of Contemporary Revolutions* 3 (Winter 1970–1971): 75–84.

3364. Shaplen, Robert. "A Reporter at Large: The Peace Talks." *New Yorker* 46 (Oct. 17, 1970): 162ff.

3365. Stone, I.F. "The Paris Peace Talks." *New York Review of Books* (June 19, 1969): 1ff.

3366. Terrill, Ross. "The Paris Negotiations." *Atlantic Monthly* 223 (May 1969): 18–22ff.

3367. Tran Van Dinh. "The Other Side of the Table." *Washington Monthly* 1 (Jan. 1970): 74–80.

3368. Wainwright, William H. "The Paris Peace Talks: Diplomacy and Stagecraft." *Antioch Review* 29 (Winter 1969): 505–514.

3369. Zubeida, Mustafa. "The Paris Peace Talks." *Pakistan Horizon* 22:1 (1969): 29–38.

Paris Talks—Final Phase

This phase (1972–1973) included the U.S. election of 1972, the mining of North Vietnamese harbors, the December bombing of Hanoi and Haiphong and the bringing of Saigon around to terms; see also Chapter 4, under "Nixon Years, 1969–1974," and Chapter 7, under "Aerial Blitz, 1972." Negotiations to work out details continued after the initial signing of the armistice; meanwhile, both the United States and the Soviet Union were charged with shipping arms to Vietnam to obtain a favorable military balance when the armistice took effect.

3370. "Getting Ready for Truce: A Rush of Arms to Vietnam." *U.S. News and World Report* 73 (Nov. 27, 1972): 18–19.

3371. Hubbard, H. "Clouds over Paris." *Newsweek* 80 (Dec. 4, 1972): 26–27.

3372. "International Conference on Vietnam Held at Paris." *U.S. Department of State Bulletin* 68 (Mar. 26, 1973): 337–347.

3373. Karnow, Stanley. "Talk and Liveried Footmen: The Looking Glass Conference." *New Republic* 168 (Mar. 17, 1973): 13–15.

3374. Kissinger, Henry A. "Dr. Kissinger Discusses Status of Negotiations Toward Vietnam Peace." *U.S. Department of State Bulletin* 67 (Nov. 13, 1972): 549–558.

3375. ———. "Dr. Kissinger Reviews Obstacles in Negotiations on Vietnam Peace." *U.S. Department of State Bulletin* 68 (Jan. 8, 1973): 33–41.

3376. ———. "Inside Story of Secret Talks with the Enemy." *U.S. News and World Report* 72 (Feb. 7, 1972): 62–66.

3377. ———. "Kissinger: 'We Believe Peace Is At Hand.'" *CQ Weekly Report* 30 (Oct. 28, 1972): 2855–2858.

3378. ———. "Presidential Assistant Kissinger Discusses Negotiations for Peace in Indochina." *U.S. Department of State Bulletin* 66 (Feb. 14, 1972): 188–198.

3379. Landon, Kenneth P. "The Impact of the Sino–American Detente on the Indochinese Conflict." In *Sino–American Detente and Its Policy Implications*, edited by G.T. Hsiao. New York: Praeger, 1974.

3380. Nixon, Richard M. "Significant Breakthrough in the Viet-Nam Negotiations—Remarks on October 26." *U.S. Department of State Bulletin* 67 (Nov. 13, 1972): 558–560. These remarks were aimed at the American electorate.

3381. Szulc, Tad. "How Kissinger Did It: Behind the Vietnam Cease-Fire Agreement." *Foreign Policy*, no. 15 (Summer 1974): 21–69.

3382. Thee, Marek. "US–Chinese Rapprochement and Vietnam." *Journal of Peace Research* 9:1 (1972): 63–67.

3383. "Thieu at the Bridge: Kissinger–Tho Discussions." *National Review* 24 (Nov. 24, 1972): 1288.

3384. "The War in Indochina: The Elusive Peace Deal." *Newsweek* 80 (Nov. 13, 1972): 42ff.

ARMISTICE, 1973

An American–Vietnamese cease-fire agreement and protocols were signed in Paris on January 27, 1973; a subsequent armistice agreement, protocols, amendments, etc. were signed in Paris on June 13, 1973, implementing the armistice.

3385. "Agreement on Ending the War and Restoring Peace in Vietnam; Protocols, Amendments, etc., June 13, 1973 ... Signed at Paris, June 13, 1973." *Treaties and Other International Acts.* Publication no. 7674. Washington, DC: GPO, 1973.

3386. "American–Vietnamese Agreement and Protocols, 27 January 1973." *Survival* 15 (Mar.–Apr. 1973): 81–97. [texts]

3387. "Communique Signed at Paris on Implementation of Vietnam Agreement." *U.S. Department of State Bulletin* 69 (July 9, 1973): 45–53.

3388. "Implementation of the Vietnam Agreement: Text of Joint Communique of June 13, 1973." *Weekly Compilation of Presidential Documents* 9 (June 18, 1973): 758–765.

3389. "Official Text of the Cease-Fire Agreement." *U.S. News and World Report* 74 (Feb. 5, 1973): 66–71.

3390. *Paris Agreement on Viet Nam: Fundamental Juridical Problems.* Hanoi: Institute of Juridical Sciences, Committee of Social Science of the DRVN, 1973.

3391. U.S. Department of State. Office of Media Services. *Documentation on the Viet-Nam Armistice.* Publication no. 8695. Washington, DC: GPO, 1973.

Evaluation

3392. "After a Cease-Fire: Stumbling Blocks to Vietnam Peace." *U.S. News and World Report* 73 (Nov. 1972): 14–17.

3393. Branfman, Fred. "Prospects for Vietnam After the Agreement Is Signed." *Bulletin of Concerned Asian Scholars* (Dec. 4, 1972): 46–48.

3394. Busch, Benjamin, Richard A. Falk, and Eugene V. Rostow. "The Justness of the Peace." *American Journal of International Law* 67 (May 1973): 258–271.

3395. "Can the U.S. Make the Truce Stick?" *U.S. News and World Report* 74 (Feb. 12, 1973): 17–20.

3396. Candlin, A.H.S. "The Truce in Vietnam." *Army Quarterly and Defence Journal* 103 (Apr. 1973): 287–293.

3397. Clark, Ramsey. "The Thoughts of Ramsey Clark on the Ending of the War in Vietnam." *Center Report* [Center for the Study of Democratic Institutions, Santa Barbara, CA] 6:1 (1973): 3–5.

3398. Clubb, Oliver E. "The Cease-Fire." *Nation* 216 (Feb. 12, 1973): 198–201.

3399. Degan, Vladimir-Duro. "The Vietnam Peace Agreement." *Review of International Affairs* [Belgrade] 24 (Feb. 20, 1973): 6–10.

3400. Duncanson, Dennis J. "The Ceasefire in Vietnam." *World Today* [London] 29 (Mar. 1973): 89–97.

3401. "For Indo-China, the War Is Far from Over." *U.S. News and World Report* 74 (Feb. 5, 1973): 20–22.

3402. Goodstadt, Leo. "The Peace No Once Believes." *Far Eastern Economic Review* 79 (Jan. 29, 1973): 11–12.

3403. Goralski, Wladyslaw. "The Paris Agreements and the Polish Contribution to the Settlement of the Vietnam Conflict." *Studies on the Developing Countries*, no. 4 (1974): 5–28.

3404. "Initial Public Reaction to Peace Settlement? We Have Achieved Peace with Honor." *Gallup Opinion Index*, no. 92 (Feb. 1973): 5–14.

3405. Jenkins, Brian. *A Route for the Enemy to Escape: Hanoi's View of the Cease-Fire.* P–5012. Santa Monica, CA: Rand Corp., May 1973.

3406. _____. *Why the North Vietnamese Will Keep Fighting.* P–4395–1. Santa Monica, CA: Rand Corp., Mar. 1972.

3407. Kaplan, Morton, et al. *Vietnam Settlement: Why 1973, Not 1969?* Washington, DC: American Enterprise Institute for Public Policy Research, 1973.

3408. Karnow, Stanley. "Truce or Peace? The Vietnam Accord." *New Republic* 168 (Jan. 27, 1973): 19–20.

3409. "Letters Between Senator Kennedy and Dr. Kissinger, March 13 and 14, 1974." *Congressional Record* 120 (Apr. 1, 1974): 9033.

3410. "Letters, Report and Interviews of Graham Martin, U.S. Ambassador to Vietnam." *U.S. News and World Report* 76 (Apr. 29, 1974): 72–74.

3411. Porter, D. Gareth. *A Peace Denied: The United*

States, Vietnam and the Paris Agreement. Bloomington: Indiana University Press, 1975.

3412. _____. "Vietnam: Politics of the Paris Agreement." *Current History* 65 (Dec. 1973): 247–251ff.

3413. Randle, Robert F. "Peace in Vietnam and Laos: 1954, 1962, 1973." In *From War to Peace: Essays in Peacemaking and War Termination*, edited by D. S. Smith. New York: Columbia University Press, 1974, 255–282.

3414. Simon, Sheldon W. "Implications of Ceasefire Pact for North Vietnamese Strategy." *International Perspectives* [Canada] (May–June 1973): 9–14.

3415. Sullivan, Marianna P. *France and the Vietnam Peace Settlement." Political Science Quarterly* 82 (June 1974): 305–324.

3416. Thompson, Robert. *Peace Is Not at Hand.* New York: McKay, 1974. Thompson argues that the U.S. allowed too easy terms.

3417. _____. "Why Did Hanoi Sign the Cease-Fire Agreement?" *Ordnance* 58 (July 8, 1973): 50–51.

3418. "The Vietnam Peace." *U.S. News and World Report* 74 (Feb. 5, 1973): 16–19.

3419. Volskii, Dmitrii A. *Great Victory of the Vietnamese People.* Moscow: Novosti, 1973.

International Commission of Control and Supervision (ICCS)

The International Commission of Control and Supervision was charged with making sure the terms of the armistice were carried out. However, it could not carry out its assignment.

3420. Culhane, Claire. "How Canada Torpedoed the Peace in Vietnam." *Canadian Dimension* 9 (July 1973): 6–7. Canada withdrew from the ICCS.

3421. Dobell, W.M. "A 'Sow's Ear' in Vietnam." *International Journal* [Toronto] 29 (Summer 1974): 356–392.

3422. Kirk, Donald. "Observers at a Continuing War: The ICCS's Impossible Mission." *New Leader* 56 (June 11, 1973): 6–9.

3423. Piotrowski, Karl P. "Negotiating with the Enemy." *Air University Review* 28 (Sept.–Oct. 1974): 53–61. The author describes the post-Armistice negotiations of the four-party Joint Military Commission.

3424. Richeson, Alfred K. "The Four-Party Joint Military Commission." *Military Review* 53 (Aug. 1973): 16–27.

3425. Van Praagh, David. "The Canadians Are Coming Home." *Nation* 216 (June 18, 1973): 779–781.

Violations of the Armistice

Violations of the cease-fire accord came quickly; the initial charge was that each side was restocking its military hardware. Fighting inside South Vietnam between ARVN and VC appears to have continued; see also "Post-Armistice Interlude, 1973–1975," in Chapter 3.

3426. Falk, Richard A. "The Paris Agreement: Breaking Faith in Vietnam." *Nation* 218 (Jan. 12, 1974): 38–41.

3427. Giardina, Andrea. "La Violazione degli Accordi di Parigi Sul Viet-Nam." *La Comunita Internazionale* 29:3 (1974): 624–640. The author describes U.S. and South Vietnamese violations.

3428. Nguyen Van Hoa. "US Violations of the Paris Agreement." *World Peace Council* 3 (May–June 1973): 24–25.

3429. "Statement by the Government of the Democratic Republic of Viet Nam concerning the Very Serious Violation of the Paris Agreement on Viet Nam by the U.S. Government and the Saigon Administration." Mimeographed. Hanoi, Feb. 26, 1973.

3430. "United States Cites Major Violations of Peace Accords by North Vietnam Text of Note to International Conference on Vietnam and to International Commission of Control and Supervision, March 15, 1974." *U.S. Department of State Bulletin* 70 (Apr. 8, 1974): 361–362.

3431. "U.S. Replies to D.R.V. Charges of Violations of Vietnam Cease-Fire." *U.S. Department of State Bulletin* 68 (May 14, 1973): 599–603.

3432. "Viet Truce Violations Documented." *Aviation Week & Space Technology* 99 (Sept. 17, 1973): 12–17. This article includes a large number of photographs.

❧ Chapter Six ❧
Strategy, Tactics and Support Efforts

"AMERICAN STRATEGISTS struck out in Vietnam," according to Colonel John M. Collins, U.S.A., retired (3545). With a self-critical attitude, he argued that Pentagon officials never grasped that America's superior military-technological advantage "was trivial rather than telling; and, the desired culmination was political, rather than military, victory."[1] While there is much to question in Collins' list of particulars, it is difficult to quarrel with his insistence that American strategists, fascinated with firepower ignored the essential political dimensions of counterinsurgency for too long.

American military leaders today are apparently still unwilling to begin the painful self-criticism necessary to create a viable counterinsurgency strategy. Led by Admiral U.S.G. Sharp's "stab-in-the-back" thesis (3507), these professionals would rather blame the failure of strategy on civilian leaders who refused to allow massive bombing of North Vietnam early in the conflict. These "strategists" insist that if Hanoi was persuaded by the aerial blitz of December 1972 to sign an armistice, an all-out bombing campaign in 1965 aimed at the North's petroleum supply, power systems and transportation network would have brought Hanoi to terms much sooner. The fallacies of this thesis are many; one of the more obvious weaknesses lies in Hanoi's unflagging determination to achieve the unification of Vietnam on their terms. If the North Vietnamese did not deviate from this objective after the 1973 armistice, why should one believe that they would have wavered after an armistice in 1965 or 1966?

Perhaps we ought to be more concerned with the not-too-implicit assumption underlying Sharp's thesis, that the military experts were prevented from achieving victory by bungling, interfering politicians. This reasoning goes hand in hand with the misguided notion that once the decision for war is made, the civilian leaders should step aside and turn the direction of the war over to the uniformed professionals. Clausewitz long ago dismissed this simplistic notion. "If a nation must go to war," this often misunderstood genius wrote, "the political object is the goal, war is the means of reaching it, and means can never be considered in isolation from their purpose."[2] How well American military leaders have digested this principle is best found in their writings; see "Admirals and Generals" later in this chapter.

Most of the "official" military histories which have appeared so far are disappointing. "Many of these efforts provide revealing data and documentation," Peter Braestrup has noted, "but they suffer from the flaws inherent in 'official' history: parochialism, heavy reliance on official papers, blandness, and a reluctance to explore error, command failure, or confusion."[3] A broad assortment of these official offerings has been listed here under "Official Histories," together with an estimate of future publication.

Other authors have not been so reluctant to level serious criticisms at the American military establishment's handling of the Vietnam War. Gabriel and Savage (3547) argue that the American Army "failed to maintain unit cohesion under conditions of combat stress" and that, if the troops had not been withdrawn by 1972, the Army eventually would have had a "military debacle in the field." They believe the major cause of this appalling situation was the decline in the quality of the officer corps, and the corps' emphasis upon "management" rather than "leadership"; too few officers died in the presence of their men to demonstrate that officers were willing to pay the price demanded of the "grunts." These serious charges, and others, are developed and expanded in, among others, the accounts of Hauser (3549) and Just (3551).

After examining strategies and tactics, this chapter focuses on personnel and support functions, depicted in Tables II through V. One of the frequently cited reasons for the increase of U.S. military personnel in Vietnam was the movement of North Vietnamese Army (NVA) units into South Vietnam. U.S. intelligence estimates of these troop deployments are shown in Table II. Estimates of South Vietnamese force totals are listed in Table III. (One essential factor that must be kept in mind in any comparison of strengths is that the VC/NVA had the very real advantage of maneuver and concentration, while ARVN forces were usually in static, defensive positions.) Table IV shows that the escalation of American forces was gradual from 1960 to the middle of 1965, and Table V lists the contributions of troops from other nations (principally South Korea) in aiding American and South Vietnamese troops.

NOTES

1. John M. Collins, "Vietnam Postmortem: A Senseless Strategy," *Parameters* 8 (Mar. 1978): 8–9.

2. See Bernard Brodie's introduction to Carl von Clausewitz, *On War*, edited by M. Howard and P. Paret (Princeton, NJ: Princeton University Press, 1976).

3. Peter Braestrup, "Vietnam as History," *Wilson Quarterly* 2 (Spring 1978): 180.

TABLE II

Estimated Deployments of North Vietnamese
Army Troops into South Vietnam

Infiltration from North Vietnam, 1964—1967

1964 —	13,400
1965 —	36,300
1966 —	92,287
1967 —	101,263

VC/NVA Personnel in Combat Battalions

1968 —	250,300
1969 —	236,800
1970 —	213,800
1971 —	197,700

Source: Guenter Lewy, *America in Vietnam* (New York: Oxford University Press, 1978), pp.66, 191.

TABLE III

Republic of Vietnam Armed Forces Strength
(in thousands)

YEAR	ARMY	AIR FORCE	NAVY	MARINE CORPS	TOTAL REGULAR	REGIONAL FORCES	POPULAR FORCES	TOTAL*	GRAND TOTAL
1954—55	170.0	3.5	2.2	1.5	177.2	54.0[a]	48.0[a]	102.0	279.2
1959—60	136.0	4.6	4.3	2.0	146.0	49.0[b]	48.0	97.0	243.0
1964	220.0	11.0	12.0	7.0	250.0	96.0	168.0	264.0	514.0
1967	303.0	16.0	16.0	8.0	343.0	151.0	149.0[b]	300.0	643.0
1968	380.0	19.0	19.0	9.0	427.0	220.0	173.0	393.0	820.0
1969	416.0	36.0	30.0	11.0	493.0	190.0	214.0	404.0	897.0
1970	416.0	46.0	40.0	13.0	515.0	207.0	246.0	453.0	968.0
1971—72	410.0[b]	50.0	42.0	14.0	516.0	284.0	248.0	532.0	1,048.0

Source: James L. Collins, Jr., *The Development and Training of the South Vietnamese Army, 1950—1972* (Washington, DC: GPO, 1975), p.151.

Note: All numerical figures are approximate.

[a] Civil Guard (later Regional Forces) and Self-Defense Corps (later Popular Forces) were not officially authorized until 1956.

[b] Decline due to increased desertions and recruiting shortfalls.

*Total Territorial.

TABLE IV

Total U.S. Military Personnel in South Vietnam

DATE	ARMY	NAVY	MARINE CORPS	AIR FORCE	COAST GUARD	TOTAL
31 Dec. 1960*	800	15	2	68	—	About 900
31 Dec. 1961	2,100	100	5	1,000	—	3,205
30 June 1962	5,900	300	700	2,100	—	9,000
31 Dec. 1962	7,900	500	500	2,400	—	11,300
30 June 1963	10,200	600	600	4,000	—	15,400
31 Dec. 1963	10,100	800	800	4,600	—	16,300
30 June 1964	9,900	1,000	600	5,000	—	16,500
31 Dec. 1964	14,700	1,100	900	6,600	—	23,300
30 June 1965	27,300	3,800	18,100	10,700	—	59,900
31 Dec. 1965	116,800	8,400	38,200	20,600	300	184,300
30 June 1966	160,000	17,000	53,700	36,400	400	267,500
31 Dec. 1966	239,400	23,300	69,200	52,900	500	385,300
30 June 1967	285,700	28,500	78,400	55,700	500	448,800
31 Dec. 1967	319,500	31,700	78,000	55,900	500	485,600
30 June 1968	354,300	35,600	83,600	60,700	500	534,700
31 Dec. 1968	359,800	36,100	81,400	58,400	400	536,100
30 April 1969	363,300	36,500	81,800	61,400	400	543,400 **
30 June 1969	360,500	35,800	81,500	60,500	400	538,700
31 Dec. 1969	331,100	30,200	55,100	58,400	400	475,200
30 June 1970	298,600	25,700	39,900	50,500	200	414,900
31 Dec. 1970	249,600	16,700	25,100	43,100	100	334,600
30 June 1971	190,500	10,700	500	37,400	100	239,200
31 Dec. 1971	119,700	7,600	600	28,800	100	156,800
30 June 1972	31,800	2,200	1,400	11,500	100	47,000
31 Dec. 1972	13,800	1,500	1,200	7,600	100	24,200
30 June 1973	***	***	***	***	***	***

Source: U.S. Department of Defense, OASD (Comptroller), Directorate for Information Operations, Mar. 19, 1974.

*Between 1954 and 1960, U.S. military strength averaged about 650 advisors.

**Peak strength.

***Totals for all five services less than 250.

TABLE V

Strength of Free World Military Assistance Forces in South Vietnam, 1964–1970

COUNTRY	1964	1965	1966	1967	1968	1969	1970
Australia							
Strength	200	1,557	4,525	6,818	7,661	7,672	6,763
Number of maneuver battalions	—	1	2	2	3	3	3
Korea							
Strength	200	20,620	45,566	47,829	50,003	48,869	48,537
Number of maneuver battalions	—	10	22	22	22	22	22
Thailand							
Strength	0	16	244	2,205	6,005	11,568	11,586
Number of maneuver battalions	—	0	0	1	3	6	6
New Zealand							
Strength	30	119	155	534	516	552	441
The Philippines							
Strength	17	72	2,061	2,020	1,576	189	74
Republic of China							
Strength	20	20	23	31	29	29	31
Spain							
Strength	0	0	13	13	12	10	7
Total strength	467	22,404	52,566	59,450	65,802	68,889	67,444
Total maneuver battalions	0	11	24	25	28	31	31

Source: S. R. Larson and J. L. Collins, Jr., *Allied Participation in Vietnam* (Washington, DC: GPO, 1975), p.23.

TABLE VI

Phoenix Operations, 1968–1971

YEAR	CAPTURED	RALLIED	KILLED	TOTAL	PERCENT KILLED
1968	11,228	2,229	2,559	15,776	16
1969	8,515	4,832	6,187	19,534	32
	SENTENCED*				
1970	6,405	7,745	8,191	22,341	37
1971 (May)	2,770	2,911	3,650	9,331	39

Source: U.S. House, Committee on Government Operations, Hearings; *U.S. Assistance Program in Vietnam,* 92d Cong., 1st Sess., July 15–Aug. 2, 1971, p.183.

*Beginning January 1970, captured VC were no longer considered neutralized until sentenced to a meaningful jail term.

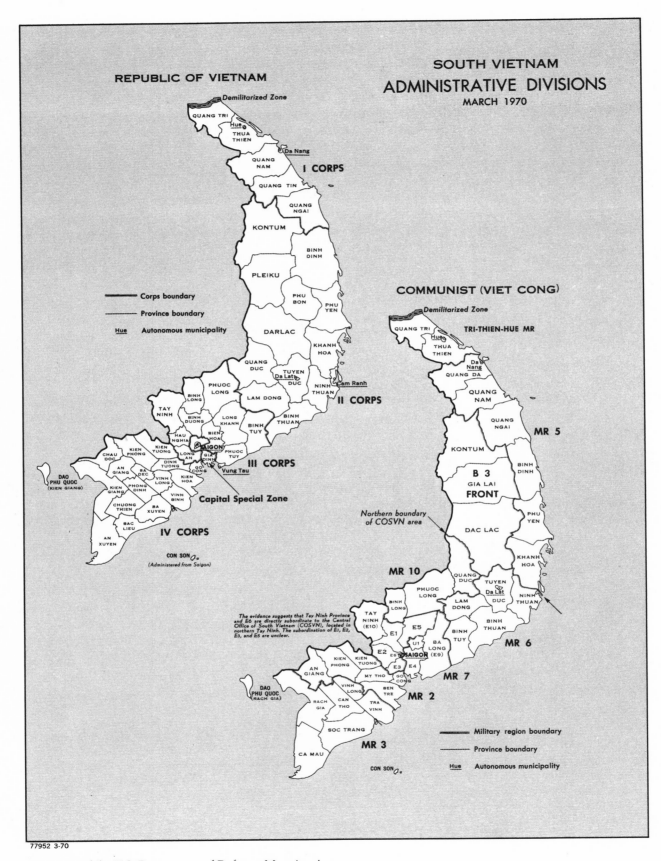

REPUBLIC OF VIETNAM

SOUTH VIETNAM
ADMINISTRATIVE DIVISIONS
MARCH 1970

Demilitarized Zone

QUANG TRI

Hue
THUA
THIEN

Da Nang

QUANG
NAM   I CORPS

QUANG TIN

QUANG
NGAI

KONTUM

BINH
DINH

PLEIKU

PHU
BON   PHU
             YEN

DARLAC

KHANH
HOA

QUANG
DUC

TUYEN
Da Lat
DUC

NINH
THUAN   Cam Ranh

II CORPS

——— Corps boundary
——— Province boundary

Hue   Autonomous municipality

BINH
LONG   PHUOC
          LONG

LAM DONG

TAY
NINH
          BINH
          DUONG   LONG
                     KHANH

BINH
TUY

BINH
THUAN

HAU
NGHIA
          BIEN
          HOA
                SAIGON
CHAU   KIEN   LONG   GIA
DOC   PHONG   AN   DINH   PHUOC
          KIEN   GO   TUY
          TUONG   DINH   CONG
AN   TUONG
GIANG   BA   Vung Tau   III CORPS
          SAC
DAO   VINH
PHU QUOC KIEN   LONG   KIEN
(KIEN GIANG) GIANG PHONG HOA
          DINH
CHUONG   VINH   Capital Special Zone
THIEN   BA   BINH
         XUYEN
         BAC
         LIEU
                        IV CORPS
AN
XUYEN

CON SON
(Administered from Saigon)

COMMUNIST (VIET CONG)

Demilitarized Zone

QUANG TRI   TRI-THIEN-HUE MR
Hue
THUA
THIEN

Da
Nang
QUANG DA

QUANG
NAM

QUANG
NGAI   MR 5

KONTUM

BINH
DINH

B 3
GIA LAI
FRONT

PHU
YEN

Northern boundary
of COSVN area

DAC LAC

KHANH
HOA

MR 10

QUANG
DUC   TUYEN
         Da Lat
         DUC   NINH
                  THUAN

PHUOC
LONG
          LAM DONG

BINH
LONG   BINH
                 TUY

TAY
NINH   BINH
(E10)   THUAN   MR 6

E1   E5

U1
E2   E6   BA
                 LONG   (E9)
         E3 E4 SAIGON
KIEN   KIEN   MY THO   GO
PHONG   TUONG   CONG   MR 7

AN
GIANG

The evidence suggests that Tay Ninh Province
and E6 are directly subordinate to the Central
Office of South Vietnam (COSVN), located in
northern Tay Ninh. The subordination of E1, E2,
E3, and E5 are unclear.

VINH
LONG   BEN
         TRE   MR 2
DAO
PHU QUOC
(RACH GIA)   RACH   CAN   TRA
             GIA   THO   VINH

SOC TRANG

CA MAU   MR 3

CON SON

——— Military region boundary
——— Province boundary

Hue   Autonomous municipality

77952 3-70

Courtesy of the U.S. Department of Defense. Mapping Agency.

Bibliographies and Guides

See Chapter 1 for additional bibliographies.

3433. Carter, G.A., et al. *User's Guide to Southeast Asia Combat Data.* R–1815–ARPA. Santa Monica, CA: Rand Corp., 1976.

3434. Center for Naval Analyses. *Naval Operations in Southeast Asia, 1964–1973: A Bibliography.* Arlington, VA, May 1974.

3435. Cresswell, Mary A., and Carl Berger, comps. *United States Air Force History: An Annotated Bibliography.* Washington, DC: Department of Defense, Office of Air Force History, 1971. See also Chapter 9.

3436. Davison, W.P. *User's Guide to Rand Interviews in Vietnam.* R–1024–ARPA. Santa Monica, CA: Rand Corp., Mar. 1972. The title refers to interviews with VC/NVA, POWs and refugees.

3437. Neufield, Jacob. *United States Air Force History: A Guide to Monographic Literature, 1943–1974.* Washington, DC: Department of Defense, Office of Air Force History, 1977.

3438. Paszek, Lawrence J. *United States Air Force History: A Guide to Documentary Sources.* Washington, DC: GPO, 1973.

3439. Slappy, Sterling. "The Vietnam War Has Been Put on the Shelf." *American Legion Monthly* 101 (Nov. 1976): 12–15. The author discusses war records at the Federal Records Center, Suitland, MD.

3440. Smith, Myron J., Jr. *Air War Southeast Asia, 1961–1973: A Bibliography and 16mm Film Guide.* Metuchen, NJ: Scarecrow, 1979.

3441. U.S. Aerospace Studies Institute. Project Corona Harvest. *USAF Activities in Southeast Asia, 1954–64.* Maxwell AFB, AL: Air University, 1973. "Corona Harvest" is the Air Force code name for its Southeast Asia historical operation.

3442. U.S. Marine Corps. *The Marines in Vietnam, 1954–1973: An Anthology and Annotated Bibliography.* Washington, DC: GPO, 1974. This is a fine introduction to operations.

3443. Willis, Roger F., and Ivy D. Cook, Jr. *Corona Harvest: Guide to Statistical Data on Air Operations in Southeast Asia, 1961–1970.* Maxwell AFB, AL: Air University, Nov. 1971.

Congressional Hearings

See index.

3444. "The May 1965 Debate on Supplemental Appropriations for South Vietnam." *Congressional Record* 111 (May 5, 1965): 9492–9507.

3445. U.S. House. Committee on Armed Services. Hearings; *Military Posture.* 91st Cong., 1st sess., Mar.–Aug. 1969.

3446. U.S. Senate. Committee on Armed Services. Hearings; *Investigation of the Preparedness Program on the Situation in South Vietnam as it Relates to: I. The Enemy Threat; II. Free World Forces (other than U.S.); III. Revolutionary Development Program; IV. The Economy of South Vietnam.* 90th Cong., 1st sess., 1967.

3447. _____. Committee on Foreign Relations. Hearings; *Moral and Military Aspects of the War in South East Asia.* 91st Cong., 2d sess., May 7, 12, 1970.

Official Histories

All of the military services have begun issuing accounts of their various activities and operations in Vietnam. The Air Force and Army are publishing two series, one of which is being prepared by professional historians and another which features accounts written by military officers. These accounts, measured against the high standards of historical professionalism found in the official military histories of World War II, are of mixed quality. Some of the first volumes appear to have met the challenge; particularly impressive is the Army Medical Department's Internal Medicine in Vietnam. Vol. I: Skin Diseases in Vietnam, 1965–72 *(3469). Other efforts, particularly volumes in the Air Force's* Southeast Asia Monograph Series *and the Army's* Vietnam Series, *are less successful; they tend to be more of a reflection of personal experiences and assessments than documented, analytical accounts.*

Listed below are the initial series planned by the various services; check your card catalog for new titles and subsequent series.

AIR FORCE

The historical efforts of the Air Force have been divided between two series. The professional historians at the Office of Air Force History are preparing, as part of their long-standing program, The Air Force in Southeast Asia Series, *a number of volumes of which have appeared, and others will be appearing shortly. At the Air University, combat-experienced officers are assisting in developing the Air War College's USAF Southeast Asia Monograph Series; it is projected to include some ten additional volumes.*

The Air Force in Southeast Asia Series

Estimated publication date is designated by a (?).

3448. Ballard, Jack S. *The U.S. Air Force in Southeast Asia: Development and Employment of Fixed-Wing Gunships, 1962–1972.* Washington, DC: GPO, 1980.

3449. Berger, Carl, ed. *The United States Air Force in Southeast Asia, 1961–1973: An Illustrated Account.* Washington, DC: GPO, 1977.

3450. Bowers, Ray L. *The Air Force in Southeast Asia: Tactical Airlift.* Washington, DC: GPO, 1982 (?).

3451. Buckingham, William A. *Ranch Hand: The United States Air Force and Herbicides in Southeast Asia, 1961–1971.* Washington, DC: GPO, 1982 (?).

3452. Eastman, James N., Jr., Walter Hanak, and Lawrence J. Paszek, eds. *Aces and Aerial Victories: The United States Air Force in Southeast Asia, 1965–1973.* Washington, DC: GPO, 1976.

3453. Fox, Roger P. *Air Base Defense in the Republic of Vietnam.* Washington, DC: GPO, 1979.

3454. Futrell, Robert F., and Martin Blumenson. *The United States Air Force in Southeast Asia: The Advisory Years to 1965.* Washington, DC: GPO, 1981.

3455. Nalty, Bernard C. *Air Power and the Fight for Khe Sanh.* Washington, DC: GPO, 1973.

3456. Tilford, Earl H., Jr. *Search and Rescue Operations in Southeast Asia, 1961–1975.* Washington, DC: GPO, 1980.

Air War College's Monograph Series

Each of the initial volumes has been produced by several officers and edited for publication by A.J.C. Lavalle.

Volume I
3457. Monograph 1: *The Tale of Two Bridges.* Washington, DC: GPO, 1977.

3458. Monograph 2: *The Battle for the Skies over North Vietnam.* Washington, DC: GPO, 1977.

Volume II
3459. Monograph 3: *Airpower and the 1972 Spring Invasion.* Washington, DC: GPO, 1977.

Volume III
3460. Monograph 4: *The Vietnamese Air Force, 1951–1975: An Analysis of Its Role in Combat.* Washington, DC: GPO, 1977.

3461. Monograph 5: *Fourteen Hours at Koh Tang.* Washington, DC: GPO, 1977.

Volume IV
3462. Monograph 6: *Last Flight from Saigon.* Washington, DC: GPO, 1978.

Volume V
3463. Monograph 7: *Airpower and the Airlift Evacuation of Kham Due.* Washington, DC: GPO, 1979.

Volume VI
3464. Monograph 8: *LineBacker II: A View from the Rock.* Washington, DC: GPO, 1979.

ARMY

The Army Chief of Staff has begun issuing the Vietnam Series, *which consists of studies by individuals of the activities they were engaged in while in Vietnam— intelligence, logistics, operations, etc. The Center of Military History, employing professional historians, is planning a multivolume series entitled* The U.S. Army in Vietnam, *which will be similar to their excellent World War II Series and will feature such topics as operations, logistics and training, among others—the initial volumes were expected in 1981.* The History of the Medical Department of the Army in Vietnam and Southeast Asia *will consist of some twenty volumes dealing with Surgery (14 volumes), Preventive Medicine (3 volumes), Aero Medical Evacuation, Nursing and Internal Medicine (3 volumes)—the first two volumes have already appeared (entries 3469 and 3470). The Army War College is preparing a volume* Strategic Lessons Learned from the Vietnam War.

Special Studies

3465. Albright, John A., John A. Cash, and Allan W. Sandstrum. *Seven Fire Fights in Vietnam.* Washington, DC: Office of the Chief of Military History, 1970.

3466. Cao Van Vien. *The Final Collapse.* Washington, DC: U.S. Army Center for Military History, 1982. The author gives a South Vietnamese perspective of the years 1972–1975.

3467. LeGro, William E. *Vietnam From Cease-Fire to Capitulation*. Washington, DC: U.S. Army Center for Military History, 1981.

3468. Scoville, Thomas W. *Reorganizing for Pacification Support*. Washington, DC: U.S. Army Center for Military History, 1982.

U.S. Army in Vietnam

3469. Allen, Alfred M. *Internal Medicine in Vietnam. Vol I: Skin Diseases in Vietnam, 1965–72*. Washington, DC: GPO, 1977. This work is invaluable in demonstrating the conditions in combat areas.

3470. Ognibene, Andre J., O'Neill Barrett, Jr., et al. *Internal Medicine in Vietnam. Vol II: Infectious Diseases and Malaria*. Washington, DC: GPO, 1982.

Vietnam Series

3471. Collins, James L., Jr. *The Development and Training of the South Vietnamese Army, 1950–1972*. Washington, DC: GPO, 1975.

3472. Dunn, Carroll H. *Base Development in South Vietnam, 1965–1970*. Washington, DC: GPO, 1972.

3473. Eckhardt, George S. *Command and Control, 1950–1969*. Washington, DC: GPO, 1974.

3474. Ewell, Julian J., and Ira A. Hunt, Jr. *Sharpening the Combat Edge: The Use of Analysis to Reinforce Military Judgment*. Washington, DC: GPO, 1975.

3475. Fulton, William B. *Riverine Operations, 1966–1969*. Washington, DC: GPO, 1973.

3476. Hay, John H., Jr. *Tactical and Material Innovations*. Washington, DC: GPO, 1974.

3477. Heiser, Joseph M., Jr. *Logistic Support*. Washington, DC: GPO, 1974.

3478. Kelly, Francis J. *U.S. Army Special Forces, 1961–1971*. Washington, DC: GPO, 1973.

3479. Larson, Stanley R., and James L. Collins, Jr. *Allied Participation in Vietnam*. Washington, DC: GPO, 1975.

3480. McChristian, Joseph A. *The Role of Military Intelligence, 1965–1967*. Washington, DC: GPO, 1974.

3481. Myer, Charles R. *Division-Level Communications*. Washington, DC: GPO, 1982.

3482. Neel, Spurgeon. *Medical Support of the U.S. Army in Vietnam, 1965–1970*. Washington, DC: GPO, 1973.

3483. Ott, David E. *Field Artillery, 1954–1973*. Washington, DC: GPO, 1975.

3484. Pearson, Willard. *The War in the Northern Provinces, 1966–1968*. Washington, DC: GPO, 1975.

3485. Ploger, Robert R. *U.S. Army Engineers, 1965–1970*. Washington, DC: GPO, 1974.

3486. Prugh, George S. *Law at War: Vietnam, 1964–1973*. Washington, DC: GPO, 1975.

3487. Rienzi, Thomas H. *Communications-Electronics, 1962–1970*. Washington, DC: GPO, 1972.

3488. Rogers, Bernard W. *Cedar Falls–Junction City: A Turning Point*. Washington, DC: GPO, 1974.

3489. Starry, Donn A. *Mounted Combat in Vietnam*. Washington, DC: GPO, 1979.

3490. Taylor, Leonard B. *Financial Management of the Vietnam Conflict, 1962–1972*. Washington, DC: GPO, 1974.

3491. Tolson, John J. *Airmobility, 1961–1971*. Washington, DC: GPO, 1974.

NAVY

The Naval Historical Center has planned a three-volume series entitled The United States Navy in the Vietnam Conflict. *Two additional volumes are expected.*

3492. Robinson, James H. "Recording Naval History in Vietnam." *U.S. Naval Institute Proceedings* 95 (Sept. 1969): 144–146.

Series

3493. Hooper, Edwin B., Dean C. Allard, and Oscar P. Fitzgerald. *The United States Navy and the Vietnam Conflict: The Setting of the Stage to 1959*. Washington, DC: GPO, 1976.

Special Studies

3494. Hooper, Edwin B. *Mobility, Support, Endurance: A Story of Naval Operational Logistics in the Vietnam War, 1965–1968*. Washington, DC: GPO, 1972.

3495. Tregaskis, Richard B. *Southeast Asia: Building*

the Bases. Washington, DC: GPO, 1975. Tregaskis tells the story of the Navy's huge construction projects.

MARINE CORPS

The History and Museums Division of the Marine Corps plans a nine-volume series entitled U.S. Marines in Vietnam, *the first two of which have appeared. The Corps has also prepared a number of more specialized accounts and bibliographies which are listed here and elsewhere in this* Guide *under the appropriate topic. For instance, see Shore,* The Battle for Khe Sanh *(4248), an anthology and bibliography (3442) and West, Small Unit Actions (4526).*

U.S. Marines in Vietnam Series

3496. Shulimson, Jack, and Charles M. Johnson. *U.S. Marines in Vietnam: The Landing and the Buildup, 1965.* Washington, DC: GPO, 1978.

3497. Whitlow, Robert H. *U.S. Marines in Vietnam: The Advisory & Combat Assistance Era, 1954–1964.* Washington, DC: GPO, 1977.

Special Studies

3498. *A Chronology of the United States Marine Corps, 1775–1969.* 4 vols. Washington, DC: Headquarters U.S. Marine Corps, Historical Division, 1965–1971. [Vol 3: *1947–1964,* and Vol 4: *1965–1969,* cover the Vietnam era]

3499. Parker, William D. *U.S. Marine Corps Civic Affairs in I Corps, Republic of South Vietnam, April 1966–April 1967.* Washington, DC: Headquarters U.S. Marine Corps, Historical Division, 1970.

3500. Stofi, Russel H. *U.S. Marine Corps Civic Action Effort in Vietnam, March 1965–March 1966.* Washington, DC: Headquarters U.S. Marine Corps, Historical Division, 1968.

Admirals and Generals

Although senior officers' views also appear in the "Official Histories," section of this chapter, the items below have been written by, or refer to, senior commanders.

GENERAL CREIGHTON W. ABRAMS

3501. Braestrup, Peter. "The Abrams Strategy in Vietnam." *New Leader* 52 (June 9, 1969): 3–5.

3502. Buckley, Kevin P. "General Abrams Deserves a Better Way." *New York Times Magazine* (Oct. 5, 1969): 34ff. [personality study]

3503. "The War: Changing the Guard." *Time* 91 (Apr. 19, 1968): 25–26ff.

3504. Weller, Jac. "Wellington against Abrams: Were the Old Ways Better?" *Army Quarterly & Defence Journal.* [Great Britain] 100:1 (1970): 60–70.

ADMIRAL ULYSSES S. G. SHARP

See his joint report with Westmoreland (3537).

3505. Sharp, Ulysses S.G. "Airpower Could Have Won in Vietnam." *Air Force Magazine* 54 (Sept. 1971): 82–83.

3506. ———. "How to Win the War in South Vietnam." *U.S. News and World Report* 60 (Mar. 28, 1966): 38–41.

3507. ———. *Strategy For Defeat: Vietnam in Retrospect.* San Rafael, CA: Presidio Press, 1978. Sharp is an outspoken proponent of the "stab-in-the-back" thesis; he believes massive bombing of North could have brought about Hanoi's surrender much sooner.

GENERAL LEWIS W. WALT

3508. Leinster, Colin. "The Two Wars of General Lew Walt." *Life* 62 (May 26, 1967): 77–84.

3509. Walt, Lewis W. *America Faces Defeat.* Boston: Houghton Mifflin, 1972.

3510. ———. *Strange War, Strange Strategy: A General's Report on Vietnam.* New York: Funk & Wagnalls, 1970.

GENERAL WILLIAM C. WESTMORELAND

See also his joint report with Admiral Sharp (3537).

3511. Clark, Blair. "Westmoreland Appraised: Questions and Answers." *Harper's* 241 (Nov. 1970): 96–101.

3512. Ferguson, Ernest B. *Westmoreland: The Inevitable General.* Boston: Little, Brown, 1968.

3513. Hamilton, A. "Westmoreland's Progress Report." *New Republic* 157 (July 8, 1967): 19–21.

3514. Westmoreland, William C. "General Westmoreland Reports on Vietnam War: Interview with the U.S. Commander." *U.S. News and World Report* 61 (Nov. 28, 1966): 44–49.

3515. _____. "Progress Report on the War in Viet-Nam." *U.S. Department of State Bulletin* 57 (Dec. 11, 1967): 785–788.

3516. _____. "A Report to the Congress by the Commander of U.S. Military Forces in Vietnam." *U.S. Department of State Bulletin* 56 (May 15, 1967): 738–741.

3517. _____. *A Soldier Reports.* New York: Doubleday, 1976. Westmoreland's own account of the war.

3518. _____. "Vietnam in Perspective." *Military Review* 59 (Jan. 1979): 34–43.

3519. _____. "Year-End Report: No Mission Impossible." *Army* 18 (Nov 1968): 27–30, 45.

OTHERS

Essays by Generals LeMay and Shoup have been included although both retired prior to the Vietnam War.

3520. "Admiral McCain Assesses the War in Southeast Asia." *Air Force Magazine* 55 (Sept. 1972): 52–59.

3521. "The Army Chief of Staff on Military Strategy in Vietnam." *Army Digest* 23 (Apr. 1968): 6–9.

3522. Devillers, Philippe. "Vietnam: The Gererals Sing an Old Song." *Nation* 205 (Sept. 18, 1967): 233–238.

3523. Johnson, Max S. "As the Military Sees It: Failure of a Strategy." *U.S. News and World Report* 62 (May 8, 1967): 33–34.

3524. Kinnard, Douglas. "Vietnam Reconsidered: An Attitudinal Survey of U.S. Army General Officers." *Public Opinion Quarterly* 39 (Winter 1975–1976): 445–456.

3525. _____. "The Vietnam War in Retrospect: The Army Generals' Views." *Journal of Political & Military Sociology* 4 (Spring 1976): 17–28.

3526. _____. *The War Managers.* Hanover, NH: University Press of New England, 1977. More than 100 generals give opinions of what went wrong; the book also covers media, strategy, professionalism and body count.

3527. Krulak, Victor H. "The Strategic Limits of Proxy War." *Strategic Review* 2 (Winter 1974): 52–57. [also in *Marine Corps Gazette* 58 (June 1974): 18–22]

3528. Larson, Stanley R. "A Report on Vietnam." *World Wars Officer Review* 6 (Nov.–Dec. 1967): 18–23.

3529. LeMay, Curtis E. "Gen. LeMay Tells How to Win the War in Vietnam." *U.S. News and World Report* 61 (Oct. 10, 1966): 36–38.

3530. _____. "How Can We Win in Viet Nam." *Human Events* 27 (Jan. 27, 1967): 56–57.

3531. McConnell, John P. "Some Reflections on a Tour of Duty." *Air University Review* 20 (Sept.–Oct. 1969): 2–11.

3532. Momyer, William W. *Airpower in Three Wars.* Washington, DC: GPO, c. 1978. Momyer describes lessons learned in World War II, Korea and Vietnam.

3533. "Retired Generals Speak on Vietnam." *Congressional Record* 116 (Mar. 26, 1970): S4628–S4631. [David M. Shoup, Samuel B. Griffin II, William W. Ford, Robert L. Hughes]

3534. Shoup, David M. "The New American Militarism." *Atlantic* 223 (Apr. 1969): 51–56. Shoup launched the first attack on officer careerism in Vietnam by a senior general.

3535. Stilwell, Richard G. "Evolution in Tactics: The Vietnam Experience." *Army* 20 (Feb. 1970): 14–23.

3536. Timmes, Charles J. "The Naive Years." *Army* 27 (May 1977): 35–40.

3537. U.S. Pacific Command. *Report on the War in Vietnam (as of June 30, 1968).* Section I: (Admiral U.S.G. Sharp, Commander in Chief, Pacific) *Report on Air and Naval Campaigns Against North Vietnam and Pacific Command-wide Support of the War, June 1964–July 1968;* Section II: (General W.C. Westmoreland, Commander, U.S. Military Assistance Command, Vietnam) *Report on Operations in South Vietnam, January 1964–June 1968.* Washington, DC: GPO, 1968.

3538. "Viet Nam: The Generals Speak." *Survival* 9 (Feb. 1967): 52–62.

3539. Weyland, Fred C, and Harry G. Summers, Jr. "Vietnam Myths and Military Realities." *Armor* 85 (Sept.–Oct. 1976): 30–36.

3540. Wheeler, Earle G. "The Challenge Came in Vietnam." *Vital Speeches* 33 (Dec. 16, 1966): 130–133.

3541. _____. "The U.S. Achievements in Viet-Nam." *U.S. Department of State Bulletin* 56 (Feb. 6, 1967): 186–192.

Evaluating the Military Dimension

For the most part, the items listed below are retrospective studies of the impact of the Vietnam War on America's military forces.

Books and Dissertations

3542. Balkind, Jonathan J. "Morale Deterioration in the United States Military During the Vietnam Period." Ph.D. dissertation, University of California, Los Angeles, 1978.

3543. Boyle, Richard. *Flower of the Dragon: The Breakdown of the U.S. Army in Vietnam.* San Francisco: Ramparts, 1972.

3544. Cincinnatus. (pseud.) *Self-Destruction: The Disintegration and Decay of the United States Army During the Vietnam Era.* New York: Norton, 1981. This book was written by a senior army officer and reviewed by John R. Galvin in *Parameters* 11 (Mar. 1981): 9–14.

3545. Collins, John M. *The Vietnam War in Perspective.* Washington, DC: National War College, Strategic Research Group, 1972.

3546. Enthoven, Allen C., and K. Wayne Smith. *How Much is Enough: Shaping the Defense Program, 1961–1968.* New York: Harper & Row, 1971. The authors defend McNamara's policies and the book is useful in understanding the broader context of Vietnam decisions.

3547. Gabriel, Richard A., and Paul L. Savage. *Crisis in Command: Mismanagement in the Army.* New York: Hill & Wang, 1978. This is a significant but flawed study which argues that officers' "managerial" careerism led to the loss of unit coherence. For a critique see *Armed Forces & Society* 3 (Spring 1977): 457–490.

3548. Gallucci, Robert L. *Neither Peace Nor Honor: The Politics of American Military Policy in Vietnam.* Baltimore: Johns Hopkins University Press, 1975.

3549. Hauser, William L. *American Army in Crisis.* Baltimore: Johns Hopkins University Press, 1976.

3550. Johnson, Haynes B., and George C. Wilson. *Army in Anguish.* New York: Pocket Books, 1971.

3551. Just, Ward. *Military Men.* New York: Knopf, 1970.

3552. King, Edward L. *The Death of the Army: A Pre-Mortem.* New York: Saturday Review Press, 1972.

3553. Lewy, Guenter. *America in Vietnam.* New York: Oxford University Press, 1978. Lewy questions many antiwar accusations about U.S. military conduct, but faults strategic assumptions; the book is highly controversial.

3554. Loory, Stuart H. *Defeated.* New York: Random House, 1973.

3555. Lovell, John P., and Philip S. Kronenberg, eds. *New Civil–Military Relations: The Agonies of Adjustment to Post-Vietnam Realities.* New York: Dutton, 1974.

3556. Palmer, Gregory. *McNamara Strategy and the Vietnam War: Program Budgeting in the Pentagon, 1960–1968.* Westport, CT: Greenwood, 1978. The Planning, Programming, Budgeting System adapted modern economic theory to military strategy, but it was disastrous in Vietnam.

3557. U.S. Army War College. *Study on Military Professionalism.* Carlisle Barracks, PA: U.S. Army War College, June 1970. [details breakdown of U.S. army in Vietnam]

3558. Walton, George. *The Tarnished Shield: A Report on Today's Army.* New York: Dodd, Mead, 1973.

Retrospective Essays
For essays that deal more with questions of strategy see "Strategy & Tactics," below, this chapter.

3559. Beaumont, Roger. "A Myth of Chivalry: Variations on a Theme by Gabriel and Savage." *Military Review* 60 (May 1980): 64–75.

3560. Fowler, John G., Jr. "Combat Cohesion in Vietnam." *Military Review* 59 (Dec. 1979): 22–32. Fowler disputes the views of Gabriel and Savage.

3561. Hersh, Seymour M. "The Decline and Near Fall of the U.S. Army." *Saturday Review* 55 (Nov. 18, 1972): 58–65.

3562. Holmes, David R. "Some Tentative Thoughts After Indochina." *Military Review* 57 (Aug. 1977): 84–87.

3563. Howze, H.H. "Vietnam . . . An Epilogue." *Army* 25 (July 1975): 12–17.

3564. Iavnov, O. "Lessons of Vietnam." *Soviet Military Review* 4 (Apr. 1976): 44–46.

3565. Kinnard, Douglas. "For the Post-Vietnam Military: No End of Advice." *Polity* 8 (Winter 1975): 297–310.

3566. Lang, Kurt. "American Military Performance in

Vietnam: Background and Analysis." *Journal of Political and Military Sociology* 8 (Fall 1980): 269–286.

3567. Powe, Marc B. "The U.S. Army After the Fall of Vietnam: A Contemporary Dilemma." *Military Review* 56 (Feb. 1976): 3–17.

3568. Spector, Ronald. "Getting Down to the Nitty-Gritty: Military History, Official History and the American Experience in Vietnam." *Military Affairs* 38 (Feb. 1974): 11–12.

3569. Yarmolinsky, Adam. "Myths and Interests." *New Republic* 172 (May 3, 1975): 14–15. [myths of hawks and doves]

3570. _____. "Picking Up the Pieces: The Impact of Vietnam on the Military Establishment." *Yale Review* 61 (June 1972): 481–495.

Strategy and Tactics

U.S. military strategy in Vietnam has come under increased criticism from antiwar critics and military analysts. While most accounts reflect this theme, the items collected here focus most directly on the issue. The "Insurgency," "Pacification" and "Vietnamization" sections which follow are also closely related to the debate over strategy.

Books
See also the "Admirals and Generals" section above, this chapter.

3571. Corson, William R. *The Betrayal*. New York: W.W. Norton, 1968. A military observer criticizes large unit operations.

3572. French, W. *Pattern for Victory*. New York: Exposition Press, 1970.

3573. Palmer, Dave R. *Summons of the Trumpet: US–Vietnam in Perspective*. Palmer criticizes the attrition strategy, but he accepts the view that civilians limited military chances of victory.

3574. Pickerell, James H. *Vietnam in the Mud*. Indianapolis: Bobbs-Merrill, 1966. This is a highly critical appraisal of U.S. tactics by a journalist.

3575. Sullivan, Cornelius D., et al. *The Vietnam War: Its Conduct and Higher Direction*. Washington, DC: Georgetown University, Center for Strategic Studies, Nov. 1968.

3576. Thompson, Robert. *No Exit from Vietnam*. Rev. ed. New York: Viking, McKay, 1970. Thompson condemns Westmoreland's "big-unit" strategy since it ignored the political fact that the U.S. was not on a collision course with the VC.

Retrospective Essays
These essays reveal at least two themes: the military's failure to grasp the necessary strategy for a limited war, and the emergence, if often oblique, of a "stab-in-the-back" thesis which believed the military was prevented from "winning" the war by Washington bureaucrats.

3577. Barrett, Raymond J. "Graduated Response and the Lessons of Vietnam. *Military Review* 52 (May 1972): 80–91.

3578. Brodie, Bernard. "Why Were We So (Strategically) Wrong." *Foreign Policy*, no. 5 (Winter 1971–1972): 151–162. [reprinted in *Military Review* 52 (June 1972): 40–46] This is must reading from the dean of U.S. strategic analysts.

3579. Clark, Wesley K. "Gradualism and American Military Strategy." *Military Review* 55 (Sept. 1975): 3–13.

3580. Collins, John M. "Vietnam Postmortem: A Senseless Strategy." *Parameters* 8 (Mar. 1978): 8–14. This is an excellent account which will not accept the "stab-in-the-back" thesis.

3581. DeWeerd, H.A. "Strategic Decision-Making in Vietnam, 1965–1968." *Yale Review* 67 (June 1978): 482–492.

3582. Ellis, Richard H., and Frank B. Horton, III. "Flexibility: A State of Mind." *Strategic Review* 4 (Winter 1976): 26–36.

3583. Ginsburgh, Robert N. "Strategy and Airpower: The Lessons of Southeast Asia." *Strategic Review* 1 (Summer 1973): 18–24.

3584. Grinter, Lawrence E. "How They Lost: Doctrines, Strategies and Outcomes of the Vietnam War." *Asian Survey* 15 (Dec. 1975): 1114–1132. [covers 1964–1975, U.S. miscalculations]

3585. Hughes, Wayne P., Jr. "Vietnam: Winnable War?" *U.S. Naval Institute Proceedings* 103 (July 1977): 60–65. Hughes makes an oblique attempt at the "stab-in-the-back" thesis.

3586. Jender, Donald. "Vietnam and the Western Military System: Two Types of War in Conflict." *Australian Army Journal*, no. 291 (Aug. 1973): 24–43.

3587. Leitenberg, Milton. "America in Vietnam: Statistics of a War." *Survival* 14 (Nov.–Dec. 1972): 268–274.

3588. Michael, Stanley, J., Jr. "Vietnam: Failure to Follow the Principles of War." *Marine Corps Gazette* 61 (Aug. 1977): 56–62.

3589. Race, Jeffrey. "Mutual Self-Limitation in Civil War: The Case of Vietnam." *Southeast Asia* 3 (Spring 1973): 211–230.

3590. Shultz, Richard. "Strategy Lessons From an Unconventional War: the U.S. Experience in Vietnam." In *Nonnuclear Conflicts in the Nuclear Age*, edited by Sam C. Sarkesian. New York: Praeger, 1980, 138–184.

3591. Staudenmaier, William O. "Vietnam, Mao and Clausewitz." *Parameters* 7 (Mar. 1977): 79–89.

3592. Thompson, Robert. "Military Victory; Political Defeat ... the Failure of U.S. Strategy in Vietnam." *International Defense Review* 7 (Dec. 1974): 727–729.

3593. Townsend, Patrick L. "Clausewitz Would Have Wondered at the Way We Fought in Vietnam." *Marine Corps Gazette* 62 (June 1978): 55–57.

3594. Wolf, Charles, Jr., *The Logic of Failure: A Vietnam "Lesson."* P-4654-1. Santa Monica, CA: Rand Corp., Oct. 1971. [reprinted in *Journal of Conflict Resolution* 14 (Sept. 1972): 397–401.] Wolf describes the failure to see the difference between limited and total war.

Contemporary Essays

3595. "As U.S. Seeks a New Strategy for Vietnam." *U.S. News and World Report* 67 (Sept. 22, 1969): 37–38.

3596. Atkinson, D.K. "Vietnam: The Unwinnable War?" *Australia Army Journal*, no. 253 (June 1970): 3–8.

3597. Beaufre, A. "Aspects stratégiques du problème Vietnamien." *International Spectator* [The Hague] 20 (Feb. 22, 1966): 260–267.

3598. "Behind the Vietnam 'Lull': The Shifts in Strategy." *U.S. News and World Report* 67 (Aug. 11, 1969): 29–31.

3599. Bennett, Ralph K. "Hitting Them Where They Live: The Ultimate Confrontation." *Data* 13 (Feb. 1968): 8–10. [the Laos and Cambodia sanctuaries]

3600. Biggio, Charles P., Jr. "Let's Learn From the French." *Military Review* 46 (Oct. 1966): 27–34.

3601. Brownlow, Cecil. "Bomb Pause Causes Major Tactics Shift." *Aviation Week & Space Technology* 84 (Feb. 14, 1966): 27–29.

3602. Butz, J.S., Jr. "Do They Want Us There? Are We Fighting Honorably? Can We Win?" *Air Force & Space Digest* 49 (Sept. 1966): 62–68.

3603. Cleland, John R.D. "Principle of the Objective and Vietnam." *Military Review* 46 (July 1966): 82–86.

3604. Davis, Vincent. "American Military Policy: Decision-making in the Executive Branch [1969]." *Naval War College Review* 22 (Nov.–Dec. 1970): 4–23.

3605. Denno, B.F. "Military Prospects in Vietnam." *Orbis* 9 (Summer 1965): 411–417.

3606. Dudman, Richard. "Military Policy in Vietnam." *Current History* 50 (Feb. 1966): 91–97, 115.

3607. Durst, Jay B. "Limited Conventional War: Can It Be Successful?" *Military Review* 50 (Jan. 1970): 56–63.

3608. Galula, David. "Military Considerations in Vietnam." *Studies on the Soviet Union* 6:2 (1966): 29–42.

3609. Galvin, John R. "Prime Tactical Lessons of the Vietnam War: Three Innovations." *Army* 22 (Mar. 1972): 16–20.

3610. Harrison, G.A. "Vietnam: How to Win the War." *New Republic* 157 (Nov. 18, 1967): 13–15. If we let the VC establish a central government, we then can fight from the hills.

3611. Hartle, A.E. "Momentum in Attack." *Army* 17 (May 1967): 35–38.

3612. Kinnard, H.W.O. "Vietnam Has Lessons for Tomorrow's Army." *Army* 18 (Nov. 1968): 77–80.

3613. Lofgren, Charles A. "How New Is Limited War?" *Military Review* 47 (July 1967): 16–23.

3614. Mallan, Lloyd. "We Can Win the War in Six Weeks!" *Science & Mechanics* 39 (Mar. 1968): 38–43ff.

3615. Marshall, S.L.A. "Fighting a Sticky War: A Strategy for Vietnam." *New Leader* 47 (Aug. 3, 1964): 12–15.

3616. ———. "The Military Mess." *New Leader* 48 (Mar. 1, 1965): 3–6.

3617. Michael, Franz. "The Stakes in Vietnam." *Orbis* 12 (Spring 1968): 121–131. Strategy.

3618. Palmer, Dave R. "Ho's Mistake." *Military Review* 47 (Apr. 1967): 35–39.

3619. Pfaff, William. "Checkmate in Vietnam." *Commonweal* 85 (Feb. 24, 1967): 585–586.

3620. Plattner, C.M. "Limited-War Concepts Weighed in Battle." *Aviation Week & Space Technology* 84 (Jan. 31, 1966): 42–46.

3621. Porter. D.G. "Is This a Limited War?" *Commonweal* 85 (Mar. 24, 1967): 9–11.

3622. Sights, Albert P., Jr. "Graduated Pressure in Theory and Practice." *U.S. Naval Institute Proceedings* 96 (July 1970): 40–45. [bombing strategy]

3623. Stennis, Senator John C. "The Enclave Theory." *Armed Forces Journal* 106 (July 12, 1969): 11–12.

3624. Stillman, Edmund. "The Bunglers' War." *Worldview* 12 (Nov. 1969): 6–9.

3625. _____. "Smart Bombs and Dumb Strategy." *Saturday Review* 55 (July 29, 1972): 27–32. Stillman felt bombing North Vietnam would not ensure favorable peace terms.

3626. Swenson, Mark E. "Vietnam: Limited-War Strategy at a Dead End?" *Air Force & Space Digest* 51 (Apr. 1968): 60–62.

3627. _____. "The Vietnamese War: A Case of Misjudged Staying Power." *Air Force & Space Digest* 50 (Dec. 1967): 42–44.

3628. Tanham, George K., and Frank N. Trager. "The Three Wars in Vietnam." *Army* 14 (May 1964): 54–59.

3629. Thompson, Robert. "'What Went Wrong?' The Failure of American Strategy in Vietnam." *Interplay* 2 (Sept. 1969): 13–16.

3630. Todd, Gary E. "Planning and Exploitation." *Marine Corps Gazette* 53 (Dec. 1969): 18–26. [battlefield tactics]

3631. Trager, Frank N. "Vietnam: The Military Requirements for Victory." *Orbis* 8 (Fall 1964): 563–583.

3632. "Viet Nam: From Tactical Victories to Strategic Defeat?" *Orbis* 11 (Spring 1967): 14–18.

3633. Wallace, James N. "Why U.S. Isn't Winning a 'Little War.'" *U.S. News and World Report* 64 (Apr. 1, 1968): 43–45ff.

3634. Warner, Denis. "Does Vietnam Need a Supreme Commander?" *Reporter* 34 (June 30, 1966): 11–17.

AIR MOBILITY

From the U.S. military side, Vietnam was a helicopter war. This emphasis has both its enthusiasts and critics. See "Airlift" below.

3635. Allgood, Frank E. "Progress and Prep Fires." *Marine Corps Gazette* 51 (Sept. 1967): 29–31. [clearing landing zones]

3636. Number not used.

3637. Bradford, Zeb B., Jr. "U.S. Tactics in Vietnam." *Military Review* 52 (Feb. 1972): 63–76. [airmobility and counterinsurgency]

3638. Burney, John C., Jr. "Chu Phong Revisited: A Combat Example of Armor Airmobile Teamwork." *Armor* 76 (Sept.–Oct. 1967): 25–29.

3639. Davis, Raymond G., and R.D. Camp, Jr. "Marines in Assault by Helicopter." *Marine Corps Gazette* 52 (Sept. 1968): 22–28.

3640. Evrard, James A. "Planning an Airmobile Assault." *Army* 18 (June 1968): 60–64.

3641. Maddox, W.J., Jr. "Airmobility in Vietnam." *Astronautics & Aeronautics* 4 (Oct. 1966): 68–73.

3642. Mertel, Kenneth D. "The Agility of Air Mobility." *Army* 17 (May 1967): 26–30.

3643. _____. "Airmobile Firepower." *Army* 18 (Jan. 1969): 55–58.

3644. Plattner, C.M. "The War in Vietnam: Airmobility Concept Proves Effectiveness in Guerrilla Fight." *Aviation Week & Space Technology* 84 (Jan. 10, 1966): 26–32.

3645. Parrino, Michael F. "The Fallacy of the Doctrine of Tactical Mobility in Vietnam." *Australian Army Journal*, no. 252 (May 1970): 36–40.

3646. Smith, Philip R., Jr. "Army Airmobility: Concept to Reality." *Army Digest* 24 (Sept. 1969): 12–19.

3647. Way, I.R. "The Influence of Mobility on Military Operations in South-East Asia." *Australian Army Journal*, no. 202 (Mar. 1966): 18–32.

FIRE SUPPORT BASE

3648. Davis, Raymond G., and Harold W. Brazier, II. "Defeat of the [NVA] 320th." *Marine Corps Gazette* 53 (Mar. 1969): 22–30. The authors describe the use of the fire support base concept in the DMZ area.

3649. Nicoli, Robert V. "Fire Support Base Development." *Marine Corps Gazette* 53 (Sept. 1969): 38–43.

3650. Piper, W.A. "Fire Support Bases: A Tactical Appraisal." *Marine Corps Gazette* 54 (Dec. 1970): 26–31.

SEARCH AND DESTROY

Although the term "search and destroy" was dropped after 1967 because of unfavorable publicity, the basic tactic continued to be employed.

3651. Bashore, B.T. "The Name of the Game is 'Search and Destroy.'" *Army* 17 (Feb. 1967): 56–59.

3652. Baxter, Gordon. *13/13, Vietnam: Search and Destroy.* Cleveland, OH: World, 1967. [a journalist's view]

3653. McEnery, John W. "'Mainstreet': A Successful Cordon and Search." *Armor* 78 (Jan.–Feb. 1969): 36–39.

3654. Schell, Jonathan. *The Village of Ben Sac.* New York: Knopf, 1967. Schell gives an eyewitness account of the impact of a search and destroy mission.

BODY COUNT

3655. Adams, Samuel A. "Vietnam Cover-Up: Playing War With Numbers." *Harper's* 245 (May 1975): 41.

3656. Sorley, Lewis. "The Body Count Revisited." *Armed Forces Journal International* 115 (Nov. 1977): 25.

3657. Truscott, Lucian K., III. "Body Count: The Degrading Illusion." *Nation* 211 (Nov. 16, 1970): 487–489.

Insurgency and Counterinsurgency

During the fighting there was considerable discussion, usually optimistic, among military officers about how to deal with "insurgency," but in retrospect it is evident they erred. "Eradicating rebel causes should have been our key goal in Vietnam," one critic noted. "Instead, we wrestled with symptoms." The studies by Andrews (3658), Race (3671) and Schell (3674) demonstrate this point.

Books and Dissertations
3658. Andrews, William R. *The Village War: Vietnamese Communist Revolutionary Activities in Dinh Tuong Province, 1960–1964.* Columbia: University of Missouri Press, 1973.

3659. Asprey, Robert B. *War in the Shadows: The Guerrilla in History.* 2 vols. Garden City, NY: Doubleday, 1975.

3660. Blaufarb, Douglas. *The Counterinsurgency Era.* New York: Free Press, 1977.

3661. Browne, Malcolm W. *The New Face of War.* New York: Bobbs-Merrill, 1965.

3662. Burchett, Wilfred G. *Vietnam: Inside Story of the Guerrilla War.* New York: International Publishers, 1965.

3663. Clutterbuck, Richard L. *The Long, Long War: Counterinsurgency in Malaya and Vietnam.* New York: Praeger, 1966.

3664. Cross, James E. *Conflict in the Shadows: The Nature and Politics of Guerrilla War.* New York: Doubleday, 1963.

3665. Greene, T.N., ed. *The Guerrilla—and How to Fight Him.* New York: Praeger, 1962.

3666. Harrison, Anthony. *A Guide to the War in Viet Nam.* Boulder, CO: Panther, 1966. [covers counterinsurgency]

3667. Kelly, Francis J. "A Problem in Counterinsurgency: Lessons Learned in Vietnam." Ph.D. dissertation, University of Denver, 1980.

3668. Meyerson, Harvey. *Vinh Long.* Boston: Houghton Mifflin, 1970. [insurgency in a province in Vietnam]

3669. Paret, Peter, and John W. Shy. *Guerrillas in the 1960s.* rev. ed. New York: Praeger, 1962.

3670. Pustay, John S. *Counterinsurgency Warfare.* New York: Free Press, 1965.

3671. Race, Jeffrey. *War Comes to Long An: Revolutionary Conflict in a Vietnamese Province.* Berkeley: University of California Press, 1972. Race provides an excellent analytical study of these themes based on documentary evidence.

3672. Rolland, Pierre. *Contre-Guerrilla.* Paris: Louvois, 1956.

3673. Sansom, Robert L. *The Economics of Insurgency in the Mekong Delta of Vietnam.* Cambridge, MA: MIT Press, 1970.

3674. Schell, Jonathan. *The Military Half: An Account of Destruction in Quang Nagai and Quang Tin.* New York: Vintage, 1968.

3675. Schultz, Richard T. "The Intellectual Origins and Development of Counter-insurgency Theory in American Foreign Policy Doctrine: The Vietnam Case Study." Ph.D. dissertation, Miami University, 1976.

3676. Taber, Robert. *The War of the Flea: A Study of Guerrilla Warfare Theory and Practice.* New York: Lyle Stuart, 1965.

3677.   Thompson, Robert. *Defeating Communist Insurgency: The Lessons of Malaya and Vietnam.* New York: Praeger, 1966.

3678.   Tringuier, Roger. *Modern Warfare: A French View of Counterinsurgency.* New York: Praeger, 1964.

INSURGENCY

While this theme is closely linked with counterinsurgency, it is also intertwined with discussions about the "Vietcong" and the "National Liberation Front," listed under "North Vietnam, 1954–1975," in Chapter 3, and "VC/NVA Operations" and "Strategy and Tactics" in Chapter 7.

Retrospective Essays

3679.   Darling, Roger. "The Unique Capacities of North Vietnam in Achieving Peasant Participation in a Revolution." *Military Review* 57 (Jan. 1977): 3–13. This is the type of material listed under "Vietcong" in Chapter 3.

3680.   Duncanson, Dennis J. "'Symbiotic Insurgency' in Vietnam Ten Years After." *International Affairs* [London] 54 (Oct. 1978): 589–601.

3681.   Paranzino, D. "Inequality and Insurgency in Vietnam: A Further Re-Analysis." *World Politics* 24 (July 1972): 565–578. See also Paige (3692) and Mitchell (3691).

3682.   Tanham, George K. "Some Insurgency Lessons from Southeast Asia." *Orbis* 16 (Fall 1972): 646–659.

3683.   Trager, Frank N. "Wars of National Liberation: Implications for U.S. Policy and Planning." *Orbis* 18 (Spring 1974): 50–105.

Contemporary Essays

3684.   Buchanan, W.J., and R.A. Hyatt. "Capitalizing on Guerrilla Vulnerabilities." *Military Review* 48 (Aug. 1968): 3–40.

3685.   Calvert, J.M. "The Pattern of Guerrilla Warfare." *Military Review* 46 (July 1966): 13–18.

3686.   Deutch, Michael J. "The Economics of Insurgency." *Vietnam Perspectives* 2:4 (1967): 3–10.

3687.   Furlong, W.B. "Training for the Front-All-Around-You War." *New York Times Magazine* (Oct. 24, 1965): 184.

3688.   Gastil, Raymond D. *Four Papers on the Vietnamese Insurgency.* 4 vols. Croton-on-Hudson, NY: Hudson Institute, 1967.

3689.   Johnson, Chalmers. "The Third Generation of Guerrilla Warfare." *Asian Survey* 8 (June 1968): 435–447.

3690.   Jones, W.M. *Predicting Insurgent and Governmental Decisions: The Power Bloc Model.* RM–6358–PR. Santa Monica, CA: Rand Corp., Dec. 1970. Jones uses VC and NVA forces among his case studies.

3691.   Mitchell, Edward J. *Inequality and Insurgency: A Statistical Study of South Vietnam.* P–3610. Santa Monica, CA: Rand Corp., June 1967. [also in *World Politics* 20 (Apr. 1968): 421–438] Subjected to reexamination, see Paige (3692) and Paranzino (3681).

3692.   Paige, Jeffrey M. "Inequality and Insurgency in Vietnam: A Re-Analysis." *World Politics* 23 (Oct. 1970): 24–37.

3693.   Prosser, L.F. "The Bloody Lessons of Indochina." *Army Combat Forces Journal* 5 (June 1955): 23–30.

3694.   Reinhardt, G.C. *Guerrilla-Combat Strategy and Deterrence in Southeast Asia.* P–2706. Santa Monica, CA: Rand Corp., Jan. 1964.

3695.   Russell, C.A., and R.E. Hildner. "The Role of Communist Ideology in Insurgency." *Air University Review* 22 (Jan.–Feb. 1971): 42–48.

3696.   Simpson, Howard R. "The Guerrilla and His World." *U.S. Naval Institute Proceedings* 95 (Aug. 1969): 42–53.

3697.   _____. "Offshore Guerrilla War." *Naval War College Review* 22 (Fall 1969): 17–20.

3698.   Sparks, Will. "Guerrillas in Vietnam." *Commonweal* 76 (June 29, 1962): 343–346.

3699.   U.S. Naval Ordinance Test Station. *Unconventional Warfare and the Vietnamese Society.* NOTS TP–3457. China Lake, CA, 1964.

3700.   Zasloff, Joseph J. *Origins of the Insurgency in South Vietnam, 1954–60: The Role of the Southern Vietminh Cadres.* RM–5163/2–ISA/ARPA. Santa Monica, CA: Rand Corp., May 1968.

COUNTERINSURGENCY

Almost all of the U.S. activities in Vietnam were part of "counterinsurgency" operations. The more general studies on the topic have been listed here.

Retrospective Essays

3701.   Boatner, Mark M., III. The Unheeded History of Counterinsurgency." *Army* 27 (Sept. 1977): 31–36.

3702. Long, William F. "Counterinsurgency: Corrupting Concept." *U.S. Naval Institute Proceedings* 105 (Apr. 1979): 56–64. This is an excellent essay by a military strategist.

3703. Mack, Andrew. "Counterinsurgency in the Third World: Theory and Practice." *British Journal of International Studies* 1:3 (1975): 226–253. Mack emphasizes the U.S. Vietnam experience from 1945 to 1975.

3704. Ott, David E. "American Artillery in Counterinsurgency: Part 7—An Overview of Work to be Done." *Field Artillery Journal* 67 (Mar.–Apr. 1977): 29–33.

3705. Race, Jeffrey. "Vietnam Intervention: Systematic Distortion in Policy Making." *Armed Forces & Society* 2 (Spring 1976): 377–396. Race discusses U.S. assumptions about counterinsurgency.

3706. Schultz, Richard T. "Breaking the Will of the Enemy During the Vietnam War: The Operationalization of the Cost-Benefit Model of Counterinsurgency Warfare." *Journal of Peace Research* 15:2 (1978): 109–130.

3707. _____. "Coercive Force and Military Strategy: Deterrence Logic and Cost-Benefit Model of Counterinsurgency Warfare." *Western Political Quarterly* 32:4 (1979): 444–466.

3708. Thompson, Robert. "The War in Vietnam: Reflections on Counterinsurgency Operations." *RUSI Journal* 118 (Mar. 1973): 20–27.

Contemporary Essays

3709. Barrett, Raymond J. "Public Information, World Opinion and Counterinsurgency." *Air University Review* 21 (July–Aug. 1970): 72–77.

3710. Bashore, Boyd T. *Diem's Counterinsurgency Strategy for Vietnam: Right or Wrong?* Carlisle Barracks, PA: U.S. Army War College, 1968. [research paper]

3711. Farmer, James. *Counterinsurgency: Principles and Practices in Viet-Nam.* P–3039. Santa Monica, CA: Rand Corp., Dec. 1964.

3712. _____. *Counterinsurgency: Vietnam 1962–1963.* P–2778. Santa Monica, CA: Rand Corp., Aug. 1963.

3713. Gastil, Raymond D. *The Problem of Counterinsurgency in South Viet-Nam.* HI–707–RR. Croton-on-Hudson, NY: Hudson Institute, 1966.

3714. Henry, T. "Techniques From Trung Lap: Small Unit Training for Counterinsurgents." *Army* 14 (Apr. 1964): 35–43.

3715. Joiner, Charles A. "The Ubiquity of the Administrative Role in Counterinsurgency." *Asian Studies* 7 (Aug. 1967): 540–554.

3716. McMahon, Richard A. "The Indirect Approach." *Army* 19 (Aug. 1969): 56–62.

3717. Smythe, Donald. "Pershing and Counterinsurgency." *Military Review* 46 (Sept. 1966): 85–92.

3718. Tanham, G.K., and D.J. Duncanson. "Some Dilemmas of Counterinsurgency." *Foreign Affairs* 48 (Oct. 1969): 113–122.

3719. Wood, John S., Jr. "Counterinsurgency Coordination at the National and Regional Level." *Military Review* 46 (Mar. 1966): 80–85.

Pacification

While pacification was the essential element of counterinsurgency, there was no commitment or support for it. The Marines sought to develop "civic action" programs, but most of their energies, as well as the Army's, were consumed in large-unit operations. See "Psychological Warfare" below, this chapter, for another dimension.

Books and Dissertations
For U.S. Marine Corps accounts, see Stofi (3500) and Parker (3499).

3720. Adams, Nina S. "The Meaning of Pacification: Thanh Hoa Under French Rule 1885–1908." Ph.D. dissertation, Yale University, 1978.

3721. Grinter, Lawrence E. "The Pacification of South Vietnam: Dilemmas of Counterinsurgency and Development." Ph.D. dissertation, University of North Carolina, Chapel Hill, 1972.

3722. Hamilton, Thomas P. "Vietnamese and American Relationships in Pacification: The Problem of Authority." Ph.D. dissertation, Claremont Graduate School, 1971.

3723. Nighswanger, William A. *Rural Pacification in Vietnam.* New York: Praeger, 1967.

3724. Tanham, George K. *War Without Guns: American Civilians in Rural Vietnam.* New York: Praeger, 1966.

3725. U.S. Army. *A Program for the Pacification and Long Term Development of South Vietnam.* 2 vols. Washington, DC: Deputy Chief of Staff for Military Operations, 1966.

3726. West, Francis J., Jr. *The Village.* New York: Harper & Row, 1972. A combined action platoon of fourteen Marines and forty militiamen shields Binh Nghia.

Retrospective Essays
3727. Heinl, Robert D., Jr. "On Basis of Pacification, Vietnam War Has Been Won." *Armed Forces Journal* 109 (Feb. 1972): 50–51. This is an example of the failure to understand the nature of pacification.

3728. Komer, Robert W. *Bureaucracy Does Its Thing: Institutional Constraints on U.S.–GVN Performance in Vietnam.* R–967–ARPA. Santa Monica, CA: Rand Corp., 1972.

3729. Pratt, Thomas M. III. "Population and Resources Control." *Marine Corps Gazette* 54 (Sept. 1970): 35–39. [for 1966–1967]

3730. Rondinelli, Dennis A. "Community Development and American Pacification Policy in Vietnam." *Philippine Journal of Public Administration* 15 (Apr. 1971): 162–174.

3731. Seiden, Matthew J. "Reality of Pacification." *New Republic* 170 (Apr. 20, 1974): 8–10.

3732. Seidenman, Paul. "Interview with William E. Colby: Pacification: A Winning Combination That Came Too Late?" *Armed Forces Journal International* 114 (Jan. 1977): 24–25.

Contemporary Essays
3733. Allen, Luther A. "The U.S. and Southeast Asia: Pacification in Quang Tri." *New Leader* 47 (June 8, 1964): 9–12.

3734. Arnison, P.M. "Civic Action in Vietnam, 1965–1966." *Australian Army Journal*, No. 200 (Sept. 1967): 3–7.

3735. Brigham, Erwin R. "Pacification Measurement." *Military Review* 50 (May 1970): 47–55.

3736. Bunker, Ellsworth. "U.S. Support of Pacification Effort in Vietnam Reorganized." *U.S. Department of State Bulletin* 56 (June 5, 1967): 844–845.

3737. Buttinger, Joseph. "How to 'Pacify' Vietnam." *War/Peace Report* 7 (June–July 1967): 8–9.

3738. Campbell, Thomas E. "South Vietnam: The First Step to Victory; Winning the People." *Iron Age* 199 (June 22, 1967): 58–63.

3739. Chamberlain, Edwin W., Jr. "Pacification." *Infantry* 58 (Nov.–Dec. 1968): 32–39.

3740. Clement, David A. "Le My: Study in Counterinsurgency." *Marine Corps Gazette* 51 (July 1967): 18–24. [civic action]

3741. Corson, William R. "Pacification Program." In *The Vietnam War: Its Conduct and Higher Management.* Washington, DC: Georgetown University, Center for Strategic Studies, 1968.

3742. Cushman, John H. "Pacification: Concepts Developed in the Field by the RVN 21st Infantry Division." *Army* 16 (Mar. 1966): 21–29.

3743. DeShazo, Thomas E. "U.S. Counterinsurgency Assistance to Rural Vietnam in 1964." *Naval War College Review* 19 (Mar. 1967): 40–53.

3744. Donnell, John C. "Pacification Reassessed." *Asian Survey* 7 (Aug. 1967): 567–576.

3745. Duncanson, Dennis J. "Pacification and Democracy in South Vietnam." *World Today* [London] 23 (Oct. 1967): 410–418.

3746. Dunn, Jerry F. "A New Look at Pacification." *Military Review* 50 (Jan. 1970): 84–87.

3747. Elliott, D.W.P., and W.A. Stewart. *Pacification and the Viet Cong System in Dinh Tuong: 1966–1967.* RM–5788–ISA/ARPA. Santa Monica, CA: Rand Corp., Jan. 1969.

3748. Ellsberg, Daniel. *The Day Loc Tien Was Pacified.* P–3793. Santa Monica, CA: Rand Corp., Feb. 1968. [reprinted in *Antioch Review* 31 (Summer 1971): 209–222]

3749. Glick, Edward B. "Military Civic Action: Thorny Art of the Peace Keepers." *Army* 17 (Sept. 1967): 67–70.

3750. Hagley, T.R. "The 'Pacification' of Phu Loi." *Progressive* 30 (June 1967): 20–22.

3751. Halberstam, David. "The Ugliest American in Vietnam." *Esquire* 62 (Nov. 1964): 37–40ff. Lt. Colonel John Paul Vann, a legendary advocate of pacification, resigned in 1963 because the U.S. military did not understand the enemy; he was killed in June 1972.

3752. Harris, Audley C. "Youth and Revolutionary Development." *Military Review* 50 (May 1970): 25–32.

3753. Head, Simon. "Pacifying Vietnam." *Far Eastern Economic Review* 56 (May 4, 1967): 259–260.

3754. _____. "Unhappy Harbingers." *Far Eastern Economic Review* 56 (June 1, 1967): 495–498.

3755. Holmberg, William C. "Civic Action." *Marine Corps Gazette* 50 (June 1966): 20–28.

3756. Honda Katsuichi. "Villages in the Battlefield: The Vietnam War and the People." *Japan Quarterly* 15 (Apr.–June 1968): 159–179.

3757. Komer, Robert W. "Clear, Hold and Rebuild." *Army* 20 (May 1970): 16–24.

3758. _____. *Impact of Pacification on Insurgency in South Vietnam.* P–4443. Santa Monica, CA: Rand Corp., Aug. 1970.

3759. _____. "Impact of Pacification on Insurgency in South Vietnam." *Journal of International Affairs* 25:1 (1971): 48–69.

3760. _____. "The Other War in Vietnam: A Progress Report." *U.S. Department of State Bulletin* 55 (Oct. 10, 1966): 549–567; (Oct. 17, 1966): 591–601.

3761. _____. "Pacification: A Look Back ... and Ahead." *Army* 20 (June 1970): 20–29.

3762. McFarlane, I.D. "Civic Action." *Australian Army Journal*, no. 214 (Mar. 1967): 19–25.

3763. Mack, Richard E. "Hold and Pacify." *Military Review* 47 (Nov. 1967): 91–95.

3764. Martin, J.A. "Operation Helping Hand." *U.S. Naval Institute Proceedings* 96 (Oct. 1970): 99–100.

3765. Maruyama Shizuo. "The Other War in Vietnam: The Revolutionary Development Program." *Japan Quarterly* 14 (July–Sept. 1967): 297–303.

3766. Mecklin, John. "The Struggle to Rescue the People." *Fortune* 75 (Apr. 1965): 126ff.

3767. Nguyen Xuan Lai. "The Failure of 'Pacification.'" *Vietnamese Studies* 20 (Dec. 1968): 191–253.

3768. Olsen, A.N. "Teaming Up to Build a Nation." *U.S. Naval Institute Proceedings* 95 (Oct. 1969): 34–43.

3769. Platt, Jonas M. "Military Civic Action." *Marine Corps Gazette* 54 (Sept. 1970): 20–26.

3770. Popkin, Samuel L. "Pacification: Politics and the Village." *Asian Survey* 10 (Aug. 1970): 662–671.

3771. "Rebuilding a Nation in the Midst of War." *Army* 20 (Oct. 1970): 111–116.

3772. Reston, James. "We May Win the War but Lose the People." *New York Times Magazine* (Sept. 12, 1965): 42–43.

3773. Rowe, T.E. "More Precious Than Bullets." *Army* 21 (Mar. 1971): 38–44.

3774. Rudd, E.A. "U.S. Military Role in Civic Action in Vietnam." *Brassey's Annual* (1966): 300–305.

3775. Shaplen, Robert. "A Reporter in Vietnam: The Delta, the Plateau, and the Mountains." *New Yorker* (Aug. 11, 1962): 48–77ff.

3776. Shaw, Edward W. "Tien Chi: Helper Task Force." *Armor* 82 (July–Aug. 1973): 11–12.

3777. Sola Pool, Ithiel de. "Further Thoughts on Rural Pacification and Insurgency." *Peace Research Society (International) Papers* 10 (1968): 23–35.

3778. Stanford, Norman K. "Bamboo Brigades." *Marine Corps Gazette* 50 (Mar. 1966): 41–47.

3779. Starner, Frances L. "Pacification in South Vietnam: A Real New Life." *Far Eastern Economic Review* 57 (Sept. 3–9, 1967): 456–457.

3780. _____, and Ben Tre. "Pacification in South Vietnam: Any Umbrellas?" *Far Eastern Economic Review* 69 (July 7, 1970): 19–20, 69–71.

3781. Synder, K.J. "Friendship: A Principle of War." *Marine Corps Gazette* 52 (Mar. 1968): 36–40. [civic action in Long Phu]

3782. Tormey, J.H. "Arteries of Pacification." *Army* 17 (Aug. 1967): 59–60.

3783. U.S. House. Committee on Armed Services. Report; *Progress of the Pacification Program.* 91st Cong., 2d sess., Feb. 9, 1970.

3784. _____. Committee on Foreign Affairs. Hearings; *Rural Development in Asia.* 2 Pts. 90th Cong., 1st sess., Feb.–May 1967.

3785. _____. Report; *Measuring Hamlet Security in Vietnam.* Rpt. no. 91–25, by J.V. Tunney, Feb. 25, 1969. 91st Cong., 1st sess., 1969.

3786. U.S. Senate. Committee on Foreign Relations. Hearings; *Vietnam: Policy and Prospects, 1970.* 91st Cong., 2d sess., 1970. [on Civil Operations and Rural Development Support Programs]

3787. Warner, Denis. "Vietnam: The Ordeal of Pacification; Revolutionary Development Program." *Reporter* 35 (Dec. 1, 1966): 24–28.

3788. Welsh, David. "Pacification in Vietnam." *Ramparts* 6 (Oct. 1967): 36–41.

3789. West, Francis J., Jr. "The Fast Rifles: A Strategy for Grassroots Pacification in Vietnam." *Public and International Affairs* 5:1 (1967): 99–109.

3790. Weyland, Fred C. "Winning the People in Hau Nghia Province." *Army* 17 (Jan. 1967): 52–55.

3791. Willoughby, William H. "Revolutionary Development." *Infantry* 58 (Nov.–Dec. 1968): 4–11.

3792. Wright, Lacy. "John Paul Vann: Portrait of an Activist." *Foreign Service Journal* 50 (Mar. 1973): 15–16, 30–32. Wright was a persistent critic of inadequate pacification programs.

3793. Wright, Robert K. "The Pacified Hamlet." *Infantry* 60 (Nov.–Dec. 1970): 24–28.

STRATEGIC HAMLET PROGRAM

Begun in February 1969 as the successor to the "agroville" program of 1959, this controversial, unsuccessful effort aimed at concentrating peasants in fortified villages away from enemy controlled areas and U.S. "free-fire" zones. The program drove reluctant peasants to hamlets which more often became simply refugee centers. See also "South Vietnam, 1954–1975" and "Rural Vietnam" in Chapter 3.

3794. Goodman, Allen E. *Government and the Countryside: Political Accommodation and South Vietnam's Communal Groups.* P–3924. Santa Monica, CA: Rand Corp., Sept. 1968.

3795. Higgins, J.W. *Temporary Villages for Refugees: Costs, Problems, and Opportunities.* RM–5444–ISA/ARPA. Santa Monica, CA: Rand Corp., Aug. 1968.

3796. O'Donnell, J.B. "The Strategic Hamlet Program in Kien Hoa Province, South Vietnam: A Case Study of Counterinsurgency." In *Southeast Asian Tribes, Minorities and Nations*, edited by Peter Kunstadter. Princeton, NJ: Princeton University Press, 1967, 703–744.

3797. Osborne, Milton E. *Strategic Hamlets in South Vietnam: A Survey and a Comparison.* Data Paper no. 55. Ithaca: Cornell University, Southeast Asia Program, Apr. 1965.

3798. Roush, Maurice D. "The Hamlet Evaluation System." *Military Review* 49 (Sept. 1969): 10–17.

3799. Smith, William A. "The Strategic Hamlet Program in Vietnam." *Military Review* 44 (May 1964): 17–23.

3800. Zasloff, Joseph J. "Rural Resettlement in South Vietnam: The Agroville Program." *Pacific Affairs* 35 (Winter 1962–1963): 327–340.

3801. ———. *Rural Resettlement in Vietnam: An Agroville in Development.* Saigon: Michigan State University, Vietnam Advisory Group, 1961.

PROJECT PHOENIX

The Phung Hoang, or Phoenix program, was designed to "neutralize" or eliminate the VC infrastructure in villages. Begun in 1967, this mixed U.S.–South Vietnamese operation was as reprehensible as the VC's selective terrorism and assassinations. For defense of the program, see Colby (3977).

3802. Drosnin, Michael. "Phoenix: The CIA's Biggest Assassination Program." *New Times* [U.S.] 5 (Aug. 22, 1975): 16ff.

3803. Klare, Michael T. "Operation Phoenix and the Failure of Pacification in South Vietnam." *Liberation* 17 (May 1973): 21–27.

3804. Knoll, Erwin. "The Mysterious Project Phoenix." *Progressive* 34 (Feb. 1970): 19–21.

3805. Lewy, Guenter. "Counterinsurgency: The Phoenix Program." In his *America in Vietnam.* New York: Oxford University Press, 1978, 279–285. Lewy provides a "defense" of the program; compare this work with Klare (3803) and Knoll (3804).

3806. Stein, Jeffrey. "From the Ashes, Phoenix: A CIA Operation." *Commonweal* 98 (Apr. 20, 1973): 154–160.

3807. U.S. Senate. Committee on Foreign Relations. Hearings; *Vietnam: Policy and Prospects, 1970.* 91st Cong., 2d sess., Feb. 17–Mar. 19, 1970, 723–727. This is a statement by former program coordinator, William E. Colby.

Vietnamization

While American policymakers repeatedly stressed that the purpose of U.S. intervention was to assist South Vietnam to defend itself, this essential insight was, in practice, ignored. Not until after the Tet offensive (1968) did a determined effort begin to turn the war back to the Vietnamese—a program called "Vietnamization." For many reasons the effort was not successful. On the military side perhaps the biggest error was the ARVN's heavy dependence on U.S.

advisors; senior ARVN officers were denied the opportunity to learn from their errors and thus become proficient in strategic and tactical maneuvers.

3808. *Analysis of Vietnamization.* 3 vols. Defense Advanced Research Projects Agency, BSR 4033A. Washington, DC: Bendix Aerospace Division, Department of Applied Science & Technology, 1973.

3809. Beecher, William. "Vietnamization: A Few Loose Ends." *Army* 20 (Nov. 1970): 12–17.

3810. "Can Vietnamization Work?" *Time* 94 (Sept. 26, 1969): 25–26.

3811. Fitzgerald, Frances. "Vietnam: The Future." *New York Review of Books* (Mar 26, 1970): 4ff. [a case of slow retreat]

3812. Fulbright, J. William. "Vietnam: The Crucial Issue." *Progressive* 34 (Feb. 1970): 16–18.

3813. "Getting Ready for Truce: A Rush of Arms to Vietnam." *U.S. News and World Report* 73 (Nov. 27, 1972): 18ff.

3814. Guelzo, Carl M. "Managing Military Assistance Support in Vietnam." *Military Review* 49 (Jan. 1969): 31–35.

3815. "How American Military Aid Helped Vietnam's National Non-Commissioned Officers Academy Produce Trained Junior Officers." *Army* 10 (Feb. 1960): 26–30.

3816. Jenkins, Brian. *A People's Army for South Vietnam: A Vietnamese Solution.* R–897–ARPA. Santa Monica, CA: Rand Corp., Nov. 1971.

3817. _____. *The Unchangeable War.* RM–6278–ARPA. Santa Monica, CA: Rand Corp., Nov. 1970. Vietnamization won't work because U.S. preparation is for conventional warfare.

3818. Johnson, Robert H. "Vietnamization: Can It Work?" *Foreign Affairs* 48 (July 1970): 629–647.

3819. Kochigian, George S. "U.S. Financial Assistance to Republic of Vietnam Armed Forces." *Armed Forces Comptroller* 12 (July 1967): 29–31.

3820. Kolko, Gabriel. "Vietnamization: The Illusion of Withdrawal." *New Republic* 165 (Oct. 2, 1971): 19–21.

3821. Laird, Melvin R. "Vietnamization: Priority Program." *Army Digest* 25 (Jan. 1970): 20–25. Laird was secretary of defense under Nixon.

3822. Lake, P.M. "About Vietnamization." *National Review* 23 (July 13, 1971): 761.

3823. Langguth, A.J. "The Vietnamization of General Di." *New York Times Magazine* (Sept. 6, 1970): 5.

3824. Levy, Charles J. "ARVN as Faggots: Inverted Warfare in Vietnam." *Trans-Action* 8 (Dec. 1971): 18–27.

3825. McCarthy, F. "Winning the Ultimate Victory through Vietnamization." *Army* 21 (Jan. 1971): 4–6.

3826. Niksch, Larry A. *Vietnamization: The Program and Its Problems.* DS 556E20 72–15F. Washington, DC: Library of Congress, Congressional Research Service, 1972.

3827. Ott, David E. "FA Assistance Program: Part IV Vietnamization." *Field Artillery Journal* 66 (Sept.–Oct. 1976): 10–17.

3828. Parker, Maynard. "The Illusion of Vietnamization." *Newsweek* 74 (Sept. 29, 1969): 32–33.

3829. Pauker, Guy J. *An Essay on Vietnamization.* R–604–ARPA. Santa Monica, CA: Rand Corp., 1971. This article may have influenced Kissinger.

3830. Podhoretz, Norman. "A Note on Vietnamization." *Commentary* 51 (May 1971): 6–9.

3831. Race, Jeffrey. "Vietnamization: The Third Time Around." *Far Eastern Economic Review* 69 (Aug. 13, 1970): 12–13.

3832. Resor, S.R. "Number One Objective Is Support of Vietnam Forces." *Armed Forces Management* 12 (Nov. 1965): 40–41.

3833. Stutzer, N.H. "Vietnamization Progress." *Ordnance* 56 (Nov.–Dec. 1971): 226–229.

3834. "Tomorrow's Leaders Are Being Trained Today: Educating Future Vietnamese Officers." *Air Force Magazine* 54 (Apr. 1971): 28–30.

3835. Treaster, Joseph B. "Paper Army: The Fraud of Vietnamization." *Harper's* 245 (July 1975): 61–65.

3836. U.S. Department of State. Bureau of Public Affairs. *Indochina Progress Report: Assessment of Vietnamization, Address to Nation; by Richard Milhous Nixon, April 7, 1971.* Washington, DC: GPO, 1971.

3837. U.S. General Accounting Office. *Department of Defense Property Disposal Operations in Vietnam.* B–15945. Washington, DC, 1974.

3838. _____. *Improvements Needed in U.S. Contractor Training of Republic of Vietnam Forces.* B–159451. Washington, DC, 1974.

3839. _____. *Logistic Aspects of Vietnamization, 1969–1972: Report to Congress on the Department of Defense.* B–159451. Washington, DC, 1973.

3840. _____. *Military Construction Equipment, Materials, Supplies, and Facilities Channeled Through the Agency for International Development Mission in Vietnam.* B–159451. Washington, DC, 1974.

3841. Vietnam Council on Foreign Relations. *The Armed Forces of the Republic of Viet Nam.* Saigon, 1969.

3842. "W. Averell Harriman Says: 'Vietnamization is Immoral.'" *Look* 34 (Nov. 17, 1970): 38–40.

3843. Weller, Jac. "Our Vietnamese Allies: An Appraisal of Their Fighting Worth." *National Guardsman* 22 (Apr. 1968): 2–10.

AIR FORCE (VNAF)

3844. Bowers, Ray L. "Americans in the Vietnam Air Force: 'Dirty Thirty.'" *Aerospace Historian* 19 (Sept. 1972): 125–131.

3845. Brownlow, Cecil. "DOD Accelerates Viet Air Force Buildup." *Aviation Week & Space Technology* 91 (July 21, 1969): 24–25.

3846. _____. "Viet Air Force Gains in Professionalism." *Aviation Week & Space Technology* 97 (Aug. 7, 1972): 16–18.

3847. DeBerry, Drue L. "Vietnamese Air Force Technical Training, 1970–1971." *Air University Review* 24 (Jan.–Feb. 1973): 43–51.

3848. Frisbee, John L. "VNAF Meets the Test." *Air Force Magazine* 55 (June 1972): 50–53.

3849. Taylor, Jim. "Helping to Build the VNAF." *Air Force & Space Digest* 53 (Dec. 1970): 47–49.

3850. Weller, Jac. "RVNAF Training: Vital Element in Vietnamization." *Military Review* 52 (Oct. 1972): 35–49.

ARMY (ARVN)

Probably the best general account of ARVN, although quite biased, is Collins (3471).

3851. Arnett, Peter. "The ARVN: Prospects for the Army of South Vietnam." *Current History* 57 (Dec. 1969): 333–338.

3852. "ARVN Army of the Republic of Vietnam." *Army Digest* 27 (July 1968): 48–53.

3853. Buckley, Tom. "ARVN is Bigger and Better, But...." *New York Times Magazine* (Oct. 12, 1969): 34–35ff.

3854. Emerson, Gloria. "A Gift From ARVN." *Esquire* 79 (Nov. 1975): 105ff. [a thirteen-foot statue of Vietnamese infantryman in Saigon]

3855. Koppel, T. "ARVN Infantry Cloth Insignia." *Military Journal* (Winter 1978): 40–42.

3856. Lanier, Donald H. "Vietnam Armed Forces Infantry School." *Infantry* 61 (Sept.–Oct. 1971): 42–43.

3857. Titley, L. "Vietnamese Special Forces on the Job." *Army Digest* 23 (Dec. 1968): 46–47.

3858. Warner, Denis. "The South Vietnamese Army: Can It Replace Our GI's?" *Look* 32 (Dec. 19, 1968): 77–86.

NAVY

3859. Croizat, Victor J. "Vietnamese Naval Forces: Origins of the Species." *U.S. Naval Institute Proceedings* 99 (Feb. 1973): 49–58.

3860. Houghton, T.C. "South Vietnam's Junk Force." *Trident* 43 (June 1966): 11–13.

3861. Madouse, R.A. "The Vietnamese Naval Academy." *U.S. Naval Institute Proceedings* 95 (Mar. 1969): 48–57.

3862. Murphy, R.P.W., and E.F. Black. "The South Vietnamese Navy." *U.S. Naval Institute Proceedings* 90 (Jan. 1964): 53–61.

3863. Slaff, Allen P. "The South Vietnamese Navy: Success Story." *Navy* 11 (Aug. 1968): 24–29.

3864. "Total of 648 River Patrol Boats to Be Given to Vietnam Navy." *U.S. Naval Institute Proceedings* 96 (Dec. 1970): 102.

3865. White, Jack M. "AcToV–The U.S. Navy's Accelerated Turnover Program." *U.S. Naval Institute Proceedings* 96 (Feb. 1970): 112–113.

U.S. ADVISORS

3866. "Advisor on the Trail." *Army Digest* 23 (Aug. 1968): 57–60.

3867. Berle, Peter A. "The Adviser's Role In South Vietnam." *Reporter* 58 (Feb. 8, 1968): 24–26.

3868. Brown, R.F. "Role of the Junk Fleet Advisor in Base Defense." *U.S. Naval Institute Proceedings* 94 (Oct. 1968): 128–130.

3869. Cook, John L. *The Advisor.* Philadelphia: Dorrance, 1973.

3870. Dacus, David M. "So, Now You're an Advisor." *Infantry* 61 (May–June 1971): 32–35.

3871. Human Resources Research Organization. *Military Advising in Vietnam, 1969–1970.* Tech Rpt 73–24. Alexandria, VA, Nov. 1973.

3872. Leftwich, William G., Jr. ". . . and a few Marines." *U.S. Naval Institute Proceedings* 94 (Aug. 1968): 34–45. [early advisory efforts]

3873. Mahan, John C. "My Counterpart." *Army* 22 (Dec. 1972): 16–20.

3874. "Naval Advisor Vietnam." *U.S. Naval Institute Proceedings* 95 (Sept. 1969): 102–104.

3875. Pickerell, James H. "Marine Advisor: Vietnam." *Marine Corps Gazette* 48 (Apr. 1964): 24–28. [Captain Donald Koelper, killed in action February 1964]

3876. Ray, James F. "The District Advisor." *Military Review* 45 (May 1965): 3–8.

3877. Slaff, Allen P. "Naval Advisor Vietnam." *U.S. Naval Institute Proceedings* 95 (Apr. 1969): 39–44.

3878. Timmes, Thomas A. "Battalion Advisor: Vietnam." *Infantry* 60 (July–Aug. 1970): 46–51.

3879. Venderbie, Jan H. *Prov Rep Vietnam: A Provincial Representative's Account of Two Years in Vietnam, 1966–1968.* Philadelphia: Dorrance, 1970.

Logistics

See Heiser (3477) for the Army's point of view.

3880. Baines, T.E. "Transportable Computers Improve Combat Support." *Signal* 23 (July 1969): 16–17.

3881. Besson, Frank S., Jr. "Army Materiel Command's Support of Our Troops in Vietnam." *Army* 17 (Oct. 1967): 57–59.

3882. ———. "Mobility in the Modern Army." *Defense Transportation Journal* 25 (Jan.–Feb. 1969): 33–38.

3883. Black, Jonas L. "The Impact of Logistics Upon Strategy." *Air University Review* 24 (Mar.–Apr. 1973): 2–21.

3884. Burke, Robert L. "Corps Logistic Planning in Vietnam." *Military Review* 49 (Aug. 1969): 3–11.

3885. Cannon, Morris C. "Direct Support Logistics." *Military Review* 51 (May 1971): 18–23.

3886. Costa, Joseph. "The FSA (Forward Support Area)." *Infantry* 58 (Sept.–Oct. 1968): 27–29.

3887. Heiser, Joseph M., Jr. "Efficiency Is Key to U.S. Logistical Success in Vietnam." *Army* 20 (Sept. 1970): 49–51.

3888. ———. "Vietnam Logistics: Past Is Prologue?" *Defense Management Journal* 12 (July 1976): 74–80.

3889. Hobson, Kenneth B. "Logistics in the Lifeline." *Air University Review* 18 (July–Aug. 1967): 2–9.

3890. Hoefling, John A. "Outflanking the Terminal Complex: The Way to Total Mobility." *Army* 17 (Apr. 1967): 34–41.

3891. Hooper, Edwin B. "The Service Force, Pacific Fleet in Action." *Naval Review* (1968): 116–127. [covers 1965–1967]

3892. Howard, James M., III. "Operating Deep Channel." *U.S. Naval Institute Proceedings* 97 (Aug. 1971): 39–49.

3893. Kendall, Lane C. "U.S. Merchant Shipping and Vietnam." *Naval Review* (1968): 129–147. [covers 1965–1967]

3894. King, Herbert T. "Naval Logistic Support, Qui Nhon to Phu Quoc." *Naval Review* (1969): 86–111.

3895. Kovit, Bernard. "Limited War Logistics." *Space/Aeronautics* 45 (Apr. 1966): 110–119.

3896. Mayor, A. Jack. "Military Containerization: Impact on Worldwide Supply." *Defense Transportation Journal* 27 (May–June 1971): 46–49.

3897. Merrell, Jack G. "Air Force Logistics Command." *Air University Review* 20 (July–Aug. 1969): 2–13.

3898. ———. "Effective Logistic Support: Key to Air Force Operational Readiness." *Defense Industry Bulletin* 5 (June 1969): 1–8.

3899. Newport, H.S. "Inventory Control in the Combat Zone." *Army* 17 (Aug. 1967): 61–64.

3900. Oliver, E.F. "A Chain of Ships." *U.S. Naval Institute Proceedings* 95 (Nov. 1969): 92–107.

3901. Polmar, Norman. "Support by Sea for War in the Air." *Aerospace International* 3 (July–Aug. 1967): 29–31.

3902. Scholin, Allen R. "Logistics: Lifeline to Southeast Asia." *Air Force & Space Digest* 48 (Dec. 1965): 42–44, 47–48.

3903. Sibley, A.K. "Mobility Support for South Vietnam." *Armed Forces Management* 11 (Jan. 1965): 62–65.

3904. Soper, James B. "A View from FMF Pac of Logistics in the Western Pacific." *U.S. Naval Institute Proceedings* 98 (May 1972): 224–239.

3905. Swindler, M.G. "Base Depot Upgrade." *Ordnance* 56 (Sept.–Oct. 1971): 143–146.

3906. U.S. Army. Materiel Command. Historical Office. *Arsenal for the Brave: A History of the U.S. Army Materiel Command, 1962–1968.* Washington, DC: GPO, 1969.

3907. U.S. General Accounting Office. *Overall Observations of Transportation and Traffic Management Activities in the Far East and Southeast Asia.* Washington, DC, Apr. 30, 1969.

3908. U.S. House. Committee on Government Operations. Hearings; *Military Supply Systems, 1969.* 91st Cong., 1st sess., 1969.

3909. _____. Report; *The Port Situation in Vietnam (Follow-up Investigation).* 6th Rpt. House Rpt no. 611. 90th Cong., 1st sess., 1967.

3910. _____. 37th Report; *Military Supply Systems: Lessons From the Vietnam Experience.* 91st Cong., 2d sess., Oct. 8, 1970.

3911. _____. 38th Report; *The Port Situation in Vietnam (Follow-up Investigation).* House Rpt no. 91–159. 91st Cong., 2d sess., 1970.

3912. _____. Committee on Merchant Marine and Fisheries. Hearings; *Vietnam: Shipping Policy Review.* 2 vols. 89th Cong., 2d sess., 1966.

3913. U.S. Joint Logistics Review Board. *Logistic Support in the Vietnam Era.* 3 vols. Washington, DC: GPO, 1970.

AIRLIFT

In addition to those materials airlifted to Vietnam from the United States, most of the supplies that moved within Vietnam were airlifted "tactical" airlift.

3914. Bornholdt, John N., Jr. "Eagle Thrust." *Army* 18 (June 1968): 30–33.

3915. Bowers, Ray L. "Air Transportation in the Northern Provinces (1968)." *Marine Corps Gazette* 60 (June 1976): 39–49.

3916. _____. "USAF Airlift and the Airmobility Idea in Vietnam." *Air University Review* 26 (Nov.–Dec. 1974): 2–18.

3917. Brownlow, Cecil. "Aircraft Variety Marks Airlift to Vietnam." *Aviation Week & Space Technology* 86 (May 15, 1967): 76–79.

3918. _____. "Tactical Air Life Vital to Forces in Field." *Aviation Week & Space Technology* 82 (May 31, 1965): 78–82.

3919. _____. "USAF Presses Advanced Airlift Concepts." *Aviation Week & Space Technology* 89 (July 29, 1968): 72–73ff.

3920. _____. "Viet Ground Effort Keyed to Airlift Base." *Aviation Week & Space Technology* 86 (May 8, 1967): 87–92.

3921. Butz, J.S., Jr. "Intratheater Airlift in Vietnam: A Question of Quantity and Control." *Air Force Magazine* 49 (July 1966): 36–40.

3922. Chapman, Roy M. "Tactical Airlift Management in Vietnam." *Signal* 24 (Aug. 1970): 35–37.

3923. Deare, C.L., Jr. "Airlift in Vietnam." *Air Force Magazine* 49 (Nov. 1966): 45–50. [315th Air Division]

3924. Eliot, George F. "Next Time We'll Have to Get There Faster." *Army* 20 (Apr. 1970): 32–36.

3925. Fremming, Donald J. "C-5: In and Out in Thirty Minutes." *Air Force Magazine* 56 (Nov. 1973): 38–42.

3926. Kennedy, Thomas B. "Airlift in Southeast Asia." *Air University Review* 16 (Jan.–Feb. 1965): 72–82.

3927. Kerby, Robert L. "Air Force Transport Operations in Southeast Asia, 1960–63." *Aerospace Historian* 22 (Mar. 1975): 6–13.

3928. Messex, Curtis L. "Airdrop Mission to Katum." *Air Force Magazine* 54 (Sept. 1971): 46–51.

3929. Prow, John W. "Airlift for a Muddy War." *Ordnance* 52 (Mar.–Apr. 1968): 490–494.

3930. Schemmer, Benjamin F. "Bien Hoa Air Base: Short on Toilet Paper But Long On Teamwork." *Armed Forces Journal* 109 (June 1972): 15–17.

3931. U.S. Air Force. Project Corona Harvest. *USAF Airlift Activities in Support of Operations in Southeast Asia, January 1, 1965–March 1968.* Maxwell AFB, AL: Air University, Aerospace Studies Institute, 1973.

3932. Wood, Horace E., Jr. "Airlift: A Balanced View." *Air University Review* 23 (May–June 1972): 62–71.

Communications

See Rienzi (3487) for Army's view.

3933. Arnold, E.R. "Signal Communications in Vietnam." *Military Review* 47 (Mar. 1967): 92–96.

3934. Axley, Robert J. "Implementation of AUTODIN in Vietnam." *Signal* 24 (Nov. 1970): 44–47.

3935. Gusmith, H.R. "Messages Sent in Symbols Will Link Multilingual Troops." *Electronics* 39 (July 25, 1966): 108–112.

3936. Hickman, W. "Vietnam Communications Network Growing Into Southeast Asia's Best." *Electronics* 39 (Oct. 3, 1966): 167–170.

3937. Hilsman, William J. "Innovations in Tactical Communications." *Signal* 22 (June 1968): 12–16.

3938. Johnson, Harold R. "Pacific Air Forces Data Communications." *Signal* 24 (Nov. 1970): 6–12.

3939. Number not used.

3940. Linnon, J.L. "Aids to Navigation in Vietnam." *U.S. Naval Institute Proceedings* 96 (Dec. 1970): 99–100.

3941. Lyerla, Floyd B. "Communications Support." *Infantry* 57 (Sept.–Oct. 1967): 49–51.

3942. McKinney, John B. "The Army's Miniature AT&T." *Military Review* 48 (Nov. 1968): 69–75.

3943. _____. "Signal Planning Needs Innovators." *Army* 18 (Mar. 1968): 36–42.

3944. Rienzi, Thomas M. "Army Communications in Vietnam." *Signal* 26 (June 1972): 42–54ff.

3945. _____. "Quality Control in Vietnam Communications." *Signal* 24 (Feb. 1970): 8–11.

3946. "Troubleshooting in Trouble Spots." *Electronics* 40 (Jan. 23, 1967): 137–140.

Construction and Engineering

See Ploger (3485) for the Army's view.

3947. Callender, Gordon W., Jr. "Seabee Bridging at Hue." *Military Engineer* 62 (Sept.–Oct. 1970): 316–319.

3948. Campbell, Herbert G. "Protective Aircraft Shelter." *Air Force Civil Engineer* 10 (May 1969): 8–9.

3949. Cassidy, W.F. "The Army's Engineers in Vietnam: A Record Unsurpassed." *Army* 17 (Oct. 1967): 61–62ff.

3950. "Construction Escalates in Vietnam." *Engineering News-Record* 176 (Feb. 3, 1966): 11–14.

3951. Curtin, R.H. "The Air Force Engineer's Problems in Southeast Asia." *Air University Review* 18 (Nov.–Dec. 1966): 76–84.

3952. Eliot, George F. "Construction in Vietnam." *Ordnance* 61 (Sept.–Oct. 1966): 159–162.

3953. Galloway, G.E. *A Historical Study of United States Army Engineer Operations in the Republic of Vietnam, January 1965–November 1967.* Fort Leavenworth, KS: U.S. Army Command and General Staff College, 1968.

3954. Garvin, David B. "Bridge Security, Vietnam." *Military Engineer* 61 (Sept.–Oct. 1969): 339–340.

3955. Hanks, Jerald. "Engineers in Vietnam: Builders and Fighters." *Army* 23 (Oct. 1968): 57–62.

3956. Huff, K.P. "Building the Advanced Base at Da Nang." *Naval Review* (1968): 89–113.

3957. Johnson, H.J. "Management of War Zone Construction." *Defense Management Journal* 5 (Summer 1969): 44–47.

3958. Kiernan, Joseph M. "Combat Engineers in the Iron Triangle." *Army* 17 (June 1967): 42–45. [Operation Cedar Falls]

3959. Lemmer, John. "Construction Management by Combat Units." *Military Engineer* 61 (Nov.–Dec. 1969): 418–420.

3960. MacGregor, A.H. "Engineers in Operations in Vietnam." *Australian Army Journal*, no. 219 (Aug. 1967): 3–17.

3961. Malley, Robert J. "Forward Airfield Construction in Vietnam." *Military Engineer* 59 (Sept.–Oct. 1967): 318–322.

3962. Mecklin, John. "Building by the Billion in Vietnam." *Fortune* 74 (Sept. 1966): 113–117.

3963. Merdinger, Charles J. "Civil Engineers, Seabees, and Bases in Vietnam." *U.S. Naval Institute Proceedings* 96 (May 1970): 256–275.

3964. Middleton, William D. "The Seabees at Dong Xozi: '... a New Kind of Fighting Man.'" *U.S. Naval Institute Proceedings* 98 (Jan. 1972): 30–36.

3965. ———. "Seabees in Vietnam." *U.S. Naval Institute Proceedings* 93 (Aug. 1967): 54–64.

3966. Patrick, D.A. "Evolution of Contract Construction in Vietnam." *Military Engineer* 62 (July–Aug. 1970): 253–254.

3967. U.S. House. Committee on Appropriations. Hearings; *Military Construction Appropriations for 1967.* 3 vols. 89th Cong., 2d sess., 1966. See Volume 3 for construction in Southeast Asia.

3968. ———. Hearings; *Military Construction Appropriations for 1970.* 3 vols. 91st Cong., 1st sess., 1969. See Volume 3, 1185–1228 for progress of Southeast Asia construction.

3969. ———. Committee on Armed Services. Report; *Military Construction Requirements in Southeast Asia.* 91st Cong., 2d sess., Mar. 11, 1970.

3970. Weyler, Michael E. "Building for Computers in Vietnam." *Military Engineer* 63 (July–Aug. 1971): 238–239.

3971. Williams, Richard C. "How to Succeed in the Construction Business by Really Trying." *U.S. Naval Institute Proceedings* 95 (Sept. 1969): 72–80. Williams discusses building port facilities in South Vietnam.

3972. Yens, David P., and John P. Clement, III. "Port Construction in Vietnam." *Military Engineer* 59 (Jan.–Feb. 1967): 20–24.

Intelligence and Reconnaissance

See McChristian (3480) for an Army view; also in Chapter 2, "Laos," for CIA activities. Colby (3977) provides information on U.S. clandestine operations against North Vietnam.

3973. Ariel. "The Stupidity of Intelligence." *Washington Monthly* 1 (Sept. 1969): 23–28.

3974. Bennett, Donald G. "Intelligence, Vietnam." *Military Review* 46 (Aug. 1966): 72–77.

3975. Carter, Marshall N. "To Kill or Capture." *Marine Corps Gazette* 57 (June 1973): 31–35. Carter explores the need to quickly exploit tactical intelligence.

3976. Cohan, Leon, Jr. "Intelligence and Vietnam." *Marine Corps Gazette* 50 (Feb. 1966): 47–49.

3977. Colby, William. *Honorable Men: My Life in the CIA.* New York: Simon & Schuster, 1978. Colby spent most of the 1960s in Vietnam and became chief of CIA operations there.

3978. Girouard, R.J. "District Intelligence in Vietnam." *Armor* 75 (Nov.–Dec. 1966): 10–14.

3979. Halloran, Bernard F. "Soviet Armor Comes to Vietnam: A Surprise that Needn't Have Been." *Army* 22 (Aug. 1972): 19–23.

3980. Heilbrun, Otto. "Tactical Intelligence in Vietnam." *Military Review* 48 (Oct. 1968): 85–87.

3981. Liberti, Joseph C. "Counterintelligence in Direct Support." *Infantry* 64 (Mar.–Apr. 1974): 39–43.

3982. Martinsen, Peter. "Interrogating Prisoners." *Liberation* 12 (Dec.–Jan. 1967–1968): 14–31.

3983. Murtha, John P. "Combat Intelligence in Vietnam." *Marine Corps Gazette* 52 (Jan. 1968): 30–34.

3984. Robbins, Christopher. *Air America.* New York: Putnam, 1978. The author describes a CIA-operated airline that was active in Laos and elsewhere in Indochina.

3985. Sahlins, Marshall. "The Best Torture: 'Once You've Broken Him Down....'" *Nation* 201 (Oct. 25, 1965): 266–269.

3986. Scott, Peter D. "The Vietnam War and the CIA Financial Establishment." In *Remaking Asia: Essays on* *the American Use of Power*, edited by Mark Selden. New York: Pantheon, 1974, 91–154.

3987. Seagraves, R.W.A. "NILO—The Naval Intelligence Liaison Officer in Vietnam." *U.S. Naval Institute Proceedings.* 94 (Dec. 1968): 145–146.

3988. Smith, Joseph B. "The CIA in Vietnam: Nation-Builders, Old Pros, Paramilitary Boys, and Misplaced Persons." *Washington Monthly* 9 (Dec. 1978): 22–31.

3989. Smith, L.D. "Facts, Not Opinions." *Army* 19 (Dec. 1969): 24–31.

3990. U.S. Central Intelligence Agency. "Capabilities of the Vietnamese Communists for Fighting in South Vietnam (Nov. 13, 1967)." In U.S. House. Select Committee on Intelligence. Hearings; *U.S. Intelligence Agencies and Activities.* 94th Cong., 1st sess., 1975, Pt. V, 1981–1991.

RECONNAISSANCE

3991. Berman, Jay M. "The Bush That Ran." *Flying Review International* 26 (Aug. 1970): 44–47. [helicopters in reconnaissance]

3992. Colby, D.A. "Four Rules for Reconnaissance in Vietnam." *Marine Corps Gazette* 50 (Dec. 1966): 48–49.

3993. Davies, R.C., and J.L. Jones, Jr. "Employing the Recon Patrol." *Marine Corps Gazette* 53 (May 1969): 40–45. [Sting Ray and Key Hole Operations by 3d Marine Division]

3994. Ducksworth, Walter L., Jr. "Dawn Recon." *U.S. Army Aviation Digest* 15 (Apr. 1969): 32–35.

3995. "Electronic Reconnaissance in Vietnam." *International Defense Review* 5 (Aug. 1972): 358–362.

3996. Hines, O.J., and Charles R. Pippitt. "Tactical Air Reconnaissance." *Infantry* 60 (Jan.–Feb. 1970): 50–53.

3997. Kaye, Richard S. "A Direction for Division Recon." *Marine Corps Gazette* 54 (Apr. 1970): 34–36.

3998. Lamm, John F. "Gang Tackling the VC." *U.S. Army Aviation Digest* 15 (Oct. 1969): 2–5.

3999. "The Lean and Hungry Eye: Navy Reconnaissance Aircraft Scan the Jungle and Sea Providing Decision Making Photos for Battle Commanders." *Skyline* 24:3 (1966): 20–29.

4000. Scholin, Allan R. "Mission: Recce North.: *Air Force & Space Digest* 51 (May 1968): 42–46.

4001. Waltz, Robert W. "Today's Thinking in Air Force Reconnaissance." *Data* 13 (May 1968): 15–19.

Psychological Warfare

Psychological warfare, designed to assist pacification efforts and to counter VC propaganda, consisted primarily of leaflet drops and loudspeaker broadcasts. Can such operations successfully oppose indigenous propaganda? See also "Vietcong" and "National Liberation Front" in Chapter 3.

Books and Dissertations
4002. Chandler, Robert W. *War of Ideas: The U.S. Propaganda Campaign in Vietnam.* Boulder, CO: Westview, 1981. [covers 1965–1972]

4003. Latimer, Harry D. *U.S. Psychological Operations in Vietnam.* Providence, RI: Brown University Press, 1973.

Essays
4004. Aaron, Harold R. "Leaflet War." *Army Digest* 22 (May 1967): 32–35.

4005. Bain, Chester A. "The Vietnamese Peasant: His Psychological World and Means of Communication." *Transition* 6 (Jan. 1966): 26–39.

4006. Bejelajac, Slavko N. "A Design for Psychological Operations in Vietnam." *Orbis* 10 (Spring 1966): 126–137.

4007. Bost, F.H. "Tool for Friendship." *Army* 18 (July 1968): 34–36.

4008. Bullard, Monte R. "Political Warfare in Vietnam." *Military Review* 49 (Oct. 1969): 54–59.

4009. Cunningham, Cleve. "A Carrot or a Stick for Charlie." *Army* 18 (Apr. 1968): 68–69.

4010. Gleason, Robert L. "Psychological Operations and Air Power: Its Hits and Misses." *Air University Review* 22 (Mar.–Apr. 1971): 34–46.

4011. Harris, Elliot. *The "Un-American" Weapon: Psychological Warfare.* New York: Lads, 1967, 13–42.

4012. Human Sciences Research, Inc. *The Use of Cultural Data in Psychological Operations Programs in Vietnam.* HSR–RR–68–1/Vs. Arlington, VA, Feb. 1968.

4013. Johnson, William F. "Neglected Deterrent: Psychological Operations in 'Liberation Wars.'" *Military Review* 48 (May 1968): 81–90.

4014. Jones, M.R. "The Polite Little Other War." *Army* 18 (Aug. 1968): 43–44.

4015. Simulmatics Corp. *Improving the Effectiveness of the Chieu Hoi Program* 3 vols. SIM/CAM/9/67. Cambridge, MA, 1967.

4016. Spencer, Wilber P., Jr. "Chieu Hoi." *Infantry* 59 (Sept.–Oct. 1969): 56–57.

4017. System Development Corporation. *Current Hoi Chanh Characteristics and Trends.* Falls Church, VA, Aug. 29, 1969.

4018. U.S. Military Assistance Command, Vietnam. *Chieu Hoi and Dai Doan Ket National Reconciliation Programs.* JUSPAO PSYOP Policy Guidance no. 75. Saigon: Joint United States Public Affairs Office, 1968.

PROPAGANDA

4019. Ardoin, Birthney, and James L. Hall. "An Analysis of Soviet and Chinese Broadcasts Concerning U.S. Involvement in Vietnam." *Southern Quarterly* 13 (Apr. 1975): 175–180. [covers 1968–1973]

4020. Bain, Chester A. "Viet Cong Propaganda Abroad." *Foreign Service Journal* 45 (Oct. 1968): 18–21ff.

4021. Herz, Martin F. "VC/NVA Propaganda Leaflets Addressed to U.S. Troops: Some Reflections." *Orbis* 22 (Winter 1978): 913–926.

4022. Labin, Suzanne. "Killing Our Ally: A Disclosure of Communist Methods Used to Discredit and Undermine the Government of South Vietnam." *Military Review* 42 (May 1962): 28–38.

4023. Offer, Thomas W. "Nguyen Van Be as Propaganda Hero of the North and South Vietnamese Governments: A Case Study of Mass Media Conflict." *Southern Speech–Communications Journal* 40 (Fall 1974): 63–80.

Personnel Policies and Problems

Themes relating to this general topic are scattered throughout the Guide; *see additionally, "Personal Experiences" in Chapter 7, "GIs against the War" in Chapter 9, "POWs and MIAs" in Chapter 8 and "Vietnam Veterans" in Chapter 9.*

Books

4024. Army Times. *American Heroes of the Asian Wars.* New York: Dodd, 1968.

4025. Bourne, Peter G. *Men, Stress and Vietnam.* Boston: Little, Brown, 1970.

4026. _____. *The Psychology and Physiology of Stress: With Special Reference to the Studies on the Viet Nam War.* New York: Academic Press, 1969.

4027. Moore, W.M. *Navy Chaplains in Vietnam, 1954–1964.* Washington, DC: Department of Navy, Bureau of Naval Personnel, Chief of Chaplains, 1968.

4028. Moskos, Charles C., Jr. *The American Enlisted Man.* New York: Russell Sage Foundation, 1970.

4029. Sack, John. *M.* New York: New American Library, 1967. Sack gives an account of a rifle company training for Vietnam.

4030. Sheehan, Neil. *The Arnheiter Affair.* New York: Random House, 1972.

4031. U.S. Senate. Committee on Armed Services. Hearings; *United States Army Combat Readiness.* 89th Cong., 2d sess., May 3–4, 1966.

4032. Vance, Samuel. *The Courageous and the Proud.* New York: Norton, 1971. Vance discusses black enlisted personnel in Vietnam.

Essays

4033. Altman, Stuart H., and Robert J. Barro. "Officer Supply: The Impact of Pay, the Draft and the Vietnam War." *American Economic Review* 61 (Sept. 1971): 649–664.

4034. "As Fighting Slows in Vietnam: Breakdown in GI Discipline." *U.S. News and World Report* 70 (June 7, 1971): 16–17.

4035. Beecher, W. "Crisis of Confidence." *Army* 17 (Jan. 1967): 45–48.

4036. Bey, Douglas R., and Vincent A. Zecchinelli. "G.I.'s Against Themselves: Factors Resulting in Explosive Violence in Vietnam." *Psychiatry* 37:3 (1974): 221–228.

4037. Bishop, Donald M. "Leadership, Followship and Unit Spirit: Reflections on a Year in Vietnam." *Air Force Magazine* 60 (Dec. 1977): 52–56.

4038. Bletz, D.F. "After Vietnam: A Professional Challenge." *Military Review* 51 (Aug. 1971): 11–15.

4039. Borus, Jonathan F. "The Impact of Military Combat." In *The Social Psychology of Military Service*, edited by Nancy L. Goldman and David R. Segal. Beverly Hills, CA: Sage, 1976, 27–44.

4040. Brown, David A. "Viet Needs: Civil Lure Pinch USAF, Army." *Aviation Week & Space Technology* 86 (May 15, 1967): 94–97.

4041. Cole, E.F. "Replacement Operations in Vietnam." *Military Review* 48 (Feb. 1968): 3–8.

4042. Ehrhart, William D. "Why I Did it." *Virginia Quarterly Review* 56:1 (1980): 19–31. Ehrhart tells why he enlisted in the Marines.

4043. Fall, Bernard B. "You Can Tell 'Em, Buddy." *New Republic* 156 (Jan. 14, 1967): 17–20. Fall describes the life style of the military in Vietnam.

4044. Fallaci, Oriana. "Working UP to Killing." *Washington Monthly* 3 (Dec. 1972): 39–46. [justification for killing]

4045. Fiman, Byron G., Jonathan F. Borus, and M. Duncan Stanton. "Black–White and American Vietnamese Relations Among Soldiers in Vietnam." *Journal of Social Issues* 31 (Fall 1975): 39–48.

4046. Grant, Zalin B. "American Defectors with the Viet Cong." *New Republic* 159 (Sept. 17, 1968): 15–16.

4047. ———. "Whites against Blacks in Vietnam." *New Republic* 160 (Jan. 18, 1969): 15–16.

4048. Greenberg, Abe, and C.H. McKeown. "Discrimination? A Minority Review [U.S. Navy]." *U.S. Naval Institute Proceedings* 92 (June 1971): 104–106.

4049. Hottell, J.A., III. "Motivation in Combat." *Army* 20 (Feb. 1970): 47–50.

4050. Just, Ward S. "West Point Rendezvous: Notes on the 'Vietnam Class.'" *Atlantic* 235 (Jan. 1975): 44–47ff.

4051. Merick, Wendell S. "Sagging Morale in Vietnam: Eyewitness Report on Drugs, Race Problems and Boredom." *U.S. News and World Report* 70 (Jan. 25, 1971): 30–33.

4052. "Military Morale in America." *Army Quarterly and Defence Journal* [Great Britain] 101:1 (1970): 70–78.

4053. Moskos, Charles C., Jr. "The American Combat Soldier in Vietnam." *Journal of Social Issues* 31 (Fall 1975): 25–37.

4054. Gabriel, Richard A. "Professionalism versus Mangerialism in Vietnam." *Air University Review* 32 (Jan.–Feb. 1981): 77–85. Comments by P.T. Bingham and others follow, 85–90.

4055. "The New Breed: Soldiers and Chaplains in Vietnam." *Army Digest* 23 (Dec. 1968): 29–41.

4056. Palmer, B., Jr. "The American Soldier in Vietnam Has Met the Challenge." *Army* 17 (Oct. 1967): 107–123.

4057. Pressler, L.L. "Civilian Personnel, Vietnam." *Military Review* 47 (Nov. 1967): 39–43.

4058. Regens, James L. "Political Attitudes and Vietnam-era Military Service." *Social Science Journal* 14 (Oct. 1977): 83–92.

4059. Sarkesian, Sam C. "Viet Nam and the Professional Military." *Orbis* 18 (Spring 1974): 252–265.

4060. Shields, Patricia M. "Enlistment During the Vietnam Era and the 'Representation' Issue of the All-Volunteer Force." *Armed Forces and Society* 7 (Fall 1980): 133–147.

4061. Summers, Harry G., Jr. "What Did You Do in Vietnam, Grandpa?" *Army* 28 (Nov. 1978): 14–19.

4062. Treaster, Joseph B. "G-Eye View of Vietnam." *New York Times Magazine* (Oct. 30, 1966): 100.

4063. U.S. General Accounting Office. *Problems Being Experienced in the Dependent Shelter Program in the Republic of Vietnam.* Washington, DC, Feb. 17, 1972.

4064. White, Jack M. "Seven Days in July." *U.S. Naval Institute Proceedings* 98 (Jan. 1972): 37–41. [racial troubles]

4065. Zinber, N.E. "G.I.'s and O.J.'s in Vietnam." *New York Times Magazine* (Dec. 5, 1971): 37.

FORCE BUILDUP AND WITHDRAWAL

President Johnson announced on March 6, 1965 that 3,500 Marines were being sent to Da Nang; President Nixon began withdrawing U.S. forces in 1971. For a table of the buildup (1960–1966), see Air Force & Space Digest 50 (Mar. 1967): 78; for U.S. military personnel (1960–1971), see Military Review 52 (May 1972): 92.

4066. "Ahead: Faster Withdrawal From Vietnam: Results of Laird Mission." *U.S. News and World Report* 68 (Feb. 23, 1970): 29–30.

4067. Greene, Fred. "The Case For and Against Military Withdrawal from Vietnam and Korea." *American Academy of Political & Social Science Annals* 390 (July 1970): 1–17.

4068.   Heilbrun, Otto. "How Many Men to Vietnam?" *Military Review* 45 (Dec. 1965): 27–33.

4069.   Loosbrock, J.F. "The High Cost of Withdrawal." *Air Force & Space Digest* 52 (Nov. 1969): 8.

4070.   McCaffrey, William J. "A Fighting Army Heads for Home: Heavy Responsibilities in 'Phased Withdrawal.'" *Army* 21 (Oct. 1971): 106–113.

4071.   Nixon, Richard M. "President Nixon Announces Increased Troop Withdrawal From Vietnam." *U.S. Department of State Bulletin* 65 (Dec. 6, 1971): 641–646.

4072.   _____. "President Nixon Announces Withdrawal of 70,000 Troops From Vietnam." *U.S. Department of State Bulletin* 66 (Jan. 31, 1972): 113–116.

4073.   _____. "The Situation in Vietnam: Troop Withdrawals." *Vital Speeches* 38 (May 15, 1972): 450–452.

4074.   Norman, Lloyd. "The '206,000 Plan': The Inside Story." *Army* 21 (Apr. 1971): 30–35.

4075.   Plattner, C.M. "The War in Vietnam: Force Buildup Keyed to Wider Escalation." *Aviation Week & Space Technology* 84 (Jan. 3, 1966): 16–21.

4076.   Pomonti, Jean-Claude. "The Other South Vietnam: Toward the Breaking Point." *Foreign Affairs* 50 (Jan. 1972): 253–269. Pomonti discusses the impact of troop withdrawal on the VC.

4077.   "U.S. Force Ceiling in Vietnam to be Cut to 27,000 by December 1; White House Announcement, August 29, 1972." *U.S. Department of State Bulletin* 67 (Sept. 18, 1972): 300.

4078.   U.S. General Accounting Office. *First Review of Phase-Down of United States Military Activities in Vietnam.* B-171579. Washington, DC, 1971.

4079.   _____. *Second Review of Phasedown of United States Military Activities in Vietnam.* B–171579. Washington, DC, 1971.

4080.   "U.S. Pullout From Vietnam: The Nixon Formula is Working, Says Rogers." *U.S. News and World Report* 67 (Oct. 27, 1969): 16ff.

4081.   "Vietnam Cutback: How Far, How Fast?" *U.S. News and World Report* 66 (June 23, 1969): 29–31.

CRIME

See also, Prugh (3486), Lewy (3553), and Gabriel and Savage (3547) for data on "fragging" (attacks on officers and noncommissioned officers).

4082.   Danto, B. L., and R.L. Sadoff. "Court-martial in Vietnam." *Corrective Psychiatry and Journal of Social Therapy* 15 (Fall 1969): 65–72.

4083.   Kroll, Jerome. "Racial Patterns of Military Crimes in Vietnam." *Psychiatry* 39 (Feb. 1976): 51–64.

4084.   Linden, Eugene. "Fragging and Other Withdrawal Symptoms." *Saturday Review* 55 (Jan. 8, 1972): 12.

4085.   Parks, W. Hays. "Crimes in Hostilities." *Marine Corps Gazette* 60 (Aug. 1976): 16–22.

4086.   Toms, James E. "Justice in the Battle Zone." *U.S. Naval Institute Proceedings* 95 (June 1969): 52–57.

4087.   U.S. Senate. Committee on Government Operations. Hearings; *Fraud and Corruption in Management of Military Club Systems, Illegal Currency Manipulations Affecting South Vietnam.* 7 vols. 91st Cong., 2d sess.; and 92d Cong., 1st sess., 1970–1971.

4088.   Westerman, George F. "Military Justice in the Republic of Vietnam." *Military Law Review* 31 (Jan. 1966): 137–158.

DRUG ABUSE

4089.   Browning, Frank, and Banning Garrett. "The New Opium War." *Ramparts* 9 (May 1971): 32–39.

4090.   Harris, T. George. "As Far as Heroin is Concerned, the Worst is Over." *Psychology Today* 7 (Aug. 1973): 68–85.

4091.   Ingraham, Larry H. "'The Nam' and 'The World': Heroin Use by U.S. Army Enlisted Men Serving in Vietnam." *Psychiatry* 37 (May 1974): 114–128.

4092.   McCoy, Alfred W., et al. "A Correspondence with the CIA." *New York Review of Books* (Sept. 21, 1972): 26ff. This correspondence concerned his book, *The Politics of Heroin in Southeast Asia.*

4093.   _____. *The Politics of Heroin in Southeast Asia.* New York: Harper & Row, 1972.

4094.   Robbins, Lee N. *The Vietnam Drug User Returns.* Washington, DC: GPO, 1974.

4095.   _____, et al. "How Permanent Was Vietnam Drug Addiction?" *American Journal of Public Health Supplement* 64 (Dec. 1974): 38–43.

4096.   Roffman, Roger A. "Addiction Concepts and the Vietnam Experience." *Urban and Social Change Review* 9:2 (1976): 16–18.

4097.   U.S. General Accounting Office. *Drug Abuse Control Activities Affecting Military Personnel.* B–164031(2). Washington, DC, Aug. 11, 1972. [a report to Congress]

4098.   U.S. House. Committee on Foreign Affairs. Report; *The International Narcotics Trade,* by Seymour Halpern. 92d Cong., 1st sess., Oct. 24, 1971.

4099.   _____. Report; *The World Heroin Problem,* by Morgan F. Murphy and Robert H. Steele. 92d Cong., 1st sess., 1971.

4100.   U.S. Senate. Committee on Armed Forces. Hearings; *Drug Abuse in the Military.* 92d Cong., 2d sess., Feb. 29, 1972.

4101.   _____. Committee on Foreign Relations. Hearings; *International Traffic in Narcotics.* 92d Cong., 1st sess., 1971.

4102.   Woolley, H.T., and L.H. Beecher. "Drug Abuse: Out in the Open." *U.S. Naval Institute Proceedings* 97 (Nov. 1971): 18–35.

4103.   Wyman, Lester P. "Reentry Stress Perceptions of Heroin Using Vietnam Era American Soldiers While Awaiting Return to Civilian Community." Ph.D. dissertation, Case Western Reserve University, 1976.

Allied Military Forces

The role of allied forces in Vietnam has not received postwar scrutiny, although Larsen and Collins (3479) have presented the Army's view.

4104.   "Allies Join the Parade Home." *U.S. News and World Report* 71 (July 19, 1971): 21.

4105.   Bernad, Miguel A. "The First Year of the PHILCAG in Vietnam." *Philippine Studies* 16 (Jan. 1968): 131–154. [Filipino forces]

4106.   Kemp, Ian. *British G.I. in Vietnam.* London: Robert Hale, 1969.

4107.   Marks, Thomas A. "Professionalism in the Royal Thai Army." *U.S. Naval Institute Proceedings* 99 (Jan. 1973): 46–53.

4108.   "Our Combat Allies in Vietnam." *Army Digest* 23 (Apr. 1968): 10–14.

4109.   "Summary of Other Nation's Assistance to South Vietnam and Summary of U.S. Assistance to Those Nations." *Congressional Record* 113 (Oct. 5, 1967): S14299.

4110.   "Total Contribution of Our 37 Allies in South Vietnam." *Congressional Record* 113 (Aug. 28, 1967): H1352–1357.

4111.   "Vietnam Troop Contributors Hold Conference at Washington: Communiqué April 23, 1971." *U.S. Department of State Bulletin* 64 (May 17, 1971): 636–638.

4112.   Weller, Jac. "New Thai Infantry." *Infantry* 59 (Jan.–Feb. 1969): 14–19.

ANZAC FORCES

A few New Zealanders and many Australians fought in Vietnam; in Australia their intervention provoked an antiwar movement. See "Other Nations View U.S. Intervention" in Chapter 5.

4113.   Battle, M.R. *The Year of the Tiger: The Second Tour of 5th Battalion, The Royal Australian Regiment in South Vietnam, 1969–1970.* Brookvale, New South Wales: Printcraft, 1970.

4114.   Braeske, Arnold W. "Aussies on the Allied Team." *Army Digest* 24 (Apr. 1969): 45–46.

4115.   Burge, M.E.P. "Australian Gunners in South Vietnam." *Journal of the Royal Artillery* 95 (Sept. 1968): 84–92.

4116.   Clunies-Ross, Anthony I., ed. *The Grey Eight in Vietnam: The History of the Eighth Battalion, the Royal Australian Regiment, November 1969–November 1970.* Brisbane, Queensland, 1971.

4117.   Crowley, John, and E.G. McNamara. "Australian Military Operations in Vietnam." *Royal United Services Institution Journal* 113 (Nov. 1968): 310–316.

4118.   Cubis, R.M.C. "With the Royal Australian Regiment of Artillery in Vietnam." *Australian Army Journal,* no. 217 (June 1967): 12–31.

4119.   MacKay, Ian. *Australians in Vietnam.* Adelaide: Rigby, 1968.

4120.   Millar, T.B. "Australia and the War in Vietnam." *Brassey's Annual 1969* (1969): 226–233.

4121.   Newman, K.E., ed. *The Anzac Battalion; A Record of the Tour of 2nd Battalion, The Royal Australian Regiment; 1st Battalion, the Royal New Zealand Infantry Regiment in South Vietnam, 1967–68.* 2 vols. Brookvale, New South Wales: Printcraft, 1968.

4122.   O'Neill, Robert J. *Vietnam Task: The 5th Bat-*

talion: *The Royal Australian Regiment, 1966/67.* Melbourne: Cassell, 1968.

4123. Roberts, A.R., ed. *The Anzac Battalion, 1970–1971.* Sydney: Printcraft, 1972.

4124. Ross, Jane. "The Conscript Experience in Vietnam." *Australian Outlook* 29 (Dec. 1975): 315–322.

4125. Stuart, R.F., ed. *3 RAR in South Vietnam, 1967–1968: A Record of the Operational Service of the Third Battalion, the Royal Australian Regiment in South Vietnam, 12th December 1967–20th November 1968.* Brookvale, New South Wales: Printcraft, 1968.

4126. Webb, J.R. *Mission in Vietnam.* Townsville, Queensland: 4th Battalion, Royal Australian Regiment, 1969.

4127. Williams, Iain M. *Vietnam: A Pictorial History of the Sixth Battalion, the Royal Australian Regiment.* Brookvale, Sydney: Printcraft, 1967.

4128. Wilms, Peter. "R.A.A.F. in Vietnam." *Royal Air Forces Quarterly* 8 (Autumn 1968): 212–214.

SOUTH KOREANS (ROKs)

4129. Baldwin, Frank. "America's Rented Troops: South Koreans in Vietnam." *Bulletin of Concerned Asian Scholars* 7 (Oct.–Dec. 1975): 33–40.

4130. Critchfield, Richard. "The 'Tigers' Pacify Binh Dinh Province." *Korean Report* 6 (Oct.–Dec. 1966): 11.

4131. Lyman, Princeton N. "Korea's Involvement in Vietnam." *Orbis* 12 (Summer 1968): 563–581.

4132. "Money for Men [Korean Troops]." *New Republic* 165 (Oct. 9, 1971): 1ff.

4133. Rasmussen, Ronald R. "ROK Operations in Central Vietnam." *Military Review* 48 (Jan. 1968): 51–55.

4134. Starner, Frances L. "The White Horses [Korean Troops in Vietnam]." *Far Eastern Economic Review* 57 (Sept. 21, 1967): 567–572.

4135. Sungjoo Han. "South Korea's Participation in the Vietnam Conflict: An Analysis of the U.S.–Korean Alliance." *Orbis* 21 (Winter 1978): 893–912.

4136. Weller, Jac. "The Fighting ROKs." *Ordnance* 53 (Jan.–Feb. 1969): 383–387.

❧ Chapter Seven ❧

Combat Operations

MILITARY OPERATIONS in South Vietnam consisted mainly of "countless small battles, skirmishes, patrol actions, ambushes, assassinations and terrorism, which were continually in progress throughout the length and breadth" of the country.[1] The Vietcong/North Vietnamese army dictated the strategy which stemmed from the VC/NVA's realization, after American intervention, that they did not have the capability of occupying, holding or denying territory in South Vietnam.

Because of the fluid, episodic nature of the fighting, no satisfactory account of combat operations has emerged. Edgar O'Ballance's useful pioneering study (4147) surveys the military dimensions and clearly demonstrates the difficulties in preparing a coherent account of that side of the war. S.L.A. Marshall's five volumes (4141–4145) reflect the early optimism of American commanders after operations in the field. The "official histories" described in the previous chapter should provide some order and clarity about the integrated nature of the combat operations.

The descriptions of Lt. General Hay may be useful in understanding the nature of VC/NVA field operations:

> The North Vietnamese Army and the Viet Cong normally defended by evading. Only occasionally would they defend a position as a feint or deception, trying to draw allied forces into a trap or to divert them from a larger unit nearby. Enemy tacticians recognized that the allied forces were superior in firepower and mobility. To overcome this superiority, the enemy attempted to mass, attack, and withdraw before allied forces could react. Each of the enemy's operations was planned in minute detail and often rehearsed.
>
> The enemy's combat forces were lightly equipped so that they could move more freely and quickly. They could not depend upon the type of supply lines used by most conventional forces. Instead, they brought supplies in before the battle and positioned them ahead of time. Extra weapons and ammunition were cached near the objective. Medical supplies, ammunition, and food were stored along the withdrawal routes. . . .
>
> The survival of the enemy forces on the battlefield depended on their ability to disengage from or avoid contact with allied forces. They considered the withdrawal phase of the operation as important as any other combat action. When necessary, they would counterattack in an attempt to disengage. If routes leading away from the battlefield were blocked, the enemy troops would try to attack a weak spot in the allied position and escape through the breach. Delaying forces would ambush and harass pursuers. If an orderly withdrawal was not possible, small unit commanders would disperse their troops in the hope of rendezvousing later at a predesigned point.[2]

American strategy could not escape its traditions. The Joint Chiefs of Staff and General William Westmoreland insisted on policies that "aimed at denying the enemy freedom of movement not just in selected areas but throughout South Vietnam, at carrying the war to the enemy, and at winning victory by the means sanctioned by the most deeply rooted historical American conceptions of strategy, the destruction of the enemy's armed forces and of his ability to wage war."[3] By waging "search and destroy" missions, rather than concentrating on pacification activities and local security, Westmoreland sought unsuccessfully to engage and defeat an illusive enemy. Gradually substituting "body count" for victory, Westmoreland persisted. He told the press on April 14, 1967: "We'll just go on bleeding them until Hanoi wakes up to the fact that they have bled their country to the point of national disaster for generations. Then they will have to reassess their position."[4]

On the ground, Army and Marine infantrymen ("grunts") learned to cope with ambushes, mines and tunnels. They gradually adapted helicopters, artillery and light-draft vessels to meet tactical needs. How this came about is described in the essays and books listed below.

One of the most controversial aspects of the Second Indochina conflict was America's heavy expenditure of munitions, delivered by artillery and aircraft. It has been charged that massive bombings and heavy-handed ground campaigns, supplemented by widespread use of "free-fire" zones, often inflicted more death and destruction on the very people whose loyalty the United States had to win if it was to be successful, than on enemy combat forces.

American use of airpower in "limited war" situations, such as Korea and Indochina, needs critical reexamination. As Table VIII indicates, the use of air-delivered munitions (mostly bombs) increased substantially in Indochina.

The use of B-52s to carry out "H&I" (harassment and interdiction) missions was a dubious tactic. According to the Air Force's own field surveys, a typical B-52 raid consisted of dropping 100 five-hundred-pound bombs which resulted in the killing of .7 to 3.5 enemy soldiers.[5] Not only is this H&I tactic questionable from a cost-effective standpoint, it is objectionable because it is highly indiscriminate and, therefore, likely to cause numerous civilian casualties.

The Air Force concentrated much of its effort on long-range interdiction tactics aimed at preventing the enemy from resupplying its combat troops. The aerial campaign against the so-called Ho Chi Minh trail in Laos was the most extensive interdiction operation, but its results were apparently less than satisfactory.

During the 1960s and early 1970s, ideological and bureaucratic commitments led to the use of a "smorgasbord" approach to military data. Now, at a calmer distance from those years, it is time that we begin to integrate the political-diplomatic dimensions with those military operations. Such studies could provide considerably more insight into the dynamics propelling insurgency warfare.

NOTES

1. Edgar O'Ballance, *The Wars in Vietnam, 1954–1973* (New Hippocrene, 1975), 10.

2. Lt. General John H. Hay, Jr., *Tactical and Material Innovations* (Washington, DC: GPO, 1974), 5.

3. Russell Weigly, *The American Way of War* (Bloomington: Indiana University Press, 1977), 464–465.

4. *The Marines in Vietnam, 1954–1973* (Washington, DC: Headquarters, U.S. Marine Corps, 1974), 71.

5. *Congressional Record* 118 (May 10–11, 1972), 16748–16836; for statistics on B-52 bombings in Vietnam, Laos and Cambodia, see SIPRI, *Antipersonnel Weapons* (London: Taylor & Francis, 1978), 26–27.

TABLE VII

U.S. Expenditure of Munitions in Indochina, 1965–1973*
(in tons)

YEAR	GROUND	AIR	SEA	TOTAL**
1965	—	285,763	—	285,763
1966	535,400	458,418	4,536	988,354
1967	1,091,824	845,604	27,216	1,964,644
1968	1,346,628	1,303,960	45,813	2,696,401
1969	1,275,341	1,258,500	27,216	2,561,057
1970	1,071,870	886,724	11,793	1,970,387
1971	755,656	692,327	4,802	1,452,785
1972	776,430	983,707	32,114	1,792,251
1973	162,581	378,098	2,722	543,401
Total	7,015,730	7,093,101	156,212	14,265,043

Source: SIPRI, *Anti-personnel Weapons* (London: Taylor & Francis, 1978), p.26.

*Includes munitions supplied by U.S.A. to its allies.

**Does not include munitions expended prior to 1965, ground or sea munitions for 1965, air munitions expended after July 1973, or ground munitions expended after June 1983.

TABLE VIII

Munitions Expended by U.S. Forces in World War II, Korea and Indochina
(in thousand metric tons)

	AIR	GROUND	TOTAL	AIR/TOTAL (PERCENT)
World War II	1,957	3,572	5,529	35.4
Korea	634	1,913	2,547	24.8
Indochina				
1966	449	535	948	47.4
1967	844	1,091	1,935	43.1
1968	1,302	1,345	2,647	49.2
1969	1,257	1,274	2,531	49.7
1970	885	1,071	1,956	45.2
1971	691	755	1,446	47.8
1972	982	776	1,758	55.8
Total Indochina*	6,410	6,847	13,221	48.5

Source: SIPRI, *Anti-personnel Weapons* (London: Taylor & Francis, 1978), p.46.

Note: Although these are the best official figures available, they are not always complete or strictly comparable. For example, World War II air munitions figures do not include rockets and aircraft cannon ammunition. Indochina figures also include allied expenditures.

*Does not include munitions expended before 1966 and 377,310 tons of air munitions and 162,550 tons of ground munitions expended in 1973.

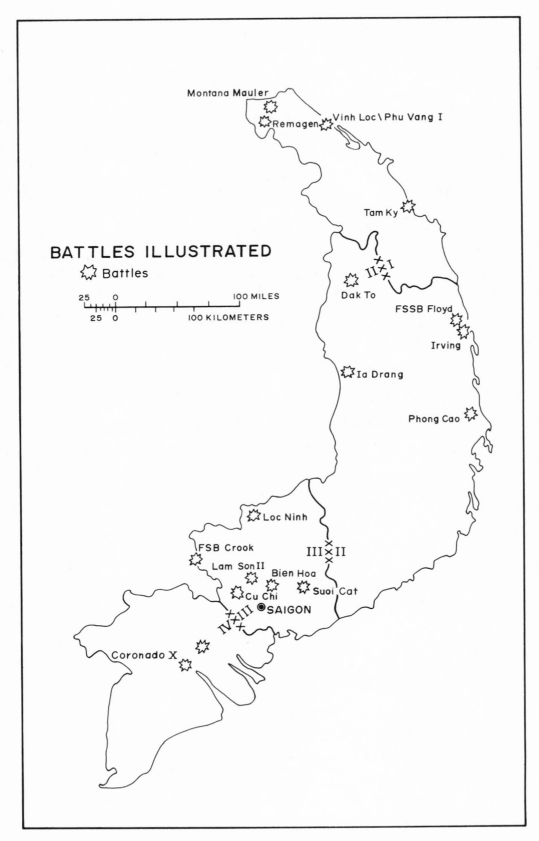

Reprinted from *Tactical and Material Innovations*, by John H. Hay, Jr. (Washington, DC: U.S. Army, 1974), p.4.

Military Operations

Books
Official histories listed in previous chapters also provide accounts of military operations.

4137. Fourniau, C. *Le Vietnam: Face à la guerre.* Paris: 1966.

4138. *From Khe Sanh to Chepone.* Hanoi: Foreign Languages Publishing House, 1971.

4139. Hirsch, P.O., ed. *Vietnam Combat.* New York: Pyramid, 1967. Hirsch has a collected battlefield accounts.

4140. Lucas, John G. *Dateline: Viet Nam.* New York: Crown, 1966. This fine account of U.S. troops in action was written by a journalist.

4141. Marshall, S.L.A. *Ambush: The Battle of Dau Tieng: Also Called the Battle of Dong Minh Chau, War Zone C, Operation Attleboro, and Other Deadfalls in South Vietnam.* New York: Cowles, 1969.

4142. ———. *Battles in the Monsoon: Campaigning in the Central Highland, South Vietnam, Summer 1966.* New York: Morrow, 1966.

4143. ———. *Bird: The Christmastide Battle.* New York: Cowles, 1968. [Binh Dinh]

4144. ———. *The Fields of Bamboo: Dong Tre, Trung Luong, and Hoa Hoi: Three Battles Just Beyond the China Sea.* New York: Dial, 1971.

4145. ———. *West to Cambodia.* New York: Cowles, 1968. Marshall's volumes reflect the optimism of the early war years.

4146. Mulligan, Hugo A. *No Place to Die: The Agony of Viet Nam.* New York: Morrow, 1967. [vignettes of U.S. and ARVN combat]

4147. O'Ballance, Edgar. *The Wars in Vietnam, 1954–1973.* New York: Hippocrene, 1975. This is a useful effort at a military history; it demonstrates the difficulties in writing about this war.

4148. Pruden, Wesley, Jr. *Vietnam: The War.* New York: National Observer, 1965.

4149. Rigg, Robert B. *How to Stay Alive in Vietnam.* Harrisburg, PA: Stackpole, 1966.

4150. Rozier, William B. *To Battle a Dragon.* New York: Vantage, 1971. [describes naval operations]

4151. Truong Son. *The Winter 1966–Spring 1967: Victory and Five Lessons Concerning the Conduct of Military Strategy.* Hanoi: Foreign Languages Publishing House, 1967.

4152. *The Vietnam War: The Illustrated History of the Conflict in South-East Asia.* London: Salamander, 1979.

4153. Weller, Jac. *Fire and Movement: Bargain Basement Warfare in the Far East.* New York: Crowell, 1967.

Essays
4154. Baldwin, Hanson W. "A Vietnam Balance Sheet." *Reporter* 37 (Oct. 19, 1967): 14–18.

4155. Browne, D.L. "Dust and Mud and the Viet Cong." *U.S. Naval Institute Proceedings* 96 (Sept. 1970): 53–57.

4156. Dalby, M.C. "Operations in Vietnam." *Royal United Services Institution Journal* 111 (Feb. 1966): 4–13.

4157. Donovan, Hedley. "Vietnam: Slow, Tough, but Coming Along." *Life* 62 (June 2, 1967): 68–77.

4158. Fitzgerald, Frances. "Life and Death of a Vietnamese Village." *New York Times Magazine* (Sept. 4, 1966): 4ff.

4159. Hackworth, David H. "Battle Analysis: The Truth of Battle Can Be Learned only from the Soldiers Who Fight It." *Army* 17 (July 1967): 33–35.

4160. McCaffrey, William J. "Vietnam in 1970: Year of Transition." *Army* 20 (Oct. 1970): 95–109.

4161. Majumbar, B.N. "The Lean and Mean War in Vietnam." *Revue Militaire Générale* 1 (Jan. 1966): 46–62.

4162. Meyers, Fred L, Jr. "Strike to Win." *Infantry* 60 (Nov.–Dec. 1970): 54–58.

4163. Mildren, Frank T. "From Mekong to DMZ: A Fighting Year for the U.S. Army's Best." *Army* 18 (Nov. 1968): 83–95.

4164. ———. "Our Troops in Vietnam: In Charge—All the Way." *Army* 19 (Oct. 1969): 96–110.

4165. Nguyen Van Hieu. "Eye-witness Report from War Zone C." *Minority of One.* 9 (July–Aug. 1967): 22–24.

4166. Pearson, B.G. William. "Day-and-Night Battle in Relief of an Outpost." *Army* 17 (Apr. 1967): 54–58.

4167. Rose, Jerry A. "I'm Hit! I'm Hit! On a Remote Asian Border, These Americans Wage a Lone Struggle Against Communism." *Saturday Evening Post* 236 (Mar. 23, 1963): 34–46.

4168. "Vietnam: State of Battle." *Economist* 225 (Nov. 18, 1967): 723–725.

Command and Control

See Eckhardt (3473) and Myer (3481) for semi-official views.

4169. Hackworth, David H. "Target Acquisition: Vietnam Style." *Military Review* 48 (Apr. 1968): 73–79.

4170. "How Command and Control Theory is Working in Practice in Vietnam." *Armed Forces Management* 13 (July 1967): 39–42.

4171. Johnson, William C. "Helicopter COC." *Marine Corps Gazette* 51 (July 1967): 25–28.

4172. Kellar, Robert S. "The Heliborne Command Post." *U.S. Army Aviation Digest* 15 (Jan. 1969): 14–21.

4173. Mack, Jerold R., and Richard M. Williams. "52 Airborne Early Warning and Control Wing in Southeast Asia: A Case Study in Airborne Command and Control." *Air University Review* 25 (Nov.–Dec. 1973): 70–78.

4174. McCaslin, Fred C., Jr. "ABCC: A Capsule View of the Men and Machines of the 7th Airborne Command and Control Squadron." *Signal* 31 (Nov.–Dec. 1976): 26–29.

Personal Experiences

See also "Admirals and Generals" and "U.S. Advisors" in Chapter 6, "U.S. Medical Support" and "POWs and MIAs" in Chapter 8, for other combat-related personal experiences. Some writers chose to depict their experiences in poetry and fiction (see final section of the Guide). Caputo's memoirs (4181) are a vivid account of what ground combat war is like, while Broughton (4180) depicts the frustrations of a professional Air Force officer.

Books
4175. Adler, Bill, ed. *Letters Form Vietnam.* New York: Dutton, 1967. [reflects soldiers' attitudes]

4176. Anderson, Charles. *The Grunts.* San Raphael, CA: Presidio, 1976.

4177. Baker, Mark. *Nam.* New York: Morrow, 1981. [oral history of experiences]

4178. Bernard, Edward. *Going Home.* Philadelphia: Dorrance, 1973.

4179. Briscoe, Edward G. *Diary of a Short-timer in Vietnam.* New York: Vantage, 1970.

4180. Broughton, Jack. *Thud Ridge.* Philadelphia: Lippincott, 1969. [Air Force pilot]

4181. Caputo, Philip. *A Rumor of War.* New York: Holt, Rinehart & Winston, 1977. [Marine officer, 1965–1966, in I-Corps]

4182. Donlon, Roger. *Outpost of Freedom, as Told to Warren Rogers.* New York: McGraw-Hill, 1965. Donlon was the first Vietnam Congressional Medal of Honor winner.

4183. Duncan, David Douglas. *This is War.* New York: Bantam, 1967.

4184. Elkins, Frank C. *The Heart of a Man.* Edited by M. R. Elkins. New York: Norton, 1973. This is a navy pilot's posthumous publication.

4185. Flood, Charles B. *The War of the Innocents.* New York: McGraw-Hill, 1970.

4186. Herrgesell, Oscar. *Dear Margaret, Today I Died ... Letters from Vietnam.* Compiled by M.R. Herrgesell. San Antonio, TX: Naylor, 1974.

4187. Hughes, Larry. *You Can See a Lot Standing under a Flare in the Republic of Vietnam: My Year at War.* New York: Morrow, 1969.

4188. Hutchens, James M. *Beyond Combat.* Chicago: Moody, 1968.

4189. Johnson, Raymond W. *Postmark: The Mekong Delta.* Westwood, NJ: Revell, 1968.

4190. Klinkowitz, Jerome, and John Sommer, eds. *Writing Under Fire: Stories of the Vietnam War.* New York: Delta, 1978.

4191. Kovic, Ron. *Born on the Fourth of July.* New York: McGraw-Hill, 1976.

4192. Marks, Richard E. *The Letters of Pfc. Richard E. Marks, USMC.* Philadelphia: Lippincott, 1967.

4193. O'Connor, John J. *A Chaplain Looks at Vietnam.* New York: World, 1968.

4194. Parks, David. *G.I. Diary.* New York: Harper & Row, 1968.

4195. Reed, David. *Up Front in Vietnam.* New York: Funk & Wagnalls, 1967.

4196. Russ, Martin. *Happy Hunting Ground.* New York: Atheneum, 1968.

4197. Sadler, Barry. *I'm a Lucky One.* New York: Macmillan, 1967.

4198. Santoli, Al. *Everything We Had.* New York: Random House, 1981. [oral history of Vietnam experiences—both military and protesters]

4199. Shepard, Elaine. *The Doom Pussy.* New York: Trident, 1967. [relates experiences of aviation unit]

4200. Tucker, James G. *Arkansas Men at War.* Little Rock, AR: Pioneer Press, 1968.

4201. Yezzo, Dominick. *A G.I.'s Vietnam Diary, 1968–1969.* New York: Watts, 1974.

Essays

4202. Duncan, Donald. "Memoirs of a Special Forces Hero: The Whole Thing Was a Lie." *Ramparts* 4 (Feb. 1966): 13–24.

4203. Emerson, Gloria. "Arms and the Woman: A Guided Tour With the Lifers in Cav Country Vietnam." *Harper's* 243 (Apr. 1973): 34ff.

4204. Herr, Michael. "Hell Sucks: Impressions from the Only War We've Got." *Esquire* 70 (Aug. 1968): 66–69, 109–110.

4205. "Images of War: An Oral History of Vietnam." *Rolling Stone* (June 19, 1975): 50–55.

4206. Rosenberger, J.W. "How the Soldiers View Vietnam." *Progressive* 32 (Mar. 1968): 22–24.

4207. "Vietnam Diary: Notes From the Journal of a Young American in Saigon." *Reporter* 34 (Jan. 13, 1966): 25–27.

Tet Offensive, 1968

The surprise VC/NVA general assault challenged the validity of President Johnson's "limited" war design and General Westmoreland's "strategy of attrition." American forces won the battles in South Vietnam, but lost the political/psychological contest at home. See "Johnson Years, 1964–1968," Chapter 4, and Braestrup's Big Story (5579) for media coverage.

4208. Brodie, Bernard. "The Tet Offensive." In *Decisive Battles of the Twentieth Century*, edited by Noble Frankland and Christopher Dowling. London: Sidgwick & Jackson, 1976, 321–334. This is an excellent survey by a noted American military strategist.

4209. "Fact vs Fantasy: The Tet Intelligence Imbroglio." *Armed Forces Journal International* 113 (Dec. 1975): 23–24.

4210. Gannett, Betty. "The NLF Offensive in Vietnam." *Political Affairs* 47 (Mar. 1968): 1–9.

4211. Hunt, David. "Remembering the Tet Offensive." *Radical America* 11:6/12:1 (1977–1978): 79–96.

4212. Kriegel, Richard C. "Tet Offensive: Victory or Defeat?" *Marine Corps Gazette* 52 (Dec. 1968): 24–28.

4213. Livingston, George D., Jr. "Pershing II: Success Amid Chaos." *Military Review* 50 (May 1970): 56–60. [U.S. operation in the provinces]

4214. Markbreiter, T.N. "A Bitter Tet." *Far Eastern Economic Review* 59 (Feb. 22, 1968): 331–333.

4215. Nossal, Frederick. "Tet: One Year Later." *Far Eastern Economic Review* 63 (Feb. 9–15, 1969): 274–276.

4216. Ott, David E. "The Holy War: Viet Nam, Part IV." *Field Artillery Journal* 66 (Jan.–Feb. 1976): 27–31. [Tet offensive]

4217. Pike, Douglas. "Giap's General Uprising." *Far Eastern Economic Review* 59 (Mar. 21, 1968): 513–515.

4218. _____. "The Tet Offensive: A Setback for Giap: But Just How Big?" *Army* 18 (Apr. 1968): 57–61.

4219. _____. "Vietnam—the Tet Offensive: Giap's General Uprising." *Far Eastern Economic Review* 59 (Mar. 17–23, 1968): 513–515.

4220. Rolph, Hammond M. "Viet Cong Seize War Initiative in Major Offensive." *Communist Affairs* 6 (Jan.–Feb. 1968): 12–14.

4221. *Scenes of the General Offensive and Uprisings.* Hanoi: Foreign Languages Publishing House, 1968.

4222. *South Viet Nam: A Month of Unprecedented Offensive and Uprising.* Hanoi: Giai Phong Publishing House, 1968.

HUE

Some of the bitterest fighting in the war occurred at Hue; Marines recaptured the city but casualties and destruction were heavy. NVA/VC troops massacred hundreds of civilians. Compare with "War Crimes," Chapter 8.

4223. Christmas, George R. "A Company Commander Reflects on Operation Hue City." *Marine Corps Gazette* 55 (Apr. 1971): 34–39.

4224. _____. "A Company Commander Remembers the Battle for Hue." *Marine Corps Gazette* 61 (Feb. 1977): 19–26.

4225. Eby, Omar. *A House in Hue.* Scottsdale, PA: Herald Press, 1969. The story of a civilian caught up in the Tet offensive.

4226. Irving, Frederick F. "The Battle of Hue." *Military Review* 49 (Jan. 1969): 56–63.

4227. Leroy, Catherine. "A Tense Interlude with the Enemy in Hue." *Life* 64 (Feb. 16, 1968): 22–29.

4228. Olson, John V. "The Battle that Regained and Ruined Hue." *Life* 64 (Mar. 8, 1968): 24–29.

4229. Smith, George W. "The Battle of Hue." *Infantry* 58 (July–Aug. 1968): 16–26.

SAIGON

The VC attack on the U.S. Embassy was fought within range of TV cameras; the battle damage was moderate, but the psychological impact in the U.S. was enormous.

4230. Pohle, Victoria. *The Viet Cong in Saigon: Tactics and Objectives During the Tet Offensive.* RM–5799–ISA/ARPA. Santa Monica, CA: Rand Corp., 1969.

4231. Tran Van Dinh. "Six Hours That Changed the Vietnam Situation." *Christian Century* 85 (Mar. 6, 1968): 289–291.

4232. Warner, Denis. "The Defense of Saigon." *Reporter* 38 (Apr. 4, 1968): 15–19.

KHE SANH/LANG VEI

The bitter and protracted NVA seige of the U.S. outpost at Khe Sanh (January 21–April 7, 1968) featured relief operations, NIAGARA I and II by the USAF and PEGASUS by the Marines, together with extensive aerial resupply which raised the seige; however, the outpost was abandoned on July 5. The media sought to compare Khe Sanh with Dien Bien Phu, but the U.S. garrison was never in that much danger of being overrun. For the USAF's role, see Nalty (3455).

4233. Althoff, David L. "Helicopter Operations at Khe Sanh." *Marine Corps Gazette* 53 (May 1969): 47–49. [interview]

4234. Bennett, Curtis D. "Khe Sanh Resupply: A Short History." *Aerospace Historian* 23 (Dec. 1976): 189–196.

4235. Brownlow, Cecil. "B-52s Prove Tactical Value During Siege of Khe Sanh." *Aviation Week & Space Technology* 88 (May 13, 1968): 26–30.

4236. Carroll, John S. "Khe Sanh." *Atlantic* 222 (Oct. 1968): 4ff.

4237. Duncan, David Douglas. "Khe Sanh." *Life* 64 (Feb. 23, 1968): 20–31.

4238. Galvin, John R. "The Relief of Khe Sanh." *Military Review* 50 (Jan. 1970): 88–94.

4239. Guay, Robert P. "The Khe Sanh Airlift: A VTOL Lesson." *Astronautics & Aeronautics* 7 (Dec. 1969): 42–49ff.

4240. Herr, Michael. "Conclusion at Khe Sanh." *Esquire* 72 (Oct. 1969): 118–123, 202. [exaggeration of U.S. peril]

4241. _____. "Khesanh." *Esquire* 72 (Sept. 1969): 118–123, 150.

4242. McLaughlin, Burl W. "Khe Sanh: Keeping an Outpost Alive: An Appraisal." *Air University Review* 20 (Jan.–Feb. 1968): 57–77. [834th Air Division]

4243. Milia, Carmelo P. "Armor Task Force (Remagen) to Khe Sanh." *Armor* 79 (May–June 1970): 42–46.

4244. Ott, David E. "The Battle of Khe Sanh, Part VI." *Field Artillery Journal* 66 (Mar.–Apr. 1976): 44–48.

4245. Pipes, K.W. "Men to Match Their Mountains." *Marine Corps Gazette* 58 (Apr. 1974): 18–24. [Marines at Khe Sanh]

4246. Sayle, M. "The Relief of Khe Sanh: How 80,000 Tons of Bombs Saved the Marines." *London Sunday Times* (Apr. 14, 1967): 6–7.

4247. Scholin, Allan R. "An Airpower Lesson For Giap." *Air Force & Space Digest* 51 (June 1968): 90–94.

4248. Shore, Moyers S., III. *The Battle for Khe Sanh.* Washington, DC: GPO, 1969. [26th Marines at Khe Sanh]

4249. Studt, John C. "Battalion in the Attack." *Marine Corps Gazette* 54 (July 1970): 39–44. [April 13, 1968, at Khe Sanh]

4250. Swearengen, Mark A. "Siege: Forty Days at Khe Sanh." *Marine Corps Gazette* 57 (Apr. 1973): 23–28.

4251. Tolson, John J. "Pegasus." *Army* 21 (Dec. 1971): 9–19. [combined U.S., ARVN and Australian air–ground relief operation]

4252. Warner, Denis. "Khe Sanh and Dien Bien Phu." *Reporter* 38 (Feb. 22, 1968): 16–19.

4253. Watts, Claudius E., III. "Aerial Resupply for Khe Sanh." *Military Review* 52 (Dec. 1972): 70–88.

Cambodian Incursion, 1970

In March 1970, U.S. officials estimated that at least 5,000 North Vietnamese troops and some 40,000 VC were in Cambodia engaged in organizational, administrative and supply activities. During the fourteen months preceding the incursion, some 3,630 B-52 bombing sorties had been secretly directed at the NVA and VC elements. The actual incursion (April 29–July 22) was an ARVN operation bolstered by U.S. troops and air support; however, results were disappointing in both the military and political sense. For the political dimensions, see, in Chapter 2, "Cambodia (Kampuchea)."

4254. O'Ballance, Edgar. "Incursion Into Cambodia—1970." In his *The Wars in Vietnam, 1954–1973.* New York: Hippocrene, 1975, 149–158. [summarizes the military operations]

Laotian Invasion, 1971

A brief (February 8–March 25), unsuccessful raid by ARVN troops, supported by U.S. airpower, occurred in the Laotian panhandle with the objective of cutting the Ho Chi Minh trail. ARVN losses were heavy: 1,445 killed, 4,016 wounded, 204 missing and 104 helicopters lost. It should have told U.S. officials something about the effectiveness of the Vietnamization program.

4255. "Balance Sheet on Laos: Victory or Defeat?" *U.S. News and World Report* 70 (Apr. 5, 1971): 15–17.

4256. "Invasion of Laos: Limited Criticism from Congress." *CQ Weekly Report* 29 (Feb. 12, 1971): 363.

4257. "Laos: The Bloody Battle To Get Out." *Time* 97 (Mar. 29, 1971): 21–22.

4258. "Laos Invasion: The U.S. Gamble." *U.S. News and World Report* 70 (Feb. 22, 1971): 15–18.

4259. "The Last Big Push: Or Wider War?" *Newsweek* 77 (Feb. 15, 1971): 20–24.

4260. O'Ballance, Edgar. "The Invasion of Laos, 1971." In his *The Wars in Vietnam, 1954–1973.* New York: Hippocrene, 1975, 159–164.

Easter Offensive, 1972

As U.S. and Allied forces withdrew from South Vietnam, the NVA and VC launched (March 30) an extensive ground attack that included a large portion of Hanoi's armored forces. U.S. responded with massive air strikes and, together with ARVN forces, repelled the invasion.

April 5– June 12:	Siege of An Loc
April 6:	U.S. bombing of North resumed
April 28:	Dong Ha captured by VC
May 1:	Quang Tri captured by NVA
May 9:	U.S. mines North Vietnamese harbors

4261. Besch, Edwin W. "North Vietnamese Offensive: Turning Point in 1972." *National Defense* 60 (Mar.–Apr. 1976): 371–373.

4262. Calvert, Michael. "Could Saigon Win With a Final Push?" *Vietnam: Yesterday & Today* 6 (May 1972): 1–4.

4263. Candlin, A.H.S. "The Spring Offensive in Vietnam." *Army Quarterly & Defence Journal* [Great Britain] 102:4 (1972): 411–418.

4264. Despuech, Jacques. *L'offensive du vendredi saint, printemps 1972; les mois les plus longs de la deuxième guerre d'Indochine.* Paris: Fayard, 1973.

4265. Elliott, D.W.P. *NLF–DRV Strategy and the 1972 Spring Offensive* Interim Rpt. no. 4. Ithaca: Cornell University, International Relations of East Asia Project, 1974.

4266. Fitzgerald, Frances. "The Offensive: I: The View From Vietnam." *New York Review of Books* (May 18, 1972): 6–14.

4267. Frisbee, John L. "Airdrop at An Loc." *Air Force Magazine* 55 (Nov. 1972): 40–42.

4268.   Hayden, Tom. "The Prospects of the North Vietnam Offensive." *Ramparts* 11 (Aug. 1972): 21–25, 51–56.

4269.   Howard, John D. "They Were Good Ole' Boys! An Infantryman Remembers An Loc and the Air Force." *Air University Review* 26 (Jan.–Feb. 1975): 26–39.

4270.   Jenkins, Brian. *Giap and the Seventh Son.* P–4851. Santa Monica, CA: Rand Corp., Sept. 1972. [strategy of 1972 offensive]

4271.   "Major North Viet Offensive Seen." *Aviation Week & Space Technology* 96 (Jan. 10, 1972): 14–15.

4272.   Miller, E.H., and W.D. Toule, Jr. "Amphibious Forces: The Turning Point." *U.S. Naval Institute Proceedings* 100 (Nov. 1974): 26–32. [use of in Spring 1972 counteroffensive]

4273.   Nixon, Richard M. "A Report on the Military Situation in Vietnam and the Role of the United States." *U.S. Department of State Bulletin* 66 (May 15, 1972): 683–686.

4274.   Prados, John. "Year of the Rat: Vietnam, 1972." *Strategy & Tactics* (Nov. 1972): 5–18.

4275.   Rothwell, Richard B. "Leadership and Tactical Reflections on the Battle for Quang Tri." *Marine Corps Gazette* 63 (Sept. 1979): 34–42. [fifty-day battle, from July 27 to September 16]

4276.   Saar, John. "Report From the Inferno." *Life* 73 (Apr. 26, 1972): 30–36; (May 12, 1972): 36–37.

4277.   Serong, F.P. *The 1972 Easter Offensive.* Southeast Asian Perspectives, no. 10. New York: American Friends of Vietnam, 1974.

4278.   "Tactical Air Action Blunts Armored Drive." *Aviation Week & Space Technology* 96 (May 15, 1972): 17–18.

4279.   Turley, G.H., and M.R. Wells. "Easter Invasion, 1972." *Marine Corps Gazette* 57 (Mar. 1973): 18–29.

4280.   Ulsamer, Edgar. "Airpower Halts an Invasion: A From-the-Scene Report." *Air Force Magazine* 55 (Sept. 1972): 60–73.

4281.   U.S. Senate. Committee on Foreign Relations. Staff Report; *Vietnam: May 1972,* by J.G. Lowenstein and R.M. Moose. 92d Cong., 2d sess., June 29, 1972.

4282.   Wallace, James N. "Why the Burst of Optimism on Ground War in Vietnam." *U.S. News and World Report* 72 (June 21, 1972): 33–35.

4283.   Ward, Ian, and Brian Crozier. "North Vietnam's Blitzkrieg: An Interim Assessment." *Conflict Studies* 4 (Oct. 1972): 1–18.

BOMBING RESUMES

U.S. bombing of North Vietnam resumed April 6, 1972 as Operation LINE BACKER I; Hanoi and Haiphong were still exempt as targets.

4284.   "Bombing Toll: How North Vietnam Is Hurting." *U.S. News and World Report* 73 (Sept. 4, 1972): 33–34.

4285.   Brown, David A. "U.S. Presses North Viet Air War." *Aviation Week & Space Technology* 97 (July 3, 1972): 12–16.

4286.   Brownlow, Cecil. "Burgeoning U.S. Use of Air Power Aimed at Forestalling Ground War With Chinese." *Aviation Week & Space Technology* 82 (Apr. 26, 1972): 26–31.

4287.   Laird, Melvin. "Secy [of Defense] Laird Explains Air War Program in Vietnam." *Commander's Digest* 12 (Sept. 7, 1972): 3–5.

4288.   Pierre, Andrew J. "Controlled Escalation in Vietnam." *Air Force Magazine* 55 (Feb. 1972): 50–53.

4289.   "Rogers, Laird Defend Resumption of Bombing." *CQ Weekly Report* 30 (Apr. 22, 1972): 896–898.

4290.   Rogers, William P. "Both Sides of Debate Over Vietnam Bombing." *U.S. News and World Report* 72 (May 1, 1972): 57–62.

4291.   "U.S. Presses Viet Air Interdiction." *Aviation Week & Space Technology* 96 (May 15, 1972): 14–16.

4292.   Wall, George. "Our Bombs Fall on People." *Washington Monthly* 4 (May 1972): 8–10.

MINING HARBORS

On May 9, 1972, Nixon ordered the mining of North Vietnamese harbors, including Haiphong, a program long urged by air and naval commanders.

4293.   "CIA, State and Defense Had Doubts About Attacking Haiphong." *New York Review of Books* (June 1, 1972): 12–13.

4294.   Kissinger, Henry A. "Presidential Assistant Kissinger Discusses Considerations Leading to President's New Decisions on Vietnam." *U.S. Department of State Bulletin* 66 (May 29, 1972): 752–760.

4295.   Laird, Melvin R. "Secretary of Defense Laird's

News Conference of May 10." *U.S. Department of State Bulletin* 66 (May 29, 1972): 761–771.

4296. McCauley, Brian. "Operation End Sweep." *U.S. Naval Institute Proceedings* 100 (Mar. 1974): 18–25. [clearing mines after Armistice from Haiphong harbor by Task Force 58]

4297. "Nixon at the Brink Over Vietnam." *Time* 99 (May 22, 1972): 11–15.

4298. Nixon, Richard M. "Denying Hanoi the Means to Continue Aggression." *U.S. Department of State Bulletin* 66 (May 29, 1972): 747–750.

4299. "North Vietnam: Nixon Action Arouses Bitter Dispute." *CQ Weekly Report* 30 (May 13, 1972): 1051–1053.

4300. Prina, L. Edgar. "Smart Bombs and Menacing Mines: Sea–Air Power Takes Spotlight as Gradualism Ends." *Sea Power* 15 (June 1972): 9–12.

4301. Robinson, Clarence A., Jr. "Viet Mine Clearing Keyed to Helicopters." *Aviation Week & Space Technology* 98 (Feb. 12, 1973): 14–17.

4302. "Soviet Statement Assails Blockade." *Current Digest of the Soviet Press* 24 (May 24, 1972): 5.

4303. Stone, I.F. "Nixon's War Gamble and Why It Won't Work." *New York Review of Books* (June 1, 1972): 11.

4304. Swayze, Frank B. "Traditional Principles of Blockade in Modern Practices: United States Mining of Internal and Territorial Waters of North Vietnam." *JAG Journal* 29 (Spring 1977): 143–173.

4305. "U.S. Imperialism's New War Escalation Denounced." *Peking Review* 15 (May 19, 1972): 13–20.

4306. Whiting, Allen S. "Nixon's Gamble: War With China?" *New Republic* 166 (May 20, 1972): 12–13.

BOMBING OF DIKES

In late June 1972 Hanoi charged the U.S. with bombing the Red River dikes—a charge that was initially leveled in 1968; see Duffett (5264), 224–236. Jane Fonda brought back films allegedly depicting such damage, and the Secretary General of United Nations Kurt Waldheim echoed the charges; however, the U.S. officially insisted that damage to dikes was caused by errant bombs, attacks on AA, SAM missile sites and fuel pipelines located on dikes, and "fall back" of errant SAM missiles.

4307. *American Aircraft Systematically Attack Dams and Dikes in the D.R.V.N.* Hanoi: Foreign Languages Publishing House, 1968.

4308. "Behind the Furor Over Bombs on Red River Dikes." *U.S. News and World Report* 73 (Aug. 14, 1972): 18–20.

4309. "English View of Nixon Bombing—Brutal." *Congressional Record* 118 (Aug. 7, 1972): 27192–27193. [*Manchester Guardian* article]

4310. Fonda, Jane. "We Have Never Built So Many Roads and Bridges." *Congressional Record* 118 (Sept. 13, 1972): 30588.

4311. Goldwater, Senator Barry. "Bombing of Red River Dikes in North Vietnam." *Congressional Record* 118 (Aug. 9, 1972): 27443. [denies charges]

4312. Hearst, William Randolph, Jr. "A Memo on Dikes." *Congressional Record* 118 (Aug. 9, 1972): 27577–27578. Hearst calls the charge communist propaganda.

4313. "International Law as it Relates to the Bombing of the Dikes and the Mining of the Ports of North Vietnam." *Congressional Record* 118 (Oct. 13, 1972): 36150–36152. [Library of Congress report]

4314. Lacoste, Yves. "Bombing the Dikes: A Geographer's On-the-Site Analysis." *Nation* 215 (Oct. 9, 1972): 298–301.

4315. Landau, David. "The Diplomacy of Terror: Behind the Decision to Bomb the Dikes." *Ramparts* 11 (Oct. 1972): 21–25, 52–56.

4316. Porter, D. Gareth. "Nixon's Next Option: Bombing the Dikes." *New Republic* 166 (Jan. 3, 1972): 19–20.

4317. Robinson, Norborne T.M., III. "Carrying the War to North Vietnam: Time to Strike the Red River Dike System." *Washington Report* [WR 68–7] (Feb. 19, 1968): Entire issue.

4318. Treaster, Joseph B. "Dike Bombing Denied by U.S. Carrier Pilots." *Congressional Record* 118 (Sept. 5, 1972): 29330–29331. [*New York Times* article of Aug. 12]

4319. U.S. Department of State. "No Major Dike Has Been Breached." *Congressional Record* 118 (Aug. 17, 1972): 29002. [July 28 statement]

4320. Yost, Charles W. "Bombing of Dikes, Dams? Argument Misses Heart of the Matter." *Congressional Record* 118 (Aug. 7, 1972): 27186–27187. [*Washington Post* article of Aug. 2]

Aerial Blitz, 1972

President Nixon authorized air strikes at previously exempt North Vietnamese targets, including Hanoi and Haiphong, in Operation LINE BACKER II (December 19–29, 1972). Some 1,000 fighter-bomber and 729 B-52 sorties were launched, with the loss of 15 B-52s, in an effort to force Hanoi to sign an armistice.

4321.   "Diplomacy by Terror: What the Bombing Did." *Newsweek* 81 (Jan. 8, 1973): 10–12.

4322.   Eade, George J. "USAF Prepares for Future Contingencies: The Lesson of Vietnam." *Air Force Magazine* 56 (June 1973): 34–40. [Operation LINE BACKER]

4323.   Francis, P.G. "The New Air Blitzkrieg." *Royal Air Forces Quarterly* 13 (Spring 1973): 31–35.

4324.   Hertz, Martin F., and Leslie Rider. *The Prestige Press and the Christmas Bombing, 1972: Images and Reality in Vietnam.* Washington, DC: Ethics and Public Policy Center, 1980.

4325.   Hopkins, Charles K. "Linebacker II: A Firsthand View." *Aerospace Historian* 23 (Sept. 1976): 128–135.

4326.   Kasler, James H. "Hanoi POL Strike." *Air University Review* 26 (Nov.–Dec. 1974): 19–28.

4327.   Moorer, Thomas H. "North Viet Bombing Held Critical." *Aviation Week & Space Technology* 98 (Mar. 5, 1973): 12–13.

4328.   Powers, Robert C. "Linebacker Strike." *U.S. Naval Institute Proceedings* 100 (Aug. 1974): 46–51.

4329.   Reynolds, Jon A. "Linebacker II: The POW Perspective." *Air Force Magazine* 62 (Sept. 1979): 93–94.

4330.   Starner, Frances L. "Negotiating With B-52s." *Far Eastern Economic Review* 78 (Dec. 30, 1972): 10–12.

4331.   Stone, I.F. "Nixon's Blitzkrieg." *New York Review of Books* (Jan. 25, 1973): 13–16.

4332.   Strickland, Donald A. *The March Upcountry: Deciding to Bomb Hanoi.* Wilmette, IL: Medina University Press International, 1973.

4333.   "The Vietnam Bombing: Senate Opposition Grows." *CQ Weekly Reports* 30 (Dec. 23, 1972): 3171–3172.

4334.   Wolff, Robert E. "Linebacker II: A Pilot's Perspective." *Air Force Magazine* 62 (Sept. 1979): 86–91.

Fall of South Vietnam, 1975

Saigon fell as a result of a full-scale frontal assault by North Vietnamese forces; this campaign (March 1–April 30) exposed the failures of Vietnamization at all levels—command, training and discipline. Snepp's book (4339) examines the collapse from the American side, while General Van Tien Dung's candid account (4342) relates North Vietnamese strategy.

Books and Documents

4335.   Bouscaren, Anthony T., ed. *All Quiet on the Eastern Front: The Death of South Vietnam.* Old Greenwich, CT: Devin-Adair, 1977.

4336.   Burchett, Wilfred G. *Grasshoppers and Elephants: Why Viet Nam Fell; The Viet Cong Account of the Last 55 Days of the War.* New York: Urizen, 1977.

4337.   Dawson, Alan. *55 Days: The Fall of South Vietnam.* Englewood Cliffs, NJ: Prentice-Hall, 1977.

4338.   Pilger, John. *The Last Day.* New York: Vintage, 1976.

4339.   Snepp, Frank. *Decent Interval: An Insider's Account of Saigon's Indecent End.* New York: Random House, 1978.

4340.   Terzani, Tiziano. *Giai Phong! The Fall and Liberation of Saigon.* Translated by John Shepley. New York: St. Martin's Press, 1976.

4341.   U.S. Senate. Committee on Armed Forces. Report; *Vietnam Aid: The Painful Options,* by Senator Sam Nunn. 94th Cong., 1st sess., Feb. 12, 1975. Was Saigon's fall hastened by U.S. failure to provide promised support?

4342.   Van Tien Dung. *Our Great Spring Victory: An Account of the Liberation of South Vietnam.* New York: Monthly Review Press, 1977. [by a North Vietnamese commander]

4343.   Vanuxem, Paul Fiedele F. *La Mort du Viet Nam: Les Faits, les causes externes et internes, les conséquences sur le Vietnam, la France et le monde.* Paris: Éditions de la Nouvelle Aurore, 1975.

4344.   *The Vietnamese People's Great Victory: Warm Congratulations to the South Vietnamese People on the Liberation of Saigon and all South Viet Nam.* Peking: Foreign Languages Press, 1975.

4345.   Vo Nguyen Giap. *Unforgettable Days.* Hanoi: Foreign Languages Publishing House, 1975.

4346. _____. *How We Won the War*. Philadelphia: RECON, 1976.

Essays

4347. Carey, Richard E., and D.A. Quinlan. "FREQUENT WIND: Organization and Assembly." *Marine Corps Gazette* 60 (Feb. 1976): 16–24.

4348. _____. "FREQUENT WIND: Planning." *Marine Corps Gazette* 60 (Mar. 1976): 35–45.

4349. _____. "FREQUENT WIND: Execution." *Marine Corps Gazette* 60 (Apr. 1976): 35–45. [the evacuation of South Vietnam]

4350. Chen, King C. "Hanoi's Three Decisions and the Escalation of the Vietnam War." *Political Science Quarterly* 90 (Summer 1975): 239–259.

4351. DeWeerd, Harvey A. "The Fall of Vietnam: An Inside View." *Army* 29 (July 1979): 14–20.

4352. Duncanson, Dennis J. "The Conquest of Indochina." *World Today* [London] 31 (June 1975): 226–231.

4353. Hayden, Tom. "Kissinger's Indochina Obsession: Will He Bomb Again." *Rolling Stone* 181 (Feb. 27, 1975): 26–30.

4354. Karnow, Stanley. "The Hasty Retreat From Saigon: Getting Out." *New Republic* 172 (May 10, 1975): 14–17.

4355. Peiris, D. "When Guns Did the Talking." *Far Eastern Economic Review* 88 (May 9, 1975): 11–13.

Mayaguez Incident, 1975

Cambodian forces seized the unarmed S.S. Mayaguez on May 12 claiming it was in their waters; the U.S. responded with air strikes and landing parties (forty-one killed and fifty wounded) in an attempt to recover the ship and crew. They were subsequently released on May 15. See also, Lavalle, Fourteen Hours at Koh Tang (3461).

4356. Behuniak, Thomas E. "The Seizure and Recovery of the S. S. Mayaquez: A Legal Analysis of United States Claims." *Military Law Review* 82 (Fall 1978), I: 3–40; 83 (Winter 1979), II: 59–130.

4357. Benjamin, M.R. "Victory at Sea." *Newsweek* 85 (May 26, 1975): 18–21.

4358. Bennett, Charles F. "The Mayaguez Re-examined: Misperception in an Information Shortage." *Fletcher Forum* 1 (Fall 1976): 15–33.

4359. Carlile, Donald E. "The Mayaguez Incident: Crisis Management." *Military Review* 56 (Oct. 1976): 3–14.

4360. Goldman, P. "Ford's Rescue Operation." *Newsweek* 85 (May 26, 1975): 16–18.

4361. Hamm, Michael J. "The Pueblo and Mayaguez Incidents: A Study of Flexible Response and Decision-Making." *Asian Survey* 17 (June 1977): 545–555.

4362. Head, Richard G., Frisco W. Short, and Robert E. McFarlane. *Crisis Resolution: Presidential Decision Making in the Mayaquez and Korean Confrontation.* Boulder, CO: Westview, 1978.

4363. Johnson, J.M., Jr., et al. "Individual Heroism Overcame Awkward Command Relationships, Confusion and Bad Information Off the Cambodian Coast." *Marine Corps Gazette* 61 (Oct. 1977): 24–34.

4364. "Machismo Diplomacy." *Nation* 220 (May 31, 1975): 642–643.

4365. "The Mayaguez: What Went Right, Wrong." *U.S. News and World Report* 78 (June 2, 1975): 78–79.

4366. "Mayaguez Incident." *Commonweal* 102 (June 6, 1975): 163–164.

4367. "Mayaguez Mistake." *Christian Century* 92 (June 4, 1975): 564–565.

4368. Morris, Roger. "What to Make of the Mayaguez." *New Republic* 173 (June 14, 1975): 9–12.

4369. Osborne, John. "Afterthoughts." *New Republic* 173 (June 28, 1975): 6–7.

4370. Paust, Jordan J. "The Seizure and Recovery of the Mayaguez." *Yale Law Journal* 85 (May 1976): 774–807.

4371. "Question and Answer Session Held by Secretary Kissinger." *U.S. Department of State Bulletin* 72 (June 2, 1975): 723–736.

4372. Rowan, Roy. *The Four Days of Mayaquez*. New York: Norton, 1975.

4373. "Story of the Rescue of Merchant Vessel Mayaguez." *U.S. News and World Report* 78 (May 26, 1975): 20–21.

4374. "A Strong But Risky Show of Force." *Time* 105 (May 26, 1975): 9–18.

4375. U.S. House. Committee on International Relations. Hearings; *Seizure of the Mayaguez*. 94th Cong., 1st sess., 1975.

4376. "U.S. Recovers Merchant Ship Seized by Cambodian Navy." *U.S. Department of State Bulletin* 72 (June 2, 1975): 719–722.

4377. Zutz, Robert. "The Recapture of the S. S. *Mayaguez*: Failure of the Consultative Clause of the War Powers Resolution." *New York University Journal of International Law* 8:3 (1976): 457–478.

Ground and Water Operations

Grouped below are the more specialized accounts of military operations involving Army, Navy and Marine forces. Helicopters are treated here because they were so frequently employed with "ground" operations. For more general volumes dealing with many of these same themes, see Marshall's (4141–4145) and Pearson's (3484) accounts.

4378. Babcock, R.S. "Stay Alert to Stay Alive." *Army Digest* 23 (Feb. 1968): 20–22.

4379. "Demilitarizing the Zone: Operation HICKORY." *Time* 89 (May 26, 1967): 24–25.

4380. Dolan, Bill. "The Battlefield, the Enemy, and You." *Army Digest* 23 (Apr. 1968): 50–56. The *Digest* printed several similar essays during 1968.

4381. Eliot, George F. "Vietnam: How the Ground War is Fought." *American Legion Magazine* 82 (May 1967): 14–18.

4382. Garland, Albert N., ed. *Combat Notes From Vietnam*. Fort Benning, GA: Infantry Magazine, 1968.

4383. Harrigan, Anthony. "Ground Warfare in Vietnam." *Military Review* 47 (Apr. 1967): 60–67.

4384. Harris, M.M. "First Team Moves South." *Army* 19 (May 1969): 43–48.

4385. Hughles, D.R. "Clean Sweep on Election Day." *Army* 18 (May 1968): 40–46.

4386. Humphrey, V.W. "The Dragoon Concept." *Military Review* 52 (Jan. 1972): 17–25.

4387. Illes, Steve J. "Combat in Caves." *Marine Corps Gazette* 50 (July 1966): 38–40.

4388. Marshall, S.L.A. "Men Facing Death: The Destruction of an American Platoon." *Harper's* 233 (Sept. 1966): 47–57.

4389. Paone, Joseph F. "Assault of Enemy Positions." *Infantry* 60 (Sept.–Oct. 1970): 9–11.

4390. Ponder, Arno L. "Trang Bang." *Army* 26 (Jan. 1976): 32–41.

4391. Pscherer, S.W. "Learning from Charlie." *Army* 18 (July 1968): 53–57.

4392. Raymond, J. "When G.I. Joe Meets Ol' Charlie." *New York Times Magazine* (July 25, 1965): 4–5.

4393. Shaver, Carl A. "Reflections of a Company Commander." *Marine Corps Gazette* 53 (Nov. 1969): 29–34. [principles of war]

4394. Smith, Richard W., and Norman L. Tiller. "Hole-Hunting for Dragon's Teeth." *Army* 19 (Aug. 1969): 50–53. [tunnels and caves]

4395. Stapleton, Homer L. "Trung Luong: Set Piece in Vietnam." *Military Review* 47 (May 1967): 36–44.

4396. Winecoff, David F. "Body Armor or Mobility." *Marine Corps Gazette* 55 (June 1941): 28–31. [Operation DEWEY CANYON, pluses and minuses of body armor]

AMBUSH

4397. Findlay, Raymond F. "Behind the Hedgerow." *Marine Corps Gazette* 53 (Apr. 1969): 22–26. [ambush tactics]

4398. Gunderman, G.L. "Ambush." *Armor* 76 (May–June 1967): 15–19.

4399. Langguth, Jack. "Ambush!" *New York Times Magazine* (June 27, 1965): 4ff.

4400. Mack, Richard E. "Ambuscade." *Marine Corps Gazette* 51 (Apr. 1967): 27–32.

4401. Maddox, Herbert R. "Surprise Party for Charlie." *Infantry* 60 (July–Aug. 1970): 12–15.

4402. McEnery, John W. "Ambush: We Can Do Better." *Infantry* 60 (Nov.–Dec. 1970): 42–45.

4403. Morris, J. "The Ambush." *Esquire* 64 (Aug. 1965): 76ff. Morris gives a cool account of how to find and kill VC.

4404. Orell, Seth R. "Caught in the Killing Zone." *Infantry* 60 (July–Aug. 1970): 15–17.

4405. Raine, David. "Vietnam: A Night Ambush." *Contemporary Review* 208 (May 1966): 237–239.

4406. Utter, Leon N. "Solid Contact for 2/7." *Marine Corps Gazette* 50 (Apr. 1966): 25–30. [Operation HARVEST MOON at Ky Phu]

ARMOR

See Starry (3489) for a general account.

4407. Ashworth, S.T., III. "Armor Can Operate in the Delta." *Armor* 76 (Mar.–Apr. 1967): 4–10.

4408. Cobb, William W., et al. "Mounted Combat Operations in Vietnam." *Armor* 78 (July–Aug. 1969): 24–40.

4409. Cole, Larry K. "Armor in Urban Combat." *Armor* 79 (May–June 1970): 27–33.

4410. Cossey, Gerald R. "Tank vs Tank." *Armor* 79 (Sept.–Oct. 1970): 16–19.

4411. MacLaren, Bruce M. "Tank Tactics for Unit Leaders." *Marine Corps Gazette* 53 (July 1969): 41–44. [employment of tanks in Vietnam]

4412. "Mounted Combat in Vietnam." *Armor* 77 (July–Aug. 1968): 9–17, 57–62.

4413. Smock, James E. "0–52–0." *Armor* 83 (Sept.–Oct. 1974): 32–36. [tank combat in Vietnam]

4414. Starry, Donn A. "Reflections [About Armor's Role in the Vietnam Conflict]." *Armor* 86 (Jan.–Feb. 1977): 14–17.

ARTILLERY

See also, Ott (3483), "Strategy and Tactics" and "Fire Support Base" in Chapter 6.

4415. Amos, H.O. "Artillery Support of Vietnamese." *Military Review* 46 (Aug. 1966): 30–41.

4416. Eliot, George F. "Fire Support in Vietnam." *Ordnance* 51 (Mar.–Apr. 1967): 470–473.

4417. Ferguson, Gilbert W. "Guns at Da Nang." *Marine Corps Gazette* 50 (Feb. 1966): 27–31. [artillery problem in the Spring of 1965]

4418. "Lessons Learned in Vietnam." *Artillery Trends* 37 (Jan. 1967): 70–80.

4419. Marshall, S.L.A. "On Heavy Artillery: American Experience in Four Wars." *Parameters* 8 (June 1978): 2–20.

4420. Ott, David E. "The Field Artillery Buildup: 1967 Combat Operations." *Field Artillery Journal* 65 (Nov.–Dec. 1975): 29–34.

KIT CARSON SCOUTS

These were former VC/NVA who changed sides under the Chieu Hoi program (see "Intelligence and Reconnaissance" in Chapter 6) and served with U.S. forces as scouts, etc.

4421. Clarkson, Edward J. "An Unknown Warrior." *Marine Corps Gazette* 54 (Aug. 1970): 38–54.

4422. Cowan, William V. "Kit Carson Scouts." *Marine Corps Gazette* 53 (Oct. 1969): 30–32.

4423. Furse, D. "Kit Carson Strikes Back." *Army Digest* 23 (Sept. 1968): 46–48.

MINES AND BOOBY TRAPS

4424. Brendt, W. "Danger: Booby Traps." *Infantry* 57 (May–June 1967): 42–43.

4425. Greene, Wallace M. "Countermeasures Against Mines and Boobytraps." *Marine Corps Gazette* 53 (Dec. 1969): 31–37.

4426. Mack, Richard E. "minbotrap." *Marine Corps Gazette* 51 (July 1967): 39–42. [unorthodox mines and booby traps]

4427. Mason, James D. "VC Trail." *Marine Corps Gazette* 53 (Apr. 1969): 38–41. [booby traps]

4428. Quinn, Woodrow L. "Dogs in Counter-mine Warfare." *Infantry* 61 (July–Aug. 1971): 16–18.

4429. U.S. Army. *Viet Cong Boobytraps, Mines and Mine Warfare Techniques.* Training Circular no. 5–31. Washington, DC: GPO, 1967.

Helicopters and Assault Gunships

Helicopters were the work-horses of the combat areas. For a discussion of carrying troops directly into combat by helicopters, see "Strategy and Tactics" and "Air Mobility" in Chapter 6.

4430. *Analysis of Combat Damage on UH-1 Helicopters in Vietnam, 1962–1964.* Memo Rpt no. 1647.

Aberdeen Proving Ground, MD: Ballistics Research Labs, 1965.

4431. Brownlow, Cecil. "Helicopter Tactics Shaped by Experience." *Aviation Week & Space Technology* 86 (May 31, 1965): 67–76.

4432. Dalby, Marion C. "Combat Hotline." *Marine Corps Gazette* 53 (Apr. 1969): 27–30. [helicopters used in 1968]

4433. Famiglietti, G. "The Chopper War in Vietnam." *Aerospace International* 3 (July–Aug. 1967): 20–28.

4434. Haid, D.J. "How to Shoot a Duck [armed helicopters]. *Military Review* 45 (Sept. 1965): 3–12.

4435. Hammer, A. "Better Guns for Choppers." *Ordnance* 56 (Sept.–Oct. 1971): 138–142.

4436. Hampe, D.E. "Tactics and the Helicopter." *Military Review* 46 (Mar. 1966): 60–63.

4437. Jackson, Senator Henry. "A Key to Victory in Vietnam." *Army* 13 (Mar. 1963): 22ff. [helicopters]

4438. McConnell, Lewis. "Copters Carry the Cargo of Men, Material, Munitions." *Army Digest* 26 (Feb. 1971): 26–30.

4439. Mertel, Kenneth D. "Combat Night Air Assault." *U.S. Army Aviation Digest* 15 (June 1969): 2–6.

4440. Meyerson, Harvey. "Choppers and the New Kind of War." *Look* 32 (Apr. 30, 1968): 92–100.

4441. Murphy, Charles J.V. "How the Battle Got Turned Around." *Fortune* 75 (Apr. 1967): 140–145. The battle of Plei Me-Ia Drang Valley established the value of helicopters.

4442. Murphy, Dennis J. "Let's Practice What We Preach About Helicopter Operations." *Marine Corps Gazette* 53 (Aug. 1969): 18024.

4443. Paquette, Dean R. "The Helicopter is the Key." *Data* 14 (Aug. 1969): 22–23ff.

4444. Rider, J.W. "Helicopters in Vietnam." *Marine Corps Gazette* 51 (Oct. 1967): 30–32. [misuse of helicopters]

4445. Sprinkle, James D. "The Hueycobra in Vietnam." *American Aviation Historical Society Journal* 20 (Fall 1965): 162–170.

4446. Terry, Frederick G. "The Armed Helicopter." *Infantry* 57 (July–Aug. 1967): 16–19.

4447. "Treetop Copter Pad Tested in Vietnam." *Army* 17 (Apr. 1967): 64–65.

4448. Trueman, H.P. "The Helicopter and Land Warfare; Applying the Vietnam Experience." *Brassey's Annual 1971* (1971): 190–204.

4449. U.S. Army. Air Mobility Research and Development Laboratory. *Operational Use of UH-IH Helicopters in Southeast Asia.* USAAMRDL Tech Rpt 73–15. Fort Eustis, VA, May 1973.

4450. Watson, William R., and John R. Dunham, Jr. "Resume of U.S. Army Helicopter Operations in Vietnam." *American Helicopter Society Journal* 13 (July 1968): 1–19.

4451. Weller, Jac. "Helicopters: The American Experience." *Army Quarterly* 103 (July 1973): 420–428.

4452. Westmoreland, William C. "A New Concept of Warfare." *Aerospace International* 3 (July–Aug. 1967): 8.

4453. Winchester, James H. "Helicopters in South Vietnam." *NATO's Fifteen Nations* 11 (Aug.–Sept. 1966): 54–58.

4454. Witze, Claude. "The U.S. Army Flies to Fight and Win." *Aerospace International* 3 (July–Aug. 1967): 13–17.

GUNSHIPS

4455. Lehnert, Richard A. "The Ghost Rider in the Sky." *Air Force Magazine* 56 (Sept. 1973): 118–122. [AC–130 gunship]

4456. Lessels, R.J., Jr. "Shadow: AC–119 Gunships In Southeast Asia." *Air Force Magazine* 54 (Nov. 1971): 38–40.

4457. Moss, Donald W. "Gunship Tactics." *Infantry* 59 (Jan.–Feb. 1969): 26–29.

4458. Record, Jeffrey. "Maximizing Cobra Utilization." *Washington Monthly* 3 (Apr. 1971): 8–12. [assault helicopter gunship]

4459. Weiss, George. "AC–130 Gunships Destroy Trucks and Cargo." *Armed Forces Journal* 109 (Sept. 1971): 18–19.

4460. Wolverton, James R. "Gunships and Guerrilla Warfare." *Tactical Air Warfare Center Quarterly Report* 2 (Sept. 1970): 22–27.

Army Operations

Included here are items dealing with battles, campaigns and army activities which do not fit under other more specialized themes.

Books

4461. *Assistant Challenge: The U.S. Infantryman in Vietnam, 1967–1970.* Edited by staff of *Fnfantry Magazine*, U.S. Army Infantry School, Fort Benning, CA. Birmingham, AL: Birmingham Publishing, 1971.

4462. Garland, Albert N., ed. *Infantry in Vietnam.* Fort Benning, GA: Infantry Magazine, 1967.

4463. Hymoff, Edward. *The First Air Cavalry Division: Vietnam.* New York: Lads, 1967.

4464. Mertel, Kenneth D. *Year of the Horse: Vietnam—1st Air Cavalry in the Highlands.* New York: Exposition Press, 1968.

Essays

4465. "Aviation. New Dimension for the U.S. Army in Vietnam." *Aerospace International* 3 (July–Aug. 1967): 7–8.

4466. Binder, L.J. "The Hundred Mile an Hour War." *Army* 19 (Mar. 1969): 16–32.

4467. Chamberlain, Edwin W., Jr. "The Assault at Ap Bac." *Army* 18 (Sept. 1968): 50–57.

4468. Coleman, J.D. "Saturation Patrolling." *Army* 17 (Dec. 1967): 54–57.

4469. Cushman, John H. "How We Did It in Thua Thien." *Army* 20 (May 1970): 48–54.

4470. Denno, B.F. "Sure Wins 1 and 2." *Army* 13 (June 1963): 43–47.

4471. Dewey, A.E. "Thrust into the Vitals of Zone D." *Army* 14 (Feb. 1964): 46–49.

4472. Donlon, Roger, and Warren Rogers. "The Battle for Nam Dong." *Saturday Evening Post* 238 (Oct. 23, 1965): 38–42, 46–53.

4473. Engler, J.E. "U.S. Army Vietnam in 1966." *Army* 16 (Oct. 1966): 105–110.

4474. Flint, Roy K. "Campaigning with the Infantry in Vietnam." *Air Force Magazine* 53 (Aug. 1970): 47–51.

4475. Garretson, R.B., Jr. "The Battle of Binh An." *Armor* 78 (July–Aug. 1969): 25–28.

4476. Gibson, James M. "The Separate Brigade." *Military Review* 50 (May 1970): 82–86.

4477. Grogan, T.L. "The Battle of An Bao II." *Armor* 78 (July–Aug. 1969): 29–31.

4478. Hackworth, David H. "Guerrilla Battalion, U.S. Style," *Infantry* 61 (Jan.–Feb. 1971): 22–28.

4479. Hartline, Franklin Y. "Route Security in the Central Highlands." *Armor* 78 (Nov.–Dec. 1969): 21–24.

4480. Harvey, T.H., Jr. "Air Cavalry in Battle: A New Concept in Action." *Armor* 77 (May–June 1968): 5–10.

4481. Heiberg, Elvin R., III. "Closing the Plei Trap Road." *Military Review* 49 (July 1969): 83–88.

4482. Hofmann, R.A. "The Affray at Slope 30." *Armor* 77 (Jan.–Feb. 1968): 13–18.

4483. Hogue, J.H. "Eagles' Eyes for the Infantry." *Army* 19 (June 1969): 61–65.

4484. Keehn, Richard C. "Night Hunter Operations." *U.S. Army Aviation Digest* 15 (May 1969): 16–20.

4485. Kinnard, H.W.O. "A Victory in the La Drang: The Triumph of a Concept." *Army* 17 (Sept. 1967): 71–91.

4486. Klein, William E. "Mechanized Infantry in Vietnam." *Infantry* 61 (Mar.–Apr. 1971): 18–21.

4487. Marshall, S.L.A. "Infantry Operations in Vietnam." *Infantry* 60 (Mar.–Apr. 1970): 6–9.

4488. Mataxis, Theodore C. "War in the Highlands." *Army* 15 (May 1965): 49–55.

4489. Meissner, Joseph P. "The Battle of Duc Lap." *Army* 19 (May 1969): 50–56.

4490. Mirsky, Jonathan. "The Tombs of Ben Suc: 'Too Blind-Stupid to See.'" *Nation* 205 (Oct. 23, 1967): 397–400.

4491. Moser, Don, and C. Rentmeester. "Battle Jump: U.S. Paratroopers in a Stepped-up War." *Life* 62 (Mar. 10, 1967): 72–77.

4492. Pepke, Donn R. "Economy of Force in the Central Highlands." *Military Review* 50 (Nov. 1970): 32–43.

4493. Pisor, R.L. "Saigon's Fighting MP's" *Army* 18 (Apr. 1968): 37–41.

4494. Rogers, R. Joe. "Army Aviation in Vietnam." *U.S.*

Naval Institute Proceedings 95 (Mar. 1969): 137–141.

4495. Sack, John M. "An Account of One Company of American Soldiers." *Esquire* 66 (Oct. 1966): 79–86, 140–164.

4496. Schlitz, William P. "The Siege of Ben Het." *Air Force & Space Digest* 52 (Aug. 1969): 48–49.

4497. Sheehan, Neil. "Letters From Hamburger Hill." *Harper's* 238 (Jan. 1969): 22–23. Also see, "Rebuttal of Hamburger Hill." *Time* 93 (June 6, 1969): 22–23.

4498. Shepherd, Jack. "American Militarism: Incident at Van Duong." *Look* 33 (Aug. 12, 1969): 26–31.

4499. Tully, W.B., Jr. "Company B." *Armor* 76 (Sept.–Oct. 1967): 12–19.

4500. Warner, Denis. "Bearing the Brunt at Con Thien." *Reporter* 37 (Oct. 19, 1967): 18–21.

4501. _____. "Fighting the Viet Cong." *Army Digest* 23 (Oct. 1968): 45–58.

DELTA OPERATIONS

See also, "Riverine Operations," below, this chapter, and Internal Medicine in Vietnam *(3469) for skin diseases.*

4502. Abrams, Arnold. "Trouble in the Delta: Return of the Vietcong." *New Leader* 53 (Feb. 2, 1970): 10–12.

4503. Burrows, Larry. "New U.S. Front in a Widening War: The Delta; Steamy, Teeming Heartland of the Vietcong." *Life* 62 (Jan. 13, 1967): 22–31.

4504. Dickerson, Sherwood. "A Taste of What's to Come in the Ugly Delta War." *Reporter* 36 (Feb. 23, 1967): 37–39.

4505. Funderburk, Raymond E. "Warfare in the Delta." *Infantry* 58 (Mar.–Apr. 1968): 41–42.

4506. Hauser, William L. "Fire and Maneuver in the Delta." *Infantry* 60 (Sept.–Oct. 1970): 12–15.

4507. Poe, William H. "Another Task for the LST." *U.S. Naval Institute Proceedings* 95 (Feb. 1969): 130–133.

4508. Smith, Albert C., Jr. "Rung Sat Special Zone, Vietnam's Mekong Delta." *U.S. Naval Institute Proceedings* 94 (Apr. 1968): 116–121.

4509. Taylor, Edmond. "Battle in the Delta." *Reporter* 34 (Jan. 13, 1966): 21–25.

4510. Warner, Denis. "The Small, Hard War in the Delta." *Reporter* 35 (Dec. 15, 1966): 27ff.

SPECIAL FORCES

See also, Kelly (3478) for an official report on Special Forces covering 1961 to 1971.

4511. Duncan, Donald. *The New Legions.* New York: Random House, 1967. [Green Berets]

4512. Prouty, L. Fletcher. "Green Berets and the CIA." *New Republic* 161 (Aug. 23, 1969): 9–10.

4513. Research Analysis Corporation. *U.S. Army Special Forces Operations Under the Civilian Irregular Defense Groups Program in Vietnam, 1961–64.* Tech. Memo RAC–T–477. McLean, VA, 1966.

4514. Sams, Kenneth. "The Fall of A Shau." *Air Force Magazine* 49 (June 1966): 70–74. [U.S. special forces base overrun]

4515. Sochurek, Howard. "American Special Forces in Vietnam." *National Geographic* 127 (Jan. 1965): 38–65.

4516. Sutton, H. "The Ghostly War of the Green Berets." *Saturday Review* 52 (Oct. 18, 1969): 23–28.

4517. Weed, A.C., II. "Army Special Forces and Vietnam." *Military Review* 49 (Aug. 1969): 63–68.

4518. Wren, Christopher S. "The Facts Behind the Green Beret Myth." *Look* 30 (Nov. 1, 1966): 28–36.

Marine Corps Operations

See also, The Marines in Vietnam, 1954–1973 *(3442) for an anthology of combat actions.*

OVERVIEWS

4519. Greene, Wallace M. "The Marines in Vietnam." *Ordnance* 52 (July–Aug. 1967): 38–42.

4520. Hymoff, Edward. *First Marine Division, Vietnam.* New York: Lads, 1967.

4521. Simmons, Edwin H. "Marine Corps Operations in Vietnam, 1965–1966." *Naval Review* (1968): 2–35.

4522. _____. "Marine Corps Operations in Vietnam, 1967." *Naval Review* (1969): 112–141.

4523. _____. "Marine Corps Operations in Vietnam, 1968." *U.S. Naval Institute Proceedings* 96 (May 1970): 290–320.

4524. _____. "Marine Corps Operations in Vietnam, 1969–1972." *U.S. Naval Institute Proceedings* 99 (May 1972): 198–223.

4525. U.S. Marine Corps. *Professional Knowledge Gained From Operational Experience in Vietnam, 1967.* Washington, DC: Department of Navy, 1968. [annual(?)]

4526. West, Francis J., Jr. *Small Unit Actions in Vietnam, Summer 1966.* Washington, DC: GPO, 1967.

SPECIFIC ACTIONS

4527. Babb, Wayne A. "The Bridge: A Study in Defense." *Marine Corps Gazette* 55 (June 1971): 16–23. [VC attack at Liberty Bridge, south of Da Nang, Mar. 19, 1969]

4528. Breslauer, Charles K. "Battle of the Northern Arizona." *Marine Corps Gazette* 61 (Jan. 1977): 47–55. [An Hoa basin, 1969]

4529. Camp, Richard D., Jr. "Cordon at Phuoc Yen." *Marine Corps Gazette* 55 (Jan. 1971): 28–31. [Northern I Corps]

4530. Davis, Crane. "Bridge at Cam Le." *Marine Corps Gazette* 54 (Feb. 1970): 33–38. [August 23, 1968 VC attack]

4531. Davis, Gordon M. "Dewey Canyon: All Weather Classic." *Marine Corps Gazette* 53 (July 1969): 32–40.

4532. Davis, Raymond G., and Sheridan W. Bell III. "Combined Operations with ARVN." *Marine Corps Gazette* 53 (Oct. 1969): 18–29. [Quang Tri province, 1968]

4533. Hammond, James W., Jr. "Combat Journal." *Marine Corps Gazette* 52 (July 1968): 20–29; 52 (Aug. 1968): 46–51. [Con Thien, near DMZ Aug.–Sept. 1967]

4534. Meyers, Bruce F. "Jungle Canopy Operations." *Marine Corps Gazette* 53 (July 1969): 20–26. [Operation MAMELUKE THRUST thirty miles west of Da Nang, May–June 1968]

4535. Peatross, O.F. "Victory at Van Tuong Village." *Naval Review* (1968): 2–13. [Operation STARLITE]

4536. _____, and W.G. Johnson. "Operation UTAH." *Marine Corps Gazette* 50 (Oct. 1966): 20–27. [south of Da Nang, Mar. 1966]

4537. Regal, John E. "Surprise for the 803d." *Marine Corps Gazette* 54 (Apr. 1970): 29–33.

4538. Sexton, Martin J., and Joseph E. Hopkins. "Assault at Mutter's Ridge." *Marine Corps Gazette* 54

(Mar. 1970): 20–25. [offensive south of DMZ, Dec. 1968]

4539. Smith, Richard B. "Leatherneck Square." *Marine Corps Gazette* 53 (Aug. 1968): 34–42. [9th Marines, Quang Tri province, 1967–1968]

4540. Warner, Denis. "Showdown in Danang." *Reporter* 34 (June 2, 1966): 14–16.

4541. Warren, George F. "Return to Conventional Warfare." *Marine Corps Gazette* 53 (Sept. 1969): 34–37.

4542. West, Francis J., Jr. "Fast Rifles." *Marine Corps Gazette* 51 (Oct. 1967): 38–44. [Binh Nghia, Quang Ngai province, summer of 1966]

AMPHIBIOUS OPERATIONS

4543. Alexander, Joseph H. "An Amphibious Operation in Vietnam." *Marine Corps Gazette* 50 (Jan. 1966): 37–40. [landings in Mar.–Apr. 1965]

4544. Hilgartner, Peter L. "Amphibious Doctrine in Vietnam." *Marine Corps Gazette* 53 (Jan. 1969): 28–31.

4545. Miller, J.E., and W.D. Toole, Jr. "Amphibious Forces: The Turning Point." *U.S. Naval Institute Proceedings* 100 (Nov. 1974): 26–32. [1972 amphibious operations]

4546. Mumford, Robert E., Jr. "Jackstay: New Dimensions in Amphibious Warfare." *Naval Review* (1968): 69–87.

4547. West, Francis J., Jr. "Stingray '70." *U.S. Naval Institute Proceedings* 95 (Nov. 1969): 26–37.

AIR OPERATIONS

4548. Bio Technology, Inc. *Biographical Factors and Activities of Marine Corps Aviation Personnel in Vietnam.* 2 vols. Falls Church, VA, 1970.

4549. Hymoff, Edward. *The First Marine Air Wing, Vietnam.* New York: Lads, 1968.

4550. McCutcheon, Keith B. "Marine Aviation in Vietnam, 1962–1970." *U.S. Naval Institute Proceedings* 97 (May 1971): 123–155.

Riverine Operations

The "Brown Water Navy," as it was often known, featured the 9th Infantry Division among its forces; see Fulton (3475) for a survey of operations, 1966–1969.

4551. Baker, J.W., and L.C. Dickson. "Army Forces in Riverine Operations." *Military Review* 47 (Aug. 1967): 64–74.

4552. Bates, C.C., G. Tselepis, and D. Von Nieda. "Needed: Shallow Thinking." *U.S. Naval Institute Proceedings* 94 (Nov. 1968): 44–51.

4553. Chapelle, Dickey. "Water War in Viet Nam." *National Geographic* 129 (Feb. 1966): 271–296.

4554. Chaplin, J.B. "The Air Cushion Vehicle." *Military Engineer* 61 (Jan.–Feb. 1969): 12–15.

4555. Conn, V. "The Brown Water Navy: A Story About U.S. Navymen Who Go Down the Rivers in Small Boats in Viet Nam." *Navy Magazine* 12 (Mar. 1969): 18–22.

4556. Dagle, Dan. "The Mobile Riverine Force, Vietnam. *U.S. Naval Institute Proceedings* 95 (Jan. 1969): 126–128.

4557. Ebersole, J.F. "Skimmer Ops." *U.S. Naval Institute Proceedings* 100 (July 1974): 40–46.

4558. Emergy, Thomas R.M. "River Power." *U.S. Naval Institute Proceedings* 96 (Aug. 1970): 117–121.

4559. Fulton, William B. "Mobile Riverine Force in Combat." *Field Artilleryman*, no. 43 (Apr. 1969): 15–28.

4560. Harrigan, Anthony. "Inshore and River Warfare." *Orbis* 10 (Fall 1966): 940–946.

4561. Malone, P.B., III. "JTEBGIG: Delta Dance of Death." *Army* 19 (July 1969): 48–52.

4562. Meyer, Richard M. "The Ground–Sea Team in River Warfare." *Military Review* 46 (Sept. 1966): 54–61.

4563. Mustin, Thomas M. "The River War." *Ordnance* 53 (Sept.–Oct. 1968): 176–178.

4564. Nossal, Frederick. "Vietnam War: The Brown Water Navy." *Far Eastern Economic Review* 64 (May 4–10, 1969): 338–339.

4565. Powers, Robert C. "Beans and Bullets for Sea Lords." *U.S. Naval Institute Proceedings* 96 (Dec. 1970): 95–97.

4566. "River Gunfire Support Ship." *U.S. Naval Institute Proceedings* 94 (Feb. 1968): 100–101.

4567. "Riverine Artillery." *Artillery Trends* 39 (Jan. 1968): 14–24.

4568. Robinette, Hillary M. "Guerrilla Warfare and Waterway Control." *Military Review* 50 (Feb. 1970): 17–23.

4569. Schreadley, Richard L. "Sea Lords." *U.S. Naval Institute Proceedings* 96 (Aug. 1970): 22–31.

4570. Searle, W.F., Jr. "The Case for Inshore Warfare." *Naval Review* (1966): 1–23.

4571. Simpson, Thomas H., and David La Boissiere. "Fire Support in Riverine Operations." *Marine Corps Gazette* 53 (Aug. 1969): 43–47.

4572. Spore, John B. "Floating Assault Force: Scourge." *Army* 18 (Feb. 1968): 28–32.

4573. Swartztrauber, S.A. "River Patrol Relearned." *U.S. Naval Institute Proceedings* 96 (May 1970): 122–157.

4574. Todaro, Donald G. "Big Weapons for Small Boats: Firepower for Riverine Warfare." *National Defense* 59 (Nov.–Dec. 1974): 215–220.

4575. "U.S. Brown Water Navy Disbanded, Heads Home." *Navy Magazine* 12 (Oct. 1969): 26–27.

4576. U.S. Office of Naval Operations. Naval History Division. *Riverine Warfare: The U.S. Navy's Operations on Inland Waters.* Washington, DC, 1969.

4577. Wallenhorst, Ralph. "Skimmers Invade 'Charlie's Country.'" *Rendezvous* 6 (May 1967): 2–8.

4578. Well, W.C. "The Riverine Force in Action, 1966–1967." *Naval Review* (1969): 48–83.

4579. Yohanan, Robert R. "Joint Training for Inshore Naval Operations." *U.S. Naval Institute Proceedings* 94 (Mar. 1968): 130–132.

Naval Operations

Items relating to the U.S. Navy's role are scattered throughout the Guide, *see Center for Naval Analyses (3434) for bibliographical references; "Logistics" in Chapter 6, for sealift activities; "Official Histories" under "Navy" in Chapter 6, for general accounts; and*

"Riverine Operations" immediately above, for Navy's role in inshore actions.

OVERVIEWS

See Rozier (4150).

4580. Berle, J.D. "The Navy in Southeast Asia: A Versatile Force." *Data* 13 (Mar. 1968): 18–21.

4581. Miller, R.T. "Fighting Boats of the United States." *Naval Review* (1968): 297–329.

4582. Moeser, Robert D. *U.S. Navy: Vietnam.* Annapolis, MD: U.S. Naval Institute, 1969.

4583. "1967 Seventh Fleet Summary." *Naval Review* (1969): 366–371.

4584. Rodgers, R.H. "America's Best Weapon." *U.S. Naval Institute Proceedings* 91 (Sept. 1968): 106–108.

4585. Schreadley, Richard L. "The Naval War in Vietnam 1950–1970." *U.S. Naval Institute Proceedings* 97 (May 1971): 182–209.

4586. "Sea Power, 1966–1967." *Naval Review* (1968): 291–292.

4587. Stillwell, Paul. "The Last Battleship." *U.S. Naval Institute Proceedings* 105 (Dec. 1979): 46–51. [*USS New Jersey*, BB–62, May to Oct. 1969]

4588. Torrance, H.S. "Naval and Maritime Events, 1 July 1967–30 June, 1968." *Naval Review* (1969): 280–338.

4589. "U.S. Naval Operations Against North Vietnam, August 1964–November 1968." *Naval Review* (1969): 360–362.

4590. U.S. Senate. Committee on Armed Services. Hearings; *Investigation of the Preparedness Program: U.S. Navy and U.S. Marine Corps in Southeast Asia.* 90th Cong., 1st sess., 1967.

OPERATIONS

4591. Cagle, M.W. "Task Force 77 in Action off Vietnam." *U.S. Naval Institute Proceedings* 98 (May 1972): 68–109.

4592. Carrison, D.J. "Influence of the Viet-Nam War." In *U.S. Navy.* New York: Praeger, 1968, 211–225.

4593. Clapp, A.J. "Shu-fly Diary." *U.S. Naval Institute Proceedings* 89 (1963): 42–53. [Marine helicopters in Mekong Delta, Apr. 1962]

4594. Collins, Frank C., Jr. "Maritime Support of the Campaign in I Corps." *U.S. Naval Institute Proceedings* 97 (May 1971): 158–179.

4595. Gayle, G.D. "Naval Operations Supporting the Commitment." In *The Vietnam War: Its Conduct and Higher Management.* Washington, DC: Georgetown University, 1968.

4596. Glickman, T.W. "Task Force 77 in Action Off Vietnam." *U.S. Naval Institute Proceedings* 98 (Sept. 1972): 90–92.

4597. Heinl, Robert D., Jr. "Welcome to the War." *U.S. Naval Institute Proceedings* 95 (Mar. 1969): 58–62. [*USS New Jersey*]

4598. Padgett, H.E., and J.A. Garrow. "Saigon—The Navy Reported Today. . . ." *U.S. Naval Institute Proceedings* 95 (Apr. 1969): 132–137.

4599. Plattner, C.M. "Combat Dictates Shift in Navy Tactics." *Aviation Week & Space Technology* 84 (Feb. 7, 1966): 65–72.

4600. Winter, R.M. "Armor Afloat in Vietnam." *U.S. Naval Institute Proceedings* 94 (Nov. 1968): 132–134.

GUNFIRE SUPPORT

4601. Bivins, Harold A. *An Annotated Bibliography of Naval Gunfire Support.* Washington, DC: Headquarters U.S. Marine Corps, Historical Division, 1971. [includes *USS New Jersey* in Vietnam]

4602. Kirk, D. "'Banging Holes in the Land': The Vietnam War from the Deck of a U.S. Cruiser." *New York Times Magazine* (June 5, 1972): 2ff.

4603. "Naval Gunfire Support." *U.S. Naval Institute Proceedings* 94 (July 1968): 95–96.

4604. "Seventh Fleet's Sea Dragons Scorch North Viet Nam with Their Fire." *Navy Magazine* 10 (June 1967): 38–39.

4605. Whitney, Craig R. "Naval Gunfire in Vietnam." *Ordnance* 53 (May–June 1969): 602–606.

MINING OPERATIONS

See also "Easter Offensive, 1972," the "Mining Harbors" section, this chapter.

4606. Falk, Jim. "Seventh Fleet Mine Warfare Officer Discusses Operations Against North Vietnam." *Navy* 10 (May 1967): 12–14.

4607. Riggs, Jerry. "U.S. Minesweeping Boats Keep

Clear the River Path to Saigon." *Navy* 10 (May 1967): 15–18.

OPERATION MARKET TIME

This operation aimed at reducing sea-borne infiltration into South Vietnam through the Gulf of Thailand.

4608. Center for Naval Analysis. Operations Evaluation Group. *Market Time: Countering Sea-Borne Infiltration in South Vietnam.* Study no. 706. Washington, DC, 1966.

4609. "Communist Weapons Trawlers Destroyed in Attempt to Run Allied Gauntlet at Sea Off South Vietnam." *Army* 11 (Apr. 1968): 40–41.

4610. Hodgman, James A. "Market Time in the Gulf of Thailand." *Naval Review* (1968): 38–67.

4611. Naval Reconnaissance and Technical Support Center. *Vietnam: U.S. and Friendly Minor Naval Ships Recognition Handbook.* 714/67–C. Washington, DC, 1967.

4612. Naval Weapons Laboratory. *"Sampans," "Junks," or "Ghes" of Vietnamese Waterways.* Dahlgren, VA, 1966.

4613. Stephan, C.R. "Trawler!" *U.S. Naval Institute Proceedings* 94 (Sept. 1968): 61–71.

NAVAL AIR ACTIVITIES

Combat activities are usually grouped with USAF activities, see Chapter 6.

4614. Brownlow, Cecil. "Air War in Vietnam: Navy Aircraft Inventory Strained." *Aviation Week & Space Technology* 89 (Aug. 26, 1968): 16–18.

4615. Bulban, E.J. "Navy Using Armed Helicopter in Vietnam." *Aviation Week & Space Technology* 88 (May 20, 1968): 69ff.

4616. Connolly, T.F. "The Attack Aircraft Carrier Shows New Potency in Vietnam." *Navy* 10 (Feb. 1967): 12–16.

4617. Haughland, Vern. "Navy Wings for Vietnam." *Ordnance* 52 (Mar.–Apr. 1968): 471–474.

4618. Moorer, Thomas H. "War in Vietnam: Combat Dictates Shift in Navy Tactics." *Aviation Week & Space Technology* 84 (Feb. 7, 1966): 64–72.

4619. "Navy's Skywarrior Has New Role: Aerial Tanker over Tonkin Gulf." *Navy Magazine* 10 (June 1967): 37.

4620. Vito, A.H., Jr. "Carrier Air and Vietnam: An Assessment." *U.S. Naval Institute Proceedings* 93 (Oct. 1967): 66–75.

COAST GUARD

4621. Kaplan, H.R. "Coast Guard Played Vital Role in Viet War." *Navy* 13 (Nov. 1970): 31–34.

4622. Moreau, J.W. "The Coast Guard in the Central and Western Pacific." *U.S. Naval Institute Proceedings* 99 (May 1973): 286–295.

ARVN Operations

For more information about South Vietnamese military activities see "Vietnamization" in Chapter 6, especially the "U.S. Advisors" section.

4623. Campbell, Thomas E. "Ambush at Song O Lau." *Marine Corps Gazette* 54 (Jan. 1970): 35–39. [South Vietnamese Marines]

4624. Cowan, William V. "Killer Forest." *Marine Corps Gazette* 54 (Aug. 1970): 31–34. A special Marine advisor talks about Rung Sat Special Zone combat.

4625. Denno, B.F. "Viet Cong Defeat at Phuoc Chau." *Marine Corps Gazette* 49 (Mar. 1965): 34–40. [northern area, 1962]

4626. Halberstam, David. "Portrait of Two Soldiers." *New York Times Magazine* (Jan. 5, 1964): 11ff. [ARVN and Vietcong]

4627. Kane, Douglas T. "Vietnamese Marines in Joint Operations." *Military Review* 48 (Nov. 1968): 26–33.

4628. Leftwich, William G. "Decision at Duc Co." *Marine Corps Gazette* 51 (Feb. 1967): 34–38. [South Vietnamese Marines, Aug. 1965]

4629. Nguyen Duc Dung. "ARVN Armor in the Battle for Ben Het." *Armor* 79 (Nov.–Dec. 1970): 24–27.

4630. Sams, Kenneth. "How the Vietnamese Are Taking Over Their Own Air War." *Air Force* 54 (Apr. 1971): 24–27.

4631. White, Michael E. "Vietnamese Riverine Forces Taking Up the Slack." *Marine Corps Gazette* 54 (Dec. 1970): 41–42.

4632. Wren, Christopher S. "The Vietnamese GI: Can He Win His Own War?" *Look* 34 (Aug. 11, 1970): 13–21.

MONTAGNARDS

4633. Booth, Waller B. "The Montagnards of Vietnam: Tragic Warriors of the Highlands." *Army* 25 (May 1975): 47–50.

4634. Fabian, David R. "Montagnards Measure Up." *Army Digest* 25 (Jan. 1970): 18–19.

4635. Jackson, Larry R. "The Vietnamese Revolution and the Montagnards." *Asian Survey* 9 (May 1969): 313–330.

4636. Johnson, Thomas M. "Montagnards Become Rangers." *Infantry* 61 (July–Aug. 1971): 50–51.

4637. Sochurek, Howard. "Viet Nam's Montagnards." *National Geographic* 133 (Apr. 1968): 443–487.

4638. Sockell, Jacques. "Après Dien-Bien-Phu: Les derniers combats au Vietnam sur les plateaux Montagnards." *Revue Historique des Armées* 3 (1977): 85–104.

4639. "Vietnam's 'Montagnards.'" *New York Times Magazine* (Dec. 9, 1962): 37.

4640. West, Richard. "The Betrayal of the Montagnards." *Atlas* 21 (Apr. 1972): 43–45.

VC/NVA Operations

Many difficulties confront any effort to separate Vietcong "military" and "political" activities; however, it is attempted here. For "political" dimensions, see "North Vietnam, 1954–1975," the "Viet Cong" and "National Liberation Front" sections in Chapter 3. VC and North Vietnamese military operations were frequently joint endeavors; references to these are obviously contained in most of the accounts of U.S. activities throughout this and other chapters dealing with the military dimension. Estimated NVA infiltration from the North between 1964 and 1967 was: 1964 (12,400); 1965 (36,300); 1966 (92,287); 1967 (101,260)—Lewy (3553), 66.

Books and Dissertations
4641. Berman, Paul. "The Liberation Armed Forces of the NLF: Compliance and Cohesion in a Revolutionary Army." Ph.D. dissertation, MIT, 1970.

4642. Gignon, F. *Les Américains face au Viet-Cong.* Paris: Flammarion, 1965.

4643. Knoeble, K. *Victor Charlie: The Face of War in Vietnam.* London: Pall Mall Press, 1967.

4644. Paignez, Y. *Le Viet-Minh et la guerre psychologique.* Paris: 1955.

4645. Pike, Douglas. *War, Peace, and the Viet Cong.* Cambridge, MA: MIT Press, 1969.

4646. Visions of Victory: *Selected Vietnamese Communist Military Writings.* Edited by P.J. McGarvey. Hoover Institution Publication no. 81. Stanford, CA: Hoover Institution, 1969.

Essays
4647. Boudarel, Georges. "Essai sur la pensée militaire Vietnamese." *L'Homme et la Société*, no. 7 (Jan.–Feb. 1968): 183–199.

4648. Chu Van Tan. *Reminiscences on the Army for National Salvation.* Data paper no. 97. Ithaca: Cornell University, Southeast Asia Program, 1974. This is the memoir of a Tho tribal chief and guerrilla leader from the northeast mountains.

4649. Duncanson, Dennis J. "The Vitality of the Viet Cong." *Survival* 9 (Jan. 1967): 14–18.

4650. Elliott, D.W.P., and M. Elliott. *Documents of an Elite Viet Cong Delta Unit: The Demolition Platoon of the 514th Battalion—Part One: Unit Composition and Personnel.* RM–5848–ISA/ARPA. Santa Monica, CA: Rand Corp., May 1969.

4651. _____. *Documents of an Elite Viet Cong Delta Unit: The Demolition Platoon of the 514th Battalion—Part Two: Party Organization.* RM–5849–ISA/ARPA. Santa Monica, CA: Rand Corp., May 1969.

4652. _____. *Documents of an Elite Viet Cong Delta Unit: The Demolition Platoon of the 514th Battalion—Part Three: Military Organization and Activities.* RM–5850–ISA/ARPA. Santa Monica, CA: Rand Corp., May 1969.

4653. _____. *Documents of an Elite Viet Cong Delta Unit: The Demolition Platoon of the 514th Battalion—Part Four: Political Indoctrination and Military Training.* RM–5851–ISA/ARPA. Santa Monica, CA: Rand Corp., May 1969.

4654. _____. *Documents of an Elite Viet Cong Delta Unit: The Demolition Platoon of the 514th Battalion—Part Five: Personal Letters.* RM–5852–ISA/ARPA. Santa Monica, CA: Rand Corp., May 1969.

4655. Pohle, V., and C. Menges. *Time and Limited*

Success as Enemies of the Viet Cong. P–3491. Santa Monica, CA: Rand Corp., Oct. 1967.

4656. Rolph, Hammond. "Viet Cong Documents on the War." *Communist Affairs* 5 (Sept.–Oct. 1967): 18–26; (Nov.–Dec. 1967): 2234; 6 (Jan.–Feb. 1968): 16–27.

4657. Warner, Denis. "Ho's Underground in South Vietnam." *Reporter* 37 (Nov. 30, 1967): 20–22.

4658. Weller, Jac. "Viet Cong Arms and Men." *Ordnance* 50 (May–June 1966): 602–610.

OPERATIONS

4659. Garland, A.B. "The First Viet Cong General Offensive." *Australian Army Journal*, no. 240 (May 1969): 24–36.

4660. _____. "The Second Viet Cong General Offensive." *Australian Army Journal*, no. 241 (June 1969): 11–22.

4661. Sexton, Martin J. "Sapper Attack." *Marine Corps Gazette* 53 (Sept. 1969): 2831. [VC attack, Feb. 24, 1969]

4662. Ulmer, Walter F., Jr. "Notes on Enemy Armor at An Loc." *Armor* 82 (Jan.–Feb. 1973): 14–20.

4663. Warner, Denis. "Hanoi's Summer Offensive: A Bigger War in Prospect." *Reporter* 36 (June 29, 1967): 31–34.

STRATEGY AND TACTICS

While NVA strategy often called for large-unit operations, the VC usually sought to concentrate their activities in hit-and-run guerrilla fashion, or in ambush tactics. For North Vietnamese strategy during the final (1975) phase, see "Final Campaign, 1975" in Chapter 3.

4664. Abrams, Arnold. "South Vietnam: Charlie Changes His Tactics." *Far Eastern Economic Review* 69 (Aug. 6, 1970): 21–22ff.

4665. Betts, R.H. *Viet Cong Village Control: Some Observations on the Origin and Dynamics of Modern Revolutionary War.* Cambridge, MA: MIT, Center for International Studies, Aug. 8, 1969.

4666. Casella, Alessandro. "Viet Cong Strategy: The Militant Mood." *Far Eastern Economic Review* 60 (May 12–18, 1968): 345–346ff.

4667. Conley, Michael C. *The Communist Insurgent Infrastructure in South Vietnam: A Study of Organization and Strategy.* Pamphlet no. 550–106. Washington, DC: Department of the Army, 1967.

4668. _____. "Communist Thought and Viet Cong Tactics." *Asian Studies* 8 (Mar. 1968): 206–222.

4669. Davison, W.P. *Some Observations on Viet Cong Operations in the Villages* RM–5267/2–ISA/ARPA. Santa Monica, CA: Rand Corp., May 1968.

4670. Gramont, Sanche de. "Under Viet Cong Control." *Saturday Evening Post* 239 (Jan. 29, 1960): 27–33, 82.

4671. Honey, P.J. "North Vietnam's Model of Strategy and Tactics for Revolution." *Studies on the Soviet Union* 6:2 (1966): 2–28.

4672. Liu Chi-chun. "Viet-cong's Strategy and Tactics." *Issues and Studies* 2 (Mar. 1966): 1–18.

4673. McFarlane, I.D. "Viet Cong Tactics." *Australian Army Journal*, no. 213 (Feb. 1967): 3–16.

4674. Modelski, George A. "The Viet Minh Complex." In *Communism and Revolution: The Strategic Uses of Violence*, edited by C.E. Black and T.P. Thornton. Princeton, NJ: Princeton University Press, 1964, 185–214.

4675. Neglia, Anthony V. "NVA and VC: Different Enemies, Different Tactics." *Infantry* 60 (Sept.–Oct. 1970): 50–55.

4676. O'Ballance, Edgar. "Viet Cong Strategy." *United Service Institution of India Journal* 96 (July–Sept. 1966): 189–194.

4677. Race, Jeffrey. "How They Won." *Asian Survey* 10 (Aug. 1970): 628–650.

4678. Rogers, Lane. "The Enemy." *Marine Corps Gazette* 50 (Mar. 1966): 51–55. [VC doctrine and tactics]

4679. Rolph, Hammond M. "Vietnamese Communism and the Protracted War." *Asian Survey* 12 (Sept. 1972): 783–792.

4680. Samson, Jack. "Viet Cong Tactics: 'Ten against One.'" *Military Review* 47 (Jan. 1967): 89–93.

4681. *A Study of Strategic Lessons Learned in Vietnam.* Vol. I: *The Enemy.* AD–AO96. Rpt no. BOM/W–78–128–TR–VOL–I. Vienna, VA: BDM Corp., Nov. 30, 1979.

4682. Turley, William S. "Origins and Development of Communist Military Leadership in Vietnam." *Armed Forces & Society* 3 (Winter 1977): 219–247.

Vo Nguyen Giap, the Strategist

For more on Giap, see Chapter 3.

4683. Clos, Max. "The Strategist Behind the Viet Cong." *New York Times Magazine* (Aug. 16, 1964): 52–55.

4684. Le Quange, Gerard. *Giap ou la guerre du peuple.* Paris: Denoel, 1973.

4685. O'Neil, Robert J. *General Giap, Politician and Strategist.* New York: Praeger, 1969.

4686. _____. *The Strategy of General Giap since 1964.* Canberra Papers on Strategy and Defense no. 6. Canberra: Australian National University, 1969.

4687. Vo Nguyen Giap. *Arm the Revolutionary Masses and Build the People's Army.* Saigon: U.S. Mission, Viet Nam Documents & Research Notes, Pts I–III, June–Oct. 1972.

4688. _____. *National Liberation War in Viet Nam: General Line, Strategy, Tactics.* Hanoi: Foreign Languages Publishing House, 1970. [distillation of Giap's previous writings]

4689. _____. *Viet Nam People's War Has Defeated U.S. War of Destruction.* Hanoi: Foreign Languages Publishing House, 1969.

PERSONNEL AND MOTIVATION

4690. Cole, R.W., III. "Portrait of an Enemy." *Armor* 76 (May–June 1967): 13–16.

4691. Denton, Frank H. *Volunteers of the Viet Cong.* RM–5647–ISA/ARPA. Santa Monica, CA: Rand Corp., Sept. 1968.

4692. Dexter, George E. "Uncle Ho Wants You! A Study of Viet Cong Motivation." *Australian Army Journal,* no. 221 (Oct. 1967): 33–39.

4693. *Diary of an Infiltrator.* Saigon: U.S. Mission in Vietnam, 1966.

4694. Fall, Bernard B. "The Adversary in Vietnam." *War/Peace Report* 4 (May 1964): 12–13.

4695. _____. "Unrepentant, Unyielding: An Interview with Viet Cong Prisoners." *New Republic* 156 (Feb. 4, 1967): 19–24.

4696. Halberstam, David. "The Face of the Enemy in Vietnam." *Harper's* 230 (Feb. 1965): 62–71.

4697. Henderson, William D. *Why the Vietcong Fought: A Study of Motivation and Control in a Modern Army in Combat.* Westport, CT: Greenwood, 1979. Henderson also provides a short critique of Gabriel and Savage, *Crisis in Command.*

4698. Kellen, Konrad. *Conversations with Enemy Soldiers in Late 1968/Early 1969: A Study of Motivation and Morale.* RM–613101–ISA/ARPA. Santa Monica, CA: Rand Corp., Sept. 1970.

4699. _____. *A View of the VC: Elements of Cohesion in the Enemy Camp in 1966–1967.* RM–5462–ISA/ARPA. Santa Monica, CA: Rand Corp., Nov. 1969.

4700. Ladd, Jonathan F. "Viet Cong Portrait." *Military Review* 44 (July 1964): 67–80.

4701. Patton, George S. "Why They Fight." *Military Review* 45 (Dec. 1965): 16–23.

4702. Pike, Douglas. "Mystique of the Viet Cong." *Army* 17 (June 1967): 25–33.

4703. Ruehl, L. "Ho's Fighting Robots." *Atlas* 11 (May 1966): 299–301.

4704. Sheehan, Susan. "The Enemy." *New Yorker* 42 (Sept. 10, 1966): 62–100.

LOGISTICS AND SUPPORT

4705. Ahearn, Arthur M. "Viet Cong Medicine." *Military Medicine* 131 (Mar. 1966): 219–221.

4706. Brown, F.C. "NVA Armor." *Military Journal* (Winter 1978): 31–33, 50.

4707. Calvert, Michael. "Engineering Aspects of Guerrilla Warfare: The Vietnamese 'Sapper.'" *Royal United Services Institution Journal* 117 (Dec. 1972): 38–42.

4708. Copeland, Peter. "Enemy Small Arms in Vietnam." *Army Digest* 24 (June 1969): 52–55.

4709. George, James A. "Primitive Weapons of the Viet Cong." *Airman* 7 (May 1963): 39–41.

4710. Grier, Samuel L. "Black Pajama Intelligence." *Marine Corps Gazette* 51 (Apr. 1967): 36–40.

4711. Higgins, J.W. *Porterage Parameters and Tables.* RM–5292–ISA/ARPA. Santa Monica, CA: Rand Corp., Aug. 1967.

4712. McLean, Donald B., ed. *Guide to Viet Cong Ammunition.* Forest Grove, OR: Normount Technical Publishing, 1971.

4713. U.S. Army. *Guide to Selected Viet Cong Equipment and Explosive Devices.* No. 381–11. Washington, DC: GPO, 1966.

4714. "Viet Cong Weapons." *TAC Intelligence Digest* 23 (June 11, 1966): 14–17. [Air Force, Tactical Air Command]

Air War

The air war in Southeast Asia ranged over Vietnam, Laos and Cambodia (see under "U.S. Activities in Laos" and "U.S. Activities in Cambodia" in Chapter 2 for the latter two countries). Most public criticism was directed at the impact of the bombing policies of the United States upon civilians, while the USAF's preference for "deep interdiction" strikes over close, or tactical, air support stirred some interservice debate. Littauer and Uphoff's account (4719) has the best summary of U.S. bombing actions, while Smith's bibliography (3440) provides an excellent survey of published materials. Willis and Cook (3443) provide a summary of official USAF statistical data on air operations from 1961 to 1970. Listed by topic in this and the other chapters dealing with the military dimensions of the war are many other citations that relate to such themes as airlift, specific combat operations, POWs, etc.

OVERVIEWS

Books

4715.   *Air War: Vietnam.* New York: Bobbs-Merrill, 1978. [covers 1965–1972]

4716.   Drendel, Lou. *The Air War in Vietnam.* New York: Arco, 1968.

4717.   Hai Thu. *North Vietnam Against U.S. Air Force.* Hanoi: Foreign Languages Publishing House, 1967.

4718.   Harvey, F. *Air War: Vietnam.* New York: Bantam Books, 1967.

4719.   Littauer, Raphael, and Norman Uphoff, eds. *The Air War in Indochina.* Rev. ed. Boston: Beacon, 1972.

4720.   Thompson, James C. *Rolling Thunder: Understanding Policy and Program Failure.* Chapel Hill: University of North Carolina Press, 1980. [covers 1965–1968]

Essays

4721.   "The Air War in Vietnam." *Air Force Magazine* 46 (May 1963): 68–73.

4722.   "The Air War in Vietnam." *Air Force & Space Digest* 45 (Mar. 1966): 35–100.

4723.   "Air War in Vietnam: The Statistical Side." *Air Force & Space Digest* 50 (Mar. 1967): 78–85.

4724.   Anthis, Rollen H. "Airpower: The Paradox in Vietnam." *Air Force & Space Digest* 50 (Apr. 1967): 34–38.

4725.   Brighton, P. "The War in South Vietnam: Some Lessons in the Use of Air Power." *Royal Air Forces Quarterly* 8 (Winter 1968): 289–293.

4726.   Brown, Harold. "Air Power in Limited War." *Air University Review* 20 (May–June 1969): 2–15.

4727.   Brownlow, Cecil. "Airpower Gives the U.S. Edge in Vietnam War." *Aviation Week & Space Technology* 82 (Jan. 9, 1967): 26–31.

4728.   Butz, J.S., Jr. "Airpower in Vietnam: The High Price of Restraint." *Air Force & Space Digest* 49 (Nov. 1966): 40–44. [political limits upon targets]

4729.   Crichton, Robert. "Our Air War." *New York Review of Books* (Jan. 4, 1968): 3–5.

4730.   Eade, George J. "Reflections on Air Power in the Vietnam War." *Air University Review* 24 (Nov.–Dec. 1973): 2–9.

4731.   Frisbee, John L. "The Air War in Vietnam: A From-the-Scene Report." *Air Force Magazine* 55 (Sept. 1972): 48–56ff.

4732.   _____. "U.S.A.F.'s Changing Role in Vietnam." *Air Force Magazine* 54 (Sept. 1971): 41–45.

4733.   Greene, Jerry. "U.S. Airpower in Vietnam: Scalpel Rather than Broadsword." *Air Force & Space Digest* 48 (May 1965): 33–36.

4734.   Harvey, F. "Air War in Vietnam: Special Feature." *Flying* 79 (Nov. 1966): 38–95.

4735.   Helmore, P.W. "Air Operations in Vietnam; I and II." *Royal United Services Institution Journal* 112 (Feb. 1967): 16–31.

4736.   McLellan, David S., and Walter Busse. "The Myth of Air Power." *Worldview* 15 (Nov. 1972): 27–34.

4737.   Menaul, S.W.B. "The Use of Air Power in Vietnam." *Royal United Services Institute for Defense Studies Journal* 116 (June 1971): 5–12.

4738.   Milton, Thomas R. "Air Power: Equalizer in Southeast Asia." *Air University Review* 15 (Nov.–Dec. 1963): 2–8.

4739.   Mitchell, James R. "The Air War in Southeast Asia: Down on the Ninety-Ninth." *Air Force Magazine* 56 (Sept. 1973): 112–116.

4740.   Olds, Robin. "The Lessons of Clobber College." *Flight International* 95 (June 26, 1969): 1053–1056.

4741. Sams, Kenneth. "Air Power: The Decisive Weapon." *Air Force & Space Digest* 49 (Mar. 1966): 69–83.

4742. _____. "The Air War in Vietnam: Countering Escalation." *Air Force & Space Digest* 48 (Dec. 1965): 72–73, 76, 79–80, 83.

4743. Scheer, Robert. "The Winner's War." *Ramparts* 4 (Dec. 1965): 19–22. Scheer argues that without airpower the U.S. is impotent in Vietnam.

4744. Teplinsky, B. "The Air War Over Indochina." *International Affairs* [Moscow] 13 (Feb. 1967): 40–47.

4745. Ulsamer, Edgar. "How USAF Prepares for Future Contingencies." *Air Force Magazine* 56 (June 1973): 34–40.

4746. Verrier, Anthony. "Strategic Bombing: The Lessons of World War II and the American Experience in Vietnam." *Royal United Services Institution Journal* 112 (May 1967): 157–161.

4747. Witze, Claude. "What Kind of Air War in Vietnam?" *Air Force & Space Digest* 50 (Oct. 1967): 42–46.

4748. Yudkin, Richard A. "Vietnam: Policy Strategy and Airpower." *Air Force Magazine* 56 (Feb. 1973): 31–35.

Miscellaneous Essays

4749. Brown, Harold. "Our Airmen in Vietnam: A Professional Team." *Air Force & Space Digest* 50 (May 1967): 48–57.

4750. Brownlow, Cecil. "Pause Cuts Soaring Loss Rates." *Aviation Week & Space Technology* 89 (July 15, 1968): 14–16.

4751. _____. "U.S. to Boost Vietnam Air Commitment." *Aviation Week & Space Technology* 84 (Feb. 7, 1966): 22–24.

4752. Butz, J.S., Jr. "Taking the Night Away From the Viet Cong." *Air Force Magazine* 49 (June 1966): 40–51.

4753. Cardenas, Robert L. "Special Operations Use of General Aviation." *Society of Experimental Test Pilots* 9:2 (1968): 179–187.

4754. de Clairmont, R.G. "The Air War in Southeast Asia: Bac Giang by Flak Light." *Air Force Magazine* 54 (Mar. 1971): 49–53.

4755. Greene, Jerry. "Airpower's Buildup in Vietnam." *Air Force & Space Digest* 48 (June 1965): 33–43.

4756. _____. "New Air Warfare Lessons Evolve From Fight in Vietnam." *Aviation Week* 77 (Aug. 20, 1962): 68–71ff. [early USAF units in a guerrilla war]

4757. Hense, Frank F.E., Jr. "Aircraft Maintenance Training for Southeast Asia." *Air University Review* 19 (Nov.–Dec. 1968): 37–41.

4758. McGlasson, W.D. "Those Gung Ho Guardsmen in Vietnam." *Air Force & Space Digest* 51 (Nov. 1968): 191–196.

4759. Plattner, C.M. "North Sortie Rate Pressed as Political Purpose Fails." *Aviation Week & Space Technology* 84 (Feb. 21, 1966): 76–85.

4760. Putz, Victor B. "The Last B-52 Mission From Guam." *Air Force Magazine* 57 (June 1974): 49–54.

4761. Ryan, Dohn D. "The USAF Support Team: Tonkin to Linebacker." *Air Force Magazine* 56 (May 1973): 52–54ff.

4762. Schlitz, William P. "Specialists in Air Base Defense: USAF's Combat Security Policy." *Air Force & Space Digest* 52 (July 1969): 38–42.

4763. Wacker, R.F. "The View from the Cockpit." *Army* 20 (July 1970): 16–25.

4764. Witze, Claude. "How Not to Win." *Air Force Magazine* 53 (Dec. 1970): 10–12.

4765. _____. "The Year Airpower Was Tested and Paid Off." *Air Force Magazine* 51 (June 1968): 110–112.

4766. Zoeller, Laurence W. "To Major Bernard F. Fisher, USAF: The Medal of Honor." *Air Force & Space Digest* 50 (Mar. 1967): 42–44. [First Air Force officer to win medal in Vietnam]

AIR COMBAT

There was relatively little air-to-air combat in Vietnam as Hanoi usually refused to commit its few fighter-interceptors to battle. For accounts of aerial victories and aces, see Eastman, et al. (3452).

4767. "Aerial Combat Tactics." *Interceptor* 14 (May 1972): 5–11.

4768. Larson, Gerald D. "How a Fighter Pilot Sees the Air War in Vietnam." *Air Force Magazine* 50 (July 1967): 45–49.

4769. Momyer, William W. "The Evolution of Fighter Tactics in SEA." *Air Force Magazine* 56 (July 1973): 58–62.

4770. Olds, Robin. "How I Got My First MIG." *Air Force Magazine* 50 (July 1967): 38–40ff.

4771. Wells, Norman E. "Air Superiority Comes First." *Air University Review* 24 (Nov.–Dec. 1972): 10–25.

ANTIAIRCRAFT DEFENSES

North Vietnam's antiaircraft defenses gradually became more sophisticated with the introduction of SAMs; see also Operation LINE BACKER II (3464).

4772. Bearden, Thomas E. "What Really Happened In the Air Defense Battle of North Vietnam?" *Air Defense Magazine* (Apr.–June 1976): 8–15.

4773. Brownlow, Cecil. "USAF Boosts North Viet ECM Jamming." *Aviation Week & Space Technology* 84 (Feb. 6, 1967): 22–24.

4774. Butz, J.S., Jr. "Our Pilots Call Hanoi 'Dodge City.'" *New York Times Magazine* (Oct. 16, 1966): 30–31ff. [extraordinary concentration of antiaircraft weapons]

4775. "Charting the Aircraft Losses." *Journal of the Armed Forces* 105 (June 15, 1968): 4–5ff. As of May 21, 1968: 1,816 lost in combat, 2,015 noncombat losses, with more than 1,600 helicopters.

4776. Plattner, C.M. "The War in Vietnam: SAMs Spur Changes in Combat Tactics, New Equipment." *Aviation Week & Space Technology* 84 (Jan. 24, 1966): 26–31.

4777. Richard, D. "In Unexpected Setting in the War Zone You'll Find Antiwar Weapons Poised to Kill." *Army Digest* 23 (Jan. 1968): 54–57.

4778. Simler, George B. "North Vietnam's Air Defense System." *Air Force & Space Digest* 50 (May 1967): 81–82.

4779. Wolfe, Tom. "The Truest Sport: Jousting With Sam and Charlie." In his *Mauve Gloves & Madmen, Clutter & Vine.* New York: Farrar, Straus & Giroux, 1976, 26–65. [excellent account]

AIR RESCUE

Air rescue units were frequently seeking out and picking up downed flyers.

4780. Armstrong, Richard. "It's Great to be Alive." *Saturday Evening Post* 239 (June 4, 1966): 21–26. [a daring rescue]

4781. Beyer, Lawrence F. "Fight to Live." *U.S. Army Aviation Digest* 15 (Mar. 1969): 36–48.

4782. Brown, Harold. "Air Rescue in Vietnam: 'That Others May Live.'" *Air Force Magazine* 50 (Mar. 1967): 86ff.

4783. Brownlow, Cecil. "U.S. to Increase Air Rescue Capability in Southeast Asia." *Aviation Week & Space Technology* 86 (May 1, 1967): 40–41.

4784. Cannon, Michael D. "Improving Search and Rescue Now!" *Data* 14 (Jan. 1969): 22–24.

4785. Del, N. "MEDCAP Missions of Mercy." *Army Digest* 23 (Dec. 1968): 57–59.

4786. Dupre, F. "Rescue at a Place Called Kham Duc." *Air Force Magazine* 52 (Mar. 1969): 98–100.

4787. Hiett, R.L. "Search and Save." *Air Force Magazine* 53 (Dec. 1970): 40–43.

4788. Shershun, Carroll S. "The Lifesavers: SEA's Air Rescuemen." *Air Force & Space Digest* 52 (June 1969): 39–44.

4789. Sochurek, Howard. "Air Rescue Behind Enemy Lines." *National Geographic* 134 (Sept. 1968): 346–369.

4790. Stovall, Dale. "The Rescue of Bengal 505 Alpha." *Air Force Magazine* 57 (Sept. 1974): 129–137.

4791. Ulsamer, Edgar. "Air Rescue in Southeast Asia: Right from Hanoi's Own Backyard." *Air Force Magazine* 55 (Oct. 1972): 30–34.

THAILAND BASES

By 1966, 75 percent of Air Force sorties over North Vietnam flew from Thai bases; see also Chapter 2 under "Thailand."

4792. Abrams, Arnold. "The Airmen in Thailand: Professionalizing the War." *New Leader* 55 (Oct. 2, 1972): 9–10.

4793. Brownlow, Cecil. "Air Force North Vietnam Effort Dependent on Thai Bases." *Aviation Week & Space Technology* 86 (Apr. 3, 1967): 26–29.

AIRCRAFT

4794. Archer, Robert D. *The Republic F-105.* Fallbrook, CA: Aero, 1969. [mainstay of Air Force operations against North Vietnam]

4795. Birdsall, Steve. *The A-1 Skyraider.* New York: Arco, 1970.

4796. Casey, W.R. "AC-119's USAF's Flying Battleship." *Air Force & Space Digest* 53 (Feb. 1970): 48–50.

4797. Clark, Robert L. "The C-130." *Aerospace History* 26:4 (1949): 223–237.

4798. Dewey, A.E. "Caribou in Vietnam." *Army* 14 (Aug. 1963): 38–39.

4799. Drendel, Lou. *Aircraft of the Vietnam War.* New York: Arco, 1971.

4800. Duncan, Scott. "The Combat History of the F-105." *Aerospace Historian* 22 (Sept. 1975): 121–128.

4801. Frisbee, John L. "How the A-7D Rewrote the Book in SEA." *Air Force Magazine* 56 (Aug. 1973): 30–36.

4802. Jackson, B.R. *Douglas Skyraider* (A-1). Fallbrook CA: Aero, 1969. [another workhorse of the Vietnam air war]

4803. McArdle, Frank H. "The KC-135 in Southeast Asia." *Air University Review* 19 (Jan.–Feb. 1968): 20–33.

4804. "A Singular Aircraft: The A-37 in Vietnam." *Air Force & Space Digest* 52 (June 1969): 49–51.

4805. "Skoshi Tiger: Evaluating the F-5 in Combat." *Air Force Magazine* 49 (Aug. 1966): 45–48.

4806. Thomis, Wayne. "Whispering Death: The F-111 in SEA." *Air Force Magazine* 56 (June 1973): 22–27.

Aerial Bombing

American bombing strategy was controversial. Many senior Air Force and Navy officers criticized presidential restrictions on targets, while civilian critics faulted the general destructiveness of the bombings. See Littauer and Uphoff (4719) for an excellent summary of bombing activities.

4807. "The American Way of Bombing." *Harper's* 244 (June 1972): 55–58.

4808. Barkinson, V.C. "Barkinson's Law on Bombing." *Columbia University Forum* 10 (Spring 1967): 37–39.

4809. Behar, Abraham. "I Bombardamenti di Objettiviv Civili nel Vietnam del Nord [The bombing of civilian objectives in North Vietnam]." *Il Porte* [Italy] 23:7/8 (1967): 897–913.

4810. Butz, J.S., Jr. "Hit 'em Where They Is!" *Air Force Magazine* 52 (Mar. 1969): 64–68.

4811. ———. "Those Bombings in North Vietnam." *Air Force & Space Digest* 49 (Apr. 1966): 42–54.

4812. Chaliand, Gerard. "Bombing of Dai Lai." *Liberation* 12 (Dec.–Jan. 1967–1968): 67–69.

4813. DeVoss, David. "Air War: To See is to Destroy." *Time* 99 (Apr. 17, 1972): 39–40.

4814. Gillette, Robert. "Smart Bombs: Air Warfare Undergoes a Reluctant Revolution." *Science* 176 (June 9, 1972): 1108–1109.

4815. "Guidance Modifications for Bombs Detailed." *Aviation Week & Space Technology* 95 (Nov. 29, 1971): 43.

4816. Meyers, Gilbert L. "Why Not More Targets in the North?" *Air Force & Space Digest* 50 (May 1967): 74, 77–78.

4817. Peterson, I. "The Bomber Pilots Like Their Work." *New York Times Magazine* (Mar. 19, 1972): 4ff.

4818. "Senate's Bombing Inquiry Finds McNamara at Fault." *U.S. News and World Report* 63 (Sept. 11, 1967): 102–103. This article is critical of presidential restrictions on North Vietnamese targets.

4819. Sights, Albert P., Jr. "Strategic Bombing and Changing Times." *Air University Review* 23 (Jan.–Feb. 1972): 14–26.

4820. Smith, Melden E., Jr. "The Strategic Bombing Debate: The Second World War and Vietnam." *Journal of Contemporary History* 12 (Jan. 1977): 175–192. Smith argues that the best North Vietnam targets were not available.

4821. Stone, Jeremy. "Why Bomb North Vietnam?" *Commonweal* 85 (Dec. 23, 1966): 339–340.

4822. Sullivan, Cornelius D. "Air War Against the North." In *The Vietnam War: Its Conduct and Higher Direction.* Washington, DC: Georgetown University, Center for Strategic Studies, Nov. 1968.

4823. "United States Bombing of Hanoi and Haiphong." *Current Notes on International Affairs* [Australia] 37 (June 1966): 397–398.

4824. "U.S. Ends Investigation of Incident Involving Soviet Ships at Haiphong." *U.S. Department of State Bulletin* 57 (Aug. 7, 1967): 170–171. This answers charges of deliberate U.S. attacks upon Soviet ships, see also (4180).

4825. U.S. Senate. Committee on Armed Services. Hearings; *Air War Against North Vietnam.* 5 Pts. 90th Cong., 1st sess., Aug. 16–29, 1967. [Critical of president's bombing restraints]

4826. U.S. Senate. Committee on Foreign Relations. Staff Study No. 5; *Bombing as a Policy Tool in Vietnam:*

Effectiveness. 92d Cong., 2d sess., 1972. [based on *Pentagon Papers*]

4827. "USAF, Navy Bombard MiG Installations at Hoa Lac, Key Bases in North Vietnam." *Aviation Week & Space Technology* 86 (May 8, 1967): 18–23.

4828. Van Dyke, Jon M. "The Bombing of Vietnam." *Center Magazine* 3 (July–Aug. 1970): 8–17.

4829. Ver Wey, W.D. "Bombing of the North after Tonkin and Pleiku: Reprisals?" *Revue Belge de Droit International* 5 (1969): 460–479.

4830. "Vietnam Bombing: Pro and Con: By a Panel of Leading Citizens." *U.S. News and World Report* 64 (Jan. 29, 1968): 36–37.

4831. Wald, George. "Our Bombs Fall on People." *Washington Monthly* 4 (May 1972): 8–10.

4832. Wilson, George C. "Congress Debates Air War Restrictions." *Aviation Week & Space Technology* 84 (Feb. 14, 1966): 28–29.

AIR INTERDICTION

This was an expensive and difficult to evaluate Air Force effort to reduce the flow of enemy personnel and material into South Vietnam. See also "Cambodia (Kampuchea)" and "Laos" in Chapter 2.

4833. Black, C.F., and L.J. Pipes. *PREMIR: A Prediction Model for Infiltration Routes.* R–656–ARPA. Santa Monica, CA: Rand Corp., Dec. 1971.

4834. Brownlow, Cecil. "Air War in Vietnam: Bombing Spurs Resupply from North." *Aviation Week & Space Technology* 88 (May 6, 1968): 22–28.

4835. Clelland, Don. "Air Interdiction: Its Changing Conditions." *Air Force & Space Digest* 52 (June 1969): 52–56.

4836. Gilster, Herman L. "Air Interdiction in Protected War: An Economic Evaluation," *Air University Review* 28 (May–June 1977): 2–18.

4837. _____. "The Commando Hunt V Interdiction Campaign: A Case Study in Constrained Optimization." *Air University Review* 29 (Jan.–Feb. 1978): 21–37. [against NVA logistics in southern Laos, 1970–1971]

4838. Higgins, J.W. *Concepts, Data Requirements, and Uses of LOC Interdiction Models as Applied to North Vietnam.* RM–6065–PR. Santa Monica, CA: Rand Corp., May 1970. Higgins analyzes attacks against NVA transport networks.

4839. Lonie, Frank R. "Interdiction in a South-East Asian Limited War." *Royal Air Forces Quarterly* 9 (Winter 1969): 293–296.

4840. Schmaltz, Robert E. "The Uncertainty of Predicting Results of an Interdiction Campaign." *Aerospace Historian* 17 (Dec. 1970): 150–153.

4841. "USAF Bombs Hit Hard at Rails, Trucks." *Aviation Week & Space Technology* 98 (Apr. 30, 1973): 14–20.

4842. Witze, Claude. "The Air War North: Interdiction: Limited but Effective." *Air Force & Space Digest* 50 (May 1967): 72–74.

HO CHI MINH TRAIL

4843. Berent, M.E. "Night Mission on the Ho Chi Minh Trail." *Air Force Magazine* 53 (Aug. 1970): 52–55.

4844. Gregory, Gene. "Hitting the Trail." *Far Eastern Economic Review* 72 (June 12, 1971): 59–60ff.

4845. Markham, J.M. "The Ho Chi Minh Trail is a Highway Now." *New York Times Magazine* (Aug. 25, 1974): 12ff.

4846. Messex, Curtis L. "Night on the Trail." *Air Force Magazine* 55 (Jan. 1972): 56–60.

4847. O'Ballance, Edgar. "The Ho Chi Minh Trail." *Army Quarterly* 94 (Apr. 1967): 105–110.

4848. "Untold Story of the Ho Chi Minh Trail." *U.S. News and World Report* 70 (Feb. 15, 1971): 23–24.

4849. Warner, Denis. "The Ho Chi Minh Trail and Our Thai Buildup." *Reporter* 34 (Jan. 27, 1966): 26–28.

4850. Weiss, George, et al. "Battle for Control of the Ho Chi Minh Trail." *Armed Forces Journal* 108 (Feb. 15, 1971): 18–22. Weiss puts emphasis on electronic warfare techniques.

LAVELLE AFFAIR

General John D. Lavelle, commander of the 7th Air Force, was charged with exceeding his authority in authorizing "protective reaction" strikes against North Vietnamese targets between November 8, 1971, and March 8, 1972, and thus interrupting the peace negotiations.

4851. "Another Tonkin Gulf Incident." *Congressional Record* 118 (June 14, 1972): 20753–20764. [a collection of newspaper articles, statements, etc]

4852. "Command and Control in the Lavelle Case." *Congressional Record* 118 (June 21, 1972): S9801–S9807.

4853. Hunter, Edward. "Unforgivable Sin Was Saving Saigon, and Us: Lavelle's Generalship Saved Us." *Congressional Record* 118 (July 27, 1972): 25875–25877. [reprinted from *Tactics*, July 20, 1972, a strong defense of General Lavelle]

4854. "Private War of General Lavelle." *Newsweek* 79 (June 26, 1972): 17–18.

4855. U.S. House. Committee on Armed Services. Hearings; *Unauthorized Bombing of Military Targets in North Vietnam*. 92d Cong., 2d sess., 1972. [Statements by General Lavelle]

4856. U.S. Senate. Committee on Armed Services. Hearings; *Nomination of John D. Lavelle, General Creighton W. Abrams, and Admiral John S. McCain*. 92d Cong., 2d sess., 1972.

4857. "Weak Link." *New Republic* 167 (July 1, 1972): 8–9.

4858. Wilson, George C. "Washington: The Lavelle Case." *Atlantic* 230 (Dec. 1972): 6ff.

4859. Witze, Claude. "Soldier or Strangelove?" *Air Force Magazine* 55 (Nov. 1972): 20–22.

Tactical Air Operations

Airpower was used extensively to provide "close air support" of the troops in the field; the items listed here relate to that activity. See also in this chapter, "Ground and Water Operations" and "Helicopters and Assault Gunships."

Bibliography
4860. Santelli, James S. *An Annotated Bibliography of the United States Marine Corps' Concept of Close Air Support*. Washington, DC: Headquarters U.S. Marine Corps, Historical Branch, 1968.

General
4861. Babich, V. "Review of Low-Elevation U.S. Air Tactics in Vietnam." *Translations on USSR Military Affairs*, JPRS, no. 1093 (Nov. 18, 1974): 1–6.

4862. Butz, J.S., Jr. "An Open Letter to Congressman Otis G. Pike." *Air Force Magazine* 49 (Apr. 1966): 34–36. [regarding hearings on close air support]

4863. _____. "Tactical Air Support: Balancing the Scales in Vietnam." *Air Force & Space Digest* 48 (Aug. 1965): 37–40. [battle for Dong Xoai]

4864. Gorton, William A. "Close Air Support; An Employment Concept." *Air University Review* 21 (Mar.–Apr. 1970): 101–108.

4865. Kipp, Robert M. "Counterinsurgency From 30,000 Feet: The B-52 in Vietnam." *Air Force Magazine* 50 (July 1967): 45–49.

4866. Loeffke, B., and R.E. Bell, Jr. "Panels Guide the Gun Ships." *Army* 17 (Jan. 1967): 48–49.

4867. McDowell, J.I. "A Day in Tuy Hoa Valley With Gunships and Slicks." *Army* 17 (Feb. 1967): 60–62. Slicks were usually unarmed troop-carrying helicopters.

4868. Mitchell, William A. "Air Power and the Protection of Mekong River Convoys." *American Aviation Historical Journal* 23 (Summer 1978): 90–98. [supplies to Phnom Penh, 1971]

4869. Momyer, William W. "Close Air Support." *Air Force Policy Letter for Commanders*. Supplement, no. 6 (June 1973): 13–21.

4870. Picou, L.J. "Call 'Falcon' for Prompt Aerial Fire Support." *Army* (June 1967): 46–54.

4871. Sams, Kenneth. "The Battle of Long My: Air Support in Action." *Air Force Magazine* 48 (Mar. 1965): 34–37.

4872. Scholin, Allan R. "U.S. Tactical Aircraft in Southeast Asia: A Gallery of Air Weapons in Vietnam." *Air Force Magazine* 50 (Mar. 1967): 118–133.

4873. _____. "When the Iron Is Hot (Tac Air)." *Air Force & Space Digest* 50 (Dec. 1967): 64–68.

4874. Sights, Albert P., Jr. "Tactical Bombing: The Unproved Element." *Air Force & Space Digest* 52 (July 1969): 39–44.

4875. U.S. House. Committee on Armed Services. Hearings and Report; *Close Air Support*. 89th Cong., 1st sess., 1966. Hearings were held Sept.–Oct. 1965; the report criticized the Air Force for failing to develop aircraft and tactics to provide close air support.

4876. U.S. Senate. Committee on Armed Services. Hearings and Report; *Close Air Support*. 92d Cong., 1st sess., 1972.

4877. _____. Hearings and Report; *U.S. Tactical Air Power Program.* 90th Cong., 2d sess., 1967.

4878. Weiss, George. "Tac Air: Present and Future Lessons, Problems, and Needs." *Armed Forces Journal* 109 (Sept. 1971): 30–36.

4879. _____. "Tactical Airpower in 1965: The Trial by Fire." *Air Force & Space Digest* 49 (Mar. 1966): 35–38.

AIR CONTROLLERS

See also "Command and Control," the first section of this chapter.

4880. Butz, J.S., Jr. "Forward Air Controllers in Vietnam: They Call the Shots." *Air Force & Space Digest* 49 (May 1966): 60–66.

4881. Evans, Douglas K. "Reinventing the FAC: Vietnam, 1962." *Air Force Magazine* 63 (Feb. 1980): 71–75.

4882. Hubbell, John G. "Brave Men in Frail Planes." *Reader's Digest* 88 (Apr. 1966): 76–80.

4883. Mulkey, Jesse. "Marine Air Observer." *Marine Corps Gazette* 53 (May 1969): 35–37.

4884. Rodwell, Robert R. "In-Country Strike." *Flight International* 91 (Jan. 12, 1967): 59–63.

4885. Rose, Jerry A. "Communique from Hill 327 at Danag." *New York Times Magazine* (Apr. 25, 1965): 10ff. [center for U.S. air strikes]

4886. Sams, Kenneth. "Return to Ap Bac." *Airpower Historian* 12 (Apr. 1965): 49–50. [air controller's mission]

4887. Schell, Orville. "Vietnam: A Day's Work." *New Republic* 158 (Mar. 2, 1968): 21–22. [a mission with an airborne controller]

4888. Taylor, Edmond. "The Battle Over Tan Hiep." *Reporter* 33 (Dec. 16, 1965): 26–29.

Bombing: Law and Morality

Much of the public criticism of U.S. bombing activities stemmed from the concern that it caused excessive and unnecessary noncombatant casualties; hence it was not only politically counterproductive, but illegal and immoral. A defense of U.S. bombing of North Vietnam (which does not deal with the bombing of South Vietnam, Laos or Cambodia) is contained in Lewy (3553), 374–417; see also, "Casualties of War," especially the two sections on refugees in Chapter 8.

4889. Perazic, Gavro. "The Theory of 'Military Necessity' in American Bombing of North Vietnam." *Review of International Affairs* [Belgrade] 23 (Nov. 5–20, 1973): 34–35.

4890. Russett, Bruce M. "Vietnam and Restraints on Aerial Warfare." *Ventures* 9 (Spring 1969): 55–61. See A.E. Berthoff, "Mumbling and Fumbling or Lying?" *Bulletin of the Atomic Scientists* 26 (Oct. 1970): 49–50.

4891. Saundby, Air Marshal Sir Robert. "The Ethics of Bombing." *Air Force & Space Digest* 50 (June 1967): 48–50, 53.

4892. Slater, Philip. "Kill Anything that Moves (a Reaction to Harvey's Air War—Vietnam)." In *The Pursuit of Loneliness: American Culture at the Breaking Point.* Boston: Beacon, 1970, 29–52.

4893. Vander Els, Theodore. "The Irresistible Weapon." *Military Review* 51 (Aug. 1971): 80–90.

4894. Wharton, John F. "En Route to a Massacre?" *Saturday Review* 50 (Nov. 4, 1967): 19–21.

Chapter Eight

The Costs of War: Ecocide, POWs, War Crimes and Casualties

MODERN WARS have usually imposed heavy penalties on victor and vanquished alike. The Second Indochina War was certainly no exception to this rule; indeed, the costs of this conflict may well extend beyond the deaths and injuries inflicted by military weapons. Future generations of Vietnamese very likely will have to pay for the serious damage done to their basic ecological system by chemicals, bomb craters and mechanized land clearing. *Ecocide*, the term used to describe deliberate ecological damage, was invented during this conflict.

In its attempt to substitute technology for manpower-intensive means of defeating the VC/NVA, the American military employed two basic techniques which injured Vietnam's ecological system: (1) local forest destruction (primarily to deny the enemy freedom of movement, staging areas and cover in general); and (2) local crop destruction (primarily to deny the enemy local sources of food and other resources). These techniques were accomplished by herbicides (or concentrated "weed killers") which killed trees, crops and other vegetation, and Rome plows (named thus because they were built in Rome, Georgia), which bulldozed the terrain clear of all foliage.

The long-range effects of America's assault upon Vietnam's ecological system is discussed by Westing (4967). Some idea of the magnitude of this activity can be seen in Table IX.

Statistics are a callous, unfeeling instrument with which to measure human suffering and death, but it is one means of computing the human toll in the Vietnam conflict which allows for historical assessment. If American and other allied losses can be assessed with considerable accuracy, Vietnamese (South and North), Cambodian and Laotian casualties cannot. Not surprisingly, therefore, the most confusing statistics are those related to civilian injuries and deaths. For example, Dr. Martin Luther King claimed that 1 million civilians had been killed by 1967; Dr. Benjamin Spock asserted that 100,000 civilian deaths per year were occurring because of the war; and a French correspondent insisted that between 1965 and 1969, some 1,116,000 civilians were killed and 2,232,000 wounded. Senator Edward Kennedy's committee (5385–5392) has explored the impact of the war on civilians, as has Lewy (3553). Table X is a composite of several reports and estimates, but draws basically from Lewy (3553) and O'Ballance (4147).

A Stockholm International Peace Research Institute (SIPRI) account, *Warfare in a Fragile World: Military Impact on the Human Environment* (London: Taylor & Francis, 1980), offers somewhat different casualty estimates (see 36). This study also provides comparative estimates of civilian fatalities for the Second Indochina War, Korean War and World War II.

The "laws of war" were obviously a recent discovery for many commentators on the Vietnam conflict. These rules, originating in the Middle Ages and finally codified in the last half of the nineteenth century, had lost considerable vitality long before the advent of the Second Indochina War. The expansion of military technology, the addiction to theories of "total war" and the augmented use of guerrilla tactics were among the forces eroding serious international commitment to the "laws of war."

Few contemporary accounts of war crimes in Vietnam, consequently, shed much light on this issue. Some writers, emphasizing the "spirit" of the nineteenth-century codes, stressed the moral aspects of American and Vietcong violations; while others, employing doctrines of mitigating circumstances (e.g., "right of reprisal," "military necessity" and "proportionality"), demonstrated the vagueness and incompleteness of the laws themselves. Ideologues voiced their outrage selectively. The antiwar dissidents castigated the behavior of American forces and virtually ignored the calculated assassination tactics of the Vietcong; interventionists reversed the focus. Before venturing far into this confusing issue, particularly the My Lai incident, one should examine Karsten's account (5208) for a useful historical perspective.

Most of the American POWs (prisoners of war) were pilots shot down during bombing raids over North Vietnam and they occupied a unique role in the war. They comprised Hanoi's best "bargaining chip" in the armistice negotiations; yet they arrived home to receive the only hero's welcome offered by the American people and their government. The individual sufferings of these unfortunate men, long imprisoned and frequently tortured, contrary to the rules of war, have been documented. However, the morality and legality of their bombing practices and the plight of their many noncombatant victims still raise questions that have rarely received postwar scrutiny. (See, in Chapter 7, "Air War" for more about U.S. bombing policies.)

Modern technology did have some positive features as far as the American soldier was concerned. U.S. casualties for the Second Indochina War were lowered by substituting firepower for manpower; and advances in medical procedures, particularly helicopter evacuation, greatly increased a wounded soldier's chances of survival. Both of these factors are demonstrated in Tables XI and XII.

The refugee problem has apparently increased since the Armistice. An initial tide of refugees accompanied Hanoi's victory in 1975, but the greater flood of homeless has been prompted by Vietnam's pursuit of the Third Indochina War. The statistics presented in Table XIII are vague, but the new refugees have that same timeless odor of misery, disease and starvation.

TABLE IX

Defoliation and Crop Destruction Coverage, 1962–1970
(in acres)

YEAR	DEFOLIATION	CROP DESTRUCTION	TOTAL
1962	4,940	741	5,681
1963	24,700	247	24,947
1964	83,486	10,374	93,860
1965	155,610	65,949	221,559
1966	741,247	103,987	845,144
1967	1,486,446	221,312	1,706,758
1968	1,267,110	63,726	1,330,836
1969	1,198,444	64,961	1,263,405
1970	220,324	32,604	252,928
Total	4,747,587	481,897	5,229,484

Source: Military Assistance Command, Vietnam, *Command History 1970*, II, pp.XIV–6; cited in Guenter Lewy, *America in Vietnam* (New York: Oxford University Press, 1978), p.258.

TABLE X

Casualties: Jan. 1, 1961–Jan. 28, 1973

U.S.
Killed in Action	45,941
Wounded	300,635
Missing, captured, interned	1,811
Died, noncombat causes	10,298

South Vietnamese
Military: Killed in Action	220,357 [a]
Military: Wounded	499,026
Civilian: Killed	415,000 [b]
Civilian: Wounded	935,000 [c]

Viet Cong/North Vietnamese
Military: Killed	666,000 [d]
Civilian: North Vietnam	65,000

Third Nation Forces
Korean	4,407
Australian/New Zealand	469
Thailand	351

Source: Guenter Lewy, *America in Vietnam* (New York: Oxford University Press, 1978); Edgar O'Ballance, *The Wars in Vietnam* (New York: Hippocrene, 1975).

[a] O'Ballance gives 183,528.
[b] Lewy estimates 300,000; Kennedy gives 430,000.
[c] Lewy estimates 913,000; Kennedy gives 1,005,000.
[d] O'Ballance suggests 924,048.

TABLE XI

**The Technological Substitution of Firepower for Manpower:
Decline in Ratio of Casualties to Manpower Deployed, U.S. Forces, 1941–1971**

	RATE PER THOUSAND MAN–YEARS OF WAR EFFORT		
	WORLD WAR II (1941–45)	KOREA (1950–53)	INDOCHINA (1966–71)*
Battle deaths**	9.3	5.6	4.5
Wounded***	21.4	17.2	15.2
Total casualties (per thousand)	30.7	22.8	19.7

Source: SIPRI, *Anti-personnel Weapons* (London: Taylor & Francis, 1978), p.47.

*U.S. fiscal years, not calendar years.

**Includes those who died of wounds.

***Includes only non-fatal wounds requiring hospital treatment.

TABLE XII

**Improvement in the Prognosis for Battle Casualties Due to Advances in Medical Treatment and
Evaluation Procedures: Decline in the Ratio of Battle Deaths to Surviving Wounded, U.S. Forces, 1941–1971
(in thousands)**

	WORLD WAR II (1941–45)	KOREA (1950–53)	INDOCHINA (1966–71)*
Battle deaths**	291.6	33.6	44.0
Wounded***	670.8	103.3	147.2
Total Casualties	962.4	136.9	191.2
Ratio of dead to wounded	1:2.3	1:3.1	1:3.5

Source: SIPRI, *Anti-personnel Weapons* (London: Taylor & Francis, 1978), p.48.

*U.S. fiscal years, not calendar years.

**Includes those who died of wounds.

***Includes only non-fatal wounds requiring hospital treatment.

TABLE XIII

Indochinese Refugees Granted Permanent Residency Since 1975

COUNTRY	NUMBER
United States	220,000
France	50,000
Australia	21,000
Canada	13,000
West Germany	3,438
United Kingdom	1,477
Japan	3

Source: U.N. High Commissioner on Refugees, cited in *Newsweek* (July 2, 1979).

TABLE XIV

VC/NVA Assassinations and Abductions, 1957—1972

YEAR	ASSASSINATED	ABDUCTED
1957—60	1,700*	2,000*
1961	1,300*	1,318
1962	1,118	1,118
1963	827	1,596
1964	516	1,525
1965	305	1,730
1966	1,732	3,810
1967	3,707	5,357
1968	5,389	8,759
1969	6,202	6,289
1970	5,951	6,872
1971	3,573	5,006
1972	4,405	13,119
Total:	36,725	58,499

Source: Douglas Pike, *The Viet-Cong Strategy of Terror* (Saigon, 1970), p.82; Guenter Lewy, *America in Vietnam* (New York: Oxford University Press, 1978), p.454.

*Estimated.

Weapons Development and Policies

The United States exploited its advantage in weapons technology to develop new antipersonnel, incendiary, electronic and chemical devices.

4895. Barkam, Stuart. "Bringing the Toys Home from Vietnam." *New Scientist* 54 (June 15, 1972): 619–621.

4896. Burshop, E.H.S. "Scientists and Soldiers." *Bulletin of the Atomic Scientists* 30 (Sept. 1974): 4–8. Burshop discusses the social responsibility of scientists.

4897. Crouch, B. "Roll Back the Curtain of the Night." *Air Force Magazine* 54 (Jan. 1971): 36–38.

4898. "DDR&E Looks for Solutions to Next Vietnam." *Space/Aeronautics* 46 (Oct. 1966): 25, 30, 34.

4899. Erikson, Arthur. "Air Force Plans with Computers, Army Sees by Starlight." *Electronics* 43 (Oct. 26, 1970): 70–77.

4900. Ezell, E.C. "The Search for a Lightweight Rifle: The M14 and M16 Rifles." Ph.D. dissertation, Case Western Reserve University, 1969.

4901. Famiglietti, G. "Hardware Being Battle-Tested in Vietnam." *Data* 12 (May 1967): 18–21.

4902. "Fighting Guerrillas from the Lab." *Time* 69 (Oct. 7, 1966): 69–70.

4903. Hamlin, R.E. "Side-Firing Weapon Systems: A New Application of an Old Concept." *Air University Review* 21 (Jan.–Feb. 1970): 77–88.

4904. Hymoff, Edward. "Stalemate in Indo-China: Technology vs. Guerrillas." *Bulletin of the Atomic Scientists* 27 (Nov. 1971): 27–30.

4905. Jaubert, A. "Zapping the Viet Cong by Computer." *New Scientist* 53 (Mar. 30, 1972): 685–688.

4906. Kalisch, R.B., and T.P. Baker, Jr. "DOD Basic Research and Limited Conflict." *Office of Aerospace Research Reviews* 7 (July 1968): 10–11.

4907. Kanegis, A., et al. *Weapons for Counterinsurgency: Chemical/Biological, Antipersonnel, Incendiary.* Philadelphia: American Friends Service Committee, 1970.

4908. Kinnard, H.W.O. "U.S. Weapons in Vietnam: Are They Good Enough?" *U.S. News and World Report* 62 (Feb. 6, 1967): 68–71.

4909. Kirchner, D.P. "Antiguerilla Armament." *Ordnance* 56 (Sept.–Oct. 1971): 127–130.

4910. Ludwigsen, E.C. "The Technology Explosion and the Coming Generation of Army Weapons and Equipment." *Army* 19 (Oct. 1969): 147–158.

4911. Mason, John F. "Jungle Fighter on Chesapeake Bay." *Electronics* 40 (Jan. 23, 1967): 153–154, 158–159.

4912. ———. "The War that Needs Electronics." *Electronics* 39 (May 16, 1966): 96–118.

4913. McEvoy, Robert W. "Limited War Lab: Development Agency for Vietnam Material." *Data* 10 (Dec. 1965): 43–45.

4914. McLean, Donald B., ed. *Guide to Combat Weapons in Southeast Asia.* Forest Grove, OR: Normount Technical Publications, 1971.

4915. "New Weapons for Vietnam War." *U.S. News and World Report* 65 (Aug. 19, 1968): 75.

4916. O'Ballance, Edgar. "The Battlefield at Night." *United Service Institution of India Journal* 99 (Apr.–June 1969): 148–152.

4917. Pay, R. "Nighttime T.V. System Gets Vietnam Use." *Technology Week* 19 (Dec. 19, 1966): 25–26.

4918. "Pentagon Stresses Tactical Gear to Meet Needs of Vietnam Conflict." *Electronics* 40 (Jan. 9, 1967): 135–138.

4919. Smith, D.A. "Educated Missiles." *Ordnance* 56 (Mar.–Apr. 1972): 384–385.

4920. U.S. House. Committee on Armed Services. Hearings; *The M-16 Rifle Program.* 90th Cong., 1st sess., May 15–Aug. 22, 1967.

4921. ———. Report; *The M-16 Rifle Program.* 90th Cong., 1st sess., Oct. 19, 1967.

4922. ———. Report; *Selected Aspects of M-16 Rifle Program Contracts.* 90th Cong., 1st sess., Oct. 11, 1968.

4923. U.S. Senate. Committee on Armed Services. Hearings: *Additional Procurement of M-16 Rifles.* 90th Cong., 2d sess., June 19–20, 1968.

4924. "U.S. Weapons in Vietnam." *Interavia* 22 (May 1967): 256–261.

4925. Weller, Jac. "Good and Bad Weapons for Vietnam." *Military Review* 48 (Oct. 1968): 57–64.

ELECTRONIC BATTLEFIELD

4926. Allman, T.D. "The Blind Bombers." *Far Eastern Economic Review* 75 (Jan. 29, 1972): 18–20.

4927. "Congress Briefed on Electronic Battlefield." *Armed Forces Journal* 108 (Dec. 21, 1970): 10–11.

4928. Deane, John R., Jr. "The Electronic Battlefield." *Congressional Record* 116 (Nov. 23, 1970): S18711–S18719.

4929. Dickson, Paul. *The Electronic Battlefield.* Bloomington: Indiana University Press, 1976. This is a popular, general account.

4930. _____., and John Rothschild. "The Electronic Battlefield: Wiring Down the War." *Washington Monthly* 3 (May 1971): 6–14.

4931. Frisbee, John L. "Igloo White." *Air Force Magazine* 54 (June 1971): 48–53.

4932. Haseltine, William. "The Automated Air War." *New Republic* 165 (Oct. 16, 1971): 15–17.

4933. Heiman, G. "Beep to Bang." *Armed Forces Management* 16 (July 1970): 36–39.

4934. Leary, F. "Finding the Enemy." *Space/Aeronautics* 47 (Apr. 1967): 92–104.

4935. McClintic, R.G. "Rolling Back the Night." *Army* 19 (Aug. 1969): 28–35.

4936. Malloy, Michael. "The Death Harvesters." *Far Eastern Economic Review* 75 (Jan. 29, 1972): 16–20.

4937. National Action/Research on the Military–Industrial Complex [NARMIC]. *The Components and Manufacture of the Electronic Battlefield.* Philadelphia: American Friends Service Committee, 1971.

4938. Norman, Lloyd. "McNamara's Fence: Our Eyes and Ears Along the DMZ." *Army* 18 (Aug. 1968): 28–32.

4939. Proxmire, Senator William. "Pentagon Conceals Facts on 3 Billion Dollar Electronic Battlefields." *Congressional Record* 117 (Mar. 23, 1971): 7453.

4940. _____. "Point of Personal Privilege [Electronic Battlefield]." *Congressional Record* 116 (July 13, 1970): 23822.

4941. Reid, M. "Turning Night into Day." *Electronics* 39 (Sept. 5, 1966): 139–141.

4942. Seigel, L. "Vietnam's Electronic Battlefield." *Pacific Research and World Empire Telegram* 2 (Sept.–Oct. 1971): 1–8.

4943. "The Silent War in Vietnam." *Atlas* 21 (Feb. 1972): 30–31.

4944. "Southeast Asia Sensor Fields: More Eyes and Ears." *Armed Forces Journal* 109 (Mar. 1, 1971): 38–39.

4945. U.S. Senate. Committee on Armed Services. Hearings; *Investigation into Electronic Battlefield Program.* 91st Cong., 2d sess., Nov. 18–24, 1970.

ANTIPERSONNEL WEAPONS

Critics of the war charged that the United States employed illegal, or at least inhumane, air-delivered fragmentation bombs and that the M-16's high velocity bullets reacted much like dum-dums. See Kanegis (4907) and SIPRI (4952) for discussions.

4946. Council on Economic Priorities. *Efficiency in Death.* New York: Harper & Row, 1970. [manufacturers of antipersonnel weapons]

4947. Dimond, F.C., and N.M. Rich. "M-16 Rifle Wounds in Vietnam." *Journal of Trauma* 7:5 (1967): 619–625.

4948. Krepon, Michael. "Weapons Potentially Inhuman: The Case of Cluster Bombs." In *The Vietnam War and International Law*, edited by R.A. Falk. 4 vols. Princeton, NJ: Princeton University Press, 1976, IV, 266–274.

4949. Members of the Japanese Scientific Committee. "Combined Report on Anti-Personnel Bombs." In *Against the Crime of Silence*, edited by J. Duffett. New York: Simon & Schuster, 1970, 258–265. [on the Cannister Bomb Unit (CBU) or pineapple bomb]

4950. Prokosch, E. "Anti-Personnel Weapons." *International Social Science Journal* 28:2 (1976): 341–358.

4951. _____. *The Simple Art of Murder: Antipersonnel Weapons and Their Developers.* National Action/Research on the Military-Industrial Complex [NARMIC]. Philadelphia: American Friends Service Committee, 1972.

4952. Stockholm International Peace Research Institute [SIPRI]. "The War in Indo-China, 1961–75." *Anti-Personnel Weapons.* London: Taylor & Francis, 1978, 25–42. This is an excellent survey of the issue beyond Vietnam.

4953. Vigier, Jean Pierre. "Technical Aspects of Fragmentation Bombs." In *Against the Crime of Silence*, edited by J. Duffett. New York: Simon & Schuster, 1970, 249–258.

Ecocide

Ecocide *came to identify those military activities which could result in long-term damage to the Southeast Asian environment. Westing (4967) and Orians and Pfeiffer (4961) are recognized authorities on this issue, and the study by Lewallen (4959) is a good summary.*

Bibliography

4954.   U.S. Environmental Science Services Administration. *An Annotated Bibliography of the Climate of the Republic of Vietnam.* Weather Bureau WB/BC–90. Silver Springs, MD, 1967.

General Accounts

4955.   Allman, T.D. "How To Kill the Earth." *Far Eastern Economic Review* 77 (Aug. 19, 1972): 12–13.

4956.   Falk, Richard A. "Environmental Warfare and Ecocide: Facts, Appraisal and Proposals." *Revue Belge de Droit International* 9:1 (1973). [also in *Bulletin of Peace Proposals* 4:1 (1973): 80–96]

4957.   Johnstone, L. Craig. "Ecocide and the Geneva Protocol." *Foreign Affairs* 49 (July 1971): 711–720.

4958.   Karnow, Stanley. "Vietnam: Legacy of Desolation." *New Republic* 170 (Mar. 16, 1974): 18–19.

4959.   Lewallen, J. *The Ecology of Devastation: Indochina.* Baltimore: Penguin, 1971.

4960.   Neilands, J.B. "Ecocide in Vietnam." In *Why Are We Still in Vietnam?*, edited by S. Brown and L. Acklund. New York: Vintage, 1970, 87–97.

4961.   Orians, Gordon H., and E.W. Pfeiffer. "Ecological Effects of the War in Vietnam." *Science* 168 (May 1, 1970): 544–554. [excellent survey]

4962.   Pfeiffer, E.W. "Ecological Effects of the Vietnam War." *Science Journal* 5 (Feb. 1969): 33–38.

4963.   Schell, Orville, Jr. "Silent Vietnam: How We Invented Ecocide and Killed a Country." *Look* 35 (July 1971): 55, 57–58.

4964.   Stockholm International Peace Research Institute. *Ecological Consequences of the Second Indochina War*, by Arthur H. Westing. Cambridge, MA: MIT Press, 1976. This is the most complete assessment of damage.

4965.   "Vietnam: Jungle Conflict Poses New R & D Problems." *Science* 152 (Apr. 8, 1966): 187–190.

4966.   Weisberg, Barry ed. *Ecocide in Indochina: The Ecology of War.* San Francisco: Canfield Press, 1970.

4967.   Westing, Arthur H. "Ecocide in Indochina." *Natural History* 80 (Mar. 1971): 56–61, 88.

4968.   _____. "Endangered Species and Habitats of Viet Nam." *Environmental Conservation* 8:1 (1981): 59–62.

4969.   _____. "Environmental Consequences of the Second Indochina War: A Case Study." *Ambio* 4:5/6 (1975): 216–222.

HERBICIDES

President Kennedy authorized the use of herbicides in Vietnam, and the Saigon government approved. Herbicides were used to kill foliage which provided VC/NVA forces with cover and to destroy crops destined for enemy forces; these operations were largely carried out under Operation RANCH HAND (1961–1967). Critics began as early as 1963 to protest that the use of these defoliates could have disastrous long-term effects on South Vietnam's terrain; see Westing account for SIPRI (4964).

Bibliography

4970.   Westing, Arthur H. *Herbicides as Weapons: A Bibliography.* Los Angeles: California State University, Center for the Study of Armament and Disarmament, 1973.

General Accounts

4971.   "AAAS Board of Directors: A Statement on the Use of Herbicides in Vietnam." *Science* 161 (July 19, 1968): 253–256.

4972.   Betts, Russell, and Frank Denton. *An Evaluation of Chemical Crop Destruction in Vietnam.* RM–5446–ISA/ARPA. Santa Monica, CA: Rand Corp., 1967.

4973.   Boffery, Philip M. "Defense Issues Summary of Defoliation Study." *Science* 159 (Feb. 9, 1968): 613.

4974.   _____. "Herbicides in Vietnam: AAAS Study Finds Widespread Devastation." *Science* 171 (Jan. 8, 1971): 43–47.

4975.   _____. "Herbicides in Vietnam: AAAS Study Runs Into a Military Roadblock." *Science* 170 (Oct. 2, 1970): 42–45.

4976.   Brightman, C. "Weed Killers and the University at the Front." *Viet Report* 2:4/5 (1966): 9–14, 33–48.

4977.   Brown, D.E. "The Use of Herbicides in War: A

Political/Military Analysis." In *The Control of Chemical and Biological Weapons.* New York: Carnegie Endowment for International Peace, 1971, 39–63.

4978. Commoner, Barry. "Toxicologic Time Bomb." *Hospital Practice* 13 (June 1978): 56–59.

4979. Constable, J., and Matthew S. Meselson. "Ecological Impact of Large Scale Defoliation in Vietnam." *Sierra Club Bulletin* 56 (Apr. 1971): 4–9.

4980. Cook, R.E., W. Haseltine, and A.W. Galston. "What Have We Done to Vietnam?" *New Republic* 162 (Jan. 10, 1970): 18–21.

4981. "Defoliants, Deformities: What Risk?" *Medical World News* 11 (Feb. 27, 1970): 15–17.

4982. "Defoliant Fallout Lingers in South Vietnam." *Science Digest* 76 (Aug. 1974): 20–21.

4983. Fair, Stanley, D. "No Place to Hide: How Defoliants Expose the Viet Cong." *Army* 14 (Feb. 1963): 54–55.

4984. Galston, A.W. "Herbicides in Vietnam." *New Republic* 157 (Nov. 25, 1967): 19–21.

4985. _____. "Military Uses of Herbicides in Vietnam." *New Scientist* 38 (June 13, 1968): 583–584.

4986. _____. "Warfare With Herbicides in Vietnam." In *Patient Earth*, edited by J. Harte and R.H. Socolow. New York: Holt, Rinehart & Winston, 1971, 136–150.

4987. Gonzalez, A.F. "Defoliation—A Controversial U.S. Mission in Vietnam." *Data on Defense and Civil Systems* 13 (Oct. 1968): 12–15.

4988. "Government Begins Buildup of Defoliants to Meet Increasing Use in Vietnam." *Chemical and Engineering News* 46 (May 27, 1968): 26–27.

4989. Gunby, Phil. "Plenty of Fuel for Agent Orange Dispute." *Journal of the American Medical Association* 242 (Aug. 17, 1979): 593–597.

4990. Holden, Constance. "Agent Orange Furor Continues to Build." *Science* 205 (Aug. 24, 1979): 770–772.

4991. Howard, J.D. "Herbicides in Support of Counterinsurgency Operations: A Cost-Effectiveness Study." M.S. thesis, U.S. Naval Postgraduate School, Monterey, CA.

4992. McConnel, A.F., Jr. "Mission: Ranch Hand." *Air University Review* 21 (Jan.–Feb. 1970): 89–94.

4993. McElheny, Victor. "Herbicides in Vietnam: Juggernaut Out of Control." *Technology Review* 73 (Mar. 1971): 12–13.

4994. Mayer, Jean. "Starvation as a Weapon: Herbicides in Vietnam." *Scientist and Citizen* 9 (Aug.–Sept. 1967): 115–121.

4995. _____, and Victor W. Sidel. "Crop Destruction in South Vietnam." *Christian Century* 83 (June 29, 1966): 829–832.

4996. National Academy of Sciences-National Research Council. *The Effects of Herbicides in South Vietnam.* 20 vols. Washington, DC: National Academy of Sciences, 1974.

4997. Nelson, Bryce. "Herbicides in Vietnam: AAAS Board Seeks Field Study." *Science* 163 (Jan. 3, 1969): 59–60.

4998. Pfeiffer, E.W. "Operation Ranch Hand: The U.S. Herbicide Program." *Bulletin of the Atomic Scientists* 38 (May 1982): 20–24.

4999. "Serious Defoliant Damage in Vietnam." *Science News* 105 (Mar. 16, 1974): 174–175.

5000. Shapley, Deborah. "Herbicides: AAAS Study Finds Dioxin in Vietnamese Fish." *Science* 180 (Apr. 20, 1973): 285–286.

5001. _____. "Herbicides: Academy Finds Damage in Vietnam After a Fight of Its Own." *Science* 183 (Mar. 22, 1974): 1177–1180.

5002. _____. "Herbicides: DOD Study of Viet Use Damns With Faint Praise." *Science* 177 (Sept. 1, 1972): 776–779.

5003. Stockholm International Peace Research Institute. *The Rise of CB Weapons.* Vol. I in *The Problem of Chemical and Biological Warfare.* 6 vols. Stockholm: Almqvist & Wiksell, 1971, 162–185. [a fine survey, use with later SIPRI study]

5004. Swanson, C.W. "Reforestation in the Republic of Vietnam." *Journal of Forestry* 73 (June 1975): 367–371.

5005. Thomas, William L., Jr. "The Use of Herbicides in South Vietnam: Resultant Economic Stress and Settlement Changes." *Pacific Viewpoint* [New Zealand] 16:1 (1975): 1–25.

5006. Thomasson, W.A. "Deadly Legacy: Dioxin and the Vietnam Veteran." *Bulletin of the Atomic Scientists* 35 (May 1979): 15–19.

5007. Tschirley, Fred H. "Defoliation in Vietnam." *Science* 163 (Feb. 21, 1969): 779–786.

5008. "2,4,5–T: Where Next." *Lancet* 2 (Nov. 24, 1979): 1114–1115. [down-plays the crisis]

5009. U.S. House. Committee on Interstate and Foreign

Commerce. Hearings; *Agent Orange: Exposure of Vietnam Veterans.* 96th Cong., 2d sess., 1980.

5010. _____. Committee on Science and Astronautics. Report; *Technology Assessment of Vietnam Defoliant Matter: A Case History*, by F.P. Huddle. 91st Cong., 1st sess., 1969.

5011. _____. Committee on Veteran's Affairs. Hearings; *Herbicide "Agent Orange."* 95th Cong., 2d sess., Oct. 11, 1978. [latent impact on veterans]

5012. U.S. Senate. Committee on Commerce. Subcommittee on Energy, Natural Resources and the Environment. Hearings; *Effects of 2,4,5–T on Man and Environment.* 91st Cong., 2d sess., Apr. 1970.

5013. "Viet Deformities: Will We Ever Know?" *Medical World News* 12 (Jan. 29, 1971): 4–5.

5014. Wade, Nicholas. "Viets and Vets Fear Herbicide Health Effects." *Science* 204 (May 25, 1979): 817.

5015. Westing, Arthur H. "Ecological Effects of Military Defoliation on the Forests of South Vietnam." *BioScience* 21 (Sept. 1, 1971): 893–898.

5016. _____. "Forestry and the War in South Vietnam." *Journal of Forestry* 69 (Nov. 1971): 777–783.

5017. _____. "Herbicides as Agents of Chemical Warfare: Their Impact in Relation to the Geneva Protocol of 1925." *Environmental Affairs* 1:3 (1971–1972): 578–586.

5018. _____. "Postwar Forestry in North Vietnam." *Journal of Forestry* 72:3 (1974): 153–156.

5019. Whiteside, Thomas. *Defoliation.* New York: Ballantine, 1970.

5020. _____. *The Withering Rain: America's Herbicidal Folly.* New York: Dutton, 1971.

WEATHER MODIFICATION

Operation PONY EXPRESS, in 1966, attempted to extend the wet season by using rainmaking techniques.

5021. "Meet the Mets: They Make Weather Work For the Army." *Army Digest* 26 (Feb. 1971): 50–51.

5022. "Military Rainmaking Confirmed by U.S." *Science News* 105 (May 25, 1974): 335.

5023. Norman, Colin. "Pentagon Admits Viet Nam Rainmaking." *Nature* 249 (May 31, 1974): 402.

5024. Ognibene, Peter J. "Making War With the Weather." *New Republic* 168 (Sept. 30, 1972): 12–14.

5025. Shapley, Deborah. "Rainmaking: Rumored Used Over Laos Alarms Arms Experts, Scientists." *Science* 176 (June 16, 1972): 1216–1220.

5026. Sheehan, L.J. "Atmospheric Visibility in Southeast Asia." *Office of Aerospace Research Reviews* 8 (May–June 1969): 12–13.

5027. Studer, T.A. "Weather Modification in Support of Military Operations." *Air University Review* 20 (Nov.–Dec. 1969): 44–50.

5028. "U.S. Military Weather Modification Activities in South-East Asia." *Congressional Record* 120 (May 20, 1974): S8574–S8575.

CRATERING

Deep bomb craters, from B-52 raids particularly, created numerous problems that included damaging the ecology.

5029. Braun, Saul. "Professor Westing Counts the Craters." *Saturday Review* 55 (Aug. 19, 1972): 18–20.

5030. Pfeiffer, E.W. "Land War, 1: Craters." *Environment* 13 (Nov. 1971): 1–5.

5031. Westing, Arthur H., and E.W. Pfeiffer. "The Cratering of Indochina." *Scientific American* 226 (May 1972): 20–29.

ROME PLOW

An example of the Army's use of Rome plows, giant earth-scrappers, is Operation PAUL BUNYAN (September 1966) carried out by special engineer units.

5032. Condominas, Georges. *We Have Eaten the Forests.* Translated by A. Foulke. New York: Hill & Wang, 1977.

5033. Draper, S.E. "Land Clearing in the Delta." *Military Engineer* 63 (July–Aug. 1971): 257–259.

5034. Kerver, Thomas J. "To Clear the Way." *National Defense* 58 (Mar.–Apr. 1974): 454–455.

5035. "Land Clearing Emerges as a Top Tactic of the War." *Engineering News Record* 184 (June 15, 1970): 27.

5036. Martin, John E. "Rome Plow Operations." *Field Artilleryman*, no. 49 (Feb. 1972): 5–8.

5037. Ploger, Robert R. "Different War—Same Old Ingenuity." *Army* 18 (Sept. 1968): 70–75.

5038. Westing, A.H. "Land War. II: Levelling the Jungle." *Environment* 13 (Nov. 1971): 8–12.

FIRE-STORMS

Apparently dissatisfied with the slow-working defoliants, the U.S. Army launched Operation SHERWOOD FOREST (1965–1966) in an attempt to burn the Boi Loi Woods north of Saigon, but American officials reported that the fire apparently created a thunderstorm which put out the flames. Operation PINK ROSE (January–April 1967) in War Zones C and D, northeast of Saigon, had the same objective, see SIPRI's Incendiary Weapons *(5088), 57–59. It is possible that some efforts were more successful than officially announced.*

5039.   Bachelder, R.B., and H.F. Hirt. *Fire in Tropical Forests and Grasslands.* ES–23. Natick, MA: Army Laboratories Earth Sciences Division, 1966.

5040.   Broido, A. "Effects of Fire on Major Ecosystems." In *Ecological Effects of Nuclear War,* edited by G.M. Woodwell. Publication no. 917. Upton, NY: Brookhaven National Laboratory, 1963, 11–19.

5041.   Kozlowski, T.T., and C.E. Ahlgren, eds. *Fire and Ecosystems.* New York: Academic Press, 1974.

5042.   Reinhold, R. "U.S. Attempted to Ignite Vietnam Forests in 66–67." *New York Times* (July 21, 1972): 1, 2.

5043.   Shapley, Deborah. "Technology in Vietnam: Fire Storm Project Fizzled Out." *Science* 177 (July 21, 1972): 239–241.

Chemical Warfare

Questions were raised about the legal and ethical use of such chemical warfare devices used in Vietnam as tear gas, herbicides (treated above), napalm and white phosphorous—see Neilands, "Vietnam: Progress of the Chemical War" (5053).

5044.   Beecher, William. "Chemicals vs. the Viet Cong: 'Right' or 'Wrong.'" *National Guardsman* 20 (Feb. 1966): 2–6.

5045.   Briantais, J.M., et al. *Massacres: la guerre chimique en Asie du sud-est.* Paris: François Maspero, 1970.

5046.   Do Xuan Sang. "U.S. Crimes of Chemical Warfare in South Vietnam." In *U.S. War Crimes in Vietnam.* Hanoi: Juridical Sciences Institute, State Commission of Social Sciences, 1968.

5047.   Etzioni, Amitai. "More 'Humane' Warfare in Vietnam." *War/Peace Report* 6 (May 1966): 5–6.

5048.   Guignard, J.P. *Vietnam: Documents sur la guerre chimique et bactériologique.* Genève: Comité National Suisse d'Aide au Vietnam, 1967.

5049.   Kahn, M.F. "CBW in Use: Vietnam." In *CBW: Chemical and Biological Warfare,* edited by Steven Rose. Boston: Beacon, 1968, 87–98.

5050.   Lederer, E. "Report on Chemical Warfare in Vietnam." In *Prevent the Crime of Silence,* edited by K. Coates et al. London: Allen Lane, 1971.

5051.   McCarthy, R.D. *The Ultimate Folly: War by Pestilence, Asphyxiation, Defoliation.* New York: Knopf, 1969.

5052.   Neilands, J.B., et al. *Harvest of Death: Chemical Warfare in Cambodia and Indochina.* New York: Free Press, 1972.

5053.   ———. "Vietnam: Progress of the Chemical War." *Asian Studies* 10 (Mar. 1970): 209–229.

5054.   Nguyen Khac Vien, ed. "Chemical Warfare." *Vietnamese Studies,* no. 29 (1971).

5055.   Pfeiffer, E.W. "Chemical Warfare in Vietnam and the American Scientific Community." *Scientific World* 12 (June 1968): 16–19.

5056.   Pham Van Bach. "Law and the Use of Chemical Warfare in Vietnam." *Scientific World* 15 (June 1971): 12–14.

5057.   Rothschild, J.H. "Chemical and Biological Warfare in Vietnam." *Science* 167 (Apr. 1967): 167–168.

5058.   "Silent Weapons: Role of Chemicals in Lower Case Warfare." *Army Digest* 23 (Nov. 1968): 6–11.

5059.   U.S. Army. Headquarters Command. *Employment of Riot Control Agents, Flame, Smoke and Herbicides in Counterguerrilla Operations.* Washington, DC: GPO, 1966.

5060.   U.S. Army, Navy, and Air Force. *Armed Forces Doctrine for Chemical and Biological Weapons Employment and Defense.* [FM 101–40; NWP 36(c); AFM 355–2; LFM 03] Washington, DC, Apr. 1964.

5061.   Ver Wey, W.D. "Chemical Warfare in Vietnam: Legal or Illegal?" *Netherlands International Law Review* 18:2 (1971): 217–244.

TEAR GAS AND OTHER GASES

5062.   *American Use of War Gases and World Public Opinion.* Hanoi: Foreign Languages Publishing House, 1966.

5063. Blumenfield, S., and Matthew S. Meselson. "The Military Value and Political Implications of the Use of Riot Control Agents in Warfare." In *The Control of Chemical and Biological Warfare*. New York: Carnegie Endowment for International Peace, 1971.

5064. Goldblat, J. "Are Tear Gas and Herbicides Permitted Weapons?" *Science and Public Affairs* 26 (Apr. 1970): 13–16.

5065. Hamm, Anthony B. *CS [tear gas] Can Save Lives.*" *Infantry* 59 (Nov.–Dec. 1969): 30–31.

5066. Harrigan, Anthony. "The Case for Gas Warfare." *Armed Forces Chemical Journal* 17:2 (1963): 12–13.

5067. "How Gas Is Being Used in Vietnam." *U.S. News and World Report* 60 (Jan. 31, 1966): 8, 10.

5068. "How the State Department Tried to Explain Away the Use of 'Non-lethal' Gases." *I.F. Stone's Weekly* 13 (Mar. 29, 1965): 2–3.

5069. Meselson, Matthew S. "Tear Gas in Vietnam and the Return of Poison Gas." *Bulletin of the Atomic Scientists* 27 (Mar. 1971): 17–19.

5070. Neilands, J.B. "Gas Warfare in Vietnam in Perspective." In his *Harvest of Death: Chemical Warfare in Vietnam and Cambodia*. New York: Free Press, 1972.

5071. Savitz, David. "Gas and Guerrillas: A Word of Caution." *New Republic* 154 (Mar. 19, 1966): 13–14.

5072. Smith, J.A. "Gas in Vietnam: Opening Wedge for 'CB' Warfare." *National Guardian* 17 (Apr. 3, 1965): 3.

5073. U.S. Army. *Employment of Riot Control Agents, Flame, Smoke, Antiplant Agents and Personnel Detectors in Counter-guerrilla Operations*. Training Circular 3–16. Washington, DC: GPO, Apr. 1969.

5074. Van Riper, Paul K. "Riot Control Agents in Offensive Operations." *Marine Corps Gazette* 56 (Apr. 1972): 18–23.

"YELLOW RAIN" CHARGES

In 1981, charges were pressed against the Soviet Union and Vietnam for using chemical/biological weapons to defeat Laotian rebels. The evidence does not appear to be as conclusive at this time as Reagan officials claim.

5075. Burt, Richard R. "Use of Chemical Weapons in Asia." *U.S. Department of State Bulletin*. 82 (Jan. 1982): 52–54.

5076. Joyce, Christopher. "New Evidence of Biological War in SE Asia." *New Scientist* (Nov. 1981): 480–481.

5077. Kalven, Jamie. "'Yellow Rain': The Public Evidence." *Bulletin of the Atomic Scientists* 38 (May 1982): 15–20.

5078. Le Moyne, James. "The 'Yellow Rain.'" *Newsweek* 98 (Sept. 28, 1981): 44.

5079. Lerner, Michael A. "Yellow Rain Dance." *New Republic* 186 (Feb. 3, 1982): 13–15.

5080. Seagrave, Sterling. *Yellow Rain: A Journey Through the Terror of Chemical Warfare*. New York: Evans, 1981. This history of chemical and biological warfare focuses on Laos and Afghanistan.

5081. United Nations. Secretariat. *Report of the Group of Experts to Investigate Reports on the Alleged Use of Chemical Weapons*. A/36/613. Nov. 20, 1981.

5082. Wade, Nicholas. "Toxin Warfare Charges May Be Premature." *Science* 214 (Oct. 2, 1981): 34.

NAPALM

Public concern centered on civilian casualties resulting from the use of napalm by U.S. aircraft.

5083. Cushmac, George E. "Enemy Napalm in Vietnam." *Army* 18 (Aug. 1968): 58–59. [used in VC/NVA flame-throwers]

5084. Dreyfus, J.C. "Napalm and Its Effects on Human Beings." In *Prevent the Crime of Silence*, edited by K. Coates, et al. London: Allen Lane, 1971, 191–198.

5085. Kusterer, D.F. *The Application of Air-Delivered Incendiary Weapons to Limited War in Southeast Asia*. NOTS Technical Publication 4229. China Lake, CA: U.S. Naval Ordance Test Station, 1966.

5086. Reich, Peter, and Victor W. Sidel. "Napalm." *New England Journal of Medicine* 277 (July 13, 1967): 87ff.

5087. Rusk, H.A. "Vietnam Medicine I. Visiting American Team . . . Reports to Johnson on Napalm Burns." *New York Times*, Oct. 1, 1967.

5088. SIPRI. *Incendiary Weapons*. Cambridge, MA: MIT Press, 1975. This is the best survey available with specifics on Vietnam.

5089. Takman, John. *Napalm: Streitschrift und Dokumentation*. Berlin: Union Verlag, 1968.

POWs and MIAs

Most of the U.S. POWs were pilots shot down over North Vietnam; they were frequently treated contrary to international law. In a political sense, they were hostages in diplomatic negotiations and in domestic affairs. For VC/NVA prisoners, see Chapter 3. Most VC defectors and those captured in the field were encouraged to enlist in the South Vietnamese armed forces.

5090.   "Ambassador Bruce Discusses Problem of U.S. Prisoners of War in Southeast Asia." *U.S. Department of State Bulletin* 63 (Dec. 21, 1970): 737–747.

5091.   Aument, Shary. *Unforgettable Faces: Drawings of American Prisoners of War and Men Missing In Action In Southeast Asia.* Kalamazoo, MI: Leaders Press, 1972.

5092.   Borman, Frank. "U.S. Prisoners of War in Southeast Asia." *U.S. Department of State Bulletin* 63 (Oct. 12, 1970): 405–418.

5093.   Branch, Taylor. "Prisoners of War, Prisoners of Peace." *Washington Monthly* 4 (Aug. 1972): 39–54.

5094.   Buckley, Priscilla L. "Prisoners of War: They Also Serve." *National Review* 22 (July 28, 1970): 786–787ff.

5095.   Carr, William K. "The Faceless P.O.W." *Naval War College Review* 30 (Fall 1977): 88–96.

5096.   Casella, A. "The Politics of Prisoners of War." *New York Times Magazine* (Apr. 28, 1972): 9ff.

5097.   Colebrook, Joan. "Prisoners of War." *Commentary* 57 (Jan. 1974): 30–37.

5098.   Cooper, Chester L. "The POWs." *New Republic* 172 (May 3, 1975): 12. [political aspects]

5099.   Dunn, J. Howard, and W. Hays Parks. "If I Become a Prisoner of War. . . ." *U.S. Naval Institute Proceedings* 102 (Aug. 1976): 18–27.

5100.   Dyke, J.M. "Nixon and the Prisoners of War." *New York Review of Books* (Jan. 7, 1971): 34ff.

5101.   Falk, Richard A. "The American POWs: Pawns in Power Politics." *Progressive* 35 (Mar. 1971): 13–21. Were POWs criminals for using illegal weapons?

5102.   Hemphill, John A. "PW and Captured Document Doctrine." *Military Review* 49 (Nov. 1969): 65–71.

5103.   Hutchinson, Simon. "Counter Insurgency: The Problem of Prisoners." *Journal of the Royal United Services Institute for Defence Studies* 116 (Sept. 1971): 48–51.

5104.   Kim, Samuel. *The American POWs.* Boston: Branden, 1978.

5105.   Krone, Robert M. "Politics and Prisoners of War." *Air University Review* 21 (Mar.–Apr. 1970): 74–86.

5106.   Lelyveld, Joseph. "Dear President Nixon: The Last 24 Hours Have Again Been Another Day of Pure Hell For Americans in Prison Camps, Cells and Cages in Southeast Asia." *New York Times Magazine* (Oct. 3, 1971): 14ff. This is from an Air Force newsletter to families of POWs or MIAs.

5107.   Lien, Maurice L. "The Plight of the Prisoners We Have Not Forgotten." *Air Force & Space Digest* 53 (June 1970): 32–37.

5108.   McCubbin, Hamilton I., et al. "Residuals of War: Families of Prisoners of War and Servicemen Missing in Action." *Journal of Social Issues* 31 (Fall 1975): 95–110.

5109.   Malloy, Michael. "Prisoners of War: Hanoi, Hurting Its Own Image." *Far Eastern Economic Review* 69 (July 30, 1970): 33–34.

5110.   Mims, Floyd C. "POWs: A Contrast of Values." *Retired Officer* 26 (July 1970): 17–20.

5111.   Neilands, J.B. "Due piloti americani ad Hanoi (Two American Pilots in Hanoi)." *Il Ponte* [Italy] 23:7/8 (1967): 926–928.

5112.   Ognibene, Peter J. "Rift in the Ranks: Politics and POWs." *New Republic* 166 (June 3, 1972): 17–19.

5113.   Reynolds, Jon A. "Question of Honor." *Air University Review* 28 (May–June 1977): 104–110.

5114.   Richardson, Walton K. "Prisoners of War as Instruments of Foreign Policy." *Naval War College Review* 23 (Sept. 1970): 47–64.

5115.   Stockstill, Louis R. "The Forgotten Americans of the Vietnam War." *Air Force & Space Digest* 52 (Oct. 1969): 38–49.

5116.   Sullivan, William H. "Department Gives Views on Proposed Congressional Resolution on U.S. Prisoners of War in Southeast Asia." *U.S. Department of State Bulletin* 62 (May 25, 1970): 668–671.

5117.   U.S. House. Committee on Armed Services. Hearings; *Problems of Prisoners of War and Their Families.* 91st Cong., 2d sess., Mar. 6, 1970.

5118.   _____. Hearings; *American Prisoners of War in Vietnam.* 91st Cong., 1st sess., Nov. 13–14, 1969.

5119. _____. Committee on Foreign Affairs. Hearings; *American Prisoners of War in Southeast Asia, 1970*. 91st Cong., 2d sess., Apr.–May, 1970.

5120. _____. Hearings; *American Prisoners of War in Southeast Asia, 1971*. 92d Cong., 1st sess., 1971.

5121. _____. Hearings; *American Prisoners of War in Southeast Asia, 1972*. 92d Cong., 2d sess., 1972.

5122. U.S. Senate. Committee on Foreign Relations. Hearings; *Bombing Operations and the Prisoners-of-War Rescue Mission in North Vietnam*. 91st Cong., 2d sess., Nov. 24, 1970.

5123. _____. Hearings; *U.S. POW's and MIA's in Southeast Asia*. 93d Cong., 2d sess., Jan. 28, 1974.

5124. _____. Report; *American Prisoners of War in Southeast Asia*. Calendar no. 698. Rpt no. 91–705. 91st Cong., 2d sess., Feb. 16, 1970.

5125. "USAF's Prisoners of War or Missing in Action." *Air Force & Space Digest* 53 (June 1970): 38–39.

5126. Wilson, Paul E. "Three C's: The Code, the Convention, the Conflict." *Marine Corps Gazette* 54 (Apr. 1970): 37–41.

MIAs

The Missing-in-Action personnel were largely pilots downed over enemy-held territory; even after the armistice and the subsequent North Vietnamese victory, Washington still pressed for an accounting of the MIAs.

5127. Clarke, Douglas L. *The Missing Man: Politics and the MIA*. National Defense University, Research Directorate. Washington, DC: GPO, 1971.

5128. Habib, Philip C. "Department Discusses Continuing Efforts to Account for American Missing in Indochina." *U.S. Department of State Bulletin* 75 (Aug. 16, 1976): 249–253.

5129. Ludwigsen, Eric C. "Missing; Dead or Captured?" *Army* 20 (Feb. 1970): 24–32.

5130. "Presidential Commission Visits Vietnam and Laos to Seek Information on Missing Americans." *U.S. Department of State Bulletin* 76 (Apr. 18, 1977): 363–374.

5131. Schlitz, William P. "MIA/POW Action Report: The Stalemated Search for Our MIAs." *Air Force Magazine* 57 (Jan. 1974): 45–49.

5132. Standerwick, Caroline. "'Missing in Action':

How Agony of Vietnam Lingers." *U.S. News and World Report* 77 (Dec. 30, 1974): 30–31.

5133. U.S. House. Committee on Foreign Affairs. Hearings; *POW/MIA's: U.S. Policies and Procedures*. 96th Cong., 1st sess., Apr. 10, May 7, June 5, 1979.

5134. U.S. House. Committee on International Affairs. Hearings; *Americans Missing in Action in Southeast Asia*. 95th Cong., 2d sess., Aug. 9, Sept. 13, 1978.

5135. U.S. House. Select Committee on Missing Persons in Southeast Asia. Hearings; *Americans Missing in Southeast Asia*. 4 Pts. 94th Cong., 1st sess., Sept. 29, 1975–June 2, 1976.

TREATMENT OF POWs

Compare with "Personal Experiences," below, this chapter.

5136. Chafee, John H. "P.O.W. Treatment: Principles versus Propaganda." *U.S. Naval Institute Proceedings* 97 (July 1971): 14–17.

5137. David, Heather. "Ill-Treated POWs Ignored at Home." *Navy* 13 (June 1970): 22–28.

5138. Denno, B.F. "The Fate of American POWs in Vietnam." *Air Force & Space Digest* 51 (Feb. 1968): 40–45.

5139. Frisbee, John L. "Surviving in Hanoi's Prisons." *Air Force Magazine* 56 (June 1973): 28–33.

5140. Hauser, Rita E. "U.S. Brings Hanoi's Treatment of American Prisoners of War to Attention of U.N. Committee." *U.S. Department of State Bulletin* 61 (Dec. 1, 1969): 471–476.

5141. Levie, Howard S. "Maltreatment of Prisoners of War in Vietnam." *Boston University Law Review* 48 (1968): 323–359. [also in Falk, Vol. III, 361–397]

5142. Lewis, Anthony. "Torture in Hanoi." *New York Review of Books* (Mar. 7, 1974): 6ff. [review article]

5143. Rogers, Warren. "P.O.W. North Vietnam: Are U.S. Prisoners Mistreated?" *Look* 31 (July 25, 1967): 53–55.

5144. Schlitz, William P. "The POWs Return," *Air Force Magazine* 56 (Apr. 1973): 25–28.

5145. Shaffer, Helen B. "Treatment of War Prisoners." *Editorial Research Reports*, no. 2 (July 12, 1967): 1ff.

5146. Sullivan, William H. "Treatment of American Prisoners of War in North Vietnam." *U.S. Department of State Bulletin* 61 (Dec. 22, 1969): 596–599.

5147. Tuohy, W. "A Big 'Dirty' Little War." *New York Times Magazine* (Nov. 28, 1965): 43ff. U.S. soldiers and civilians were dragged by VC through villages and sometimes executed.

5148. "U.S. Prisoners in North Vietnam." *Life* 63 (Oct. 20, 1967): 21–34.

5149. Van Dyke, Jon M. "Prisoners from Hanoi: Were They Tortured?" *Nation* 209 (Oct. 6, 1969): 332, 334–335.

GENEVA CONVENTION AND POWs

5150. Falk, Richard A. "International Law Aspects of Repatriation of Prisoners of War During Hostilities." *American Journal of International Law* 67 (July 1973): 465–478.

5151. "The Geneva Convention and the Treatment of Prisoners of War in Vietnam." *Harvard Law Review* 80 (Feb. 1967): 851–868.

5152. Havens, Charles W., III. "Release and Repatriation of Vietnam Prisoners." *American Bar Association Journal* 57 (Jan. 1971): 41–44.

5153. "International Conference of the Red Cross Calls For Observance of the Geneva Convention on Prisoners of War...." *U.S. Department of State Bulletin* 61 (Oct. 13, 1969): 323–325.

5154. Kelly, Joseph B. "PW's as War Criminals." *Military Review* 52 (Jan. 1972): 91–96.

5155. Kornblit, Mitchell. "The Third Geneva Convention and Prisoners of War in Vietnam." *SAIS Review* 16 (Spring 1972): 35–51.

5156. Landen, Walter J. "Geneva Conventions: The Broken Rules." *U.S. Naval Institute Proceedings* 99 (Feb. 1973): 34–39.

5157. Levie, Howard S. "International Law Aspects of Repatriation of Prisoners of War During Hostilities: A Reply." *American Journal of International Law* 67 (Oct. 1973): 693–710.

5158. _____. "Procedures for the Protection of Prisoners of War in Viet-Nam: A Four Way Problem." *American Journal of International Law* 65 (Oct. 1971): 637ff.

5159. Pradelle, P. de la. "Le Nord-Viet Nam et les conventions humanitaires de Genève." *Revue Générale de Droit Internationale Public* (Apr.–June 1971): 313–332.

SONTAY RAID

U.S. commandos raided an abandoned former POW camp in North Vietnam on November 21, 1970.

5160. "Back to the Hills." *Economist* 237 (Nov. 28, 1970): 14–16.

5161. David, Heather. *Operation Rescue*. New York: Pinnacle, 1971.

5162. Schemmer, Benjamin F. *The Raid*. New York: Harper & Row, 1976.

PERSONAL EXPERIENCES

The following are personal accounts by POWs.

5163. Blakely, Scott. *Prisoner at War: The Survival of Commander Richard A. Stratton*. Garden City, NY: Doubleday, 1978.

5164. Chesley, Larry. *Seven Years in Hanoi: A POW Tells His Story*. Salt Lake City: Bookcraft, 1973.

5165. Daly, James, and Lee Bergman. *A Hero's Welcome*. New York: Bobbs-Merrill, 1975. [an enlisted man]

5166. Denton, Jeremiah A., Jr. *When Hell Was In Session*. New York: Reader's Digest Press, 1976.

5167. Dramesi, John A. *Code of Honor*. New York: Norton, 1975.

5168. Dudman, Richard. *Forty Days with the Enemy*. New York: Liveright, 1971.

5169. Fallaci, Oriana. "From North Vietnam: Two American POW's." *Look* 33 (July 15, 1969): 30–35.

5170. Gaither, Ralph, and Steve Henry. *With God in a P.O.W. Camp*. Nashville: Broadman, 1973.

5171. Grant, Zalin B. *Survivors*. New York: Norton, 1975. [returning POWs]

5172. Heslop, J.M., and Dell R. Van Orden. *From the Shadow of Death: Stories of POWs*. Salt Lake City: Deseret Books, 1973.

5173. Hubbell, John G. *P.O.W.: A Definitive History of the American Prisoner-of-War Experience in Vietnam, 1964–1973*. New York: Reader's Digest Press, 1977.

5174. Jensen, Jay R. *Six Years in Hell: A Returned POW Views Captivity, Country, and the Nation's Future*. Bountiful, UT: Horizon, 1974.

5175. McGrath, John M. *Prisoner of War: Six Years in Hanoi*. Annapolis, MD: Naval Institute Press, 1975.

5176. Mulligan, James A. *The Hanoi Commitment*. Virginia Beach, VA: RIF Marketing, 1981.

5177. Overly, Norris M. "Held Captive in Hanoi: An Ex-POW Tells How It Was." *Air Force & Space Digest* 53 (Nov. 1970): 86–90.

5178. Pitzer, D.L., and Warren Rogers. "The Animal Called POW: My Years in a Vietcong Prison." *Look* 33 (Feb. 18, 1969): 46–51.

5179. Plumb, Charlie. *The Last Domino? A POW Looks Ahead*. Independence, MO: Independence Press, 1975.

5180. _____, and Gen. DeWerff. *I'm No Hero: A POW Story*. Independence MO: Independence Press, 1973.

5181. Risner, Robinson. *The Passing of the Night: My Seven Years as a Prisoner of the North Vietnamese*. New York: Random House, 1974.

5182. Rowan, Stephen A. *They Wouldn't Let Us Die: 26 Prisoners of War Tell Their Story*. Middle Village, NY: Jonathan David, 1973.

5183. Rowe, James N. *Five Years to Freedom*. Boston: Little, Brown, 1971.

5184. Rutledge, Howard, et al. *In the Presence of Mine Enemies, 1965–1973: A Prisoner of War*. Old Tappen, NJ: Revell, 1973.

5185. Smith, George E. *P.O.W.: Two Years With the Vietcong*. Berkeley, CA: Ramparts Press, 1971.

5186. Stockdale, James B. "Experiences as a POW in Vietnam." *Naval War College Review* 26 (Jan.–Feb. 1974): 2–6.

5187. Webb, Kate. *On the Other Side: 23 Days With the Viet Cong*. New York: Quadrangle, 1972. [captured in Cambodia]

Lessons of the Experience

5188. Alvarez, Everett, Jr. "Sound: A POW's Weapon." *U.S. Institute Proceedings* 102 (Aug. 1976): 91–93.

5189. Mulligan, Jim. "Communications: The Key to P.O.W. Survival." *Signal* 32 (Sept. 1977): 18–22.

5190. Wagnon, Bobby D. "Communication: The Key to Prisoner of War Survival." *Air University Review* 27 (May–June 1976): 33–46.

OPERATION HOMECOMING AND AFTER

5191. Anderson, Robert S. "Operation Homecoming: Psychological Observations of Repatriated Vietnam Prisoners of War." *Psychiatry* 38:1 (1975): 65–74.

5192. Fellowes, Jack H., and Lisa Hellman. "Operation Homecoming." *U.S. Naval Institute Proceedings* 102 (Dec. 1976): 30–38.

5193. Green, Jesse L., and James K. Phillips III. "Intelligence Test Performance of Vietnam Prisoners of War, 2 Years Post-Return." *Aviation, Space & Environmental Medicine* 47 (Nov. 1976): 1210–1213.

5194. Hunter, Edna J., et al. "Resistance Posture and the Vietnam Prisoner of War." *Journal of Political and Military Sociology* 4 (Fall 1976): 295–308.

5195. Morgan, Cindy. "U.S. Vietnam POW's . . . Where Did They Go From There?" *Countermeasures* 2 (May 1976): 42–46.

5196. Segal, Julius. "Therapeutic Considerations in Planning the Return of American POWs to Continental United States." *Military Medicine* 138 (Feb. 1973): 73–77.

5197. Stratton, Alice. "The Stress of Separation." *U.S. Naval Institute Proceedings* 104 (July 1978): 52–59.

5198. U.S. House. Committee on Armed Services. Hearings; *Full Committee Briefing on Project Egress Recap*. 92d Cong., 2d sess., 1972.

War Crimes

Acts of wanton destruction, assassination, torture and mutilation were committed by forces on both sides in Vietnam. Whether these crimes were worse in Indochina than in other wars can be argued. The awesome military technology of the United States spawned a massive expenditure of munitions, resulting in substantial noncombatant casualties, refugees and ecocide that raise serious ethical and legal questions. Insurgency and the Vietcong's deliberate assassination program pose especially difficult problems. Lewy (3553) and Ramsey (5250) argue that insurgents initiating violence must accept considerable responsibility; Falk (5206) and others argue that insurgents be granted the rights of belligerency. Perhaps the most balanced effort to date is Farer's (5232). Antiwar rhetoric—moved by conscience and ideology—greatly diminished the meaning of genocide (South Vietnam's population actually increased during the American intervention).

Bibliographies

5199. Lewis, John R. "The Vietnam War, 1946–1975." *Uncertain Judgment: A Bibliography of War Crimes Trials.* Santa Barbara, CA: ABC-Clio, 1979, 161–169.

5200. Sacharoff, M. "Bibliography of Recent and Forthcoming Books on U.S. War Crimes in Indochina." *New Republic* 164 (Jan. 2, 1971): 29ff.

Books

5201. Bo Ngoia Giao, and Vu Thong Tin Bao Chi. *U.S. War Crimes in North Viet Nam.* Hanoi: Foreign Languages Publishing House, 1966.

5202. Browning, Frank, and Dorothy Forman, eds. *The Wasted Nations: Report of the International Commission of Enquiry Into United States Crimes in Indochina, June 20–25, 1971.* New York: Harper & Row, 1972.

5203. Carey, A.E. *Australian Atrocities in Vietnam.* Sydney: Gould, Convenor, Vietnam Action Campaign, 1968.

5204. Chomsky, Noam, and Edward S. Herman. *Counterrevolutionary Violence: Bloodbaths in Fact and Propaganda.* Andover, MA: Warner Modular Publishing, 1973.

5205. *The Dellums Committee: Hearing on War Crimes in Vietnam, An Inquiry into Command Responsibility in Southeast Asia.* Edited with introduction by the Citizens Commission of Inquiry. New York: Vintage, 1972.

5206. Falk, Richard A., et al., eds. *Crimes of War.* New York: Random House, 1971.

5207. Herman, Edward S. *"Atrocities" in Vietnam: Myths and Realities.* Boston: Pilgrim Press, 1970.

5208. Karsten, Peter. *Law, Soldiers and Combat.* Westport, CT: Greenwood, 1978. This is an excellent introduction to war crimes, especially My Lai.

5209. Knoll, Erwin, and Judith N. McFadden, eds. *War Crimes and the American Conscience.* New York: Holt, Rinehart & Winston, 1970.

5210. Kunen, James S. *Standard Operating Procedure: Notes of a Draft-Age American.* New York: Avon, 1971.

5211. Lane, Mark. *Conversations With Americans.* New York: Simon & Schuster, 1970. [concerns atrocities]

5212. Lang, Daniel. *Casualties of War.* New York: McGraw-Hill, 1970. [from *New Yorker*, Oct. 18, 1969; appeared in England as *Incident on Hill 192*—relates a single incident]

5213. *Livre noir des crimes américains au Vietnam.* Paris: Payard, 1970.

5214. Melman, Seymour, et al. *In the Name of America: The Conduct of the War in Vietnam by the Armed Forces of the United States....* New York: Clergy and Layman Concerned About Vietnam, 1968.

5215. *New Facts: Phu Loi Mass Murder in South Viet Nam.* Hanoi: Foreign Languages Publishing House, 1959.

5216. Russell, Bertrand, and S. Russell. *War and Atrocity in Vietnam.* London: Bertrand Russell Peace Foundation, 1964.

5217. Syme, Anthony V. *Vietnam: The Cruel War.* London: Horwitz, 1966.

5218. Taylor, Telford. *Nuremberg and Vietnam: An American Tragedy.* Chicago: Quadrangle Books, 1970.

5219. Trooboff, Peter D., ed. *Law and Responsibility in Warfare: The Vietnam Experience.* Chapel Hill: University of North Carolina Press, 1975. [tactics and weapons]

5220. Uhl, Michael. *Vietnam: A Soldier's View.* Wellington: New Zealand University Press, 1971. [pamphlet on atrocities]

5221. *U.S. War Crimes in Viet Nam.* Hanoi: Juridical Science Institute, State Commission of Social Sciences, 1968.

5222. Vietnam Veterans Against the War. *The Winter Soldier Investigation: An Inquiry Into American War Crimes.* Boston: Beacon, 1972.

Essays

5223. Bedau, Hugo A. "Genocide in Vietnam?" In *Philosophy, Morality and International Affairs*, edited by V. Held, S. Morgenbesser, and T. Nagel. New York: Oxford University Press, 1974, 5–46.

5224. _____. "Genocide in Vietnam: The Line Between Legal Argument and Moral Judgment." *Worldview* 17 (Feb. 1974): 40–45.

5225. Bishop, Joseph W., Jr. "The Question of War Crimes." *Commentary* 54 (Dec. 1972): 85–92.

5226. Chomsky, Noam. "After Pinkville." *New York Review of Books* (Jan. 1, 1970): 3–14.

5227. Davidson, A.L. "Vietnam: When Terror Is Not Statistics." *American Opinion* 11 (Feb. 1968): 73–84.

5228. Dellinger, Dave. "Unmasking Genocide." *Liberation* 12 (Dec.–Jan. 1967–1968): 3–12.

5229. Falk, Richard A. "Ecocide, Genocide, and the Nuremberg Tradition of Individual Responsibility." In *Philosophy, Morality and International Affairs*, edited by V. Held, S. Morgenbesser, and T. Nagel. New York: Oxford University Press, 1974, 123–137.

5230. _____. "Law and Responsibility in Warfare: The Vietnam Experience." *Instant Research on Peace and Violence*, no. 1 (1974): 1–13.

5231. _____. "War Crimes: The Circle of Responsibility." *Nation* 210 (Jan. 26, 1970): 77–82.

5232. Farer, T.J. "Laws of Wars 25 Years after Nuremberg." *International Conciliation* 583 (May 1971): 5–54.

5233. Ferencz, B.B. "War Crimes Law and the Vietnam War." *American University Law Review* 17 (June 1968): 403–420.

5234. "Geneva Convention of 1949: Application in the Vietnamese Conflict." *Virginia Journal of International Law* 5 (1965): 243–265. [also in Falk (5206), I, 416–438]

5235. Hart, Franklin A. "Yamashita, Nuremberg and Vietnam: Command Responsibility Reappraisal." *Naval War College Review* 25 (Sept.–Oct. 1972): 19–36.

5236. Hoopes, Townsend. "The Nuremberg Suggestion." *Washington Monthly* 1 (Jan. 1970): 18–21.

5237. International Commission of Jurists. "Human Rights in Armed Conflict: Vietnam." *Bulletin* 34 (June 1968): 41–45.

5238. "International Law and Military Operations Against Insurgents in Neutral Territory." *Columbia Law Review* 68 (June 1968): 1127–1148.

5239. Leifer, Michael. "The Bounds of Conflict in Indochina." *Journal of Asian Studies* 31 (Nov. 1972): 121–124.

5240. Lewy, Guenter. "The Punishment of War Crimes: Have We Learned the Lessons of Vietnam?" *Parameters* 9 (Dec. 1979): 12–19.

5241. Luce, Don. "Torture in Three Countries: Vietnam." *New York Review of Books* (May 31, 1973): 44–45.

5242. McWilliams, Wilson Carey. *Military Honor after Mylai*. Special Studies no. 213. New York: Council on Religion & International Affairs, 1972.

5243. Meyrowtiz, Henri. "Le Droit de la guerre dans le conflit vietnamien." *Annuaire Français de Droit International* 13 (1967): 143–201.

5244. Miller, R.H. "Convention on the Non-applicability of Statutory Limitations to War Crimes and Crimes against Humanity." *American Journal of International Law* 65 (July 1971): 476.

5245. Norden, Eric. "American Atrocities in Vietnam." *Liberation* 10 (Feb. 1966): 14–27.

5246. Norman, Lloyd. "Fighting a War Where There Are No Rules." *Army* 21 (Feb. 1971): 52–55.

5247. O'Brien, William V. "The Law of War, Command Responsibility and Vietnam." *Georgetown Law Journal* 60 (Feb. 1972): 605ff.

5248. Parks, W. Hays. "Command Responsibility for War Crimes." *Military Law Review* 62 (Fall 1973): 1–104.

5249. Pham Cuong. "War Crimes and Genocide." *Vietnamese Studies* 18/19 (Sept. 1968): 275–302.

5250. Ramsey, Paul. *The Just War, Force and Political Responsibility*. New York: Scribner's, 1968, 432–440. Ramsey argues that insurgents have a basic responsibility to follow the "rules" because they initiate the violence.

5251. Reel, A. Frank. "Must We Hang Nixon Too?" *Progressive* 34 (Mar. 1970): 26–29.

5252. Reston, James, Jr. "Is Nuremberg Coming Back to Haunt Us?" *Saturday Review* 53 (July 18, 1970): 14–17, 61.

5253. Saburo Kugai. "The Root of U.S. War Crimes in Vietnam." *No More Hiroshimas* 17:1 (Jan. 2, 1970): 5–10.

5254. Sahlins, Marshall. "The Destruction of Conscience in Vietnam." *Dissent* 13 (Jan.–Feb. 1966): 36–62.

5255. Schirmer, D.B. "Mylai Was Not the First Time." *New Republic* 164 (Apr. 24, 1971): 17–21.

5256. Sheehan, Neil. "Should We Have War Crime Trials?" *New York Times Book Review* (Mar. 29, 1971): 1–3, 30ff.

5257. "Tan Am Base Vietnam: Feb. 12—1000 Hrs." *Scanlan's* 1 (Apr. 1970): 1–11. [Lt. James B. Duffy's trial]

5258. Wald, George. "Corporate Responsibility for War Crimes." *New York Review of Books* (July 2, 1970): 4–6.

5259. Wilson, Andrew. "The War in Vietnam: How

Relevant Are the Rules of War?" *Current* 114 (Jan. 1970): 3–6.

5260. Woodward, Beverley. "Nuremberg Law and U.S. Courts." *Dissent* 16 (Mar.–Apr. 1969): 128–136.

STOCKHOLM (RUSSELL) TRIBUNAL

A private "war crimes tribunal" was organized by antiwar critics under Lord Bertrand Russell's name at Stockholm; it was criticized by Lynd (5266) and Lewy (3553), 311–321.

5261. Aptheker, Herbert. "The Stockholm Conference on Vietnam." *Political Affairs* 46 (Aug. 1967): 47–58.

5262. Coats, Kenneth, et al. *Prevent the Crime of Silence: Reports from the Sessions of the International War Crimes Tribunal Founded by Bertrand Russell.* Baltimore: Penguin, 1971.

5263. DeWeerd, H.A. *Lord Russell's War Crimes Tribunal.* P–3561. Santa Monica, CA: Rand Corp., Mar. 1967.

5264. The International War Crimes Tribunal. *Stockholm and Copenhagen, 1967: Against the Crime of Silence: Proceedings of the Russell International War Crimes Tribunal.* New York: Bertrand Russell Peace Foundation, 1968. [also published as: Duffet, J., ed. *Against the Crime of Silence. Proceedings of the Russell International War Crimes Tribunal.* Flanders, NJ: O'Hare Books, 1968, and as a Clarion Book, NY: Simon & Schuster, 1970]

5265. Jack, Homer A. "Confrontation in Stockholm." *War/Peace Report* 7 (Aug.–Sept. 1967): 7–9.

5266. Lynd, Staughton. "The War Crimes Tribunal: A Dissent." *Liberation* 12 (Dec.–Jan. 1967–1968): 76–79. Lynd wants to try both sides.

5267. Russell, Bertrand. *War Crimes in Vietnam.* London: Allen & Unwin, 1967.

5268. Sartre, Jean-Paul. *On Genocide: And a Summary of the Evidence and the Judgments of the International War Crimes Tribunal.* Boston: Beacon, 1968. This work was adopted by the tribunal as part of its findings.

5269. Viet-Nam. Republique du Livre Blanc. Vol. 1: *Le Judgement de Stockholm;* Vol. 2: *Le Judgement final.* Tribunal Russell. Paris: N.R.F., 1968.

MY LAI (PINKVILLE) INCIDENT

Captain Medina and Lieutenant Calley led Task Force Bravo of the 11th Brigade, American Division, into Son My, a hamlet of My Lai IV, on March 16, 1968, and killed some 300 to 400 civilians. General Peer's report of March 14, 1970, charged fourteen officers—ranging from captain to major general—of covering up the incident; subsequently, Medina and Calley were tried and Calley was convicted.

Books

5270. Calley, William L., and John Sack. *Lieutenant Calley: His Own Story.* New York: Viking, 1971. [published in Great Britain as *Body Count*]

5271. Everett, Arthur, et al. *Calley.* New York: Dell, 1971.

5272. French, Peter A. *Individual and Collective Responsibility: The Massacre at My Lai.* Cambridge, MA: Schenkman, 1972.

5273. Gershen, Martin. *Destroy or Die: The True Story of Mylai.* New Rochelle, NY: Arlington House, 1971.

5274. Giles, Barbara M. "My Lai and the Law: An Analysis of How International Law Relates to the My Lai Incident and Its Cover-up." Ph.D. dissertation, University of Tennessee, 1978.

5275. Goldstein, Joseph, et al, eds. *The My Lai Massacre and Its Cover-Up: Beyond the Reach of Law? The Peers Commission Report With a Supplement and Introductory Essay on the Limits of Law.* New York: Free Press, 1976.

5276. Greenhaw, Wayne. *The Making of a Hero: The Story of Lt. William Calley, Jr.* Louisville: Touchstone, 1971.

5277. Hammer, Richard. *The Court-Martial of Lt. Calley.* New York: Coward, McCann & Geoghegan, 1971.

5278. _____. *One Morning in the War: The Tragedy at Son My.* London: Hart-Davis, 1970.

5279. Hersh, Seymour. *Cover-Up: The Army's Secret Investigation of the Massacre at My Lai 4.* New York: Random House, 1972.

5280. _____. *My Lai 4.* New York: Random House, 1970.

5281. Kelman, Herbert C., and Lee H. Lawrence. "American Response to the Trial of Lt. William L. Calley." In *The Military in America: From the Colonial Era to the Present,* edited by Peter Karsten. New York: Free Press, 1980, 431–446.

5282. McCarthy, Mary. *Medina.* New York: Harcourt, Brace & Jovanovich, 1972.

5283. Peer, W.R. *The My Lai Inquiry*. New York: Norton, 1979. General Peer conducted the official inquiry; here he analyzes the cover-up.

5284. Tiede, Tom. *Calley: Soldier or Killer?* New York: Pinnacle Books, 1971.

5285. U.S. Army. *Report of the Department of the Army Review of the Preliminary Investigations Into the My Lai Incident* (1970). Washington, DC: GPO, 1974.

5286. U.S. House. Committee on Armed Services. Hearings; *Investigation of the My Lai Incident*. 91st Cong., 2d sess., July 15, 1970.

5287. Winn, Larry J. "My Lai: Birth and Death of a Rhetorical Symbol." Ph.D. dissertation, Indiana University, 1973.

Essays
5288. "An American Atrocity." *Esquire* 72 (Aug. 1969): 59–63, 132.

5289. Barthelmes, Wes. "Mylai and the National Conscience-II: Cry, Our Beloved Country." *Commonweal* 94 (Apr. 30, 1971): 186–187.

5290. "Calley and Company." *New Republic* 164 (Apr. 10, 1971): 10–11.

5291. Cooper, Norman G. "My Lai and Military Justice: To What Effect?" *Military Law Review* 59 (Winter 1973): 93–127.

5292. Deutcher, Irwin. "Buchenwald, Mai Lai, and Charles van Doren: Social Psychology as Explanation." *Sociological Quarterly* 11 (Fall 1970): 533–540.

5293. Falk, Richard A. "Circle of Responsibility." *Nation* 210 (Jan. 27, 1970): 37–42.

5294. ———. "Songmy: War Crimes and Individual Responsibility, a Legal Memorandum." *Trans-Action* 7 (Jan. 1970): 33–40.

5295. Goldstein, Joseph. "The Meaning of Calley." *New Republic* 164 (May 8, 1971): 13–14.

5296. Heinl, Robert D., Jr. "My Lai in Perspective: The Court-Martial of William L. Calley." *Armed Forces Journal* 108 (Dec. 21, 1970): 38–39.

5297. Hersh, Seymour M. "My Lai 4: A Report on the Massacre and Its Aftermath." *Harper's* 240 (May 1970): 53–84.

5298. "House Panel Charges 'Cover-up' of My Lai Massacre." *CQ Weekly Report* 28 (July 17, 1970): 1796–1797.

5299. "Is There a Bit of Calley in Us?" *Look* 35 (June 1, 1971): 76–77.

5300. Kelman, Herbert C., and Lee H. Lawrence. "Assignment of Responsibility in the Case of Lt. Calley: Preliminary Report on a National Survey." *Journal of Social Issues* 28 (Winter 1972): 177–212. [public opinion]

5301. Lesher, S. "The Calley Case Re-Examined." *New York Times Magazine* (July 11, 1971): 6ff.

5302. "The Massacre at Mylai." *Life* 67 (Dec. 5, 1969): 36–44.

5303. "My Lai Massacre: Grim Details, Unanswered Questions." *CQ Weekly Report* 27 (Dec. 5, 1969): 2464–2473.

5304. Novak, Michael. "Mylai and the National Conscience-I: The Battle Hymn of Lt. Calley ... and the Republic." *Commonweal* (Apr. 30, 1971): 183–186.

5305. Opton, E.M., Jr., and R. Duckles. "Mental Gymnastics on Mylai." *New Republic* 162 (Feb. 21, 1970): 14–16.

5306. Paust, Jordan J. "MyLai and Vietnam: Norms, Myths and Leader Responsibility." *Military Law Review* 57 (Summer 1972): 99–187.

5307. "Punishment for War Crimes: Duty or Discretion?" *Michigan Law Review* 69 (June 1971): 1312–1346.

5308. Quinn, Robert E., and William H. Darden. "Opinion: United States Court of Military Appeals: United States, Appelle v. William L. Calley, Jr., First Lieutenant, U.S. Army, Appellant." *International Lawyer* 8 (July 1974): 523–539.

5309. Rowe, Terry E. "Nevada Reacts to My Lai." *Nevada Historical Society Quarterly* 17 (Summer 1974): 60–103.

5310. Russell, Kent A. "My Lai Massacre: The Need for an International Investigation." *California Law Review* 58 (May 1970): 703–729.

5311. Taylor, Jack. "Army's Records Dispute My Lai Findings." *Congressional Record* 118 (Aug. 31, 1972): 29235–29236.

5312. Thompson, Kenrick S., et al. "Reactions to My-Lai: A Visual-Verbal Approach." *Sociology and Social Research* 58 (Jan. 1974): 122–129.

COLONEL HERBERT AFFAIR

Colonel Herbert complained of twenty-one incidents of war crimes alledged to have occurred in Vietnam in

1968 and 1969. Dissatisfied with the Army's investigations, he filed charges against his superiors for failing to report the incidents.

5313. Ewing, Lee. "Col. Anthony Herbert: The Unmaking of an Accuser." *Columbia Journalism Review* 12 (Sept.–Oct. 1973): 8–14. TV's "60 Minutes" challenged the accuracy of Herbert's statements.

5314. Herbert, Anthony B., with James Wooten. *Soldier.* New York: Holt, Rinehart & Winston, 1972.

5315. _____. "Soldier—A Memoir." *Ramparts* 11 (Jan. 1973): 27–32, 50–52.

5316. "The Herbert Case and the Record." *Army* 22 (Feb. 1972): 6–11.

5317. *The Herbert v. Lando*: Reporter's Privilege From Revealing the Editorial Process in a Defamation Suit." *Columbia Law Review* 78 (Mar. 1978): 448–467. Herbert won the initial phase of his slander suit against CBS and "60 Minutes."

5318. Lando, Barry. "The Herbert Affair." *Atlantic* 231 (May 1973): 73–81.

VC/NVA WAR CRIMES

The terrorist tactics of the Vietcong, which clearly violated the rules of war, received little attention from the U.S. media. The VC, and to a lesser extent the NVA, conducted an organized assassination program designed to eliminate opponents. South Vietnam and the CIA countered with the "Phoenix" program; see Chapter 6. At Hue during the Tet offensive of 1968, VC/NVA forces ruthlessly killed hundreds of civilians; see Chapter 7.

5319. "The Bloody Hands of the Viet Cong." *Army* 12 (July 1962): 67–77.

5320. Bo Ngoai Giao. *The Communist Policy of Terror.* Saigon: Ministry of Foreign Affairs, 1972.

5321. "Communist Terror Attacks on Civilians in Vietnam." *Congressional Record* 119 (Jan. 22, 1973): E327–E328.

5322. Eppridge, Bill, and Don Moser. "Vietcong Terror in a Village." *Life* 59 (Sept. 3, 1965): 28–33, 68–70.

5323. Fallaci, Oriana. "An Interview with a Vietcong Terrorist." *Look* 32 (Apr. 16, 1968): 36–42.

5324. Joiner, Charles A. *The Politics of Massacre: Political Processes in South Viet Nam.* Philadelphia: Temple University Press, 1973.

5325. Jones, James. "In the Shadow of Peace: Effects of

1968 Hue Massacre." *New York Times Magazine* (June 10, 1973): 15ff.

5326. Mallin, Jay. *Terror in Viet Nam.* Princeton, NJ: Van Nostrand, 1966.

5327. "The Massacre of Dak Son." *Time* 92 (Dec. 15, 1967): 32–34. [VC murder of 252 Montagnards]

5328. Pike, Douglas. "The Kind of War That Is Vietnam: 'People's War' with Terror as the Tool." *Air Force & Space Digest* 53 (June 1970): 78–81.

5329. _____. *The Viet-Cong Strategy of Terror.* Cambridge, MA: MIT Press, 1970.

5330. Rolph, Hammond M. "The Viet Cong Strategy of Terror." *Communist Affairs* 4 (July–Aug. 1966): 3–13.

5331. Treaster, Joseph B. "Enemy is Said to Execute Hundreds in South Vietnam." *Congressional Record* 118 (Aug. 4, 1972): 26933–26934. This is a *New York Times* summary of episodes in Binh Dinh province.

Casualties of the War

The human toll of any war is usually difficult to tally, but it is especially so for the Second Indochina conflict. While American losses are probably quite accurate, South Vietnamese, Cambodian and Laotian casualties—killed, injured and displaced—can only be crudely estimated. North Vietnam has not announced its losses, so they must also remain estimates. For a compilation of these estimates, see the introduction to this chapter.

U.S. CASUALTIES

5332. Badillo, Gilbert, and David G. Curry. "The Social Incidence of Vietnam Casualties: Social Class or Race?" *Armed Forces & Society* 2 (Spring 1976): 397–406.

5333. Canova, Pamela, and James D. Hessman. "The Casualty Reports: Some Startling Statistics." *Armed Forces Journal* 106 (Aug. 2, 1969): 16–18.

5334. Fiedler, Leslie. "Who Really Died in Vietnam?" *Saturday Review* 55 (Dec. 1972): 40–43.

5335. Hessman, James D., and Louis R. Stockstill. "The Casualty List: Disturbing but Distorted." *Armed Forces Journal* 105 (Mar. 30, 1968): 2–3ff.

5336. Hessman, James D., and Margaret Berkowitz.

"Vietnam Casualty Report: The Downward Trend." *Armed Forces Journal* 107 (Feb. 14, 1970): 19–21.

5337. Kovaric, J.J., et al. "Vietnam Casualty Statistics: February–November 1967." *Archives of Surgery* 98 (Feb. 1969): 150–152.

5338. Lieberman, E. James. "Statement on the Effects of U.S. Casualties in Vietnam on American Families." *Journal of Marriage & the Family* 32 (May 1970): 197–199.

5339. Research Analysis Corporation. *Combat Operations Loss and Expenditure Data: Vietnam (COLED-V)*. Rpt RAC–R–131. McLean, VA, Aug. 1971.

5340. "Toll of the War." *U.S. News and World Report* 73 (Dec. 18, 1972): 27. [By age, cause of death, etc.]

5341. Truscott, Lucian K., IV. "Who Dies in Vietnam?" *Nation* 211 (Oct. 12, 1970): 326–327.

5342. U.S. Department of Defense. Directorate for Information Operations. *List of Casualties Incurred by U.S. Military Personnel in Connection With the Conflict in Vietnam; Deaths from 1 January 1961 thru 31 December 1971*. 2 vols. Washington, DC, 1972.

5343. Willis, John M. "Variations in State Casualty Rates in World War II and the Vietnam War." *Social Problems* 22 (Apr. 1975): 558–568.

5344. _____. "Who Died in Vietnam? An Analysis of the Social Background of Vietnam Casualties." Ph.D. dissertation, Purdue University, 1975.

5345. Zeitlin, Maurice, et al. "Death in Vietnam: Class, Poverty, and the Risks of War." *Politics and Society* 3 (Spring 1973): 313–328.

U.S. MEDICAL SUPPORT

For U.S. soldiers the time between being wounded and being evacuated to treatment facilities was 10.5 hours in World War II, 6.3 in Korea and 2.8 in Vietnam (up to 1967), the decrease being mainly due to the use of helicopters. Between 1965 and 1967, 1.6 percent of the wounded who reached hospitals died within 24 hours; only a further 0.9 percent died of wounds after that initial day—a truly remarkable accomplishment. See Neel (3482), for an Army Medical Corps account.

Books

5346. Browne, Corinne. *Body Shop: Recuperating From Vietnam*. New York: Stein & Day, 1973. Browne describes amputees at Letterman General Hospital learning to live again.

5347. Glasser, Ronald J. *365 Days*. New York: Braziller, 1971. Glasser gives a doctor's account of his tour in Vietnam.

5348. Herrera, Barbara H. *Medics in Action*. Mountain View, CA: Pacific Press, 1968.

5349. Parrish, John A. *12, 20 & 5: A Doctor's Year in Vietnam*. New York: Dutton, 1972.

5350. U.S. Army. Office of the Surgeon General and Center of Military History. *Internal Medicine in Vietnam*. Vol. 1: *Skin Diseases in Vietnam, 1965–72*, by A.M. Allen. Washington, DC: GPO, 1977.

5351. Williams, Fenton A. *Just Before the Dawn: A Doctor's Experiences in Vietnam*. New York: Exposition Press, 1971.

Essays

5352. Arnold, Keith, and Robert T. Cutting. "Causes of Death in United States Military Personnel Hospitalized in Vietnam." *Military Medicine* 143 (Mar. 1978): 161–164.

5353. Bezreh, Anthony A. "Injuries Resulting From Hostile Action Against Army Aircrew Members in Flight Over Vietnam." *Aerospace Medicine* 41 (July 1970): 763–769.

5354. Bjornson, J. "A Psychiatrist in Vietnam." *Progressive* 30 (Feb. 1966): 13–15.

5355. Brady, Eugene P. "Dust Off Operations." *Army Logistics* 5 (July–Aug. 1973): 18–23. [helicopter ambulances]

5356. _____. "The Thread of a Concept." *Marine Corps Gazette* 55 (May 1971): 35–42. [air medical evacuation]

5357. Glasser, Ronald J. "The Burn Ward." *Washington Monthly* 3 (Apr. 1971): 25–35.

5358. Hammon, W.M. "Analysis of 2187 Consecutive Wounds of the Brain From Vietnam." *Journal of Neurosurgery* 34 (Feb. 1971): 127–131.

5359. Heaton, L.D. "Medical Support in Vietnam." *Army* 16 (Oct. 1966): 125–128.

5360. Jones, E.L., et al. "Early Management of Battle Casualties in Vietnam." *Archives of Surgery* 97:1 (1968): 1–26.

5361. Jones, Franklin D., and Arnold W. Johnson, Jr. "Medical and Psychiatric Treatment Policy and Practice in Vietnam." *Journal of Social Issues* 31 (Fall 1975): 49–65.

5362. Lee, Richard, et al. "Surveillance of Some Infectious Diseases Among Aircrew Personnel in Southeast

Asia." *Aviation, Space & Environmental Medicine* 46 (Sept. 1975): 1152–1154.

5363.   McClendon, F.O., Jr. "Doctors and Dentists, Nurses and Corpsmen in Vietnam." *U.S. Naval Institute Proceedings* 96 (May 1970): 276–289.

5364.   Maughon, J.S. "An Inquiry Into the Nature of Wounds Resulting in Killed in Action in Vietnam." *Military Medicine* 135 (Jan. 1970): 8–13.

5365.   Rich, N.M., et al. "Wounding Power of Missiles Used in the Republic of Vietnam." *Journal of the American Medical Association* 199 (Jan. 1967): 157–168.

5366.   Savitz, David. "New Medical War in Vietnam." *Medical Opinion & Review* 3 (Aug. 1967): 78–86.

5367.   Shannon, Robert H., and Arthur N. Till, Jr. "Combat Use of Life Support Systems in Southeast Asia, 1 Jan. 1967–31 Dec. 1968." *SAFE Engineering* 3 (Oct.–Nov. 1969): 13–16.

5368.   Tarrow, Arthur B. "USAF Hospital Clark and the Vietnam Casualties." *Air University Review* 18 (Nov.–Dec. 1966): 85–89.

5369.   U.S. Army. Edgewood Arsenal. *Analysis of 210 U.S. Army Deaths in Vietnam from July to September 1967.* Technical Rpt. EATR 4357. Edgewood Arsenal, MD, Mar. 1970.

5370.   _____. *Head Trauma: Analysis of 120 Casualties in Vietnam from July 1967 to January 1968.* Technical Rpt. EATR 4359. Edgewood Arsenal, MD, Mar. 1970.

5371.   _____. *Injuries of the Extremities in 369 U.S. Army and Marine Corps Casualties in Vietnam.* Technical Rpt. EATR 4402. Edgewood Arsenal, MD, Apr. 1970.

5372.   _____. *Thoracic Trauma: Analysis of 140 U.S. Army Casualties in Vietnam from July to September 1967.* Technical Rpt. EATR 4358. Edgewood Arsenal, MD, Mar. 1970.

5373.   White, M.S., et al. "Results of Early Aeromedical Evacuation of Vietnam Casualties." *Aerospace Medicine* 42 (July 1971): 780–784.

CIVILIAN CASUALTIES

These items range from personal accounts to concern about postwar damage.

Books—Personal Accounts
5374.   Brass, Alister, J.D. *Bleeding Earth: A Doctor Looks at Vietnam.* Melbourne: Heineman, 1968.

5375.   Evans, Barbara. *Caduceus in Saigon: A Medical Mission to South Vietnam.* London: Hutchinson, 1968.

5376.   Ford, Herbert. *No Guns on Their Shoulders.* Nashville, TN: Southern Publishing Association, 1968. These Seventh Day Adventists worked with medical and sanitation problems.

5377.   Gloechner, Fred. *A Civilian Doctor In Vietnam.* Philadelphia: Winchell, 1972.

5378.   Schulze, Gene. *The Third Face of War (Medical and Sanitary Operations).* Austin, TX: Pemberton, 1970.

5379.   Schwinn, Monika, and Bernhard Diehl. *We Came to Help.* New York: Harcourt, Brace & Jovanovich, 1976. [nurses captured by NVA]

5380.   Sunderland, Sydney. *Australian Civilian Medical Aid to Viet-Nam: Report, March 1969.* Canberra: Department of External Affairs, 1969.

5381.   Terry, Susan. *House of Love: Life in a Vietnamese Hospital.* London: Newnes, 1967.

5382.   Turpin, James W. *Vietnam Doctor: The Story of Project Concern.* New York: McGraw-Hill, 1966.

Reports
See also, "Refugees: Pre-Armistice" and "Refugees: Post-Armistics," below, this chapter.

5383.   U.S. General Accounting Office. *Problems in the Khmer Republic (Cambodia) Concerning War Victims, Civilian Health, and War-Related Casualties.* B–169832. Washington, DC, 1972.

5384.   U.S. Senate. Committee on Foreign Relations. Hearings; *Vietnam Children's Care Agency.* 92d Cong., 2d sess., Apr. 5, 1972.

5385.   U.S. Senate. Committee on the Judiciary. Hearings; *Civilian Casualty, Social Welfare, and Refugee Problems in South Vietnam.* 90th Cong., 1st sess., May–Oct. 1968.

5386.   _____. Hearings; *Problems of War Victims in Indochina.* 4 vols. 92d Cong., 2d sess., 1972.

5387.   _____. Hearings; *Refugees and Civilian War Casualty Problems in Laos and Cambodia.* 91st Cong., 2d sess., May 7, 1970.

5388.   _____. Hearings; *War-Related Civilian Problems in Indochina.* 3 vols. 92d Cong., 1st sess., 1971.

5389.   _____. Report; *Civilian Casualty and Refugee Problems in South Vietnam: Findings and Recommendations.* 90th Cong., 2d sess., May 9, 1968.

5390. _____. Report; *Refugee Problems in South Vietnam: Report Pursuant to S. Res. 49.* Senate Rpt no. 1058. 89th Cong., 2d sess., 1966.

5391. _____. Staff Report; *The Human Cost of Communism in Vietnam: A Compendium.* 92d Cong., 2d sess., 1972.

5392. _____. Staff Report; *Refugees and Civilian War Casualties Problem in Indochina.* 91st Cong., 2d sess., Sept. 28, 1970.

Essays

5393. Alcock, N.Z., and K. Lowe. "The Vietnam War as a Richardson Process." *Journal of Peace Research* 6:2 (1969): 105–112.

5394. Cutting, Robert T., et al. *Congenital Malformations, Hydatidiform Moles and Stillbirths in the Republic of Vietnam, 1960–1969.* Washington, DC: Department of Defense, 1970.

5395. Dudley, H.A., et al. "Civilian Battle Casualties in South Vietnam." *British Journal of Surgery* 55:5 (1968): 332–334.

5396. *Epidemiological Situation in Vietnam.* World Health Organization. 41/42. (Jan. 1968).

5397. Grant, Zalin B. "Civilians Caught in the Vietnam Crossfire." *New Republic* 159 (Aug. 17, 1968): 11–12.

5398. Hayes, Marcia. "Plague Goes to War." *Far Eastern Economic Review* 59 (Mar. 7, 1968): 418–420.

5399. Iden, George. "Human Resource Cost of the War." *Journal of Peace Research* 7:3–4 (1971): 293–298.

5400. Kelman, R.B. "Vietnam: A Current Issue in Child Welfare." *Social Work* 13:4 (Oct. 1968): 15–20.

5401. Kennedy, Edward M. "The Indochina War." *Congressional Record* 118 (May 3, 1972): 15577. [people problems of the war]

5402. Smilkstein, Gabriel. "Volunteer Physicians for Vietnam: A Six Year Review." *Journal of the American Medical Association* 219 (Jan. 24, 1972): 495–499.

5403. "Sorry 'Bout That." *New Republic* 156 (Jan. 7, 1967): 7–9. [inaccuracy in information about civilian casualties]

5404. "To Make Children Whole Again." *Look* 32 (July 23, 1968): 30–34.

5405. "Viet Deformities: Will We Ever Know?" *Medical World News* 12 (Jan. 29, 1971): 4–5.

5406. "The War Victims of South Vietnam." *Congressional Record* 119 (Feb. 28, 1973): S3608–S3610.

REFUGEES: PRE-ARMISTICE

5407. Chun-Hoon, William C. "The Migration of Indochinese Refugees and Its Impact on an Urban School District." Ph.D. dissertation, Claremont Graduate School, 1978.

5408. Conn, Harry. "Refugees: The World's Forgotten People." *American Federationist* 73 (Sept. 1966): 17–20.

5409. Geyelin, Philip. "The Vietnamese Refugee Problem." *Reporter* 33 (Sept. 23, 1965): 43–45.

5410. Jenkins, Loren. "Vietnam's War-Torn Children." *Newsweek* 81 (May 28, 1973): 52–61.

5411. Kennedy, Edward M. "The Forgotten Casualties." *Commonweal* 93 (Oct. 30, 1970): 119–121.

5412. Luce, Don. "No Way Home: Vietnam's Refugees." *Christian Century* 84 (Oct. 11, 1967): 1279–1281.

5413. Marks, E.B. "Saigon: The Impact of the Refugees." *Reporter* 36 (Jan. 12, 1967): 33–36.

5414. Murfin, Gary D. "War, Life and Stress: The Forced Relocation of the Vietnamese People." Ph.D. dissertation, University of Hawaii, 1975.

5415. Peabody, J.C. "The Refugees of Vietnam." *Think* 33 (Mar.–Apr. 1967): 29–32.

5416. Rambo, A. Terry, et al. *The Refugee Situation in Phu-yen Province, Viet-Nam.* McLean, VA: Human Sciences Research, 1967.

5417. Tinker, J.M. *Refugee Situation in Dinh Tuone Province.* Memorandum no. 6. McLean, VA: Human Sciences Research, Aug. 1967.

5418. U.S. Senate. Committee on the Judiciary. Hearings; *Refugee Problems in South Vietnam and Laos.* 89th Cong., 1st sess., 1965.

REFUGEES: POST-ARMISTICE

For accounts of the Vietnamese escapees ("boat people"), see, in Chapter 3, "Third Indochina War" and "Vietnam: Reunification and Rebuilding."

5419. Frank, Kurt W. "The Resettlement of a Vietnamese Refugee Family by the Drexel Hill Baptist Church (a Case Study)." Doctor Ministry dissertation, Eastern Baptist Theological Seminary, 1978.

5420.   Hammond, James W., Jr. "Operation New Arrivals." *Marine Corps Gazette* 59 (Aug. 1975): 20–32.

5421.   Le Thi Que, A. Terry Rambo, and Gary D. Murfin. "Why They Fled: Refugee Movement During the Spring 1975 Communist Offensive in S. Vietnam." *Asian Survey* 16 (Sept. 1976): 855–863.

5422.   Moos, Felix, and C.S. Morrison. "The Vietnamese Refugees at Our Doorstep: Political Ambiguity and Successful Improvisation." *Policy Studies Review* 1 (Aug. 1981): 28–46.

5423.   Paley, G. "We Were Strong Enough To Kill the Parents in Vietnam: Does That Make Us Good Enough to Raise the Orphans?" *Ms.* 4 (Sept. 1975): 68ff.

5424.   Shaplen, Robert. "Survivors." *New Yorker* 53 (Sept. 5, 1977): 33. A reporter at large discusses Indochinese refugees.

5425.   Shaver, William D. "New Arrivals: An Operation of Human Concern and Compassion." *Aerospace Historian* 25 (Mar. 1978): 19–24.

5426.   Silverman, Edwin B. "The Indochina Legacy: The Refugee Act of 1980." *Publius* 10 (Winter 1980): 27–42.

5427.   Suhrke, Astri. "Indochinese Refugees and American Policy." *World Today* 37 (Feb. 1981): 54–62.

5428.   Townsend, Patrick L. "The Hand of Hope: Vietnamese Refugee Camp at Camp Pendleton, California." *U.S. Naval Institute Proceedings* 102 (Sept. 1976): 38–45.

5429.   U.S. General Accounting Office. *U.S. Provides Safe Haven for Indochina Refugees.* ID–75–71. Washington, DC, June 17, 1975.

5430.   U.S. Department of State. "The Indochinese Refugees: A Status Report." *Current Policy*, no. 30 (Aug. 1978): 1–6.

5431.   U.S. House. Committee on Foreign Affairs. Hearings; *Indochinese Refugees.* 96th Cong., 1st sess., Apr. 5, 25, May 22, June 13, 1979.

5432.   _____. Hearings; *1979—Tragedy in Indochina: War, Refugees, and Famine.* 96th Cong., 1st sess., 1980.

5433.   _____. Hearings; *1980—The Tragedy in Indochina Continues: War, Refugees, and Famine.* 96th Cong., 2d sess., 1980.

5434.   _____. Committee on International Relations. Hearings; *Refugee Crisis in Indochina, 1978.* 95th Cong., 2d sess., 1978.

5435.   _____. Committee on the Judiciary. Hearings; *Extension of Indochina Refugee Assistance Program.* 95th Cong., 1st sess., Sept. 23, 27, 1977.

5436.   _____. Hearings; *The Indochinese Refugee Problem.* 96th Cong., 1st sess., 1979.

5437.   U.S. Senate. Committee on Foreign Relations. Hearings; *The Current Situation in Indochina.* 95th Cong., 2d sess., 1978. [Cambodia–Vietnamese conflict, refugees and human rights in Cambodia]

5438.   _____. Committee on Human Resources. Hearings; *Indochina Migration and Refugee Assistance Amendments of 1978.* 95th Cong., 2d sess., 1978.

5439.   _____. Committee on the Judiciary. Hearings; *Indochina Evacuation and Refugee Problems.* 94th Cong., 1st sess., Apr. 15–30, 1975.

5440.   _____. Hearings; *Refugee Crisis in Cambodia.* 96th Cong., 1st sess., 1980.

5441.   _____. Report; *Humanitarian Problems in South Vietnam and Cambodia: Two Years After the Cease-Fire: A Study Mission.* 94th Cong., 1st sess., Jan. 27, 1975.

5442.   _____. Report; *Relief and Rehabilitation of War Victims in Indochina: One Year After the Cease-Fire.* 93d Cong., 2d sess., Jan. 27, 1974.

5443.   _____. Staff Report; *Aftermath of War: Humanitarian Problems of Southeast Asia.* 94th Cong., 2d sess., 1976.

5444.   _____. Staff Report; *Indochina Evacuation and Refugee Problems.* 94th Cong., 1st sess., 1975.

Economic Costs

The fiscal costs of the Second Indochina War to the United States are very difficult to measure. Estimates vary greatly, as the following indicates:

Clayton (1969) – $353 billion
Duke (1970) – $750 billion
Lekaachman (1972) – $400 billion
Riddell (1973) – $676 billion
Stevens (1976) – $526 billion

These are all estimates of "total costs": original wartime expenditure as well as subsequent costs yet to be spent such as veterans benefits, debt interest, etc.

Past U.S. experiences suggest that such "total costs" for wars eventually reach three times the initial wartime expenditure.

Books, Dissertation, and Reports

5445.   Caton, Christopher N. "The Impact of the War in Vietnam on the U.S. Economy." Ph.D. dissertation, University of Pennsylvania, 1974.

5446.   Hamilton-Paterson, James. *A Very Personal War: The Story of Cornelius Hawkridge.* London: Hodder & Stoughton, 1971. [blackmarket operations, U.S. edition entitled *The Greedy War*]

5447.   King, Christopher T. "The Unemployment Impact of the Vietnam Years." Ph.D. dissertation, Michigan State University, 1976.

5448.   Perlo, Victor. *The Vietnam Profiteers.* New York: New Outlook Publishers, 1966.

5449.   Riddell, Thomas A. "A Political Economy of the American War in Indo-China: Its Costs and Consequences." Ph.D. dissertation, American University, 1975.

5450.   Stevens, Robert W. *Vain Hopes, Grim Realities: The Economic Consequences of the Vietnam War.* New York: New Viewpoints, 1976.

5451.   U.S. Arms Control and Disarmament Agency. *The Economic Impact of Reductions in Defense Spending.* Washington, DC: July 1972.

5452.   U.S. Congress. Joint Economic Committee. Hearings; *Economic Effect of Vietnam Spending.* 2 vols. 90th Cong., 1st sess., 1967.

5453.   _____. Report; *Economic Effect of Vietnam Spending; Together with Supplementary Views.* 90th Cong., 1st sess., July 7, 1967.

5454.   U.S. Department of Labor. Bureau of Statistics. *Projections of the Post-Vietnam Economy.* Washington, DC: GPO, 1972.

5455.   U.S. Library of Congress. *Impact of the Vietnam War.* Prepared for the Committee on Foreign Relations, U.S. Senate. 92d Cong., 1st sess., 1971.

5456.   U.S. Senate. Committee on Foreign Relations. Hearings; *Impact of the War in Southeast Asia on the U.S. Economy.* 91st Cong., 2d sess., Apr.–Aug. 1970.

5457.   Weidenbaum, Murray. *Economic Impact of the Vietnam War.* New York: Renaissance Editions, 1967.

Essays

5458.   Benoit, Emile. "Cutting Back Military Spending: The Vietnam Withdrawal and the Recession." *Annals of the American Academy of Political and Social Sciences,* no. 406 (Mar. 1973): 73–79.

5459.   Bernstein, Peter L. "Vietnam and the Gold Drain." *Nation* 206 (Apr. 1, 1968): 430–431.

5460.   Bowen, William. "The Vietnam War: A Cost Accounting." *Fortune* 73 (Apr. 1966): 119–123ff.

5461.   Brand, H. "Vietnam and the U.S. Economy: Can the Freedom Budget Solve Our Problems?" *Dissent* 15 (Mar.–Apr. 1968): 171–176.

5462.   Chamber of Commerce of the United States of America. *After Vietnam: A Report of the Ad Hoc Committee on the Economic Impact of Peace After Vietnam.* Washington, DC, 1968.

5463.   Clayton, James. "The Ultimate Cost of the Vietnam Conflict." In U.S. Congress. Joint Economic Committee. Hearings; *The Military Budget and National Priorities.* 91st Cong., 1st sess., 1969, Pt I, 146ff.

5464.   Cohen, B.J. *Vietnam, The Impact on American Business.* Princeton, NJ: Princeton University, Department of Economics, Dec. 1969.

5465.   Cook, Fred J. "Greedy War." *Nation* 215 (Sept. 11, 1972): 177–179.

5466.   "Defense Budget Anticipates Further Vietnam Escalation." *Armed Forces Management* 12 (Mar. 1966): 47–50.

5467.   Dowd, D.F. "Political Economy of War." *Nation* 212 (June 28, 1971): 811–815.

5468.   Dudley, Leonard, and Peter Passell. "The War in Vietnam and the U.S. Balance of Payments." *Review of Economics and Statistics* 50 (Nov. 1968): 437–442.

5469.   Duke, Keith. *Cost of the War in Vietnam.* Carlisle Barracks, PA: U.S. Army War College, 1970.

5470.   Eisner, Robert. "The War and the Economy." In *Why Are We Still in Vietnam?,* edited by S. Brown and L. Ackland. New York: Random House, 1970.

5471.   Lee, D.B., Jr., and J.W. Dyckman. "Economic Impact of the Vietnam War: A Primer." *Journal of the American Institute of Planners* 36 (Sept. 1970): 298–309.

5472.   Lekaachmann, Robert. "The Cost in National Treasure: $400 Billion Plus." *Saturday Review* 55 (Dec. 1972): 11–12, 46–49.

5473.   Lynch, John E. "Regional Impact of the Vietnam War (1965–71)." *Quarterly Review of Economics & Business* 16 (Summer 1976): 37–50.

5474. McCarthy, Terence. "What the Vietnam War Has Cost." *New University Thought* 6 (Summer 1968): 1–17.

5475. Murray, Martin J. "The Post Colonial State: Investment and Intervention in Vietnam." *Politics and Society* 3:4 (1973): 437–461.

5476. Oliver, Richard P. "Increase in Defense-Related Employment During Vietnam Buildup." *Monthly Labor Review* 93 (Feb. 1970): 3–10.

5477. Riddle, Thomas A. "The $676 Billion Quagmire." *Progressive* 37 (Oct. 1973): 33–37.

5478. Schultze, C.L. "The Fiscal Dividend After Vietnam: Military versus Civilian Spending." In U.S. Congress. Joint Economic Committee. Hearings; *The Military Budget and National Economic Priorities*. 91st Cong., 1st sess., 1969. Pt. 1, 45–86.

5479. "Vietnam and the Peace Dividend." In *Setting National Priorities: The 1972 Budget*, edited by C.L. Schultze, et al. Washington, DC: Brookings Institution, 1971, 102–107.

5480. "War Costs: Budget Figures Easy, Others Impossible." *CQ Weekly Report* 31 (Jan. 27, 1973): 148–150.

❋ Chapter Nine ❋
The War at Home

AMERICAN OFFICIALS, both civilian and military, apparently failed to comprehend the important role the "home front" would play in determining America's Vietnam strategies.[1] The generals, presidents and their advisors guiding America's Southeast Asian policies had come to political maturity in the 1940s and early 1950s. They had been schooled, by books or experience, in the politics of international power which they defined largely in military terms. Unfortunately for their aspirations, they ignored a vital element of power—morals and morale. In the end, "public will," more than military or economic power, determined America's final strategy—withdrawal.

Wars waged by democratic societies require public approval of policy and goals, according to Alonzo Hamby (5499). He reports that the Korean and Vietnam wars "appear to demonstrate that the American people are unlikely to support extended limited wars that promise neither a decisive victory or a quick end." But then, how many peoples will? The dynamics of the "national will" have been widely studied, as the selections below will reveal.

Television and the antiwar movement did much to shape Americans' view of the war. The antiwar movement took many forms and involved many individuals of widely differing political philosophies. Yet the leadership and direction of the mass protests against the war came from traditional pacifists, youthful campus "radicals" and the ideologically committed Left. For an excellent overview of the antiwar movement's organization, and for an introduction to "movement" personalities, see Fred Halstead's account (5707). The campus scene is caught in Ken Hurwitz's poignant memoir (5713), and there are other fine personal accounts. (For congressional antiwar attitudes, see Chapter 5.)

No adequate reassessment of the broad impact of the antiwar movement on American foreign policy, or on American society itself, is yet available. Such a reassessment should begin with an examination of the political and social currents that inspired those individuals and groups who led the mass protest movement. Halstead's reconstruction of the politics of the various national antiwar coordinating committees dispells any doubt that many of these activists hoped their efforts would lead to more than an "end to the war." Consequently, some of the questions that need to be addressed are: Who were the protesters? Was there any concensus between the antiwar majority (those who did not attend rallies) and the platforms and speakers of the antiwar movement? How many of the protesters underwent any substantial change in their political, social and economic values?

The role of the media in presenting the "facts" of the Indochina War is still a matter of considerable controversy. Peter Braestrup's massive study (5579) on the reporting of the 1968 Tet offensive raises serious questions about the manner and motives of reporting.

However, any final evaluation of media activities must also take into consideration the government's self-serving, frequently inhibiting, role in providing information to the American public.

Issues of the Vietnam conflict remain with us today. Should amnesty be given to draft evaders and deserters? Are we adequately providing for Vietnam veterans? The question of amnesty has often been embroiled in politically inspired emotions and semantic confusion. To extend amnesty does not mean to forgive past behavior, which both draft resisters and the American Legion denounce, but rather it means to forget past actions and to begin anew. Moreover, military and draft "offenders" may not be who they have been thought to be. Baskir and Strauss (5924) report that President Ford's clemency board "had expected to find intensely political, well-educated, antiwar activists; instead, the typical cases involved high school dropouts from low-income families whose offenses were often the result of severe personal problems.

Public indifference or hostility to Vietnam veterans, rather prevalent in the early and middle 1970s, appeared to be waning at the end of the decade. A great deal has been made of the fact that these veterans returned to neither victory parades nor popular adulation, and that this missing glory has left a personal burden of emotional torment. Perhaps the more balanced portrait of the Vietnam veteran, shown in Table XV, that has begun to appear in films, books and television will help ease that emotional burden.

Books by Levy (6068) and Lifton (6069) contributed to the creation of the infamous, incorrect stereotype that earlier plagued the veteran; see Ladinsky's essay (6096) for a much needed correction and evaluation of other accounts. Perhaps the most balanced account of the Vietnam veteran's plight is told by Starr (6073), while the question of drug usage is best handled in Robins (6072).

NOTE

1. See Bernard Brodie, *War and Politics* (New York: Macmillan, 1973).

TABLE XV

A Statistical Portrait of the Vietnam Veteran

Number of Veterans		
Vietnam era, 1964–75	8.7	million
Service in Vietnam	2.6	million
In Vietnam Combat	1	million (est)
Vital Statistics, 1977–78		
Average Age	32	years
Education (median year)	12.9	years
Utilizing G.I. Bill	65	percent[*]
Income, ages 20–39	$12,680[**]	
Unemployment, ages 20–34	5.5	percent
Disabled veterans (512,000)	50	percent (est)
In VA hospitals	9,652	
For Psychiatric problems	60	percent

Source: Compilation from Veterans Administration, Department of Defense and Public Reports.

[*]higher than for World War II or Korean veterans

[**]some $2,800 higher than non-veteran

Chronology of
Major Antiwar Activities

1964   *May:* May Second Movement (M–2–M) begins collecting signatures on a pledge to refuse to fight in Vietnam

1965   *March 24–25:* First "teach-in" at the University of Michigan
April 17: SDS-inspired "March on Washington" draws 20,000*
May 15: TV "national teach-in" at Washington, DC
May 21–22: Berkeley "teach-in" attracts 30,000
August 6: National Coordinating Committee to End War in Vietnam (NCC) established at Madison, Wisconsin
August 9: "Declaration of Peace" march in Washington to Congressional building
August 30: Congress passed and Johnson signed law prohibiting mutilation of draft cards
October 15–16: International Days of Protest; New York City "Fifth Avenue Vietnam Peace Parade" draws 30,000
November 25–28: First convention of NCC; March on Washington for Peace in Vietnam (Nov. 27) inspired by SANE

1966   *January 6:* Student National Coordinating Committee (SNCC) and a civil rights group come out against the war
March 26: Second International Days of Protest with demonstrations on a worldwide scale; demonstrations in over 100 cities, a New York City march draws 50,000
June–July: "Fort Hood Three" refuse reassignment to Vietnam

July 4: Los Angeles demonstration sponsored by Peace Action Council
August 6–9: Demonstrations held in several cities; Cleveland, Atlanta, and San Diego have largest antiwar actions yet
November 5–8: Nationwide demonstrations, most with modest participation
November 9: Dearborn, Michigan referendum on Vietnam; 40 percent of middle-class voters call for immediate withdrawal
November 26: Organization of Spring Mobilization committee to End the War in Vietnam at Cleveland, Ohio; headquarters to be in New York City
December 8: SANE rally against the war held in Madison Square Garden draws 20,000
Mid-December: Harrison Salisbury's dispatches from Hanoi for the *New York Times* mark the first shift in the major media; King Broadcasting (TV) in the Pacific Northwest also begins criticizing LBJ
December 28–30: "Student Mobilization Committee to End the War in Vietnam" organized in Chicago; headquarters in New York City

1967   *February 25:* Dr. Martin Luther King endorses the antiwar movement
April 15: Nationwide demonstrations; New York City has 125,000 demonstraters, San Francisco 75,000; also end of Boston-to-Pentagon walk

*Crowd sizes are estimates; figures vary.

June 23: Century Plaza, Los Angeles, saw 20,000 protest LBJ's visit; police break up the protest in first such confrontation in U.S. during antiwar movement

August 6: 10,000 people turn out in Los Angeles for another march; this time no police confrontation

October 16–20: San Francisco Bay Area "Stop the Draft Week" with draft card turn-in

October 21: March on the Pentagon draws 100,000

November 7: San Francisco referendum on the war

December 4–8: Second "Stop the Draft Week"; this time in New York City

1968

January 27–29: New York City conference of Student Mobilization Committee brings together 900 leaders from 110 colleges and 40 high schools

April 23: Columbia University strike begins

April 26: Student antiwar strikes and public demonstrations draw over 1 million participants

August 28–30: Police battle rioters at the Chicago Democratic Convention

1969

January 20: First Counter-Inaugural in Washington and New York City, with ball and parade, draws 10,000

March 29: Federal grand jury in Chicago indicts eight for inciting convention riot

April 5: Easter GI-civilian demonstrations with largest turn-outs in Chicago (30,000), New York City (100,000) and San Francisco (40,000)

July 4–5: Formation of New Mobilization Committee to End War in Vietnam ("New Mobe") at Chicago

October 8–11: Weathermen's "Days of Rage" end in rioting in Chicago

October 15: Vietnam Moratorium at colleges and public meetings

November 13–15: March Against Death and Vietnam Moratorium in Washington and San Francisco

1970

April 15: Vietnam Moratorium, student strikes and anti-ROTC actions occur in major cities and on many college campuses

May 1–13: General campus strikes protesting the Cambodian intervention

May 4: Kent State University students shot by national guardsmen

May 9: Widespread demonstrations

May 13: Jackson State University students shot by police

August 29: Chicano Moratorium in Los Angeles

October 31: Call for nationwide protests, small turn-out

1971

April 19–24: National Peace Action Week, largest crowds in Washington (200,000–500,000) and San Francisco (150,000–350,000)

May 1–3: Demonstrations in Washington, 7,000 people arrested

November 6: General antiwar demonstrations, crowds small

1972

January 19–20: Second Counter-Inaugural in Washington, large crowd

General Accounts

These two accounts are solid surveys of the "home front" during the Vietnam conflict.

5481. Kendrick, Alexander. *The Wound Within: America in the Vietnam Years, 1954–1974.* Boston: Little, Brown, 1974.

5482. Powers, Thomas. *The War at Home: Vietnam and the American People, 1964–1968.* New York: Grossman, 1973.

Public Opinion

Opinions about "public opinion" were, and are, plentiful; accurate measurement of it and its impact upon policy are more difficult to discern. The Gallup Poll (see monthly issued Gallup Political Index Report) *began in early 1965, asking periodically two questions: 1) did the public have confidence in the President's handling of the war? and 2) did the U.S. make a mistake sending troops to fight in Vietnam? By July 1967, a majority began expressing the view that we had made a mistake in intervening in Vietnam. Of the many good accounts, see Gallup's collected polls (5484), and the essays by Verba and Brody (5508) and Robinson and Jacobson (5541).*

Books and Dissertations

5483. Andrews, Bruce. *Public Constraint and American Policy in Vietnam.* Sage Progressional Papers 4. Beverly Hills, CA: Sage, 1976. Policymakers did not want to recognize antiwar opposition.

5484. Gallup, George H. *The Gallup Poll: Public Opinion, 1935–1971.* 3 vols. New York: Random House, 1972. [indexed]

5485. Harris, Louis. *The Anguish of Change.* New York: Norton, 1973. [opinion polls]

5486. Leites, Nathan. *Edwin Reischauer and the Choice on the War.* P–3715. Santa Monica, CA: Rand Corp., Oct. 1967.

5487. Lubell, Samuel. *The Hidden Crisis in American Politics.* New York: Norton, 1971. Lubell has a chapter on public reaction to the war.

5488. Mueller, John E. *War, Presidents and Public Opinion.* New York: Wiley, 1973.

5489. Simon, Jeffrey D. "Public Opinion and American Foreign Policy, 1952–1972." Ph.D. dissertation, University of Southern California, 1978.

5490. Weaver, G.R. *The American Public and Vietnam: An In-Depth Study of the American People in Times of International Conflict.* Ph.D. dissertation, American University, 1970.

5491. Weiler, H. *Vietnam: Eine Volkerrechtliche Analyse des Amerikanishen Krieges und Seiner Vorgeschichte.* Marburg: Marburger Abhandlunge zur Politishen Wissenschaft, 1973–1974.

5492. Wood, Hugh G. "American Reaction to Limited War in Asia: Korea and Vietnam, 1950–1968." Ph.D. dissertation, University of Colorado, 1974.

Retrospective Essays

5493. Brody, Richard A., and Sidney Verba. "Hawk and Dove: The Search for an Explanation of Vietnam Policy Preferences." *Acta Politica* 7 (July 1972): 285–322.

5494. Burstein, Paul, and William Freudenburg. "Changing Public Policy: The Impact of Public Opinion, Antiwar Demonstrations, and War Costs on Senate Voting on Vietnam War Motions." *American Journal of Sociology* 83 (July 1978): 99–122.

5495. Granberg, Donald. "Jewish–non-Jewish Differences on the Vietnam War: A Study of Social Psychologists." *American Sociologist* 8 (Aug. 1973): 101–106.

5496. _____, and Gail Corrigan. "Authoritarianism, Dogmatism and Orientations Toward the Vietnam War." *Sociometry* 35 (Sept. 1972): 468–476.

5497. Granberg, Donald, and John Seidel. "Social Judgments of the Urban and Vietnam Issues in 1968 and 1972." *Social Forces* 55 (Sept. 1976): 1–15.

5498. Gray, Colin S. "Hawks and Doves: Values and Policy." *Journal of Political and Military Sociology* 3 (Spring 1975): 85–94.

5499. Hamby, Alonzo L. "Public Opinion: Korea and Vietnam." *Wilson Quarterly* 2 (Summer 1978): 137–141.

5500. Herzon, Frederick D., et al. "Personality and Public Opinion: The Case of Authoritarianism, Prejudice and Support for the Korean and Vietnam Wars." *Polity* 11 (Fall 1978): 92–113.

5501. Hollander, Neil. "Adolescents and the War: the Sources of Socialization." *Journalism Quarterly* 48 (Autumn 1971): 472–279. [impact of mass media]

5502.   Lau, Richard R., et al. "Self-Interest and Civilian's Attitudes Toward the Vietnam War." *Public Opinion Quarterly* 42 (Winter 1978): 464–483.

5503.   Lunch, William M., and Peter W. Sperlich. "American Public Opinion and the War in Vietnam." *Western Political Quarterly* 32 (Mar. 1979): 21–44.

5504.   Mullady, Brian. "The Military Implications of Public Opinion." *Air University Review* 29 (May–June 1978): 51–59.

5505.   Page, Benjamin I., and Richard A. Brody. "Policy Voting and the Electoral Process: the Vietnam War Issue." *American Political Science Review* 66 (Sept. 1972): 979–995.

5506.   Rothbart, Myron, and James C.M. Johnson. "Social Class and the Vietnam War: Some Discrepant Motives for Supporting or Opposing United States Involvement in Southeast Asia." *Pacific Sociological Review* 17 (Jan. 1974): 46–59.

5507.   Sigelman, Lee. "Rallying to the President's Support: A Reappraisal of the Evidence." *Polity* 11:4 (1979): 542–561.

5508.   Verba, Sidney, and Richard A. Brody. "Participation, Policy Preferences, and the War in Vietnam." *Public Opinion Quarterly* 34 (Fall 1970): 325–332.

5509.   Welch, Susan K. and Walter B. Oliver. "Interest Groups, Ideology and the Costs of Participation." *Rocky Mountain Social Science Journal* 12 (Apr. 1975): 81–98.

Contemporary Essays
5510.   Appleton, Sheldon. "The Public, the Polls, and the War." *Vietnam Perspectives* 1:4 (May 1966): 3–13.

5511.   Brogan, Dennis W. "Americans and the War in Vietnam." *Listener* 75 (Apr. 7, 1966): 493–495, 509.

5512.   Browne, R.S. "The Freedom Movement and the War in Vietnam." *Freedom-Ways* 5 (Fall 1965): 467–480.

5513.   Burnham, W.D. "Vietnam and the Voter." *Commonweal* 84 (Sept. 30, 1966): 635–637.

5514.   Caine, P.D. "The United States in Korea and Vietnam: A Study in Public Opinion." *Air University Review* 20 (Jan.–Feb. 1968): 49–55.

5515.   Converse, Philip E., and Howard Schuman. "Silent Majorities and the Vietnam War." *Scientific American* 222 (June 1970): 17–25.

5516.   "The Current American Mood: Its Consciousness

of Vietnam." *Round Table* 55 (Sept. 1965): 342–347.

5517.   Erskine, Hazel. "The Polls: Is War a Mistake?" *Public Opinion Quarterly* 34 (Spring 1970): 134–150.

5518.   Fall, Bernard B. "Vietnam 'Hawks' and 'Doves.'" *New Republic* 152 (Jan. 16, 1965): 7–8.

5519.   Finn, James. "The Debate on Vietnam." *Catholic World* 203 (May 1966): 76–80.

5520.   Friedman, A., and Henry S. Commager. "Debate on Vietnam Policy." *Massachusetts Review* 7 (Spring 1966): 407–419.

5521.   Gelb, Leslie H. "The Essential Domino: American Politics and Vietnam." *Foreign Affairs* 50 (Apr. 1972): 459–475.

5522.   Hahn, Harlan. "Correlates of Public Sentiments about War: Local Referenda on the Vietnam Issue." *American Political Science Review* 64 (Dec. 1970): 1186–1198.

5523.   Halberstam, David. "The Questions Which Tear Us Apart." *Harper's* 240 (Feb. 1970): 70–76.

5524.   Halle, L.J. "After Vietnam—Another Witchhunt?" *New York Times Magazine* (June 6, 1971): 36ff.

5525.   Hamilton, Richard F. "A Research Note on the Mass Support for 'Tough' Military Initiatives." *American Sociological Review* 38 (June 1968): 439–445. [Korea and Vietnam]

5526.   Heckscher, August. "Democracy and Foreign Policy: The Case of Vietnam." *American Scholar* 35 (Autumn 1966): 613–620.

5527.   Howe, Irving. "When Grave Issues Like Vietnam Are up to Debate, the Writer Can't Keep to His Attic." *New York Times Magazine* (Dec. 5, 1965): 43.

5528.   Iglitzin, L.P. "Democracy and the Radical Challenge." *Midwest Quarterly* 12 (Nov. 1970): 59–77.

5529.   Kroef, Justus M. van der. "[American Opinion on the Vietnam War]." *Contemporary Review:* "I: The Doves" 206 (1965): 295–299; "II: The Hawks" 207 (July 1965): 22–25.

5530.   Labin, Suzanne. "Survey of American Public Opinion on the Vietnam War." *NATO's Fifteen Nations* 13 (Apr.–May 1968): 46–49ff.

5531.   Larson, Allan. "Politics, Social Change, and the Conflict of Generations." *Midwest Quarterly* 11 (Jan. 1970): 123–137.

5532.   Lipset, Seymour M. "Polls and Protests." *Foreign Affairs* 49 (Apr. 1971): 548–555.

5533. ———. "The President, the Polls, and Vietnam." *Trans-Action* 3 (Sept.–Oct. 1966): 19–24.

5534. Lowry, C.W. "American Intellectual and U.S. Vietnam Policy." *World Affairs* 128 (Apr.–June 1965): 21–27.

5535. McWilliams, Wilson C. "Democracy, Publics and Protest: The Problem of Foreign Policy." *Journal of International Affairs* 23:2 (1969): 189–209.

5536. Markel, Lester. "Public Opinion and the War in Vietnam." *New York Times Magazine* (Aug. 8, 1965): 9.

5537. Mueller, John E. "Trends in Popular Support for the Wars in Korea and Vietnam." *American Political Science Review* 65 (June 1971): 358–375.

5538. Nuveen, John. "Vietnam: The Neglected Debate." *Christian Century* 84 (Mar. 29, 1967): 399–403.

5539. "Public Opinion and the Vietnam War, 1964–1967." *Gallup Opinion Index*, no. 30 (Dec. 1967): 6–35.

5540. "Public Opinion on the Vietnam War, 1964–1969: A Special Report." *Gallup Opinion Index*, no. 52 (Oct. 1969): 1–15.

5541. Robinson, J.P., and S.G. Jacobson. "American Public Opinion about Vietnam." Peace Research Society (International) *Papers* 10 (1968): 63–79. [also in W. Isard, ed. *Vietnam: Issues and Alternatives*. Cambridge, MA: Schenkman, 1969]

5542. Stahnke, P.K. "The New Left and Its Implications for Strategy in the Seventies." *Naval War College Review* 22 (Summer 1969): 20–42.

5543. "The State of the Vietnam Protest." *War–Peace Report* 7 (June–July 1967): 14–15.

5544. Taylor, Clyde. "Black Consciousness and the Vietnam War." *Black Scholar* 5 (Oct. 1973): 2–8.

5545. Trillin, Calvin. "A Reporter at Large: The War in Kansas." *New Yorker* 43 (Apr. 1967): 56–145.

5546. Verba, Sidney, et al. "Public Opinion and the War in Vietnam." *American Political Science Review* 61 (June 1967): 317–333.

5547. Windmiller, Marshall. "U.S. Public Opinion and the Vietnam War." *Review of International Affairs* [Belgrade] 18 (Jan. 20, 1967): 5–7.

ISSUES: MORALITY AND CONSCIENCE

Critics focused on the moral and ethical issues involved in U.S. involvement in the Vietnam conflict.

5548. Brown, Robert M. "The Church and Vietnam." *Commonweal* 87 (Oct. 13, 1967): 52–54.

5549. ———. "Vietnam: Crisis of Conscience." *Catholic World* 206 (Oct. 1967): 5–10.

5550. ———, Abraham J. Heschel, and Michael Novak. *Vietnam: Crisis of Conscience*. New York: Association Press, 1967.

5551. Brzezinski, Zbigniew. "Peace, Morality and Vietnam." *New Leader* 48 (Apr. 12, 1965): 8–9.

5552. Campbell, Keith E. "Religiosity and Attitude Toward Selected Wars: A Correlation Study." Ph.D. dissertation, University of Missouri— Columbia, 1977.

5553. Capps, Walter H. "The Vietnam War and American Values." *Center Magazine* 11 (July–Aug. 1978): 17–39.

5554. Colenback, Don F. "Christian Moral Argument and United States Policy in Viet Nam." Ph.D. dissertation, Yale University, 1975.

5555. Drinan, Robert F. *Vietnam and Armageddon: Peace, War and the Christian Conscience*. New York: Sheed & Ward, 1970.

5556. England, Eugene. "The Tragedy of Vietnam and the Responsibility of Mormons." *Dialogue: A Journal of Mormon Thought* 2:4 (1967): 71–91.

5557. Granberg, Donald, and Keith E. Campbell. "Certain Aspects of Religiosity and Orientations Toward the Vietnam War Among Missouri Undergraduates." *Sociological Analysis* 34 (Spring 1973): 40–49.

5558. Hamilton, Michael P., ed. *The Vietnam War: Christian Perspectives*. Grand Rapids, MI: Eerdmans, 1967.

5559. Harris, W.H. "Morality, Moralism and Vietnam." *Christian Century* 82 (Sept. 22, 1965): 1155–1157.

5560. Menzel, Paul, ed. *Moral Argument and the War in Vietnam*. Nashville: Aurora, 1971.

5561. Minogue, K.R. "On the Fashionable Idea of National Guilt." *American Scholar* 39 (Spring 1970): 211–218.

5562. Myrdal, Gunnar. "The Vietnam War and the

Political and Moral Isolation of America." *New University Thought* 5 (Spring 1967): 3–12.

5563. Neuhaus, Richard J. "The War, the Churches, and Civil Religion." *Annals of the American Academy of Political and Social Science* 387 (Jan. 1970): 128–140.

5564. Porter, Ethel M. "Vietnam and the Collapse of the American Democratic Faith: The Meeting of Ethics and Ideology in History, 1963–1969." Ph.D. dissertation, Yale University, 1978.

5565. Quinley, Harold E. "The Protestant Clergy and the War in Vietnam." *Public Opinion Quarterly* 34 (Spring 1970): 43–52.

5566. Russell, Bertrand. "Appeal to the American Conscience." *Liberation* 11 (Aug. 1966): 15–18.

5567. Schevitz, Jeffery M. *The Weaponsmakers: Personal and Professional Crisis During the Vietnam War.* Cambridge, MA: Schenkman, 1978.

5568. Smylie, James H. "American Religious Bodies, Just War, and Vietnam." *Journal of Church and State* 11 (Autumn 1969): 383–408.

5569. Starr, Jerold M. "Religious Preference, Religiosity and Opposition to War." *Sociological Analysis* 36 (Winter 1975): 323–334.

5570. Swomley, John M., Jr. "Who Speaks for the Church." *Christian Century* 85 (Mar. 6, 1968): 291–293.

5571. United Presbyterian Church. U.S.A. General Assembly. *Vietnam: The Christian, the Gospel, the Church.* Philadelphia, PA, 1967.

5572. Wermuth, Anthony L. "Deputies of Zeus: Morality and the Vietnam War." *U.S. Naval Institute Proceedings* 100 (Aug. 1974): 26–34. Wermuth questions the moral arguments.

5573. Wogman, Philip. "A Moral Reassessment of Our War in Vietnam." *Christian Century* 84 (Jan. 4, 1967): 7–9.

5574. Wolf, Donald J. "Vietnam Morality: Who Judges What, When, How." *Catholic World* 207 (June 1968): 107–110.

ISSUES: TRUST IN GOVERNMENT

How much did the Vietnam conflict contribute to the American public's decline of confidence in their government?

5575. Bachman, Jerald G., and M. Kent Jennings. "The

Impact of Vietnam on Trust in Government." *Journal of Social Issues* 31 (Fall 1975): 141–156.

5576. Cantril, Albert. *The American People, Viet-Nam and the Presidency.* Princeton: Institute for International Social Research, 1970.

5577. Jukam, Thomas O. "The Effects of Vietnam Policy on the Decline of Political Trust in American Political Life." Ph.D. dissertation, Michigan State University, 1978.

Media: Reporting the War

Press and TV coverage of the war has been, and will likely continue to be, a controversial matter. Did the American press corps in Saigon develop an anti-South Vietnamese and anti-U.S. involvement bias? How accurately did press and TV accounts reflect "reality"? Did American officials attempt to mislead the press corps? Peter Braestrup's Big Story (5579) is a critical, retrospective look at the problem. (See also, in Chapter 4, "Personal Experiences in Vietnam" for some reporters' accounts.)

Books and Documents
5578. Bagdikian, Ben H. *The Information Machine.* New York: Harper & Row, 1971.

5579. Braestrup, Peter. *Big Story: How the American Press and Television Reported and Interpreted the Crisis of Tet 1968 in Vietnam and in Washington.* 2 vols. Boulder, CO: Westview Press, 1977.

5580. Clews, John C. *Communist Propaganda Techniques.* New York: Praeger, 1964.

5581. Efron, Edith. *The News Twisters.* Los Angeles: Nash, 1971.

5582. Hallin, Daniel C. "The Mass Media and the Crisis in American Politics: The Case of Vietnam." Ph.D. dissertation, University of California, Berkeley, 1980.

5583. Jaeggi, Urs T.V., et al. *Der Vietnamkrieg und die Presse.* Zurich: EVA-Verlag, 1965.

5584. Knightley, Phillip. *The First Casualty: From the Crimea to Vietnam: The War Correspondent as Hero, Propagandist, and Myth Maker.* New York: Harcourt, Brace, Jovanovich, 1975.

5585. Lee, Richard W., ed. *Politics and the Press.* Washington, DC: Acropolis, 1970.

5586.   MacDonald, Glenn. *Report or Distort? The Inside Story of the Media's Coverage of the Vietnam War.* New York: Exposition, 1973.

5587.   Norris, Benjamin P. "Transnational Perception, An Ideal Typical Approach: An Examination of Ten Influential American Journals of Political Opinion Concerning Their Image of the Democratic Republic of Vietnam and Its Allies, 1954–1973." Ph.D. dissertation, University of Pittsburgh, 1976.

5588.   Small, William T. *Political Power and the Press.* New York: Norton, 1972.

5589.   Stein, Robert. *Media Power: Who Is Shaping Your Picture of the World?* Boston: Houghton Mifflin, 1972.

5590.   U.S. House. Committee on Government Operations. Hearings; *U.S. Government Information Policies and Practices: The Pentagon Papers.* 92d Cong., 1st sess., 1971.

5591.   U.S. Senate. Committee on Foreign Relations. Hearings; *News Policies in Vietnam.* 89th Cong., 2d sess., Aug. 17, 31, 1966.

Essays

5592.   Aronson, James. "The Media and the Message." In *The Senator Gravel Edition: The Pentagon Papers.* Vol. 5: *Critical Essays.* Boston: Beacon, 1972, 41–59.

5593.   "As Newsmen See the Vietnam War." *War/Peace Report* 8 (Mar. 1968): 6–11.

5594.   Baldwin, Hanson W. "The Information War in Saigon." *Reporter* 34 (Feb. 24, 1966): 29–31.

5595.   Blanchard, Ralph W. "The Newsman in Vietnam." *U.S. Naval Institute Proceedings* 95 (Feb. 1969): 50–57.

5596.   _____. "The Newsman in Vietnam: Responsible or Irresponsible?" *Naval War College Review* 20 (June 1968): 14–42.

5597.   Braestrup, Peter. "Covering the Vietnam War." *Nieman Reports* 23 (Dec. 1969): 8–13.

5598.   _____. "The Press Corps in Vietnam." *Freedom At Issue*, no. 41 (1977): 9–11.

5599.   Browne, Malcolm W. "Viet Nam Reporting: Three Years of Crisis." *Columbia Journalism Review* 3 (Fall 1964): 4–9.

5600.   Chomsky, Noam. "Reporting Indochina: The News Media and the Legitimation of Lies." *Social Policy* 4 (Sept.–Oct 1973): 4–19.

5601.   Cleary, T.J., Jr. "Aid and Comfort to the Enemy." *Military Review* 48 (Aug. 1968): 51–55.

5602.   Davison, W. Phillips. "Making Sense of Vietnam News." *Columbia Journalism Review* 5 (Winter 1966–1967): 5–9.

5603.   Fox, Tom. "The Word From the Front: The Unreported War, Army vs the Press." *Commonweal* 90 (Aug. 8, 1969): 485–486.

5604.   Fritchey, Clayton. "Are We Being Told the Truth About Vietnam?" *Harper's* 234 (Mar. 1967): 121–122.

5605.   Goodman, G.J.W. "Our Man in Saigon [David Halberstam]." *Esquire* 61 (June 1964): 57–60, 144–146.

5606.   Halberstam, David. "Getting the Story in Vietnam." *Commentary* 39 (Jan. 1968): 30–34.

5607.   Hui Yeh. "A Television Cameraman in South Vietnam." *China Reconstructs* [Peking] 15 (June 1966): 8–11.

5608.   Johnson, DeWayne B. "Vietnam: Report Card on the Press Corps at War." *Journalism Quarterly* 46 (Spring 1969): 9–19.

5609.   Karnow, Stanley. "The Newsmen's War in Vietnam." *Nieman Reports* 17 (Dec. 1963): 3–8.

5610.   Kennedy, William W. "It Takes More Than Talent to Cover a War." *Army* 28 (June 1978): 23–26.

5611.   Lang, Daniel. "A Reporter at Large: Home Again." *New Yorker* 47 (Sept. 4, 1971): 35ff.

5612.   Lawrence, David. "What's Become of Voluntary Censorship?" *U.S. News and World Report* 67 (Sept. 8, 1969): 92.

5613.   Marshall, S.L.A. "Press Failure in Vietnam." *New Leader* 49 (Oct. 10, 1966): 3–5. For a response by eight war correspondents, see *New Leader* 49 (Nov. 21, 1966): 3–16.

5614.   Padgett, Harry E. "A Close Look at the Controversial U.S. Press Corps in Vietnam." *Navy* 11 (May 1968): 8–14.

5615.   Polsby, Nelson W. "Political Science and the Press: Notes on the Coverage of a Public Opinion Survey on the Vietnam War." *Western Political Quarterly* 22 (Mar. 1969): 47–60.

5616.   "Press Sees Vietnam [Tet] Offensive as U.S. Defeat." *Current Digest of the Soviet Press* 20 (Feb. 28, 1968): 3–6.

5617.   Rigg, Robert B. "How Not to Report a War." *Military Review* 49 (June 1969): 14–24.

5618.   Scott-Barnet, D.W. "The Media and the Armed Services." *Military Review* 52 (Apr. 1972): 62–76.

5619.   Stone, I.F. "Vietnam: An Exercise in Self-Delusion." *New York Review of Books* (Apr. 22, 1965): 4–6.

5620.   Turnbull, G.S., Jr. "Reporting of the War in Indo-China: A Critique." *Journalism Quarterly* 34 (Winter 1957): 87–89.

5621.   "Vietnam and the Press: A Critical Analysis." *Columbia Journalism Review* 9 (Winter 1971): 7–47.

5622.   Wechsler, J.A. "The Press and the War." *Progressive* 30 (June 1967): 18–19.

5623.   Welch, Susan K. "The American Press and Indochina, 1950–56." In *Communication in International Politics*, edited by R.L. Merritt. Urbana: University of Illinois Press, 1972, 207–231.

5624.   ———. "Vietnam: How the Press Went Along." *Nation* 213 (Oct. 11, 1971): 32–33.

5625.   Young, Perry D. "Two of the Missing." *Harper's* 245 (Dec. 1972): 84–100.

GOVERNMENT AND PUBLIC INFORMATION

5626.   Arnold, Hugh M. "Official Justifications for America's Role in Indo-China, 1949–67." *Asian Affairs* [U.S.] 3 (Sept.–Oct. 1975): 31–48.

5627.   Bunge, Walter, Robert V. Hudson, and Chung Woo Suh. "Johnson's Information Strategy in Vietnam: An Evaluation." *Journalism Quarterly* 45 (Autumn 1968): 419–425.

5628.   Chittick, William O. "American Foreign Policy Elites: Attitudes Toward Secrecy and Publicity." *Journalism Quarterly* 47 (Winter 1970): 689–695.

5629.   Effros, William O. *Quotations—Vietnam: 1945–1970*. New York: Random House, 1970.

5630.   Elterman, Howard A. "The State, the Mass Media and Ideological Hegemony: United States Policy Decisions in Indochina, 1954–1975—Historical Record, Government Pronouncements and Press Coverage." Ph.D. dissertation, New York University, 1978.

5631.   Faulkner, Francis D. "Bao Chi: The American News Media in Vietnam, 1960–1975." Ph.D. dissertation, University of Massachusetts, 1981.

5632.   Goulding, Phil G. *Confirm or Deny: Informing the People on National Security*. New York: Harpers, 1970. The assistant secretary of defense discusses government secrecy and bombing policy.

5633.   Heise, Juergen A. *Minimum Disclosure: How the Pentagon Manipulates the News*. New York: Norton, 1979.

5634.   Huynk Kim Khanh. "The War in Vietnam: The U.S. Official Line: A Review Article." *Pacific Affairs* 42 (Spring 1969): 58–67.

5635.   Joseph, Paul I. "The Politics of "Good" and "Bad" Information: The National Security Bureaucracy and the Vietnam War." *Politics and Society* 7:1 (1977): 105–126.

5636.   Ladd, Bruce. *Crisis in Credibility*. New York: New American Library, 1968.

5637.   MacDonald, C.B. "Official History and the War in Vietnam." *Military Affairs* 32 (Spring 1968): 2–11.

5638.   McGaffin, William, and Erwin Knoll. *Anything But the Truth: The Credibility Gap: How the News is Managed in Washington*. New York: Putnam, 1968.

5639.   Moody, Randall J. "The Armed Forces Broadcast News System: Vietnam Version." *Journalism Quarterly* 47:1 (1970): 27–30.

5640.   Nguyen To-Thi. "A Content Analysis of Voice of America News Broadcasts to Vietnam (May 8–17, 1972)." Ph.D. dissertation, Ohio State University, 1977.

5641.   Wise, David. *The Politics of Lying: Government Deception, Secrecy and Power*. Garden City, NY: Doubleday, 1973.

TELEVISION

5642.   Adams, Anthony A. "A Study of Veteran Viewpoints on TV Coverage of the Vietnam War." *Journalism Quarterly* 54 (Summer 1977): 248–253. This is a study of 300 combat veterans and their views on news coverage.

5643.   Arlen, Michael J. *Living-Room War*. New York: Viking, 1969.

5644.   Bailey, George A. "Television War: Trends in Network Coverage of Vietnam, 1965–1970." *Journal of Broadcasting* 20 (Spring 1976): 147–158.

5645.   ———. "The Vietnam War According to Chet, David, Walter, Harry, Peter, Bob, Howard and Frank: A Content Analysis of Journalistic Performance by the Network Television Evening News Anchormen, 1965–1970." Ph.D. dissertation, University of Wisconsin, Madison, 1973.

5646. _____, and Lawrence W. Lichty. "Rough Justice on a Saigon Street: A Gatekeeper Study of NBC's Execution Film." *Journalism Quarterly* 49 (Summer 1972): 221–229.

5647. Browne, Don R. "An American Image as Presented Abroad by U.S. Television." *Journalism Quarterly* 45 (Summer 1968): 307–316.

5648. Compton, Neil. "Consensus Television." *Commentary* 40 (Oct. 1965): 67–72.

5649. Day, Robin. "Troubled Reflections of a TV Journalist." *Encounter* 34 (May 1970): 78–88.

5650. Frank, Robert S. "The IAS Case Against CBS." *Journal of Communication* 25 (Autumn 1975): 186–189.

5651. Gitlin, Todd A. "'The Whole World is Watching': Mass Media and the New Left, 1965–1970." Ph.D. dissertation, University of California, Berkeley, 1977.

5652. Hofstetter, C. Richard, and David W. Moore. "Watching TV News and Supporting the Military: A Surprising Impact of the News Media." *Armed Forces and Society* 5:2 (1979): 261–269.

5653. Jacobsen, K.C. "Television and the War: The Small Picture." *U.S. Naval Institute Proceedings* 101 (Mar. 1975): 54–60.

5654. Kirk, Gerry. "Heads They Win . . . Tails We Lose: TV and the War." *New Guard* 12 (Dec. 1972): 8–10.

5655. Lafever, Ernest W. "CBS and National Defense, 1972–1973." *Journal of Communication* 25 (Autumn 1975): 181–185.

5656. Lichty, Lawrence, and Murray Fromson. "Comparing Notes on Television's Coverage of the War." *Center Magazine* [Center for the Study of Democratic Institutions, Santa Barbara, CA] 12 (May 1979): 42–49.

5657. McNulty, Thomas M. "Network Television Documentary Treatment of the Vietnam War, 1965–1969." Ph.D. dissertation, Indiana University, 1974.

5658. _____. "Vietnam Specials: Policy and Content." *Journal of Communication* 25 (Autumn 1975): 173–180.

5659. "Pictures in Our Minds." *New Republic* 156 (Jan. 7, 1967): 9–10. [NBC news documentary "The Battle for Asia"]

5660. Rollins, Peter C. "Television's Vietnam: The Visual Language of Television News." *Journal of American Culture* 4:2 (1981): 114–135.

5661. Russo, Frank D. "A Study of Bias in TV Coverage of the Vietnam War, 1969–1970." *Public Opinion Quarterly* 35 (Winter 1971–1972): 539–543.

5662. Singer, Benjamin D. "Violence, Protest, and War in Television News: The U.S. and Canada Compared." *Public Opinion Quarterly* 34 (Winter 1970–1971): 611–616.

THE PRESS

Many of the essays listed under "Media: Reporting the War," above, pertain to activities of print-news journalists.

5663. Dibacco, Thomas V. "The Business Press and Vietnam: Ecstacy or Agony?" *Journalism Quarterly* 45 (Autumn 1968): 426–435.

5664. Hunter, William H. "The War in Vietnam, Luce Version." *New Republic* 148 (Mar. 23, 1963): 15–17.

5665. McDougall, Derek. "The Australian Press Coverage of the Vietnam War in 1965." *Australian Outlook* 20 (Dec. 1966): 303–310.

5666. *Vietnam: Articles and Editorials From the New Republic, 1955–1962.* Washington, DC: New Republic, 1966.

5667. "A Viet Nam Register: Journalism and a Year in the War." *Columbia Journalism Review* 6 (Winter 1967–1968): 4–13.

5668. Wright, James D. "Life, Time and the Fortunes of War." *Trans-Action* 9 (Jan. 1972): 42–52. [shifting opinion, 1964–1968]

CARTOONISTS VIEW THE WAR

5669. Abu, comp. *Verdicts on Vietnam: A World Collection of Cartoons.* London: Pemberton, 1968.

5670. Lee, Bill. *Absolutely No U.S. Personnel Permitted Beyond This Point.* New York: Dell, 1972.

5671. Pratt, Don, and Lee Blair. *Salmagundi Vietnam.* Rutland, VT: Tuttle, 1970.

5672. Steward, George. *What's So Funny About Vietnam?* Tampa, FL: Tampa Art & Publishing, 1968.

5673. Trudeau, G.B. *But This War Had Such Promise.* New York: Holt, Rinehart & Winston, 1973. [a Doonesbury book]

PHOTO ESSAYS

5674. Biberman, Edward. "Vietnam: An Artist's View of War." *Mankind* 2:3 (1969): 24–34.

5675. Brelis, Dean. *The Face of South Vietnam.* Boston: Houghton Mifflin, 1968.

5676. Cherry, Dick. "The Vietnam War as Filmed by U.S. Air Force Cameramen." *American Cinematographer* 49 (Sept. 1968): 658–661ff.

5677. Duncan, David Douglas. *I Protest!* New York: New American Library, 1968. [U.S. Marine operations around Khe Sanh]

5678. Gould, Donna, and Dave Dellinger, eds. *In the Teeth of War.* New York: Fifth Avenue Vietnam Peace Parade Committee, 1966. [Mar. 26, 1966 New York City demonstration]

5679. Greene, Felix. *Vietnam! Vietnam!* Palo Alto, CA: Fulton, 1966. Indictment of U.S. bombing of North Vietnam.

5680. Griffiths, Philip J. *Vietnam, Inc.* New York: Macmillan, 1971.

5681. Jury, Mark. *The Vietnam Photo Book.* New York: Grossman, 1971.

5682. Morris, Marjorie, and Don Sauers. *And/Or: Antonyms for Our Age.* New York: Harper & Row, 1967.

5683. Ribound, Marc, with text by Philippe Devillers. *Face of North Vietnam.* New York: Holt, Rinehart & Winston, 1970.

5684. Waterhouse, Charles H. *Vietnam Sketchbook: Drawings from Delta to DMZ.* Rutland, VT: Tuttle, 1968.

5685. _____. *Vietnam War Sketches: From the Air, Land and Sea.* Rutland, VT: Tuttle, 1970.

Antiwar Movement

The materials listed below emphasize the individuals and activities of the antiwar movement. Other dissenting arguments by activists can be found in "Issues: Morality and Conscience," above, this chapter. Halstead (5707) is a fine survey of the organization of the movement; Dellinger (5697) presents another retrospective view; and Vogelgesang (5729) evaluates the "mood of the U.S. intellectual left" during LBJ's term. For those who want to see the "literature" of various antiwar groups, Heath (5709) has preserved 118 pieces; his book also contains the names of many antiwar leaders around the country, and an extensive chronology of activities and events. A shorter chronology of major demonstrations follows the introduction to this chapter.

Books and Dissertations

5686. American Civil Liberties Union. Southern California Branch. *Day of Protest, Night of Violence: The Century City Peace March: A Report.* Los Angeles: Sawyer, 1967. This report describes the first major police confrontation with antiwar demonstrators, June 23, 1967.

5687. Bannan, John F., and Rosemary S. Bannan. *Law, Morality, and Vietnam: The Peace Militants and the Courts.* Bloomington: Indiana University Press, 1974.

5688. Berrigan, Daniel. *Trial of the Catonsville Nine.* Boston: Beacon, 1970.

5689. Berrigan, Philip. *Prison Journals of a Priest Revolutionary.* New York: Holt, Rinehart & Winston, 1970.

5690. Bloom Lynn Z. *Dr. Spock: Biography of a Conservative Radical.* Indianapolis: Bobbs-Merrill, 1972.

5691. Bryan, C.D.B. *Friendly Fire.* New York: Putnam, 1976.

5692. Burton, Michael G. "Elite Disunity and Political Instability: A Study of American Opposition to the Vietnam War." Ph.D. dissertation, University of Texas, Austin, 1974.

5693. Butwin, Miriam, and Patricia Pirmantgen. *Protest II: Civil Rights and Black Liberation, the Antiwar Movement.* Minneapolis: Lerner, 1972.

5694. Carl, William J., III. "Old Testament Prophecy and the Question of Prophetic Preaching: A Perspective of Ecclesiastical Protest to the Vietnam War and the Participation of William Sloane Coffin, Jr." Ph.D. dissertation, University of Pittsburgh, 1977.

5695. Cox, James R., Jr. "The Rhetorical Structure of Mass Protest: A Criticism of Selected Speeches of the Vietnam Antiwar Movement." Ph.D. dissertation, University of Pittsburgh, 1973.

5696. Dane, Barbara, comp. *The Vietnam Songbook.* New York: The Guardian, distributed by Monthly Review Press, 1969.

5697. Dellinger, Dave. *More Power Than We Know: The People's Movement Toward Democracy.* Garden City, NY: Anchor, 1975.

5698. Denardo, James D. "The Political Strategy of Protest and Rebellion." Ph.D. dissertation, Yale University, 1977. [SDS and antiwar movement]

5699. *Dr. Martin Luther King, Dr. John C. Bennet, Dr.*

Henry Steel Commager, Rabbi Abraham Heschel Speak on the War in Vietnam. New York: Clergy and Laymen Concerned About Vietnam, 1967.

5700.   Donovan, James A. *Militarism, U.S.A.* New York: Scribner's, 1970.

5701.   Duncan, David Douglas. *War Without Heroes.* New York: Harper & Row, 1970.

5702.   Duncan, Donald. *The New Legions.* London: Gollancz, 1967.

5703.   Fernandez, Benedict J. *In Opposition: Images of American Dissent in the Sixties.* New York: Da Capo, 1968.

5704.   Finan, John J. *Guns and Blood for Butter.* New York: Vantage, 1969.

5705.   Foner, Philip. *American Labor and the Indochina War: The Growth of Union Opposition.* New York: International Publishers, 1971.

5706.   Fortas, Abe. *Concerning Dissent and Civil Disobedience.* New York: Signet, 1968.

5707.   Halstead, Fred. *Out Now! A Participant's Account of the American Movement Against the Vietnam War (1965–1975).* New York: Monad, 1978. [an excellent survey]

5708.   Haskins, James. *The War and the Protest: Vietnam.* Garden City, NY: Doubleday, 1971.

5709.   Heath, G. Louis, ed. *Mutiny Does Not Happen Lightly: The Literature of the American Resistance to the Vietnam War.* Metuchen, NJ: Scarecrow, 1976. [valuable research source of ephemeral pamphlets]

5710.   Hensley, William E. "The Vietnam Anti-War Movement: History and Criticism." Ph.D. dissertation, University of Oregon, 1979.

5711.   Hentoff, Nat. *Peace Agitator: The Story of A.J. Muste.* New York: Macmillan, 1963. [senior "statesman" of the movement]

5712.   Hoffman, Paul. *Moratorium: An American Protest.* New York: Belmont-Tower, 1970.

5713.   Hurwitz, Ken. *Marching Nowhere.* New York: Norton, 1971. [Vietnam Moratorium Committee]

5714.   Jackson, Lester. "The Neutrality of the American Political System: An Analysis of Opportunities Afforded Left of Center Activists, with Emphasis on How They Could Have Ended the Vietnam War By 1970." Ph.D. dissertation, New York University, 1975.

5715.   Jacobs, Harold, ed. *Weatherman.* Palo Alto, CA: Ramparts, 1970. The Weathermen were a violent wing of the SDS responsible for many bombings.

5716.   Katz, Milton S. "Peace, Politics, and Protest: SANE and the American Peace Movement, 1957–1972." Ph.D. dissertation, Saint Louis University, 1973.

5717.   Lang, Daniel. *Patriotism Without Flags.* New York: Norton, 1974. The essays discuss the trial of Dr. Spock, U.S. deserters in Sweden, and many other topics.

5718.   Long, Ellis E. "Communication and Social Change: The Verbal and Nonverbal Protest of Selected Clerical Activists Opposed to the Vietnam War, 1965–1970." Ph.D. dissertation, Florida State University, 1971.

5719.   Mailer, Norman. *Armies of the Night.* Cleveland, OH: World, 1968. [Pentagon protest march, Oct. 21, 1967]

5720.   Miller, A.H. "Perceptions and Recommendations of the Vietnam Peace Movement: A Case Study of Activists in Pittsburgh." Ph.D. dissertation, University of Pittsburgh, 1969.

5721.   O'Rourke, William. *Harrisburg 7 and the New Catholic Left.* Binghamton, NY: Apollo Editions, 1973.

5722.   Rosenberg, Milton J., et al. *Vietnam and the Silent Majority: The Dove's Guide.* New York: Harper & Row, 1970.

5723.   Schultz, John. *Motion Will Be Denied: A New Report on the Chicago Conspiracy Trial.* New York: Morrow, 1972. This trial was an outgrowth of the 1968 riots.

5724.   Skolnick, Jerome H., ed. *The Politics of Protest: A Task Force Report Submitted to the National Commission on the Causes and Prevention of Violence.* New York: Simon & Schuster, 1970.

5725.   Spock, Benjamin M., and Mitchell Zimmerman. *Dr. Spock on Vietnam.* New York: Dell, 1968.

5726.   Taylor, Clyde, comp. *Vietnam and Black America: An Anthology of Protest and Resistance.* Garden City, NY: Anchor, 1973.

5727.   *Trials of the Resistance.* New York: Vintage, 1970.

5728.   Velvel, Lawrence R. *Undeclared War and Civil Disobedience: The American System in Crisis.* New York: Dunellen, 1970.

5729.   Vogelgesang, Sandy. *The Long Dark Night of the Soul: The American Intellectual Left and the Vietnam War.* New York: Harper & Row, 1974. This has an excellent bibliography of antiwar literature.

5730. *We Accuse: The Vietnam Day Protest in Berkeley, California.* Berkeley, CA: Diablo Press, 1965.

5731. Woodstone, Norma S. *Up Against the War: A Personal Introduction to U.S. Soldiers and Civilians Fighting Against the War in Vietnam.* New York: Tower, 1970.

5732. Zinn, Howard. *Disobedience and Democracy: Nine Fallacies on Law and Order.* New York: Random House, 1968.

Retrospective Essays

5733. Baral, Jaya Krishna. "Anti-Vietnam War Student Movement in America, 1965–1971." *Indian Political Science Review* [India] 12:1 (1978): 43–58.

5734. Berkowitz, William R. "Impact of Anti-Vietnam Demonstrations upon National Public Opinion and Military Indicators." *Social Research* 2 (Mar. 1973): 1–14.

5735. Burton, Michael G. "Elite Disunity and Collective Protest: the Vietnam Case." *Journal of Political and Military Sociology* 5 (Fall 1977): 169–183.

5736. Cox, James Robert, Jr. "Perspectives in Rhetorical Criticism on Movements: Antiwar Dissent, 1964–1970." *Western Speech* 38 (Fall 1974): 254–268.

5737. Fallows, James. "What Did You Do in the Class War, Daddy?" *Washington Monthly* 7 (Aug. 1975): 5–19. Fallows argues that the antiwar movement left a rich heritage for class warfare.

5738. Jacobson, Julius. "Neo-Stalinism: The Achilles Heel of the Peace Movement and the American Left." *New Politics* 11 (Summer 1976): 49–58.

5739. Mantell, David M. "Doves vs Hawks: Guess Who Had the Authoritarian Parents?" *Psychology Today* 8 (Sept. 1974): 56–62.

5740. Morse, Stanley J. "A Study of Participants in an Anti-Vietnam War Demonstration." *Journal of Social Issues* 27 (Fall 1971): 113–136.

5741. O'Brien, James. "The Antiwar Movement and the War." *Radical America* 8 (May–June 1974): 53–86.

5742. Pugh, M.D., et al. "Participation in Anti-War Demonstrations: A Test of the Parental Continuity Hypothesis." *Sociology and Social Research* 56 (Oct. 1971): 19–28.

5743. Schreiber, E.M. "Anti-war Demonstrations and American Public Opinion on the War in Vietnam." *British Journal of Sociology* 27 (June 1976): 225–236.

5744. _____. "Vietnam: Demonstrations and Votes in USA." *Politics* [Australia] 10 (Nov. 1975): 207–209.

5745. Schuman, Howard. "Two Sources of Antiwar Sentiment in America." *American Journal of Sociology* 78 (Nov. 1972): 513–536.

5746. Shippee, John. "Do Movements Learn? A Commentary on 'A Learning Theory of the American Anti-Vietnam War Movement' by John Vasquez." *Journal of Peace Research* 14:3 (1977): 261–266.

5747. Stohl, Michael. "War and Domestic Political Violence: The Case of the United States, 1890–1970." *Journal of Conflict Resolution* 19 (Sept. 1975): 379–416.

5748. Thorne, Barrie. "Protest and the Problems of Credibility: Uses of Knowledge and Risk-Taking in the Draft Resistance Movement of the 1960s." *Social Problems* 23:2 (1975): 111–123.

5749. Tygart, Clarence E. "Social Movement Participation: Clergy and the Anti-Vietnam War Movement." *Sociological Analysis* 34 (Fall 1973): 202–211.

5750. Vasquez, John A. "A Learning Theory of the American Anti-Vietnam War Movement." *Journal of Peace Research* 13:4 (1976): 299–314.

Contemporary Essays

5751. "The Audible Minority and the Price of Protest." *Army* 19 (Dec. 1969): 9–11.

5752. Barnes, P. "Withholding War Taxes." *New Republic* 164 (Apr. 10, 1971): 15–17.

5753. Beisner, Robert L. "1898 and 1968: The Anti-Imperialists and the Doves." *Political Science Quarterly* 85 (June 1970): 187–216.

5754. Bickel, Alexander M. "Judging the Chicago Trial." *Commentary* 51 (Jan. 1971): 31–40. [Chicago convention riots trial, 1969–1970]

5755. "The Biggest Bust." *Newsweek* 77 (May 17, 1971): 24–29. [review of antiwar tactics]

5756. Cicchetti, Charles J., et al. "On the Economics of Mass Demonstrations: A Case Study of the November 1969 March on Washington." *American Economic Review* 61 (Sept. 1971): 719–724.

5757. Crawford, Mary. "Peg Mullen and the Military: The Bureaucracy of Death." *Ms.* 5 (Jan. 1977): 70–73, 95. [cf. *Friendly Fire*]

5758. Dellinger, Dave. "Resistance: Vietnam and America." *Liberation* 12 (Nov. 1967): 3–7.

5759. "Far-Reaching Consequences Seen for War Dissent." *CQ Weekly Report* 25 (June 2, 1967): 935–937.

5760. Gannon, Thomas M. "A Report on the Vietnam Moratorium." *America* 121 (Nov. 7, 1969): 380–383.

5761. Goodman, William. "The New Mobe (I): Who's Who? What's What?" *New York Times Magazine* (Nov. 30, 1969): 25ff.

5762. Gottlieb, Gidon. "Vietnam and Civil Disobedience." *1967 Annual Survey of American Law* (1967): 699–716.

5763. Grauman, L., Jr. "Goals of Dissent: Evaluation of the Vietnam Protest Movement." *Nation* 205 (Dec. 11, 1967): 617–621.

5764. Guttmann, Allen. "Protest Against the War in Vietnam." *Annals of the American Academy of Political and Social Sciences* 382 (May 1969): 56–63.

5765. Halberstam, David. "The Vast Backfire of Activism." *Saturday Review* 55 (Dec. 1972): 28–32.

5766. Harries, Owen. "After the Moratorium." *Quadrant*, 65 14:3 (1970): 40–43.

5767. Harrington, Michael. "The Peace Movement is Using the Wrong Strategy." *New York Times Magazine* (May 30, 1971): 10–11, 20–23.

5768. _____. "Strategies for Opposition: The Draft-Tax Refusal- 'Resistance.'" *Dissent* 15 (Mar.–Apr. 1968): 119–130.

5769. Hartley, Anthony. "Antimilitarism Can Be Too Much of a Good Thing." *New York Times Magazine* (Oct. 19, 1969): 30–31ff.

5770. Howe, Irving, et al. "The Vietnam Protest." *New York Review of Books* (Nov. 25, 1965): 12–13.

5771. "Huge Moratorium Protest Divides Congress." *CQ Weekly Report* 27 (Oct. 17, 1969): 1971–1974ff.

5772. Ions, Edmund. "Dissent in America: The Constraints on Foreign Policy." *Conflict Studies* 18 (Dec. 1971): 1–14.

5773. Jackson, Bruce. "The Battle of the Pentagon." *Atlantic Monthly* 221 (Jan. 1968): 35–42. [Oct. 1967 march and news media]

5774. Kempton, Murray. "Washington After Dark." *New York Review of Books* (Dec. 18, 1969): 10ff. [mobilization march of Nov. 1969]

5775. McWilliams, Wilson C. "Civilian Disobedience and Contemporary Constitutionalism: The American Case." *Comparative Politics* 1 (Jan. 1969): 211–227.

5776. _____. "Opportunities and Dangers: Growing Public and Church Anti-Vietnamese War Attitude." *Nation* 214 (June 5, 1972): 706–708.

5777. Mander, John. "Letter from New York." *Encounter* [Great Britain] 34 (Jan. 1970): 3–10.

5778. Mitchell, Edward J. *Relating Rebellion To the Environment: An Econometric Approach.* P–3726. Santa Monica, CA: Rand Corp., Nov. 1967.

5779. Mongillo, Larry. "Ellsberg at Stanford: Performing the New Morality." *New Guard* 12 (June 1972): 8–9.

5780. Murdock, Steve. "Labor for Peace: The Unions Find Consensus." *Nation* 215 (July 10, 1972): 11–14.

5781. Muste, A.J. "Last Words: Report on a Visit to North Vietnam." *Liberation* 11 (Feb. 1967): 8–11.

5782. Ogburn, C. "Mr. Katzenbach's Puzzle." *New Republic* 157 (Nov. 4, 1967): 13–14. Why did liberals who supported the Korean War oppose Vietnam.

5783. Pemberton, P. "Translating Antiwar Protest into Political Power." *Christian Century* 85 (Jan. 3, 1968): 11–14.

5784. Perkins, Dexter. "Dissent in Time of War (1789 to the Present)." *Virginia Quarterly Review* 47 (Spring 1971): 161–174.

5785. Rachlin, Carl. "Draft Cards and Burning the Constitution." *Brooklyn Law Review* 32 (Apr. 1966): 334–352.

5786. Rose, R.C. "Busted Flat in Washington, Waiting: Clergy and Laymen Concerned Demonstration." *Christian Century* 89 (May 31, 1972): 625–626.

5787. Rostow, Eugene V. "Three Questions for President Brewster and Mayor Lee." *National Review* 21 (Nov. 4, 1969): 1113–1114ff.

5788. Schlesinger, Arthur, Jr., et al. "A Talk-In on Vietnam." *New York Times Magazine* (Feb. 6, 1966): 12ff. [a debate]

5789. Serfaty, Simon. "No More Dissent?" *Foreign Policy* 11 (Summer 1973): 144–158.

5790. Shinn, Roger L. "Our Cause Is Not Just." *Christian Century* 89 (Nov. 1, 1972): 1099–1103.

5791. Steinfels, P. "Once again into the Streets." *Commonweal* 96 (May 26, 1972): 279.

5792. "Vietnam Controversy Grows in Capitol and Nation." *CQ Weekly Report* 37 (Oct. 10, 1969): 1897–1901.

5793. "The Vietnam Protest Movement." *Dissent* 13 (Jan.–Feb. 1966): 7–9.

5794. Welch, E.H. "What Did You Write about the War, Daddy?" *Wilson Library Bulletin* 46 (June 1972): 912–917.

5795. Wilson, Richard B. "The Arrogance of Constitutional Power." *Colorado Quarterly* 16 (Winter 1968): 267–285.

5796. Woodward, Beverly. "Vietnam and the Law: The Theory and Practice of Civil Challenge." *Commentary* 46 (Nov. 1968): 75–86.

CAMPUS PROTEST

The American college and university campuses were a major source of ideas, leadership and manpower for the antiwar movement from 1965 to 1970; they also were often the scene of violence—Columbia University and Kent State were prime examples. See also Hurwitz (5713).

Books
5797. Asinof, Eliot. *Craig and Joan: Two Lives for Peace.* New York: Viking, 1971. [suicide protest]

5798. *Crisis at Columbia: Report of the Fact-Finding Commission Appointed to Investigate the Disturbances at Columbia University in April and May 1968.* New York: Vintage, 1968.

5799. Divale, W.T., with James Joseph. *I Lived Inside the Campus Revolution.* New York: College Notes & Texts, 1970.

5800. Eszterhas, Joe, and M.D. Roberts. *Confrontation at Kent State: 13 Seconds.* New York: College Notes & Texts, 1970.

5801. Harris, Janet. *Students in Revolt.* New York: McGraw-Hill, 1970.

5802. Jacobs, Paul, and Saul Landan. *The New Radicals.* New York: Vintage, 1966.

5803. Katz, J. *The Student Activist.* Washington, DC: U.S. Office of Education, 1967.

5804. Kelman, Steven. *Push Comes to Shove: The Escalation of Student Protest.* Boston: Houghton Mifflin, 1970.

5805. Lipset, Seymour M., ed. *Student Politics.* New York: Basic Books, 1967.

5806. *May 1970: Birth of the Antiwar University.* New York: Pathfinder, 1971.

5807. Menashe, Louis, and Ronald Radosh, eds. *Teach-Ins USA: Reports, Opinions, Documents.* New York: Praeger, 1967.

5808. Michener, James A. *Kent State.* New York: Fawcett, 1972.

5809. Peterson, R.E. *The Scope of Organized Student Protest in 1967–68.* Princeton, NJ: Educational Testing Service, 1968.

5810. Potter, Paul. *A Name for Ourselves.* Boston: Little, Brown, 1971. [a president of SDS]

5811. Rader, Dotson. *I Ain't Marchin' Anymore!* New York: McKay, 1969.

5812. Sale, Kirkpatrick. *SDS.* New York: Vintage, 1974. [Students for a Democratic Society]

5813. Stone, I.F. *Killings at Kent State: How Murder Went Unpunished.* New York: Random House, 1971.

5814. U.S. Senate. Committee on the Judiciary. Hearings; *The Anti-Vietnam Agitation and the Teach-in Movement: The Problem of Communist Infiltration and Exploitation.* 89th Cong., 1st sess., 1965.

Retrospective Essays
5815. Adamek, Raymond J., and Jerry M. Lewis. "Social Control, Violence and Radicalization: The Kent State Case." *Social Forces* 51 (Mar. 1973): 342–347.

5816. Brown, Michael L. "Student Protest and Political Attitudes." *Youth & Society* 4 (June 1973): 413–442.

5817. Handberg, Robert B., Jr. "The 'Vietnam Analogy': Student Attitudes on War." *Public Opinion Quarterly* 26 (Winter 1972–1973): 612–615.

5818. Levine, Mark H., and Serge R. Denisoff. "Draft Susceptibility and Vietnam War Attitudes." *Youth & Society* 4 (Dec. 1972): 169–176.

5819. Longino, Charles F., Jr. "Draft Lottery Numbers and Student Opposition to War." *Sociology of Education* 46 (Fall 1973): 499–506.

5820. McCaughey, Robert A. "American University Teachers and Opposition to the Vietnam War: A Reconsideration." *Minerva* 14 (Autumn 1976): 307–329.

5821. Rothman, Jack. "The Radical Liberal Strategy in Action: Arnold Kaufman and the First Teach-In." *Social Theory & Practice* 2 (Spring 1972): 33–45. [Michigan, 1965]

5822. Schreiber, E.M. "Opposition to the Vietnam War Among American University Students and Faculty." *British Journal of Sociology* 24 (Sept. 1973): 288–302.

Contemporary Essays

5823. Altbach, P.G. "Commitment and Powerlessness on the American Campus: The Case of the Graduate Student." *Liberal Education* 56 (Dec. 1970): 562–582.

5824. Armor, David J., et al. "Professors' Attitudes toward the Vietnam War." *Public Opinion Quarterly* 31 (Summer 1967): 159–175.

5825. Asbury, B.A., et al. "The Role of Campus Ministers in Protest and Dissent." *Liberal Education* 56 (May 1970): 317–338.

5826. Barton, Allan H., "The Columbia Crisis: Campus, Vietnam, and the Ghetto." *Public Opinion Quarterly* 32 (Fall 1968): 333–351.

5827. Beisner, Robert L. "On Student Reaction to the Indochina Crisis." *North American Review* 255 (Fall 1970): 55–58.

5828. Bell, Daniel. "Columbia and the New Left." *Public Interest* 13 (Fall 1968): 61–101.

5829. Berreman, Gerald D. "Racism, the War and the University." *Kroeber Anthropological Society, Papers*, no. 43 (1970): 1–9.

5830. Bickel, Alexander M. "The Tolerance of Violence on the Campus." *New Republic* 163 (June 13, 1970): 15–17. [a liberal critic]

5831. Bitner, John W. "ROTC: The Universities' Stake in National Defense." *Liberal Education* 56 (Oct. 1970): 454–457.

5832. Brennan, Robert V. "SDS Tactics as an Indicator of Aims Designed to Influence U.S. Foreign Policy." *Naval War College Review* 23 (Summer 1970): 65–78.

5833. Brogan, Dennis W. "The Student Revolt." *Encounter* 31 (July 1968): 20–25.

5834. Brooks, T.R. "Voice of the New Campus 'Underclass.'" *New York Times Magazine* (Nov. 7, 1965): 25.

5835. Caldwell, Dan. "Campus Unrest." *U.S. Naval Institute Proceedings* 95 (June 1969): 58–62.

5836. Casey, Thomas A. "Some Reflections on Student Rights." *Catholic Education Review* 66 (May 1968): 297–306.

5837. Clecak, Peter. "The Snare of Preparation." *American Scholar* 38 (Autumn 1969): 657–667.

5838. Downing, Lyle A., and Jerome J. Salomone. "Professors of the Silent Generation." *Trans-Action* 6 (Aug. 1969): 43–54. [a survey]

5839. Eckhardt, William. "The Black Arm Band Story." *Journal of Human Relations* 17:4 (1969): 495–515. [1965 high school protest]

5840. Ferguson, John. "Student Protest and Power in the United States." *British Journal of Education Studies* 18 (Feb. 1970): 32–41.

5841. Feuer, Lewis S. "Student Unrest in the United States." *Annuals* of the American Academy of Political and Social Science, no. 404 (1972): 170–182.

5842. Flacks, Richard. "The Liberated Generation." *Journal of Social Issues* 23 (July 1967).

5843. Glick, Edward B. "ROTC: From Riot to Reason." *Air Force & Space Digest* 53 (Oct. 1970): 70–73.

5844. Greeley, Andrew M. "The End of the Movement." *Change* 4:3 (1972): 42–47.

5845. Hausknecht, Murray. "Sources of Student Rebellion: How Shall We Understand the Columbia Uprising?" *Dissent* 15 (Sept.–Oct. 1968): 389–395.

5846. Hayes, Samuel P. "Right Face, Left Face: the Columbia Strike." *Political Science Quarterly* 84 (June 1969): 311–327.

5847. Hesburgh, Theodore M. "Comments on Campus Unrest." *Social Science* 44 (Oct. 1969): 195–199.

5848. Howe, Irving. "The Agony of the Campus." *Dissent* 16 (Sept.–Oct. 1969): 387–394.

5849. Jencks, Christopher. "Limits of the New Left." *New Republic* 157 (Oct. 21, 1967): 19–21.

5850. Joy, Ted. "Espionage at Kent State." *Nation* 216 (Jan. 29, 1973): 144–148.

5851. Kateb, George. "The Campus and Its Critics." *Commentary* 47 (Apr. 1969): 40–48.

5852. Kazin, Michael. "Some Notes on S.D.S." *American Scholar* 38 (Autumn 1969): 644–655.

5853. Kelman, Steven J. "Youth and Foreign Policy: Youth of the 'New Left' and Their Opposition to United States Policies in the Vietnamese War." *Foreign Affairs* 48 (Apr. 1970): 414–426.

5854. Kryske, L.M. "NROTC at UCLA: The Colors Still Fly." *U.S. Naval Institute Proceedings* 97 (Dec. 1971): 18–25.

5855. Langer, E. "National Teach-In: Professors Debating Viet Nam, Question Role of Scholarship in Policy-Making." *Science* 148 (May 21, 1965): 1075–1077.

5856. Laqueur, Walter. "Reflections on Youth Movements." *Commentary* 47 (June 1969): 33–41.

5857. Lipset, Seymour M. "The Activists: a Profile." *Public Interest*, no. 13 (1968): 39–51.

5858. ———. "Rebellion on Campus." *American Education* 4 (Oct. 1968): 28–31.

5859. Lubell, Samuel. "That Generation Gap." *Public Interest* (Fall 1968): 52–61.

5860. McNamara, R.J. "Students and Power: A Fordham Reflection." *Thought* [Fordham Univ. Q.] 43 (Summer 1968): 202–210.

5861. Mahaffrey, Fred K. "Student Antimilitarism and Its Impact on National Security." *Forum*, no. 13 (Fall 1971): 26–51.

5862. Neugeborn, D. "Letter From Stanford: Humphrey and the Now Generation." *New Republic* 156 (Mar. 18, 1967): 32–35.

5863. Parsons, J.S. "Students in Conflict." *SAIS Review* 10 (Winter 1966): 20–26.

5864. Rabinowitz, Dorothy. "Power in the Academy: A Reminiscence and a Parable." *Commentary* 47 (June 1969): 42–49.

5865. Schurmann, Franz. "The NLF Asks the American Left: Where Are You Now That We Really Need You?" *Ramparts* 8 (Aug. 1969): 14–22.

5866. Scott, J.W., and Mohamed El-Assad. "Multiversity, University Size, University Quality and Student Protest: An Empirical Study." *American Sociology Review* 34 (Oct. 1969): 702–709.

5867. Selby, H. "Vietnamese Students Talk About the War." *New York Times Magazine* (Oct. 31, 1965): 104ff.

5868. Skolnick, Jerome H. "Student Protest." *AAUP Bulletin* 55 (Sept. 1969): 309–326.

5869. Slek, Merry. "Styles of Handling Student Demonstrations." *Bulletin of the Atomic Scientists* 25 (June 1969): 36–38.

5870. Smith, Robert B. "The Vietnam War and Student Militancy." *Social Science Quarterly* 52 (June 1971): 133–156.

5871. "Special Issue on the American University and Student Protest." *American Behavioral Scientist* 11 (May–June 1968).

5872. Strait, Roger. "We Can Become Responsible." *Journal: Division of Higher Education, United Church of Christ* 9:4 (1971): 4–11.

5873. Trachtenberg, Alan. "Culture and Rebellion: Dilemmas of Radical Teachers." *Dissent* 16 (Nov.–Dec. 1969): 497–504.

5874. Turner, Floyd. "The Student Movement as a Force for Educational Change." *Liberal Education* 56 (Mar. 1970): 39–50.

5875. "Vietnam Critics in Perspective." *Communist Affairs* 4 (May–June 1966): 7–9.

5876. Westly, D., and R.G. Braungart. "Class and Politics in the Family Backgrounds of Student Political Activists." *American Sociological Review* 31 (Oct. 1966): 690–692.

VETERANS AGAINST THE WAR

5877. Goldberg, Art. "Vietnam Vets: The Anti-War Army." *Ramparts* 10 (July 1971): 11–17.

5878. Kerry, John F. "Where Are the Leaders of Our Country?" *New Republic* 164 (May 8, 1971): 15–18.

5879. ———, and the Vietnam Veterans against the War. *The New Soldier*. New York: Macmillan, 1971.

5880. Kovic, Ron. *Born on the Fourth of July*. New York: McGraw-Hill, 1976. A Vietnam veteran.

5881. Michelson, P. "Bringing the War Home: Veterans Testify Against the Atrocity in Indochina." *New Republic* 164 (Feb. 27, 1971): 21–25.

5882. Retzer, Joseph D. "War and Political Ideology: The Roots of Radicalism Among Vietnam Veterans." Ph.D. dissertation, Yale University, 1976.

5883. Truscott, Lucian K., IV. "Vietnam Veterans Against the War." *Saturday Review* 55 (Oct. 1972): 7–8ff.

GIs AGAINST THE WAR

5884. Connally, Orabelle. "Anti-war Work by Discouragement of Warriors: A Critique of Anti-war Tactics Used Among Naval Personnel in the Vietnam War." *Journal of Sociology and Social Welfare* 4 (Jan.–Mar. 1977): 626–638.

5885. Cortright, David. *Soldiers in Revolt; The American Military Today*. Garden City, NY: Anchor, 1975. Several additional topics.

5886. Gardner, Fred. *The Unlawful Concert: An Account of the Presidio Meeting Case.* New York: Viking, 1970.

5887. "The GI Anti-war Movement: Little Action and Money: And Few G.I.'s." *Armed Forces Journal* 108 (Sept. 7, 1970): 32–33ff.

5888. Halstead, Fred. *GIs Speak Out Against the War: The Case of the Ft. Jackson 8.* New York: Pathfinder, 1970.

5889. Hayes, James R. "The Dialectics of Resistance: An Analysis of the GI Movement." *Journal of Social Issues* 31 (Fall 1975): 125–139.

5890. _____. "The War Within a War: Dissent in the Military With an Emphasis Upon the Vietnam War." Ph.D. dissertation, University of Connecticut, 1975.

5891. Mataxis, Theodore C. "This Far, No Farther. How the Army Handles Dissenters in Uniform." *Military Review* 50 (Mar. 1970): 74–82.

5892. Noyd, Dale. "Letter of Resignation From an Air Force Officer." In *The Military in America: From the Colonial Era to the Present Day*, edited by Peter Karsten. New York: Free Press, 1980, 452–455. Resigned in 1966.

5893. Rinaldi, Matthew. "The Olive-Drab Rebels: Military Organizing During the Vietnam Era." *Radical America* 8 (May–June 1974): 17–52.

5894. Sherman, E.F. "Bureaucracy Adrift: Anti-War Dissent within the U.S. Military." *Nation* 212 (Mar. 1, 1971): 265–275.

5895. U.S. House. Committee on Internal Security. Hearings; *Investigation of Attempts to Subvert the United States Armed Forces.* 92d Cong., 2d sess., 1972.

5896. Waterhouse, Larry G., and Mariann G. Wizard. *Turning the Guns Around: Notes on the G.I. Movement.* New York: Praeger, 1971.

FBI Counterintelligence Operation

The Federal Bureau of Investigation, as well as other government agencies, undertook surveillance of dissenters; their methods and motives were questionable in terms of constitutional guarantees. The FBI's "Cointelpro" or Counterintelligence Program (1968–1971) was aimed primarily at the "New Left" and antiwar leaders. The CIA (1967–1972) created a special unit with its counterintelligence office to seek possible foreign links to American antiwar activists; it compiled about 10,000 files on U.S. citizens. The Army, some National Guard units, and local police forces also participated or developed their own files. The subsequent congressional investigation of these activities (1974–1976) presumably terminated them.

Books, Dissertations and Reports
5897. Berrigan, Daniel. *America Is Hard to Find.* Garden City, NY: Doubleday, 1972, 33–92. [antiwar leader's report]

5898. Blum, Richard H., ed. *Surveillance and Espionage in a Free Society: A Report by the Planning Group to the Policy Council of the Democratic National Committee.* New York: Praeger, 1972.

5899. Cowan, Paul. *State Secrets: Police Surveillance in America.* New York: Holt, Rinehart & Winston, 1974.

5900. Nelson, Jack, and Ronald J. Ostrow. *The FBI and the Berrigans: The Making of a Conspiracy.* New York: Coward, McCann & Geoghegan, 1972. Nelson refers to the Berrigans' indictment and trial.

5901. Perkus, Cathy, ed. *Cointelpro: The FBI's Secret War on Political Freedom.* New York: Monad, 1976.

5902. Pyle, Christopher H. "Military Surveillance of Civilian Politics, 1967–1970." Ph.D. dissertation, Columbia University, 1974.

5903. U.S. House. Committee on the Judiciary. Hearings; *FBI Counterintelligence Programs.* 93d Cong., 2d sess., 1974.

5904. U.S. Senate. Committee on Government Operations. Hearings; *Intelligence Activities.* 94th Cong., 1st sess., 1975.

5905. _____. Report; *Intelligence Activities and the Rights of Americans.* Bk 2, Rpt no. 94–755. 94th Cong., 2d sess., 1976.

5906. _____. Report; *Supplementary Detailed Staff Reports on Intelligence Activities and the Rights of Americans.* Bk 3, Rpt no. 94–755. 94th Cong., 2d sess., 1976.

Essays
5907. Baskir, Lawrence M. "Reflections on the Senate Investigation of Army Surveillance." *Indiana Law Journal* 49 (Summer 1974): 618–653.

5908. Blackstock, Paul W. "Political Surveillance and

the Constitutional Order." *Worldview* 14 (May 1971): 11–14.

5909. Burlingham, B. "Paranoia in Power: [Tom C.] Huston's Domestic Spy Plan." *Harper's* 249 (Oct. 1974): 26ff. In Nixon administration.

5910. "The CIA: An Attack and a Reply." *U.S. News and World Report* 71 (Oct. 11, 1971): 78–82.

5911. Donner, Frank. "The Confession of an FBI Informer." *Harper's* 245 (Dec. 1972): 54–62.

5912. _____. "Domestic Political Intelligence." In *Uncloaking the CIA*, edited by Howard Frazier. New York: Free Press, 1978, 165–173.

5913. The FBI's Political Abuses: Full Text of Official Report." *U.S. News and World Report* 79 (Dec. 15, 1975): 61–64.

5914. "How the U.S. Army Spies on Citizens." *Life* 70 (May 26, 1971): 20–27.

5915. Meisel, Alan. "Political Surveillance and the Fourth Amendment." *University of Pittsburgh Law Review* 35 (Fall 1973): 53–71.

5916. Nathanson, Nathaniel L. "Freedom of Association and the Quest for Internal Security: Conspiracy From Dennis to Dr. Spock." *Northwestern University Law Review* 65 (May–June 1970): 153–192.

5917. Powers, Thomas. "The Government is Watching: Is There Anything the Police Don't Want to Know?" *Atlantic* 230 (Oct. 1972): 51–63. [FBI and CIA]

5918. Theoharis, Athan G. "Political Counterintelligence." In his *Spying on Americans: Political Surveillance from Hoover to the Houston Plan.* Philadelphia: Temple University Press, 1978, 133–156.

5919. _____. "Political Use of Surveillance." In *ibid.*: 156–196.

The Draft: Protest and Resistence

Also see Chapter 6, "Personnel Policies and Problems." Selective Service (the draft) was increasingly criticized as the war lengthened. Questions arose over "equality"—did deferments mean that only lower class, non-college males had to serve? The best account

account to date is Baskir and Strauss's *Chance and Circumstance (5924).*

5920. Anderson, Martin, comp. *Conscription: A Select and Annotated Bibliography.* Stanford, CA: Hoover Institution Press, 1976. Anderson deals with most aspects; international issues, "all-volunteer" military, amnesty, etc.

GENERAL

5921. Alden, J.D. "National Strength through National Service." *U.S. Naval Institute Proceedings* 95 (July 1969): 68–78.

5922. American Friends Service Committee. *The Draft?* New York: Hill & Wang, 1968.

5923. Barnett, Correlli. "On the Raising of Armies." *Horizon* 10 (Summer 1968): 40–47.

5924. Baskir, Lawrence M., and William A. Strauss. *Chance and Circumstance: The Draft, the War, and the Vietnam Generation.* New York: Vintage, 1978.

5925. Berger, E., et al. "ROTC, Mylai and the Volunteer Army." *Foreign Policy*, no. 2 (Spring 1971): 135–160.

5926. Carper, Jean. *Bitter Greetings: The Scandal of the Military Draft.* New York: Grossman, 1967.

5927. Flacks, Richard, et al. "On the Draft." In *The Triple Revolution*, edited by R. Perucci, and M. Pilisuk, et al. Boston: Little, Brown, 1968.

5928. Jacobs, Clyde E., and John F. Gallagher. *The Selective Service Act: A Case Study of the Governmental Process.* New York: Dodd, Mead, 1967.

5929. Kendall, David, and Leonard Ross. *The Lottery and the Draft: Where Do I Stand?* New York: Harper & Row, 1970.

5930. Minot, S. "On Aiding and Abetting: The Anguish of Draft Counseling." *Harper's* 237 (Sept. 1968): 47–50.

5931. National Advisory Commission on Selective Service. *In Pursuit of Equity: Who Serves When Not All Serve?* Washington, DC: GPO, 1967.

5932. "National Service Plan Wins Approval of Large Majority." *Gallup Opinion Index*, no. 103 (Jan. 1974): 24–25. The "all-volunteer" military may not be the answer.

5933. Peck, Harry F., Jr. "Selective Service: Right to Counsel, Due Process and the First Amendment." *Marquette Law Review* 51 (Spring 1968): 407–425.

5934. Sander, Jacquin. *The Draft and the Vietnam War.* New York: Walker, 1966.

5935. Shields, Patricia M. "The Burden of the Draft: the Vietnam Years." *Journal of Political and Military Sociology* 9 (Fall 1981): 215–228.

5936. Shields, Patricia M. "The Determinants of Service in the Armed Forces During the Vietnam Era." Ph.D. dissertation, Ohio State University, 1978. [draft avoidance connected with high wages, not race]

5937. Suttler, David. *IV-F: A Guide to Draft Exemption.* New York: Grove, 1970.

5938. Tarr, Curtis W. "The Obligation to Serve." *Air University Review* 23 (Sept.–Oct. 1972): 2–11.

5939. Useem, Michael. "The Educational and Military Experience of Young Men During the Vietnam Era: Non-Linear Effects of Parental Social Class." *Journal of Political and Military Sociology* 8 (Spring 1980): 15–29.

5940. Vetter, B.M. "The Draft—and its Consequences...." *Scientific Research* 3 (Sept. 2, 1968): 38–41.

5941. Walton, Richard J. "*Chance and Circumstance: The Draft, the War, and the Vietnam Generation* by L.M. Baskir and W.A. Strauss: (a review)." *New Republic* 179 (Apr. 29, 1978): 33–35.

CONSCIENTIOUS OBJECTORS

Major changes in this "status" gradually took place— no longer was the "belief in god" required for exemption.

Books and Dissertations

5942. Bressler, Marion A., and Leo A. Bressler. *Country, Conscience, and Conscription: Can They Be Reconciled?* Englewood Cliffs, NJ: Prentice-Hall, 1970.

5943. Cornell, Julien D. *The Conscientious Objector.* New York: Da Capo, 1970.

5944. Finn, James. *A Conflict of Loyalties: The Case for Selective Conscientious Objection.* New York: Pegasus, 1968.

5945. Forest, James H. *Catholics and Conscientious Objection.* New York: Catholic Peace Fellowship, 1966.

5946. Heath, Robert C., ed. *Statements of Religious Bodies on the Conscientious Objector.* Washington, DC: National Service Board for Religious Objectors, 1966.

5947. Paris, John J. "Toward an Understanding of the Supreme Court's Approach to Religion in Conscientious Objector Cases." Ph.D. dissertation, University of Southern California, 1972.

5948. Ramsey, Paul. *War and the Christian Conscience.* Durham, NC: Duke University Press, 1961.

5949. Rohr, John A. *Prophets Without Honor: Public Policy and the Selective Conscientious Objector.* New York: Abingdon, 1971.

5950. Showalter, Stuart W. "Coverage of Conscientious Objectors to the Vietnam War: An Analysis of Editorial Content of American Magazines, 1964–1972." Ph.D. dissertation, University of Texas, Austin, 1975 [summarized in *Journalism Quarterly* 53:4 (1976): 648–653].

Essays

5951. Bartley, William C. "Armed Services—Conscientious Objectors—Belief in Orthodox Concept of God Not Required for Exemption." *Duquesne Law Review* 9 (Fall 1970): 113–122.

5952. Beitler, Roger R. "Conscientious Objector Exemption: Still Unsettled." *George Washington Law Review* 33 (June 1965): 1108–1126.

5953. Brandon, Robert M. "Conscientious Objector Exemption; Discrimination Against the Disadvantaged." *George Washington Law Review* 40 (Dec. 1971): 274–311.

5954. Brotsky, Allen. "Trial of a Conscientious Objector." In *The Relevant Lawyers,* edited by A.F. Ginger. New York: Simon & Schuster, 1972, 98–115.

5955. Cain, Edward R. "Conscientious Objection in France, Britain, and the United States." *Comparative Politics* 2 (Jan. 1970): 275–307.

5956. Cohen, David M., and Robert Greenspan. "Conscientious Objection, Democratic Theory, and the Constitution." *University of Pittsburgh Law Review* 29 (Mar. 1968): 389–413.

5957. "Conscience and War." *Intercom* 11 (Nov.–Dec. 1969): 21–60.

5958. "The Conscientious Objector and the First Amendment: There But For the Grace of God...." *University of Chicago Law Review* 34 (Autumn 1966): 79–105.

5959. Denno, Theodore F. "Conscience and Conscientious Objection: Win the Case and Lose the Issue." *Albany Law Review* 33 (Winter 1969): 267–279.

5960. Field, Martha A. "Problems of Proof in Conscientious Objector Cases." *University of Pennsylvania Law Review* 120 (May 1972): 870–950.

5961.   Good, P. "Legal Aspects of Conscientious Objectors." *Nation* 204 (Mar. 1967): 365–370.

5962.   Goodman, William. "Choose Your War: Or the Case of the Selective Conscientious Objector." *New York Times Magazine* (Mar. 23, 1969): 34–35ff.

5963.   Houston, Bruce R. "Conscientious Objectors: the Aftermath of United States v. Seeger, 85 Sup. Ct. 850." *Albany Law Review* 30 (June 1966): 304–316.

5964.   Lurie, Howard R. "Conscientious Objection: The Constitutional Questions." *West Virginia Law Review* 73 (May 1971): 138–156.

5965.   Marcin, Raymond B. "The Conscientious Objector Exemption as an Establishment and an Accommodation of Religion." *Connecticut Bar Journal* 40 (Spring 1966): 426–439.

5966.   Newton, Jerry. "Conscientious Objection: a New Avenue of Escape?" *California Western Law Review* 6 (Spring 1970): 267–287.

5967.   Pemberton, John de J., et al. "War and the Christian Conscience: Old and New Issues." *Social Action* 32 (Apr. 1966): 4–32.

5968.   Potts, Linda F. "Conscientious Objector: From the Pearly Gates to Walden." *Tennessee Law Review* 37 (Spring 1970): 595–627.

5969.   Rabin, Robert L. "Do You Believe in a Supreme Being? The Administration of the Conscientious Objector Exemption." *Wisconsin Law Review* 19 (Summer 1967): 642–684.

5970.   Rice, Charles E. "Conscientious Objection: A Conservative View." *Modern Age* 13 (Winter 1968–1969): 67–68.

5971.   Sharp, Malcolm P. "Reflections on Conscientious Objection to War." *Guild Practitioner* 25 (Fall 1966): 115–124.

5972.   Sherk, J.H. "Position of the Conscientious Objector." *Current History* 55 (July 1968): 18–22.

5973.   Silva, Ruth C. "The Constitution, the Conscientious Objector, and the 'Just' War." *Dickinson Law Review* 75 (Fall 1970): 1–61.

5974.   Tower, R.P. "Conscientious Objector Exemption After Welsh." *Houston Law Review* 8 (Nov. 1970): 358–370.

5975.   Winter, Harold E. "Non-Religious Conscientious Objector." *Gonzaga Law Review* 6 (Fall 1970): 65–78.

DRAFT RESISTERS

Individuals took different measures to resist the draft, including draft card burnings and destroying draft board records; for an example of the latter, see D. Berrigan's Trial of the Catonsville Nine *(5688).*

5976.   "A Call to Resist Illegitimate Authority." *New Republic* 157 (Oct. 7, 1967): 34–35.

5977.   Chandler, Richard, and Frank Femia. "War Resisters: Notes from Prison." *Peace and Change* 1 (Fall 1972): 79–81.

5978.   D'Amato, A.A. "War Crimes and Vietnam: The Nuremberg Defense and the Military Service Resister." *California Law Review* 57 (Nov. 1969): 1055–1110.

5979.   Ferber, Michael and Staughton Lynd. *The Resistance*. Boston: Beacon, 1971.

5980.   Gray, Francine du Plessix. "The Ultra-Resistance." *New York Review of Books* (Sept. 25, 1969): 11–12. Draft resistence movement.

5981.   Gross, Harriet E. "Micro and Macro Level Implications for a Sociology of Virtue: The Case of Draft Protesters to the Vietnam War." *Sociological Quarterly* 18 (Summer 1977): 319–339.

5982.   Hall, Clarence W. "Must Our Churches Finance Revolution?" *Reader's Digest* 99 (Oct. 1971): 95–100.

5983.   Hoagland, Edward. "The Draft Card Gesture." *Commentary* 45 (Feb. 1968): 77–79.

5984.   Lynd, Alice. *We Won't Go: Personal Accounts of War Objectors*. Boston: Beacon, 1968.

5985.   "The Resistance Movement." *New Republic* 156 (May 27, 1967): 5–6.

5986.   Stevens, Franklin. *If This Be Treason: Your Sons Tell Their Own Stories of Why They Won't Fight For Their Country*. New York: Wyden, 1970.

5987.   Useem, Michael. *Conscription, Protest, and Social Conflict: The Life and Death of a Draft Resistance Movement*. New York: Wiley, 1973.

EXILES, EXPATRIATES AND DESERTERS

How many males went to Canada to avoid the draft? The figures are often inflated, according to Nye (6005).

5988.   Beavers, Roy L. "They Are Not Heroes." *U.S. Naval Institute Proceedings* 99 (Apr. 1973): 46–51.

5989.   Beeson, Trevor. "Britain: No Haven for U.S. Deserters." *Christian Century* 88 (Jan. 13, 1971): 37.

5990.   Bell, D. Bruce, and Beverly W. Bell. "Desertion and Antiwar Protest: Findings From the Ford Clemency Program." *Armed Forces and Society* 3 (Spring 1977): 433–444.

5991.   Christy, Jim, ed. *The New Refugees: American Voices in Canada*. Toronto: Peter Martin Assoc., 1972.

5992.   Cooney, John, and Dana Spitzer. "'Hell No, We Won't Go!' Deserters and Draft Dodgers in Canada and Sweden." *Trans-Action* 6 (Oct. 1969): 53–62.

5993.   Emerick, Kenneth F. *War Resisters in Canada*. Knox, PA: Pennsylvania Free Press, 1972.

5994.   Epp, Frank H., ed. *I Would Like to Dodge the Draft-Dodgers, But....* Winnipeg, Canada: Conrad Press, 1970.

5995.   Fleming, Karl. "America's Sad Young Exiles." *Newsweek* 77 (Feb. 15, 1971): 28–30.

5996.   Franks, Lucinda. *Waiting Out a War: The Exile of Private John Picciano*. New York: Coward, McCann & Geoghesan, 1974.

5997.   Gooding, Richard. "An Exile in My Own Country." *Look* 34 (Feb. 24, 1970): 19–23.

5998.   Hayes, Thomas L. *American Deserters in Sweden: The Men and Their Challenge*. New York: Association Press, 1971.

5999.   Kasinsky, Renée G. "The Continental Channeling of American Vietnam War Refugees." *Crime and Social Justice* 6 (Fall 1976): 28–40. [draft resisters and immigration]

6000.   Killmer, Richard, Robert S. Leaky, and Deborah S. Wiley. *They Can't Go Home Again: The Story of America's Political Refugees*. Philadelphia: United Church Press, 1971.

6001.   Lang, Daniel "AWOL." *New Yorker* 48 (Oct. 21, 1972): 96–133. Underground refugees, Pt 4.

6002.   Levine, Saul V. "American Exiles in Canada: A Social and Psychological Follow-up." *Psychiatric Opinion* 11 (Nov. 1974): 20–31.

6003.   _____. "Draft Dodgers: Coping With Stress, Adapting to Exile." *American Journal of Orthopsychiatry* 42 (Apr. 1972): 431–440.

6004.   Musil, Robert K. "The Truth About Deserters." *Nation* 216 (Apr. 16, 1973): 495–499.

6005.   Nye, Russel B. "All Those Draft Resisters Up There (Canada)." *Progressive* 36 (May 1972): 42–43. [newspaper figures are grossly inflated]

6006.   Prasad, David. *They Love It But Leave It: American Deserters*. London: War Resister's International, 1971.

6007.   Shils, Edward. "A Profile of a Military Deserter." *Armed Forces and Society* 3 (Spring 1977): 427–432.

6008.   Surrey, David S. "The Assimilation of Vietnam Era Draft Dodgers and Deserters into Canada: A Matter of Class." Ph.D. dissertation, New School for Social Research, 1980.

6009.   U.S. Senate. Committee on Armed Services. Report; *Treatment of Deserters From Military Service* 91st Cong., 1st sess., Mar. 11, 1969.

6010.   Whitmore, Terry, and Richard Weber. *Memphis, Nam, Sweden: The Autobiography of a Black American Exile*. Garden City, NY: Doubleday, 1971.

6011.   Williams, Roger N. *The New Exiles: American War Resisters In Canada*. New York: Liveright, 1971.

6012.   _____. "The New Exodus: Go North, Young Man." *New Republic* 162 (May 16, 1970): 15–16.

PUNISHMENT OF DRAFT RESISTERS

See also, "Draft Resisters" section above, and "Presidential Clemency Program" below, this chapter.

6013.   Gaylin, Willard. *In the Service of Their Country: War Resisters in Prison*. New York: Viking, 1970.

6014.   "How the Courts are Treating Draft Dodgers and Deserters." *U.S. News and World Report* 74 (Jan. 15, 1973): 26–27.

6015.   Merklin, Lewis, Jr. *They Chose Honor: The Problem of Conscience in Custody*. New York: Harper & Row, 1974. [what it was like in jail]

6016.   Sax, J.L. "Conscience and Anarchy: The Prosecution of War Resisters." *Yale Review* 57 (June 1968): 481–494.

Amnesty

Amnesty is another unresolved issue. Do the debaters recognize that amnesty, by definition, means "to forget" the past, not "to forgive"? For an excellent summary see Polner (6019), 203–246.

6017. Lamkin, David. *The "Amnesty" Issue and Conscientious Objection: A Selected Bibliography.* Los Angeles: California State University, Center for the Study of Armament & Disarmament, 1973.

6018. Sherman, Morris, comp. *Amnesty in America: An Annotated Bibliography.* Passaic: New Jersey Library Association, 1974.

Books and Hearings

6019. Polner, Murray, ed. *When Can I Come Home? A Debate on Amnesty for Exiles, Antiwar Prisoners and Others.* Garden City, NY: Anchor, 1972.

6020. Reston, James, Jr. *The Amnesty of John David Herndon.* New York: McGraw-Hill, 1973.

6021. Schardt, Arlie, William A. Russher, and Mark O. Hatfield. *Amnesty? The Unsettled Question of Vietnam.* New York: Sun River Press, 1973. Three different positions.

6022. U.S. Senate. Committee on the Judiciary. Hearings; *Selective Service and Amnesty.* 92d Cong., 2d sess., Feb. 28, 29; Mar. 1, 1972.

Essays

6023. "Amnesty: An Act of Grace." *St. Louis University Law Journal* 17 (Summer 1973): 501–524.

6024. "Amnesty: Latest in a Hot Debate: Should Men Who Refused To Be Drafted or To Fight in Vietnam Get Full Pardon?" *U.S. News and World Report* 74 (Mar. 12, 1973): 34–35.

6025. "Amnesty as Controversial as the Vietnam War." *CQ Weekly Report* 30 (Oct. 14, 1972): 2661–2663.

6026. "Amnesty For Draft Fugitives?" *Army* 19 (Dec. 1969): 11–12.

6027. "Amnesty For the War Exiles." *Newsweek* 79 (Jan. 17, 1972): 19–26.

6028. "Amnesty Now (editorial)." *Commonweal* 98 (Mar. 16, 1973): 27–28.

6029. "The Amnesty Problem (editorial)." *Nation* 214 (Jan. 17, 1972): 67–68.

6030. Barnette, Henlee. "Agony and Amnesty." *Christian Century* 88 (Sept. 29, 1971): 1133–1134.

6031. Bennett, John C. "The Case For Amnesty." *Christianity and Crisis* 32 (Dec. 11, 1972): 267–270.

6032. Buckley, William F., Jr. "Amnesty." *National Review* 24 (Feb. 4, 1972): 118–119.

6033. "Case For a National Amnesty (editorial)." *America* 126 (Mar. 18, 1972): 278–279.

6034. Commager, Henry Steele. "The Case For Amnesty." *New York Review of Books* (Apr. 6, 1972): 23–25.

6035. Damico, Alfonson J. "In Defense of Amnesty." *Dissent* 21 (Winter 1974): 90–93.

6036. Ebel, Wilfred L. "The Amnesty Issue: a Historical Perspective." *Parameters* 4:1 (1974): 67–77.

6037. Finn, James. "The Issue of Amnesty: What Are the Questions?" *Current*, no. 1 (Jan. 1973): 33–39.

6038. Fitt, A. "Amnesty." *New York Times Magazine* (Sept. 8, 1974): 27ff.

6039. Fleming, Karl. "How the Exiles View the Issue." *Newsweek* 79 (Jan. 17, 1972): 24–25.

6040. Freeman, Harrop A. "What Nixon Forgets: Congress Bestows Amnesty." *Nation* 216 (Mar. 26, 1973): 401–403.

6041. Gardner, Robert. "Amnesty When? A Canadian Perspective." *New Republic* 165 (Dec. 25, 1971): 12–13.

6042. "A History and Discussion of Amnesty." *Columbia Human Rights Law Review* 4 (Fall 1972): 529–540.

6043. Howay, Jack W. "Amnesty: An Old Gift in New Wrappings." *Naval War College Review* 25 (Mar.–Apr. 1973): 46–57.

6044. Jones, Douglas W., and David L. Raish. "American Deserters and Draft Evaders: Exile, Punishment, or Amnesty?" *Harvard International Law Journal* 13 (Winter 1972): 88–131.

6045. Loh, Wallace D. "National Loyalties and Amnesty: A Legal and Social Psychological Analysis." *Journal of Social Issues* 31 (Fall 1975): 157–170.

6046. Lusky, L. "Congressional Amnesty for War Resisters: Policy Considerations and Constitutional Problems." *Vanderbilt Law Review* 25 (Apr. 1972): 525–555.

6047. Neuhaus, Richard J. "The Good Sense of Amnesty." *Nation* 210 (Feb. 9, 1970): 145–148.

6048. "Unconditional Amnesty For Men Who Left the U.S. to Avoid Military Service in Vietnam." *Gallup Opinion Index* (Mar. 1973): 16–20.

6049. Wick, William D. "Case For an Unconditional,

Universal Amnesty For Draft Evaders and Armed Forces Deserters." *Buffalo Law Review* 22 (Fall 1972): 311–334.

PRESIDENTIAL CLEMENCY PROGRAMS

Presidents Ford and Carter initiated programs of limited forgiveness. For best summary, see Baskir and Strauss (5924), 203–246.

6050. Baskir, Lawrence M., and William A. Strauss. *Reconciliation After Vietnam: A Program of Relief for Vietnam-Era Draft and Military Offenders.* Notre Dame, IN: University of Notre Dame Press, 1977. [Ford's program]

6051. Bell, D. Bruce, and Thomas J. Houston. *The Vietnam Era Deserter: Characteristics of Unconvicted Army Deserters Participating In the Presidential Clemency Program.* Washington, DC: U.S. Army Research Institute for the Behavioral & Social Sciences, July 1976.

6052. Cowlishaw, Patrick R. "The Conditional Presidential Pardon." *Stanford Law Review* 28 (Nov. 1975): 149–177. [Ford's program]

6053. Maxfield, David M. "Clemency Program: Should It Be Extended?" *CQ Weekly Report* 33 (Sept. 20, 1975): 2012–2016.

6054. Miller, Judith. "Amnesty: Eddie McNally Comes Home." *Progressive* 38 (Feb. 1974): 17–21.

6055. Shichor, David, and Donald R. Ranish. "President Carter's Vietnam Amnesty; An Analysis of a Public Policy Decision." *Presidential Studies Quarterly* 10 (Summer 1980): 443–450.

6056. U.S. House. Committee on Judiciary. Hearings; *Amnesty.* 93d Cong., 2d sess., Mar. 8, 11, 13, 1974.

6057. ———. Hearings; *The Presidential Clemency Program.* 94th Cong., 1st sess., Apr. 14, 17, 18, 1975.

6058. ———. Report; *The Presidential Clemency Program.* 94th Cong., 1st sess., Aug. 1975.

6059. U.S. Senate. Committee on Judiciary. Hearings; *Clemency Program: Practices and Procedures.* 93d Cong., 2d sess., Dec. 18–19, 1974.

Vietnam Veterans

Increasing attention is being paid to Vietnam veterans by academics, if not always by the government. Jack Ladinsky's essay (6096) provides a good introduction to materials related to the veteran's problems and complaints. Also see Chapter 8, "Herbicides," for possible latent reaction in veterans.

Books and Dissertations

6060. Abel, Frederick J. "Vietnam Era Veterans: A Cross-Sectional Study of Attitudes." Ph.D. dissertation, University of Northern Colorado, 1976.

6061. Borchard, David C. "Self-Actualization in Vietnam Veteran and Non-Veteran Male College Students." Ph.D. dissertation, George Washington University, 1976.

6062. Collins, Jimmie L. "A Post-Hoc Analysis of Veterans Administration Guidance Counseling: Allan Hancock College, 1972–1977." Ph.D. dissertation, U.S. International University, 1978.

6063. Educational Testing Service. *Final Report on Educational Assistance to Veterans: A Comparative Study of Three G.I. Bills.* Submitted to U.S. Senate. Committee on Veteran's Affairs. Committee Print no. 18. 93d Cong., 1st sess., Sept. 20, 1973.

6064. Helmer, John. *Bringing the War Home: The American Soldier in Vietnam and After.* New York: Free Press, 1974. See Ladinsky's review (6096).

6065. Ingham, Donald F. "The Physically Disabled Vietnam Era Veteran: Anomie and Social Adjustment." Ph.D. dissertation, University of Utah, 1976.

6066. Levitan, Sara, and Joyce K. Zickler. *Swords Into Plowsharers: Our G.I. Bill.* Salt Lake City: Olympus, 1973.

6067. Levitan, Sara, and Karen Cleary. *Old Wars Remain Unfinished: The Veteran Benefit System.* Baltimore, MD: Johns Hopkins University Press, 1973.

6068. Levy, Charles J. *Spoils of War.* Boston: Houghton Mifflin, 1974. Levy discusses the dubious theory of veterans' "war guilt."

6069. Lifton, Robert J. *Home From the War: Vietnam Veterans: Neither Victims Nor Executioners.* New York: Simon & Schuster, 1973. Lifton's work is related to Levy's theme (6068).

6070. Miliano, Fred A. "The Generational Divide: A Study of Italian-American Veterans and Non-Veterans of the Vietnam Era." Ph.D. dissertation, Pennsylvania State University, 1977.

6071.   Polner, Murray. *No Victory Parades: The Return of the Vietnam Veteran.* New York: Holt, Rinehart & Winston, 1971.

6072.   Robins, Lee N. *The Vietnam Drug User Returns.* Special Action Office for Drug Abuse Prevention. Executive Office of the President. Monograph Series A. no. 2. Washington, DC: GPO, May 1974.

6073.   Starr, Paul, with assistance of James F. Henry and Raymond P. Bonner. *The Discarded Army: Veterans After Vietnam: The Nader Report on Vietnam Veterans and the Veterans Administration.* New York: Charterhouse, 1973. [fine survey]

6074.   Taussig, Michael K. *Those Who Served.* Twentieth Century Fund Task Force on Policies Toward Veterans, Background Paper. New York: Twentieth Century Fund, 1974.

6075.   U.S. Department of Defense. *Project One Hundred Thousand; Characteristics and Performance of "New Standards" Men.* Washington, DC: Asst. Secretary of Defense. Manpower & Reserve Affairs, Dec. 1969. This report describes efforts to use men not meeting mental and physical standards between 1966 and 1971.

6076.   U.S. Senate. Committee on Labor and Public Welfare. Hearings; *Unemployment and Overall Readjustment Problems of Returning Veterans.* [Nov. 25, Dec. 3, 1970]. 91st Cong., 2d sess., 1971.

6077.   _____. Committee on Veterans' Affairs. Report; *A Study of the Problems Facing Vietnam Era Veterans on Their Readjustment to Civilian Life.* 92d Cong., 2d sess., Jan. 31, 1972.

6078.   _____. Staff Report; *Source Material on the Vietnam Era Veteran.* Committee Print no. 26. 93d Cong., 2d sess., Feb. 12, 1974. [935 pages of reprinted items related to Vietnam veterans; excellent source]

6079.   Wikler, Norma J. "Vietnam and the Veterans Consciousness: Pre-Political Thinking Among American Soldiers." Ph.D. dissertation, University of California, Berkeley, 1973.

6080.   Worthington, Elliott R. "The Vietnam Era Veteran: Adjustment and Anomie." Ph.D. dissertation, University of Utah, 1973.

Essays
6081.   Borus, Jonathan F. "Incidence of Maladjustment in Vietnam Returnees." *Archives of General Psychiatry* 30 (Apr. 1974): 554–557.

6082.   _____. "The Reentry Transition of the Vietnam Veteran." *Armed Forces and Society* 2 (Fall 1975): 97–114.

6083.   _____. "Reentry, III: Facilitating Healthy Readjustments in Vietnam Veterans." *Psychiatry* 36 (Nov. 1973): 428–439.

6084.   Boulanger, Raymond P. "The Undesirable Veteran." *Commonweal* 98 (Sept. 21, 1973): 500–510. ["undesirable" discharges]

6085.   Egendorf, Arthur. "Vietnam Veteran Rap Groups and Themes of Postwar Life." *Journal of Social Issues* 31 (Fall 1975): 111–124.

6086.   Fendrich, James M. "The Returning Black Vietnam-Era Veterans." *Social Service Review* 46 (Mar. 1972): 60–75.

6087.   "From Vietnam to a VA Hospital: Assignment to Neglect." *Life* 68 (May 22, 1970): 25–31.

6088.   Furlong, W.B. "The Re-Entry Problem of the Vietvets." *New York Times Magazine* (May 7, 1967): 23.

6089.   Gelman, David. "Vietnam Marches Home." *Newsweek* 91 (Feb. 13, 1978): 85–86.

6090.   Gray, Glenn J. "Back [Review of R.J. Lifton's *Home From the War*]." *New York Review of Books* (June 28, 1973): 22–24.

6091.   "Home From Vietnam: For 2.3 Million U.S. Veterans—a New Way of Life." *U.S. News and World Report* 74 (Feb. 12, 1973): 21–23.

6092.   Horowitz, Mardi J., and George F. Solomon. "A Prediction of Delayed Stress Response Syndromes in Vietnam Veterans." *Journal of Social Issues* 31 (Fall 1975): 67–80.

6093.   Jay, Jeffery A. "After Vietnam: I: In Pursuit of Scapegoats." *Harper's* 248 (July 1978): 14ff.

6094.   Jennings, M. Kent, and Gregory B. Markus. "Political Participation and Vietnam War Veterans: A Longitudinal Study." In *The Social Psychology of Military Service,* edited by Nancy L. Goldmand and David R. Segal. Beverly Hills, CA: Sage, 1976, 175–200.

6095.   Johnson, Loch. "Political Alienation Among Vietnam Veterans." *Western Political Quarterly* 29 (Sept. 1976): 398–409.

6096.   Ladinsky, Jack. "Vietnam, the Veterans, and the Veterans Administration." *Armed Forces and Society* 2 (Spring 1976): 435–467. [excellent review of the literature]

6097. Leventman, Seymour. "Official Neglect of Vietnam Veterans." *Journal of Social Issues* 31 (Fall 1975): 171–180.

6098. Lifton, Robert J. "The Postwar War." *Journal of Social Issues* 31 (Fall 1975): 181–195. [POWs and antiwar veterans compared]

6099. Lorr, Maurice, et al. "Interpersonal Styles of Vietnam Era Veterans." *Journal of Personality Assessment* 39 (Oct. 1975): 507–510.

6100. Martindale, Melanie, and Dudley L. Poston, Jr. "Variations in Veteran/Nonveteran Earnings Patterns Among World War II, Korea and Vietnam War Cohorts." *Armed Forces and Society* 5 (Winter 1979): 219–243.

6101. Mattila, J. Peter. "G.I. Bill Benefits and Enrollments: How Did Vietnam Veterans Fare?" *Social Science Quarterly* 59 (Dec. 1978): 535–545.

6102. Michelotti, Kopp, and Kathryn R. Gover. "The Employment Situation of Vietnam Era Veterans." *Monthly Labor Review* 95 (Dec. 1972): 7–15.

6103. Perlman, Michael S. "Basic Problems of Military Psychiatry: Delayed Reaction in Vietnam Veterans." *International Journal of Offender Therapy and Comparative Criminology* 19:2 (1975): 129–138.

6104. Pilisuk, Marc. "The Legacy of the Vietnam Veteran." *Journal of Social Issues* 31 (Fall 1975): 312.

6105. Strayer, Richard, and Lewis Ellenhorn. "Vietnam Veterans: A Study Exploring Adjustment Patterns and Attitudes." *Journal of Social Issues* 31 (Fall 1975): 81–94.

6106. Thomasson, W.A. "Deadly Legacy: Dioxin and the Vietnam Veteran." *Bulletin of the Atomic Scientists* 35 (May 1979): 15–19. Thomasson describes the latent effects of herbicides used in Vietnam.

6107. Villemez, Wayne J., and John D. Kasarda. "Veteran Status and Socioeconomic Attainment." *Armed Forces and Society* 2 (Spring 1976): 407–420.

6108. Waldman, Elizabeth. "Vietnam War Veterans: Transition to Civilian Life." *Monthly Labor Review* 93 (Nov. 1970): 21–29.

Artists and the War

During the days of protest, young and not so young poets and dramatists frequently joined students in protesting the war—some may recall the "guerrilla theater" which often appeared on campuses. Although novelists and moviemakers have become more prominent in this area since the war ended, there were earlier efforts to create fictional heroes and heroines. (For cartoonists and photographic essays, see "Media: Reporting the War," Chapter 9.)

DRAMA AND FILMS

6109. Gessner, Peter. "Films From the Vietnam Congress." *Nation* 202 (Jan. 24, 1966): 110–111.

6110. Horowitz, Irving Louis. "On Reliving the Deformities of Our Transgressions." *Society* 16 (May 1979): 80–83. [reviews the film *Deer Hunter* and public reaction to it]

6111. Mills, Nicolaus. "Memories of the Vietnam War." *Dissent* 26 (Summer 1979): 334–350. [Movies reviewed]

6112. Shafer, George W. "Rhetorical Dramaturgy of Anti-Vietnam War Drama." Ph.D. dissertation, Kent State University, 1976.

6113. Smith, Julian. "Look Away, Look Away, Look Away, Movie Land." *Journal of Popular Film* 2:1 (1973): 29–43.

6114. ———. *Looking Away: Hollywood and Vietnam.* New York: Scribner's, 1975.

6115. Suid, Lawrence H. "The Film Industry and the Vietnam War." Ph.D. dissertation, Case Western Reserve University, 1980.

6116. "Theater Goes to War: Anti-War Plays...." *America* 116 (May 20, 1967): 759–761.

6117. Winner, Carole A. "A Study of American Dramatic Productions Dealing With the War in Vietnam." Ph.D. dissertation, University of Denver, 1975.

POETRY

6118. Barry, Jan, ed. *Peace is Our Profession.* New York: East River Anthology, 1981. [recollections and poetry about the Vietnam War]

6119. Casey, Michael. *Obscenities*. New Haven: Yale University Press, 1972.

6120. Floyd, Bryan A. *The Long War Dead*. New York: Avon, 1976.

6121. Lowenfels, Walter, comp. *Where Is Vietnam? American Poets Respond; an Anthology*. Garden City, NY: Anchor, 1967.

6122. Luce, Don, John C. Schafer, and Jacquelyn Chasnon, eds. *We Promise One Another: Poems From an Asian War*. Washington, DC: Indochina Mobile Education Project, 1971.

6123. Mersmann, James F. *Out of the Vietnam Vortex: A Study of Poets and Poetry Against the War*. Lawrence: University Press of Kansas, 1974.

6124. Nelson, Cary. "Whitman in Vietnam: Poetry and History in Contemporary America." *Massachusetts Review* 16:1 (1975): 55–71.

6125. Rottman, Larry, et al. *Winning Hearts and Minds: War Poems by Vietnam Veterans*. Brooklyn, NY: 1st Casualty Press, 1972.

6126. Spender, Stephen. "Poetry of the Unspeakable." *New York Review of Books* (Feb. 8, 1973): 3. [review of *Winning Hearts and Minds*]

NOVELS

6127. Beidler, Philip D. "Truth-Telling and Literary Values in the Vietnam Novel." *South Atlantic Quarterly* 72:2 (1979): 141–156.

6128. _____. "The Vietnam Novel: An Overview With a Brief Checklist of Vietnam War Narrative." *Southern Humanities Review* 12:1 (1978): 45–55.

6129. Robinson, Jo Ann. "Novels and Vietnam." *Peace and Change* 4 (Fall 1976): 12–18. [with bibliography]

6130. Sanders, Clinton R. "The Portrayal of War and the Fighting Man in Novels of the Vietnam War." *Journal of Popular Culture* 3:3 (1969): 553–564.

6131. Stromberg, Peter L. "A Long War's Writing: American Novels about the Fighting in Vietnam While Americans Fought." Ph.D. dissertation, Cornell University, 1974.

6132. Taylor, Gordon O. "American Personal Narrative of the War in Vietnam." *American Literature* 52:2 (1980): 294–308.

List of Titles

This list was compiled, in part, with the generous assistance of Myron J. Smith, Jr., and drawn from his Men at War: A Fiction Guide *(Metuchen, NJ: Scarecrow, 1979), and* The Sea Fiction Guide, *with R.C. Weller (Metuchen, NJ: Scarecrow, 1976). See also Robinson (6129).*

6133. Anderson, William C. *The Gooney Bird*. New York: Crown, 1968. [U.S. helicopter crew, woman reporter and the VC]

6134. Blacker, Irwin K. *Search and Destroy*. New York: Random House, 1966. [Special Forces team raids installation at Hanoi]

6135. Boatman, Alan. *Comrades in Arms*. New York: Harper, 1974. [reminiscences by wounded Marines in stateside hospital]

6136. Boulle, Pierre. *Ears of the Jungle*. Translated by M. Dobry and L. Cole. New York: Vanguard, 1972. The North Vietnamese seek countermeasures to U.S. electronic sensors along the Ho Chi Minh trail.

6137. Briley, John. *The Traitors*. New York: Putnam, 1969. Survivors of a U.S. patrol are persuaded by an American renegade to join the VC.

6138. Bunting, Josiah. *The Lionheads*. New York: Braziller, 1972. A bitter account of search and destroy missions in the delta.

6139. Butterworth, W.E. *Stop and Search: A Novel of Small Boat Warfare Off Vietnam*. Boston: Little, Brown, 1969.

6140. Chandler, David P. *Captain Hollister*. New York: Macmillan, 1973. Reporting casualties bends the mind of an officer during his second tour.

6141. Clark, Alan. *The Lion Heart*. New York: Morrow, 1969. U.S. "grunts" fight the VC in the mid–1960s.

6142. Crowther, John. *Fire Base*. New York: St. Martin's Press, 1976. Racial problems pit black against white at an artillery post.

6143. Crumley, James. *One to Count Cadence*. New York: Random House, 1969. At a U.S. airbase in 1962, a sergeant learns the value of friendship and the horrors of war.

6144. Derrig, Peter. *Pride of the Green Berets*. New York: Paperback Books, 1966. [super commandos]

6145. Dibner, Martin. *The Trouble With Heroes*. Garden City, NY: Doubleday, 1971. A destroyer captain refuses to shell a Vietnamese village.

6146.   Downs, Hunton. *The Compassionate Tiger*. New York: Putnam, 1960. The story of a U.S. soldier of fortune in the First Indochina War.

6147.   Durden, Charles. *No Bugles, No Drums*. Garden City, NY: Doubleday, 1973. [firefights and psychological warfare]

6148.   Eastlake, William. *The Bamboo Bed*. New York; Simon & Schuster, 1970. [Army helicopter pilot's adventures]

6149.   Field, Della. *Vietnam Nurse*. New York: Avon, 1966. [a love story, little combat]

6150.   Ford, Daniel. *Incident at Muc Wa*. Garden City, NY: Doubleday, 1967. [combat and atrocities]

6151.   Garfield, Brian. *The Last Bridge*. New York: Dale, 1978. [mission behind North Vietnamese lines]

6152.   Giovannitti, Len. *The Man Who Won the Medal of Honor*. New York: Random House, 1973. On trial, a soldier recalls his Vietnam combat experiences.

6153.   Groom, Winston. *Better Times Than These*. New York: Simon & Schuster, 1978. This book takes a vivid look at 1966–1967 skirmishes of Bravo Company.

6154.   Grossback, Robert. *Easy and Hard Ways Out*. New York: Harper, 1975. A pilot tests a new, but flawed, navy plane in Vietnamese combat.

6155.   Halberstam, David. *One Very Hot Day*. Boston: Houghton Mifflin, 1968. Halberstam gives a detailed description of a U.S.–ARVN raid, from briefing to body count.

6156.   Haldeman, Joe W. *War Year*. New York: Holt, 1972. Haldeman describes the experiences of a nineteen-year-old "grunt."

6157.   Hardy, Rondl. *Place of the Jackels*. Garden City, NY: Doubleday, 1955. A chaplain experiences war with French troops in the 1954 conflict with the Vietminh.

6158.   Heinemann, Larry. *Close Quarters*. New York: Farrar, 1974; reprint 1978. Heinemann describes battle and boredom east of Saigon in 1967–1968.

6159.   Hempstone, Smith. *A Tract of Time*. Boston: Houghton Mifflin, 1966. An American advisor to Montagnard tribes is caught between VC and ARVN.

6160.   Huggett, William T. *Body Count*. New York: Putnam, 1973. A Marine lieutenant leads his platoon on blood patrols.

6161.   Just, Ward. *Stringer*. Boston: Little, Brown, 1974. The last mission of a U.S. civilian guerrilla is to destroy an enemy convoy.

6162.   Karlin, Wayne, et al. *Free Fire Zone: Short Stories by Vietnam Veterans*. New York: McGraw-Hill, 1973. [horrors of combat]

6163.   Kempley, Walter. *The Invaders*. New York: Saturday Review Press, 1976. A fanatical North Vietnamese colonel and a brainwashed U.S. deserter plot to set up rocket launchers in Harlem.

6164.   Klose, Kevin. *The Typhoon Shipments*. New York: Norton, 1974. A plot is concocted to ship heroin stateside in the body bags of dead servicemen.

6165.   Kolpacoff, Victor. *The Prisoners of Quai Dong*. New York: New American Library, 1967. Kolpacoff gives a savage view of U.S. stockades and interrogation methods in Vietnam.

6166.   Kruger, Carl. *Wings of the Tiger*. New York: Fell, 1964. [USAF operations against North Vietnam]

6167.   Lartegy, Jean. *The Centurions*. New York: Avon, 1961. [romantic novel of French troops in Indochina, 1950–1954]

6168.   _____. *Yellow Fever*. New York: Dutton, 1966. [last days of French efforts against Vietminh]

6169.   Layne, McAvoy. *How Audie Murphy Died in Vietnam*. Garden City, NY: Doubleday, 1973. An alienated Marine is captured by VC after receiving an unearned Silver Cross.

6170.   Lederer, William J., and Eugene Burdick. *Sarkhan*. New York: McGraw-Hill, 1965. The authors describe the U.S. military response to communist subversion in a small Southeast Asian nation.

6171.   Little, Lloyd. *Parthian Shot*. New York: Viking, 1975. Forgotten by the bureaucrats, a small group of U.S. soldiers open a textile factory on the Cambodian border, dealing with both the VC and South Vietnamese.

6172.   Maggio, Joe. *Company Man*. New York: Putnam, 1972. [CIA mercenaries at work]

6173.   Mailer, Norman. *Why Are We In Vietnam? A Novel*. New York: Putnam, 1967. An eighteen-year-old disc jockey discusses his impending departure for Vietnam.

6174.   Mayer, Tom. *The Weary Falcon*. Boston: Houghton Mifflin, 1971. [collection of short combat stories]

6175.   Moore, Gene D. *The Killing at Ngo-Tho*. New York: Norton, 1967. [life and times of a U.S. advisor in Vietnam, 1964]

6176.   Moore, Robert L. *The Country Team*, by Robin Moore (pseud.). New York: Crown, 1967. Drastic measures are required when a Southeast Asian nation is besieged by guerrillas.

6177. _____. *The Green Berets*, by Robin Moore (pseud.). New York: Crown, 1965. [short stories about counterinsurgency operations in Vietnam]

6178. _____, and Henry Rothblatt. *Court-Martial.* Garden City, NY: Doubleday, 1971. [semi-fictionalized tale of Special Forces liquidators on trial]

6179. Moore, Robert L., and June Collins. *The Khaki Mafia.* New York: Crown, 1971. This work is based on facts involving corruption in U.S. support services.

6180. Morris, Edita. *Love to Vietnam.* New York: Monthly Review Press, 1968. A Vietnamese girl is badly burned by American napalm.

6181. O'Brien, Tim. *Going After Cacciato.* New York: Delacorte, 1978. U.S. soldiers pursue a deserter from Vietnam.

6182. _____. *If I Die in a Combat Zone, Box Me Up and Ship Me Home.* New York: Delacorte, 1973. [semi-fictional, a draftee in the Americal Division]

6183. Patterson, Henry. *Toll For the Brave*, by Jack Higgins, (pseud.). New York: Fawcett, 1976. English mercenary leaves his VC captors only to find himself tailed upon return to Great Britain.

6184. Pratt, John C. *The Laotian Fragments.* New York: Viking, 1974. [a forward air controller over Laos]

6185. Proud, Franklin M., and Alfred F. Eberhardt. *Tiger in the Mountain.* New York: St. Martin's Press, 1977. A Vietnam veteran hijacks a C–141 to rescue captured U.S. pilots in North Vietnam.

6186. Rivers, Gayle, and James Hudson. *The Five Fingers.* Garden City, NY: Doubleday, 1978. Special Forces teams are sent to kill eleven top Chinese and North Vietnamese leaders.

6187. Roth, Robert. *Sand in the Wind.* Boston: Little, Brown, 1973. [experiences of Marine officers and enlisted men]

6188. Rubin, Jonathan. *The Barking Deer.* New York: Braziller, 1974. Rubin contrasts a Montagnard legend with the arrival of twelve American soldiers to protect a village from the VC.

6189. Simpson, Howard R. *To a Silent Valley.* New York: Knopf, 1962. French paratroopers besiege, and are besieged in, a North Vietnamese valley.

6190. Sloan, James P. *War Games.* Boston: Houghton Mifflin, 1971. Repelled by the behavior of fellow Rangers, a U.S. soldier kills an entire VC patrol; his actions are misconstrued and he is decorated.

6191. Smith, Steven P. *American Boys.* New York: Putnam, 1975. [four GIs volunteer for Vietnam]

6192. Stone, Robert. *Dog Soldiers.* Boston: Houghton Mifflin, 1974.

6193. Strahs, James. *Seed Journal.* New York: Harper & Row, 1973. [semi-fiction]

6194. Taylor, Thomas. *A–18.* New York: Crown, 1967. [tale of Vietnam combat]

6195. _____. *A Piece of This Country.* New York: Norton, 1970. [problems of a black U.S. advisor]

6196. Tiede, Tom. *The Coward.* New York: Trident, 1968. A soldier convicted of cowardice is sent to Vietnam and is killed.

6197. Vaughan, Robert. *The Valkyrie Mandate.* New York: Simon & Schuster, 1974. [Buddhists, Madame Nhu and U.S. Army in conflict, 1961–1963]

6198. Webb, James H., Jr. *Fields of Fire.* Englewood Cliffs, NJ: Prentice-Hall, 1978. Marines slogging through rice paddies evoke the ambiguous and gruesome nature of this war.

6199. Wilson, William. *The LBJ Brigade.* New York: Apocalypse, 1967. A college graduate recalls his first firefight.

6200. Wolfe, Michael. *The Chinese Fire Drill.* New York: Harper, 1976. Vietnamese irregulars kidnap an American general.

6201. _____. *Man on a String.* New York: Harper, 1973. A cameraman undertakes one last mission.

6202. _____. *Two-Star Pigeon.* New York: Harper, 1975. A U.S. general tries to restore the Vietnamese monarchy.

Glossary

Additional glossaries may be found in Noam Chomsky and Howard Zinn, eds. The Pentagon Papers: Senator Gravel Edition, *vol. 5 (Boston: Beacon, 1972), and Guenter Lewy,* American In Vietnam *(New York: Oxford University Press, 1978).*

AirCav—Air Cavalry

AMERICAL—U.S. 23d Infantry Division

Angel's Wing—The area west of Saigon, along the Cambodian border which forms a salient pointing towards the city; also known as Duckbill and Parrot's Beak

ANZAC—Australian and New Zealand Army Corps

Annamite—The mountain range forming part of the boundary between Laos and Vietnam

ARC LIGHT—B-52 operations in Southeast Asia, flown from Guam, Kadena and U-Tapao (Thailand)

ARVN—Army of the Republic of Vietnam

BIG RED ONE—U.S. 1st Infantry Division

BLACK HORSE—U.S. 11th Cavalry Regiment (11th Cavalry Airmobile)

Black Virgin Mountain—(Nui Ba Den) An isolated mountain northeast of Tay Ninh

Boi Loi Woods—A heavily wooded VC/NVA base area in west-central III Corps

Catcher's Mitt—VC staging area west-northwest of Bien Hoa

Chieu Hoi—"Open Arms" program designed to persuade VC to rally to South Vietnamese government; a returnee was called a Hoi Chanh

Chinook—U.S. helicopter (CH-47) used to airlift cargo and personnel

Citadel—A geographic area west of Saigon in III Corps

Claymore—A directional antipersonnel mine

COIN—Counterinsurgency

Combat hamlet—A VC term for a strategic village captured and fortified for VC purposes

Corona Harvest—The U.S. Air Force project to collect documents for historical purposes

COSVN—Central Office for South Vietnam—North Vietnamese leadership in South Vietnam

Daisy Cutter—MK-82 (500 pound HE) or MK-84 (2,000 pound HE) with fuse extenders designed to explode at the surface to kill personnel and to defoliate land and forests

DMZ—Demilitarized Zone along the 17th parallel between North and South Vietnam

Dog's Face—Prominent geographic feature near the Cambodian border in MR 3, northwest of Tay Ninh city

Dragonship—AC-47 gunship (Spooky) with 3 miniguns

DRV (DRVN)—Democratic Republic of Vietnam, government of North Vietnam (NVN)

EGRESS RECAP—Plan for processing released U.S. POWs

FIRST TEAM—U.S. 1st Cavalry Division

Flat Iron—Straight portion of the border between Cambodia and Binh Long Province

Garlic—Explosive fuel-air munitions, the 1,000 pound bomb

Gunship—An armed helicopter; also, any of several modified fixed wing transport aircraft equipped with side-firing machine guns and cannons

GVN—Government of South Vietnam

HE—High explosive

Heartland (NVN)—Greater Hanoi/Haiphong/Ninh Binh area of the lower Red River Valley, which had the major concentrations of population, agriculture, industry and transportation networks in NVN

Ho Chi Minh Trail—NVN logistic supply route through the Nape, Mu Gia and Ban Karai Passes into Laos, down the eastern Laotian panhandle where roads and trails turn eastward into RVN

Hobo Woods—VC/NVA base area northwest of Saigon

Huey—U.S. army helicopter (UH-1)

ICC—International Control Commission (established by Geneva Accords of 1954)

IGLOO WHITE—Surveillance system consisting of air-dropped sensors, relay aircraft and an infiltration surveillance center; a project strongly supported by Secretary of Defense McNamara

IRON AGE—USAF assistance to the French in Indochina, from December 5, 1953 to August 1, 1954

Iron Triangle—A VC stronghold in the dense jungle, about twenty miles north-northwest of Saigon

IVY DIVISION—U.S. 4th Infantry Division

JUNGLE JIM—Original covert training and reconnaissance in RVN (1961)

La Nga Base Area—Area along La Nga River, south of Dinh Quan, east central Long Khanh Province, used by enemy forces

Lazy Dog—MK-44 bombs containing 10,000 small missiles which spread over a very large area

Lao Dong—NVN Communist Party

MAAG—Military Assistance Advisory Group

Marble Mountain—South of Da Nang, on South China Sea

Michelin Plantation—Rubber plantation thirty KM east of Tay Ninh in III Corps, used extensively by enemy as a safe area

Mike Force—Companies of Nung Chinese Mercenary soldiers, also called CHINA BOY I, II, etc.

Monkey Mountain—(Mon Ky) west of Da Nang on South China Sea

Montagnard—Primitive mountain tribesmen (approximately 800,000) with a history of antipathy towards Vietnamese

NVA—North Vietnamese Army (also known as People's Army, North Vietnam)

NVAF—North Vietnamese Air Force

NVN—North Vietnam(ese)

Orange—A herbicide composed of 2,4-D and 2,4,5-T, effective against broadleaf vegetation and used in defoliation operations

Parrot's Beak—See Angel's Wing

PAVN—People's Army, North Vietnam (also known as NVA)

Pathet Lao—Laotian communist military or civil group

Phoenix, Operation—A program to "neutralize" VC throughout South Vietnam; later called Phung Hoang

Plaines des Jars—A militarily strategic area north-northeast of Vientiane in Laos

POW—Prisoner of War

PRG—Provisional Revolutionary Government (NC)

PSYWAR—Psychological warfare

Ranch Hand—UC-123 defoliation, herbicide operations

Rat Fink Valley—A valley west of Ban Karai Pass in the central portion of the Laotian panhandle, noted for its extremely heavy antiaircraft fire

Razor Back—An isolated range of hills north of Dau Tieng in extreme northern Binh Duong Province

Rice Bowl—An area in western Binh Tuy Province noted for high rice production

Rung Sat Special Zone—A VC infested mangrove and saw grass swamp which bounded the ship channel to Saigon

RVN—Republic of Vietnam

Santa Fe Trail—Nickname for NVN infiltration route leaving the west end of the DMZ and turning south near Tchepone to join the Ho Chi Minh Trail

Seven Mountains—In western IV Corps, southwestern Chau Doc Province

Sihanouk Trail—VC/NVN logistic route which began at Sihanoukville and came out of Cambodia in the trib-order area near Dak To and Ban Het (Route L10)

Straight Edge Woods—A wooded area southwest of Tay Ninh City, near Cambodian border

Strategic hamlet—RVN constructed village in South Vietnam, organized and fortified to resist VC attack; rural citizens were often forced to leave their hamlets to live here

Three Sisters—Three isolated mountains in southwestern IV Corps along the coast of Kien Giang Province

VC—Vietcong, south Vietnamese communist forces which ranged from guerrillas to well-equipped and well-trained main forces

Vietminh—Described Vietnamese communists prior to 1954, later they became known as VC

War Zone C—A VC redoubt northwest of Saigon, roughly encompassing northwestern Tay Ninh Province

War Zone D—A VC redoubt north-northwest of Saigon encompassing an area centered on the intersection of Binh Long, Phuoc Long and Bin Duong Provinces

White—A herbicide composed of 2,4-D and pichloram, effective against broadleaf vegetation

YANKEE STATION—U.S. naval forces in Gulf of Tonkin which launched attacks on NVN

Author Index

Aaron, Harold R., 4004
Abel, Elie, 311
Abel Frederick J., 6060
Abel, Lionel, 2271, 2272
Abrams, Arnold, 784, 4502, 4664, 4792
Abu, 5669
Acheson, Dean, 2412, 3280
Ackland, Len A., 2159
Ackland, Len E., 1962
Adamek, Raymond J., 5815
Adams, A., 1789
Adams, Anthony A., 5642
Adams, John, 1082
Adams, Nina S., 683, 775, 1669, 3720
Adams, Samuel A., 3655
Adler, Bill, 4175
Adloff, R., 504, 747
Adloff, Richard, 212
Aertker, Samuel R., 978
Ahearn, Arthur M., 4705
Ahlgren, C.E., 5041
Air War College, 3457–3464
Ajalbert, Jean, 222
Alberti, Jean B., 223
Albertson, Dean, 2443
Albinski, Henry S., 1806, 3097
Albright, John A., 3465
Alcock, N.Z., 5393
Alden, J.D., 5921
Alexander, Joseph H., 4543
Alexeyev, E., 423
Alford, Neill H., Jr., 3072
Ali, Mehrunnisa, 445
Ali, S.M., 979
Allard, Dean C., 3493
Allen, Alfred M., 3469
Allen, Gary, 2818
Allen, Luther A., 1469, 3733
Allgood, Frank E., 3635
Allison, John M., 248
Allman, T.D., 544, 559, 594, 629, 630, 748, 749, 4926, 4955
Allman, Timothy, 1013
Alpern, Stephen I., 955

Altbach, P.G., 5823
Althoff, David L., 4233
Altman, Stuart H., 4033
Alvarez, Everett, Jr., 5188
Ambekar, G.V., 406
American Civil Liberties Union, 5686
American Enterprise Institute for Public Policy Research, 2944
American Friends Service Committee, 3217, 3218, 5922
American Historical Association, 64
American University, 883
Amnesty International Report, 1965
Amos, H.O., 4415
Andelman, David A., 866
Anderson, Charles, 4176
Anderson, K.P., 1514
Anderson, P., 2529
Anderson, Martin, 5920
Anderson, Robert S., 5191
Anderson, William C., 6133
Andonian, J.K., 3073
Andres, Gunther, 2228
Andrews, Bruce, 5483
Andrews, S., 1470
Andrews, William R., 3658
Andrus, David J., 2910
Anley, Henry, 1185
Anthis, Rollen H., 4724
Anthony, William H., 2891
Appleton, Sheldon, 5510
Aptheker, Herbert, 2327, 5261
Archer, Robert D., 4794
Ardoin, Birthney, 4019
Ariel, 3973
Arlen, Michael J., 5643
Armbruster, Frank E., 1471, 2229
Armor, David J., 5824
Armstrong, Hamilton Fish, 2647
Armstrong, John P., 545
Armstrong, Richard, 4780
Army Times, 4024
Arnett, P., 2844
Arnett, Peter, 1787, 3851
Arnison, P.M., 3734

Arnold, E.R., 3933
Arnold, Hugh M., 5626
Arnold, Keith, 5352
Arnold, M., 2928
Aronson, James, 5592
Arrowsmith, P., 2328
Ascoli, Max, 1325
Asbury, B.A., 5825
Ashmore, Harry, 2648, 3186
Ashmore, Harry S., 2845
Ashworth, S.T., III, 4407
Asinof, Eliot, 5797
Asprey, Robert B., 3659
Association of Asian Studies, 6–9
Astri Suhrki, 956
Atkinson, D.K., 3596
Attwood, William, 1843
Audric, John, 494, 495
Aument, Shary, 5091
Austerlitz, M., 1945
Austin, Anthony, 2759
Australia. Department of External Affairs, 121, 1261, 3098–3100, 3101
Auvade, Robert, 10
Axelrod, Robert, 1857
Axley, Robert J., 3934
Ayal, Eliezer B., 949
Ayme, G., 1086
Azeau, H., 1670

Babb, Wayne A., 4527
Babcock, R.S., 4378
Babich, V., 4861
Bachelder, R.B., 5039
Bachman, Jerald G., 5575
Backlund, Donald R., 1217
Baczynskyj, Boris, 560
Bader, W.B., 2945
Badillo, Gilbert, 5332
Bagdikian, Ben H., 5578
Baggs, Andrew H., 1745
Bagguley, John, 3162
Bailey, George A., 5644–5646

Shy, John W., 3669
Si Kuen Lee, 1111
Sibley, A.K., 3903
Sibley, M.Q., 3090
Sidel, Victor W., 4995, 5086
Sidey, Hugh, 2576, 2907
Siffin, William, J., 40, 893
Sigelman, Lee, 2569, 2577, 5507
Sigford, Rolf N., 2390
Sights, Albert P., Jr., 3622, 4819, 4874
Sihanouk, Norodom, 552–557
Silcock, T.H., 945
Silva, Ruth C., 5973
Silverman, Edwin B., 5426
Silverman, Jerry M., 378, 1393–1395,
    1412, 1888, 3270
Simcock, William, 1229
Simler, George B., 4778
Simmonds, E.H.S., 689, 745, 766, 767
Simmons, Edwin H., 4521–4523,
    4524
Simon, Jean-Pierre, 537
Simon, Sheldon W., 458, 459, 519,
    538, 663, 664, 2048, 2049,
    2070, 3414
Simonet, P.A., 953
Simpson, Howard R., 2516, 3696,
    3697, 6189
Simpson, Thomas H., 4571
Simulmatics Corporation, 4015
Singer, Benjamin D., 5662
Singh, L.P., 3119
SIPRI *see* Stockholm International
    Peace Research Institute
Siracusa, Joseph M., 2214, 2215
Sirikrai, Surachai, 1027
Sisouk Na Champassak, 680
Sivaram, M., 2261
Skinner, G. William, 946
Skolnick, Jerome H., 5724, 5868
Skorov, A., 2711
Slaff, Allen P., 3863, 3877
Slappy, Sterling, 3439
Slater, Jerome, 2225
Slater, Philip, 4892
Slek, Merry, 5869
Slingsby, H.G., 1112
Sloan, James P., 6190
Small, William, T., 5588
Smilkstein, Gabriel, 5402
Smith, Albert C., Jr., 4508
Smith, Charles, 768
Smith, D.A., 4919
Smith, Desmond, 1536
Smith, Gaines, 2879
Smith, George E., 5185
Smith, George W., 4229
Smith, H., 3236
Smith, Harvey H., 1324
Smith, J.A., 5072
Smith, Jessica, 1853
Smith, Joseph B., 3988
Smith, Julian, 6113, 6114
Smith, K. Wayne, 3546
Smith, L.D., 3939
Smith, Melden E., Jr., 4820
Smith, Myron J., Jr., 3440

Smith, N.I., 1468
Smith, Nelle Van D., 2754
Smith, Philip R., Jr., 3646
Smith, R.L., 1594
Smith, R.M., 211
Smith, R.S., 2712
Smith, Ralph B., 1078, 1164
Smith, Richard B., 4539
Smith, Richard M., 1992
Smith, Richard W., 4394
Smith, Robert B., 5870
Smith, Roger M., 520, 539, 540
Smith, Rolph, 2009
Smith, Russell H., 611
Smith, Steven P., 6191
Smith, William A., 3799
Smock, James E., 4413
Smocker, P., 3116
Smuckler, Ralph H., 1396
Smylie, James H., 5568
Smythe, Donald, 3717
Snepp, Frank, 4339
Snitowsky, Mike, 643
Snow, Edgar, 1838
Snyder, Joel J., 489
Snyder, Wayne W., 1476
Sobel, Lester A., 2175
Sochurek, Howard, 1343, 4515, 4637,
    4789
Sochwick, Howard, 2374
Sockell, Jacques, 4638
Soedjatmoko, 460
Sokan, I.U., 588
Sola Pool, Ithiel de, 1397, 3777
Solomon, George F., 6092
Solomon, Robert L., 286
Soloveytchik, G., 2713, 2714
Sommer, John, 2254, 4190
Sontag, Susan, 2356
Soper, James B., 3904
Sorenson, Theodore C., 2486
Sorenson, John L., 3094
Sorley, Lewis, 3656
Sosmena, Gaudioso C., Jr., 1398
Soustelle, Jacques, 1183
South Viet Nam National Front for
    Liberation, 1783
Souvann Phouma, 731
Spanier, John W., 2181
Sparks, Will, 1498, 3698
Spector, Ronald, 3568
Speed, F.W., 401, 3109
Spencer, Wilber P., Jr., 4016
Spender, Stephen, 6126
Sperlich, Peter W., 5503
Spinks, Charles N., 1662
Spitz, Allan, 1739
Spitzer, Dana, 5992
Spock, Benjamin M., 5725
Spore, John B., 4572
Springer, W.L., 1964
Sprinkle, James D., 4445
Sproule, James M., 2578
Spruille, Jane Polk, 2357
Spurr, Russell, 1913, 1993
Staaversen, Van J., 4
Stahnke, P.K., 5542

Standerwick, Caroline, 5132
Stanford, Norman K., 3778
Stanley, G.F.C., 1230
Stanton, M. Duncan, 4045
Stanton, Thomas H., 469
Stapleton, Homer L., 4395
Stapleton, Margaret L., 2410
Stark, Gail D., 541
Starner, Frances L., 644, 800, 1004,
    1537, 1889, 2715, 3779, 3780,
    4134, 4330
Starobin, Joseph R., 1135, 3350
Starr, Jerold M., 5569
Starr, Paul, 6073
Starry, Donn A., 3489, 4414
Staudenmaier, William O., 3591
Stavins, R., 2262
Stavins, Ralph, 2487
Stavis, Ben, 2796
Steel, Ronald, 1941, 3137
Stein, Jeffrey, 3806
Stein, Robert, 5589
Steinburg, Alfred, 2579
Steiner, H.A., 1740
Steinfels, P., 5791
Steinhaus, Kurt, 126
Stempel, John D., 2391
Stennis, Senator John C., 3623
Stephan, C.R., 4613
Stephen, Jacobs, 3179
Stephens, Michael D., 690
Stern, S., 1804
Stevens, Franklin, 5986
Stevens, Robert W., 5450
Stevenson, Adlai E., 3180
Stevenson, Charles A., 781
Stevenson, John R., 612
Steward, George, 5672
Stewart, W.A., 3747
Stewart, William J., 2411
Stifel, Laurence D., 954
Stillman, Edmund, 3624, 3625
Stillwell, Paul, 4587
Stilwell, Richard G., 3535
Stirling, John, 461
Stockdale, James B., 5186
Stockholm International Peace Research
    Institute (SIPRI), 4952, 4964,
    5003, 5088
Stockstill, Louis R., 5115, 5335
Stockwin, H., 287
Stoessinger, John G., 2816
Stofi, Russel H., 3500
Stohl, Michael, 5747
Stoler, Mark A., 3027
Stone, I.F., 1914, 2770, 2880, 3237,
    3351, 3365, 4303, 4331, 5619,
    5813
Stone, Isidor F., 2149
Stone, Jeremy, 4821
Stone, Marvin L., 2716
Stone, Robert, 6192, 6193
Storry, Richard, 3158
Stovall, Dale, 4790
Strahs, James, 6193
Strait, Roger, 5872
Stratton, Alice, 5197